C000115356

EUROPE BY TRAIN

Katie Wood was born and educated in Edinburgh, where she read Communications then English at university. After a short spell in Public Relations she spotted the gap in the market for a guide on training round Europe on a budget. *Europe by Train* allowed her to combine her two greatest loves, travelling and writing, and the first edition of this now-classic book was published in 1983. Since then she has written some 34 guidebooks on topics ranging from family holidays to the environmental and social impacts of tourism. Her books have been universally praised for their practical, down-to-earth approach and the quality of her research.

A fellow of the Royal Geographical Society, Katie continues to write freelance on travel for various publications and is the national Travel Editor of *The Sun* newspaper.

She currently lives in Perthshire with her husband and two children, but rail travel remains her first love and she takes to the train with her backpack to update *Europe by Train* whenever she can.

EUROPE BY TRAIN 1998

KATIE WOOD

RESEARCHERS:
Daniel Gooding,
Stephen Frost,
Kevin Jenkins

In memory of Kevin Jenkins

EBURY PRESS
LONDON

First published by Fontana 1983

Sixteenth edition published in the United Kingdom in 1998 by
Ebury Press
Random House UK Ltd
Random House
20 Vauxhall Bridge Road
London SW1V 2SA

Random House Australia (Pty) Lt
20 Alfred Street
Milsons Point, Sydney
New South Wales 2061, Australia

Random House New Zealand Lin
18 Poland Road, Glenfield
Auckland 10, New Zealand

Random House South Africa (Pty)
Endulini, 5a Jubilee Road
Parktown 2193, South Africa

Random House UK Limited Reg. No. 954009

A CIP catalogue record for this book is available from the British Library.
11 13 15 17 19 20 18 16 14 12

ISBN 0 09 186077 6

Printed and bound in Great Britain by
Cox & Wyman Ltd, Reading, Berkshire

CONTENTS

FOREWORD

What makes this book different from other guidebooks on Europe is that it's train-orientated and economy-minded. Research for this guide stems from travel all over Europe on a very tight budget, backed up by thorough investigation. This is the only guide of its kind, giving train and station information as well as details of accommodation and sights. It was written because I, like thousands of others, needed such a book and it didn't exist.

Europe by Train is now in its 16th year and I hope you'll be able to learn from my mistakes and benefit from my experiences. The book (updated annually) tells of the finds made when travelling around Europe in recent years and explains the different ways of using various rail passes which offer an exceptional opportunity to see the sights, meet new people and broaden your horizons – all at a low price.

PRICES AND EXCHANGE RATES

Because these fluctuate, we can only give a rough guide. As a reference, this book uses £1 = $1.50, but this rate (and all prices listed herein) is subject to change. The cost of living in former communist countries is particularly vulnerable to inflation as these countries move further towards a market economy.

FREE BOOKS FOR THE MOST HELPFUL LETTERS

Please feel free to write in with your comments and suggestions. Obviously, in a book containing the amount of data that this one does, information and prices quickly go out of date. Though I try to update as thoroughly as possible every year, I would appreciate your assistance if you find something that has changed or if you feel a place deserves more detailed treatment. While I enjoy reading about your experiences, please keep your letters brief and concise (2 sides of A4 maximum, preferably typed). Try and give me as much detail as possible (i.e. full address, telephone number and directions), and quote the relevant page numbers from *Europe by Train*. The writers of the 6 best letters of 1998 will each receive a free copy of the updated 1999 guide.

All correspondence should be addressed to me, care of my publishers, at the address on p.4.

ANY POTENTIAL RESEARCHERS OR BUDDING JOURNALISTS OUT THERE?

Many of you write asking if I need researchers to help me update my guides. I do; however, there are stringent rules that apply.

RESEARCHER CRITERIA:

1. You must have travelled very extensively.
2. You must be very interested in travel. I mean maniacally interested, not just keen on going to foreign parts. Are you the type who never misses a travel programme; who immediately turns to the travel sections of newspapers and magazines; who yearns for foreign travel more than anything else?
3. Do you know, or are you prepared to learn, all about the travel industry?
4. Do you write well? You need to be up to A-level English at least, preferably degree level, and be competent in your use of language. You will need to be concise yet interesting. Can you read a tourist booklet and translate it into a couple of sentences? Could you pick out the most salient points? This is what guide-book writing is all about.
5. Can you work to deadlines? Publishing schedules wait for no one, and if a guide isn't on the shelves by the holiday season, forget it. I work to very strict deadlines and I am a hard task mistress! And the fact that you had to stay up half the night to finish your piece should not be obvious to the reader. Could you deliver in time? You will be contractually bound to do so.

If, after reading the requirements, you still feel you have what it takes, please send me a fully typed CV, photo, list of where you've travelled and samples of any published writing or any travel writing to me care of the publishers (the address is on p.4). If you do not comply with these rules, no reply will be sent. Sorry, but each year I'm inundated with enquiries and can only respond to those who have shown that they can follow instructions.

INTRODUCTION

This is the 16th edition of Europe by Train and during the last decade and a half Europe and rail travel have altered dramatically.

This year has seen major changes in the different ticket option available to the traveller in Europe and this 98 edition offers the most up-to-date information available. So before you lash out hundreds of pounds on a ticket, spend some time wading through Part One of this guide and make sure you get the best pass for your needs – and at the best price! There's also information in Part One on getting fully organised before your trip and ensuring you have all the right kit and correct paperwork.

Europe by Train 1998 is still the same budget-minded guide it always has been. Throughout the book I have assumed the traveller is looking for the very cheapest deals for accommodation, eating out and sightseeing–whilst still ensuring good value for money.

This year's researchers have worked incredibly hard to ensure our info is as up to the minute as possible – not easy in a continent which is still in a state of flux. My thanks to them.

And thank you for continuing to make *Europe by Train* the best-selling rail guide. Thank you for all your letters. Thanks for the praise and constructive criticism. Enjoy your travels.

Katie Wood
January 1998

Cheap Sleeps Europe

Every year, the most common question I am asked is how to make finding accommodation easier. From years of experience on the rails of Europe, I can sympathize, and agree that finding a bed is the one drawback of flexible rail travel. Booking too many beds ahead decidedly cramps your style, yet spending a night in a station or park leaves you vulnerable, exhausted the next day, and is far from ideal.

There are enough hostels, pensions and campsites to go around in Europe (supply does keep pace with the demand) – it's just a case of knowing where to go and in which areas to look. This is fine if you have spent the last 10 years doing it, but most eurorailers need a little guidance. Such was the reasoning behind my *Cheap Sleeps Europe* guide. The first edition came out in 1992 and was an immediate success. The 1998 edition has been completely revised to complement the updated *Europe by Train*. Every major city and tourist location throughout Europe is covered, especially those areas where readers have had trouble finding a bed. International youth hostels, privately run hostels, pensions, campsites and sleep-ins are all covered. Buying this book will save you shelling out on the *Youth Hostels Handbook* and the *Campsite Directory*, not to mention time and aggravation at Tourist Offices trying to get recommendations and bookings for places to stay.

With a copy of *Europe by Train* and *Cheap Sleeps Europe*, you will have all you need (apart from the *Thomas Cook European Timetable*) to plan your European trip.

Your input and suggestions are, as always, welcome. If an establishment seems to you unworthy of its recommendation, or if you come up with a new find, please drop me a letter (the address is on p.4) and share the benefits of your experience with other eurorailers. The writers of the three best letters of 1998 will each receive a free copy of the updated 1999 guide.

PART ONE

EURORAILING

THE ADVANTAGES OF TRAIN TRAVEL

So why should you want to whizz round Europe by train when you can lie comatose on a Spanish beach for 2 weeks or buy a new electric guitar for around the same amount of money? Well, besides the fact that travelling round Europe by train is a real bargain, there are many other advantages that this lifestyle has over normal ways of burning holes in your pocket.

Firstly there's the dream. We all love the freedom of being able to wake up one morning in Paris, give the sky the once over and get on a train to Barcelona. With a rail pass, this dream becomes a reality, something which may not become available to you again or an option which you haven't had before. For the independent traveller this is the sort of stuff which holidays are made of, an opportunity to be grasped and not to be missed. Without a doubt then, the train is the safest, most convenient and most interesting means of transport to discover the hidden corners of Europe that hitchhiking can never show you while covering a lot of ground in a very short time.

Compared to hitching or being in a car, or even flying the advantages are enormous. For starters you will invariably leave from and arrive at stations which are located in city centres and you will avoid leaving yourself open to the vagaries of the weather. You also cut out the frustration of being caught in the inevitable traffic jams which occur on Europe's roads during high seasons. Then there's the obvious: you can actually spend more time at your chosen destination to relax or sightsee. If you think that railway lines are too restrictive for the route you want to take, remember that virtually all tourist centres in Europe can be conveniently reached by rail, and the few exceptions can be reached by bus or by using bicycle rental facilities which are available at an increasing number of stations. Every year Europe's main roads become more congested and road improvements move at a slow pace, compared to the investments continually being made to the European rail network. In northern Europe, second-class seats today are comparable to the first-class of 20 years ago. Speeds in excess of 120mph are now common in France, Great Britain and Germany, and as the networks are expanded this will become the norm everywhere. As new, simplified, direct routes between cities emerge, it is more likely that you will find a train to take you direct to your final destination rather than having to change.

Europe's rail renaissance has meant that letting the train take the strain is now a serious alternative to flying. Travelling by train means avoiding Europe's increasingly congested airports and their confusing, time-consuming check-in procedures. Compared to flying, the train (assuming you can take a high-speed express and not a local shunt-about) can actually travel faster than a plane on a distance of under 400 miles, allowing for the time it takes to commute to and from airports. It's also becoming a much cheaper alternative to high-price European short hops. Germany's ICE between Frankfurt and Basle for example, is ten minutes faster and £100 cheaper than the plane.

Eurostar is at the forefront of the European rail revolution and is making serious inroads into airlines' business. Last year Eurostar carried some 5 million people on its twice-a-day Waterloo–Paris and Brussels service. There are now 17 daily round trips to Paris and eight to Brussels. From Paris it's easy to reach Eurostar's hub station at Lille and tap into French Railways' network of TGVs for all points south and on to Italy and Spain. Change at Brussels for connections to destinations anywhere in Belgium, Holland and Germany. As prices come down so do journey times, London–Brussels takes just 2 hours 45 minutes. Paris–Lyon trains run on the hour in each direction from 6 a.m. to 10 p.m. and journey time is a speedy 2 hours. By 2003, the British high-speed line from St Pancras will knock a further half hour off journey times to France.

For the record, almost all European trains are driven by diesel or electric power and are government-owned. The main exceptions to this are some of the mountain lines in Switzerland and the various privatised sections of what was once British Railways. Also remember that if you're on a train you can walk about and stretch your legs, go for a meal or a snack and, providing you aren't travelling on a reserved seat, you can plant yourself wherever you want. The informality of the train means that it's almost impossible to make a trip on one of the more popular routes in the summer months and not end up swapping stories and yarns with fellow travellers. On overnight journeys, the intimacy of the train compartment makes it quite impossible!

Other advantages are so plentiful we could fill the book with them! For starters there's the standard of service. Anyone who has travelled in North America will notice the difference straight away: European trains are faster, more plentiful, more punctual, serving many more destinations. Historically, the European network has not been maintained on a profit-making basis and few countries' networks actually make any money. They are essentially a public service, as the Inter-Rail and Eurail passes demonstrate. For example, though you may pay £159 for an Inter-Rail pass it can easily save you that much, or more, off the standard point-to-point fares. Having said all that, there is more of a trend nowadays for public sector businesses to be more financially accountable so things may change.

From an environmentalist's point of view, trains are good news when you bear in mind they consume up to 17 times less energy than aeroplanes and 5 times less than cars to transport the same volume of people. A train carries more people per square metre than cars can – and with fewer pollution problems.

One of the greatest attractions of travelling Europe by train – and the main pleasure you'll look back on – is the immense feeling of freedom you will enjoy. It's entirely up to you where you spend your time, when you move on and how you choose to get there. It's quite a heady feeling, never really knowing where you will be tomorrow. To preserve this, it is advisable not to book too many nights' accommodation or train journeys in advance – if you bother to book any. However, to counteract the negative side-effects of total flexibility, it's a good idea to arrive in major cities as early in the morning as possible in order to find yourself a bed for the night. The best option is pick up a copy of *Cheap Sleeps Europe* (see p. 11) or to get to the tourist accommodation office, which is often located in the station, before noon. However, almost every town has affordable places to stay within a few blocks of the station, so don't despair if you arrive late at night as you should be able to find somewhere within walking distance.

See 'When You're There' (p. 65) for more tips and advice, and pp. 38–51 for all rail pass information.

Before You Go

GETTING TO EUROPE BY PLANE

Whether you're flying to Europe from the Americas, Australasia, Ireland or the UK, you want to do it cheaply. The basic rule is: the more you pay, the greater the flexibility; the less you pay, the more restrictions. A little preplanning will save money and buy you extra time on your trip. It is therefore important to choose the right city as your starting point so you can visit the countries not covered by your rail pass either before your pass starts or after it expires; there is no sense in wasting precious days of your pass where you can't use it.

There is no shortage of airlines or different types of tickets available, so take your time and do your homework before buying. Once you've found the best deal, go to a good, reliable travel agent and tell them where, when and how much you can afford. Most travel agency services are free and they may come up with some new ideas, so use them to the full. Contact your local student travel office:

this can be a goldmine of information, sometimes offering special flights open to everyone, not just students or the under-26s.

If you don't know where the local student travel office is, consult the listing of CIEE offices in Appendix IV or check with the information office at a nearby college or university.

TICKET TYPES

Most reduced airfares must be purchased up to 30 days in advance, so try to book as far ahead as possible. Scan the travel supplements of the major newspapers in your area and talk to as many other travellers as you can to pick up tips. Don't forget to check the smaller or less popular airlines and ticket routings – a good example of this is Icelandair's New York to Frankfurt run via Reykjavik.

SCHEDULED FLIGHTS

APEX. On scheduled flights the only possible option for the budget traveller is, if you can afford it, an APEX (Advanced Purchase Excursion fare) ticket. A Super-APEX fare is also available on some routings and this allows you even more freedom. Check the small print on any ticket purchase as many allow you to arrive and depart from different cities (and countries), use different airlines for the separate legs of your journey, or even postpone your return flight – for a small fee of course. Also ask whether your fare has any 'student' or 'youth' discounts as this may provide further savings.

STANDBY During the peak season (June to September) you can expect all the airlines to be fully booked. Unless you reserve well in advance, you could be forced to fly standby – if it's even available. Not all airlines offer standby and your choice of destinations is restricted, as are the number of seats available. Tickets are sold on a 'first come, first served' basis the day of the flight, so it pays to be organized. You stand a better chance of getting a flight midweek rather than at the weekend. Call the airline a few days before you want to leave and check seat availability (don't mention the word 'standby', though, as some agents may become suddenly unhelpful).

The night before the flight, call once more to confirm that there are still open seats. Get to the airport early (6 or 7 a.m.) before the ticket counter opens. Once you've bought your ticket, go straight to the gate and get your name on the standby list. Once this is done, it becomes a waiting game which could last all night.

BUDGET FARES These are similar to standby tickets, except that you have the security of a confirmed seat reservation. First, call the airline and tell them which week you want to leave and return (if so desired). Seven days or so before the day of your flight the airline will get back to you with the exact details. This way the airline gets to choose the date and time most convenient for them, not you. Usually the savings aren't much better than a good APEX fare, but if you don't want to risk a standby flight and you're too late to buy an APEX ticket it's worth a shot.

CHARTER FLIGHTS

If cash is tight and you can't afford flexibility, go for a charter flight. This gives you the luxury of a seat reservation at a lower cost, but will involve backtracking to the airport you arrived at. But beware – some countries will not allow you to use the return half of the ticket if you have left the country during your stay. Greece is notorious for this – a day-trip to Turkey can cost you a full-fare ticket home if you're not careful. We know, it almost happened to one of our researchers! Check with the charter company first and make sure to read the 'owner-participant' contract so you are aware of all the rules.

PACKAGE HOLIDAYS

A similar option is to buy a low-cost 'package' holiday to your destination. This gives you a flight and a place to stay while you familiarize yourself with the area and local routines. During the winter, you can find long-stay holidays (e.g. 4–6 weeks) including a flight and room for as little as £300. This can be a great way to provide yourself with a base from which to explore a country in depth; and if you get low on cash, you have a room until your return flight home. As the flights on package holidays are usually charters, the same restrictions on leaving the country may apply; check it out with the company first.

CROSSING THE CHANNEL

Many travellers of Europe by train start their trip in Britain and use the ports of Dover and Folkestone to cross over into France. There are, however, many alternatives to these routes that you should consider. Of course, not all ferry ports have rail connections, but those without a rail link usually have bus connections run by the ferry operators. These bus services sometimes require an additional reservation and or fare, so check with the ferry company. Bear in mind that some services are seasonal (e.g. Truckline's Poole to Cherbourg service runs only from May to September).

There are over a dozen ferry routes between the UK, Ireland and the Continent, many of which have special rail connections (boat trains) that meet the ferry, allowing you to walk straight off the boat and on to a waiting train. Ostend and Hoek van Holland both have boat train connections to Germany, and Dieppe has one to Paris via northern France.

From Dover, there are frequent services to Calais and Boulogne operated all year round by P&O European Ferries, Stenalines (formerly Stena Sealink) and Hoverspeed. Hoverspeed's Seacat service makes the crossing in under an hour. P&O also runs ships from Dover to Ostend and Zeebrugge, and has a fast Jetfoil service to Ostend. From Portsmouth you can take P&O to Cherbourg and Le Havre or Brittany Ferries to St Malo and Ouistreham. For the really adventurous, Brittany Ferries also operate a service between Plymouth and Santander in Spain.

If you're in Ireland, or planning to go there, Irish Ferries run services from Rosslare and Cork to Cherbourg and Le Havre. Boat trains connect London and Dublin via Holyhead–Dun Laoghaire or Holyhead–Dublin Harbour. Stenalines and Seacat operate between Belfast in Northern Ireland and Stranraer in Scotland though the shortest crossing on the Irish Sea is P&O's super new Jetliner service between Larne and Cairnryan. Although there is no railway station on the Scottish side, there's a fairly decent bus service to nearby Stranraer.

A summary of the main cross-channel and Irish Sea ferries is contained in Appendix II with the approximate journey times and frequency. For a complete listing, check the 'international shipping' section of the Thomas Cook guide for cross-channel ferries and tables 620–627 for the Irish Sea crossings.

THE CHANNEL TUNNEL

Work first started back in 1881, but was abandoned for fear of a French (military) invasion. A century later, a fixed link was again proposed. An unprecedented trans-European finance consortium was set up, and in 1987 engineers set to work. On May 6 1994, after years of delay, the Channel Tunnel was officially inaugurated by the Queen and President Mitterrand and it was hoped that a regular service would soon follow. At the time of going to press, Eurostar are operating 17 trains a day to Paris and eight to Brussels. The Cheriton (nr Folkestone)–Coquelles (nr Calais) car-transporter service, Le Shuttle, is now running a full service. They offer four trains every hour, 24 hours a day, 365 days a year. It's only 35 minutes platform to platform.

EUROSTAR Half of the people travelling from London to Paris now go by train. Last year more than 60% of those going to the

French capital chose Eurostar. Eurostar focuses on 2 routes: London Waterloo–Paris Nord and London Waterloo–Lille Europe–Brussels Midi/Zuidi (regular trains in each direction to each destination; journey time around 2 hrs 45 mins). Change at Brussels for trains to the Netherlands and Germany etc., and at Lille for TGVs to the rest of France and south Italy and Spain. Eurostar has been at the forefront of the European rail revolution and will soon launch through trains from the North of England and Scotland. Two routes will be in operation; one, starting at Glasgow, will go through Edinburgh, Newcastle, Darlington, York, Doncaster, Newark, Peterborough to the tunnel. The other train will start at Manchester and go via Stockport, Crewe, Stafford, Birmingham, Coventry and Milton Keynes. Both trains will by-pass London and will pick up on the Paris and Brussels routings. There are a range of fares starting at £69 return for rail pass holders London–Paris or Brussels. A range of discounts also are in operation such as summer savers and these currently offer savings of up to 40%. Eurostar also operates a winter ski service. Travel direct from Waterloo and Ashford to the French Alps. There are even daily trains from London to Disneyland, Paris. For reservations, phone Eurostar (Tel. 0990 300 003) or contact a major international rail agent.

PREPLANNNG

To ensure you get the most out of your time abroad, start by planning out a rough itinerary of where you want to visit. Once this is done, look at a map of Europe and sketch a route between the cities, checking its feasibility against a timetable. Make sure that you use the appropriate timetable for the season you want to travel in (summer services run from mid-May until mid-September). If the schedule you need isn't out yet, try to find a copy of last year's edition rather than using the winter schedule.

When planning an itinerary for a complete tour of Europe, there are 3 main considerations to take into account: the interesting destinations you'd like to see, how much time you want to spend at each one and the most scenic route to get there.

TIME ALLOCATION For those who want to do a whistle-stop tour taking in as many countries as possible, time is crucial. Most cities require a minimum of 2 days to see everything; this means spending at least 1 night there. You can maximize your time by sleeping on trains, arriving early (7 a.m.) and leaving late (10 p.m.). This saves you time and money, but you could miss out on some great scenery.

DESTINATIONS AND ROUTES Most travellers of Europe by train have a few special places in mind before they set off. By using a timetable and the information in this book, you'll be able to work out the quickest and best routes between destinations. There are often 2 or 3 routes to choose from, and one is bound to appeal to you more than another.

WHEN TO GO For obvious reasons, most eurorailers find themselves on the road (or rail) between June and September. Travelling in the high season gives you the advantages of encountering more people, better weather and being sure that everything is open. However, prices are higher, the character of a place may be swamped by crowds of tourists, accommodation is harder to find, tourist industry people have less time for you and there are generally more hassles on the trains. For the lucky few who can choose when to travel, I'd recommend spring to early summer.

TIME DIFFERENCES Bear in mind the different time zones you will pass through and allow for this when making connections. Timetables usually list departures and arrivals in the local time; the notable exception to this is the former Soviet republics, where all times listed in Russian timetables are Moscow time, regardless of which zone the city is actually in. The table below lists the various time zones for the countries covered in this book:

COUNTRY	TIME	COUNTRY	TIME	COUNTRY	TIME
Albania	CET	Greece	EET	Portugal	GMT
Austria	CET	Hungary	CET	Romania	EET
Belgium	CET	Ireland*	GMT	Russia	MST
Belarus	EET	Italy	CET	Slovakia	CET
Bosnia-		Latvia	EET	Slovenia	CET
Hercegovina	CET	Liechtenstein	EET	Spain	CET
Bulgaria	EET	Lithuania	CET	Sweden	CET
Croatia	CET	Luxembourg	CET	Switzerland	CET
Czech Rebulic	CET	Macedonia	CET	Turkey	EET
Denmark	CET	Malta	CET	Ukraine	EET
Estonia	EET	Morocco	GMT	UK	GMT
Finland	EET	Netherlands	CET	Yugoslavia ?	CET
France	CET	Norway	CET	(Serbie)	
Germany	CET	Poland	CET	broken up? ou Kosovo?	

GMT is the standard time zone, all others are calculated as follows: CET adds 1 hour to GMT, EET adds 2 hours to GMT and MST adds 3 hours to GMT. From the end of March to the end of September all time zones add 1 hour for Daylight Savings Time except that marked by a *, where Daylight Savings Time continues until the end of October.

ADVANCE TOURIST INFORMATION If you know which countries you want to visit, contact the appropriate Tourist Office in your own country before you leave. They'll be glad to send you booklets and maps to whet your appetite and give you an idea of what to see and, more importantly, what you can afford to miss. While most offices provide these services for free, there is an unfortunate trend for Tourist Offices to 'pay their way' by charging for literature and their time. An increasing number, including British Rail International and French Railways, now operate premium-rate 0891 pay-per-call phone lines to handle enquiries and others may ask for a small 'donation' to cover postage costs. Of the offices listed in Appendix V, only the Netherlands Tourist Board in London charges for its services, but expect others to follow suit. In the meantime, most information is free and there's nothing to lose by writing in to ask. Remember, though, Tourist Offices are in the business of selling their country, so take claims like 'the most beautiful city in Europe' with a pinch of salt.

PASSPORTS AND VISAS

If you already have a passport, make sure the photo is up to date and actually looks like you. If the picture was taken when you were 16 and you're now 23 and sporting a beard, you will have problems at borders in eastern Europe. If you don't have a passport, make sure to apply a couple of months in advance to allow plenty of time to get any visas you may need.

Try to get all the necessary visas before you leave your home country, as it is often harder to get a visa when you're abroad. There are several reasons for this: the embassy staff may not speak English, they may be unfamiliar with visa procedures for your nationality, or even impose restrictions on you that would not be required at home (e.g. having a certain amount of money). Before you leave, be sure to double check with the embassies of all the countries you plan to visit to make sure their entry requirements haven't changed.

UK RED TAPE Same-day passport applications can be made in person at the London Passport Office. Applications by mail take from 10 days to a month. Passports are valid for 10 years and application forms can be found in post offices. You will need your birth certificate, a photo ID card, 2 recent photos and £18. Note that the old British Visitor's Passport which used to be valid for 1 year has now been withdrawn.

Bulgaria, Romania and Turkey issue visas at the border, usually for a small fee. British nationals also require visas (in advance) for: Belarus, Russia, the Ukraine and the new Yugoslavia. No visas are required for the Baltic states, eastern Europe or Morocco, but the duration of your stay may well be restricted.

There are a number of agencies that will advise you on visa requirements and application procedures. One of the friendliest is the Passport and Visa Service in London (Tel. 0171 833 2709). Do remember that they are agents and out to make a quick buck or two, it is better to contact the embassy concerned directly.

IRISH RED TAPE Passports are valid for 10 years. Applications can be made through the Passport Office or by mail; you will need your birth certificate, a photo ID, 2 recent photos and £47.

Croatia and Turkey issue visas at the border, usually for a small fee. In addition, Irish Nationals require visas (in advance) for: Belarus, Bulgaria, Estonia, Latvia, Lithuania, Romania, Russia, the Ukraine and the new Yugoslavia.

AMERICAN RED TAPE Passport applications can be made at any Passport Office and are valid for 10 years (5 years for those under 18). Applications by mail will only be accepted if you live in a remote area or if you have an expired passport and are applying for a replacement. You will need your birth certificate, state driver's licence or ID card and 2 recent photos. Replacement passports and passports for renewal cost US$55, first-time passport applications cost US$65.

Croatian and Macedonian visas are issued at the border. In addition, Americans require visas (in advance) for: Belarus, Latvia, Lithuania, Romania, Russia, the Ukraine and the new Yugoslavia.

Contact the Visa Center at 507 Fifth Avenue, Suite 904, New York, NY 10017 (Tel. 212 986 0924) for up-to-the-minute information.

CANADIAN RED TAPE Applications can be made at any Passport Office or the Passport Section, Department of Foreign and International Trade, 125 Sussex Drive, Ottawa, ON KIA 0G3. Passports are valid for 5 years only. You will need your birth certificate or citizenship card, a photo ID, 2 recent photos and CDN$35 for your application.

Croatian and Macedonian visas are issued at the border. In addition, Canadians require visas (in advance) for: Belarus, Bulgaria, the Czech Republic, Latvia, Lithuania, Poland, Romania, Russia, Slovakia, the Ukraine and the new Yugoslavia.

AUSTRALIAN RED TAPE Passports can be applied for at either a Passport Office or post office and are valid for 10 years (5 years for those under 18). You need your birth certificate or nationality papers, a photo ID, 2 recent photos and Aus$120.

Croatian and Macedonian visas are issued at the border. In addition, Australians require visas (in advance) for: Belarus, Bosnia-Hercegovina, Bulgaria, the Czech Republic, France, Hungary, Latvia, Lithuania, Poland, Romania, Russia, Slovakia, Spain, the Ukraine and the new Yugoslavia.

NEW ZEALAND RED TAPE Passport applications can be made at any Passport or Link Office. You need your birth certificate or nationality papers, a photo ID, 2 recent photos and NZ$60.

Croatian visas are issued at the border. In addition, New Zealanders require visas (in advance) for: Belarus, Bosnia-Hercegovina, Bulgaria, the Czech Republic, Hungary, Latvia, Lithuania, Poland, Romania, Russia, Slovakia, the Ukraine and the new Yugoslavia.

HEALTH

Before you leave, ask your doctor to refer you to a travel clinic or specialist who can check the current requirements and advisories for the regions you intend to visit. (They should also be able to provide you with recommendations about taking care of your health while abroad.) Health literature and information is available free in the UK from the Department of Health by telephoning 0800 555 777.

None of the countries covered in this guide imposes any vaccination requirements unless you are arriving from an 'Infected Area'. Unfortunately, the World Health Organization until 1993 classified the Ukraine as an 'Infected Area' because of an outbreak of cholera and diphtheria of epidemic proportions. Though these are now officially under control, the Crimea continues to wage war with cholera and diphtheria is still rife throughout. A diphtheria booster is strongly recommended, and you should be particularly choosy about whom you kiss. Another Ukrainian quirk is their heavy-handed AIDS policy. In the past, visitors planning to visit for more than 3 months, or those returning to the Ukraine after an absence of more than a month, were sometimes asked to have an AIDS test at the border. However, an up-to-date WHO certificate from your home doctor should suffice.

Those planning a trip to southern Morocco or the wilds of eastern Turkey are advised to get a typhoid vaccination and some anti-malaria pills. You should also check that your inoculations for tetanus, MMR (mumps, measles and rubella) and polio are up to date – not as a requirement of entry, but as a matter of common sense.

A few preventative measures could not only save your trip from disaster, but also save you a packet on doctor's bills or hospital fees.

NB: Make sure that you get all vaccinations recorded on a World Health Certificate to avoid any complications.

If you're only travelling in EEA countries (that is, the EC, Austria and Scandinavia) and you're an EEA citizen, go along to your local post office and get form E111. This service is often neglected by travellers of Europe by train, which is surprising as it provides medical cover in EEA countries to the same level that a national of that country enjoys. In theory it takes a few days to obtain, but usually can be granted there and then. Take your NI number with you. You may, however, have to pay part or all of your treatment and drugs. Keep receipts and claim back the cost from the DSS when you return home.

Doctors in Europe can be very expensive and often a chemist can give just as good advice – free! To find a 24-hour chemist, either ask at a police station or go to the nearest chemist's shop and look in the window, as there's often a notice saying where one is open.

If you've got to carry prescribed drugs or injection needles for medical reasons, take a prescription or doctor's note about them, as you could otherwise be prevented from carrying the medicine through customs, especially in eastern Europe and Turkey.

Whether or not you can drink the tap water while travelling depends on where you go and your personal constitution. As a general rule, problems mainly occur in the more remote areas or less developed countries. However, if you have a weak stomach, stick to bottled water throughout your trip. Make sure that seals on bottled water are unbroken, or you will probably be getting the local tap water in a recycled bottle. If you plan to camp, carry water purification tablets or boil all water before you drink it.

Avoid eating raw, unpeeled fruit or vegetables and steer clear of under-cooked meat. Take along some multivitamin pills to keep body and soul together during those long hauls. Remember to pack indigestion and anti-diarrhoea tablets, just in case you eat something that doesn't agree with you.

The further south you go the more mosquitoes and other undesirables you'll encounter, take some insect repellent and, if you're a scratcher, something to soothe the bites. A small pack of plasters and a supply of painkillers won't go amiss either. Don't forget sun-screen and sunglasses, and try to stay out of the midday sun in places around the Mediterranean.

Watch out, girls, in eastern Europe it's still difficult to get hold of tampons or sanitary towels, so take a supply along with you. Also, if you'll need contraceptives, take them from home.

Essential Preparation

WHAT TO TAKE

Obviously this very much depends on where you're going and at what time of the year: if you're off to Scandinavia in the spring, an extra jumper will certainly come in very useful. However, there are various points to remember, irrespective of where you are going or the time of the year. Unless you're visiting family or friends in Europe and expect to be met at every station, we strongly advise that you use an internal-frame rucksack. The advantages are manifold: it gives one the feeling of membership of a eurorail club and this stimulates conversation and communication which otherwise might not take place. Also – and more importantly – both your hands will be free, allowing you to produce your maps, passport, etc., at the right moment.

Shops specializing in outdoor equipment are an invaluable source of information and help. They will, in most cases, give free objective advice on what you really need for your trip and which brand names to look out for to suit your budget. If you're starting from scratch it'll take about £200 to get together all the basic gear required to camp your way round Europe, but once bought this will see you through future trips and you'd easily spend that much on grotty accommodation in just one Inter-Rail trip. Names to look out for in the UK are Milletts and the YHA shops and Field & Trek Equipment (catalogue from 3 Waters Way, Brentwood, Essex, CM15 9TB and from many branches of W. H. Smith – it costs a couple of quid). In the US, check out REI stores, which carry just about everything.

PACKING Every summer Europe is full of backpackers wishing they hadn't taken so much. Before you set out, put out on the bed everything you want to take with you – then halve it. Before you finally make up your mind, try wearing your rucksack with everything you intend to take in it on a good walk. Remember, you'll be returning with more than you left with in the way of presents and souvenirs, so leave room for them. All this is common sense really; however, we all need reminding from time to time, as it can make the difference between a relaxing and an exhausting holiday.

ESSENTIALS
THE RUCKSACK Without doubt this will be your most important single piece of equipment, so it is essential to ensure that it is both

comfortable and light. The 3 most important features you should look out for are: it sits just above your hips and has a support belt for round your waist; the shoulder-straps are well padded and the tension can be adjusted; and (most important of all) that your pack is 'high' rather than 'wide' when packed to capacity. I wish I had a pound for every eurorailer I've seen creating havoc along the all too narrow train corridors. If they're not pulling the door shut on someone's leg, they're laying out the natives with swinging cameras and boots hanging from the sides.

DAYPACK A small daypack is invaluable when sightseeing as it will hold your maps, guidebook, camera, films, food, etc., all conveniently together and waterproof. It will solve a lot of problems and saves you walking around all the time with a large rucksack. It's a good idea to put your name and address in the inside of your pack, just in case – something which many travellers overlook.

VALUABLES Keep a separate note of your ticket and passport numbers. If you do lose your passport, notify the police and get a copy of the report the police make out then go along to your country's nearest consulate or embassy. A photocopy of both your passport and your birth certificate, kept separately, may help your case. Another very useful thing to have with you are a couple of passport photos, which can come in handy for impromptu visas, replacement ISICs or passports.

One idea, very popular with the Scandinavians, is to buy a pouch to hang round your neck with all your tickets in it. Keep your cash separate – in a safe inside pocket, perhaps. Another good idea is a moneybelt. You can pick up one of these in most camping or travel orientated stores.

SLEEPING BAG Unless you plan to spend all your time staying with friends or in hotels you'll need a good bag. Hostels charge for bedding and many in northern Europe won't allow you to use your bag, which is very frustrating – but the rule. If taking a sheet sleeping bag, ensure it is to YHA standards. Note: At some hostels you may find it compulsory to hire sheets, even if you do have your own. Also, at some stage in your travels, it's likely you'll be a deck passenger on an overnight ferry somewhere. If you don't have a sleeping bag and can't borrow one from a friend, go along to your local camping shop and get the best you can afford. When you're shopping around for a bag, price is likely to be your main criterion, as it's not difficult to spend more on your sleeping bag than on your ticket. Size when packed down is a factor worth bearing in mind. If you're going to northern Europe it's a good investment to go for a good duck-down sleeping bag. Although the initial cost is steep, you get back the value over the years and if you can afford it it's well worth the extra cash. Do not make cutbacks in this: there are few things worse than a cold sleepless night before a hard day's sightseeing. Buying a cheap bag is a classic false economy and hopeless if you are going to do lots of walking around with it.

If you're taking a bag and plan to do a lot of camping or sleeping out on southern beaches, then a foam pad is also advisable. Try and get one that is long enough but not too wide (remember those train corridors). Lie down on it in the shop to check it out. Print your name on it as you'll find pads disappear with remarkable frequency.

COMFORTABLE WALKING SHOES (already broken in) are essential as you can expect to spend as much time walking as you will on trains. Don't go over the top and wear boots that would look better on Everest than strolling round the Vatican. If you're heading south, a pair of sandals is a necessity to give your feet a chance to breathe. If you don't have any, don't worry: they're cheap in southern Europe.

CAMPING GEAR If you're heading for northern Europe and plan to camp a lot, get a sturdy tent with a fly-sheet; however, if you'll be mainly in the south, pick a light one, preferably of nylon. A small Calor gas stove can save you a lot of money, especially in places like Norway where buying a cup of tea or coffee can be expensive. Gas refills are widely available, so don't bother carrying spares. Unless you're camping non-stop for a month, don't carry a lot of food supplies and camping equipment with you, but do take cutlery. Shopping from the local supermarkets makes much more sense. Remember to take a torch for those late-night pitches.

CLOTHES Obviously it depends on where you're going and the time of year. Use your common sense, but don't take anything you don't absolutely need and remember, though you may look terrific in your white jeans when they're newly washed, you'll look terrible after you've sat up all night in them on a train. Take dark comfortable clothes that won't show the battering you're giving them. Laundries are often expensive, so take a little washing powder or liquid detergent and wash your own clothes. Washaway tablets from Boots the chemist are particularly handy.

BUDGETING

Exactly how much money you have to spend will affect your lifestyle in many ways. I'm making the general assumption that the average traveller of Europe by train is short of cash and won't ever be keen to spend more than necessary on basics such as accommodation and food. There's no shortage of information for those wishing to spend more – other 'budget' guides to Europe you can buy will list hotels for £30 ($54) a night, or restaurants for £20–25 ($36–45) meals. I'm not interested in that. After all, who needs advice on how to spend money in Europe? Also, you experience more of the real country when living like the locals on a budget.

It's a straight fact that £30 ($45) a day in Norway will just about get you a hostel bed and a cafeteria meal; the same £30 in Spain will give you a hotel bed and a restaurant meal, so take into consideration the countries you want to go to and budget accordingly.

The most expensive countries are: Norway, Sweden, Finland, Denmark, Switzerland and Austria; the intermediate ones are: Germany, the United Kingdom, Ireland, the Netherlands, Belgium, Luxembourg, France and Italy; and the cheap ones are: Spain, Greece, Portugal, Turkey, eastern Europe and Morocco. The southern part of Europe remains much cheaper than the north, but to take full advantage of this cheapness you have to be prepared to accept the local standards of hygiene, cuisine, etc. Eastern Europe is cheap for food, drink and entertainment, but hotel accommodation is expensive, so hostel or camp – though watch out for escalating camping prices in Hungary and Poland. The basic fact of the matter is that camping and hostelling are cheap all over Europe, and if you are prepared to do this and buy your food in the local shops and markets to make your own picnics, you can travel for very little money.

On average, for your bed and daily food, you'll need at least £30 ($45) a day for the expensive countries, £20 ($30) a day for the intermediate ones, and £15 ($22.50) a day for the cheap ones. Remember, if you're travelling on your own and you insist on a single bedroom in a cheap hotel, it can double your costs, so double up with fellow travellers where at all possible.

DISCOUNT CARDS

One way to save money in Europe is to take advantage of an expanding network of discount card schemes for those under 26. In Scotland, there's the Young Scot card, in England the Euro Under 26 card, in Belgium the Cultureel Jonger en Passport, in France the Carte Jeune, and so on. The cards cost £6, can be bought from a variety of outlets, and offer literally thousands of discounts on meals, clothes, souvenirs and other goods. The cards can all be used interchangeably – so you can buy a Scottish card and use it to get discounts in France, for example.

INTERNATIONAL STUDENT IDENTITY CARD This offers worldwide discounts on venues, flights and accommodation in 88 countries. It can save you as much as 75% on museums and art galleries, etc., and, in some cases, gives free entry. It also entitles up to 30% discount on rail travel (Eurostar included), and on some air fares, discounts on YHA goods and accommodation, as well as reduced entry into some pubs and clubs. You need a certificate from your college or university, a photograph and £5. The ID card, when purchased in the USA, even provides you with automatic accident/sickness insurance anywhere you travel (outside the US) for the entire validity period of the ID card. ISIC can be purchased through Student Union branches in the UK, student travel offices or from one of these addresses:

UK ISIC PO Box 36, Glossop, Derbyshire, SK13 8HT or Campus Travel, 52 Grosvenor Gardens, London SW1W 0AG (Tel. 0171 730 3402).

REP. OF IRELAND Usit, 19–21 Aston Quay, Dublin 2 (Tel. 01 6798833).

N. IRELAND Usit, College Street, Belfast (Tel. 1232 324 073).

USA CIEE, New York Student Center, 895 Amsterdam Ave., New York, NY 10025 (Tel. 212 666 4177).

CANADA Travel Cuts, 187 College Street, Toronto M5T 1P7 (Tel. 416 979 2406).

AUSTRALIA Australian Student Travel/STA, 220 Faraday Street, Carlton, Melbourne VIC 3053 (Tel. 3 9349 2411).

NEW ZEALAND Student Travel Bureau, Students' Union, University of Auckland, Princes Street, Auckland (Tel. 375 265). STA Travel, 233 Cuba Street, Wellington (Tel. 4 385 0561).

For further information contact ISIC on 01457 890902.

STUDENT TRAVEL OFFICES

Geared specifically to the needs of young budget travellers, Campus Travel (UK), Council (US), CUTS (Canada) as well as STA and WST (worldwide) are the market leaders. They nearly all sell BIJ, Inter-Rail and Eurail tickets, and the staff will work out the cheapest alternative for you. They also sell ISICs and are usually found in university or college campuses. Note: They offer their services to anyone under 26, not just students.

THE COUNCIL ON INTERNATIONAL EDUCATIONAL EXCHANGE CIEE

The CIEE is a non-profit, membership organization based in the US. Their travel experts, Council Travel, are one of the foremost organizations concerned with budget travel and to help travellers of all ages with low-cost travel (air, train, etc.) as well as accommodation problems. In fact, they cover every aspect of your trip from your Student ID card to your airline ticket and reservations. Get hold of their *1998 Student Travel Catalogue* by writing to CIEE, 205 East 42nd Street, New York, NY 10017-5706 (Tel. 212 822 2600). They also have offices in other US and European cities (see Appendix IV). The catalogue provides information on Student ID cards, travel, study and work abroad. Use the council's expertise as much as possible to get the lowest possible air fares, rail passes and other travel packages.

A USEFUL TIP
Go to your local library and explore the world of travel grants to see what's available. It's amazing what funds are around and it pays off to do your research well in advance. Try Rotary International (Tel. 0171 487 5429), Lion Club International (Tel. 01245 813 661), Round Table (Tel. 0121 456 4402) or The Chamber of Commerce (Tel. 0171 248 4444).

MONEY

There's a 'Catch 22' situation with money in Europe. Undoubtedly, with violence and crime the way it is at present in Europe, it's a big risk to carry around all your cash in ready notes on you, even in a money-belt. To be weighed against this is the fact that by taking traveller's cheques you lay yourself open to continual queueing, especially in the summer, not to mention the problems trying to find a bank or travel agent to cash them. Credit or debit cards are OK in towns and cities, but you'll be hard-pushed to find a cash dispenser in remote areas, and the risk of losing cards or having them stolen is serious. You are also at the mercy of fluctuating exchange rates. This can work to your benefit in a country with high inflation where the local currency is falling against your home currency – but it works both ways.

If you decide to play safe and take most of your money in traveller's cheques, get them from VISA, Thomas Cook or American Express. Don't find yourself trying to cash an obscure brand of traveller's cheque. When buying your traveller's cheques, always buy some in small denominations as this is more economical on a tight budget. If you offer a £50 cheque and ask for £30 in French francs and £20 in Italian lire, most banks will charge you first to change into francs, then again into lire. It's better to get traveller's cheques in denominations of £10 ($20). Anyone from the USA or a major European country should buy cheques in their own currency – unless you're planning to spend 99% of your time in one country.

In general, it's a good idea to take some bank notes of the countries you know you'll end up in, especially if there's a chance you will arrive late at night or at the weekend. As a rule, I take £25 ($45) cash in 4 or

5 currencies in case there's no opportunity to change money on arrival and you have to pay for your room in advance. For more obscure currencies it's best to order cash from your bank at least 2 weeks in advance. However, banks do not always give the best rate – shop around. It's always worth while taking along a few US dollar notes as a standby as they will be accepted in most countries, particularly in eastern Europe where goods and services may be priced in US dollars.

You can cash a personal cheque of up to £100 or sometimes more in any European bank displaying the EC symbol if you've got a Eurocheque Encashment card and cheque book. Eurocheques are normally written in the local currency (US dollars in parts of eastern Europe) and no commission should be charged when cashing them (it's deducted from your account). Girobank plc no longer runs its Postcheque service.

Credit and debit cards can be useful, providing you keep them for emergencies. They are not as widely accepted abroad as in the UK and US, but can help if you need to pay for something but don't want to use cash or traveller's cheques. It goes without saying that you should be very careful indeed and keep cards separate, so that if you are robbed you don't lose them as well. You may want to pay money into your credit card account before you leave so that it is in credit and you run less risk of paying interest. It is also becoming increasingly easy to find cashpoints from which you can withdraw cash using Visa/Mastercard (you'll need a PIN number).

Remember, if you use a credit card to buy your traveller's cheques from a bank before leaving home this will be treated as a cash advance and you start paying interest right away. However, if you have a Thomas Cook credit card and buy your cheques from them, you have up to 55 days to settle the bill before paying interest. One advantage of using credit cards to pay for your initial ticket, or any other tickets *en route*, is that there is often some kind of travel insurance built in. Check it out and remember that these 'incentives' vary from card to card and from time to time.

Beware: French credit cards have an electronic chip in them instead of just a magnetic chip, so automatic card-reading machines in France may not accept UK and US cards.

BANKING

Banks in all countries open in the morning from Monday to Friday, but beware of public holidays and the siestas in Mediterranean countries (see individual country details for banking hours). In some countries, such as Germany, post offices (which have longer opening hours) will change money for a lower commission rate than banks.

MONEY IN EASTERN EUROPE

'Hard' currency from the West helps strengthen the local stuff; as a result some countries insist on a minimum exchange requirement. This is nearly always more than is strictly necessary, and in some cases you'll have difficulty trying to get rid of it. To discourage black-market dealings, you may have to declare all your hard currency and any valuables. This declaration is normally carried out on the train at the border. If you're thinking of playing the black market you will have to 'forget' to declare some of your hard currency because if, on departure, you cannot account for the missing money or produce the required receipts, you will be in trouble.

BLACK MARKET

The freeing up of exchange mechanisms is starting to finish off the black market (as in Poland). The authorities in parts of eastern Europe still come down with a heavy hand on those caught in the act – and in some cases this means imprisonment. Hard currency is very much in demand and many private citizens are prepared to pay far more than the official rate to get it. Some people are still prepared to pay high prices for jeans, pocket calculators, etc., though this is becoming less common. In general, never have any dealings with anyone who approaches you in the street; at best, you're likely to get poor rates and, at worst, they could be plain-clothes police or an informer. A final word: tipping is not general practice here, so hang on to your cash.

MONEY TIPS:

1. Take a money belt or neck pouch.
2. Sending money abroad is expensive, so take ample with you.
3. Banks tend to offer better rates than station, hotel or 24-hour exchange bureaux. A similar rule applies to commission rates.
4. Check commission rates to see if it is a fixed amount per transaction or a percentage. Also beware of places charging commission individually on traveller's cheques. Thomas Cook cheques can be exchanged with no commission at any Thomas Cook *bureau de change.*
5. In some countries, notably in eastern Europe and Italy, ripped or damaged notes may not be taken.
6. If taking your Eurocheque guarantee card or credit card, remember your PIN number; there are many cashpoints in Western Europe where you can get cash advances.
7. If you spot travellers arriving when you are leaving a country, offer your spare currency. It is a useful way of getting rid of that

loose change and gets you small change for another country. Be discreet in countries where currency control exists.

INSURANCE

Whether or not to get insurance cover depends very much on where you're going, and for how long. If you've a lot of expensive new camping gear and photographic equipment then undoubtedly it's worth it. Shop around for the best deal; call in at your local student travel centre and see what they have to offer. STA Travel (tel. 0171 361 6161) offer a range of policies designed especially for Back-packers. Prices start at £19 for 1 months cover in Europe. 'Standard' and 'Premier' policies are also available. 'Premier' covers lost Interrail tickets. It could be you're already insured through your home policy (your parents' or your own), so check up first. Eurotrain offer a travel insurance scheme. It's worth bearing in mind that train travel is very safe and it's highly unlikely that you'll end up in hospital because of an accident, but your health and your valuables are a different matter. Still, after food poisoning in Morocco and with a doctor being called out at 2 a.m., the bill for one of us was less than the insurance premium would have been.

As mentioned earlier, some credit card companies include travel insurance if you pay for your ticket with their card.

AMERICAN AND CANADIAN TRAVELLERS If your personal policies don't provide adequate cover abroad, check with your travel agent or CIEE office to see what options are available.

POLITICS

It makes sense to find out something about the local political situation before you travel. Read the newspapers and watch TV. Once there, take advice from reliable sources – local police, consulates, airlines and other travellers. If you are planning on visiting a volatile area, let the local embassy or police know. Avoid provoking controversy. You may have strong political beliefs, but keep quiet about them, especially close to local election times, even if you seem to have a sympathetic audience. Listen and learn from other people's beliefs and dress and speak with respect for local customs and religions.

General safety rules apply – avoid ghetto areas, stick to well-lit streets and be cautious about accepting offers of help from strangers. Keep an eye out for suspicious packages and don't leave your own luggage lying around unattended. If you are confronted by criminals, terrorists or armed thugs, offer no resistance. Trying to be a hero isn't clever and may prove fatal.

LAST-MINUTE REMINDERS

1. Photocopies of all documents (passport, visas, tickets, etc.) may be useful – best packed separately or kept by a friend. A photocopy of your Inter-Rail card is a requirement for some ferries.
2. A pre-filled water bottle for long thirsty journeys. Prices of drinks on trains are high.
3. A Swiss Army knife with as many functions as possible, including corkscrew, tin and bottle opener, comes in handy. You may also want some camping cutlery and a sharp knife for cutting bread.
4. Take toilet paper, soap and a small towel.
5. Plastic bags are good for containing potentially leaky liquids or separating off dirty washing etc.
6. A torch can come in handy if you want to go to the toilet without waking everyone else in the dorm.
7. A notepad and pen. Get shopkeepers to write down prices before saying yes, if you don't know the language. That way you'll know when you're being ripped off.
8. A calculator for working out exchange rates. The cheapest one you can find will do.
9. A travelling alarm clock or a watch with an alarm is handy, especially if you have early trains to catch.
10. A small padlock and chain may be useful when hostelling (for lockers) or to secure your bag if sleeping on a train. A spare cycle chain is essential if cycling.
11. A good book or a Walkman for when you get temporarily fed up with your travelling companions and want a bit of solitude.
12. Alternatively, if you want to be sociable, how about a pack of cards or a travel chess set?
13. Ear plugs can come in handy to help you sleep.
14. A small sewing kit and safety pins: very useful for mending those burst buttons.
15. A small first-aid kit; see the health section (pp. 26–27) for suggestions.
16. Insect repellent is a very good idea if you are visiting countries like Scotland or Scandinavia.
17. A warm sweater for air-conditioned trains or breezy ferry crossings.
18. Women: Take a scarf or shawl to cover your head and shoulders, as often you'll be refused entry to churches and cathedrals if your arms and shoulders are bare. Shorts are also prohibited in many churches.
19. Photos of your family or postcards of your home town are a good ice-breaker. Let foreigners see where you're from, you could even boost home town tourism!

20. If you're taking a tent, a length of string can be useful. It can be used as a makeshift clothes line, an extra guy rope or to bundle up bits and bobs.
21. Are you carrying sufficient information – including *Cheap Sleeps Europe* (see p. 11)?

Travelling Europe by Train: Options

There are 3 basic schemes you can choose from: a BIJ/rover ticket following a set route, an Inter-Rail/Eurail pass (depending on where you live – Inter-Rail tickets may be purchased by residents of Europe, Eurail is available to non-Europeans) or an individual country's national rail pass.

Your ticket, whatever method you choose, is non-transferable and non-refundable if lost or stolen, so be sure to keep it close at hand and never let it out of your sight! Ideally, keep your ticket hidden away somewhere separate from your passport and money.

Check that your name and other details are correct before you leave the issuing agent's office. A simple mistake such as transposing 2 letters in your name could lead to your pass being confiscated by an over-zealous conductor, leaving you stranded in the middle of nowhere.

If you plan to see a lot of Europe, Inter-Rail/Eurail is the best option as it lets you take in as much as is physically possible in the allotted time. On the other hand, if you want to focus on a certain area – Greece, for example – it may work out cheaper to purchase a BIJ ticket and/or a Greek rail pass. Before handing over any money, sit down and define your objectives. Do you want to:

i)   see as many countries as possible, sampling each country a little and visiting only a few cities;
ii) head for a specific area, taking in some of the sights along the way; or
iii) concentrate on one country, touring it in depth and immersing yourself in the culture?

All 3 methods are equally enjoyable and great fun in their own may; the choice is yours.

WHAT ISN'T COVERED? Seat reservations, meals, 'fast train' supplements (such as EuroCity/InterCity and TGVs), Jetfoil and catamaran supplements (on BIJ tickets), accommodation and port taxes – on certain ferries – are extras not included in the price of your ticket.

In many cases, these 'extras' are obligatory (e.g. all Spanish expresses require a seat reservation), so check before you set foot on that train or ship. Trains marked with 'EC' or 'IC' at the top of the timetable column require a supplement (usually only £2–£5). Some long-haul ferries require you to book a berth (can be avoided by taking a shorter crossing and a connecting train).

If you plan on buying a first-class option, check first that it's going to be worth your while: many trains do not have first-class accommodation.

BIJ

The BIJ scheme (*Billet International pour Jeunes*) operates under the auspices of the continental railways and offers reduced fares to people under 26. Eurotrain is the largest company in this scheme followed by Wasteels and British Rail International, now Rail Europe. Between them these companies offer fares to over 2,000 different destinations throughout Europe, the CIS, Turkey and North Africa with discounts of up to 40%.

BIJ tickets are valid for up to 2 months (6 months for returns to Morocco and Turkey) and allow you to break your journey anywhere along your route. For example, if your final destination is Rome, you could travel out via Paris, Lyon and Turin and return via Florence, Lucerne, Luxembourg and Belgium.

In addition, there are often 7 or 8 routings to a particular city, so it's possible to go out via 1 route and return by another. The cost difference between purchasing 2 singles and a return is usually only £10 to £20, so pick the routes which take in the places you most want to see.

EUROTRAIN

Eurotrain is the leading UK operator in continental rail travel for the 'under 26' crowd and, in addition to BIJ fares, they offer several 'Circle route' tickets taking in a variety of cities. The Dutch Explorer, for example, covers London, Amsterdam and Brussels. Other Explorer passes include the Venetian, Eastern, Riviera and Spanish Explorer. The Explorer pass provides individual country rail passes for certain eastern European countries such as the Baltic States (Estonia, Latvia, Lithuania), Czech Republic, Slovakia, Hungary, Poland, Portugal and Spain.

Validity of the passes is 7 days or more, with the exception of the Spanish regional pass, which is valid for 5 days from £11. The 7-day passes start from £19 for the Czech Republic.

Explorer passes are available to under-26s, full-time students holding an ISIC, teachers or academic staff, accompanying spouse and children of eligible persons. For further information, contact their handling agents: Campus Travel, 52 Grosvenor Gardens, London SW1W 0AG (Tel. 0171 730 3402).

WASTEELS

Wasteels UK is part of the international Wasteels group, Europe's largest rail operator with over 200 local offices in 22 countries throughout Europe. Their BIJ scheme operates in the UK under the name Route-26. They act as agents for Italian Railways, offering a variety of Italian passes and travel bargains.

The Kilometric Ticket is valid for 2 months and allows up to 20 journeys (to a maximum of 3,000 kilometres) throughout Italy. One advantage of this ticket is that it can be used by up to 5 people, the mileage for each person being deducted from the total allowable. It costs £150 for first class and £88 for second.

Another option is the Italy Rail Card which covers the entire Italian network including seat reservations and supplements. Current prices are:

	8 days	15 days	21 days	30 days
1st class	£178	£224	£260	£312
2nd class	£122	£150	£176	£210

Wasteels also supply passes for other countries, sell international rail tickets and make reservations. They are agents for the German Rail Network, the Paris métro and Eurostar youth fares. Current specials for under-26s with an ISIC card from London to Paris are from £49, Amsterdam from £75 and Milan from £140. Their special 'mini-tour' tickets combine several major European cities and places of interest. For more information, contact Wasteels next to platform 2, Victoria Station, London SW1V 1JT (Tel. 0171 834 7066).

BRITISH RAIL INTERNATIONAL/RAIL EUROPE

Following SNCF's purchase of British Rail International, the latter's European ticket sales activity and SNCF's Rail Europe Ltd have merged. This has created the new and bigger Rail Europe.

As well as Inter-Rail Passes, Rail Europe sell Euro Domino tickets. These are flexible passes giving you unlimited travel for 3, 5 or 10 days in a 1-month period in up to 26 European countries, plus Morocco.

You buy a coupon for each country you wish to visit and you are free to travel on the trains of your choice. Fast train supplements (e.g. TGVs in France and Talgos in Spain) are included and you can opt for second- or first-class travel. The French ticket gives special fares on Eurostar services to Paris. At the time of going to press the 1998 prices for these tickets were unavailable so we have listed the 1997 prices here:

EURO DOMINO PRICES 1997

Country	3 days			5 days			10 days		
	1st Adult	2nd Adult	Youth	1st Adult	2nd Adult	Youth	1st Adult	2nd Adult	Youth
ADN/HML	89	69	59	89	69	59	89	69	59
Austria	139	99	79	159	109	79	279	189	149
Belgium	NA	49	39	79	59	39	149	99	79
Bulgaria	59	39	29	69	49	39	119	79	69
Croatia	49	39	29	59	49	39	109	69	59
Czech Republic	59	39	29	79	59	39	129	89	69
Denmark	99	69	49	139	89	69	179	119	89
Finland	119	79	59	159	109	79	209	139	109
France	NA	105	85	195	135	110	310	205	175
Germany	209	139	109	229	159	119	309	209	159
Greece	79	59	49	109	69	49	159	109	79
Hungary	59	39	39	89	59	49	169	109	89
Ireland	NA	49	39	NA	69	69	NA	109	99
Italy	159	119	89	199	149	109	329	239	179
Luxembourg	29	19	19	34	24	24	59	39	29
Morocco	49	29	29	59	49	49	119	89	89
Netherlands	59	39	29	89	69	49	159	109	79
Norway	NA	89	69	NA	129	99	NA	169	129
Poland	59	39	39	69	49	49	99	79	59
Portugal	149	99	79	179	129	99	269	189	139
Romania	59	39	29	79	49	39	139	89	69
Slovakia	49	29	29	59	39	39	79	59	49
Slovenia	39	29	19	59	39	29	89	59	39
Spain	119	89	69	169	139	109	299	249	199
Sweden	139	109	79	179	149	109	269	199	149
Switzerland	159	109	79	179	119	89	229	159	119
Turkey	39	29	19	59	39	29	99	69	49

ADN = Adriatica di Navigazione
HML = Hellenic Mediterranean Lines
There are ferry services between Brindisi and Patras. NB: It is cheaper to buy this pass than the normal return ticket.
Netherlands pass also includes unlimited transport on all public systems – buses, trains, trams and the metro service.

For more information contact 0990 848 848. Or find the website (http://www.britrail.com). Euro Domino Passes are also available from Wasteels. Pass holders qualify for discounts on Eurostar and P&O Ferries.

INTER-RAIL

A BRIEF HISTORY

The Inter-Rail scheme was devised in 1972 by the UIC (Union of International Railways) to commemorate 50 years of international transport law. The pass, valid for 1 month, allowed those under 26 to travel at a discount in the country of purchase, with free travel over an unlimited distance in other participating countries. By May 1991 the programme had been expanded to include a special pass (Inter-Rail 26) for those over 26, and though the year's combined youth and adult sales exceeded half a million, this phenomenal success did not please everyone.

At the end of 1992 official complaints from the French, Italian, Portuguese and Spanish rail authorities were lodged! Their trains were more packed than ever, but they were receiving far less of the proceeds than their north European counterparts, and the consequent squabbling led to a massive price hike on the youth pass and to several countries abandoning the adult scheme altogether.

And 1993 was no less turbulent: new zoned passes were introduced for the under-26s (more on this later) whilst others were deleted, and the adult pass seemed once again to be in danger of total disintegration. Trying to get over a dozen countries to agree on new prices and formats was more fraught than ever. And yet, by 1994, a greater selection of passes emerged than in the whole of Inter-Rail's history.

This year's changes are fairly radical: the various under-26 Inter-Rail passes have changed their structure and prices have actually fallen!

The Inter-Rail 26+ scheme is great for the over 26s and now runs in a similar way. It's now zoned too.

UNDER-26 PASSES

First, there is the all-Europe (26 railways) Inter-Rail for those under 26, which will sell at £259. In addition, there are now 8 zoned Inter-Rail passes. These can be bought as single or multiple zones, so that you can make up your own itinerary. They make a lot of sense for those wishing to tour part of Europe in depth and offer more flexibility than the individual country passes, Euro Domino or Euro Youth.

The 8 Inter-Rail zones are:

A. The Republic of Ireland
B. Sweden, Norway and Finland
C. Denmark, Germany, Switzerland and Austria
D. Poland, the Czech Republic, Slovakia, Hungary and Croatia
E. France, Belgium, The Netherlands and Luxembourg
F. Spain, Portugal and Morocco
G. Italy, Slovenia, Greece, Turkey and boats between Brindisi (Italy) and Patras (Greece).
H. Bulgaria, Romania, Yugoslavia, Bosnia-Hercegovina and Macedonia.

A card for a single zone is valid for 22 days and costs £159. Monthly passes for any 2 zones will be sold at the fixed price of £209, any 3 zones at £229 and all zones at £259.

All cards offer unlimited travel during their validity, but normal supplements are payable, except on lightly loaded TGV services.

Countries participating in the all-Europe Inter-Rail youth scheme are: Austria, Belgium, Bulgaria, Croatia, the Czech Republic, Denmark, Finland, France, Germany, Greece, Hungary, the Republic of Ireland, Italy, Luxembourg, Macedonia, Morocco, the Netherlands, Norway, Poland, Portugal, Romania, Slovakia, Slovenia, Spain, Sweden, Switzerland, Turkey and the new 'Yugoslavia'. Also included in the deal is the Brindisi–Patras ferry crossing.

WHO QUALIFIES? Anyone living in Europe for 6 months who is under the age of 26 on the first day the pass becomes valid. It's up to you to decide when the pass will start. If you want to travel for more than 1 month, buy 2 or more passes and get the dates to run consecutively.

BUYING AN INTER-RAIL: Inter-Rail passes can only be sold through the offices of national railway authorities or their duly appointed agents. In the UK, this means directly from British Rail International selected stations or authorized travel agents. Do not buy a pass from someone on the street as the rail authorities carry out rigorous checks; your pass may be confiscated and you could be ejected from the train. If in doubt, check with the rail authority in your country before you buy.

USING AN INTER-RAIL: You can purchase a youth Inter-Rail pass up to 2 months in advance, provided you will still be under 26 on the first day of use. Since you can't change the start date, however, it's a good idea not to purchase a ticket until your plans are finalized. Take care when choosing your start date: the pass runs from 12.01 a.m. on the first day to midnight on the preceding day of the next month, so a pass starting on 14 February will be valid until midnight on 13

March. Unfortunately, since February has only 28 days (3 years out of 4, at any rate) you get 28 days of travel rather than 31.

REDUCTIONS: An all-Europe Inter-Rail pass in the UK entitles you to discounts of 34% on trains in Britain and Northern Ireland and 50% on most Channel ferry services to the continental ports although these percentages are subject to change.

Many ferry companies offer reduced rates for Inter-Rail ticket holders. Both Sealink and P&O ferries give 30% discounts on most of their services, while B&I and Irish Continental (Rosslare–Cherbourg or Rosslare–Le Havre) offer a 50% reduction. See the individual country sections and Appendix I for further details of ferry discounts.

OVER-26 PASS

The Inter-Rail 26 pass has been extended to cover the same countries and zones as the under 26 pass. A one zone pass costs £229, two zones costs £279, three zones costs £309 and a 'global' pass covering all zones costs £349.

Countries participating in the Inter-Rail 26 scheme are: Austria, Belgium, Bulgaria, Croatia, the Czech Republic, Denmark, Finland, France, Germany, Greece, Hungary, Republic of Ireland, Italy, Luxembourg, the Netherlands, Norway, Poland, Romania, Slovakia, Slovenia, Spain, Sweden, Turkey and the new 'Yugoslavia'. It also includes the Brindisi–Patras ferry crossing.

WHO QUALIFIES? Anyone of any age holding a current passport (though presumably not under 26) who has been resident in Europe for more than 6 months on the first day that pass becomes valid.

BUYING AND USING AN INTER-RAIL 26 PASS: The rules are the same as for the youth pass. Don't be tempted by cheap imitations because they are bound to be duds; don't book too far ahead as start dates once confirmed cannot be altered; do treat your pass with great care – stolen, lost or disfigured passes will not be replaced.

REDUCTIONS: Passes bought in the non-participating countries (such as Belgium, France and the UK) may allow for discounted returns to the frontiers of countries that are covered by the pass. For instance, in the UK, discounted rail and ferry passage from London to Hoek van Holland or Scandinavia with Stena Line or Scandinavian Seaways, or cheap fares across Belgium are available. But for full details check the Guidance Notes on the back of the pass or ask a rail agent for some help.

EURAIL

A BRIEF HISTORY

Eurail came into existence because Europe had a new and expensive network of intercity trains that needed riders. Its purpose was to entice potential passengers from the other side of the Atlantic by offering 2 months of second-class travel on any or all of the member rail systems. The first pass was issued in 1959 and 5,000 tickets were sold that year. Subsequently the range of passes on offer was expanded to include 1- and 3-month passes, 15-day passes, first-class travel, and such fringe benefits as free access to many ferry and steamer connections and free or discounted bus transportation. In 1966 a 21-day pass was introduced to complement air excursion fares. The Eurail Youthpass, aimed at those under the age of 26, was such a success that Europe developed its own youthpass system, Inter-Rail, followed closely by the country passes.

WHO QUALIFIES? The Eurail Passes are available to anyone who resides outside Europe and North Africa or has arrived in Europe no more than 6 months ago. The Eurail Pass is not valid in Great Britain and Northern Ireland or on cross-Channel ferries.

PASSES AVAILABLE The Eurail Youth Flexipass is open to anyone under 26 and gives unlimited second-class travel in 17 countries and allows either 10 or 15 days of travel in a 2-month period. The Eurail Youth Consecutive Pass is also available to under 26s and is valid for 15 days, 21 days, 1, 2 or 3 months.

The Eurail Pass has no age restriction and comes in first-class only; again 15-day, 21-day, 1-, 2- and 3-month Eurail Passes are available. The Eurail Flexipass is a first-class version of the Youth Flexipass, without the age restriction, and allows 10 or 15 days of travel in a 2-month period.

The Eurail Saver Pass is a first-class pass for 2 or more persons each holding a Saver Pass travelling together between 1 October and 31 March. For the rest of the year 3 people must travel together; it works out about 15% cheaper than a regular Eurail Pass.

The 1998 prices for Eurail passes are:

	Eurail Pass	Saver Pass	Eurail Youthpass
15 days	$538	$458	$376
21 days	$698	$594	$489
1 month	$864	$734	$605
2 months	$1224	$1040	$857
3 months	$1512	$1286	$1059
	Eurail Flexipass	Eurail Saver Flexipass	Eurail Youth Flexipass
10 days in 2 months	$634	$540	$444
15 days in 2 months	$836	$710	$585

If you were unable to purchase your pass before leaving home, it is possible to buy one in Europe from the French Railways office (SNCF) in London, or from any Eurail Aid office in any participating country, but you must do so within 6 months of your arrival. Passes purchased in Europe cost 20% more than those purchased outside. The countries currently participating in the Eurail scheme are: Austria, Belgium, Denmark, Eire, Finland, France, Germany, Greece, Hungary, Italy, Luxembourg, the Netherlands, Norway, Portugal, Spain, Sweden and Switzerland. This is not as wide-ranging as the Inter-Rail card, but many of the countries not covered by the Eurail scheme are in eastern Europe and have their own passes, which can be very cheap.

FREE TRAVEL UNDER THE EURAIL SCHEME: Reductions on some of Europe's private railways are also included (many of these are Swiss mountain railways). Children aged between 4 and 11 benefit from a 50% reduction on first-class passes only. Children under 4 travel free.

REFUNDS: Refunds are subject to a 15% surcharge. You can only get a refund from the office at which you bought your pass.

CAR RENTAL: Eurail Drive and European Drive combine rail travel and car rental. Eurail Drive starts at $350 per person for 2 people – 4 rail days and 3 car days. European Drive starts at $265 per person for 2 people – 3 rail days and 2 car days.

Other Eurail options:

THE EUROPASS

The Europass makes sense for those wishing to make an in-depth tour of a few European countries, rather than a whistle-stop tour of all 17. The 5 main countries in the scheme are France, Germany,

Italy, Spain and Switzerland. You can travel on any 5 days in a 2-month period, visiting any or all of these countries. On payment of a specified supplement, the reach of the pass can be extended to include any or all of the associate zones, Austria/Hungary, Belgium/Luxembourg/the Netherlands, Portugal and Greece. On payment of a further supplement additional travel days (up to 10) can be added.

Europass – 1st class

	2 Adults*	Adult
Any 5 days in 2 months	US$261	US$326
with 1 associate country	US$309	US$386
with 2 associate countries	US$333	US$416
with 3 associate countries	US$349	US$436
with 4 associate countries	US$357	US$446
Additional rail day	US$33.50	US$42

*Prices per person based on 2 people travelling together, i.e. 40% partner discount.

Europass Youth – (under 26) 2nd class

Any 5 days in 2 months	US$216
with 1 associate country	US$261
with 2 associate countries	US$286
with 3 associate countries	US$301
with 4 associate countries	US$309
Additional rail day	US$29

COUNTRY PASSES

Many countries offer passes giving you the freedom of their rail network. The obvious disadvantage is that it can cost more to get to the country in question than to purchase an Inter-Rail card. One option is to buy a BIJ ticket to the first city inside the border of your target country and then use the country's rail pass to get around. Another is to combine a country pass with a cheap flight (see p.18). Another drawback is that most country passes do not cover buses and ferries, whereas BIJ tickets include ferry crossings and Inter-Rail offers reductions on both.

If you really want to explore a country in depth, however, this is an excellent way to do so.

Most country passes offer a more flexible timescale (with tickets valid from 4 days to 1 month) and are usually open to anyone, not just those under 26. Some passes are excellent value, but others aren't worth the money – it all depends on your currency's staying power against the country in question and what you want to do. Before committing yourself, find out how extensive the rail network is, how useful the pass will be to you, and what it will cost to get to that country.

BRITRAIL PASS

Since Great Britain is not covered in the Eurail or Inter-Rail scheme, if you are from North America your best option is to purchase a BritRail Pass. This is valid for unlimited travel throughout Great Britain (England, Scotland and Wales), with the notable exception of the London Underground.

Prices for 1998 BritRail Classic Pass (consecutive days travel) are:

	Under 26 2nd (only)	Adult		Senior (60+) 2nd (only)
		2nd	1st	
8 days	US$205	US$259	US$375	US$319
15 days	US$318	US$395	US$575	US$489
22 days	US$410	US$510	US$740	US$630
1 month	US$475	US$590	US$860	US$730

The BritRail Flexipass allows travel on a certain number of days within a set period. Prices for 1998 are:

	Under 26 2nd (only)	Adult		Senior (60+) 1st (only)
		2nd	1st	
4 days in 1 month	US$175	US$219	US$315	US$269
8 days in 1 month	US$253	US$315	US$459	US$390
15 days in 1 month	n/a	US$480	US$698	US$590
15 days in 2 months	US$385	n/a	n/a	n/a

When 3 or more adults travel together using a BritRail Flexi or Classic Pass, a fourth adult can travel at half price.

Also the Just For Families scheme allows anyone buying one adult or Senior Pass to take one accompanying child (5–15).

If you wish to explore the area around London, the London Visitors Travel Card offers unlimited travel within London on London Transport. There are also a number of regional rover passes that can be purchased within the UK. Passes are available for Scotland, Ireland and the South East. '(See the UK section for further details.)

London Visitors Travel Card

	Adults	Child
3 days	US$29	US$12
4 days	US$39	US$15
7 days	US$59	US$22

BritRail passes can only be purchased in North America, where they are available from most reputable travel agents or direct from BritRail Travel International at 500 Mamaroneck Harrison, New York NY 10528.

CARTE 12-25
This is France's under-26 discount railcard. It is available to anyone aged between 12 and 25 and costs £28. It offers up to 50% reduction on off-peak (blue) and ordinary (white) trains, 50% on TGV's (subject to availability) and 25% at all other times.

POLRAIL PASS
Valid on Polish Railways trains, including express services and trains where reservations are obligatory, the pass entitles the holder to a free seat reservation, which can be booked at your departure station, at any rail booking office, or on the train. In the UK you can get it at Wasteels. Current prices are:

Days	Adult		Youth (Under 26)	
	1st	2nd	1st	2nd
8 days	£61	£42	£44	£29
15 days	£71	£49	£50	£34
21 days	£84	£55	£58	£39
1 month	£103	£71	£71	£50

SCANRAIL PASS
The ScanRail Pass allows you 1 month's unlimited travel throughout the rail networks of Denmark, Finland, Norway and Sweden.

Several ferry crossings are included (many others offer 50% reduction) as well as some free bus runs and free travel on Copenhagen's local rail services. For a complete breakdown see the Norway section or contact Wasteels. Current prices are:

	Under 26		Adult	
	2nd	1st	2nd	1st
ScanRail Flexi				
5 days in 15	£99	£120	£132	£160
10 days in 1 month	£135	£165	£180	£220
ScanRail				
21 days consecutive	£149	£198	£198	£264
1 month consecutive	£195	£243	£260	£324

SPECIAL TRAINS

If you have the opportunity, there are some trains which are a delight to travel. All are accessible with a first-class rail pass, though the majority have both first- and second-class carriages and are therefore available to Inter-Rail, Eurail Youthpass and BIJ ticket holders (though there may be a supplement). A complete list of these trains is contained in the *Thomas Cook European Rail Timetable*, but our particular favourites are as follows:

TRAIN NAME	CITIES
BLAUER ENZIAN	Dortmund–Cologne–Stuttgart–Munich–Salzburg–Klagenfurt
CATALAN TALGO	Barcelona–Port Bou–Avignon–Geneva
CISALPIN	Paris–Lausanne–Brig–Milan
COLOSSEUM	Basle–Lucerne–Milan–Florence–Rome
ÉTOILE DU NORD	Paris–Brussels–Amsterdam
FRANZ HALS	Amsterdam–Munich
L'ARBALETE	Zürich–Paris
LIGURE	Marseille–Nice–Genoa–Milan
MERKUR	Copenhagen–Frankfurt
MONTEVERDI	Basle–Berne–Brig–Milan–Venice
NORDPILEN	Stockholm–Boden–Kiruna–Narvik
PERNILLE EXPRESS	Oslo–Bergen
REMBRANDT	Amsterdam–Cologne–Basle–Zürich–Chur
ROMULUS	Vienna–Klagenfurt–Venice–Florence–Rome
TRANSALPIN	Basle–Zürich–Innsbruck–Salzburg–Vienna

OTHER SERVICES

YOUTH HOSTEL ASSOCIATION: The Youth Hostel Association offers a variety of excellent value packages based on combined rail travel and YHA accommodation. The scheme currently operates in 15 different countries including Iceland, Israel, Japan, Australia and New Zealand. For further information write to YHA Travel, Trevelyan House, 8 St. Stephen's Hill, St. Albans, Herts. AL1 2DY (Tel. 01727 855215).

THE EURORAILERS CLUB: Based in Sweden, the club's *raison d'être* is to provide a network of contacts to enable eurorailers over the age of 26 and no longer eligible for Inter-Rail to find out about the various passes available to them. Its Swedish members are also helpful to travellers of Europe by train visiting Sweden. Monthly meetings take place in Stockholm, but postal membership is possible for £5 a year. For more information write to Club 26, Nybrogatan 51, 11440 Stockholm, Sweden.

ODYSSEY TRAVEL CLUB: This UK-based organization was started in 1987 to act as an introduction service between fellow adventurers. The main purpose is to match up people who are interested in taking similar trips, whether a day-trip from London or a round-the-world tour. Their advice line helps with visa information, vaccinations, and general information on foreign destinations.

Information for this service is provided by members who have returned from trips of their own. A year's membership costs around £25. Contact Odyssey Travel Club, 21 Cambridge Road, Waterbeach, Cambridge, CB5 9NJ, England (Tel. 01223 861079) for further information.

SENIOR CARDS: The British Senior Railcard gives a 30% discount on UK fares to those over 60. The Rail Europe Senior Pass, combined with a senior card from another country, will entitle the bearer to 30–50% discounts on first- and second-class cross-border travel between any of the following: Austria, Belgium, Croatia, the Czech Republic, Denmark, Finland, France, Germany, Greece, Hungary, Ireland, Italy, Luxembourg, the Netherlands, Norway, Portugal, Slovakia, Slovenia, Spain, Sweden, Switzerland (most lines) and the UK. Information on further discounts can be obtained through Thomas Cook Travel offices or Rail Europe (Tel. 0990 300 003).

Train Information

NIGHT TRAVEL

Travelling at night has distinct advantages for the eurorailer who doesn't mind missing the scenery of a particular area or the fact that night trains invariably take longer to get to their destinations. The advantage of night travel is that in effect you save money on accommodation and at the same time add an extra day to your stay by arriving in the morning, ready to start your tour. Of course, how you spend the night and the consequent amount of sleep you manage to get depends largely on which of the sleeping arrangements you opt for (and how good a sleeper you are). Basically there are 4 ways of travelling at night:

1. **Sit up all night** in a seat. It's free, but not guaranteed to find you fresh enough for a full day's sightseeing the next day. In this case, a neck air cushion is a good idea, but be careful as guards often get upset if they see your footwear on the seats.

2. **Pull-down seats.** These are great when you can find them, as they're free yet still allow you to stretch out, thus increasing the chances of sleep. Once all 6 seats are pulled down, they join together to form a massive bed. How much room you end up with depends on how full the compartment was originally; if there are only 2 or 3 of you in the compartment, you're home for a good night's free sleep. Reserve one if you can.

3. **Couchettes.** This is a seat by daytime, which at night is converted into a proper full berth. There are six to a compartment in second class and four in first class. There is no sex segregation (see p. 74) as the couchettes are nearly always full. For your £9–12 ($14–18) (average cost, but see under individual countries) you get a sheet, blanket and pillow, and there's a bed-light. You can use the washroom next to the toilets for washing. Each couchette has a luggage rack, but it's always wise to take your valuables to bed with you. Standards of couchettes vary enormously as they're run by the individual national rail networks, so that in Germany they're very good, while in Spain and Italy they could be better. Reservations for couchettes are more or less essential in the summer. You are required to book at least five hours before the train leaves the station.

4. **Cabines.** French Railways operate Cabine 8, a compartment (in new air-conditioned coaches) with 8 semi-reclined bunks enabling you to stretch out in your own sleeping bag. They are completely free, but as they are very popular you will find it worthwhile reserving ahead.

5. **Sleepers.** Sleeping cars are a great step up in comfort from couchettes, but they're also a lot more expensive. As in Britain, European sleepers come in 2 classes and offer: a proper bed with all the trimmings, a sink with soap, towels and warm water, an electrical outlet and occasionally your own WC.

Sleepers are operated either by the Wagons-Lits Company (an international concern) or by a subsidiary of the railway. Many of these are developing into combined groups, collectively calling themselves Trans Euro Nuit/Nacht/Notte. The Scandinavian and East European countries operate their own sleepers. The average 2- or 3-berth sleeper is £20–40 ($36–72) a person, but price is dependent on the distance you're covering.

Very often, your train gets into the station an hour before departure; if you've had a hard day, this is good to know as you can get yourself bedded down earlier. If you take the train right through to its final destination, you can often lie in for another half-hour or so in the morning, once it arrives, before getting ousted. If the train is packed, it might be worth asking the guard for permission to sleep in first-class.

If you're reserving a couchette or sleeper, try for the top berths as they're roomier, there's more air and they afford you a slightly greater degree of privacy. Watch out when the train enters for the yellow stripe along the outside of the carriage, just below roof level; this indicates first-class.

If you're going by sleeper or couchette on an international trip (or even for some internal ones in Italy), the attendant will take your passport, visa and ticket from you so that, in theory anyway, you won't need to be woken up at the border in the middle of the night. Don't worry, they will be returned the next morning.

Once you're all in, lock the door and hope you've not landed yourself – as I have so often in the past – with a collection of snorers! When you get into the couchette check for ticketless passengers hiding in the compartment (under the bunks).

The best trains for a good night's sleep are those that don't cross international borders (difficult to avoid) or stop every couple of hours at stations *en route*, otherwise you'll have customs officials coming in for a nose-around at 3 a.m., or train announcements blaring out all night long (you can bet it'll be your carriage that stops right beneath the loudspeaker). My advice to insomniacs is to have a heavy meal before the journey, take some ear plugs, and don't hold back on the local vino.

WARNING: A few years ago, many travellers on Italian and Spanish trains accepted the 'hospitality' of their fellow travellers in the form of doped orange juice and other drinks, and woke up many hours later to find they had been robbed. Some copycat incidents occurred, but following arrests, this worrying trend seems to be over (but be warned). Thieves have also been known to use a knock-out spray, sprayed through compartment vents, to steal belongings, though such incidents are very rare.

Most night trains do not have a bar or eating facilities on board so if you're the type of person who enjoys a midnight feast or gets thirsty in the night, you had better bring your own supplies along or you'll wake up with an empty stomach and a throat like a vacuum cleaner.

MAIN NIGHT TRAINS
Below is a list of just some of the many good night trains in Europe. Remember you can save money by sleeping on these night trains and cover more ground during your vacation.

Amsterdam–Copenhagen
Amsterdam–Munich
Barcelona–Geneva
Barcelona–Madrid
Barcelona–Nice
Barcelona–Paris
Barcelona–Pamplona
Basle–Hamburg
Belgrade–Thessaloniki
Brussels–Genoa
Brussels–Munich
Copenhagen–Hamburg
Hamburg–Munich
Heidelberg–Lugano
London–Edinburgh
Madrid–Algeciras
Madrid–Lisbon
Madrid–Santander
Malmö–Stockholm
Milan–Paris
Nice–Geneva
Ostend–Munich
Paris–Amsterdam
Paris–Copenhagen
Paris–Munich
Paris–Nice
Rome–Nice
Vienna–Cologne
Vienna–Frankfurt
Vienna–Lindau
Vienna–Venice

Don't forget it is often preferable to sleep in a good compartment than in a crowded youth hostel. Try pretending you're sound asleep when the train pulls in to stations and you'll raise the chances of being left undisturbed.

EATING

Few travellers of Europe by train can afford to indulge in buffet or restaurant meals on the trains because they're never cheap. The majority of the dining services offered on European trains are run by the Wagons-Lits Company. The quality of the food and service varies from country to country though, as it really depends on the staff and hygiene of the host country. Don't be fooled by the mobile minibars that wheel temptingly past you – they are extremely expensive, with coffee costing anything from £1. On top of that the food and drink is of very poor quality. Stock up with food from a supermarket before you leave and treat yourself to a good picnic on the train.

As a general rule all Eurocity and most Intercity and long-distance express trains have a separate dining car with set-price meals from £5–15 ($9–27) or a bar/buffet car serving drinks, sandwiches and light snacks. It's a very satisfying experience having a leisurely meal along one of the scenic routes even if you can only afford it once. Remember: You can't drink the water from the train washrooms anywhere in Europe; buy your drink before you get aboard.

TRAIN SPLITTING

Trains in Europe undertake some pretty complicated routes and use one another's rolling stock. Consequently, trains on long international journeys often split into various sections at certain points, so it's obviously important to check that you get on the relevant part of the train. The best policy is to ask and make sure you're on the right segment before you settle down. If your coach is going to be shunted about on to another train, find out at which station it's due to happen and at what time. It's all made quite easy by the signs posted on the doors and windows at intervals along the train, e.g.:

PARIS	CALAIS	MILANO
(Nord)	VENEZIA	(Centrale)

This shows that the coach starts at Calais, stops at Paris (Nord) and Milan (Centrale) and terminates in Venice. There will also be a '1' or '2' to tell you the class of the carriage; and often a symbol indicating smoking or non-smoking. Whatever happens, don't get out of a train which is due to split up, and then get back on another car with the intention of walking along to your seat – you could find you're no longer connected to that bit of the train! Just in case you do get separated from your fellow travellers, carry your own money, ticket and passport at all times. This advice is also relevant in case one of you gets mugged – that way you won't lose everything at once.

In some stations, mainly terminals, you'll find the train reversing and going back in the direction you've just come. This is often the case in Switzerland. Don't worry about it, as it's just a standard shunting procedure. This often takes place on the last stop before, or the first after, an international frontier, and is used to reduce the number of carriages or add on extra ones. If you have any doubts, ask the ticket inspector as soon as you are on board.

SUPPLEMENTS

An Inter-Rail or BIJ ticket alone is not sufficient to travel on many of the express trains, or the EuroCity services. If you want to use these trains, you'll have to pay a supplement, which is calculated on the distance you're travelling and the type of express you've chosen (unless you have a regular Eurail). Some countries, notably the Scandinavian ones, do not charge supplements as such, but make seat reservations compulsory on expresses. (Full details are found under the individual country chapters.)

It's often worth inquiring how much the additional first-class supplement is, particularly if you're feeling under the weather and the train's packed. (As a survivor of the Spanish olive oil epidemic of '81 trying to get home, I can vouch for it!)

TIMETABLES

One of the best timetables is *Thomas Cook's European Timetable*. This is published on the first day of each month. The June to September issues have a full summer schedule and there are summer service forecasts from February to May. The full winter schedule appears in the October to May issues, with forecasts in August and September. Although it seems expensive, the timetable is worth its weight in gold and can save you hours of queueing (particularly at Italian stations). It also has a table of airport city centre links.

The timetable is available from all Thomas Cook travel agents (price £8.40) or direct from Thomas Cook Publishing (Tel. 01733 505821, price £9.80, including UK postage and packing).

Also worth thinking about is their *Rail Map of Europe* which costs £4.95 (or £5.70 by post), published biennially. Write to Thomas Cook Publishing Office, PO Box 227, Thorpe Wood, Peterborough, PE3 6PU. Back issues are available at half price, but be sure to ask for one with the appropriate summer or winter schedules.

Another good idea is Thomas Cook's excellent *Guide to Greek Island Hopping*. The latest edition is more comprehensive (and longer) than ever, and costs £12.95 (or £14.70 by post).

The best value is the free UIC international timetable on ABC lines, though copies are like gold in most travel agents'. Also good to have is the Eurail timetable free from any Eurail issuing office.

If you want the more detailed national timetable and rail map for a particular country (often hard to find), contact the SBB Timetable Shop, Office 224, Hauptbahnhof, CH-9001 St Gallen, Switzerland, which runs a mail order service, though check first with Thomas Cook Publishing, by sending them a self-addressed envelope and asking for their list.

Bear in mind the change from winter to summer schedules: all European rail networks start their summer schedules on the last Sunday in May and the winter schedules on the last Sunday in September, except in Britain. Also check the time zone the country's in and keep an eye out for local and national holidays.

INTERNATIONAL TIMETABLE SYMBOLS:

R	Reservations compulsory
⎰	Trains running on certain days only
1,2	1st/2nd class
∟	Couchette
◆	Trains subject to special regulations stated in the information notes of the relevant timetable
🛏	Sleeping car
✗	Restaurant car
🍴	Buffet/Cafeteria
⊞	Frontier border station; customs and passport checks
⎐	Drinks service and snacks
✗	Except Sundays and public holidays

①,② Mondays, Tuesdays, etc.

🚌 Connection by bus

🚢 Connection by boat

PUBLIC HOLIDAYS AFFECTING TRAINS

At public holiday times, you'll find services are amended, and those trains that are operating will be busier than usual and with more reservations. Check with stations for details and turn up earlier for the train. We list all the relevant holidays under the individual country chapters. In many countries the day, or at least the half-day, preceding an official public holiday is also regarded as a holiday. We give below a calendar of moving holidays for 1998:

Shrove Tuesday	24 February
Ash Wednesday	25 February
Good Friday	10 April
Easter Day	12 April
Ascension Day	21 May
Whit Monday	24 May

MUSLIM HOLIDAYS:

Ramadan begins	11 January
Id-ul-Fitr	10 February
Id-ul-Adha	18 April
New Year (1417)	8 May

HAZARDS

On those long hot runs in southern Europe, where temperatures are high and trains aren't air-conditioned, the temptation is to stick your head out of the window to cool off. Be warned: you may cool off more than you anticipated. When you feel that unexpected drop of rain upon your face, you may fear the worst... someone's been to the loo further up. Moreover, don't be reassured by the notices announcing that it's illegal to throw rubbish out of the window. Expect anything, and be on your guard, especially for cans and bottles. Most importantly of all, always be on your guard for open or unsecured doors; even the safety-conscious DB (Deutsche Bundesbahn) estimates that nearly 225 people were killed in 5 years by falling from trains.

Always carry your valuables with you when you go to the loo and be extra careful on night trains, as this is where most theft occurs. Often a small padlock securing your bag to a fixed point is enough to deter a thief. The importance of keeping your passport on you at all times cannot be stressed enough. Obtaining an emergency passport involves considerable red tape and can restrict the options on your journey.

TRAINS IN EASTERN EUROPE

Train travel in eastern Europe has improved immeasurably since the overthrow of the various communist regimes. Increasingly, the eastern European stations are being re-modelled on Western lines, but don't expect comparable standards yet awhile. The station facilities are basic, so don't expect luxuries like showers or permanently staffed Tourist Information booths. To avoid unbelievable anxiety and frustration while travelling in eastern Europe, it's useful to remember the following:

1. Tickets are often only valid for the specific date and class stated on your ticket. To change your date is more trouble than it's worth, so always be sure of the exact date and time you wish to leave before buying your ticket or making a reservation.
2. Queueing is a fact of life, so try to buy tickets and make reservations at odd hours: one of the best times is late at night, since queues begin long before offices open in the morning. Whenever possible, try to buy your ticket/make your reservation from western Europe at the appropriate student office.
3. For all international journeys, tickets and reservations are often obtained through the official government travel agents (listed under each country). Otherwise use the train stations where queues are slightly shorter.
4. Make sure you're in the right queue. There's often one queue for journeys over 100 kilometres, another for reservations, etc. These are not immediately obvious as often there are no signs and it's quite possible to stand for up to an hour in the wrong line.
5. When you reach the front of the queue try and get everything possible done in one go, so you don't have to queue again later: buy your ticket, make your reservation, ask what platform the train leaves from, etc. Write it all down first, in case the assistant doesn't speak English.
6. Try to view the whole exercise as an initiative test, and always be prepared for any eventuality. It's not uncommon to discover that all second-class seats are fully booked so, unless you fancy another

hour's wait at the end of the queue, it's best to have considered alternative trains or routes and whether you are prepared to pay the extra. Compared to the West, you'll find that train fares are cheaper, but this is changing. It is often worth the extra cost to go first class for the added comfort, space and – sometimes – cleanliness.

TRAIN AND BIKE TRAVEL

Those wishing to combine a cycling and train holiday will find the situation very different in the various countries. In some it is easy to arrange transport for your bike with you, in others almost impossible. Many railway systems publish leaflets giving details of trains on which cycles can be accommodated, with costs where relevant. You can take your bike free on Sealink Stena Ferries to France and Northern Ireland. For routes to Eire, Holland and on Hoverspeed services, there is a charge. In some countries it is possible to hire bikes.

For advice and details contact the Cyclists' Touring Club, Cotterell House, 69 Meadrow, Godalming, Surrey, GU7 3HS (Tel. 01483 417217). They publish loads of information including very useful Country Information Sheets and also have many other services, including cycle insurance – but you must be a member to benefit. If you take your cycling seriously it's a bargain at £25, half price for students.

Station Information

The average station in a major European city will have most of the following facilities:

1. **Ticket desk:** At large stations, tickets for domestic and international trains are usually purchased at different windows, so make sure you're in the right line.
2. **Information office:** Marked with a blue letter 'i'; you can find out times and availability of trains here. If the office is packed, check outside for posted timetables. There are normally separate posters for arrivals (white background) and departures (yellow background) with all fast trains listed in red. Each listing will show the arrival/departure time (in 24-hour format), the train number, name, routing information (point of origin, final destination and important stops) and the track or platform number. In addition, major stations often have computerized information boards showing the arriving and departing trains

for the next few hours. Each platform will also have a 'train composition board' showing where each car goes and the class of service it contains.

3. **Left luggage:** Big stations will have a manned depot (usually open from around 5 a.m. to midnight) and/or automatic lockers. Check that the depot will be open when your train is due to leave and if not, use a locker. Before you put any money in the slot, make sure that your bag fits into the locker.

4. **Lost property office:** Usually open from 9 a.m. to 5 p.m. on Mondays to Fridays only. If it's an emergency (e.g. you've lost your rucksack or passport), go to the station master's office.

5. **Station master's office:** In theory this official is in charge of the trains, not the passengers. However, since the station master runs the station, this is your best bet in an emergency.

6. **Telephones and post-boxes:** Most stations are equipped with these, and major terminals will have international telephone booths and post offices operating in them. In the smaller ones, stamps can usually be bought from machines or newsagents, and international calls placed through the local operator.

7. **Shops and newsagents.**

8. **First aid offices:** Most stations have some sort of first aid station. For those that don't, find the station master's office where they should have a first aid kit at least. In Germany and France, there are special travellers' aid offices called Bahnhofsmission and Bureau d'accueil where multilingual staff will help you if you're ill, lost or generally in distress.

9. **Toilets:** These will vary dramatically in cleanliness and are not always free of charge.

10. **Waiting rooms:** As with toilets, they vary in cleanliness but are obviously useful to eurorailers. Many close at night, so don't count on sleeping there, though the ones in city terminals are often open 24 hours.

11. **Baths and showers:** Most large stations have these facilities and you can often buy or rent towels, soap and shampoo. The cost is usually around £2 ($3) for a bath or £1.50 ($2.25) for a shower.

12. **Bureau de change:** Unless you are really desperate, these are a bad idea as their exchange rates are usually extortionate! You are better off looking for a cash machine (which most major stations have) and taking money off your credit card.

13. **Tourist Information office:** These offices frequently hand out free maps and guides of the local area and, for a small charge of £1 to £2 ($1.50 to $3), will book accommodation for you somewhere.

If there are any outstanding features to a particular station (like a good, cheap snack bar), they will be listed under the 'Station Facilities' section of the particular city.

PICTOGRAMS

The majority of stations are clearly signposted with universal pictograms which overcome the language barrier. Most are extremely straightforward; however, there are some which may cause confusion:

Meeting Point

Lost and Found

Luggage and baggage storage pictograms can even catch old hands in the wrong line. For example, the signs for self-service luggage-carts and the porter are very similar:

Self-Service Luggage-Cart

Call for Porter

In some stations, you will have enough trouble fighting the porters off without going looking for them, especially in Morocco!

Confusion can also occur between the luggage registration office (for sending luggage through to your next destination) and the left-luggage or baggage check room:

Luggage Registration Office

Baggage Check Room

At both of these offices, you will receive a ticket which must be presented when you pick up your luggage. Make sure that you get one before you leave since it can be almost impossible to retrieve your bag without it.

Automatic lockers may be marked by either a pictogram:

Locker

or a written sign similar to the following:

CONSIGNE DES BAGGAGES (French)
GEPÄCKAUFBEWAHRUNG (German)
CONSIGNA DE EQUIPAJES (Spanish)
DEPOSITO BAGAGLIO (Italian)

RESERVATIONS

Unless you don't mind slouching in the corridor for hours on end, a seat reservation is common sense during the summer months. On many services, reservations are compulsory (marked with an 'R' on the timetable) and you could face a fine for boarding a train without one. For the equivalent of £2 to £3 ($3 to $4.50), a seat reservation is worth the effort.

When making a reservation, be sure to tell the clerk exactly what you want. More often than not they won't ask you, so make your wishes clearly known when booking (e.g. if you do not specify non-smoking it will usually be presumed you are a smoker). Try writing down all the details before getting to the counter, bearing in mind:

1. Class: Make sure you do not end up in first class unintentionally.
2. Smoking/non-smoking.
3. Which side of the train: This can make a big difference, for example if you wind up on the north side for a Riviera journey you will miss all the views.
4. Facing backwards or forwards: Some people prefer to be looking either in the direction of travel or away from it.
5. Aisle or window seat: Window seats often have pull-out tables which can be handy for eating or writing, whereas the aisle seats afford more leg room.

If you choose not to reserve a seat (or for some reason cannot), check at the information office how busy the train will be. In many western European countries, you can make reservations up to 2 months in advance, while sometimes in eastern Europe you cannot make a reservation until the day of departure. In the latter case, get to the station as soon as the ticket office opens. Requirements regarding reservations are covered in the individual country chapters later on.

When making a reservation, try to get to the office between 9 and 11 a.m. or 3 and 5 p.m. during the week. You would be amazed at how many people show up at lunch time on a weekday when all the locals are out in force trying to make their own reservations for the weekend.

If you find yourself on a train without a reserved seat, quickly shoot down the corridors looking for spaces on the reservation boards outside each compartment or on the seats themselves. If this fails, find the conductor or a guard as soon as possible and check to see if any more carriages are being added or if any reservations have been cancelled or unused.

SOME HELPFUL TIPS

Always check the name of the station you're dealing with if a city has more than one. Don't assume that a northbound train will leave from the northern station; it doesn't always follow. The following list shows cities with more than one station. A * indicates that a station other than the main one is used for connecting ferry services.

ANTWERP	COMO	LIÈGE	PORTSMOUTH
ATHENS	DOVER	LISBON	PRAGUE
BARCELONA	DUBLIN	LONDON	ROME
BASLE	ESSEN	LYON	ROTTERDAM
BELFAST	EXETER	MADRID	SAN SEBASTIÁN
BELGRADE	FOLKESTONE	MALMÖ	SEVILLE
BERLIN	GENEVA	MANCHESTER	STOCKHOLM
BILBAO	GLASGOW	MARSEILLE	TILBURY
BOULOGNE*	HAMBURG	MILAN	TOURS
BRUSSELS	HARWICH*	MUNICH	TURIN
BUCHAREST	HELSINGBORG*	NAPLES	VENICE
BUDAPEST	HENDAYE	NEWHAVEN*	VIENNA
CALAIS*	IRÚN	OPORTO	WARSAW
CASABLANCA*	ISTANBUL	PARIS	ZÜRICH

The city-centre maps on the reverse side of the *Thomas Cook European Rail Map* indicate which cities have more than one mainline station. Also, bear in mind that the distances between stations in these cities can be quite substantial (in London, for example, Paddington and Liverpool Street stations are about 8 km apart; in Paris the Gare de Lyon and Gare St Lazare are about 6.5 km apart). The moral is: don't count on split-second connections, especially between stations.

When You're There

ACCOMMODATION

As accommodation is the largest potential headache for eurorailers and I'm limited for space, I'm restricting suggestions to the main tourist centres. If you plan to travel off the beaten track or arrive late in peak season, I strongly recommend you buy my *Cheap Sleeps Europe 1998* (Ebury Press). For the price of a tourist board booking, it will save you a lot of time, trouble and money in the end. It is the only publication out to contain hundreds of recommendations in all categories with everything from where to sleep rough in safety to cost of B&Bs. Remember those travelling in July and August will end up paying more for accommodation, as prices often go up with demand.

My suggestions tend to be biased towards hostels and to places located near stations. There are basically 4 types of accommodation open to you: cheap hotels; youth or student hostels; camping and private accommodation. Theoretically, there is a fifth option – and it will certainly ensure you get round Europe at a phenomenal rate – to sleep on the trains, not just in couchettes or sleepers which vary in price from £5 to £40 ($8–64) for a night's sleep, but for free in the seats. As we've discussed night travel already and I don't really recommend you spend your trip doing this, we'll concentrate on the others.

CHEAP HOTELS/PENSIONS

If you're travelling with your girlfriend/boyfriend or husband/wife, don't fancy camping and can't get into private accommodation, this is your only real alternative if you want to spend the night together. The advantages are obvious: relative comfort and convenience. If you're in a city and you haven't long to be there, it's best to try for one located near the centre, to save on bus journeys and hassles.

The disadvantages are: it's more expensive, and if you're in a really cheap hotel, you often find a sort of 'skid row' atmosphere. The hotels I list under each country are the best compromise I could find between clean, pleasant surroundings and a fair price.

If there are 2 or more of you, it's a good idea for 1 person to wait in the Tourist Office queue with all the luggage, while the other goes looking for a room. You invariably find hotels close to the stations, the rooms in these places are generally cheap and, of course, very convenient. If you all want to go off to hunt together, leave your heavy packs in left luggage. You won't regret the £1 ($1.50) or so you spend for the extra comfort and speed you'll get out of it.

Once you've found a suitable place and have been told the price, ask the receptionist again if she has nothing cheaper. Often this works and you get a cheaper room tucked away near the top. The luxury of taking a room with a private bath or shower is bought at a high price, so you do best to use the communal one. Always ask how much a bath or shower costs. If you're travelling in a group it can be cheaper to have a room with a bath than to pay for 4 showers. In the vast majority of cheap hotels it's not included in the price, and it can come as a nasty shock when you get the bill.

Unfortunately the British institution of B&B is rare in Europe. Breakfast is often extra and rarely does it merit the name or the cost. Anyway, it's far cheaper and more entertaining to find a coffee bar or café: where the locals go.

Pensions (guest houses) are often far more attractive and friendly than hotels. A double bed is usually cheaper than 2 singles. Remember to check all the following before deciding on a room in a hotel: the price of the room, including all taxes; whether breakfast is included; whether a bath/shower is included; whether there is nothing cheaper; whether the hotelier would mind if 3 or 4 people used a double room; and finally, when you must check out the next day, to avoid paying for another night's accommodation.

HOSTELS
YOUTH HOSTELS: Hostels run by the International Youth Hostel Federation are good value and an ideal place to meet up with other travellers. They're the next cheapest alternative to camping, ranging from £3 to £18 ($4.50 to $27) a night, though most are £5–10 ($7.50 –$15). You need to be a member of your own country's YHA or that of the country you're in, though often you can buy temporary membership on the spot. If you're already a member of the YHA, attach a photo of yourself to your YHA card to allow you to hostel in Europe.

Youth hostels offer simple basic accommodation for men and women in separate dormitory-style bedrooms, washing and toilet facilities, and a common room. Many hostels have their own communal kitchen. In this way you can buy food at supermarket prices and cater for yourself for next to no cost at all. Economical meals (including vegetarian options) are laid on at many hostels (we list these under each country). Nowadays hostellers are not expected to do domestic chores, but any help offered is appreciated. At the least respect other hosteller's health and hygiene. Even if you bring your own sleeping bag, most hostels still insist you hire their sheets – a pain, but nothing you can do about it. Some hostels will accept standard YHA sheet sleeping bags, however.

The general rule is that you can't stay more than 3 nights at any one hostel, but it is up to the hosteller. If you've never hostelled before, go round a couple at home so you get to know what it's like. If you're expecting room service or breakfast in bed, forget hostelling. Average cost in the UK is around £6.50 ($10) a night and average meal £2–3.50 ($3.60–6.30).

BOOKING AHEAD: During July and August it's a good idea to book your hostel bed ahead in the major tourist cities. Try phoning ahead, but often they will tell you they are full, even when they aren't. If you're going to be doing a lot of hostelling in Europe, a useful system is International Multi-Lingual Booking Cards: they cost 5p each and allow one or more people to reserve beds and meals. You should be able to buy them at your local hostel or from your country's Youth Hostel Association head office. You post the cards on to the hostel concerned with an International Reply Coupon (60p at post offices). Beds reserved through this scheme are held until 6 p.m. Scottish Hostels offer a free Fax Ahead reservation service.

Another option is to take advantage of the International Booking Network (IBN). Telephone one of the main national access numbers listed below (have your credit card handy) and you can reserve a bed at least for the first night of your trip from home. Some of the more remote hostels are not covered by the IBN, however.

AUSTRALIA	02 9261111
ENGLAND	0171 836 1036
NEW ZEALAND	09 379 4224
REP. OF IRELAND	01 3017 266
NORTHERN IRELAND	01232 324733
SCOTLAND	0141 332 3004
UNITED STATES	0202 783 6161

Hostels vary a tremendous amount; though generally the further south you go in Europe, the less strict the rules tend to be and the more basic the accommodation becomes. Some hostels insist on midnight curfews and lock you out between 10 a.m. and 4 p.m., while others are far more liberal. If in doubt, it's always a good move to phone ahead from the station and check out if there's space and what rules, if any, apply. Many hostels are open only in the summer.

Some good news is that, following a worldwide inspection of their hostels – many of which were found to be way below par – the IYHF have decided to implement an international Assured Standards scheme. Accordingly, hostels must meet prescribed levels of comfort, cleanliness, security, privacy and welcome, and those failing to comply will be struck off the list. Those in Austria, the Netherlands, Sweden, Switzerland and the United Kingdom were to have been shipshape by the end of 1997, with the rest of the world's 5,000 hostels set for refurbishment by the end of this year. Our findings are that this seems more or less to be the case, especially in Scandinavia where you can expect some spectacular hostels.

Beware of the increasing number of unofficial hostels which are springing up, especially in southern Europe. Many call themselves 'Student Youth Hostels' and, though they impose no curfews or sex segregation, the facilities they offer are often very poor and the charges are more than those of official youth hostels.

If you intend to stay in youth hostels frequently, get a full list of all YHA hostels in Europe or buy *Cheap Sleeps Europe*, which lists the best ones, along with other accommodation options.

If you need more hostelling information, the London office of the YHA is: 14 Southampton Street, London WC2E 7HY (Tel. 0171 836 1036). Go along in person. Written or telephone enquiries should be addressed to their head office: Trevelyan House, 8 St Stephen's Hill, St Albans, Herts AL1 2DY (Tel. 01727 855215). Check out the Internet site: http://www.iyhf.org

STUDENT HOSTELS: Student hostels are similar to youth hostels, but instead of a YHA card you need an international student ID card. Many student hostels are unused student dorms and only open during university vacations.

YMCA INTER-POINTS: YMCA Interpoint is a summer programme running throughout Europe between July and September. Offering cheap accommodation, Interpoints are run by young people for young people and also help with the social needs of young travellers. Leaders organize activities (sightseeing, excursions, parties, etc.) and they are useful, cheap and very friendly places to stay.

They are also good in a crisis, helping out if you lose your passport etc. Costs vary but about £5 a night is average. There are Interpoints available in the following cities:

Denmark – Copenhagen (2), Odense
England – Nottingham, St Leonard's-on-Sea, Dover
Finland – Helsinki, Tampere
France – Toulouse
Ireland – Dublin (2), Newcastle (2)
Latvia – Riga
Netherlands – Enschede, Utrecht
Norway – Bergen, Bodø, Oslo
Poland – Gdynia
Scotland – Aberdeen
Slovakia – Bratislava, Kremnica
Sweden – Gothenburg, Stockholm, Sundsvall
Switzerland – Geneva, Zürich

For further info, including directions from the stations, write to National Council of YMCAs in Ireland Ltd, St George's Building, 37–41 High St, Belfast. Most of them are listed in this guide, and all of them are in my book *Cheap Sleeps Europe*. To use the centres you need to buy a YMCA Interpoint Pass. These are available at any Interpoint and cost about £2. They can also be bought from the YMCA International Co-ordinator.

CAMPING
If you're keen on the 'great outdoors', then camping in conjunction with a rail pass is ideal for you. There's no shortage of scenic sites, and even the major cities of Europe have campgrounds on their outskirts. But as a general rule we advise against it for big cities. The advantages of camping are obvious: it's cheap, if you're on a campsite you have all necessary facilities to hand, and it adds a dash of 'pioneering spirit' to your holiday. Prices on official campsites range from £2 to £6 ($3–9) a tent, and £2 to £7 ($3–11) per person.

The International Camping Carnet is only useful if you're doing a lot of camping at the various European campgrounds which insist on it, such as those in the state forests of France and Denmark. You can buy the carnet at most sites.

The disadvantages of official camping that spring to mind are: other people, cars, radios, tents all around, queueing for showers, etc. Unofficial camping, however, removes all these problems and can be a memorable experience. Remember to check with the farmer or landowner before pitching tent for the night, and observe strict hygiene.

It's quite feasible to camp throughout your entire trip. A tent, gas stove, utensils, sleeping bag and foam mattress will solve all your accommodation problems at once. Don't skimp too much on equipment, however; a good tent is far and away the most important thing. (For more information, see p. 30.)

PRIVATE ACCOMMODATION

This is an interesting and, in many ways, preferable alternative to hotels. Pricewise, it's slightly cheaper than hotels, but more expensive than hostels or camping. Individuals arrange through local tourist authorities for tourists to come and stay at their houses for any period of time from a night to the whole summer. It's an excellent way to meet the locals and get a home-from-home atmosphere. It also provides the perfect opportunity to ask all the questions you want about the country, but otherwise could not. Understanding the locals gives you a much better insight into the country, and, for my money, this is the best form of accommodation.

Ask at the Tourist Office and they will arrange the details for you. The only problem is that you may find all the places full in the high season as in many cities there are more prospective guests than recipient hosts.

ACCOMMODATION – EASTERN EUROPE

Since the collapse of the communist regimes, many of the former tourist-grade hotels have gone beyond the budget traveller's price range, as the authorities take advantage of increased demand. This coupled with the lack of infrastructure has not made your accommodation problems any easier. Your best choice is private accommodation. It is cheaper, gives you a better idea of eastern European life, and can be arranged at Tourist Offices, or negotiated in the street. You will often find women meeting trains to offer their flats or rooms. This is common and perfectly acceptable, but use your own judgement if you are worried about the safety aspects of this. Camping is another good option but, as always, check how far out the site is and check on the public transport situation, especially if you need an early morning connection.

At the official Tourist Offices expect long queues, especially in summer, as demand is increasing faster than the bureaucracy is improving. However, some of the old rules take a long time to go; for instance, you may still be told that all the youth hostels were booked up months ahead by large parties. In some places, such as Prague, several unofficial Tourist Offices have sprung up, which should help to relieve demand.

EATING

Whenever possible sample the local cuisine. Apart from being an extremely enjoyable way of learning about another culture, it's often a lot cheaper and more appetizing than eating more familiar food. If the restaurants are too expensive, don't despair; you'll find nearly every supermarket has a section devoted to regional specialities where, with a little bit of imagination, you can prepare yourself a veritable feast. Like everything else, a little background knowledge can add greatly to one's enjoyment. Here are the basic rules, accumulated over years of good and bad eating out:

1. Avoid expensive, pretentious-looking restaurants and cafés with no prices displayed.
2. Read the menu first, then add up the cost of your choices and all taxes and service charges before ordering.
3. Go for 'menus of the day' or tourist menus with fixed prices.
4. Serve yourself whenever you can.
5. Don't buy food or drink from vendors on the trains or from stalls in the stations. Buy it in advance from supermarkets.
6. If you've an addiction to something like coffee in the morning, take your supplies with you in the form of a camping stove, a small pan and some instant coffee.
7. When it comes to cheeses, wines, meats, biscuits, etc., buy the local stuff. Imports are always more expensive and it's good to sample the local produce.
8. Use fast-food chains if nothing else is available for cheap, reliable snacks. They're often far better and cheaper than local snack bars, especially in southern Europe where hygiene is often suspect.
9. Be adventurous and try something new. Ask for the house wine: it's always cheaper than listed wines and there's a good chance it's the popular wine of the region.
10. Eat breakfast out when it's optional at your hotel, as it's nearly always cheaper in a local café.
11. Make lunch your main meal of the day. Prepare yourself a big picnic whenever possible. Even when you eat at restaurants, it's at least 15% cheaper than in the evening. Avoid tourist areas, where the prices are always higher; search out university areas, where prices are more reasonable.
12. Look out in the stations for drinking water taps and fill your

bottles for free when you get the chance.
13. Vegetarian travellers and others with special dietary requirements might need some advance organization. There are various specialist publications available. Contact The Vegetarian Society, Parkdale, Dunham Road, Altrincham, Cheshire, WA14 4QG (Tel. 0161 928 0793).

CITY TRANSPORT

If you're going to stay in one place for more than a day or so, find out about the cheap travel passes on offer. Some cities offer day passes, others weekly ones and, if your accommodation is out of town, they can save you quite a bit. Before rushing off to buy one, however, check on a map for the location of the main sights you're interested in, as in many towns these are all within easy walking distance of one another and you won't need a bus pass. If you're not in a rush, using the buses as opposed to the underground lets you see a bit more of the city – which is worth bearing in mind.

Tickets for the buses and underground can often be bought at tobacco kiosks, or from machines in central locations. Also beware of large on-the-spot fines for non-ticket holders. *Thomas Cook's Railpass Guide* is particularly good on local transport.

COMMUNICATIONS

You will usually find both these facilities at the general post office. Some countries also offer special telephone kiosks for international calls. Find out the international dialling code before you start and remember to drop the leading zero from area codes.

Since April 1995 all UK area codes have a '1' added after the initial '0'. The international access code has become '00' instead of '010', thus bringing it into line with other European countries.

Always try to dial direct as it's much cheaper. Direct dialling codes to and from each country can be found in the basic information for the country or in Appendix VI. Never telephone via the switchboard at hotels or hostels as they invariably add on a lot – sometimes as much as the call itself – for themselves. Throughout Europe it's pretty standard that calls after business hours (7 p.m.–8 a.m.) are charged at a cheaper rate. In nearly every country, dialling instructions in either English or pictograms are to be found inside telephone boxes.

One of the most recent and recommended means of keeping in touch with friends and family is by Voice Mail. On subscription you are given your own phone number which can be accessed from asanywhere in the world using a personalised security code. You can then leave a recored message for anyone who is following your travels and pick up any messages from them. Travellers' Connections (Tel. 0181 286 3065) offer monthly subscriptions (£15) or yearly rates (£75). You may also consider using a BT Chargecard on your travels and pick up the bill on return.

Another option is the growing number of Internet cafés which are gracing most cities and large towns. As well as giving you something to do for an hour if it's raining cats and dogs, it could be a cheap way of keeping in touch with anybody who's equally tuned in.

Telegrams are expensive and in almost every case you'll find it cheaper making a quick phone call; but if that's impossible, write out your message and hand it to the clerk to avoid spelling mistakes.

MAIL

Airmail letters from major west European cities to the USA and Britain usually arrive within a week. Those from southern or eastern Europe tend to take longer, and postcards are even worse. Use surface mail (by ship) for posting home any books or clothes you don't fancy carrying around. It's usually very cheap – but very slow.

Trying to collect mail in Europe is more often than not a nerve-racking business. If you've no fixed address, the best method to use (and it's free or costs very little) is *poste restante*. This means your mail is sent to you c/o the main post office in any city or town. Depending on the country's domestic postal system, your mail should be at the *poste restante* office filed under your surname. Just produce your passport or equivalent proof of identity and pick it up. If the clerk says there's nothing for you, get him to check under your first name.

In eastern Europe, get the sender to put a '1' after the city's name to ensure it goes to the main post office.

Holders of American Express cards or traveller's cheques can get mail sent to AMEX offices to await collection.

SHOPPING

Unlike many other guidebooks, I don't include details on shopping. I take it for granted that most people won't have spare cash to blow in the shops, and if you do, you'll have enough common sense to head for the centre and find the main shopping areas for yourselves.

In general, the student area of a city is cheaper, and for food the large supermarkets are your best bet.

Shopping hours vary from country to country but they're all based round the 8–6 routine, though lunch hours can range from none at all to 3 hours. As a basic rule, the further south you go, the longer the 'siesta', and you can count on only a half day on Saturday.

TIPPING

Tipping is anything but an exact science. In western Europe, most restaurants and cafés usually include a service charge and technically one shouldn't feel under pressure to tip over and above that. In practice though, a lot of people, albeit mainly locals, tend to do just that, sometimes even up to an additional 10–15%.

In eastern Europe, the old idea of taking 20 Western cigarettes as a tip is gradually dying out. If you're in an area where it is clear that you are more wealthy than the locals, tip generously but not patronizingly. In most countries it is standard to throw some loose change to lavatory attendants.

WOMEN TRAVELLERS

Each year I receive letters from women travellers who have encountered problems when travelling alone. It's a sickening fact of life that women are victims of harassment, verbal at best and physical all too often; so it makes sense to take certain precautions to help avoid problems. The further south and east you get in Europe, the less emancipated women are, and the more men will look on you as a sophisticated westerner, and easy game.

The single most important thing to do is to dress appropriately. In Muslim countries especially, any large area of naked flesh (including arms, lower legs and shoulders) is read as the equivalent of a green light. Even a T-shirt and jeans can be construed as seductive clothing there. A cover-up shawl in light cotton is a good investment. Never mind that the other European women don't seem to bother with this. If you are travelling alone, or could be in a situation where you are with just 1 or 2 other women and a lot of men, heed this advice.

No mini-skirts, always wear a bra, and no shorts. Wear sloppy loose cotton trousers/skirts and tops. Clothes that don't show your shape are more comfortable for travelling anyway. Save showing off your curves (if you must) for the West, where they will be quietly appreciated, not read as an open invitation.

On trains, especially on the type with no corridor and with entrance from outside compartment doors, do not necessarily choose an empty compartment. Choose one with other women in it. It might be less private, but empty compartments can soon fill up with men, and then you've no control over the situation. It's a good idea to meet other women travellers anyway.

Couchettes that are not allocated on a single sex or family basis are another potential headache. Always have a word with your attendant to ensure you're in with a family or other women. Simply do not accept a couchette with a male majority – it's unreasonable to expect you to. You'd be better spending the night sitting up in a public compartment.

Do not sleep in parks or stations, ever. Women on their own are at great risk if they do this. Who's going to know if anything happens to you? Throw yourself on the mercy of the station master, police, embassy, local church, anywhere, but don't sleep rough. Plan ahead and get into town in time to find a room.

I have travelled in every continent as a lone woman, and I do understand the problems. These rules are the tip of the iceberg.

LONE TRAVELLERS

Travelling alone in Europe is an adventure which some people would prefer to forgo, but it has its compensations, which make it worth considering. During a month travelling you could make many new friends, of many nationalities, quite easily. Staying in youth hostels is an excellent way of meeting people; it is easy to strike up a conversation whilst stringing up a makeshift washing line between bunks! During the summer it is easy to spot other lone travellers on the popular routes, who may wish to have a chat. Another great advantage of going alone is that you have more freedom to go where you want, when you want, with no arguing over the next destination.

The main problem of travelling alone is that you have to be even more careful with your belongings, as you have no one to fall back on. The same rules apply as to groups, but with more emphasis. A good policy is to leave an idea of your route with relatives or friends, even if it is only a rough idea.

GAY AND LESBIAN TRAVELLERS

The general rule of thumb is that the gay scene is further developed and more tolerant in western and particularly northern Europe than in the old Eastern Bloc countries and parts of southern Europe. The major gay cities are universally known and certainly include London, Paris, Amsterdam, Berlin and Madrid, though as one would expect, any large European metropolis is going to have at least some sort of an area where the gay scene is developed.

Be aware of the fact that the age of consent in most cases will be higher than the heterosexual age and that Romania is the only country left in Europe where it is still illegal to practise homosexuality.

A useful contact in the UK is the London Lesbian and Gay Switchboard (Tel. 0171 837 7324) who operate a 24-hour service or The International Gay Travel Association, PO Box 4974, Key West, FL 33041 (Tel. 1 800/448 8550).

DISABLED TRAVELLERS

The facilities available for disabled travellers vary widely across Europe, as you would expect. In general the best facilities are available in the north of Europe and in Italy. However, even the countries with well advertised facilities are not always up to scratch, relying as they do on the staff to be available to help.

In the UK wheelchairs can be accommodated on many trains, but to guarantee this it is advisable to contact the station first, to ensure that ramps and a space are available. In France a similar situation exists on TGV services. For other trains SNCF publish a booklet with the disabled traveller in mind. Elsewhere you may end up having to fold your wheelchair away.

There are several important things to consider when travelling by train, the first being the platform access. In many places the access to platforms requires steps up to a bridge or down to an underpass. Lifts are often hidden away from sight and can only be operated by a member of staff, with the appropriate key. Another problem, especially at smaller continental stations, is the height of the train compared with the platform. Planning in advance, to ensure staff are available to help, is the only solution here.

Be familiar with your condition. Medical terms are precise and internationally understood whereas colloquialisms are not always meaningful to foreign medical personnel. The generic name of a medicine can be obtained from a doctor or pharmacist: a particular brand name may not be available but generic formulae will be.

Check the accessibility of sites with Tourist Information centres. It may be more expensive to join a tour, but the guide may provide a helping hand or know of a more accessible route. Roads may be unpaved and unlit, pavements, if any, uneven and kerbstones steep: the wheelchair/pram pusher is rarely catered for away from main centres and you should be physically able to cope with the terrain.

Certain foods may be unavailable in some countries. The Maltese use little fresh milk and foods for young babies are harder to find where prolonged breastfeeding is the norm, e.g. southern Spain.

Attitudes to disability vary. The disabled may, on one hand, be treated as a normal part of society (which, of course, they are) or they may be closely questioned about their condition. This may seem impertinent but is often only genuine interest in the disabled person's welfare, and, in time, may lead to a greater understanding of the disabled traveller's needs.

Bathroom facilities may be unsuitable for the disabled in southern Europe: toilets are often of the eastern 'squat' type in Turkey and parts of Greece. Ask around – people are very understanding and will always direct one to Western-style facilities. Hot water may be restricted to certain times of the day and, in time of drought, may be rationed and turned off for intervals. Be flexible: alternatives may turn out better than the original plan. Try to meet obstructive people with charm and, above all, remember, 'Where there's a will, there's a way!'

Good sources of information on accessibility and services are provided by the British, French and Italian national Tourist Offices, but ask at the others as well – you may be lucky. Any of the disabled pressure groups will also be willing to help, with several of them producing guidebooks – try contacting RADAR, 12 City Forum, 250 City Road, London EC1V 8AF (Tel. 0171 250 3222), The Society for the Advancement of Travel for the Handicapped, 347 5th Ave, New York, NY 10016 (Tel. 212/447 7284), or ACORD, PO Box 60, Curtain, Canberra, ACT 2605 (Tel. 06/682 4333). Also listen to Radio 4's programmes, such as *Does He Take Sugar?*, which feature field tests of accessibility.

NOTES

PART TWO

THE COUNTRIES

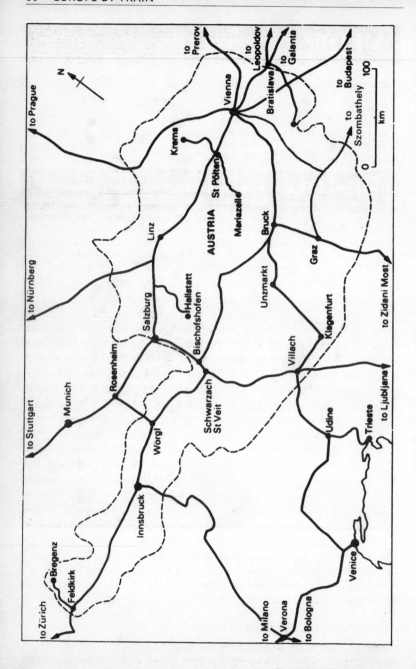

Europe -

1st Europe by I rain 1998

Kotu Wood   p. 23

No. 1 Croatia 22

No. abutting Germany (10) Clothing Denmark K. Netherlands.

No. visited by OH and WZ ishona.

NB. Word ...refen K. Yuga- p. 23 Serbia p. ?

AUSTRIA (Österreich)

Entry requirements	Passport
Population	7,800,000
Capital	Vienna (pop.: 1,500,000)
Currency	Austrian Schilling
	£1 = approx. AS19
Political system	Federal Republic
Religion	Roman Catholic
Language	German (English spoken)
Public holidays	New Year's Day, Epiphany, Easter Monday, Labour Day, Ascension Day, Whit Monday, Corpus Christi, Assumption, National Holiday, All Saints' Day, Immaculate Conception, Christmas Day and Boxing Day
International dialling codes	To Austria: int'l 43 number
	From Austria: 00 + country code number

Austria would have been no place for eurorailing during its early history, certainly not for sleeping out at the station, as one power struggle followed another until the Habsburgs emerged victorious at the end of the 13th century. They ruled the changing empire from 1278 to 1918. As good Catholics and Holy Roman Emperors for 4 centuries, they spent most of their time fighting the Turks as well as keeping everyone at home in order. As a result of this, they provided a strong monarchy, but it was no fun to be in the army as Austria continued to be involved in political struggles till the 18th century. By then, Vienna had become the home of Europe's finest musicians such as Mozart, Beethoven and, of course, later on, Strauss. With the First World War the monarchy came to an end and Austria's empire folded up. She had a hard time in the Second World War as she was forcibly annexed by Germany, and suffered heavily from Allied bombing. In 1955, Austria obtained independence, declared neutrality and has since made a spectacular economic recovery. This is particularly so with Vienna, which has been lovingly restored and once again fulfils its ancient role as a stopover place. The alpine scenery and distinctive villages in many provinces, including the well-known Tyrolean ones, make Austria one of Europe's most attractive countries and a perfect destination for those seeking the great outdoors.

AUSTRIAN FEDERAL RAILWAYS
(ÖSTERREICHISCHE BUNDESBAHNEN, ÖBB)
As you might expect, trains run on time. They are clean and comfort-

able, as are the stations. However, there's generally a lot of queueing in summer, so be warned. Most intercities run 2 hours apart.

Train types are: long-distance expresses (*Expresszüge*), expresses (*Schnellzüge*), semi-fast services (*Eilzüge* or *Regionalzüge*), and EuroCity trains. Apart from on some EuroCity trains, you can get by without supplements. Avoid local trains unless you have plenty of time as they tend to be slow, especially if you're on a mountainous route.

PASSES AVAILABLE The Austrian Rail Pass (*Bundesnetzkarte*) is available to anyone. It gives unlimited first- or second-class travel for a month on ÖBB, the Schneeberg and Schafbergspitze rack railways and ÖBB ships. Also it gives 50% reductions on Bodensee and DDSG ships, and a number of private railways. Cost AS5,900 first class, AS4,300 second class. There is also a 1-year ticket (*VORTEILScard*) available. It is valid on the whole Austrian Rail network (including most private railways), it also gives reductions on some shipping services, as well as bike and car hire. Also available are Regional Puzzle tickets giving unlimited travel for 4 days in 10, within any one of 4 regions (north, east, south or west). The ticket also gives 50% reductions on a number of private railways. Cost AS1,740 first class and AS1,090 second class (over 26) or AS1,060 first class, AS660 second class (under 26), 50% reduction for children. A Euro Domino ticket is also available for Austria, see p. 41.

Both Eurail and Inter-Rail passes are valid. Austria is in Inter-Rail Zone C, along with Germany, Switzerland and Denmark. For details of the 8 Inter-Rail zones, see the Inter-Rail section in Part One of this guide.

INTER-RAIL BONUSES See Appendix I for reductions.

EURAIL BONUSES The following services are free:
Puchberg am Schneeberg–Hochschneeberg rack railway.
St Wolfgang–Schafbergspitze rack railway.
Steamers on Lake Wolfgang.

REDUCED FARES
50% reduction on steamers operated by steamship companies on Lake Constance.
50% reduction on steamer day trips operated between Linz and Passau or vice versa by Wurm & Köck.
10% reduction on steamer trips operated by Erste Donau-Dampf-schiffahrts-Gesellschaft.

TRAIN INFORMATION

Austrian Federal Railways main information for the whole country is at Elisabethstrasse 9, A-1010 in Vienna (Tel. (from Britain) 0043-1-580 00)

Information officers are nearly all multilingual, while most other rail staff speak at least a little English. You can easily tell the information officers: they wear yellow cap bands. Luggage lockers use 10-Schilling pieces. Children under 6 travel free on ÖBB. Groups of 6 plus qualify for reductions, special booking procedures necessary.

RESERVATIONS Are not necessary. If you want to make one, it can be done until 2 hours before your train leaves (cost: AS30).

NIGHT TRAVEL Austria's too small for an extensive service. Sleepers and couchettes are clean and comfortable. Reserve at least 5 hours beforehand. Couchettes cost from AS200. There are also compartments with pull-down seats which cost nothing.

LEFT LUGGAGE You can leave your luggage at any station in Austria for AS20 per piece per day. Some stations have luggage lockers; these cost AS20–AS40 per day and are open 24 hours.

EATING ON TRAINS For those with money, there are dining cars on all intercity trains. Mini-bars are to be found on all trains except locals. As always, we advise picnics, but if you don't have time to go to a supermarket before the train leaves, there are kiosks at most stations. Vienna's stations, in particular, have well-stocked delicatessens which are open long hours, including Sundays.

SCENIC TIPS The main Innsbruck–Zell am See–Salzburg line is one of the most scenic in the country. If you're going from Innsbruck to Italy, take the train to Brennero for beautiful mountainous scenery. If you're heading towards Slovenia, try Vienna–Trieste – this goes via Klagenfurt and Udine. If you're travelling from Innsbruck to Munich or vice versa, try the route via Garmisch – again, the mountain scenery is beautiful. Bregenz, situated on the Bodensee in the west of Austria, is a good place to sail across to Germany. From here you can go to Konstanz over the border (ask about reductions for train pass holders). Also at Bregenz you can take the Pfanderbahn up to the top for a wonderful view of the Alps and over the Bodensee. Go to the Vorarlberg Tourist Office in Bregenz on Anton-Schneider-Strasse for information on alpine villages and excursions. You can sail the Danube from the German–Austrian border (Passau) to Vienna or from Vienna to Passau. The trip lasts 1½ days, stopping overnight at Linz. Alternatively, there's the Linz–Vienna trip or vice versa. The prettiest part of the trip is from Krems to Melk. The train runs from both Melk and Krems. Further information from DDSG, Reisedienst 2, Handelskai 265. In Passau, go to DDSG-Schiffsstation, Im Ort 14a, Dreiflusseck. Get off the boat and take a look around as often as possible as many of the stopping-off places are well-preserved medieval or baroque towns. If you're leaving Vienna for Salzburg, stop off at the village of MARIAZELL. It's beautiful. Surrounded by mountains, it was a religious pilgrimage site. Take the cable-car for the view. From Vienna take the train to St Pölten from the Westbahnhof, then change there to a train for Mariazell.

BIKES You can rent out a bike in nearly every important station in Austria – *Fahrrad am Bahnhof*. Take a quick look at the traffic situation before committing yourself. Prices are normally around AS90, but your train ticket should get you half price.

TOURIST INFORMATION

There's a local Tourist Office (*Verkehrsverein*) in every large town which will give you the addresses of the provincial tourist boards if required.

ISIC BONUSES 50% reductions on most art galleries and museums. 10% on Rosen Hotels. For further information, contact Ökista at Türkenstrasse 4–6, Vienna (Tel. 3475260).

MONEY MATTERS 1 Austrian Schilling (AS) = 100 groschen (gr).
  Banking hours are Mon.–Wed., Fri.: 8 a.m.–12.30 p.m., 1.30 p.m.–3 p.m., Thurs.: 8 a.m.–12.30 p.m., 1.30 p.m.–5.30 p.m. The main banks in Vienna stay open over lunch. It's best to cash your traveller's cheques in large denominations as commission charges are high. You can cash Eurocheques without paying commission if you are staying at the Ruthensteiner hostel near the Westbahnhof.

POST OFFICES Open Mon.–Fri.: 8 a.m.–12 noon, 2 p.m.–6 p.m., Sat.: 8 a.m.–10 a.m. Stamps can also be bought from Tabak-Trafik shops.

SHOPS Generally keep to the same hours as the post offices, closing on Saturday afternoons. Food shops usually open before 8 a.m., but close for lunch 12.30–3 p.m.

MUSEUMS Tend to close on Mondays.

TIPPING 10–15% is added to bills in restaurants but a tip is also expected. Look out for *Einschliesslich Bedienung,* which means 'service included'.

SLEEPING

HOSTELS To stay at any Austrian youth hostel, you need an International Youth Hostel Association membership card, though guest cards are always available. In general, they're open about 6 a.m.–10 p.m. and charge about AS100–200 for bed and breakfast, from AS60 for just bed, and about AS60–120 for a meal, adding on an extra charge where cooking facilities are available.

At many hostels breakfast is compulsory; check first. Provided space is available, you can stay more than 3 nights at most hostels unless you're travelling in a large group. If you are, write in advance to the warden and book your space. A number of hostels are only open May–mid-September, so consider this when planning your journey.

HOTELS Hotels are nearly always clean but wildly expensive, particularly in Vienna and Salzburg. If you travel off-season, prices are 20–40% cheaper; also in May, June and September they can be 15–25% cheaper than in July and August. You can expect to pay at least AS400 for a double, from AS600 in Vienna and other cities. Bear this in mind if you're approached by an Austrian hotelier trying to fill his hotel – he may be offering you a bargain. Don't be put off by this approach as it's a buyer's market; ask the price and location and what's included. You're under no obligation.

PRIVATE HOUSES (*Privat Zimmer/Zimmer Frei*): Rooms are around AS160 per person and make an interesting alternative.

CAMPING The International Camping Carnet is not obligatory, but it'll get you preferential treatment on most sites. Generally, the sites are very good: clean, efficient and well laid out. Austrians are keen campers themselves, so in peak season you might find it advisable to get to the site and pitch as early in the day as you can. Charges are from AS25 per person and AS25 per tent, with Vienna at around AS55 per person and per tent.

EATING AND NIGHTLIFE

Austrian food is wholesome stuff and great if you've a soft spot for pastries. In general, the pork (*Schwein*) and fish dishes are better value than lamb and beef. *Tafelspitz* (boiled beef) is good and cheap, and this with a noodle or dumpling soup is a filling, inexpensive meal. The coffee-and-cakes scene is good news all round, except for the price. *Strudel* is excellent, as is *Sachertorte*. Having said all this, you may well end up eating from fast-food chains most of the time, since restaurant prices are similar to those in Britain. If so, try and eat the local dishes at least once, you won't regret it.

The nightlife is centred round coffee houses and the opera, rather than heavy-metal gigs and bars. You have to remember that discos and bars cost money in Austria and anyway they tend to be a bit smooth. The best advice is to head towards a wine tavern or beer cellar in the student areas where possible, as prices tend to be more realistic there. The east of the country is best for wine. However, if you're into opera, Vienna's the place. The season runs from September to June, and whilst most prices are very high, cheap standby tickets (AS50) can sometimes be obtained 2 hours before a performance if you're prepared to queue.

Vienna (Wien) city phone code: 01

Gateway between the East and West for over 2,000 years, Vienna's middle-European flavour makes it unique among all capital cities. Its position as ruler of half of Europe for over 6 centuries has left behind a legacy of impressive buildings and an atmosphere of solid institutionalism. This is probably helped by the fact that a third of Vienna's 1.6 million population are pensioners.

The city is divided into 23 districts, with the 'Ring' in the city centre as no. 1. Vienna's not actually on the Danube – the river only runs through its suburbs – but the Danube canal is part of the city. If you want to sail on the Danube and are heading for Hungary, it is a fraction of the price in Budapest.

Use this book and do your sums carefully in Vienna to avoid its high costs during your stay. It's a great place, but at a price.

STATION FACILITIES

Vienna has 2 large main stations: the Westbahnhof and the Südbahnhof, with trains leaving daily from Westbahnhof at Europaplatz to France, Switzerland and Germany. Trains for Eastern European countries, southern Austria, former Yugoslavian states and Italy leave from Südbahnhof. Trains to Budapest leave from either

Westbahnhof or Südbahnhof. Trains for Berlin and Prague leave from Franz Josef Bahnhof or Wien Mitte Bahnhof. For further info, telephone (1) 1717.

TOURIST INFORMATION.

The main office is at Kärntnerstrasse 38, behind the Opera (Tel. 5138892). Open Mon.–Sat.: 9 a.m.–7 p.m., closed Sunday. There are also Tourist Offices at Westbahnhof and Südbahnhof and they, like any other in Austria, can provide an accommodation-finding service. Pick up the city map, transport map and the students' magazine *Jugend/Youth Scene*. There is also an information centre for young people at Bellaria-Passage, open Mon.–Fri. noon–7p.m. and 10a.m.–5p.m. Sat. (Tel. 1799). Tourist information for all of Austria is available at Margaretenstrasse 1 (Tel. 5872000), open Mon.–Fri.: 9 a.m.–5 p.m.

The 3 main stations in the city all have train information, reservations desks and left-luggage lockers. The South (*Südbahnhof*) and West (*Westbahnhof*) stations have post offices, Tourist Information and foreign exchange bureaux as well as shower facilities and a greater range of other commercial concessions.

Trams 6 and 18 connect the South and West stations. To get to the city centre from Südbahnhof take tram D or S-Bahn 1, 2 or 3 to Südtiroler Platz (1 stop), then U-Bahn 1. From Westbahnhof take Tram 58 or 52, or U-Bahn 3. From Franz Josef, turn left down Althastrasse to Alserbachstrasse, turn left again, and walk to Friedensbrücke, on U-Bahn 4.

ADDRESSES

POST OFFICE Fleischmarkt 19. Poste restante. Open 24 hours.

AMEX Kärntnerstrasse 21–23, Mon.–Fri.: 9 a.m.–5.30 p.m., Sat.: 9 a.m.–12 noon (Tel. 515400)

UK EMBASSY Jauresgasse 12 (Tel. 7131575)

IRISH EMBASSY Landstrasser Hauptstrasse 2, Hilton Centre (Tel. 7154246)

US EMBASSY Boltzmanngasse 16 (Tel. 31339)

CANADIAN EMBASSY Laurenzerberg 2 (Tel. 5138300)

AUSTRALIAN EMBASSY Mattiellistrasse 2–4 (Tel. 5128580)

NEW ZEALAND Springsiedlergasse 28, (Tel. 3188505)

POLICE EMERGENCY Tel. 133

MEDICAL EMERGENCY Tel. 144/141

ÖKISTA (Student travel) Türkenstrasse 4–6, Mon.–Fri.: 9.30 a.m.–5 p.m. (Tel. 401480). Help with any accommodation and train tickets.

GETTING ABOUT

Information on city transport is available at Karlsplatz U-Bahn station, where they can also provide a leaflet in English called *Exploring Vienna by Train*, which gives information on ticket details and how to use the system. There are various passes on offer, but remember you can see most of Vienna on foot.

Tickets for a single journey, within the central zone, on buses, trams, U-Bahn and S-Bahn (free on Inter-Rail) cost a few Schillings more from the driver than the vending machines. Strip tickets for 4 or 8 journeys, within 1 zone, are also available and more than 1 person can use them by just cancelling the relevant number of strips in the machine and Bob's your uncle. The 8-day environment pass is used like the strip tickets, but is valid for 1 full day for each strip cancelled. Other possible tickets are a 24-hour or 72-hour explorer ticket, the Vienna Card (AS120). Late-night theatre or concert goers can use their tickets to travel anywhere on any line for 2 hours before and 6 hours after the start of the performance.

Tickets can also be purchased from automatic machines in stations and on some trams, so have AS5 and AS10 coins to hand. Night buses radiate from Schwedenplatz. Forget the city tours, taxis and *Fiakers* (2-horse coaches at AS400 a go), as they'll cripple your budget.

SEEING

Pick up leaflets from Tourist Information offices. These will give you all the history, details, opening times, etc. At the heart of Vienna is St Stephan's Cathedral and its square, Stephansplatz, at the intersection of Graben and Kärntnerstrasse – it's a good place to sit and watch Viennese life go by. Rather than suggest a walking tour with everyone tramping round exactly the same treadmill like guinea pigs, we list the major sights and you can devise your own route by using the map. If you plan on doing some serious culture trekking, consider a VIENNA CARD, it's AS180 and will get you into 30 or so of the main attractions.

ST STEPHAN'S CATHEDRAL: Built in the 13th and 14th centuries, it's the most important Gothic building in Vienna. Climb the 340 steps of the south steeple (or take the lift up the north steeple, AS40) for a good view of Vienna, or descend to the catacombs and look at the Habsburgs' innards in the Old Prince's Vault.

THE HOFBURG: The old imperial winter palace sprawling all over the heart of the city and encompassing every architectural style from the 13th to the 20th century; it includes the Spanish Riding School (training may be watched in the mornings) and the Hofburgkapelle where the Vienna Boys' Choir performs – though, crazily, both close down for periods in summer. Entry to the Hofburg is AS30 (reductions for ISIC holders).

SCHÖNBRUNN PALACE: This was the Habsburgs' summer palace. Situated at Schönbrunner Schloss-Strasse in the outskirts, south-west from Westbahnhof, U-bahn 4. There are a limited number of English tours for AS95, which are worth it. Also see the Gloriette, the gardens and the butterfly collection.

THE BELVEDERE: Includes the Austrian gallery of modern art and a museum of medieval art.

THE KUNSTHISTORISCHES MUSEUM, Maria-Theresien Platz: one of the great art collections and the 4th largest gallery in the world. All the treasures the Habsburgs could get their imperial hands on are here. The Breughel room contains over half the artist's remaining pictures.

There's also the new KUNSTHAUSWIEN at Untere Weissgerberstrasse 13, open 10 a.m.–7 p.m. daily, which houses international art and interesting contemporary exhibitions.

The above are the main sights but, if you've any time left, take in the FREUD MUSEUM. Followers of the master can visit his house at Berggasse 19 (AS60), small but well documented.

Of interest to musicians will be: HAYDN MUSEUM at Haydngasse 19; MOZART ERINNERUNGSRAUM, Domgasse 5; SCHUBERT MUSEUM, Nussdorferstrasse 54; and SCHUBERT STERBEZIMMER, Kettenbrückengasse 6; JOHANN STRAUSS MUSEUM, Praterstrasse 54. At all these addresses, the composers' original houses are still standing. The charges for entrance seem to be constantly changing, but municipal museums should be free for all on Friday mornings and national museums offer reductions for all students and ISIC holders. But don't be surprised if the rules change – especially outside the high season. Pick up the leaflet *Museums Wien* from the Tourist Office.

Alternatively, as a break take a walk and a picnic in the Vienna Woods, which border the city on its southern and western sides. Take tram 38 to its terminus at Grinzing, then bus 38a to Kahlenberg.

If you are feeling energetic and are after a novel way of seeing Vienna, check out Pedal Power at Ausstellungersstrasse 3 (Tel. 729 7234). Their cycle tours start at 10 a.m., cost AS230 for students' AS280 otherwise, and include a flying visit to a wine cellar.

SLEEPING

Write in advance if at all possible, as cheap beds are few and far between in the summer. This is mainly due to the fact that they don't open their student hostels till July (making late June a particularly bad time); hotels are ridiculously expensive and the cheap pensions get full quickly. Use *Cheap Sleeps Europe* (see p. 11) or the ISIC accommodation booklet as these list all the best places.

There are 2 main accommodation-finding services in Vienna: the travel agencies at the stations, and the student organization Ökista. If you want to save the commission charge, try phoning yourself. Most hoteliers speak English, or you can try out your phrase-book German.

HOSTELS A novel hostel is in the bell tower of a church at Türmherberge on Bosco, Lechnerstrasse 12 (Tel. 7131494). Take Tram 18 from Westbahnhof or Südbahnhof to the end or U-Bahn 3. Men only. Costs AS60. Don't confuse with hotel Don Bosco. No catering, and don't expect a long lie in – the alarm bell is very loud and very close!

YOUTH HOSTELS Ruthensteiner, Robert Hamerlinggasse 24 (Tel. 8934202 and 8932796). Offers 77 beds with all facilities, near Westbahnhof: turn right out of Westbahnhof, right into Mariahilferstrasse, left into Palmgasse and right into Hamerlinggasse. Costs from AS129 for dormitory to AS219 for a single room. Free showers, but no lockers. They will store extra luggage free of charge (at your risk) if space permits. No curfew. Breakfast available at AS25.

Jugendherberge, Myrthengasse 7 (Tel. 5236316). 241 beds and all facilities. All rooms have showers, near centre. Midnight curfew. AS140. B&B, but you must be an IYHF member. Advance booking is essential. Walkable from Westbahnhof, or U-bahn 6 to Burggasse, then bus 48a to Neubaugasse, hostel nearby.

Jugendgasthaus, Friedrich-Engels Platz 24 (Tel. 33282940). 330 beds, all facilities, curfew at 12.30 a.m. Near the Danube. Must be IYHF member. Tram N from Schwedenplatz (U-bahn 1 or 4) to Friedrich-Engels Platz.

Hütteldorf, Schlossberggasse 8 (Tel. 8770263). 271 beds and all facilities. Must be IYHF member. Take S-Bahn 50 or U-Bahn 4 from Westbahnhof to Hütteldorf, then a signposted 10-minute walk. AS137 B&B, AS75 for evening meal.

The YMCA, Kenyongasse 15 (Tel. 936304), July–Aug. Cost is around AS150 (breakfast is compulsory). Bring your own sleeping bag.

PENSIONS Pension Columbia, Kochgasse 9 (Tel. 426757), quiet with doubles from AS630 to AS670, including breakfast. Tram 5 from outside Westbahnhof.

Another option is Pension zur Stadthalle, Hackengasse 35 (Tel. 9824272). The cheapest singles are from AS520 and the cheapest doubles start from AS780. All prices include breakfast, and they will give you a 10% discount if you show this book! Turn left outside Westbahnhof and then left again; Hackengasse is on your right.

PRIVATE ROOMS Private rooms are available, owned by Hedwig Gally, near the Westbahnhof at Arnsteingasse 25/10 (Tel. 8929073/8931028). Prices start at AS400 for a double, AS500 for a double with shower.

Try the rooms owned by Irmgard Lauria at Kaiserstrasse 77/8, close to the Westbahnhof (Tel. 5222555). Costs AS200 including showers and cooking facilities. Shared rooms at AS160. Beware though, there have been some disparaging reports about this hostel.

Irene Hamminger, Türkenschanzstrasse 34 (Tel. 3450305) offers rooms in a Viennese villa for AS400–500 for 2 people – 15 minutes from the city centre.

Frank Heberling runs an establishment at Siccardsburggasse 42 (Tel. 6040229), phone first. Very friendly, walkable from Südbahnhof.

The city Tourist Offices can also arrange private rooms, for a small fee.

CAMPING All grounds are located well out of the city with an average price of AS58 per person and AS52 per tent.

Wien West II, Hüttelbergstrasse 80 (Tel. 9142314). Get off train at Hütteldorf, then bus 52b. Open April–October.

Wien West I, just up the same street (Tel. 9142314). Open mid-July–end-August. But I've had terrible reports of declining standards in Wien West I and II, and despite promised improvement I would not advise them.

Camping Süd (Tel. 869218), open August, close to the Atzgersdorf-Mauer S-Bahn station. Noisy.

Quite near this site is the Rodaun-Schwimmbad site at An der Au 2 (Tel. 884154). Take tram 58 from Westbahnhof to Hietzing, then tram 60 to the end. Hot showers are AS5, and there is a free swimming pool. Open end March–mid-Nov.

Also ask at the Tourist Office for details of other sites, further out, but worth a try if it's really busy. If you are really desperate, sleep out at the Prater Park, but it is not to be recommended.

EATING AND NIGHTLIFE

There's no shortage of places to eat in Vienna – the only problem's the prices. As usual, though, if you know where to look you will be all right. The Hungarian and Turkish restaurants are usually good value.

The *Schnell-Imbiss* counters (quick snacks) dotted all over the city serve cheap filling snacks (AS40–80), and of course there's always McDonald's, one of them very convenient for the Westbahnhof on Mariahilferstrasse heading towards the city, on the left-hand side.

Cafés are a Viennese institution, serving up their delicious pastries and cakes, but they're expensive, so make your café visit on a wet afternoon when you can hang around reading the papers, playing cards and generally getting your money's worth. Try Freud's one-time watering hole, Cafe Landtmann, 1 Karl Lueger Ring 4 or the popular student haunt Cafe Stein, 9 Wahringerstrasse 6.

For picnics, use the self-service supermarkets. There's no shortage of good breads, sausages, cheeses, fruits and wines, so a picnic is easy. Vienna's largest market, the NASCHMARKT, lying from the 4th to the 6th districts, has a few food bargains and plenty more besides. Get to it by the underground to Kettenbrückengasse.

SUGGESTIONS There is nowhere really cheap in the centre of Vienna to eat, but scrutinize any 'menu of the day' you see. Places worth trying include the Naschmarkt restaurant chain, with one on Schwarzenberg Platz. The best place to head for is the 7th district around the Neustiftgasse where you will find the Phoenixhof and Puppenstube restaurants. You can expect a good meal and wine for around AS140 and if these are full there are other places in the vicinity. The student restaurant Mensa is at Universitätsstrasse 7. It's open for lunch and dinner, Mon.–Fri., and there's no problem getting in as long as you look like a student. Prices from AS45 to AS50 for a basic meal, good value for money.

Vegetarians should try Gasthaus Wrenkh, Hollergasse 9 (15th district) or at Bauernmarkt 10 (1st district).

The Viennese are happier at the opera or the theatre than engaged in active nightlife. Young people tend to congregate in the coffee houses (*Kaffeekonditorei*) rather than in pubs or discos, but Vienna still has a few surprises up its sleeve. A good night out can be had at the Prater – Vienna's large amusement park on the outskirts of the city. Entrance is free and the rides average AS15–25, although the big wheel, built in 1895 by British engineer Walter Bassett, costs AS30. Open from Easter to October. Take tram 21 or U-bahn 1, it's reasonably obvious where to get off.

Bars and nightclubs can be sleazy and expensive, so watch out. For techno dance floor try U4 Disco, Schönbrunnerstrasse 222; it's very popular with the young Viennese and it's easy to get to, or look at the latest *Youth Scene*. In general, though, you're better off heading for a wine tavern or beer cellar. These represent best value by far. Try: Esterhazykeller, Haarhof, good student crowd with the best prices in town; or Zwölf-Apostelkeller, Sonnenfelsgasse 3, near St Stephan's, so low down from street level, the walls are covered with straw to diminish the dampness. Go down to the lowest level – it's the liveliest. Open Sundays, but closed all July. There's a good atmosphere here. And for the connoisseur, Melkerkeller, Schottengasse 3, run by Benedictine monks, has excellent wine.

For enthusiasts, Europe's largest bowling alley is in Vienna. It's the Bowling-Brunswick at Hauptallee 124 and costs around AS25 a line. Plenty of students congregate here.

Fans of opera or ballet should head for the *Staatsoper*, 1 Openring 2. Whilst the principal venue for classical music is the *Musikverein* at 1 Karlsplatz 6, home of the Vienna Philharmonic. Check with Tourist Information for up-to-date programmes, but when buying tickets don't use an agency, as they charge a 30% commission. Tickets are sometimes available on the night. Standing room is available at the opera; queue and tie a scarf around the barrier to reserve your place.

Southern Austria

If you're travelling south on to Italy or the former Yugoslavia, you'll pass through the southern regions of Burgenland, Steiermark and Kärnten.

BURGENLAND is the province next to the Hungarian border and is famous for its wines. EISENSTADT is its capital and between late August and early September this turns into a pretty lively place, thanks to its Weinwoche (wine week).

STEIERMARK is in the south-eastern area of Austria, along the Slovenian border which the Weinstrasse (wine road) runs through. Its capital is Graz. The journey between Salzburg and Villach is particularly scenic and if you fancy visiting a typical alpine town you could do worse than to choose BADGASTEIN. Although expensive, it is worth while spending a relaxing few hours here, taking in the wonderful views down the valley from the station and seeing the powerful waterfall at close range.

KÄRNTEN (Carinthia) has as its capital KLAGENFURT. This is an attractive region with lakes, wildlife parks and rolling hills. Klagenfurt itself has 2 campsites, and a youth hostel in its centre, and is a good place to base yourself to explore the surrounding Naturpark Kreuzbergl.

Graz

Compact Graz is Austria's second city and most of it can be seen on foot. Go to the Hauptplatz, which is the main market square, to start your rambles. Worth seeing are the 16th-century LANDHAUS and the ZEUGHAUS and there are also a couple of decent museums and art galleries. There's a CATHEDRAL and a BURG which is now government offices.

TOURIST INFORMATION
There's a Tourist Office at the station but if you head down town for 200m, there's a much bigger one at Herrengasse 16. The train station is on the periphery of the town so you have to walk or get a short tram ride (no. 6) to and from the central Hauptplatz.

SLEEPING AND EATING
Any private rooms booked are likely to be in the suburbs, but the youth hostel is more central at Idlhofgasse 74 (Tel. 914876).

There's not much in the way of cheap hotels, but the Pension Iris, on Bergmanngasse, is one of the more highly recommended ones.

For decent entertainment, head to the alleys off the Hauptplatz or look for the cafés and bars which line the streets close to the university, east of the Stadtpark.

Central Austria

South of the Linz–Salzburg line lies a region of Austria that the tourist hordes haven't as yet discovered or spoilt. It consists mainly of mountains, lakes and tiny old villages – the sort of Austria you'd optimistically imagined. Not being commercialized, prices are low, so it's really got everything going for it.

From Vienna or Salzburg catch a train to Attnang Puchheim, then take a local train going in the direction of Stainach Irdning, passing through Gmunden, Hallstatt and Obertraun.

GMUNDEN, a town at the northernmost end of the Traunsee, the largest lake of the region, is particularly lovely. Tourist Information is at Am Graben 2. Traunsteinstrasse is one of the best streets in which to look for accommodation.

HALLSTATT is the third stop after Bad Goisern. It is a particularly beautiful village with lakes, cliffs and a waterfall as the backdrop to your views. The small youth hostel at Lahn 50 (Tel. 06134 279) is open May–mid-September (excellent facilities), and there's camping at Campingplatz Häll (Tel. 06134 329). Tourist information is in the Prähistorisches Museum just off Seestrasse; they'll advise on accommodation. The oldest salt mines in the world (they claim) are here, as well as an incredible graveyard. This area is rich in walks and sails; you can rent a small boat from AS105 an hour. There's a ferry into the town from the station after each train arrives, but you have to pay about AS20, there's no other way round it.

OBERTRAUN, the next stop along, has an interesting ice cave, and 2 other large caves, but the admission cost is quite high. Their youth hostel is at Winkl 26 (Tel. 06131 360) and opens at 5 p.m.; it is more pleasant than the hostel in Hallstatt; AS100 for B&B. Again, open peak season only.

Salzburg city phone code: 662

Extremely expensive, touristy, but beautiful. The prince-archbishops who ruled over the town built many fine churches, palaces, mansions and gardens until it became known as the 'Rome of the North'. The town is famous for its festival (late July–end August), which attracts all the big international names in music and fills every hotel, hostel and campsite with the thousands who flock to this event.

Luckily, Salzburg is a university town, so this slightly eases some of the financial problems eurorailers may encounter. There are some student hostels and restaurants which are less than half the price of their commercial counterparts, but basically Salzburg is a town which caters for the middle-aged and middle-class.

Salzburg is 3¼ hours from Vienna, 2 hours from Munich in Germany, 2½ hours from Innsbruck and 5 hours from Zürich; there are daily trains to Cologne, Hamburg and Copenhagen. The Tourist Information office at the station will help you find a room for AS30. It is to the left side of the building facing you as you come out of passport control.

STATION FACILITIES
Train information is available daily: 7 a.m.–8.30 p.m. (Tel. 1717) and reservations Mon.–Fri.: 9 a.m.–5.30 p.m.; Sat.: 9 a.m.–12.30 p.m. Tourist information is also available daily 8.30 a.m.–8 p.m. (Tel. 871712).

There are all the usual amenities, including 24-hour left-luggage lockers.

TOURIST INFORMATION AND ADDRESSES

The city's main Tourist Information offices are at Mozartplatz 5 (Tel. 847568, 88987330) (open all year Mon.–Sat.: 9 a.m.–6 p.m., Sun.: 9 a.m.–6 p.m., summer only) and at the station. There is an information centre for young travellers, Jugend-Service-Stelle, at Hubert-Sattler-Gasse 7 (Tel. 80722592) open Mon. and Wed.: 10 a.m.–7 p.m., Tues., Thurs. and Sat.: 10 a.m.–4.30 p.m., and Fri.: 10 a.m.–2 p.m. City transport information and free maps are obtained from the bus drivers. Single fares are AS20, with 24-hour and 72-hour passes available at AS180 and AS350. These passes give free entry to the railway for the castle, the Salzburg–Bergheim tramway and the lift to the Mönchsberg terrace. However, most sights are within walking distance of the centre.

POST OFFICE Residenzplatz 9, Mon.–Fri.: 7 a.m.–7 p.m., Sat.: 8 a.m.–10 a.m. or 24-hour service; main railway station.
AMEX Mozartplatz 5–7 (Tel. 842501)
ÖKISTA (Student travel service) Wolf-Dietrich-Strasse. 31 (Tel. 883252), Mon.–Fri.: 9.30 a.m.–5.30 p.m.

SEEING

Gone are the days when Salzburg depended on its salt; tourists now come in their thousands to see the impressive baroque legacy of the powerful archbishops. They weren't all good, though; they did their fair share of expelling the Jews, pillaging and persecuting the local Protestants – all the usual stuff. The HOHENSALZBURG FORTRESS (their residence) shouldn't be missed. Take the funicular up 534m and kill 2 birds with 1 stone, as the view from the top over the city is tremendous. If you're getting fed up with your travelling companion, check out the torture section of the MUSEUM there.

The other 4 main sites are the RESIDENZ (17th-century archbishops' palace), SCHLOSS MIRABELL, the CATHEDRAL and MOZART'S BIRTHPLACE at Getreidegasse 9. Slightly outside Salzburg is SCHLOSS HELLBRUNN, the baroque castle built by a prince-archbishop, surrounded by Salzburg's Hellbrunn zoo. Take bus 55 from the station.

If you've had enough of tourists, there are several escape routes: 2 of them a short bus or train ride away over the border in Bavaria. The first is a visit to Hitler's retreat, the 'EAGLE'S NEST', and the second is a visit to the salt mines. Organized excursions to the salt mines run several times a day from Mirabellplatz, although you can do both trips independently. The starting-off point for both trips is Berchtes-gaden. You might find it more convenient to take the bus as it runs more frequently than the train, and since the journey is quite short the cost is reasonable at around AS40. (Discount with Inter-Rail, free on Eurail.) Once you are at Berchtesgaden you need to take a bus to the mines where you can hire protective clothing for around 25DM. Check to see if your bus passes the mine entrance on the way to Berchtesgaden. For the 'Eagle's Nest' you will need a local service bus to the entrance road, where you change to special buses for the trip up to the car park. Don't even think about going any further if you suffer from vertigo, for the bus seems to be suspended in mid-air for most of the tortuous journey up the single-track mountain road. You then walk into the middle of the mountain before going up to the eyrie in a brass-panelled lift. Total cost about 20DM. The view is quite spectacular, although you might be just as happy to take a cable car up to the top of the Untersberg (1,740m), which will give you fine views of the alpine scenery without the same expense in time and money, but even this is relatively expensive at AS190 return. Alternatively, take one of the regular *Sound of Music* tours round the locations of this popular musical. Details from Tourist Information.

SLEEPING

Your best bet here is to go for private accommodation: ask at Tourist Information for their list of private rooms. Forget hotels, especially during Easter and the summer arts festivals, and try one of the hostels or campsites. If you've no luck here, go to the Tourist Office and tell them the most you can afford, then wait and see what they can come up with. If all else fails, consider going out to one of the villages on the outskirts. For instance, Maria Plan, a few minutes by train, is quiet, well connected to the city and has several pensions to choose from.

YOUTH HOSTELS The Jugendgastehaus Salzburg at Josef-Preis Allee 18 (Tel. 8426700) has 390 beds and all facilities, but fills up quickly so go early or book in advance. It closes 9 a.m.–11 a.m. and at midnight. Reports on cleanliness vary. Take bus 5 to Justizgebäude then a short walk.

The YO-HO International Hostel at Paracelsusstrasse 9 (Tel. 879649) is only a few blocks away from the station. It is reasonably well kept, but noisy, with a washing machine and drier on-site. Although showers and breakfast are extra, you can choose from Continental, British or American. There is also a cheap restaurant/bar which serves an excellent Wiener Schnitzel. Expect to pay around AS150 for a bed.

Near the centre of town is the Jugendherberge Aigen hostel at Aignerstrasse 34 (Tel. 623248-14). Buses 5 or 6 and change to 49 at Zentrum. It can get very busy and noisy.

The hostel at Glockengasse 8 (Tel. 876241) can be reached by bus 29; get off at Hofwirtstrasse. Open Apr.–Oct. only.

PENSIONS Zum Junger Fuchs, Linzergasse 54 (Tel. 875496). AS220-400. Very good. Walk from the Staatsbrücke bridge along Linzer -gasse.

Also try the Elizabeth at Vogelweiderstrasse 52 (Tel. 871664). Doubles about AS350–520.

CAMPING There are several campsites; most are open May–30 September and prices vary from AS50–75 per person and tent. If visiting the sights near Berchtesgaden, try Camping Allwegehein on Untersalzberg mountain (Tel. 08652 2396).

Camping Gnigl Ost, 5023 Salzburg, Parscherstrasse 4 (Tel. 643060) is situated on the side of a football pitch and is very cheap. It is only AS80 for 2 people sharing a tent with the use of the facilities in the club house free – a bargain as the showers are possibly the hottest and cleanest you could find.

Another option is Camping Nordsam, Samstrasse 22a (Tel. 660494). Take bus 33 from the station and set off by the camping sign. It's a 3-minute walk round the corner. A little more expensive at AS100 per person and AS95 per tent, the location makes it worthwhile.

EATING AND NIGHTLIFE

There are plenty of flash restaurants in Salzburg and no shortage of ways to blow your money if you have any. Try Pitterkeller, Rainerstrasse 6, near the station. The food's not bad and it's cheap by Salzburg standards. Recently renovated.

For picnic food, there's a good open-air market on Thursday mornings by St Andrew's church, and there are 2 every weekday on Universitätsplatz and Franz-Josef Strasse. There is a cheap stand-up Imbiss place, with a larger range than most, at Judengasse 10, where Wiener Schnitzel and chips can be had for around AS100.

Beer Gardens: Salzburg is a bit more orientated towards beer than wine, probably due to its proximity to the German border. The beer cellars invariably offer good value in eating, drinking and entertainment. Try Augustiner Bräustübl, Augustinergasse 4 – there are several small stalls in this building where you can treat yourself.

If it's just a drink you're after, try Stiegl Beer Cellar, Festungsgasse 10, which has a great atmosphere and views over the city to match (but closed during the winter), or Students' Centre, Gstättengasse 16, weekdays 9 a.m.–12 noon and 1 p.m.–6 p.m.

Western Austria

The route from Liechtenstein through the Arlberg Tunnel to the Vorarlberg Alps is particularly scenic: mountains, chalets, green fields, etc. The best towns to base yourself in to explore this region are Feldkirch and Bregenz.

FELDKIRCH is an old town with many reminders of its Gothic heyday. The Tourist Office is at Herrengasse 12 (Mon.–Fri.: 8.30 a.m.–12 noon, 2 p.m.–6 p.m., Sat.: 9 a.m.–12 noon). They'll suggest walking tours. There's a youth hostel (Tel. 05522 73181) at Reichsstrasse 111 and a campsite.

BREGENZ, on the shores of Lake Constance (or Bodensee), with its medieval old quarter, is the capital of the Vorarlberg region. It is well known for its opera festival from July 20 to Aug. 21. The information office is at Inselstrasse 15 (Tel. 05574 43391). There's a youth hostel at Belruptstrasse 16a (Tel. 05574 42867) and 4 campsites.

Innsbruck city phone code: 0512

As capital of the Tyrol and the Austrian ski scene, Innsbruck is busy all the year round. It is beautifully situated and well worth a day or two of your time.

STATION FACILITIES

Train information daily 7 a.m.–9.30 p.m. (Tel. 1717) and reservations daily 8 a.m.–7.30 p.m. (Tel. 1700). There's a Tourist Information kiosk and all the other amenities, including 24-hour left-luggage lockers.

For food and provisions, head towards the Maria-Theresienstrasse area, 2 streets straight ahead from the station.

There are daily trains from Innsbruck to Cologne, Hamburg, Munich (2½ hours), Salzburg (2½ hours), Vienna (5½ hours), Milan, Rome, Venice and Zürich (4 hours).

There's a centre for young travellers at the station (open 9 a.m.–10 p.m.). It's wonderful. Seize this opportunity to be treated like a human being and use it.

TOURIST INFORMATION AND ADDRESSES

At the station, open daily 9 a.m.–10 p.m. They'll find you a room and change your cash. There's another office at Burggraben 3, in the city centre, open daily 8 a.m.–7 p.m. The post office is at Maximilianstrasse 2 (one block away from the Triumphal Arch).

The AMEX office is at Brixnerstrasse 3, and the student travel service, Ökista, is at Josef-Hirnstrasse 7/2.

ALPINE INFORMATION As you're in one of the best alpine centres in Europe, you may feel inclined to head for the hills. Check up on conditions before setting off at Wilhelm-Greilstrasse 17 (Tel. 5320 171) or, if you prefer to take an organized hike, contact Tourismusverband at Burggraben 3 (Tel. 59850). Some free hikes are available; persistence at the Tourist Office should get you information on these.

MOUNTAIN HUT SCHEME There are over 700 huts up in the mountains surrounding Innsbruck. They belong to various local and national alpine associations, and doing a tour of them, or even just staying the night in one, is very rewarding, cheap and provides a good memory of Austria. Many of the huts have some cooking facilities and some even serve up hot food. Prices range from about AS150 to AS300 for a night. Washing facilities tend to be basic.

Before setting out, make sure you have emergency food supplies, a waterproof and are wearing good climbing boots. The distress call in this neck of the woods is 6 visible or audible signals spaced evenly over a minute, followed by a minute's break, then the 6 signals again.

SEEING

The Nordkette mountains dominate the main shopping street, Maria-Theresienstrasse. At one end is the TRIUMPHAL ARCH and at the other the old Gothic town. The GOLDEN ROOF is the symbol of Innsbruck; it's an ornate Gothic balcony built in 1500 from 2,657 gilded copper tiles. The ski jump, on the hillside above the town, is a good viewpoint. You could also visit the rather small Olympic Museum here. The HOFBURG (Imperial Palace) is the other major sight.

For an all-round perspective, take the cable car up to HAFELEKAR. At 2,250m, the view is quite spectacular. Take tram 1 to the Hungerburg funicular, then the cable car, but be warned, it is expensive to go all the way. There are also 2 other cable car routes. The 1964 and 1976 Winter Olympics were held at IGLS near Innsbruck, and if you're in the ski set you can still go and see the set-up (bus J from Innsbruck station or tram 6). Enjoy the view but stay out of the cafés there.

If you want to see a pretty alpine village, despite the commercialism, go to the village of FULPMES, in good picnic country. Take tram 1 to Stubaitalbahnhof where the mountain train leaves. An alternative is to take the tram direct from the main station. Buy a hiking map (*Wanderkarte*) and try the rewarding walk from Fulpmes to the Pfarrachalm mountain inn.

SLEEPING

The Glockenhaus Hostel at Weiherburggasse 3 (Tel. 286515) is situated 10 minutes' walk from the town centre and 20 minutes' from the station, although there is a pick-up service from the station if you arrange in advance, or alternatively use bus K. Beds are limited but they also have a building at Innstrasse 95 (Tel. 286515) where they will send you if you want dormitory accommodation. Neither of these takes phone reservations, and there have been complaints about them. The owners lay on ski rental and organize skiing, hiking, river rafting and wind surfing excursions. A typical price is AS310 for a double; there are also singles and larger rooms.

The Pension Tautemann, at Stamser Feld 5 (Tel. 281572), charges AS450–550 for a double room with shower, en suite WC, and includes breakfast. Very comfortable.

There is also a small hostel at Sillgasse 8a, although reports on its cleanliness vary and it is only open peak season. Only 5 minutes' walk from the station, it charges AS190 for bed, breakfast and shower (Tel. 571 311).

There's the youth hostel at Reichenauerstrasse 147, which is a long way from the town centre, has a 10 p.m. curfew, is reportedly unfriendly and has strict rules. Take bus O or R to Campingplatz or a 30-minute walk. Cost is around AS120 (Tel. 46179). Alternatively, try the hostel, Torsten-Arneus Schwedenhaus, at 17b Rennweg (Tel. 585814). Open July and August only. Small rooms at AS165 including breakfast.

The only campsite is Kranebitten, an hour's walk from the station, or bus LK from Bozner Platz.

Avoid eating evening meals in the pensions. The meal may be 'fixed price', but the extras can be expensive.

EATING AND NIGHTLIFE

Head towards the university area. Try Gasthaus Gruber, Innrain 160 (between university and Old Town). Also, the Mensa (off Innrain) at Herzog-Siegmund Ufer 15, 2nd floor, offers cheap meals for ISIC holders, lunchtimes only. Good value meals are available in many old town restaurants, on the way from Maria-Theresienstrasse to the Golden Roof – and the bars/restaurants around here are lively in the evening.

There's a free Tyrolean evening in front of the Golden Roof most Thursday evenings in season at 8.30 p.m. For a pleasant short excursion out of town, try HALL, 8 km down river. Drive up the 1,500m Hinterhornam then walk on to the Walderalm dairy farm and have a meal with the Inn river valley stretching beneath you – great stuff!

NOTES

....

....

....

....

....

....

....

....

....

....

....

....

....

NOTES

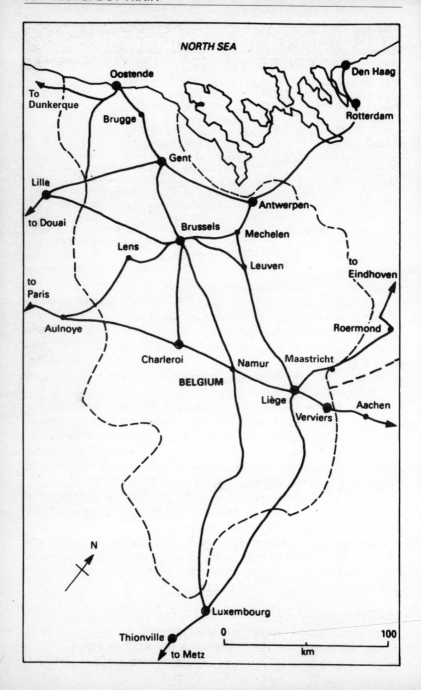

BELGIUM (Belgie; Belgique)

Entry requirements	Passport
Population	10,000,000
Capital	Brussels (pop.: 1,200,000)
Currency	Belgian Franc
	£1 = approx. 55BF
Political system	Constitutional Monarchy
Religion	Roman Catholic
Language	French and Flemish (English widely spoken)
Public holidays	New Year's Day, Easter, Labour Day, Ascension, Whit Monday, Flemish Community Day, Assumption, Assumption, All Saints' Day, Armistice, the King's Birthday, Christmas
International dialling codes	To Belgium: int'l code 32 number
	From Belgium: 00 + country code number

To confuse the Flemish with the Walloons is like calling the Scots or Welsh English – it is a mistake to be avoided in a country where the 2 major ethnic groups each speak their own language and are equally proud of their historical and cultural differences. The Flemish speak their own language closely akin to Dutch, live in the north and west, and still carry the hard-working characteristics of their Germanic forebears. The Walloons, on the other hand, speak French, often in the old French dialect, and are in every way more like their French neighbours.

During the early Middle Ages, trade and commerce created a rich town life unrivalled in northern Europe. All this was to change, however, as Belgium got caught up in the crossfire of European affairs through marriage and alliance. The French, Spanish and Austrians all fought to secure her strategic ports and the fertile lands of Flanders, until she gained independence in 1830.

In the 20th century Belgium was the scene of fierce fighting in both world wars, in particular that of 1914–18, when a generation of men was decimated in the fields of Flanders.

The 4 main centres of interest are: Bruges, Brussels, Antwerp and Ghent, and although Belgium is the second most densely populated country in Europe, it's still possible to find solitude among the forests and hills of the Ardennes in the south.

BELGIAN NATIONAL RAILWAYS

(NATIONALE MAATSCHAPPIJ DER BELGISCHE SPOORWEGEN, NMBS)
(SOCIÉTÉ NATIONALE DES CHEMINS DE FER BELGES, SNCB)

Belgium's train network is one of the most reliable and extensive in

Europe. The trains are frequent and go just about everywhere. To cross the country takes only 3½ hours, and trains leave for most internal destinations every hour. The fastest services are the Euro-City services and the Inter-City services (IC), and the semi-fast services are 'Inter-regional' (IR numbers). No supplements are charged for any trains running wholly within Belgium, but supplements are payable for travel by certain international trains.

Inter-Railers and Eurail pass holders have an extra bonus as it's possible – and often advisable – to use one city as a base and tour the rest of the country from it (it only takes 1 hour from Bruges to Brussels).

PASSES AVAILABLE There are 3 types of ticket which can be purchased for rover travel within Belgium. The 50% reduction card, for 570BF, allows you to buy an unlimited number of single journey tickets at half normal price. It is valid for 1 month on the whole of the Belgian network.

The 5-day Tourrail Card is valid for 5 days of your own choice within a 1-month period. For adults over 26, the second-class card is 1,995BF. First class costs 50% extra.

The Benelux Tourrail card, valid in Belgium, the Netherlands and Luxembourg, works very much like the Tourrail card, costs 4,040BF for adults, and 3,030BF for under 26s. First class 50% extra.

A Euro Domino ticket is also available for Belgium, see p. 41.

The Inter-Rail pass has been broken down into zones, so that a careful selection of zones means you don't have to pay for travel to areas you have no intention of visiting. For £159 you can spend 22 days in a zone. Belgium is in Zone E, along with France, Luxembourg and the Netherlands. (For further details of the 8 Inter-Rail zones, refer to the Inter-Rail section in Part One of this guide.)

INTER-RAIL BONUSES See Appendix I.

EURAIL BONUSES 35% reduction on normal fares for the ferry crossing Ostend–Ramsgate operated by Régie Belge des Transports Maritimes. Reduced fare tickets only at the principal Belgian stations and the ports of Ostend and Dover.

The following half-price reductions are granted by Europabus on transportation costs only and by local offices in Europe:

> Antwerp–Brussels–Menton
> Antwerp–Brussels–Barcelona
> Ostend–Brussels–Frankfurt-am-Main
> Ostend–Lille
> Antwerp–Brussels–Le Havre–Lisieux

TRAIN INFORMATION

Information officers speak good English, other rail staff speak both Flemish and French. If you're spending any time in Belgium, buy a copy of the official SNCB timetable (*indicateur/spoor-boekje*) from any station. It has an introduction in English and explains all you need to know about schedules and supplements. There is also a free pocket-sized booklet giving details of the main services. If you don't get either, don't worry, as there are large posters everywhere, giving departure and arrival information. Most stations have coin-operated lockers, or use the luggage offices, at 60BF per item per day.

RESERVATIONS Are not necessary, or even possible, on inland routes. International reservations cost 80BF and can be made up to 2 months in advance, if you're that highly organized. If you are, you'd probably also like to know that you can reserve seats on trains leaving for Austria, Denmark, France, Germany, Italy and Switzerland at most large stations, as the SNCB's computer is linked up with these countries.

NIGHT TRAVEL Belgium is too small to warrant inland services, but SNCB have couchettes and Wagons-Lits sleepers on international routes. (Look out for the German rolling stock with pull-down seats, to save a bit of money.)

EATING ON TRAINS There are not many services on inland trains; some have a mini-bar and a few have a buffet. Don't let that worry you, though, as Belgium's supermarkets are renowned for their food. International trains have all the usual expensive facilities, so either way prepare a picnic in advance, and don't count on station shops to supply it, as there aren't any, except in major cities.

BIKES SNCB run a scheme called *Train Vélo* (*Trein Fiets* in Flemish) which allows you to take advantage of Belgium's perfect cycling conditions. You can rent a bike from upwards of 160BF per day (with a rail pass) from 35 stations. Most roads have cycle tracks and it's flat going all the way to explore the surrounding countryside. (Don't forget to ask for a free tour map.)

TOURIST INFORMATION

Local Tourist Offices are to be found in every large town. For any extra information on the provinces and the country, ask at the main office in Brussels. If you've any problems Tourist Information can't help out with, try the Info-Jeunes (Info-Jeugd) office. There are branches in most large towns.

ISIC BONUSES 50% off most museums, reductions on rail and bus tickets. For further information, contact Connections, 13 rue Marché au Charbon, 1000 Brussels (also a Eurotrain office), or ACOTRA, rue de la Madeleine 51, 1000 Brussels.

MONEY MATTERS 1 Belgian franc (BF) = 100 centimes.

Banking hours are Mon.–Fri.: 9 a.m.–12 noon, 2 p.m.–4 p.m. Late opening, Friday till 4.30 p.m. AMEX are the only bank that do not charge high commissions on transactions involving traveller's cheques. Eurocheques are thus the preferred means of payment. The station exchanges take no commission, but their rate of exchange is about 10% below the official one. The ferries give a good rate and their commission is considerably less.

POST OFFICES Open Mon.–Fri.: 9 a.m.–5 p.m., tend to shut for lunch but this practice is dying out in cities and popular tourist destinations.

SHOPS AND MUSEUMS There are no hard-and-fast rules here, but museums tend to shut either on Mondays or Fridays, and some in the afternoons. Shops open 10 a.m.–6/7 p.m., Mon.–Sat., with lunch 12 noon–2 p.m. Bakers and newsagents open early in the morning, and you can also find a grocer open on Sunday somewhere. Many shops stay open till 9 p.m. Late night Friday.

TIPPING The Belgians have a bit of a reputation for keeping their hand outstretched if they want a tip. Although this may be somewhat exaggerated, do expect a tipping culture. Restaurants and such-like normally include this on the bill so you're not under pressure to add any more, but it is acceptable practice to 'round up'.

SLEEPING

Apart from Tourist Information, the Info-Jeunes offices also give help with accommodation. Unmarried couples wanting to sleep together might find problems if they are under 18 as hoteliers can be imprisoned for up to 3 years under Belgian law for allowing this.

Hostels are your best bet – either the IYHF ones or those run by an organization called Amis de la Nature/Natuurvrienden. There are two IYHF organizations, one for the French region, one for the Flemish. There are a few unofficial ones, as well as student hostels which offer a more relaxed atmosphere. All of these are given in the *Budget Holi-*

day booklet which you can pick up at any Tourist Information office.

Hotels tend to be expensive (absolute minimum 1,000BF double) but clean, and offer an inclusive continental breakfast.

EATING AND NIGHTLIFE

The Belgians love their food and take eating very seriously, a fact which is borne out by the well-stocked supermarkets you will find even in the small towns. Always be prepared for an impromptu picnic. If you're eating out, go for your main meal at lunchtime as the fixed menu is not available at night, so making dinner a more expensive affair. Belgian cuisine is similar to French, both in quality and in price. If possible, try some local specialities: *carbonnades flamandes* (beef stewed in beer) and *waterzooi* (chicken and vegetables stewed in sauce). Don't miss the Belgian waffles served with fruit or cream, or the excellent pastry and cakes, and if you think the Swiss are the only Europeans who know how to make delicious chocolates, try the Belgian pralines (especially the fresh-cream-filled white chocolates, available from any branch of Leonidas).

Apologies for making your mouth water if you're really broke, but there are always Belgian chips, which are small, thin and delicious and are served with mayonnaise. In fact, the *friterie/frituur* is the cheapest and most prolific source of fast food in Belgium. There's always one near a station, and they serve kebabs, sausages, etc., too.

Belgium's selection of bars would satisfy the most demanding drinker. While wine is good and cheaper than in the UK, you'll do best to try what they're famous for: beer. In the cities, it's quite common to find pubs serving up to 50 varieties (La Houblonnière in Brussels boasts 100). Try one of the Trappist brews, a good nightcap, or for those willing to try anything once, *kriek*, a cherry-flavoured beer.

There is no shortage of theatres, cinemas or discos, and the set-up is very similar to the UK. Don't waste your time looking for cheap seats or student discounts, as they do not exist.

Ostend (Oostende) city phone code: 059

If you're coming from England by ferry or Jetfoil, chances are you will land here. There's not much to see, but if you want to stop overnight, the youth hostel De Ploate at Langestraat 82 (Tel. 059 805 297) is only 5 minutes from the docks and station and is very good. It is, however, difficult to get a bed during summer, so try to book in advance.

Bruges (Brugge – Flemish; Bruges – French)
city phone code: 050

This beautifully preserved medieval town is more like an open-air museum than a 20th-century city. If you're going to stop off anywhere in Belgium, make sure it's Bruges, as this is definitely one of the most attractive towns in Europe. For over 200 years, Bruges was one of the most important commercial centres in western Europe, and the Counts of Flanders spent their money making the town's guildhalls, palaces and churches as impressive as they could. All this glory came to an end when their harbour silted up and made trade impossible. Bruges is known as the 'Venice of the North', and its network of canals, bridges (*brugge* means 'bridge') and tall Gothic buildings reminds you very much of its Italian counterpart.

STATION FACILITIES
The station is on the southern edge of the town, 1½ km from the city centre. If you don't feel like a walk (although it is quite pleasant through the large park) get any of the buses going to the Markt, close to where the main Tourist Information is situated. There's train information daily: 6.30 a.m.–10.30 p.m. (Tel. 382 382, multi-lingual) and all the usual amenities including cycle hire and a post office. The station shuts 1 a.m.–4.30 a.m.

Daily trains to: Amsterdam, Cologne, Vienna, Koblenz, Berlin, Belgrade, London (via Ramsgate), Munich, Salzburg, Basle, Brig, Milan, Brussels, Paris.

TOURIST INFORMATION AND ADDRESSES
The Tourist Office is at Burg 11 (Tel. 448686) and is open Apr.–Sept., Mon.–Fri.: 9.30 a.m.–6.30 p.m., Sat.: and Sun.: 10 a.m.–12 p.m., 2 p.m.–6.30 p.m. and Oct.–Mar., Mon.–Fri.: 9.30 a.m.–5 p.m., Sat.: 9.30 a.m.–1.15 p.m. and 2–5 p.m. Closed Sunday. They will sell you a map, give you leaflets and fix up a bed for you. There is an exchange bureau in the building Apr.–Oct., daily except Wednesdays.

The post office is nearby at the Markt.

The Youth Information Centre, JAC, on Kleine Hertsbergerstraat 1 (Tel. 33 83 06), amongst other things, has lists of cheap rooms.

SEEING
The main things to see are: THE BELFRY on the Markt, built from the

13th to the 15th century. Climb up for a good view of the layout of the old town and listen out for the CARILLON (bell concert). Two museums right next door to each other on the Dyver are GRUUTHUSE and GROENINGE (closed at lunchtime, and on Tuesdays in winter). Gruuthuse is a museum of applied arts, housed in a particularly beautiful 15th-century mansion, while Groeninge is devoted to Flemish painting and contemporary art. Joined on to Gruuthuse is the 13th-century CHURCH OF OUR LADY, containing Michelangelo's *Madonna and Child*. The BEGIJNHOF (a Belgian type of convent) is in a peaceful location off the Wijngaardplein. You can wander around the interior and the grounds for free or pay a few francs to visit the museum.

The canal boat trips may seem a rip-off at around 200BF a go, but they're actually quite good value as you get an added perspective on the town and they don't rush. Bus fares are a set fee for any distance, but as you can see most of Bruges on foot, you shouldn't need to use them much. If you're wanting to see 'alternative Flanders', try taking one of the cheap bus tours offered by Quasimodo's. They are very good, covering everything from beer tasting to the World War I and II cemeteries, expertly guided (Tel. 370470 or call at 52 Engelendalelaan, 8310 St-Kruis, or Poortersstraat 47).

If you are feeling fairly active and have 3 hours or so to spare, hire a bike at the station from upwards of 150BF per day and cycle to SLUIS, just over the Dutch border. Take the road Noorweegsie Kaai and follow the Bruges–Sluis canal for 15 km till you reach Sluis. It's real biking country and is worth the effort to see the windmill at Sluis itself.

SLEEPING

Try and stay central, as all the sights in Bruges are close together; bear in mind that the town gets its fair share of visitors in summer, so get there early.

The youth hostel Europa is at Baron Ruzettelaan 143 (Tel. 352679). It's not too central, can be crowded, but is reasonable, if a little more expensive than some of the other hostels in town. There is an 11 p.m. curfew and you'll need an IYHF card and 375–470BF for B&B in dorms. Closed Mon.–Sat.: 10 a.m.–1 p.m., Sun.: 10 a.m.–5 p.m., and over Christmas and the New Year. Take bus 2 to Steenbrugge and get off shortly after the canal. The driver will point it out.

Some good private hostels are in Bruges as well. Try The Passage, Dweersstraat 26 (Tel. 340232) or Hotel Lybeer, Korte Vulderstraat 31 (Tel. 334355).

The Snuffel Travellers' Inn is also good value, 300–350BF for B&B,

based on sharing a 4-person room. It's at Ezelstraat 47–49 (Tel. 333133). Though not exactly luxurious, it is comfortable, central and friendly, and has recently been renovated. There is a good choice of reasonably priced meals and the bar has a happy hour each evening. Get there early as there are only 50 beds.

Bauhaus at Langestraat 135–137 has 105 beds (Tel. 341093). Cost from 380BF for dorms, or 950BF for a double with B&B. Five minutes from market place, near the windmills.

Camping St Michiel is at Tillegemstraat 55, St Michiels (Tel. 380819), from 95BF per person, 135BF per tent. Quite a way out: take bus 7 from the station or 't Zand. Change traveller's cheques here free of commission.

EATING AND NIGHTLIFE

As Bruges is not a university town, there's no specific cheap student area, but you can get by. The Lotus at Wapenmakerstraat does a good *plat du jour* for lunch and serves vegetarian dishes. The Ganzespel at Ganzestraat 37 do a cheapish *menu du jour*. There are late-night cafés dotted around the old town; Vlissinge on Blekerstraat claims to be among the oldest in Europe.

EXCURSIONS FROM BRUGES

50 km south of Bruges are the Battlefields of YPRES. During the four long years of the Great War 'Flanders Fields' witnessed the loss of a generation. Visit 'some corner of a foreign field' with Salient Tours. Contact 051 505788.

Brussels (Brussel – Flemish; Bruxelles – French)
city phone code: 02

Brussels is a real patchwork of old and new: a city of extreme contrasts, from the 17th-century GRAND' PLACE to the modern skyscrapers of the multinationals and the EC headquarters. The main part of this capital which is worth seeing is enclosed in quite a small area of the old town; don't waste your time on the new 'cement heap', as predictably there's nothing unique or particularly Belgian about it. The city revolves round 'the most beautiful square in Europe' – the Grand' Place. Try to view it in daytime and then again when it's floodlit at night.

STATION FACILITIES

Brussels has 3 main stations: Gare du Nord, Gare du Midi and Gare Centrale. Though Centrale handles few international trains, it is conveniently located for the Grand' Place area, and there are inter-connecting trains between the 3 stations every 15–20 minutes. Trains leave daily for Holland, Denmark, Germany, Switzerland, Italy and France. It takes less than 3 hours to get to Cologne, Paris or Amsterdam from Brussels.

There are some booths near the Gare du Midi selling food, and friteries in the nearby rue de France. For Tourist Information go to Gare Centrale and walk across Place de l'Europe for 3 blocks.

There's a post office near Gare du Midi (open 24 hours) and at Centrale. You'll find social segregation at the Midi station in the form of the Brussels Tavern, which provides a snack bar, etc. Officially, these are only for the use of EuroCity or IC passengers, but in practice you can get in if reasonably dressed. Don't be tempted to buy anything, as the prices are roughly double what you can pay elsewhere in the station.

For information on city transport, head down to the metro station at Gare du Midi.

Finally, if you arrive late at night when the Tourist Office is shut, head for the Gare du Nord, as there are several student hostels in this area.

TOURIST INFORMATION

Is at 61 rue de Marché-aux-Herbes (Tel. 504 0390). The TIB on Grand' Place (Tel. 513 8940) is also OK but gets very busy. Hours of both the city's Tourist Offices are, Mar.–Sept.: 9 a.m.–6 p.m. daily; Oct.–Nov.: 9 a.m.–4 p.m. Mon.–Sat., 10 a.m.–2 p.m. Sundays; Dec.–Feb.: 10 a.m.–2 p.m. Mon.–Sat., closed Sunday.

They'll fix you up with accommodation and give you maps and all the usual handouts.

Other organizations providing help are:

ACOTRA, rue de la Madeleine 51 (Tel. 512 8607 and 512 5540). This youth organization provides a free room-finding service. They're open weekdays 10 a.m.–5.30 p.m. (Tel. 070 233444).

INFO-JEUGDJEUNES, rue Marché-aux-Herbes 27 (Tel. 512 3274) is near the Grand' Place and is open Mon.–Fri.: 12 a.m.–6 p.m.

ADDRESSES

POST OFFICE First floor of tall building at Place de la Monnaie, poste restante here.

AMEX Place Louise 2 (Tel. 512 1740), open Mon.–Fri.: 9 a.m.–5 p.m., Sat.: 9.30 a.m.–noon.

UK EMBASSY Britannia House, 85 rue d'Arlon (Tel. 287 6211)

IRISH EMBASSY 19 rue Luxembourg (Te.l 513 6633)

US EMBASSY 27 blvd du Régent (Tel. 513 3830)

CANADIAN EMBASSY 2 av. de Tervuren (Tel. 735 6040)

AUSTRALIAN EMBASSY 6 rue Guimard (Tel. 231 0500)

NEW ZEALAND EMBASSY 47 blvd du Régent (Tel. 512 1040)

AMBULANCE Tel. 100

POLICE Tel. 101

24-HOUR CHEMIST 99 av. Houba (Tel. 479 1818)

GETTING ABOUT

Basically, there's a flat rate of around 50BF within the city which is valid for transfers between métro, bus and tram for 1 hour. There's also a tourist pass which gives unlimited travel for 1 day, costing 120BF. You can also buy a 10-trip pass from métro stations for 305BF, or a 5-trip pass for 220BF. For information on city transport, there are offices under the Place Rogier, Porte de Namur and Gare du Midi.

One tip – if using the métro take a map with you, there is limited information posted, and it is hard to understand.

SEEING

If you have only a single day, a bus tour is the best bet. But try to avoid the traditional ones in luxury coaches and 6 languages which end your tour at a lace shop where the driver gets a back-hander – there's usually a much better alternative with Chatterbus. It's run by the former manager of one of the city's youth hostels and is aimed at the young eurorail type of customer. Chatterbus takes in all the places you want to see in Brussels – and a few of the ones the city authorities would rather you didn't. You'll get a good tour of the city and an honest assessment of the places not worth exploring further. The cost is around 650BF, or 500BF if you are staying at one of the youth hostels. The same group also runs 'Brussels on Foot' tours during the summer at around 250BF each. If you're in a group they will arrange off-beat tours such as hijacking a tram, or a beer-tasting night, including beer-flavoured food, and they also have lists of ordinary Brussels residents who are prepared to act as guides for the price of the telephone call to book them. Book through youth hostels, or call Chatterbus directly (Tel. 673 1835). As Chatterbus is more of an informal service than a profit-making business, you may find it only runs on certain days and at certain times. But it is well worth making the effort to try to catch one of these tours.

If you've a bit more time or like to be independent, head for the GRAND' PLACE, which is *the* sight of Brussels – a well-preserved collection of Gothic guildhalls and public buildings from the 17th century. In the mornings, except Mondays, a flower market is held there, Apr.–Nov., and at night it's floodlit. Opposite the MAISON DU ROI (the city museum) is the Gothic TOWN HALL, considered Brussels' most elegant building. MANNEKEN-PIS (a small statue of a boy having a pee) is the symbol of Brussels and is situated behind the town hall on rue l'Étuve. There are several stories as to his origin, the main one being that he saved the city by damping down some dynamite – in a natural and effective fashion.

The MUSÉE DES BEAUX ARTS has a good collection of early Flemish masters, including Rubens (free; closed Monday). In contrast, next door is the modern art gallery, THE MUSEUM OF ART AND HISTORY, one of the largest in Europe, covering absolutely everything (closed Monday). It is situated at the Parc du Cinquantenaire. The MUSICAL INSTRUMENT MUSEUM has the largest collection in the world (over 4,000).

If you've any time left, try and see the PALAIS DE JUSTICE, closed weekends, ST MICHAEL'S CATHEDRAL and ERASMUS'S HOUSE.

Paris has the Eiffel Tower and London Big Ben, but Brussels' big monument (apart from Manneken-Pis) is the ATOMIUM, an immense model of an iron molecule, which was built to celebrate the 1958 International Exhibition at Heysel. At the foot of the Atomium is MINI-EUROPE, a collection of 350 models of well-known European sights. Spot the places you have seen, but at a price: 380BF. Open 25 Mar.–7 Jan. Also in the same area, known as Bruparck, there are a water theme park, a planetarium, an IMAX cinema and a 27-screen cinema, claimed to be the world's biggest.

A few interesting day trips from Brussels are: LEUVEN, a medieval university town (20 minutes by train); WATERLOO, site of the battle, now with museums; and BOKRIJK, the largest open-air museum in Europe with over 100 reconstructions of medieval buildings (Apr.–Oct.). Trains from any Brussels station (90 minutes). Note that it is quite a walk from the Waterloo station to the Wellington Museum – and too far to walk to the battlefield (though a bus runs in peak season) so a better bet is to take the bus which runs from Place Rouppe every 30 minutes, all year round, directly to the battlefield. Place Rouppe is between Gare du Midi and Grand' Place.

There is a good amusement park at BIERGES, a half-hour from Gare du Nord, called WALIBI. For a more relaxed day trip head to LOUVIAN, thirty minutes away by train and littered with ornate houses and some excellent coffee shops.

SLEEPING

Unless you're prepared to go a long way out of town, your choice is limited to hostelling or hotelling (the campsites are a long way out). There's not much difficulty getting a bed in Brussels, even in summer, and things are getting easier. The best area to concentrate your efforts on is round the Gare du Nord. If you have any trouble, ACOTRA (see under tourist info) will find a bed for you.

STUDENT HOSTELS Sleep Well at rue Damier 23 (Tel. 218 5050) is the best value in the city. It's clean, central (near Gare du Nord, in the direction of Place Rogier), cheap and has a good atmosphere. It makes an effort to be different, and in fact the piped background music is all classical. Dormitory beds are around 360BF, singles 620BF and doubles 980BF. Open 7 a.m.–1 a.m. Try to reserve ahead as it's popular. In summer, it arranges city tours by local students.

Another student hostel which offers good value is CHAB at 8 rue Traversière (Tel. 217 0158) close to the Botanique metro station, or 10 minutes' walk from the Gare du Nord. It has 180 beds in dorms (use own sleeping bag) (380BF), 3/4 bedded rooms (430BF), twins (510BF) and singles (620BF). 10% reduction with ISIC. Although school groups are accepted in low season, the preferred age range in summer is 18–35. Open 7.30 a.m.–2 a.m. This hostel also has kitchen, laundry and locker facilities. They organize walking tours of Brussels and free, or cheap, music and art events, plus there is an open-air cinema at the nearby Botanique Culture Centre.

YOUTH HOSTELS There's a hostel at Heilige Geeststraat 2 (Tel. 511 0436) near the Kappelle Kerk/Église de la Chapelle; head down Keizerslaan from Centrale station. It's known as the Breugel and costs from 395BF to 660BF including breakfast. You'll need an IYHF card.

The International Accommodation Centre Jacques Brel is at rue de la Sablonnière 30 (Tel. 218 0187). It has 134 beds and charges between 395BF and 660BF, including breakfast. It is open all year round, but booking is essential. Has a cafeteria, information and TV room; métro Botanique or Madou.

Hostel La Fonderie, at 4 rue de l'Eléphant, has 130 beds, and charges 395BF to 660BF (Tel. 410 3858). Take métro to Comtes de Flandres.

PENSIONS/HOTELS There are a few at Avenue Fonsny (opposite Gare du Midi): the Merlo is OK and reasonably priced by Brussels standards.

Hôtel Sabina at 78 rue du Nord (Tel. 218 2637) and Hôtel de l'Yser, 913 rue d'Edinbourg (Tel. 511 7459) are worth investigating.

The Hôtel du Grand Colombier at rue du Colombier 10 (Tel. 217 9622 or 219 5136) charges around 1,100BF for a double, with shower, including breakfast. The Sleepwell, 27 rue de la Blanchisserie (Tel. 218 5050) offers a 10% reduction with ISIC. Ask at TIB for other suggestions.

CAMPING Try Beersel, Steenweg op Ukkel 75 (Tel. 331 0561 or 378 1977), 9 km south of the city, or Paul Rosmant, at Warandeberg 52 (Tel. 782 1009) although the latter, while nearer town, is only open between April and the end of September. Metro to Kraainem, then bus 30 to Place St Pierre.

Also Grimbergen at Veldkanstraat 64 (Tel. 269 2597), open Jan.–Oct., bus G from Gare du Nord to terminus, then walk.

EATING AND NIGHTLIFE

It's easy to eat cheaply and well in Brussels. Use the stalls on the main shopping streets for waffles. There are plenty of fast-food chains and no shortage of cheap restaurants with fixed-price meals. For a splash out, go along the rue des Bouchers, trying the varieties of *moules marinières* (400–500BF). The department stores offer good food at reasonable prices and the shopping centre, City 2, located off Place Rogier (5 minutes from Gare du Nord), has several cafés; the one on the top floor does soup and as much salad as you can get on your plate for around 100BF. Open 9 a.m.–8.30 p.m. The Vietnamese and African restaurants are also good value and Le Breton, 59 rue des Drapiers, offers authentic Belgian food, beer and wines in a studenty atmosphere.

Head for the Gare du Midi – the student quarter – for pubs, clubs, etc. Discos are expensive, so make do with a lively pub if you can. Try Le Dolle Mol, 52 rue des Éperonniers, for the young crowd. To meet the locals go to La Mort Subite at rue Montagne aux Herbes Potagères, or Bierodrome at Place Fernand Cocq 21. Films are good value (usually 180BF for students), and the Styx, 72 rue de l'Arbre Bénit, shows revival films with midnight meals, which usually attract an interesting crowd.

Southern Belgium

The main line to Luxembourg passes through Namur and the Ardennes. To explore the area, it's best to base yourself at NAMUR; the regional Tourist Office is at rue Notre Dame 3 (Tel. 081 22 29 98). For information on the city, go to the pavilion next to the station or the Info-Jeunes at the belfry in the town (Tel. 081 71 47 40). Namur has one of the friendliest youth hostels in Europe at rue Félicien Rops, 8 La Plante (Tel. 081 22 36 88, bus 3 or 4 from the station).

Antwerp (Antwerpen – Flemish; Anvers – French)
city phone code: 03

Belgium's second city is famous for its flourishing diamond trade, its shipping and fine art. There are 2 stations: Berchem and Central; international trains stop only at Berchem, except those from Amsterdam. The Tourist Office is at Grote Markt 15, open Mon.–Sat.: 9 a.m.–6 p.m.; Sun. and holidays: 9 a.m.–5 p.m. Most sights are concentrated in the old town: for example, OUR LADY'S CATHEDRAL, and PETER PAUL RUBENS' HOUSE. There is also the GROTE MARKT, with over 2,500 paintings and an excellent exhibition of 8 centuries of northern painting, as well as ST CHARLES BORROMEO'S CHURCH, the PLANTIN-MORETUS MUSEUM of 16th-century printing and CASTLE STEEN, a maritime museum. Most of the museums are shut on Mondays. There are free diamond-cutting exhibitions and tours of diamond works; ask at Tourist Information.

The student hostel Boomerang at Volkstraat 49 (Tel. 2384782) is centrally located and reasonably priced, though reports of standards vary. Take bus 23 from Central station to the Museum stop, or tram 8 from Berchem station. Hôtel Florida, at De Keyserlei 59, is right in front of Central Station.

The New International Youth Hostel at 256 Provinciestraat (Tel. 2300522) is clean, friendly and near the station, down Pelikaanstraat, 20 minutes to Provinciestraat. The youth hostel (IYHF) is at Eric Sasselaan 2 (Tel. 2380273). Tram 2 or bus 27 from Central station, to just after bridge across main road.

There is a campsite at Vogelzanglaan (Tel. 2385717), bus 17 to the Holiday Inn Crowne Plaza hotel, which is cheap. Another site is located at St-Annastrand, on the left bank of the river (Tel. 2196090).

Don't be taken in by the 'rooms for tourists' advertised in cafés around the station – they're brothels!

For food, the Prinsstraat area (round the university) has several cafés doing fixed-price menus. The local dish is worth trying, it's mussels with chips and mayonnaise. The old town is lively in the evenings and round the Grote Markt there are bars and restaurants – but they're rather expensive.

Ghent (Gent – Flemish; Gand – French)
city phone code: 09

Renowned for its art and flowers and a glut of historic buildings. Day trippers from Antwerp should get off at Dampoort station, which is nearer the centre, but from all other destinations you go on to St Pieter's station which is a 24-hour station but train information is obviously only available (daily) 7 a.m.–9 p.m. (Tel. 222 4444). Reservations have much the same hours and there are all the usual other facilities. Daily trains to: Cologne, Vienna, Koblenz, Berlin, Belgrade, Munich, Salzburg, Basle, Brig, Milan, Brussels, Paris.

Tram 1 will take you to the centre, Korenmarkt. Tourist Information is at Botermarkt Crypt, Town Hall (Tel. 225 3641 and 224 1555) 2 Apr.–6 Nov.: Mon.–Sun.: 9.30 a.m.–6.30 p.m.; 7 Nov.–14 April: Mon.–Sun.: 9.30 a.m.–4.30 p.m.

All the sights are central and within easy walking distance of one another. The main sights are: the CATHEDRAL OF ST BAVO, containing Van Eyck's *The Mystic Lamb*; next door is the BELFRY, 'S'GRAVENSTEEN – the 12th-century FLEMISH COUNTS' CASTLE – and the guildhouses by Graslei.

The new youth hostel De Droecke is at Sint-Widostraat, 9000 Gent (Tel. 233 7050). Alternatively, use pensions or the university halls of residence during holidays which are at Stalhof 6 (Tel. 264 7100), just off Overpoortstraat (open 24 hours, all single rooms). The university at Overpoortstraat is also your best bet for eats and nightlife, and has the added advantage of being near the station – take bus 9, 70, 71 or 90.

There is camping at Camping Blaarmeersen, Zuiderlaan 12 (Tel. 221 5399), bus 51, 52 or 53 to the Europaburg, then bus 38, or a 30-minute walk from St Pieter's station.

BOSNIA-HERCEGOVINA

The normal country information you would find at the beginning of each section has been omitted here since the country is still in such a state of turmoil that much of it is irrelevant. Few people (if any) will visit Bosnia-Hercegovina in the near future, but the information given here represents as clear a picture as we are able to give in the circumstances.

You will probably not require a visa to enter Bosnia-Hercegovina and if you do cross the border, chances are a soldier will decide whether or not to let you in. The population count is indeterminate but, at the last count, it was around 4,500,000. The capital, or what is left of it, is Sarajevo and the political system depends on which town you are in.

Currency, generally speaking, is worthless regardless of the type – though Deutschmarks may come in handy; food is the main 'currency' people want. The country used to be comprised of 49% Muslims, 32% Orthodox Serbs and 19% Catholic Croats, but what is left now is anybody's guess. Languages include Serbian and Croatian, which are written and pronounced differently (see the language notes under Croatia and Yugoslavia), and if you can find a phone that works, dial 99 country code number to call the outside world. Needless to say, both train system and Tourist Offices are non-existent at present or, at least, not operative.

In March 1992, the population of Bosnia-Hercegovina voted for independence with a 99% majority – the Serbs abstained. The country was officially recognized by both the EC and USA on 6 April (even though the elected government went out of its way to secure rights for Muslims, Croats and Serbs alike). Belgrade's propaganda of a 'Greater Serbia' helped incite Serb extremists to fight for control. The situation is far from resolved and the country is considered unsafe by every government in the world. As such, we do not encourage travel there but include the information below for the sake of completeness.

Sarajevo

The official capital of Bosnia-Hercegovina was shaped by its 500 years of Turkish rule. There used to be 73 mosques here and the river front was virtually unchanged since 1914, when Archduke Ferdinand was assassinated. Sarajevo was the only oriental city in Europe and the Turkish bazaar of Bascarsija was one of the great bazaars of the world (2 others being Marrakech and Istanbul). Unfortunately, continued shelling from Serb guerrillas in the hills has left little of this city and its culture.

Mostar

This town used to be quite beautiful, though touristy, with a magnificent Turkish-built bridge stretching across the river Neretva. There was also a well-preserved old town, though reports from EC monitors say that little remains.

The nearby city of BLAGAJ lies in the shadow of the castle from which Herceg Stjepan Vukcic (for whom Hercegovina was named) ruled much of what is now southern Bosnia-Hercegovina. This *was* a lovely town, but it's impossible to guarantee what it will be like by the time the fighting comes to an end.

Medujorde

This town is a modern pilgrimage site for Catholics who maintain that visions of the Virgin Mary have been, and are still, seen here. Much of this region is under Croat control (being Catholics, the Croats have struggled to keep the area from being destroyed or desecrated). While travelling in Dalmatia in early 1992, I met several devout pilgrims on their way to, and returning from, this site. Those who returned claimed that everything was safe and the site preserved, but I would not recommend a visit.

NOTES

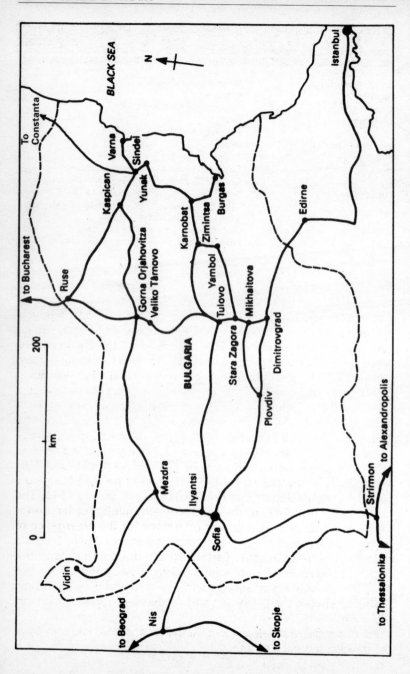

BULGARIA

Entry requirements	Passport and visa
Population	9,300,000
Capital	Sofia (pop.: 1,000,000)
Currency	Leva
	£1 = approx. 90 Leva
Political system	Republic
Religion	Eastern Orthodox
Language	Bulgarian (Russian widely spoken; some German, French and English understood)
Public holidays	New Year's Day, Liberation Day (3 Mar.), Easter, Labour Day, Bulgarian Culture Day (24 May), Saints' Day, Christmas
International dialling codes	To Bulgaria: int'l code 359 number
	From Bulgaria: 00 + country code number

Every year, swarms of tourists from East and West alike flock to the Black Sea coast for the sun. Few venture far from their hotels, leaving much of the country's interior unspoilt. The original Bulgars were an Asiatic tribe who were eventually conquered by Slavs from the north. By the 10th century, Bulgaria had her own empire in which literature and the arts flourished. This continued till the 14th century, while trade helped Bulgaria to become the leader in south-eastern Europe. In 1396, the Ottomans became worried at what was going on and moved in. For the next 500 years they hung about to keep a check on things, and only left after the Russo–Turkish war of 1877 obliged them to do so. Fortunately during this long period the Bulgarians managed to preserve their native culture by giving refuge to writers and artists in their monasteries, many of which survive.

The Bulgarians were allied with the Germans in both World Wars and Bulgaria was occupied by the USSR in 1944 before becoming a Socialist People's Republic in the Russian mould during 1946. The ousting, during 1989, of the hard-line communist leader, Todor Zhivkov, led towards democratic reforms. With the emergence of political parties and the free elections of summer 1990, Bulgaria followed the trend in other Eastern European countries, with the reformed and renamed communists holding power. Along with new freedoms came rising inflation, unemployment and renewed ethnic tensions between the Bulgarians and the formerly repressed Turkish Muslim minority.

Prices are still relatively low but rising fast, and hard currency buys the traveller less each month.

BULGARIAN STATE RAILWAYS (BDZ)

Trains tend to be overcrowded and slow in Bulgaria. Occasionally things come together and they run on time, but this is the exception rather than the rule. There are 3 types of trains: express (*Ekspresen*), fast (*Brzi*) and slow (*Putnichki*). Avoid the latter at all costs. Unfortunately, BIJ only run as far as Sofia. In theory, it should be possible to cross the country to the Black Sea coast and return again late the same day – trains leave Sofia early every morning, arriving at Burgas in the early afternoon. In practice, there are often delays at intermediate stations. Whenever possible, buy your ticket at least a day before setting off. Reservations are compulsory on most expresses, or arrive early at the station to be sure of a seat. An alternative would be to take the overnight sleeper trains. Fortunately for eurorailers, Sofia is not too far across the Serbian border: take an express from Belgrade to Dimitrovgrad, at the border, then the normal fare to Sofia.

During recent years, many of the services between Bulgaria and former Yugoslav states were suspended due to the civil war. Try to buy your ticket before getting the train, if possible in other Eastern countries, as the fare charged once your're on board the train is higher. It is also advisable to buy a return ticket outside the country, as Bulgarian Railways tend to overcharge for international journeys.

PASSES AVAILABLE The Inter-Rail pass has been broken down into zones, so that you pay only for travel within the area you want to visit. For £159 you can spend 22 days touring a zone. Bulgaria is now in Zone H, along with Yugoslavia, Bosnia-Hercegovinia, Romania and Macedonia. For details of the 8 Inter-Rail zones, see the Inter-Rail section in Part One of this guide.

A Euro-Domino ticket is also available for Bulgaria, see p. 41.

Those wishing to explore further afield should enquire about a Balkan Flexi Pass which covers Bulgaria, Greece, Macedonia, Romania and Serbia and Turkey. Under-26s can travel for 5 days in 1 month for US$90, 10 days for US$126, 15 days for US$190. Tickets for those over 26 are US$152, US$264 and US$317 respectively.

TRAIN INFORMATION

Few of the staff speak English, so you might find German and French more helpful. Timetables are given in the Cyrillic alphabet (see p. 128), but there is a Latin equivalent shown against international trains. If you're stuck, try: *Ot koi peron zaminava vlaka za… ?* (From which platform does the train to… leave?) Depend on your *Thomas Cook European Timetable* for most of the time.

RESERVATIONS To be sure of a seat you'll have to reserve at least one day in advance. Reservations are obligatory on international expresses, but are not available on the Sofia–Istanbul leg of the Munich express. They can be made through BalkanTourist or RILA offices. They may be available for foreign travellers at stations by this year, but do not count on this.

NIGHT TRAVEL All couchettes and sleepers are operated by the state railways and fall well short of Western standards.

EATING ON TRAINS There's either a buffet car or mini-bar on all fast trains.

TOURIST INFORMATION

There are BalkanTourist Offices in nearly every large town. They answer all your travel and accommodation problems as well as giving out tourist information. Balkantourist is in the process of being broken up – expect its name to change regionally, and private tourist agencies to be set up, like *Varnenski bryag* in the Varna region. With the recent political upheaval some street names have changed, in some cases more than once. Best bet is to find information before you go.

Try Independent Travel Line, Sofia House, 19 Conduit St, London W1 (Tel. 0171 493 8612), they're the non-package holiday part of Balkan Tours.

ISIC BONUSES With an ISIC card (obtainable from ORBITA Youth Travel Bureau, 45a Boulevard Stambolijski, Sofia), cheap entrance charges to many museums and galleries are available.

MONEY MATTERS 1 leva = 100 stotinki
Banking hours are 8 a.m.–12.30 a.m. and 1 p.m.–3 p.m. Mon.–Fri. As usual, forget the blackmarketeers; you risk being ripped off. Be sure to keep hold of your exchange receipts.

SHOPS Open 8 a.m.–5 or 7 p.m. with a siesta from 1 p.m. to 2 p.m.

MUSEUMS Tend to shut on Mondays, but there's no fixed pattern; opening times also tend to vary.

LANGUAGE Like the Russian language, Bulgarian is written with the Cyrillic alphabet, with some variations.
It is also useful to remember that in Bulgaria a nod means 'No'

(*Ne*), and that a horizontal shake means 'Yes' (*Da*), though as contact with the West increases, expect confusion.

CYRILLIC ALPHABET		ENGLISH EQUIVALENT	SOUND VALUE		CYRILLIC ALPHABET		ENGLISH EQUIVALENT	SOUND VALUE	
А	а	A	for **Anglia**		П	п	P	for **Park**	
Б	б	B	for **Bed**		Р	р	R	for **Road**	
В	в	V	for **Vault**		С	с	S	for **Soft**	
Г	г	G	for **Garage**		Т	т	T	for **Trail**	
Д	д	D	for **Day**		У	у	Ou	for **Cool**	
Е	е	E	for **Engine**		Ф	ф	F	for **Fair**	
Ж	ж	Zh	for **Azure**		Х	х	H	for **Hot**	
З	з	Z	for **Zebra**		Ц	ц	Ts	for **Tsar**	
И	и	I	for **In**		Ч	ч	Ch	for **Cheese**	
Й	й	Y	for **Yes**		Ш	ш	Sh	for **Ship**	
К	к	K	for **Kerb**		Щ	щ	Sht	for **Ashtray**	
Л	л	L	for **Lip**		Ъ	ъ	U	for **Under**	
М	м	M	for **Morris**		Ь	ь	J	for **Yodel**	
Н	н	N	for **Nut**		Ю	ю	Yu	for **You**	
О	о	O	for **Austin**		Я	я	Ya	for **Yard**	

TIPPING As in all Eastern European countries, it is good manners to round up your bill at the end, especially in the poorer countries or regions when it is blatantly obvious that as a tourist you have a lot more money than them.

SLEEPING

When dealing with BalkanTourist Offices and its successors, bear in mind that they always try to fill up their own hotels first. These are often more expensive and offer a poor service. Ask for a room in a private home whenever possible, as they're always a lot cheaper and more interesting. If you decide to bypass the Tourist Office and take up a local on the offer of a room, you're still supposed to register this with the police. There's no real need to do this if you've already got a couple of official stamps on the card you were given at the border. Be careful here, for if you cannot account for several nights, you could still face a fine. As time goes on, this bureaucracy is diminishing and you probably will not be bothered. ORBITA, the student travel service, will find you a cheap bed in one of their hostels any time between mid-July and mid-September. For advance bookings, try writing to International Tourist Relations, ORBITA Youth Travel Bureau, 45a Boulevard Stambolijski, Sofia. ISIC holders making reservations through ORBITA can get reductions of up to 50%.

Camping costs about £1.50 ($2.40) per tent and similar per

person on any of the 100 or so official campsites. Beware, though: recent reports suggest that some campsites are slowly being neglected by the authorities. Freelance camping is illegal, with a fine if caught. Most accommodation still has to be paid for in hard currency, but this is slowly changing.

EATING AND NIGHTLIFE

Eat as much as you can in Bulgaria, as food is tasty and cheap. National dishes have a strong Turkish influence, with lamb and pork the most common meats. Try *haiduchki kebab* (lamb cooked with onions, white wine and pepper) or one of their wonderful meat and vegetable dishes, slowly cooked in an earthenware pot, known as *gyuvech*. You cannot go wrong with any of the charcoal-roasted meat dishes with fresh salad. Yoghurt originated here and the Bulgarians are addicted to it: the thick sheep's milk type is particularly good, but not always available. Their ice cream is excellent, too. Vegetarian travellers should try *shopska* salad, vegetarian versions of *gyuvech*, or one of several aubergine dishes, including *iman bayaldu*. For drinks try any *slivova*, a spirit made from plums. Bulgarian wine has become well known in the West, and can be enjoyed cheaply here. Avoid the Bulgarian beer; it has little to recommend it. Upset stomachs are not uncommon when in Bulgaria and very few loos supply paper, so bring plenty with you! If buying for a picnic don't be put off by the possibility of coupons etc., the natives won't bite, and can, in fact, be very helpful.

Most Bulgarian towns have at least one theatre, several cities having open-air ones. A range of plays, operas and ballet can be seen. See the local BalkanTourist Office for details and tickets. They will also give information on arranged folklore events. Also look out for occasional rock concerts with local bands.

Sofia city phone code: 02

The 5,000-year-old city of Sofia lies in the middle of the Balkan peninsula. It's got a lot going for it: it's the 'greenest city in Europe', has skiing (Dec.–Apr.) less than half an hour away, and has some fascinating buildings – mosques, museums and churches which range from Byzantine to Roman, Turkish and Greek architecture. But this is offset by the many communist-inspired concrete piles around the city.

STATION INFORMATION

Sofia has one of the most modern and impressive stations you are ever likely to find with all facilities. However, washing and toilet facilities are grim, as are the restaurant and café. It is open 4 a.m.–1 a.m., but do be prepared to wait if requiring train information. The BalkanTourist money exchange office is open 8 a.m.–9 p.m. The station has a confusing system of platform numbering that

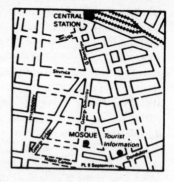

divides them into *zapad* (west) and *istok* (east) sections, so allow plenty of time for your train. It has also become noticeable that the station attracts vagrants and criminals, so do not think about sleeping there and keep hold of your luggage at all times.

TOURIST INFORMATION

The BalkanTourist Office at the station (open 8 a.m.–9 p.m.) is just one of many dotted all over the city, though a very poor example. The main office is on Dondukov Ulica 37 (open 8 a.m.–9 p.m. daily); they can organize private rooms, guided tours at good rates, and will provide general information. Take tram 1, 7 or 15 from the station and get off after 4 stops. The BalkanTourist Office is a short walk away, down the side of the large Central Department Store (TSUM). The branch at Boulevard Vitosha 1 (Tel. 43331) houses the AMERICAN EXPRESS office (open Mon.–Fri.: 8 a.m.–8 p.m.; Sat.: 8.30 a.m.–1.30 p.m.). Credit card holders can obtain leva here for a 4% commission. Try also the Bulgarian Foreign Trade Bank opposite the Sheraton Hotel.

For train information telephone 311111.

ADDRESSES

CENTRAL POST OFFICE Gurko Ulitsa 2, open daily 7 a.m.–9 p.m. Also poste restante here.

ORBITA – STUDENT TRAVEL OFFICE Will grudgingly find you a room in a student hostel. 45a Boulevard Stambolijski (Tel. 879552). Continue along Georgi Dimitrov to ploshtad Lenin, then head down Stambolijski away from Balkan-Sheraton hotel. Open daily 9 a.m.–12 noon and 1 p.m.–5 p.m., but times unreliable.

RILA International Railway Bureau, Gurko Ulitsa 5 (Tel. 870777). All tickets for international journeys, except those wanted for same day's travel, can be bought here. Open daily 8 a.m.–11.30 a.m., 12 noon–4 p.m. Make sure you have your exchange forms with you.

UK EMBASSY 65 Vasil Levski Boulevard (Tel. 885361).
US EMBASSY 1a Ulica Suborna (Tel. 884801). Americans are advised to register with Consular section of the embassy upon arrival in Bulgaria. Go to Kapitan Andreev 1.
AUSTRALIA, CANADA, IRELAND, NEW ZEALAND These countries have no diplomatic presence in Bulgaria. Informally we are told that the UK embassy may help out. Alternatively, try your own embassy in Athens.
24-HOUR CHEMIST Alabin Ulitsa 29 (Tel. 879029). Dial 178 for current information.

GETTING ABOUT

The city buses and trams are reasonably priced. One-or 5-day cards are available if you plan to use them a lot. Buy your tickets in advance from the special kiosks, also grocery stalls. There's a flat fare of 10 leva. Remember to cancel the tickets in the machines on board. The main area worth seeing, however, is easily walked around. A metro system is under construction; expect changes to bus/tram routes as more sections are opened. If you want a taxi get your hotel to call the cheaper state-operated firm.

SEEING

The two main churches of Sofia are the 20th-century neo-Byzantine ALEXANDER NEVSKY, and the 6th-century, early Byzantine ST SOPHIA on Nevski Square. The former, topped with its golden domes, is dedicated to the Russians who fell liberating Bulgaria from the Ottoman Empire. The fascinating crypt is stuffed full of beautiful icons from all over the country (closed Tues.). Also worth seeing is the BOYANA CHURCH, at the foot of Mount Vitosha, with its restored medieval frescoes. In the courtyard of the Sheraton Hotel is the 4th-century ST GEORGE ROTUNDA, the oldest standing building in Sofia. Built during the late Roman period, it has been used as both church and mosque. The St George church is closed for restoration, for an unspecified length of time, and has been for some time.

The church of SAINT PETKA SAMARDZHIYSKA, situated below street level, was built in the 14th century, in a plain style so as not to upset the Ottoman conquerors.

The NATIONAL ARCHAEOLOGICAL MUSEUM, Boulevard Stambolijski (closed Mon.), is in the former Buyuk mosque, with Roman, Greek, Thracian and Turkish finds. The NATIONAL HISTORY MUSEUM at 2 Boulevard Vitosha, in the former Palace of Justice, contains the national treasures, including Thracian gold and ecclesiastical art plus much more. Probably the best one to visit, open 10.30 a.m.–6 p.m., Fri.

2.30 p.m.–6.30 p.m., closed Mondays. This may move if the building regains its former function.

At one end of Boulevard Russki is the September 9th Square, with, on the south side, the MAUSOLEUM OF GEORGI DIMITROV, the first leader of the former People's Republic. His body has now been removed, and the building is due to be re-used or demolished.

On the opposite side of the square is the former royal palace, built during the Ottoman empire. This now houses the NATIONAL ETHNO-LOGICAL MUSEUM. The NATIONAL GALLERY OF PAINTING AND SCULPTURE, also here, may be relocated to Alexander Nevski Square, open 9 a.m.–6 p.m., closed Mondays.

On Georgi Dimitrov Boulevard there is the 16th-century BANYA BASHI MOSQUE, behind which is the run-down mineral baths building. Both of these have been recently undergoing renovation; the mosque is now reopened, the baths sometime in the future. Opposite the mosque is the HALI market hall, built in the National Revival style in 1910; due to 'restoration' the inside has been spoilt, and it is currently closed for 're-restoration'.

SLEEPING

Use either BalkanTourist on Stambolijski 27 or ORBITA for private accommodation and expect to pay 150–200 leva for a double through BalkanTourist, less through ORBITA. Do not be surprised if Balkan-Tourist give you the keys of the house and there is no one there, and be aware that your host will probably not speak English. If you're arriving late and these offices are shut, stay in the station and look 'lost'. You'll find locals coming up to you and offering a place in their house for about 100 leva per person. People have halved the price by *discreetly* paying in hard currency (sterling, dollars, marks, francs). If you want hotel accommodation and BalkanTourist is closed, go to the hotels directly. If the trend in Bulgaria follows that in other eastern European countries, expect the cost of accommodation to soar.

ORBITA Student Hostel, Boulevard James Bauchar 76 (Tel. 657447/655138) is OK and not too far out from the centre, tram 9.

There are several hostels in the Vitosha National Park. Book via the PIRIN agency at 30 Boulevard Stambolijski, who will give you directions.

Worth a try is Hotel Bulgaria at 4 Boulevard Russki, near the Dimitrov Mausoleum (Tel. 871977) or Hotel Slaviya at Ulica Sofijski Geroi 2 (Tel. 443 441), tram 13 from station, about three stops down General Totleben. Be warned – prices are rising rapidly and former cheap hotels suddenly become 4-star ones. These hotels now cost upwards of £20 for a double.

If things look desperate, make your way to the university, set in a park off Boulevard Lenin (trams 1, 2, 7, 9, 14 and 18, then change to 4 or 10), and ask around for a student to let you share.

Camping Vrana (Tel. 781213) is on Boulevard Lenin and offers campsites and bungalows. Bus 313, 213 or 305 from station to Orlow Most and then bus 5. Another site is Cherniya Kos (Tel. 571129); take tram 5 from the city to the end of the route, then bus 58 or 59. Bungalows are also available and the site is at the base of the mountains. Both sites open May–Oct.

EATING AND NIGHTLIFE

Food's cheap and good, and eating out in Sofia can cost far less than a picnic in western Europe, although the price is expected to rise rapidly. Count on around 500 leva for a full and excellent meal. For Bulgarian specialities, try Koprivshtitsa, on 3 Boulevard Vitosha; for Russian food, try Krim, Slavyanska 17; and for German food, Berlin on 2 Boulevard V. Zaimor. There are new 'European' restaurants too, as well as Forum and Havana which claim to be Cuban. They are both centrally located.

If you're really cutting corners, there are plenty of self-service places and an open-air market on Georgi Kirkov Ulica near the station. There are also Bulgarian-style fast-food places on Vitosha.

BalkanTourist fill you in on what shows and concerts are on. These tend to be more classical than popular, but the National Folk Ensemble put on some good things.

EXCURSIONS

If your long journey to Sofia has filled your lungs with smoke, hike up to the VITOSHA MOUNTAINS NATIONAL PARK, a winter ski resort area 8 km from Sofia. Take tram 5 to its last stop, in the Kinyazevo district, then a short uphill walk to the cable car. Alternatively there are several bus routes up to Vitosha; ask at BalkanTourist. The mountain air will do you good, and if you're feeling energetic ZLATNIY MOSTOVE, the glacial moraine, should provide the necessary challenge.

As Bulgaria is known for its monasteries, another possible excursion from Sofia is to the RILA MONASTERY with its hundreds of medieval icons, around 121 km south. BalkanTourist arrange costly day trips; alternatively, you can get yourself there, with difficulty, by occasional bus from the Ouchna Koucha terminus, or by train to Kocherinovo station, then bus. If dressed respectfully and carrying your passport, you may spend the night here. Camping Bor is within walking distance of Rila. Ask at BalkanTourist or the bus station for the services, and book accommodation in advance.

Plovdiv city phone code: 032

Plovdiv is only 2½ hours from Sofia by train and is Bulgaria's second largest city. Whilst much of this city is now industrialized, with many modern grey apartments, there is a great deal worth seeing in the old town. From the station take bus 1 or 7 to the central square.

For information go to Puldin Tour at Boulevard Balgariya 106 (Tel. 55 38 48), trolley-bus 102 from the railway station, to just over the river. Pick up a map here, but they are of little help with accommodation, except for private rooms. Try Hotel Leipzig (Tel. 23 22 50), 76 Russki Boulevard, expensive at around £10 ($) per person in a double. Or Hotel Bulgaria, Patriarch Evtimii 13 (Tel. 22 60 64) The nearest campsite is Trakiya (Tel. 55 13 60), 4 km west, bus 4 or 23.

For food try the cafés around the 19 Noemvri Square or the restaurants in the old town or in the cheaper hotels. If you are really cutting costs, there is also a self-service canteen on Maksim Gorki and another opposite the railway station.

The main attractions are in the old town, located on the 3 hills which gave rise to Plovdiv's Roman name of Trimontium. Around the maze of cobbled streets rise houses of the National Revival Period and the remains of the old fortress walls. A restored portion of a ROMAN AMPHITHEATRE is situated in this area, and is now used for theatrical performances. Also in the old town is the ETHNOGRAPHICAL MUSEUM and an Icon Exhibition.

The partial remains of a Roman stadium may be seen in 19 Noemvri Square and other ROMAN REMAINS in the Tsentralen Square. Also in 19 Noemvri Square is the 15th-century DJOUMAYA MOSQUE. The ARCHAEOLOGICAL MUSEUM in Saedinenie Square has many relics of ancient Plovdiv. However, much of its excellent collection of Thracian gold has recently been moved to the National History Museum in Sofia and replaced with mock-ups.

South of Plovdiv is the working BACHKOVO MONASTERY. Founded in 1083 and with early 16th-century structures, the Monastery is an easy trip on a Smolyan-bound bus from the Rodopi bus terminal.

Veliąko Tąrnovo city phone code: 062

The capital of Bulgaria until the Ottoman invasion of 1396, this old city on the Jantra river is stunning and well worth the trouble of getting there. Take the train from Sofia towards Varna and change at Gorna-Orjahovitza, using table 963 of Thomas Cook's timetable. You will arrive at the station, on the southern outskirts, at the foot of the Sveta Gora hill. Take one of the many buses to the city centre.

BalkanTourist is at 1 Vasil Levski (Tel. 2 18 36). Try Motel-camping Sveta Gora for tents and chalets, bus 14 from Balkantourist, or bus 15 from the station. A moderate price hotel in the old town is Hotel Yantra, I Velohova Zavera Square (Tel. 2 03 91), alternatively try Hotel Etar, I Ivailo or Orbita, Hirsto Botev 15.

The two main areas of interest are VAROSHA and TSAREVETS. Walk around these to get the best from them, but prepare for tired legs – it is not exactly flat. From BalkanTourist head into Varosha, the old Ottoman town, armed with your map. The National Revival Museum is on the site of the Ottoman town hall, or *Konak*, with the Revolutionary Museum nearby, in a former Turkish prison. All museums are shut on Mondays.

Tsarevets, almost completely enclosed in a loop of the river, is approached by a stone causeway. The continuing digs turn up more each year. Parts of the impressive ramparts are on view, as are the palace ruins. The views from Tsarevets make the uphill struggle, literally, well worth while, even for those not interested in old stones. One of the views, in an adjacent loop of the river, is the Trapezica hill. Here excavation of several of the old Bulgarian rulers' churches and other buildings is in progress.

Black Sea Coast – Varna and Bourgas

The two main cities are VARNA and BOURGAS, each reachable by around 6 trains a day from Sofia. Along the whole coast accommodation is difficult, if not impossible, to find during the summer, due to the increasing popularity of the area, both to Eastern and Western tourists. Varna has more going for it, with Roman remains, an early Christian basilica and several reasonable museums. Buses can be taken from either Varna or Bourgas along the coast. If you are along the coast at the Sunny Beach resort and get bored with soaking up the rays, visit the Nessebur museum town. This is a UNESCO listed heritage centre, with ruins of over 40 medieval churches.

In Varna there is a former BalkanTourist Office, open all year, opposite the railway station, at Ulitsa Musala (Tel. 222389), open 8 a.m.–6.00 p.m. A hotel worth trying is next door: the Musala (Tel. 0523925).

The nearest campsite is Camping Panorama, which is at the eastern edge of the Golden Sands resort, about 25 km from town. It can be reached by most buses stopping adjacent to the park in the centre of Varna. There's also camping at Galata, bus 17 from Boulevard Botev.

Bourgas has a Primoretz Tourist Office at 2 Ul Alexsandrovska (Tel. 45553). Ask about accommodation. The cheapest hotel is probably Primonets at 1 Liliana Dimitrova (Tel. 44117).

NOTES

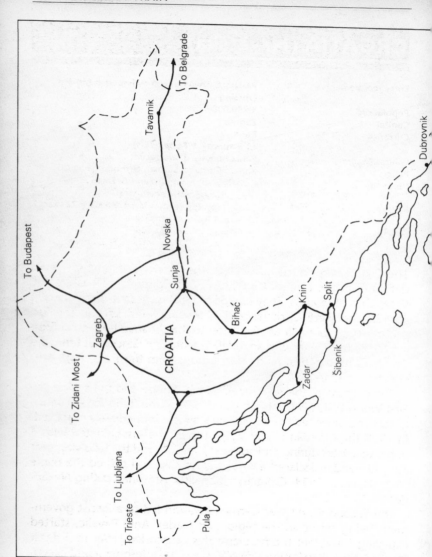

CROATIA (Hrvatska)

Entry requirements	Passport. Any visas can by issued at border crossing.
Population	4,760,000
Capital	Zagreb
Currency	Kuna
	£1 = approx. 9 Kuna (HKN)
Political system	Parliamentary democracy
Religions	Roman Catholic, Serbian Orthodox and Muslim.
Language	Croatian, some English and German in tourist areas, Italian in the north-west
Public holidays	1, 6, 7 Jan.; Easter Monday; 1, 30 May; 22 June, 15 Aug; 1 Nov.; 25, 26 Dec.
International dialling codes	To Croatia: int'l code 00385
	From Croatia: 99 + country code number

The Croats can be traced back to the Jordan valley where relics dating from the time of Christ have been discovered bearing the Croatian coat of arms. They moved to what is present-day Croatia in AD 625 and were Christianized 175 years later. Late in the 9th century, Pope John VIII wrote a letter to the Croatian leader, confirming the country's status as an independent state. Since that time, the Croatians have had to fend off incursions from the Turks, Austrians, Venetians and Italians.

The collapse of the Austro-Hungarian empire and the end of the First World War saw Croatia become part of the 'Kingdom of Serbs, Croats and Slovenes', a decision they almost immediately regretted. In 1928 the Croatian leader Stjepan Radic was assassinated with 4 of his associates during parliamentary session, and the following year King Alexander declared a royal dictatorship and coined the name 'Yugoslavia'. In 1934, Croatian nationalists assassinated King Alexander.

The Second World War German invasion led to a fascist government being set up in the region. Its leader, Ante Pavelic, started expelling Serbs, but the problems this caused led Hitler to order it stopped. One devastating side-effect was the internment and execution of over 350,000 Serbs and Jews.

After the war, Marshal Tito (a Croat) seized control and set up a communist government based in Belgrade. Though Serbs only accounted for 30% of the population, they controlled 80% of all positions of power, including the police and military. This imbalance meant Serbian interests were given preferential treatment, which caused increasing resentment among the non-Serbs.

With the death of Tito, many expected Yugoslavia to finally break up, but the Serbs had other ideas. The nationalist drive in Croatia frightened the 600,000 ethnic Serbs there and when the country declared independence in 1991, without first securing the rights of the ethnic Serbs, the Serbian majority in Krajina declared its independence from Croatia. All this helped to contribute to the increasing tensions in the region which eventually erupted into full-scale war.

After EC intervention, the Croats agreed to postpone their declaration of independence for 3 months to avoid more bloodshed. The only real effect of this was to allow the Serbian-dominated Federal Army to take over a third of Croatia's territory. Germany put pressure on its EC colleagues to recognize Croatia's independence and after the 3-month postponement, Croatia re-declared independence and was immediately recognized by the EC.

CROATIAN STATE RAILWAYS

(HRVASTSKE ZELJEZNICE, HZ)

The railway was hit hard during the war and many lines were destroyed or heavily damaged by the retreating Serbs. Train services in the north are intact from the coast all the way to Nasice and use rolling stock left over from the former Yugoslav railways. Expresses are mostly modern, comfortable and cost no more than the slower local trains.

There are still major plans for the railways including new high-speed lines for Rijeka–Budapest and Paris–Istanbul. The latter line will travel down the coast of Croatia, through Albania and Greece, cutting 600 km off the current route *and* travelling at 220 km/h. The project is being co-ordinated by all the railway boards of Europe.

HZ's main head office is at 12 Mihanoviceva St, 10000 Zagreb (Tel. 457 7111 or 9830).

TRAIN INFORMATION

In Zagreb and Pula, you should find someone who speaks English; otherwise it's Italian in Istria and German everywhere else. As usual, a note with the city, train, date and time is usually enough to get you where you want to go regardless of the language barrier.

RESERVATIONS Required only on international trains to countries other than Slovenia.

NIGHT TRAVEL Only international overnight trains have sleeping accommodation. Most trains drop their first-class cars at the border and carry only second-class couchettes. Normal compartments have pull-down seats and are rarely full during the off season.

EATING ON TRAINS Internal trains have a trolley service while the international trains have the normal range of snack bars and dining cars.

SCENIC ROUTES The only scenic route still open is the line from Ogulin to Rijeka, which is worth the time if you are heading for Istria.

BUSES Extensive damage to the rail lines means this may be the only way to see certain areas of the country. The bus lines are extensive and a little more expensive than the train but are very good.

TOURIST INFORMATION

Croatia was the tourism hub in the old Yugoslavia, so almost every city has a Tourist Office of some sort. These are still being reorganized into separate offices for national, regional and local affairs, though any office should be able to give you the basics. Most have free maps and inexpensive guides to the sights in the city or region and there's usually someone who speaks a little English.

ISIC BONUSES Discounts are given for many sights, so always show your ISIC card before buying tickets.

MONEY MATTERS The currency is the Croatian Kuna (HKN).
    Banking hours are generally Mon.–Sat: 7 a.m.–7 p.m. In smaller towns and in coastal resorts during the summer, some premises may close for a siesta from 2 p.m. to 5 p.m. You may also find that some banks will close earlier on a Saturday. People waiting in front of banks will ask if you want to change money. This is generally not a good idea since you won't actually get that much more and you may find yourself stuck with old Yugoslav dinar, which are worthless.

POST OFFICES Open Mon.–Sat. 8.30 a.m.–5 p.m. with the same pattern for siestas and Saturdays as banks and shops. Stamps can be bought at newsagents', though without an airmail sticker post will go by surface. Post offices in tourist areas open on Sundays and will remain open until 10 p.m. on weekdays.

SHOPS Open Mon.–Sat. 7a.m.–8 p.m. During the summer months in most towns, a lunch break will not be taken. In the evening you may also find that some premises will open until 9 p.m. or occasionally, 10 p.m. On Saturday expect to find some shops shutting around mid-afternoon.

MUSEUMS Many of these were closed during the war and the exhibits moved to underground storage for safety. Check with the Tourist Offices to see which ones have reopened.

MEDIA
English language radio news broadcasts at 8 and 10 a.m. and 2 and 11 p.m.

SLEEPING
The *Studenski Dom* and youth hostels (open May–Sept.) are the best value at £3.50-£4, $5–6 with a 50% increase in July and August. There are also several campsites along the coast, though most cater to auto-caravans and are quite expensive. Camping illegally is strongly discouraged.

The only other option is private rooms. These can be arranged by the Tourist Office, for a fee, and require a minimum stay. Alternatively, look for *sobe* or *Zimmer* signs in people's windows.

EATING AND NIGHTLIFE
The variety of takeaway shops and self-service cafeterias means there is never a shortage of cheap places to eat. Every town has some sort of 'farmers' market' which often has produce grown in the locals' back gardens. Between these and the bakeries, you can make excellent picnics for next to nothing. Snack on *bureks* (greasy pastry stuffed with cheese or meat), a local favourite. In Istria, Italian dishes are not only very good but half the price they are in Italy. Anywhere on the Adriatic you will find great seafood dishes.

The nightlife here is somewhat subdued since most of these people have lost a great deal more than their jobs in recent years. However, if you wander the towns at night, you will hear loud music drifting out of the cafés where the young people hang out.

LANGUAGE
Regardless of what any linguist tells you, Serbo-Croat is not a language but a mix of Serbian and Croatian words. Serbian and Croatian are not only written using 2 different alphabets (Cyrillic and Latin) but also pronounced differently.

Before arriving, I purchased a Serbo-Croat phrase-book. I was met by scowls and worse until someone told me that 80% of what was in the book was actually Serbian. Most people here speak a second language; English is common amongst the young and German amongst the old. Here are some basic Croatian phrases to help break the ice:

Good morning	*Dobar dan*	one	*jedan*
Goodbye	*Do videnja*	two	*dva*
Yes	*Da*	three	*tri*
No	*Ne*	four	*četiri*
Please	*Molim*	five	*pet*
Thank you	*Hvala*	six	*šest*
Excuse me	*Izvinete*	seven	*sedam*
I would like...	*Zelim...*	eight	*osam*
Where is...	*Gde...*	nine	*devet*
I'm looking for...	*Trazim...*	ten	*deset*

Zagreb city phone code: 01

This is not only the political capital of the country, but also the cultural capital. The town is much like any other city in western Europe and being here it is hard to imagine the horrific fighting going on nearby.

The train station is in the middle of the new town and has a full range of facilities, including left luggage, a restaurant, a bureau de change and information office. The main post office is next door, to the right as you leave the station, and the police station is to the left. There are not always Croatian guards on the trains and you may arrive in Zagreb without a visa. If this is the case, soldiers on the platform may escort you to the police station, where they should issue you with one in about 15 minutes.

TOURIST INFORMATION AND ADDRESSES

TOURIST OFFICE Trg Josipa Jelacica 11, open Mon.–Fri.: 8 a.m.–8 p.m.; Sat.–Sun.: 9 a.m.–6 p.m. Tel. 272 530, 278 855, 278 910. And Ilicia 1a (Tel. 4556 455).

POST OFFICE Next to the railway station, open Mon.–Sat.: 8 a.m.–8 p.m.; with poste restante open round the clock.

UK EMBASSY 121 Vlaska, Zagreb (Tel. 455 5310)
IRISH EMBASSY Contact nearest embassy – Zürich, Switzerland
US EMBASSY 2 Andrije Hebranga, Zagreb (Tel. 455 6000)
CANADIAN EMBASSY Consular service in Hotel Esplanade, Zagreb (Tel. 455 0785)
AUSTRALIAN EMBASSY Consular service in Hotel Esplanade, Zagreb (Tel. 455 1663)
NEW ZEALAND EMBASSY Contact nearest embassy – Rome, Italy.
AMEX c/o Atlas Travel, Zrinjevac 17, open Mon.–Fri. 8 a.m.–7 p.m.; Sat. 10 a.m.–5 p.m.
MEDICAL ASSISTANCE 24-hour pharmacy at 3 Trg Josipa Jelacica, Zagreb
EMERGENCY NUMBERS Police 92, Fire Brigade 93, Ambulance 94

SEEING

The city is divided into 3 main areas: the upper town, the lower town and the new town. Concentrate your efforts on the upper town, taking in ST STEPHEN'S CATHEDRAL, ST MARK'S and the CROATIAN NATIONAL MUSEUM. Check with the Tourist Office on Trg Jelacica to find out which museums are currently open and what is going on in town. Ask about the Zagreb Welcome Card offering discounts and free travel on the city's transport network.

TIPPING Round up bills in cafés with a few loose coins.

SLEEPING

The only campsites are outside of town and this is not a city where you want to be far from the centre. The only hostel is near the train station on Petrinjska 77 and costs about £7 (Tel. 434 964). Alternatively, check with the Centar Turist Biro on Savska cesta 25, which may be able to put you up in a student dorm in the summer, or try the Tourist Office on Trg Jelacica for private rooms. If you're young, try the Centre for International Youth Co-operation (Information and Accommodation section), Dezmanov prolaz 9, 10000 Zagreb (Tel. 278 239).

EATING

The area to look for cheap food is near the cathedral. This is also where you will find the local farmers and fish markets. There are lots of little cafés to the north of Trg Jelacica on Tkalcicva, which is where all the young people hang out and socialize of an evening. It's expensive by local standards but affordable by Western standards. There are a variety of takeaway stalls and there is even a Hard Rock

Café off Gajeva in a small shopping arcade. For excellent cheap sweets, try Croatia's premier chocolate maker, Kras. If you're really in a tight spot there's a Jabuka 24-hour supermarket just by the main railway station.

Dalmatian Coast

SPLIT

This is the regional capital of Dalmatia and dates back to the Romans. The local Tourist Information is inside the city walls at Preporoda, and Dalmatiatourist is on the waterfront at the west end of the palace. The PALACE was built by Diocletian in the 3rd century, and later developed into a medieval town with the apartments becoming houses and the corridors the streets. Enter the city via the palace's basement entrance, which faces the harbour, and you will come out in the PERISTYLE, a large courtyard with old Roman columns. To the right is the impressive CATHEDRAL and TOWER, which you can climb for spectacular views, while to the left is the TEMPLE OF JUPITER. Continue straight on to the modern glass and steel bank, the interior of which is amazing. Because the law prevents artefacts from being moved, the bank has had to leave a column, part of a wall and a beautiful mosaic in the middle of its lobby.

The city itself is one great big museum, but while strolling around, look out for the ARCHAEOLOGICAL MUSEUM and markets just outside the east gate. Don't miss the statue of GREGORIUS NIN which was cut in half and buried by the Serbians. If you touch the toe it is supposed to bring good luck and grant you your heart's desire (the lack of oxidation testifies to the locals' beliefs!).

You will have to travel here by bus because the rail lines were destroyed during the war. For accommodation you'll have to rely on private rooms. Check with the Tourist Office or look for signs saying *sobe* or *Zimmer*. Expect to pay around £6 and haggle if they ask for more.

Dubrovnik

Dubrovnik's old city is listed as a historical site and is protected by UNESCO. Unfortunately that didn't stop the Serbs from bombing it heavily. Much of the city has been rebuilt, but you can still see the mortar holes in the main street. Make sure to walk along the CITY WALLS and look at the roofs of the city. All the dark red tiles are original, but the bright red ones are replacements since the bombing. It will give you an idea of how extensive the damage was. Check out the FRANCISCAN MONASTERY and the DOMINICAN MONASTERY. You will either have to get here by bus or ferry from Split. Check with the Tourist Office on Placa to see if the hostels are open and if not, have them fix you up with a private room. There is a Youth Hostel at Bana Jelacica 15–17 (Tel. 412592).

Istrian Peninsula

PULA

Pula is primarily a resort town and, being in Istria, it has been completely left out of the fighting. Having once belonged to Italy, the region has a decidedly Italian flavour to it and many people here speak Italian instead of their native Croatian.

This is an excellent place to base yourself for exploring the region and visiting the island of BRIJUNI. There is a very well preserved Roman amphitheatre here which is still used for concerts and open-air plays in the summer. Under the amphitheatre is the ARCHAEOLOGICAL MUSEUM, which is interesting, even though everything is written in Croatian. Also check out the TEMPLE OF AUGUSTUS which was completely destroyed during the Second World War (and rebuilt stone by stone) and the TOWN HALL.

There is a hostel on Zhljev Valsaline (Tel. 52 34211) which is only open in summer, or try the Tourist Office on Trg Bratstva i Jedinstva for private rooms.

NOTES

....

....

....

....

....

....

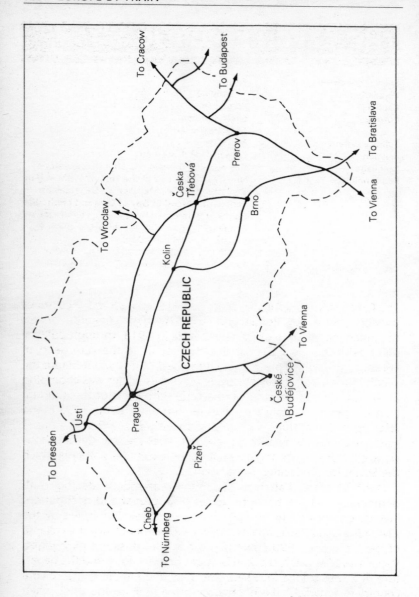

THE CZECH REPUBLIC

Entry requirements	Passport
Population	12,000,000
Capital	Prague (pop.: 1,500,000)
Currency	Czech Koruna
	£1 = approx. 47Kčs
Political system	Republic
Religion	Catholic and Protestant
Language	Czech (some German and English understood)
Public holidays	New Year's Day, Day of the Three Wise Men (Jan 6), Easter Monday, May Day, VE Day (May 8), Pentecostal Monday, Day of Cyril and Methodius (July 5), Death of Jan Hus (July 6), Foundation of Republic Day (Oct. 28), All Souls' Day (Nov. 1), Christmas and Boxing Days
International dialling codes	To the Czech Republic: int'l code 42 number
	From the Czech Republic: 00 + country code number

The Czech lands of Bohemia, Moravia and Silesia, for many centuries provinces of the Holy Roman and Austro-Hungarian Empires, formed the independent state of Czechoslovakia in 1918, through political union with Slovakia. Geographically they lie at the very heart of Europe – not a good place to be at the best of times, but before the Second World War it was positively disastrous. Hitler was chomping at the bit, demanding the German-speaking parts of the country. France, Britain and Italy agreed to let him have them in 1939, and after Poland and Hungary had also taken parts, a Slovak puppet state, under German control, remained. After the war, Czechoslovakia was restored to its original boundaries, except for Ruthenia which the Soviet Union decided to hang on to.

Dubček's ill-fated attempt to combine communist ideology with democracy in 1968 brought Soviet disapproval and occupation. Twenty-one years later the peaceful 'velvet' revolution, led by the Civic Forum and Public against Violence movements, saw the collapse of the old order. 1990 confirmed the former dissident playwright, Vaclav Havel, as president, and brought free elections, and the departure of Soviet troops followed. The slow and painful course of the country to a market-led economy was given a jolt in June 1992, when the election result prompted the Slovaks to form their own government in Bratislava and to declare Slovakia an independent nation. The 'Velvet Divorce' was confirmed on January 1, 1993. This continues to have considerable economic repercussions, so expect the exchange rate and other facilities to be constantly changing.

CZECH STATE RAILWAYS (ČSD)

The service is a hot contender for the title of slowest in Europe, but if you're lucky you may find you have no complaints at all. Like Britain, the Czechs have their own 125 – the only trouble is it's 12.5 mph. However, the system is relatively dense and so most places can be reached by rail. Trains are frequent and tickets are sold according to the speed of the train. Don't cut corners here as it's generally recognized that even buses are faster than the expresses. Go for the fastest possible (*Expresní* or *Rychlík*). Unfortunately, these require seat reservations and supplements, and that may mean queues. Generally avoid travel on Friday and Sunday afternoons. Price rises (up to 60% in some cases) in the last few years mean that rail travel is not as cheap as it once was.

PASSES AVAILABLE The Inter-Rail pass has been broken down into zones, so that you pay only for travel within the area you want to visit. For £159 you can spend 22 days touring a zone. The Czech Republic is in Zone D, along with Slovakia, Poland, Hungary, and Croatia. For details of the 8 Inter-Rail zones, see the Inter-Rail section in Part One of this guide. A Euro-Domino ticket is also available for the Czech Republic, see p. 41. The Czech Explorer Pass offers 7 consecutive days of unlimited travel on the Czech Republic rail services of CD. 2nd class at £19, first, £26. There is also a 7-day Explorer pass covering the Czech and Slovak Republics, 2nd class £26, first £40. Czech Railways have recently introduced rail passes but these are only of real value to those planning a lengthy stay; a 6-month Junior Pass costs 390Kč, 12 months 690Kč and gives a 20% discount.

TRAIN INFORMATION

Take it for granted that the staff will be friendly but won't speak English at information offices so have the German vocabulary and/or a pen and paper with your request at the ready. If you still haven't any success, try: *Z kterého nástupiště odjíždí...vlak do...?* (From which platform does the train to...leave?) However, there are generally plenty of timetable boards available, though they can be a bit confusing. Express trains are marked in bold or red letters: Arrival – *Příjezd*, Departure – *Odjezd*. Many of the left-luggage lockers in the main towns are vandalized – it's not that you've got the combination wrong. The left-luggage offices normally cost 5–10Kčs, depending on weight.

RESERVATIONS Try to reserve well ahead of time to be sure of a seat, as trains are always busy. This is obligatory on some expresses marked with an R or *míst*. Use the ARES office located at many stations. If you are going on to Hungary, it is essential to specify which of the routes you are taking and get your ticket from the appropriate counter. The crossing points are Štúrovo and Komárom in Slovakia.

NIGHT TRAVEL Sleepers and couchettes are operated by the state railway and run on all long journeys. Avoid sleepers, as they tend to be expensive. Beware – numerous thefts from couchette compartments on international routes have been reported in recent years.

EATING ON TRAINS There's either a restaurant car or buffet on selected fast trains.

ROVER TICKETS The European East pass, available in North America from several outlets, is valid here.

SCENIC TRIPS Along the Labé river between Lovosice and Děčín; and along the Berounka River south-west of Prague.

TOURIST INFORMATION

The official state-run agency was Čedok, who now operate as a private travel agency rather than an information office. They suggest tours and book accommadation etc. ISIC holders can get discounts of up to 50% on international tickets bought at their offices. The student travel offices (CKM) are staffed by students and issue ISIC and IYHF cards. They are normally very good.

MONEY MATTERS 1 Czech koruna (Kčs) = 100 haléřů (hal).

Beware: the Czech Republic and Slovakia now each have their own individual currencies and it is not possible to use Slovakian money in the Czech Republic (or vice versa).

Banking hours are Mon.–Fri.: 9 a.m.–5 p.m. with a break at lunchtime. There is no longer any minimum currency exchange and the black market has died down. Avoid the remains of the black market; you will be ripped off, and are likely to be given worthless Polish Zloty, not Koruna. Private exchange offices are now flourishing, permitted under new laws. The best rate is from feeding notes directly into an electronic machine inside the Czech National Bank in Na Příkopě (1% compared to hotels' 8% commmission).

POST OFFICES Open 8 a.m.–5 p.m, at noon on Saturdays.

SHOPS Follow the usual pattern, opening at 9 a.m. and shutting at 6 p.m. on weekdays and at noon on Saturdays.

MUSEUMS Open Tues.–Sun.: 10 a.m.–5 p.m. Generally closed Mondays.

TIPPING Round up the price of your meal.

SLEEPING

Despite the revolution, the accommodation situation has not really improved. This is due to increased demand and lack of infrastructure; however, the situation will improve as new developments are financed. The prices below are likely to be subject to inflation. For advance booking use CKM (address in Prague section, p.156), or the National Federation of Hotels and Restaurants, Senovazne nàmĕstí. 23 11201 Prague (Tel. 2414 2676) but allow for a long wait and a booking fee. In Vienna, the CKM office is at Parkring 12 (Tel. 513 2609). Hotels are graded from C (1-star) to deluxe A (5-star). The rare 2-star doubles should cost about 500Kčs per night, though bargains can still be found outside the main towns. Make sure you have agreed beforehand on the cost. In a country where the main language is Czech, the second Russian and the third German, your chances of winning an argument in English are somewhat minimal.

The Czechs are keen campers. There are over 400 sites in the country and they average 175Kčs.

Staying at a private home also works out a lot cheaper than hotels. In Prague, Pragotur is the main official agency for this form of accommodation. New private agencies are coming forward to supplement Pragotur and Čedok. Don't be surprised if you are approached in the station or even on the street by a budding host, take the usual precautions. Advance accommodation can also be arranged from the UK through Czechbook, Japes Mill, Trebrown-bridge, Cornwall PL14 3PX (Tel. 01503 240629).

Apart from Čedok offices, it's also possible to find accommodation through the student travel offices (CKM) during July and August.

In Prague avoid the AVE accommodation service in the station as they charge a hefty commission.

Dormitories (*internáty* or *koleje*) are converted into youth hostels (*střediska*), many of which have good 2-bedded rooms from only 400–600Kčs per person on an IYHF card, more without.

There has been an increase in the numbers of independent hostels in the main centres. Finding out about these may be a problem, as Čedok and other agencies will direct you to their own hostels. Look in the stations for notices, or ask fellow travellers.

EATING AND NIGHTLIFE

Food is generally pretty uninspiring: lots of pork and few salads and veggies. Dinner is eaten early. If you go after 8.30 p.m. you're likely to have very little choice. Specialities include *zeleninová* (a vegetable and cream soup) and any dish made from pork (*vepřové*). For cheap meals, try any of the self-service stand-up restaurants (*automaty*).

A lot of the grade-1 and 2 restaurants have dancing, but apart from this things are very quiet by Western standards. Čedok should be able to help out on what open-air concerts, etc., there might be. The best way to find out what's happening is to ask any young locals. They will probably advise you to head towards a wine bar (*vinárna*) or beer hall (*pivnice*), where most young people meet. Try Budvar, Prazdroj or any other beer you're recommended, for not only is Czech beer among the best in Europe, it's also the cheapest.

Brno city phone code: 05

The capital of Moravia and the republic's second city has quite a lot to offer. A royal city, founded in the 13th century, on the rail line between Prague and Bratislava.

The new Taxatour Brno information desk in the station, the Tourist Information Centre at Radnicka 8 (Tel. 42 2110 90), and CKM at Česká 11 (Tel. 21 31 47), are the best bets for accommodation suggestions. The city fills up, during the several exhibitions and trade fairs held every year. The summer student hostels are at Purkyňova 93 and Kohontova 55; apply to the CKM office. The nearest camping site is the Obora, 15 km from Brno (Tel. 79 11 05), not easily reached by public transport. There is another site at Modrice though private accommodation may be your best bet.

The ŠPILBERK CASTLE, founded 1277 and rebuilt in the 18th century, houses the MUNICIPAL MUSEUM and ART GALLERY. See the display of torture instruments in the museum. Dominating the city and castle is the CATHEDRAL OF ST PETER AND ST PAUL. Also worth seeing is the OLD TOWN HALL and the CAPUCIN MONASTERY, complete with mummified monks on display. Also see the colourful outdoor CABBAGE MARKET (*Zelny Trh*).

České Budějovice

Like Pilsen, this town is renowned for its beer – Budvar or Budweiser – and its salt trade, and is located in the beautiful region of south Bohemia. It can be reached from Prague by a couple of trains a day, taking around 2 hours. The more frequent buses from Prague may be a better bet.

Budéjovice was founded in 1265 as a Royal Borough, at the strategic meeting point of the Vltava and Malše rivers. The town is centred on the large Zižkova nàměstí, surrounded by painted baroque buildings. The TOWN HALL, dating from 1555, was modified in the early 18th century, to give its current frontage. The 72m high BLACK TOWER, also on this square, dates from the 16th century, built as a watch tower and belfry for the ST NICHOLAS CHURCH. The tower is a good viewpoint, open Tues.–Sun., 10 a.m.–4 p.m. Close to the Malše river bank are the remains of the original Gothic city defences. The Tourist Office is at Otakara II on the main square (Tel. 594 80) and they can arrange accommodation. Try also CKM at Karla IV which has student hostel information. The Stromovka campsite (Tel. 38308) is on Na Dlouhé Lávce, open Apr.–Oct. The large Masné Krámy beer hall is lively and is an ideal place for trying the local beer and to get some basic food if hungry. Canoe trips are one of the Czechs' favourite summer pastimes and some of the best trips are in this area. Ask at the Tourist Office.

Pilsen (Plzeň)

Basically, this is an ugly, uninspiring place, the regional centre of western Bohemia and that other great cultural icon, the Skoda car. If, on the other hand, you're a beer fan, then it's pilgrimage country, for this is the birthplace of Pilsner Urquell beer. See the BURGHER'S BREWERY (tours start at 12.30 Mon.–Fri.), the BREWING MUSEUM on Veleslavínova Street (Tues.–Sun.; 10 a.m.–6 p.m.). The ABBEY OF THE VIRGIN MARY and ST BARTHOLOMEW'S CHURCH are the town's other saving graces.

The Tourist Information Office (MIS) is on Republic 41 (Tel. 723 6393). Čedok are on Sedláčkova 12, close to the town centre, on the corner of Sedláčkova and Prešovská, open Mon.–Fri., 9 a.m.–6 p.m. (shuts for lunch). No IYHF hostel but try the university for student rooms on Bolevecka. The nearest campsite is Bílá Hora (Tel. 35611/62850) which also lets chalets; take bus 20 from the centre.

Prague (Praha) city phone code: 02

Prague, the 14th-century capital of the Holy Roman Empire, is where to go if you want to step back into medieval life and have all your preconceptions of an Eastern European city shattered. As far as sights are concerned, many consider Prague to be on a par with, if not better than, Paris, London or Rome. It lies in central Bohemia and is a riot of bridges, parks, hills and a fascinating array of architectural styles. Prague is the capital of Bohemia and the Czech Republic.

STATION FACILITIES

There are 3 main stations in Prague: Praha-Hlavní (Wilsonovo), Masarykovo and Holešovice. The first 2 are located close to the centre, with the latter to the north, across the Vltava river. Hlavní (Wilsonovo) is used by domestic services and international trains to Germany, Poland, Russia and Hungary; Masarykovo is mainly for domestic services. Holešovice has international trains for Germany, Russia and Hungary. Some trains from Germany call at Holešovice before getting to Hlavní (Wilsonovo). All these stations are served by the metro system, and have the usual facilities, including an influx of exchange offices. The left-luggage facilities at Holešovice are available 24 hours. Take care when setting locker combinations and with left-luggage receipts; theft at stations is common.

TOURIST INFORMATION

There is a Tourist Information office in the main concourse at Hlavní (Wilsonovo) station, which hands out basic information. The AVE office, also at the station, will also help out with accommodation, but charges a hefty commission.

Alternatively, from the main station (Praha-Hlavní) or Praha-Masarykovo, walk up Hybernská to the Prague Information Service at Na Příkopě 20 (Tel. 544444) and also Panská 4 (Tel. 224311) and Staromcštské 22 (Tel. 223411). They'll give you a free map, *What's On* and general information (open Mon.–Fri.: 9 a.m.–7 p.m., Sat.–Sun.: 9 a.m.–6 p.m.). Čedok has 2 main offices: Na Příkopě 18 (Tel. 212111) change money and operate a room-finding service round the corner at Panská 5 (open Mon.–Fri.: 9 a.m.–8 p.m., Sat.: 8.30 a.m.–2 p.m.,

Sun.: 9 a.m.–2 p.m.), Tel. 227004 or 225657.

There are also a number of privately run 'Tourist Offices' set up around the city. AVE Agency will book accommodation ahead. You can also try the Pragotur room-finding service at Sokolska 56 (Tel. 2491 3331). In general be careful, some of the private agencies have 'i' signs which is a bit misleading as they're only trying to let their own rooms.

ADDRESSES

POST OFFICE: Jindřišská 14, 24-hour service. Also *poste restante* here (closes 1 p.m. on Saturdays). International phone calls from here.

CKM (THE STUDENT AGENCY): Žitná Ulice 12, 12105 Prague 2. Open Mon.–Fri.: 8 a.m.–5 p.m. (Tel. 2491 5767)

FIRST AID Palackého 5 (Tel. 2422 2521 or 2422 2520)

POLYCLINIC FOR FOREIGNERS Roentgenova (Tel. 526040)

UK EMBASSY Thunovská Ulice 14, Malá Strana (Tel. 2451 0439)

IRISH EMBASSY No diplomatic representation in the Czech Republic; try the Irish embassy in Vienna or Berlin. In an emergency the UK or any other EU embassy may help.

US EMBASSY Tržiště 15, Malá Strana (Tel. 2451 0847)

CANADIAN EMBASSY Hradčany, Mickiewiczova 6 (Tel. 2431 1108)

AUSTRALIAN EMBASSY Use UK for emergencies, otherwise try own embassy in Vienna.

NEW ZEALAND EMBASSY As Australia.

PRAGOTUR U Obecního domu 2; also operate a room-finding service. Open Mon.–Fri.: 8 a.m.–8.30 p.m., Sat.: 9.15 a.m.–6 p.m., Sun.: 8.30 a.m.–3 p.m. (Tel. 2312 5128).

INFORMATION SERVICES Na Příkopě 20 (Tel. 544 444); Panská 4 (Tel. 224311).

TELEPHONES Can be found at post offices and in most metro and train stations. Phonecards (100 Kčs) are available from post offices and newsagents.

GETTING ABOUT

The underground is efficient and cheap, and the bus and tram network covers every corner of the city. Buy tickets in advance from news-stands, hotels, machines and tobacconists, and stamp them on the buses. The basic single ticket costs 10Kčs and is valid for 60 mins. Non transfer tickets cost 6Kčs and are valid for 4 stops on one metro line or for 15 mins on a tram or bus. There are special tourist tickets valid on the metro, trams, buses and the Petřín funicular, one-day passes for 90Kčs. For 350Kčs you can buy a calendar month pass or 130 for 3 days and 190 for a week. The metro, and most trains, stop at midnight. Punch all single tickets in the yellow machines at the metro entrance, or on the tram or bus. Be warned: the on-the-spot fine for having the wrong ticket is high – 200Kčs – and ignorance of the rules will not be accepted. Forget taxis altogether.

SEEING

Don't judge the city by its station. I nearly boarded the first train out again on my first visit, but it is in 2 halves – the platforms ancient, crowded and dirty, and the rest of it like an airport terminal. Had I done so, I'd have missed a city with as much to see and do as Paris. Prague started off as 5 separate towns, and each merits a visit: the New Town (Nové Město), the 19th-century commercial centre; the Old Town (Staré Město), medieval buildings and fascinating Jewish Quarter; the Lesser Town (Malá Strana), the baroque area of palaces and churches; Hradčany, the area round Prague Castle; and Vyšehrad, the 9th-century fortress-town opposite the castle.

A good way to get your bearings is to take a boat trip on the Vltava. Leave from Vltava Quay in the New Town and rather than return by boat take metro line B from Palacky Bridge (Most Palack-ého). Also worth a visit is the National Technical Museum, which is open 10 a.m. to 5 p.m. except Mondays and costs 20Kčs admission. The main hall has a large selection of cars made by Czech manufac-turers in the 1920s and 1930s. Beneath, there are guided tours along reconstructed mining galleries.

NOVÉ MĚSTO The main sights are WENCESLAS SQUARE, locally known as *Václavské náměsi*, the main boulevard, the NATIONAL MUSEUM and CHARLES SQUARE (*Karlovo náměsi*), the largest square in Prague, with a park in its centre and the NEW TOWN HALL on its north side. Also DVOŘÁK'S MUSEUM, Ke Karlovu 20, is in this vicinity.

STARÉ MĚSTO The Old Town dates back to 1120 – and you can feel it. The POWDER TOWER, used to store gunpowder in the 15th century, gives a good view from the top (if it is not covered in scaffolding), while the OLD TOWN SQUARE was at the centre of medieval Prague. Here is to be found the 1490 Astronomical Clock of the OLD TOWN HALL which performs every hour. Tour round the Town Hall, and then see the TYN CHURCH on the east side of the square. This twin-Gothic-spired church has a baroque interior and dates from 1365. Connecting the Old Town with the right bank of the Vltara is the beautiful baroque CHARLES BRIDGE.

The JEWISH QUARTER houses the oldest synagogue in Europe (1270) and the 15th-century JEWISH CEMETERY with its 12,000 tombstones piled on top of one another. The museum in KLAUS SYNAGOGUE tells of the extermination of Jews in the Second World War. A single combination ticket permits entry into all the exhibits in the Jewish Quarter.

Bordering the New Town is the BETHLEHEM CHAPEL where the Czech hero John Hus preached, and the baroque CHARLES BRIDGE has superb views of the castle, the island of Kampa and the River Vltava.

MALÁ STRANA The rich 17th- and 18th-century merchants spent their money on this town. The lesser town square and Neruda St are testament to that. ST NICHOLAS' CHURCH is the finest baroque building in Prague (admission 20Kčs) and just north of it is the palace of the Habsburg general, Albrecht Wallenstein.

HRADČANY PRAGUE CASTLE today is the seat of the Czech president, but it used to be the palace of the kings of Bohemia. Try to get on a tour round it; ask for details at the information stand in ST VITUS' CATHEDRAL. A good view over the city can be had from the adjacent terrace. Also in this 'royal city' is St Vitus' Cathedral itself, which is quite incredible, and is certainly the most detailed Gothic church in central Europe, with amazing stained-glass windows. The National Gallery is in the ŠTERNBERK PALACE in the castle square and has an excellent collection of French Impressionists.

A charming walk can be taken down the GOLDEN LANE where the alchemists tried to turn their lead into gold. The STRAHOV MONASTERY, west of the castle, houses the Museum of Czech Literature. For a good view over the whole of Prague, take a walk along the observation paths to Petřín Hill, where the slopes are covered in orchards.

VYŠEHRAD The VYŠEHRAD FORTRESS has in its grounds the 11th-century Rotunda of St Martin, and in its cemetery Dvořák, Smetana and other Czech 'greats' are buried. If you have a couple of hours to spend, the zoo in the north of the city at Trojá (Tel. 84 14 41) is well worth a visit.

RIVER VLTAVA Sightseeing trips on the Vltava leave from the Jiraskuv Most quay and are well worth taking.

SLEEPING

This is your main headache in Prague. As the number of tourists has increased drastically, the situation has got worse. Pragotur, AVE, CKM, Čedok or private agencies or a private arrangement are your best bets for finding a room. Prepare yourself for the inevitable long queues and insist on somewhere central and cheap. They often charge a hefty commission. Private accommodation is cheaper, so ask for this or, better still, the student hostels. You will probably do best contacting the campsites yourself; you will be pleasantly surprised by the sites' quantity and quality. Get a list from Prague Information Service.

HOSTELS There are four IYHF hostels; CKM Junior Hotel, Zitna 12 (Tel. 292984) near to Hlavni Nádraží station; Hotel Beta, Roskotova 1225 (Tel. 61262158) bus 124, 205 from metro Budějovická line C (good reductions with ISIC); Hostel Branik, SOU Vrbova (Tel. 4021682), metro Smichovske nádraží line B; and Hotel Standart, Vodni Stavby (Tel. 2875258), 10 mins from metro Nádraží. IYHF Hostels in Prague are open 24 hours, expect to pay between 150 and 500Kčs.

Other student hostels can work out slightly cheaper. Go in person as official offices often charge hefty commissions. Čedok's hostels are booked through Panská 5, where there is a clean hostel serving breakfast and snacks. They don't make waves about unmarried couples, but cost more than the others. Do try, though, to avoid any hostels being plugged at the station, as they tend to be a bit unsavoury.

Try: Domov Mladeze, Dykova 20, tram 16 from Náměstí Miru metro; ESTEC Kolej Strahov, Vaničkova 5, tram 22 from metro Malostranska. Hostel Sokol, Helichova 1, Malá Strana.

STUDENT ROOMS Try Rooseveltova Kolej, Strojnická 7, take tram 12, 5 or 7 from Holešovice metro station to the Universal Exhibition site. This is an extremely cheap stopover and includes showers. TJ Sokol Karlin, Maleho 1, metro Florenc but only if desperate.

1-STAR HOTELS
Every year they get thinner on the ground and those which are left all charge about the same rate. The cost of these has risen significantly over the last few years.

Hotel Balkan, Svornosti 28 (Tel. 540777) offers good pub grub.

The 3 'botels' moored on the River Vltava are now very expensive and cramped. They are the Admiral (Tel. 548685), Albatros (Tel. 2316996) and the Racek (Tel. 426051).

PRIVATE ROOMS Try Věra Hlaváčová, Na Bálkaně 126/2116 (Tel. 2/66314166). Take tram 9 from Hlávní nádraží for the 15-minute ride to Spojovací. Comfortable rooms with kitchen facilities and English-speaking hostess.

Also recommended: Mrs Rotingova, Thunovská 16, Prahal, Malá Strana (1200Kčs). Another option is at Jitka Erhardová, Dolnokriská 16 (Tel. 4721917). From Budějovická metro take bus 192 and get off at the fourth stop. Doubles and triples available.

NB: Don't be reluctant to accept offers from those selling private rooms at the stations. Settle a price and go for it!

CAMPING There are several sites around Prague. Try: Sokol Trojá at Trojská 171 (Tel. 842 833), Sokol Dolní Počernice at Dolní Počernice Nárhrdinu (Tel. 718 034) and Kotva at U Ledáren 55 (Tel. 466 085/461 397).

Camp Fremunt (Tel. 688 0641), almost next door to Sokol Trojá, offers discounts to Inter-Railers. From the terminal station 'Nádraží Holešouice' of metro line "C" go either five stops with bus no 112 or one stop across the river with tram no 5, 17 or 25.

EATING AND NIGHTLIFE

Beer halls (*pivnice*) and wine cellars (*vinárny*) are dotted all over the city. Take advantage of the Czech beer while you can. Popular favourites are U Prince, Old Town Square, opposite the town hall, good but pricey in a wonderful setting, open daily; U. Fleku, Křemencova 11, much akin to a Munich beer hall (Germans are supplied free of charge); also, U Hrocha, Thunovská 10, Malá Strana. The strongest beer can be found at U Supa, Celetná 22. These are safe bets for cheap food and drink, as are the stand-up snack places. Don't expect a huge menu, but what's there is usually OK. There are plenty of *automaty* – self-service restaurants – in the Wenceslas Square area, which are good and cheap, try the Staropraška Rychta or the Halaligrill. Homesick Westerners could head for the pizzas, MTV and endless coffee of the American Hospitality Center, off Wenceslas Square, at Malé náměstí. 14, open daily 10 a.m.–11 p.m. Or, for a cheap splurge, head for the Akademii Restaurant at Karlova 26, where a fixed 3-course meal costs from 99Kčs. Internet heads can get a fix at the Internet café, Stepanska 18 (Tel. 23 30 24). Temporary eMail facilities can be set up for you.

The Prague Spring Festival (12 May–4 June) is a big draw for music and drama lovers, but note that the official programme is printed in September so misses over half the last-minute productions. Always ask at the time. Prices vary enormously with local artists offering the best value. The monthly *What's On* can be had from PIS, Na Příkopě 20. The Laterna Magiká, Národní 40, is a review of films, ballet and drama which deserves a mention, but you usually need reservations of up to a month.

The citizens of Prague love their ice-cream (*zmrzlina*), and everybody seems to be licking furiously away. One of the best ice-cream places we have found outside Italy is in Prague, on Vodičkova in the shadow of the new town hall. You can join the queue outside on the pavement to buy one to enjoy in the nearby Charles Square (*Karlovo náměstí*) or queue up inside for a seat in this popular café.

Cafés and smaller bars are the most likely places to meet Czech students. Try: Hogo Fogo, Staromeštska 4, Lavka, Novotneho lavka, Staré Město or the UPM, 17 Lisopadu, metro Staromeštska. U Malvaze, Karlova 10, is a big student dive. At night, the places to be are the Old Town Square and Charles Bridge – both have illuminations and street entertainment. Best clubs are Radhost, Belehradska 120, metro I.P. Pavlova or Bunkr, Lodecka 2, Nové Město. For live music head to Arcadia, Na Příkopě 22, Nové Město, or Agaharta Jazz Centrum on Krakovska, Nové Město. Don't forget to try Absinthe, a dangerous green concoction only available in Prague. It's hallucinogenic properties (and vile aftertaste) allegedly have led to several gruesome murders. Try it at your peril.

EXCURSIONS FROM PRAGUE

Half an hour in the train is all it takes to get to the amazing 14th-century castle of KARLŠTEIN – Bohemia's finest example. Take the train from Smíchovske station – on the metro. Visit Karlštein as a day trip from Prague. You might consider going as part of a guided tour, find out when the next one in your language is as soon as you arrive.

The famous spa of KARLOVY VARY (Karlsbad) also makes an interesting trip. Trains take about 3 hours to get there. Čedok is at Tržiště 23.

Another castle of note is KŘIVOKLÁT, medieval seat of Bohemia's kings, located above the Berounka river, a worthwhile sight in its own right. Take the train from Prague-Smíchov, change at Beroun, then on to Křivoklát. The site where St Wenceslas was murdered is in the church complex of Stara Boleslav, to the north of Prague. To get there take the half-hour bus journey from Florenc or Palmovka bus stations in Prague.

Olomouc city phone code: 068

The Czech Republic boasts many beautiful historic towns, and Olomouc is one which you might consider visiting. The town is on the direct line from Praha-Hlavní, the journey taking around 3½ hours. Olomouc became an important city in Moravia as early as the

11th century, and today is a tourist's delight. From the station, the centre is a 15-minute walk and on several tram routes. Tourist information, ATIS, is at Horní náměstí. (Tel. 551 3385), located in the city central square, providing the usual facilities. CKM is at Denisova 4 (Tel. 29009). Čedok is at Horní náměstí 2 (Tel. 28831). Try these for accommodation suggestions, or in July and August the Studencentrum, at Křížkovského 14, may help to find a room. Hostelovy drm, Volgogradska (Tel. 29671) is the cheapest hotel in town and thus often full. Take bus 16 from the terminus near the station. There are no campsites in the town, but half an hour away by train, in Šternberk, there is a Grade A site. Make sure you get precise directions before heading off.

There are plenty of beer halls, wine cellars and restaurants, so there should be no problems. To meet local students try Mikulovská vináarna and U Trojice wine cellars, in the city centre.

The town is a protected urban reservation. The main sight is the superb 12th-century ST WENCESLAS CATHEDRAL, with the PRZEMYSL CASTLE, ST ANN'S CHAPEL and CHAPTER DEANERY nearby. The Renaissance TOWN HALL is also worth a look, as are some of the buildings of the university, the second oldest in Czechoslovakia. A trip on bus 11 from the railway station will bring you to the Kopeček hill, with a good view of the town, and site of the 17th-century VIRGIN MARY CHURCH and MONASTERY.

NOTES

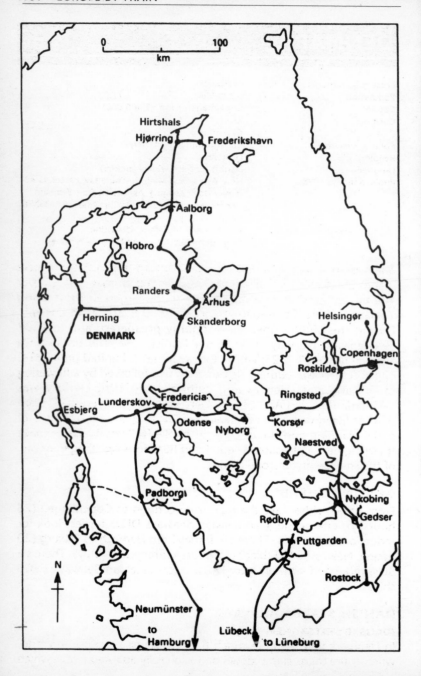

DENMARK

Entry requirements	Passport
Population	5,200,000
Capital	Copenhagen (pop.: 1,400,000)
Currency	Krone
	£1 = approx. 11kr
Political system	Constitutional monarchy
Religion	Lutheran
Language	Danish (English widely spoken)
Public holidays 1998	New Year's Day, Maundy Thursday, Easter, Great Prayer Day (25 Apr.), Ascension Day, Whitsun, Constitution Day (5 June), Christmas (24, 25, 26 Dec.)
International dialling codes	To Denmark: int'l code 45 number
	From Denmark: 00 + country code number

The country is split up as follows: the mainland (Jutland); the 2 main islands of Funen and Zealand; and innumerable smaller islands. Over 100 of Denmark's islands are inhabited, the largest of these being Zealand, where Copenhagen was founded in the 12th century. During the Middle Ages the economy prospered, and in 1397 Sweden and Norway came under Danish rule. The union with Sweden lasted till 1523, while Norway remained united until 1814. The acceptance of Luther's Reformation was followed by a flowering of the arts and sciences and culturally the 19th century was Denmark's 'Golden Age'. Today Denmark enjoys a very high standard of living; from a eurorailer's perspective, the high degree of social planning and the number of public facilities available make travelling here a pleasure, whether you head for Copenhagen or one of the smaller, picturesque islands.

GETTING THERE

From Britain either take the train from London to Copenhagen (26 hours) or one of the Scandinavian Seaways DFDS ferries; look for reductions off-season. There are ferries from Harwich to Esbjerg (20 hours), Newcastle to Esbjerg (19 hours, summertime only). There's a 50% reduction with an Inter-Rail on Scandinavian Seaways DFDS ships.

DANISH STATE RAILWAYS

(DANSKE STATSBANER, DSB)

In Denmark you spend as much time on water as you do on land, when entire trains clamp down on to specially adapted ferries which connect the islands with one another. With hourly intercity trains, they've had plenty of practice and have got the whole operation down to a fine art. There's a great feeling of camaraderie once you're on board. Passengers are free to get out and wander about. This is particularly true on the Kalundborg–Århus crossing (3 hours). A fixed rail link across the Great Belt has just been completed linking the main islands and the Jutland peninsula. This new system has ended the Nyborg–Korsør train ferries, thus revolutionizing train travel in Denmark by cutting an hour off journey times between Copenhagen and the major cities in Fyn and Jylland initially, InterCity trains will retain their hourly frequency but regional trains will be extended through to Odense. From the winter both InterCity and regional trains are expected to become half-hourly, and there will be further limited-stop Lyntog trains.

The rail network is divided into 4 categories:

1. *Lyntog* (Lightning trains) *L*. Almost as luxurious as EuroCity and used on long hauls, such as Copenhagen to Frederikshavn. The new DSB IC3 InterCity trains are now in service; they serve all major cities.
2. *InterCity IC*. Equally fast, serving the shorter distances between large towns.
3. *Regionaltoget*. Slower regional trains, connecting up the smaller towns with the main network.
4. *S-tog*. Copenhagen's underground, connecting the city with the suburbs.

PASSES AVAILABLE The best ticket to go for is the ScanRail pass. It allows a certain number of days' travel within a limited period of time. It is valid on trains operated by the Danish, Norwegian, Swedish and Finnish state railways, and also grants either free travel or with up to 50% reduction on inter-Scandanivian ferry and bus routes, as well as discounts on some inter-island sailings. See Part One of this guide for details.

If you are travelling with at least 3 paying passengers (adults and children), there are discounts of 20% available on 1st- and 2nd-class tickets.

The NorthStar ticket offers reductions on 2nd-class return travel from Copenhagen to Oslo, Stockholm, Sweden, Gothenburg, Oster-sund and Kiruna. Buy the ticket 2 days prior to departure.

Monthly tickets for unlimited travel on Danish domestic rail and ferry services cost 1,340kr.

In Denmark children under 4 travel free and those between 4 and 11 at half price. Children travelling on an ordinary children's ticket can take an adult on 2nd class for the price of a child.

Both Eurail and Inter-Rail passes are valid. Denmark is in Inter-Rail Zone C, along with Germany, Austria and Switzerland. For details of the 8 Inter-Rail zones, see the Inter-Rail section in Part One of this guide.

A Euro-Domino ticket is also available for Denmark, see p. 41.

INTER-RAIL BONUSES See Appendix I.

EURAIL BONUSES The following services are free:
Ferry crossings Århus to Kalundborg, Knudshoved to Halskov, Nyborg to Korsør, Fynshavn to Bøjden.
Ferry crossings Rødby Faerge to Puttgarden (Germany) and Gedser to Warnemünde (Germany).
Ferry crossings operated by the Danish and Swedish State Railways between Helsingør and Helsingborg (Sweden).

REDUCED FARES
25% reduction for Eurail Youthpass holders on the hydrofoil of the Fly-vebadene Company between Copenhagen and Malmö.
50% reduction for Eurailpass holders on the ferries of Stena Line between Frederikshavn and Göteborg.
30% reduction between Hirtshals and Kristiansand (Norway) on the normal fares of the steamship company Color Line.
20% reduction on the normal fares of the Steamship Company DFDS between Esbjerg–Harwich, Esbjerg–Newcastle, Esbjerg–Faroe Islands, Copenhagen–Oslo.
50% reduction on the Hjørring–Hirtshals private railroad.

TRAIN INFORMATION
Timetables are dotted everywhere around the stations and all the staff seem to speak fluent English. If you're spending some time in Denmark, ask for the *Køreplan*, a timetable for all the ferries, trains and buses.

RESERVATIONS Are compulsory on any IC or Lyntog train crossing the Great Belt between Sjaelland and Fyn (that is, from Korsør to Nyborg). The cost is 30kr. You can pay on the train. Reservations can also be made for other Lyntog and IC trains.

NIGHT TRAVEL Couchettes/sleepers cost *relatively* less in Scandinavia than elsewhere in Europe. A couchette costs around 65kr and a bed in a 2-berth sleeper 160kr. Within Denmark, they operate between

Copenhagen and Esbjerg as well as to Struer and Frederikshavn and cost less than on international journeys.

EATING ON TRAINS There are no dining cars, even if you could afford them, though on L and IC trains there are buffets and trolleys selling snacks. The coffee is reasonably priced, but the sandwiches are as expensive here as they are everywhere else. If you're starving, try to survive till you get aboard the ferries as they have self-service cafeterias. The Puttgarden–Rødby service usually does a good choice at reasonable prices.

If you're on an international crossing, don't forget to check out the duty-free shops. They have good prices for cheese, wine, cigarettes and chocolates. Don't forget that in Scandinavia prices are high.

SCENIC TIPS There's good coastline scenery if you're on your way to Frederikshavn from Copenhagen or vice versa. Take the route which goes via Odense and Fredericia. If you're heading for Stockholm from Copenhagen, your best route is to train it to Helsingør (1 hour) then take the ferry to Helsingborg (free on Inter-Rail).

BIKES You can hire a bike in the summer at most of the larger stations, with the exception of Copenhagen, for 30 to 50kr per day, plus deposit of 100–200kr. Ask at stations for leaflet *Take a Train – Rent a Bike*. Bikes are allowed on most regional, interregional and S trains but not on InterCity or EuroCity trains. A special ticket is required at 110kr.

TOURIST INFORMATION

In Denmark the Tourist Offices are the best in Europe, particularly for the under-26s. They are both friendly and efficient, and if every tourist board were like them we would be out of a job.

If you tune in a radio to Radio Denmark programme 3 on 93.8 MHz at 8.30 a.m., Mon.–Fri., you'll hear news in English, and information about exhibitions and other events in Copenhagen for that day.

ISIC BONUSES 50% off some films, theatres and museums. For further information, contact DIS Skindergade 28, Copenhagen.

MONEY MATTERS 1 krone (kr) = 100 øre.

Banking hours are Mon., Tues., Wed., Fri.: 9.30 a.m.–4 p.m., Thurs.: 9.30 a.m.–6 p.m. Bank commission varies from 10 to 18kr.

For late-night service there are facilities at Central station and Tivoli park in Copenhagen. Some Tourist Offices may exchange money out of banking hours. Those with credit cards can use cash dispensers labelled *Kontanten*, coloured red and valid for Mastercard and Visa.

POST OFFICE Opens Mon.–Thurs.: 9 a.m.–5 p.m., Fri.: 9 a.m.–7 or 8 p.m., Sat.: 9 a.m.–12 noon, with variations out of large towns.

TELEPHONES Either fully automatic or through the operator if the number starts with letters. Insert 1kr for local calls or 2kr for long distance. You do not get change from 25 øre coins and with older machines get no change at all.

SHOPS Hours vary from town to town; in general: Mon.–Thurs.: 9 a.m.–5.30 p.m., Fri. to 7 or 8 p.m., Sat. to 1 p.m. or 2 p.m. First Sat. of each month to 5 p.m. in larger towns. New opening hours are being introduced, expect extensions.

TIPPING
Tips are normally included in most bills but it is customary to add a few more loose coins. Give a krone or two to an attendant in public lavatories.

SLEEPING
Youth hostels require you to register before 9 p.m. and have IYHF membership. n maximum charge is 85kr per night in a dorm or between 150 and 340kr in a private room. In most hostels breakfast can be had for around 40kr, dinner for 60kr. Outside Copenhagen an 11 p.m. curfew is the norm. Hostelling International Denmark have introduced a national star rating system, five-star hostels offer the best facilities. Most hostels are 4-berth rooms rather than dormitories. A free booklet listing all of Denmark's hostels and many campsites is available from the Tourist Office. There are over 500 campsites and the Camping Carnet (30kr) is required. An average overnight stay will cost 35kr. Town mission hostels are excellent, clean and cheap. If you can't get into a hostel and don't want to be bothered with camping, stay in a private home (anything but a hotel, as these really are very expensive). Tourist information will put you in touch with a Danish family who'll put you up. This costs 100–200kr and can be organized before you set foot in the country. Any Tourist Office in Denmark can do it, their UK agent is the Host and Guest Service, 27 Effie Rd, London, SW6 1CN (Tel. 0171 731

5340). Also consider 'Sleep-Ins', open in the main towns during the summer a good, cheap option.

EATING AND NIGHTLIFE

Danish food is expensive, but don't despair: shop at the well-stocked supermarkets and prepare your own *smørrebrød* (open sandwiches). *Pølser* (hot dog) stands are on most street corners, and the famous Danish brews round off picnics in style. Look out for cafés with signs *Madkurve kan Medbringes* (literally, 'Bring your own food'), so just buy a coffee.

ISIC gives you 50% off films, theatres, etc., and there's no shortage of pubs in Denmark. For Copenhagen, Use It have leaflets which give you a rundown on what's on, and if that's not enough they also have special information sheets on entertainment.

Copenhagen (København)

The largest city in Scandinavia, situated on the north-eastern shore of Zealand, Copenhagen is a well-run, exciting place with lots going for it and an almost Parisian *joie de vivre*. The Danes are a socially-minded lot, and this shows particularly in their capital where they operate 2 free services for young travellers which are almost too good to be true.

The YMCA and YWCA get together and open a centre for euro-railers in high summer where you can go for advice on what to see, where to go and for help with problems. Inter-point is at Valdemars-gade 15 (Tel. 3131 1574). Open 8 a.m.–10.00 a.m. and 2.30 p.m.–5.30 p.m., late June–early August. You can also stay there for 65kr (25kr for breakfast).

The second organization, called Use It, is much larger, is open all year, and is sponsored by the city youth organization. It offers countless free or non-profit-making services: free maps, tourist information and advice, a series of leaflets on cheap restaurants and hostels, and free luggage storage. The Use It centre is located at Rådhusstraede 13 (Tel. 3315 6518), a 10-minute walk from the central station along Tietgensgade, down one side of the Tivoli Gardens, on into Storm-gade, then left into Rådhusstraede. There is a restaurant, jazz club, rock/folk club and cinema where you can meet fellow travellers and young Danes. Use It will also find you a bed you can afford, or help you out if you've an emergency or crisis. They're open in summer 10 a.m.–7 p.m. and off-season 10 a.m.–4 p.m.

Bear in mind: the YMCA/YWCA set-up is a Christian organization and can be quite strict – even in Copenhagen – so if you're after advice on the hottest places for evening entertainment, etc., go to Use It.

For an off-beat tour of Copenhagen contact GuideNet, Norrebrogade 52 (Tel. 3536 1516). Their young guides will show you 'the' places to eat, drink and be merry, all for 20kr.

These sort of facilities are unique in Europe, make the most of them whilst you're there and don't expect anything remotely like it in southern Europe.

STATION FACILITIES

Copenhagen's Hovedbanegård is the terminus for all main-line trains. Information is available 8 a.m.–10 p.m. (Tel. 33 14 17 01) and reservations 8 a.m.–9 p.m. The station is closed 1.30 a.m.–4.30 a.m.

You should be able to get something to eat from some of the many buffets, snack bars or restaurants up until late evening and there's a supermarket by the station which is open 8 a.m.–midnight. There is also a foreign exchange, a post office and left-luggage locker facilities. It's a particularly fine station with many facilities, including the recently introduced Inter-Rail Centre (Tel. 3314 0400 ext. 13467), which is open July–mid-Sept., 7 a.m.–midnight daily. Anyone with a youth Inter-Rail, Eurail Youthpass or BIJ ticket can use its excellent facilities. It's very useful for information (throughout the day, there are news bulletins in English, German and French, and tape-recorded tourist information in the same languages), or you can relax for a coffee, a chat, or even a shower.

The platforms are below ground level. The 'S' trains (suburban electrics) also use the station. Look out for drunks.

It takes 40 minutes from Copenhagen to Malmö, 5 hours to Gothenburg, 5/7 hours to Hamburg, and 6 hours to Stockholm.

The nearest room-finding service is at Bernstoffsgade 1 but since their commission is 15kr, it is best to go to Use It, who offer the same service for free.

TOURIST INFORMATION

Danmarks Turistråd – Tourist Information – (Tel. 3311 1325) is located at Bernstoffsgade 1, opposite the railway station. Open May: Mon.–Fri.: 9 a.m.–6 p.m., Sat.: 9 a.m.–2 p.m., Sun. and holidays: 9 a.m.–1 p.m; June–mid-Sept.: daily 9 a.m.–6 p.m.; off season: Mon.–Fri.: 9 a.m.–5 p.m., Sat.: 9 a.m.–noon. Their service is excellent and helpful and there are leaflets on everything you could possibly need to know. Be specific and ask for everything you might need, for instance camping, walking, other parts of Denmark, etc. Don't forget to pick up their free map and a copy of *Copenhagen This Week*.

ADDRESSES

USE IT Rådhusstraede 13 (Tel. 3315 6518). They help out eurorailers with everything and will even hold your mail and find you a bed for the night. Not always over-friendly, but useful!

POST OFFICE Tietgensgade 37 (behind Central station). *Poste restante* also here. 10 a.m.– 6 p.m., 9 a.m.– 1 p.m. on Saturday.

AMEX Amagertorv 18 (Tel. 3312 2301)

UK EMBASSY Kastelsvej 36–40 (Tel. 3526 4600)

IRISH EMBASSY 21 Ostbanegade (Tel. 3142 3233)

US EMBASSY Dag Hammarskjölds Allé 24 (Tel. 3142 3144)

CANADIAN EMBASSY Kristen Bernikowsgade 1 (Tel. 3312 2299)

AUSTRALIAN EMBASSY Kristianiasgade 21 (Tel. 3526 2244)

NEW ZEALAND EMBASSY See Australia. UK may also help.

24-HOUR CHEMIST Steno Apotek, Vesterbrogade 6C (Tel. 3314 8266)

GETTING ABOUT

The S-tog is free with any rail pass. If you haven't got one, the buses are a better bet at 10kr a ride. All tickets are interchangeable between buses and trains providing they are used within the hour. The best way of all, however, is to invest in a Copenhagen Card which gives you unlimited travel by bus and rail in the whole of the metropolitan area and includes North Zealand. It also gives free admission to many sights, attractions and museums. If you don't have a pass which gives free or reduced ferry crossings to Sweden, the Copenhagen Card allows a 50% reduction. It is valid for 1, 2 or 3 days and costs 140kr, 230kr and 295kr respectively. Children aged 5 to 11 pay half-price.

For 70kr you can buy a 24hr ticket valid for just train and bus travel within the metropolitan area.

The Copenhagen Zone travel card is handy as most of Copenhagen's museums and sights lie within the central traffic area. This is part of the broader joint zone fare system that embraces all HT/Copenhagen Transport buses and DSB/State Railways and S-trains in metropolitan Copenhagen and North Zealand as well as some privately operated railway routes in the area. It is therefore possible to interchange between trains and bus routes on the same ticket. Go to a rail station to get a timetable and brochure (in English) explaining the joint zone rail and bus rebate fare system. The discount cards with 10 fares are available and are valid for unlimited travel in the zone that you start in and its adjacent zones. Fares for 2 zones cost 70kr, an all-zone card will cost 240kr. Note that clip cards are stamped face up in automatic machines.

Feeling fit? Then take advantage of City Bike Copenhagen. Supermarket sponsors 'Netto' have provided 1000 bikes for communal use. Insert your 20K coin into one of the 120 racks in the city and pedal away. When you return the bike you get your money back. Simple!

If you're thinking of going to Malmö in Sweden, carefully compare the ferry lines on offer. Prices vary considerably; bonuses for Inter-Rail may be available. The jetfoil saves you 45 minutes travelling with an Inter-Rail reduction, otherwise the trip takes 1½ hours.

SEEING

Copenhagen is a great walking city and most of the sights can easily be negotiated on foot. There are 6 well-planned city walking tours which last about 2 hours (ask Tourist Information or Use It). TIVOLI (the famous amusement park) is in the centre across from the station and has, over the years, become rather too commercial for our liking. Entrance 44kr, with rides from 8kr but generally overpriced; a Tour Pass ticket at 160kr allows unlimited rides. Avoid eating here. Open May–mid-Sept., 10 a.m.–midnight.

An alternative is the free entry amusement park of BAKKEN. Take the S-tog to KLAMPENBORG (free on Inter-Rail and Eurail) and walk through the park. Open Apr.–end Aug., 12 noon–12 midnight.

The CARLSBERG and TUBORG breweries run a good deal (a classic favourite for thirsty eurorailers): tours of the breweries with free samples afterwards (beware of the time limit on your sampling), closed weekends. Carlsberg tours at 11 a.m. and 2 p.m. Take bus 6 or 18. Tuborg tours at 10 a.m., 12.30 p.m. and 2.30 p.m. S-tog line A to Svanemøllen or Hellerup, or bus 6, 21, or 23. Tuborg brewery have opened the EKSPERIMENTARIUM, an interactive science museum, in an old bottling hall, entrance fee around 59kr.

As you will be on foot, you will not miss STRASÖXGET, a series of streets throbbing with life. The area around the university is host to a multitude of bookshops, *bric-à-brac,* a good selection of cafés and the VOR FRUE KIRKE, Copenhagen's cathedral. See also the RUNDETÅRN, the summit of which affords a great view of the old town and is curiously reached by a continuous spiral ramp.

Another good view of the town can be obtained by climbing the unusual tower of VOR FRELSERS KIRKE on Prinsessegade and Torvegade. The spiral staircase is on the outside of the church's spire and gets progressively steeper and more uneven. Not recommended in high winds or rain! It costs 10kr to climb it. The tower is still undergoing renovation and may be closed.

'Alternative' Copenhagen can be experienced at CHRISTIANA on Prinsessegade. Occupied in 1971 by a group of hippies who enjoyed the free Danish attitudes to pot, drinking and nudism, it makes an interesting visit! The veggie café and craft stalls are worthwhile and it is safe to look round. Restaurants, bars and shops are cheaper than in the rest of the town. Avoid taking photographs of the inhabitants to avoid any unpleasantness.

Copenhagen has a multitude of museums and perhaps the best are the WORKERS' MUSEUM and the NATIONAL MUSEUM which is best on Danish history and the Vikings. Also worth a look are the THORVALD-SEN'S MUSEUM for the work of Denmark's famous sculptor, the interesting RESISTANCE MUSEUM, tracing the growth of opposition to the German occupation during the Second World War, and NY CARLSBERG GLYPTOTEK (with free admission on Wed. and Sun.) for classical art.

The Bellevue is a beach between Copenhagen and Helsingør, known locally as *Fluepapiret* (fly-paper) for its ability to draw the bikini-clad blondes and the local likely lads.

The walk to the Little Mermaid, along the LANGELINIE, is the best part of the trip, as the statue's nothing special. Look out for the nearby GEFION FOUNTAIN. The comprehensive leaflet provided with the Copenhagen Card gives full details of opening times, locations and other facilities. Most of the sights, including the Little Mermaid, can be seen during the good 36kr boat trips round the harbour and canals.

Your best day trip from Copenhagen is 40 km north to FREDERIKS-BORG CASTLE at Hillerød (35 minutes by S-tog, leaving from the main station).

SLEEPING

Hotels in Copenhagen are busy all year round, with prices starting at 400kr; you are better investigating the city hostels, private house schemes and campsites. If you are organized in advance try the apartment booking agency Citi-Let, at Fortunstrade 4, DK-1065, Copenhagen K (Tel. 3325 2129; Fax. 3391 3077).

HOSTELS These are busy in summer, so don't waste time touring round them yourself. Use It will help you find a bed (when their office is shut, they often post up the latest bed situation just outside their office).

The main youth hostel (you'll need an IYHF card), Bellahøj at Herbergvejen 8 (Tel. 3128 9715), is very good and situated in a park in a nice suburb about 15–20 minutes from the city centre. The cost is 85kr. Take bus 2 from the station almost to the end of the route.

Security can be a problem, so use the lockers in the basement.

The Copenhagen Youth Hostel (IYHF) at Vejlandsallé 200 is very clean and modern. Book in after 1 p.m. (Tel. 3252 2908). Take bus 13 or train to Valby station, changing to bus 37.

Vesterbro Ungdomsgård, Absalonsgzide 8 (Tel. 31 31 2070), is more expensive than the other hostels, due to its good location. Take bus 16 from the station, or a 10-minute walk along Vesterbrogade. Cost: 95kr.

There is a YMCA hostel in Copenhagen which costs 65kr. A 15-minute walk from the station to Valdemarsgade 15 (Tel. 3131 1574; open mid-July to mid-Aug.).

SLEEP-INS Are another option and can be found in converted ice-rinks or gymnasiums at various changing locations throughout the city. Check *Copenhagen This Week*, Tourist Information, or telephone 3526 5059. Very few restrictions; IYHF cards are not required; co-ed dorms; bring your own sleeping bag. The cost is 75kr–115kr, including breakfast. Current options include Ajax Copenhagen, Bavnehoj Allé 30 (Tel. 3121 2456), Sleep-In Heaven, Frederiksberg C (Tel. 3536 6016) or the Sleep-In at Blegdamsvej 132 (Tel. 3526 5059).

PRIVATE ACCOMMODATION Go to any Tourist Office to find yourself a room in a private house and expect to pay up to 250kr for a single, 350kr a double. They also take about 15kr commission per person.

HOTELS If you have no alternative and want to stay in a hotel, try the Amager in Amagerbrogade (Tel. 3154 4008). It's handy to the airport and it's got the oldest lift in Denmark, which is rather funky.

You will also find places in the area behind the central station on Helgolandsgade (Absalon Hotel) and Colbjørnsensgade (Ansgar Hotel), but expect to pay anything from 500kr for even the cheapest hotels in the capital.

CAMPING There are 7 sites costing around 36kr per person with Danish camping pass. The all-year site is at Absalon Camping, 132 Korsdalsvej (Tel. 3641 0600): take the S-tog, line B or H, to Brøndyøster station. Cabins are available for up to 5 people, but the shop here is expensive.

EATING AND NIGHTLIFE

This is varied, interesting and there is no shortage of places to choose from. For meals, you can't do much better than the set menus at Chinese restaurants. To keep you going there are *pølser* (hot dog) stalls, fast-food chains, daily specials (*dagens ret*) and *smørrebrød*. (See the Use It brochure *Where to Eat*.) One of the most popular places for *smørrebrød* is Smørrebrødførretning at Gothersgade 10, open 8 a.m.–10 p.m.

Universitetspoppen (university refectory), 52 Kobmagergade, charge 65kr for huge lunchtime meals. You'll need an ISIC, but they are closed July and Aug. At Pasta Basta, Valkendorfsgade 22, eat as much spaghetti as you can for a fixed price. There are good 'eat as much as you can' places, at reasonable prices. Try Alexander's Pizza House: pizza and salad for around 50kr, at Lille Kannikestraede 5. Spisehuset, Rådhusstraede 13 (part of Use It). Or try all you can eat reasonably cheaply (noon–3 p.m.). In the evenings it's a pub (serving food). Or DSB Bistro, Banegardspladsen 7, for a Danish food fiesta.

There are hundreds of pubs, clubs and discos in Copenhagen. NYHAVN (the dock district) makes an interesting nocturnal wander – but it is not advisable for girls to go there alone. The Use It house is as good and cheap a place for a drink as any, and Frederiksberggade comes alive at night. Good jazz can normally be found on Norregade. For live music listings see music mags like *Hust*, *Neon Guiden* or *Gaffa*, pick these up in music stores. Basically though, you won't need to look hard for nightlife in Copenhagen.

Århus

Denmark's second city is a busy industrial and commercial centre and yet fully deserves its reputation as Denmark's cultural centre. See the Old Town (*Den gamle By*) OPEN AIR MUSEUM, a reconstructed 16th-century village, the CITY PREHISTORIC MUSEUM with the amazing red-headed mummy of the Grauballe man, the 12th-century CATHE-DRAL and the VIKING MUSEUM.

Tourist information is in the Town Hall, one block from the station, and is open 9.30 a.m.–7 p.m. Shorter hours out of season, small charge to book accommodation (Tel. 8612 1600). It's a university town and the student centre is at 84 Niels Juelsgade. The IYHA hostel is Vandrerhjemmet Pavillonen at Marienlundsvej 10 (Tel. 8616 7298); closed 12 noon–4 p.m. It's good and well situated in a forest, near beaches. Take bus or tram nos 1, 2, 6 or 8 to the terminus, then follow signs. There is a sleep-in at Fredericks Allé 20.

The campsite (Tel. 8627 0207) is 7 km out at Blommehaven, Ørneredevej, bus 6 or 19.

For nightlife, try Kulturgyngen, Mejlgade 53, or if you're a bit of an owl you could visit the Café Paradis – it's open to 6 a.m. on weekends.

Your cheapest lunch is at the Matematiske Fakultet (university) off Langelandsgade; closed after 1 p.m. and all July. Even better is the Use It Youth Centre at 15 Vester Allé. They also give free concerts and plays. Musik café at Mejlgade 53 is worth a try in the evenings as is Blitz, Klostergade 34.

Odense

En route from Copenhagen to Jutland, Odense is one of Denmark's oldest towns. It's the home town of Hans Christian Andersen; you can visit his house at Hans Jensens Straede 37–45 (20kr, no reductions).

Tourist Information is in the town hall, south of the station (Tel. 6612 7520), open in summer 9 a.m.–7 p.m., Sun. 11 a.m.–7 p.m. The Odense Fairy Tale Card gives free admission to museums and other sights, costs 90kr for 2 days – good value, if a tacky name. ST CANUTE'S 13th-century cathedral and the OPEN-AIR FOLK MUSEUM, plus an operational farm on the outskirts of Odense are interesting.

At Ladby (20 km north-east of Odense) is the coffin ship of a 10th-century Viking chief.

The youth hostel is at 121 Kragsbjergvej (Tel. 6613 0425). It has 170 beds, and is on bus route 61 or 62 from the station (cost 75kr). There is a campsite at Odensevej 102 (Tel. 6611 4702), bus 1.

Aalborg

The 1,000-year-old centre of north Jutland. The main sights include the remains of a Viking village and mass grave (at Nørresundby, just outside Aalborg), the well-preserved OLD TOWN, the 15th-century MONASTERY OF THE HOLY GHOST, AABORGHUS CASTLE, ST BOTOLPH'S CATHEDRAL, and the baby brother of Tivoli, TIVOLILAND. There is a new museum at the Viking site, with many artefacts from the area. Tourist Information is at Østeragade 8 (Tel. 9812 1900).

All Americans in Aalborg on 4 July should make their way to the Rebild National Park, 30 km south of the city, for the most extensive Independence Day celebrations outside the USA.

The Aalborg Vandrerhjem hostel is at Skydebanevej 50 (Tel. 9811

6044) and costs 85kr per night. Two campsites are located nearby: Fjordparken (Tel. 9811 6044) and Strandparken (Tel. 9812 7629). Bus 2 or 178 from centre or railway station, to terminus.

Legoland

One of Denmark's most famous exports is Lego, the children's plastic building brick. At BILLUND in mid-Jutland there is a mini-town of houses, railway, harbour, boats and cars – all made out of the stuff. Legoland is open May–Oct., with some indoor exhibitions from Easter to mid-Dec. Take the train to Vejle and then bus 912 from the station to Billund (around 40kr each way). Journey takes about an hour. A 1-day pass is available for 110kr and this include all rides. Another option is a 1-day combined ticket with return coach travel and admission for around 170kr. Legoland opens at 10 a.m. and closes at 8 p.m. Reduced entrance fees may be offered later in the day. Call Legoland on 7533 1333 for more information. There are also aviation and motor vehicle museums close by, open daily 10 a.m.–8 p.m.

There is a campsite very near Legoland, at Nordmarksvej 2 (Tel. 7533 1521) or another option is the Billund Hostel, Ellerhammers Allé (Tel. 7533 2777).

NOTES
....

....

....

....

....

....

....

....

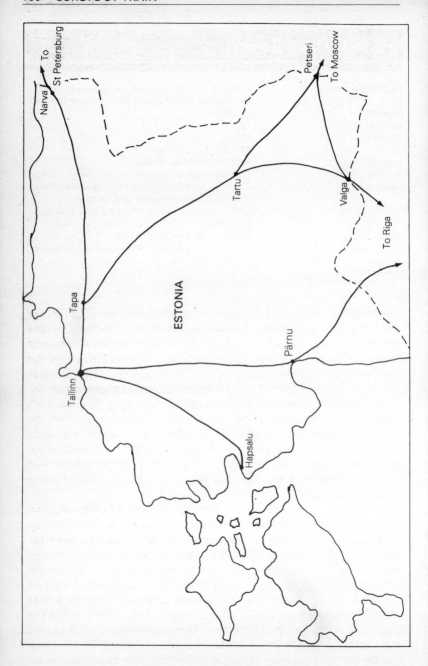

ESTONIA (Eesti)

Entry requirements	Passport. No visa required for citizens of USA, UK, Ireland, Canada, Australia and New Zealand.
Population	1,500,000
Capital	Tallinn
Currency	Kroon
	£1 = approx. 20 kroon
Political system	Parliamentary Democracy
Religion	Protestantism, Lutheranism & Russian Orthodox
Language	Estonian, Russian widely spoken (see note on languages), some English and German
Public holidays	New Year's Day, Independence Day (24 Feb.), Good Friday, Easter Sunday, May Day (1 May), Whitsun, Victory Day (23 June), St John's Day (24 June), Rebirth Day (16 Nov.), Christmas and Boxing Day.
International dialling codes	To Estonia: int'l code 372 number
	From Estonia: dial 8 00

The people of Estonia led a peaceful existence until the 12th century when the Pope launched a crusade against them. Shortly after, the country was divided when the crusaders took the south and the Danes the north. In 1346, Denmark sold northern Estonia to the Teutonic Knights, who retained control of the entire country for over 200 years, during which time the coastal towns prospered but the inland population was little more than slave labour. In the mid-16th century, Sweden captured the northern half of the country from the Hanseatic league and managed to conquer the remainder by 1620. Estonian historians have taken to calling this period of Swedish occupation the country's 'Golden Age'. Unfortunately, when Sweden was defeated in the Great Northern War of the early 18th century, Estonia fell under Russian rule.

While most of the indentured servants were freed under Russian rule, the central government in Moscow was so repressive that they were worse off than before, and many Estonians began to yearn for independence. During the First World War, Russia gave the Baltics to Germany as part of the Brest–Litovsk Treaty in an effort to stave off further German aggression. Estonia declared independence just before the treaty, but no one noticed and they had to repeat it later when Germany surrendered. Russia stepped in to try and retake the Baltics but met with opposition from the locals (who received some international help). The country floundered until 1933 when Konstantin Pats took over as one of the world's few innocuous dictators. Things went smoothly until Nazi Germany and the USSR secretly divided Europe between them in the 1939 Molotov–Ribbentrop non-aggression pact, placing the Baltics once again under Russian rule.

It was 1988 before pressure for democratic change resurfaced and in August of 1989 over 2 million people formed a human chain across the borders with Latvia and Lithuania in a plea for independence. This time it worked. Two years later Estonia declared itself a sovereign state and within 3 weeks was recognized by the West *and* the former USSR.

GETTING THERE

Tallink Express ferry services operate several crossings daily between Tallinn and Helsinki (Finland). There is a 30% ISIC discount.

TRAIN INFORMATION

There is usually someone at the station in Tallinn who speaks English, but don't count on finding English speakers outside the capital. The years of Soviet occupation mean that Russian is widely understood, but there's a strong anti-Russian sentiment in Estonia, so exercise a little discretion before practising your Russian on the locals. Information signs are being changed to Estonian, though some Russian ones remain.

PASSES AVAILABLE The Baltic States Explorer Pass provides 7, 14 or 21 consecutive days of unlimited 2nd-class travel on the national rail networks of Estonia, Latvia and Lithuania; 7 days, US$38; 14 days, US$56; 21 days, US$75. Sample journeys might be Riga–Tallinn (7 hours) 2 trains a day; Vilnius–Riga (6.5 hours) 4 trains a day.

RESERVATIONS While only mandatory on international trains, the normal trains are always packed, so you should try to book a day or two in advance. When available, first class is not much more expensive than second class, but it's less crowded and well worth the extra money.

NIGHT TRAVEL Trains are slow enough here without taking an overnighter and most of the carriages are not conducive to a good sleep.

EATING ON THE TRAIN There are sporadic trolley services but the food often looks dodgy, so stock up with picnic supplies before you leave.

TOURIST INFORMATION

There are Tourist Offices in most towns, with a main one in Tallinn. Although the amount of information may seem scant, compared to even a couple of years ago, it has really improved. They do a good free map and also a useful *Tallinn This Week*.

ISIC BONUSES Discounts on Airlines, ferries to Finland and Sweden and national buses. Show your card when you buy a ticket for *anything*.

MONEY MATTERS Banking hours are generally 9 a.m.–4 p.m. and banks are closed at weekends. Outside the best hotels, traveller's cheques and credit cards are not widely used here, so bring cash. The best currencies are US dollars and Deutschmarks which you can change at the bank for kroon or use directly. Currency exchange offices are open Mon.–Fri. 9 a.m.–7 or 8 p.m., Sat. 9 a.m.–5 p.m. Some open Sun.

SHOPS Generally open 9 a.m.–6 p.m. If there is no marked price, you run a risk of getting ripped off. There would appear to be 2 prices for everything: one for the locals and a higher sum for the tourists. With few tourists until recently, the general attitude here was that those who came could afford whatever was charged.

MUSEUMS Hours fluctuate wildly, but most are open 11 a.m.–4 p.m.

LANGUAGE Estonian is the national language, but you're unlikely to find a phrase-book in your local bookshop. Many younger people learn English or German and almost everyone speaks Russian (small wonder). People may not react warmly, though, if you confront them in Russian, so make an attempt at Estonian with these useful phrases:

Hello	*Tere*	Thank you	*Tänan*
Goodbye	*Head aega*	Excuse me	*Vabandage*
Yes	*Jah*	Do you speak	*Kas teie räägite*
No	*Ei*	English?	*inglise keelt?*
Please	*Palun*	Russian?	*rooski keelt?*

TIPPING As is usual in Eastern Europe, waiters and waitresses are paid buttons, so any tips are very much appreciated. Some restaurants will have a service charge included, in which case round up your bill with loose change.

SLEEPING AND EATING

The youth hostel project here was started in 1991 and there are 10 hostels across the country which charge £2–4. The Estonian Youth Hostel Association at Tatari 39, Tallinn (Tel. 6461 457), will book accommodation for you. Unfortunately, they recommend that you reserve 4 weeks in advance! Another option is the student dorms (open in summer) at around £4–6. Camping is really at its best here, with most sites charging less than £1 per person.

There are lots of cheap cafés and restaurants around and when it becomes evident you're a Westerner you will be treated well. Of course it also means you may be taken advantage of, so be sure you get a menu. Vegetarians may experience difficulties, but the bakeries and vegetable markets are fairly well stocked and you should be able to put together good picnics.

Tallinn

The old city was almost levelled by Soviet bombing during the Second World War. Though some cobbled streets and historic buildings remain, the metropolis which arose in its place is primarily industrial. This, coupled with the forced migration of people from other Soviet Republics under communist rule, has created a unique city which is nothing like the Tallinn of even 50 years ago.

Tourist Information is on 18 Raekoja Plats in the centre of the old town (Tel. 63 13940). There is also an office at Tallinn Harbour. The British Embassy (Tel. 63 13462) and the American Embassy (Tel. 63 12021) are both at Kentmanni 20 while the Canadian Embassy is on Tolli 3 (Tel. 63 13570). Irish nationals needing consular service should contact the Irish embassy in Helsinki, Australians should contact their Swedish embassy in Stockholm and New Zealand nationals should use their embassy in Moscow.

GETTING ABOUT

There is a good system of buses, trams and trolley buses. Buy tickets or a multi-journey card (9 kroon) from street kiosks before getting on and have them stamped when you board.

SEEING

The city is split into 3 distinct areas: the lower town, the upper town and the new town.

In the LOWER TOWN, check out the GREAT COAST GATE and FAT MARGARET, built to guard the gate but now home to the SEA MUSEUM. From here, follow Pikk Street South taking in the medieval houses and guildhalls on either side. At the other end of Pikk is OLEVISTE CHURCH, the town symbol. On 17 Lai, the next street over, is the APPLIED ART MUSEUM in a 17th-century barn (open Wed.–Sun.).

Enter the UPPER TOWN via Pikk and continue on to the ALEXANDER NEVSKY CATHEDRAL. Behind the cathedral is the TOOMPEA CASTLE and the 14th-century tower PIKK HERMANN. Another interesting place is the museum housed in the KIEK-IN-DE-KOK tower at the southern end of Komandandi.

SLEEPING AND EATING

Check with the Tourist Information office on Raekoja Plats for lists of campsites and other accommodation, but they will probably suggest the Family Hotel Association on Mere pst 6. There's also a B&B at Sadama 11 (Tel. 602 091). The central Youth Hostel is at Viru 1 (Tel. 631 3853); another, further out, is at Vikerlase 15.

There are 3 Peetri Pizza places around town where you can eat for just over £2. One is at the rail station, which also has a decent snack bar where you can really fill up for around £1. The best Indian restaurant for miles around is on Raekoja 13. You can get a good meal here until 1 a.m. for around £4. More traditional fare can be found at Eeslitall Restoran, Dunkri 4.

NOTES

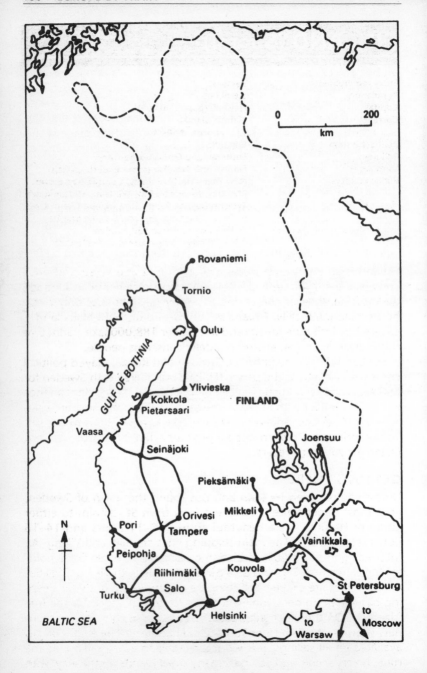

FINLAND (Suomi)

Entry requirements	Passport
Population	5,000,000
Capital	Helsinki (pop.: 500,000)
Currency	Finnish Markka
	£1 = approx. 8.50mk
Political system	Republic
Religions	Lutheran and Orthodox ministry
Languages	Finnish and Swedish (some English spoken)
Public holidays	New Year's Day, Epiphany, Good Friday, Easter, May Day, Ascension Day, Whitsun, Midsummer's Eve and Day, All Saints' Day, Independence Day (6 Dec.), Christmas Eve and Day, Boxing Day
International dialling codes	To Finland: int'l code 358 number
	From Finland: 990 + country code number

Finland is an interesting mixture of both East and West, and once you reach there you really do feel a long way from home. In summer, darkness hardly ever comes and in winter daylight lasts only a few hours. Geographically, Finland is very beautiful: 70% of its land is covered by lush pine forests and it has over 188,000 lakes; added to this is clear air and an environmentally conscious people.

For centuries, its neighbours, Sweden and Russia, played political chess with Finland as the pawn. (Finland was linked with Sweden for 650 years and with Russia for 100 before proclaiming independence in 1917.) Conflict with Russia in the Second World War lost her valuable territories and landed her with large war reparations to pay off. Today, prices are reasonable by Scandinavian standards, i.e. not cheap for young travellers.

GETTING THERE

Unless you're going by train and bus round the north of Sweden, your most direct route is to take a ferry from Stockholm to either Turku or Helsinki. It's a beautiful cruise (10–11 hours and 14–16 hours respectively). The main shipping lines are Silja and Viking. An Inter-Rail gets you a 50% reduction on both lines, while Eurail holders travel free with Silja and on a 50% reduction with Viking. Facilities on both lines are excellent. Cabins are expensive, so get your sleeping bag down on deck somewhere, or, better still, head for the free 'sleep-in'. On the older ships these have 60 beds, but the excellent new ships on the Silja Lines Turku–Stockholm route have 200 places available on all sailings. It is worthwhile taking a day sailing, as the route is very scenic and you pass many small islands on the way, with the ship constantly zigzagging to keep in deep water. Snacks and coffee on the ship are reasonably priced as are the duty-free goods – by Scandinavian standards. There are several services each day, with prices varying depending on the crossing. The Helsinki ferries leave at 6 p.m. or 7 p.m. and cost a minimum 84mk on Viking Line, or 235mk on Silja Line. The Turku ferries leave at 10 a.m., 8 p.m. and 9.15 p.m. during high season, and cost a minimum of 69mk on Viking Line, and 110mk on Silja Line. There are also regular daily ferry crossings to Tallinn (Estonia). For travel with a difference contact Mr Rolf Tubenthal in Hamburg (Tel. 4940 3705 2593) who arranges trips on container ships.

FINNISH STATE RAILWAYS

(VALTIONRAUTATIET, VR)

Big, solid and reliable (like the Finns!), the majority of the rolling stock is new. There are 4 types of trains: IC-trains (*IC-juna*), special expresses (*Erikoispikajuna*), regular expresses (*Pikajuna*) and locals (*Henkilöjuna*). Their service extends as far north as Lapland and includes nearly 6,000 km of line.

PASSES AVAILABLE The Finnrail Pass entitles you to 3, 5 or 10 days of travel within 1 month for 540mk, 730mk or 995mk respectively (second class). Under-26s are eligible for a 25% discount, under-17s travel half-price. A first-class Finnrail Pass is available.

The ScanRail Pass is valid for travel anywhere in Scandinavia and allows 1 month of consecutive travel for £260, or 21-days travel for £198, or 5 days of travel within 15 days for £132. The ticket should be purchased outside Scandinavia, as more restrictions apply if it is bought on arrival. Under-26s are entitled to around 25% discount; a first-class ScanRail Pass is available for a supplement of 20%.

The Inter-Rail pass has been broken down into zones, so that a careful selection of zones means you do not have to pay for travel to areas you have no intention of visiting. For £159 you can tour a single zone for 22 days. Finland is in Zone B, along with Sweden and Norway. (For further details of the 8 Inter-Rail zones, refer to the Inter-Rail section in Part One of this guide.)

A Euro Domino ticket is also available for Finland, see p. 41.

INTER-RAIL BONUSES See Appendix I, plus free entry to the VR Railway Museum in Hyvinkää, and Narrow Gauge Railway Museum in Jokioinen (Gare Minkio).

EURAIL BONUSES Free services:

Buses, particularly those which operate during certain hours of the day as train substitutes.

Ferry crossings operated by Silja Line between Vaasa and Umea.

Note that the service between Vaasa and Sundsvall has been withdrawn.

REDUCTIONS 50% reduction on the normal adult rate for the ferry crossing from Helsinki to Travemünde on the Finnjet (bookings earliest 7 days before departure).

TRAIN INFORMATION

At the major stations you'll find the staff speak English. Contact the Neuvonta at the station if you've problems.

RESERVATIONS Obligatory on the IC-trains and special expresses (marked 'EP' in timetable); optional on other trains. Oddly, reserved seats are not marked, making it difficult to tell if a seat is free. Costs are 18mk on the special expresses, 25mk on IC-trains (second class) and 15mk on other trains.

NIGHT TRAVEL There are no couchettes, only sleepers, which are reasonably priced, 60–90mk in a 3-berth compartment or 100–150mk in 2-berth. Reductions off-peak. During the peak periods (Easter and July/August) try and reserve sleepers as far ahead as possible.

TOURIST INFORMATION

City offices, *Matkailutoimistot*, provide excellent maps and leaflets on their locality. For Finland as a whole, the Finnish Tourist Board, MEK, has its base in Helsinki. Museums tend to close on Mon.

ISIC BONUSES Student discounts on museums, art galleries and theatres. 50% discount on *Scanhotel* chain between June and mid August, weekends rest of the year.

MONEY MATTERS 1 Finnish markka (mk) = 100 penni (p).

Banking hours are Mon.–Fri.:, 9.15 a.m.–4.15 p.m., but vary by locality. Banks give the best rate of exchange. All banks and exchange bureaux close over the midsummer weekend holiday.

POST OFFICES Open 9 a.m.–5 p.m., Mon.–Fri. Stamps are also sold at bookshops, newsagents' and stations. Post boxes are yellow.

SHOPS Mon.–Fri.: 9 a.m.–5 p.m. or 6 p.m. (with department stores staying open to 8 p.m. summer weekdays). Saturday hours 9 a.m.– 2 p.m. or 3 p.m. (department stores to 6 p.m.).

TELEPHONES Accept 1 and 5mk coins only, returned if no reply. There are also card phones which accept all major credit cards, and variously priced phonecards are sold for use in special booths.

TIPPING In Finland, tips are normally only given in fairly smart restaurants.

SLEEPING

Youth hostels and campsites are graded on a star basis with 5 grades. There's no age limit to Finland's 160 hostels and you don't need IYHF membership, except in the most expensive category, which often have saunas. Prices 60–150mk, though most cost around 80mk. For further information about youth hostels in Finland, contact Suomen Retkeilymajäjarjestö (SRM), Yrjön-katu 38 B, SF-00100 Helsinki (Tel. 6931 347/6940 377).

There are something like 340 campsites, varying in price from 25 to 80mk per night (for a family with max. 3 adults plus children with tents, a caravan or trailer). For more details on hostelling and camping, ask at Tourist Information for the excellent current leaflet *Finland Budget Accommodation*.

Private accommodation and small boarding houses are also available. Summer hotels are often made out of student dorms, and they're usually clean, modern and reasonably priced. The cheapest you'll get for a hotel room (double) with breakfast is 100–150mk per person.

If organized in advance and you have a preference for hotels, ask at the Finnish Tourist Office in your country about the FinnCheque advance booking discount system.

EATING AND NIGHTLIFE

The *baaris*, *grillis*, *krouvis* or *kahvilas* are a mixture of café and fast-food chains. They're OK but vary dramatically in quality. The student-run cafés are your best bet. Finnish specialities include salted Baltic herring, rye bread, crayfish and fruit-filled pancakes. Various fish dishes are common and if you eat meat, watch out for dried reindeer.

Nearly all restaurants have set lunch and dinner menus, but you're better advised to starve yourself and look out for a *Voileipäpöytä or Smörgåsbord* (Scandinavian cold table) for a set price, usually available at lunchtime. This often includes hot dishes as well, and you work on the basis of eating as much as you like for a set price.

Heavy tax on alcohol means consequently high prices, e.g. a pint of beer is 15–25mk. Alcohol sales are controlled by a state organization, and only beer and non-alcoholic drinks are available elsewhere.

Finns are keen on dancing and there's plenty of that going on on Vappu Night (30 April). This is the students' spring festival which is a good excuse for Helsinki's 20,000 students to let rip and have a knees-up after the long winter.

Whether you've been sleeping on deck or going by train and bus round the north, there's nothing like a real Finnish sauna to relax you. Most hotels welcome non-residents. (Rub birch-leaves with the Finns – it's cheaper to take a sauna in a group but do not expect mixed saunas!)

Helsinki city phone code: 90

A clean, bright, modern capital city. Your first impression will probably be of the colourful harbourside market, a daily event in front of the City Hall and President's Palace. Helsinki particularly reminds one visually of its geographical location: the solid eastern-looking buildings contrast with the modern department stores selling endless well-designed consumer goods. In some ways, you feel closer to Russia in Helsinki than you do in Budapest.

STATION FACILITIES
There are daily trains from Helsinki to Turku, Tampere, Kontiomäki, Oulu, Kemi and Rovaniemi (10–13 hours). If you have a Russian visa, there are also 2 daily trains to St Petersburg and 2 to Moscow.

Helsinki Central is one of the world's few architecturally famous stations. It's a classic example of *Art Nouveau*, designed by Eliel Saarinen.

Train information is available Mon.–Sat: 7 a.m.–10 p.m., Sun.: 9 a.m.–10 p.m. (Tel. 0100121, International queries west Tel. 664849, east Tel. 625216)

The station shuts during the following hours: Mon.–Thurs., Sun.: 1 a.m.–5 am. Fri.–Sat.: 12 midnight–5 a.m.

There are left-luggage lockers on both the lower and upper floors. The small ones on the upper level are too small for packs and cost 10mk. You may get a pack in the larger ones on the lower level. Hotellikeskus is the accommodation-finding service in a building between the station and the nearby post office, at Asema-aukio 3 (Tel. 171133). They take 10mk commission per find. Summer hours: Mon.–Sat.: 9 a.m.–7 p.m., Sun.: 10 a.m.–6 p.m.; off-season Mon.–Fri.: 9 a.m.–5 p.m. They also have a list of all the IYHF youth hostels in Finland.

TOURIST INFORMATION

The city Tourist Office is west of the market at Pohjoisesplanadi 19 (Tel. 169 3757). Open mid-May–mid-Sept., Mon.–Fri.: 9 a.m.–7 p.m., Sat.–Sun: 9 a.m.–3 p.m., mid-Sept.–mid-May, Mon.–Fri.: 9 a.m.–5 p.m. Sat.–Sun.: 9 a.m.–3 p.m. They produce very comprehensive leaflets and are incredibly helpful. Pick up a tourist map, *Helsinki This Week*, *Helsinki Guide* and *Helsinki on Foot*, which includes 6 self-guiding tours. If you're staying for a while, ask them about the city transport passes.

Another possibility is the Helsinki Card, which is valid for either 24 hours at 95mk, 48 hours at 135mk, or 72 hours at 165mk. Not only does it allow you free travel on all public transport, but it also entitles you to free entry to various museums and other discounts.

If it's a wet day or you're fed up with walking, tram 3T does an excellent round trip from the station. It takes about an hour and all the main sights are pointed out.

ADDRESSES

FINNISH TOURIST BOARD Eteläesplanadi 4 (Tel. 41769300) for information on all of Finland. Open Mon.–Fri.: 9 a.m.–5 p.m., Sat.: 9 a.m.–1 p.m. during the summer.

POST OFFICE Mannerheimintie 11, open Mon.–Fri.: 9 a.m.–5 p.m. *Poste restante* is here.

AMEX Pohjoisesplanadi 2, open Mon.–Fri.: 9 a.m.–1 p.m., Sat.: 10 a.m.–2 p.m.

UK EMBASSY Itäinen Puistotie 17 (Tel. 661293)

IRISH EMBASSY Erottajankatu 7 (Tel. 646 006)

US EMBASSY Itäinen Puistotie 14a (Tel. 171931)

CANADIAN EMBASSY Pohjoisesplanadi 25b (Tel. 171141)

AUSTRALIAN EMBASSY Use the embassy in Stockholm.

NEW ZEALAND EMBASSY Use the Australian embassy in Stockholm.

24-HOUR CHEMIST Yloipiston Apteekki, Mannerheimintie 96

STUDENT TRAVEL AGENCY Travela, Mannerheimintie 5c (Tel. 624 101). Near the train station.
HELSINKI TODAY Tel. 058 for information and events in English, 040 for news and weather.

SEEING

The neoclassical centre of town, around the Senate Square, built after a fire which devastated Helsinki, makes a good starting point. On the square stand the Lutheran CATHEDRAL, UNIVERSITY and GOVERN-MENT PALACE, all built in the early 19th century. Heading down towards the sea front, the PRESIDENT'S PALACE, CITY HALL and ORTHODOX CATHEDRAL can be seen. The Tourist Office's walking tours take you around the sights. The NATIONAL MUSEUM, north of Mannerheimintie from the station, is worth a visit on route to the ROCK or TEMPPELIA UKIO CHURCH. From the museum head down Aurorankatu, then along Temppelikatu. Two island locations of note are the SEURASAARI OPEN-AIR MUSEUM, bus 24 to its terminus, and the SUOMENLINNA FORTRESS ISLAND, reached by ferry from near the Tourist Information.

Finland is also rightly acclaimed for being a world leader in manufacturing design, and the MUSEUM OF APPLIED ARTS at Korkeavuorenkatu 23 brings together all the best the country has to offer.

SLEEPING

You'll find the Hotel Booking Centre in the west wing of the main station. Open Sept. 1–May 31: 9 a.m.–5p.m., Mon.–Fri. (closed Sat.. Sun.) and June 1–Aug. 31: 9 a.m.–7 p.m., Mon.–Sat. and 10 a.m.–6 p.m. Sun. Hotels in Helsinki are often fully booked in summer, hostelling is a better bet.

HOSTELS Try youth hostel Stadionin Maja, Pohjoinen Stadiontie 3b (Tel. 496071), 45–100mk with IYHF card. Located in the Olympic Stadium complex and reached by tram 3T or 7A from Mannerheimintie, just out of the station.

Eurohostel, at Linnankatu 9 (Tel. 622 0470) is open all year, price 110–160mk. ISIC reductions.

There's a YMCA Interpoint hostel at Vuorikatu 17 (Tel. 173 441) open 15 July–15 Aug. It costs 45mk.

Also try the Academica, Hietaniemenkatu 14 (Tel. 4020206). Head across Mannerheimintie from the station, and down Arkadiankatu, then Pohjoinen Rautatiekatu to the junction with Hietaniemenkatu.

During the summer the Hotelli Satakuntalo, Lapinrinne 1a (Tel. 695851) has dorm facilities and single rooms. Near the station. Fenno-Finnapartment, Franzeninkatu 26 (Tel. 773 1661) offers ISIC discounts.

CAMPING The nearest campsite is Rastila (Tel. 316551). Take the metro from the station to Östra centrum, then bus 90, 90a, 96 or 98, first stop after the bridge. Open May–Sept., around 25mk per person.

EATING AND NIGHTLIFE

There are plenty of stalls, takeaways and cafés, as well as the excellent markets, so eating is no problem. Stockmann's department store have a good basement food hall, and if you're going for a restaurant meal, you've the usual choice of Chinese, Indian, etc., or Russian.

Try Vanhan Kellari, Mannerheimintie 3, a good self-service, popular with students. Open till 1 a.m. Also Kasvisravintola, Korkeavuorenkatu 3, for good vegetarian food. Open Mon.–Fri.: 11 a.m.–6 p.m., Sat.–Sun.: 12 p.m.–6 p.m. Closes 5 p.m. in summer.

Finns really come to life in the pub, of which Helsinki has no shortage. You don't have to look far for them. Try the following pubs: Hamlet at Vilhonkatu 6; Konig at Mikonkatu 4; or Kaarle XII on Kasarmikatu 40. KY Exit at Pohjoinen Rautatiekatu 21 is popular with students; also worth trying is the Café Adlon at Fabianinkatu 14. There is an Irish pub, O'Malley's, at Hotel Torni, Yrjonkatu 26.

For jazz, try Storyville, Museokatu 8.

If you're in Helsinki on 30 April or Midsummer's Eve, prepare yourself for a late night as they stay up all night dancing and drinking.

Turku (Åbo) city phone code: 21

The oldest town and former capital of Finland. If arriving on the ferry from Sweden, take the train or bus to the city centre, from outside the terminus.

TOURIST INFORMATION

Käsityöläiskatu 3, open Mon.–Fri.: 8 a.m.–4 p.m., from 8.30 a.m. in winter. Also at Aurakatu 4 (Tel. 233 6366), open June–mid-Sept., Mon.–Fri.: 8.30 a.m.–7.30 p.m., Sat.–Sun.: 10 a.m.–5 p.m.; mid-Sept.–end May, Mon.–Fri.: 8.30 a.m.–6 p.m., Sat.–Sun.: 10 a.m.–5 p.m.

SEEING

The main sights are the 12th-century CASTLE, originally a Swedish stronghold, which now houses part of the PROVINCIAL MUSEUM entry is 15mk, but get off the train at the harbour station to see it and save a 25-minute walk;. TURKU CATHEDRAL, dating from the 13th century; the SIBELIUS MUSEUM, containing many instruments and his personal possessions; and the LUOSTARINMÄKI MUSEUM where craftsmen put on live demonstrations of their skills in an old-style street. SUOMEN JOUT-SEN, a sailing vessel open to the public, is anchored in the Aura River and worth a look, as is the museum ship *Sigyn* nearby. Also, there are boat excursions through the archipelago to the neighbouring town of NAANTALI.

SLEEPING

HOSTELS Kaupungin Retkeilymaja at Linnankatu 39 (Tel. 316578). 128 beds in dorms and small rooms. Take bus 10 or 20 from the station to the Market Square; from here or the ferry terminus, take bus 30, getting off at the Martinsilta bridge. Reception open 3 p.m. to midnight, 35–95mk and 20mk for sheets.

Turisti-Aula (Tel. 334484) is central and very good. One block north of city Tourist Office at Käsityöläiskatu 11, from 160mk single to 250mk double.

CAMPING Island of Ruissalo (Tel. 589249), bus 8 from Market Square. Buses are not too frequent and it is a 20-minute ride. Facilities are good with a worthwhile restaurant and beach nearby, also has sauna facilities.

EATING

Go to the MARKETPLACE (8 a.m.–2 p.m.) where the food's good, as cheap as you can expect to find and is a sight in itself. There is also an evening market in summer until 8 p.m.

Just up the road is the KAUPPAHALLI (covered market). It's open 8 a.m.–5 p.m. and Saturday morning, and is full of delights. There are several pizza places and the department stores have good cafés.

Tampere city phone code: 31

Located on the isthmus between 2 lakes, Tampere is Finland's second city. Although an industrial centre, it has plenty going for it to make it worth a visit.

TOURIST INFORMATION

At Verkatehtaankatu 2. Open weekdays 8.30 a.m.–8 p.m., Sat. 8.30 a.m.–6 p.m., Sun. 11.30 a.m.–6 p.m.; weekdays only off season, 8.30 a.m.–5 p.m. (Tel. 212 6652).

SEEING

SÄRKÄNNIEMI not only has an amusement park, but also an aquarium, dolphinarium, planetarium, children's zoo and the NÄSINNEULA OBSERVATION TOWER, which affords a good view of Tampere and its surroundings. The SARA HILDÉN modern art museum is also nearby (open 11 a.m.–6 p.m. daily, closed Mon.).

The LENIN MUSEUM at Hämeenpuisto 28 (open Mon.–Fri.: 9 a.m.–5 p.m., Sat.–Sun: 11 a.m.–4 p.m.) is possibly unique as the only museum outside Eastern Europe dedicated to the life of V. I. Lenin.

The CATHEDRAL, built 1907, is worth a look for its altarpiece and frescoes, as is the ORTHODOX CHURCH at Tuomiokirkonkatu 27, which, although it is the only neo-Byzantine church in the Nordic countries, has the largest bells in Finland.

SLEEPING

HOSTELS Uimahallin Maja at Pirkankatu 10–12 (Tel. 229460) is central for most of the sights and about 1 km from the railway station. Head down Hämeenkatu and bear right at the end.

An alternative is the hostel and summer hotel Domus, at Pellervonkatu 9 (Tel. 255 0000). Take bus 25 from the station; only open 1 June–31 Aug.

The Interpoint Hämeenpuisto at Hämeenpuisto 14 is also fairly central and nearer the station. Head down Hämeenkatu and Hameenpuisto, but only open 15 July–15 Aug. It costs 35mk.

The YWCA at Tuomiokirkonkatu 12a is close to the station. Open mid-June–late Aug. (Tel. 225446).

CAMPING Härmälä camping has 400 beds in cabins for 3 to 5 persons, open early May–late Aug. only (Tel. 651250). Take bus 1 from outside Tourist Office.

Northern Finland

If you want to sail in the midnight sun and walk in the forests of Europe's remotest northern land, prepare yourself for a minimum of 20 hours' train travel from Helsinki and buses and ferries which don't always connect up as smoothly as one would like. The end goal is a unique experience, but to be honest it's easier to get up to the Arctic tundra through Norway or Sweden.

Oulu and Rovaniemi

These are the most attractive of the northern towns. The trip from Helsinki to Rovaniemi isn't too bad – a direct 12-hour train journey – and this takes you to a convenient starting point for your Lapland excursions. The Tourist Offices at Oulu and Rovaniemi will supply you with all you need to know and suggest accommodation.

The Rovaniemi youth hostel, at Hallituskatu 16 (Tel. (960) 344644) is good and clean and costs 70–80mk. Turn right outside the station and follow the signs.

Southern Finland

The lakes and woods of the south make this area an outdoor recreation paradise and one of Europe's last wildernesses. Savonlinna is a good centre to base yourself at. In this neck of the woods you really ought to camp to get the feel of Finland. The Tourist Office can arrange canoes and bikes for you.

Savonlinna

Near the Russian border, 6 hours from Helsinki, has more charm than the other towns in the Lake Region. Don't wait on the train for the main station at Savonlinna, get off at the stop near the centre, Savonlinna Kauppatori, as you're nearer the Tourist Office there. It's at Puistokatu 1 and is open in early June and late Aug. 8 a.m.–6 p.m.

every day, late June–late Aug. to 10 p.m. every day, and 9 a.m.–4 p.m. Mon.–Fri. on other dates (Tel. 273977).

At the heart of the town is OLAVINLINNA, on a small island, the medieval castle with the old wooden houses of Linnankatu surrounding it. Take the English guided tour of the castle.

During most of July, the opera festival takes place, and it fills up beds at an incredible rate and is expensive to participate in.

Use the open-air markets to picnic from, and try to stay at the excellent Malakias youth hostel at Pihlajavedenkuja 6 (Tel. 23283), 70mk, either a 15-minute walk along Tulliportinkatu and Savonkatu, or bus 2 or 3 from centre. Camp at Savonlinna Camping (Tel. 537353) at Vuohimäki, 6 km from the centre, take bus 3. It costs from 70mk per tent.

Imatra

Almost on the Russian border, and on the route to Savonlinna, is the small town of Imatra, on the Vuoksi river. The youth hostel and campsite are on the sandy shore of a lake in the forest. Despite the 3 km walk, or bus ride, it is a great place to relax.

NOTES

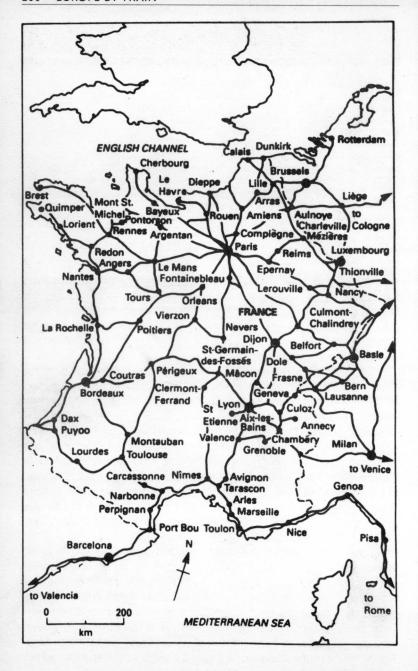

FRANCE

Entry requirements	Passport
Population	56,600,000
Capital	Paris (pop.: 10,825,000)
Currency	Franc £1 = approx. 9.39F
Political system	Republic
Religion	Mainly Roman Catholic
Language	French
Public holidays	New Year's Day, Easter, Labour Day, Bastille Day, VE Day, Ascension Day, Whitsun, Bastille Day, Assumption Day, All Saints' Day, Remembrance Day, Christmas Day
International dialling codes	To France: int'l code 33 number
	From France: 00 + country code number
	Important – France has been re-coded, see section, p.207.

France is a country of great diversity whose long and eventful history has left behind a wealth of attractions and pleasures to experience. Because of the efficient rail network, you can make as much or as little of France as you want: it's just as possible to explore each region in depth as it is to take an overnight express straight to the Riviera, if time and tanning are of the essence.

France (Gaul) was part of the Roman Empire till the Germanic Franks moved in during the 5th century. Charlemagne was crowned by the Pope on Christmas Day 800, but after his death the French nobles tried to go it alone. More successful than most were the Dukes of Burgundy and Normandy. In 987 the Capetian dynasty began to centralize power, which led to a period of prosperity and trade, and the eventual growth of Paris as the intellectual centre of Europe in the 13th century. England's Norman kings held vast estates in France till the Hundred Years' War sent them packing. This further strengthened the French monarchy; a process which continued under the Valois and Bourbon kings, till Louis XIV said it all: *'L'état, c'est moi'* ('I am the state').

Under the Sun King (Louis XIV), literature and the arts flourished and all the stylish people in Europe wanted to speak French. From this high point things gradually turned sour. and heads began to roll with the revolution in 1789. The First Republic didn't last long; then out of the chaos emerged Napoleon and dictatorship. During the 19th century the French Empire continued to grow, with power constantly changing hands between democracy and dictatorship. The revolution of 1848 brought about the Second Republic, which was followed by a *coup d'état* and the dictatorship of Napoleon III (nephew of the first). The Third Republic of 1870 survived until the German occupation of France in 1940. After Liberation the Fourth was created, and de Gaulle got the Fifth off the ground in 1958.

FRENCH NATIONAL RAILWAYS

(Société Nationale des Chemins de Fer Français, SNCF)

Arguably, Europe's best railway, with the most luxurious carriages travelling at the fastest speeds on the most extensive rail network. On the Sud-Est and Atlantique routes the TGVs (*trains à grande vitesse*) offer the only convenient services (Paris–Lyon–Marseille–Toulon and Nice), and are well worth the supplement. In general, though, supplements are only required on about 40% of journeys. The high-speed network is being expanded with huge investment, not only within France but to neighbouring countries, including the Channel link with England. Strasbourg is only 4 hours away from Paris, with Berne only 4½ hours and Nice under 7 hours. Bordeaux is now 3 hours from Paris, and the Spanish border just over 5 hours away. Lille and the Channel Tunnel are connected by the TGV Nord route, the tunnel being under 2 hours from Paris. The next development is the TGV Est route, to bring Strasbourg to 2½ hours from Paris, with onward connections into the heart of Europe. There's been a breakthrough too for Eurostar passengers using Lille as a TGV hub. Without having to stop at Paris, passengers coming from London (and Brussels) can go direct from Lille to Brittany and the southwest. This makes the journey time of, for example, London–Bordeaux only 7 hours. Further improvements to the TGV will give more powerful units and will include sleepers. The non-supplement Corail trains are almost indistinguishable from the Eurocity in comfort and in many cases run at the same speed.

The network serves over 2,500 destinations using 4 different types of trains: TGV; Eurocity; Corail; and Turbo-train.

There are 2 special overnight trains from Calais to the French Riviera. Depending on the season they may call at Paris Nord, but no change is required, see Thomas Cook 12, l2a and 12b. These trains have no seating accommodation, so you will have to go for either a sleeper or a couchette at about £9 extra.

As with most other aspects of French life, the train network is centred round Paris, so if your route is via Paris, generally you're OK, but if you're crossing France from east to west, your impression of SNCF will be somewhat less glowing.

PASSES AVAILABLE The Inter-Rail pass has been broken down into zones, so that a careful selection of zones means you don't have to pay for travel to areas you have no intention of visiting. For £159 you can spend 15 days in a zone. France is in Zone E, along with Luxembourg, Belgium and the Netherlands. (For further details of the 8 Inter-Rail zones, refer to the Inter-Rail section in Part One of this guide.)

CARTE 12-25 This new card scheme for the under-26s has replaced the old Carrissimo Card. It offers up to 50% reductions on TGVs (depending on availability) and up to 50% reductions on off-peak ('blue period') and 'white period' travel and 25% off tickets at other times. Valid tor 1 year from the date of the first journey, it costs £28. The card is valid in first or second class, for up to 4 people travelling together. Similar schemes, called Carte Kiwi and Carte Vemeil, are available for those under 16 and over 60 respectively. Couples (married or cohabiting) can take advantage of Carte Couple which is free of charge, ask at SNCF offices.

THE 'BLUE' AND 'WHITE' TARIFF CALENDAR The French Railways tariff calendar is colour coded as follows:

'Blue' (off-peak) period: generally 12 noon Mon.–12 noon Fri. and 12 noon Sat.–3 p.m. Sun.
'White' (standard) period: generally 12 noon Fri.–12 noon Sat. and 3 p.m. Sun.–12 noon Mon., plus some French public holidays.

To help you plan your trip(s), you are supplied with a copy of the tariff calendar when you buy your Carrissimo.

WHERE TO BUY YOUR RAILCARD You can buy your Carrissimo at French Railways' Rail Shop, 179 Piccadilly, London W1V OBA (Tel. enquiries: 0990 300 003), upon presentation of your passport, as proof of your age, accompanied by a passport-size photograph. The 4-journey card can also be bought at any railway station in France.

FAMILY TRAINS Another novel idea from SNCF is the 'family train', which runs on 11 long-distance routes, mainly from Paris, but also from Nice and Nantes. Each train has fully-equipped play areas where young children can while away the journey as their parents look on. Special menus are available for family groups and there are even power points for baby's bottle-warmer. There is no additional cost and children under 4 travel free if they don't occupy a seat. If they do, quarter-price fares are charged – but this only applies to family trains. Provided at least 4 full-fare-paying passengers, including at least one under 12, are in a group, a whole compartment may be reserved.

ROVER TICKETS Those resident outside France and Britain could consider the new BritRail Pass + Eurostar (details p. 48). The popular France Vacances pass has now been replaced with the Euro Domino scheme (see p. 41). There is also a France Railpass for USA residents.

EURAIL BONUSES Free: Digne–Nice or vice versa on the Chemins de Fer de la Provence.

REDUCTIONS The following half-price reductions are granted by Europabus on transportation costs only and by local offices in Europe.

253 Besançon–Lausanne
254 Chamonix–Evian–Geneva
255 Geneva–Nice
256 Grenoble–Nice
257 Grenoble–Briançon
258 Thonon–Evian–Stresa
446 Best of Brittany

P&O European Ferries offer the following discounts to passengers: 50% reduction on normal fares for the ferry crossings Calais–Dover, Dieppe–Newhaven, Cherbourg–Southampton and 30% reduction on the normal fare of the Le Havre/Cherbourg–Portsmouth sailing. Channiland ferries offer a 25% reduction on services between St. Malo and Jersey, Guernsey, and Granville.

TRAIN INFORMATION

English is spoken by rail staff at the major stations. *Agents d'accueil* ('welcome officers') wear orange caps and armbands and are in the stations to help with travel queries and any problems you've encountered on your journey, i.e. if you've had your rucksack stolen. They tour round as opposed to sitting in the information offices. At the ticket barriers in all French stations you'll see a bright orange machine. Use this to validate your ticket only if you've bought it in France. Otherwise ignore it. But if you have a French-purchased ticket, including *Résa* reservation/supplement cards (see below), you must validate it, or face a fine.

RESERVATIONS Obligatory on all Eurocity and TGVs as well as a few of the Rapide trains. If you are taking a Eurocity you'll find the reservation charge is included in the supplement you'll have to pay. The supplement depends on distance – between 50F and 75F. Other optional reservations cost about 14F. Reservations can be made up to noon, for trains between 5 p.m. and midnight on that day, and up to 8 p.m. for trains from midnight to 5 p.m. the following day. For trains to or from Paris, give yourself 2–3 days if possible. If you are very well prepared you can reserve up to 4 months in advance. Eurocity are reservable up to 1 hour before departure. Generally, it's a good idea to reserve on international trains and on days before public holidays. On some services the reservation ticket is known as *Résa*. Note that on these services you must validate the reservation ticket along with the main ticket.

NIGHT TRAVEL A sleeper or couchette in France will cost you more than anywhere else in Europe. Granted the service is good, but at a price. SNCF offer both first- and second-class couchettes with 4 and 6 berths respectively. Couchettes cost about 80F and must be reserved in advance, not later than 8 p.m.

French Railways have introduced a super new concept in budget night travel, the Cabine 8. This is a second-class air-conditioned coach with compartments containing 8 semi-reclined bunks which are completely free of charge to use. If you are contemplating a long-haul overnight journey in France, check to see if Cabine 8 coaches have been added to the train you intend to use (check this in the Thomas Cook timetable, in the French section). In view of their success, it is advisable to reserve your bunk, for the standard seat reservation fee.

Unless you're loaded with cash, avoid the TEN (Trans Euro Nuit) sleepers. Second-class sleepers are either (T3), 3 beds, or (T2), 2 beds.

EATING ON TRAINS Surprisingly, few stations have tempting delicatessens selling fresh croissants, pâtés and cheeses, so you must come prepared if you want to picnic. There are restaurants and bars at stations which are good but pricey. If you're going to have a blowout, you'd do far better going for a meal which you can at least be sure will be good, rather than for a snack from the ridiculously priced mini-bar trolleys, from which a coffee, for example, will cost about 12F.

SCENIC TIPS Take a train anywhere in southern France and you won't be disappointed. Not surprisingly the Alps provide a spectacular backdrop on any run. If you just want to breeze through, consider the Paris–Turin route (10 hours) which goes via the Mont Cenis tunnel (14 km long). For those who aren't happy with anything but the best, change at Culoz or Aix-les-Bains, for Chamonix.

If you want to head down to the coast, we recommend the run from Grenoble to Marseille (5 hours), then Marseille–Genoa (be sure to sit on the right-hand side of the train on the Riviera stretch). All this journey along the Côte d'Azur is beautiful.

On the other side of the country, the lines between Clermont-Ferrand and Béziers, and Limoges and Toulouse provide fine upland scenery. The Perpignan–La Tour de Carol is another favourite, as is Valence–Briançon.

BIKES The scheme's called *Train et Vélo*, and bikes can be hired at many stations from upwards of 50F a day, plus around 1,000F deposit. Note, SNCF has complex rules for taking bikes on trains, generally avoid rush hours in towns and remember in regional areas there will only be room for a couple of bikes. Where trains allow bikes on with no cost, the timetable will have a blue cycle symbol on it.

ADVANCE TICKETS Tickets to and for within France can be purchased at British Rail Travel Centres and at French Railways Rail Shop, 179 Piccadilly, London W1V 0BA. Telephone the SNCF Rail Shop on 0990 300 003 for travel information and credit card bookings.

TOURIST INFORMATION

There are over 5,000 Tourist Information offices in France. They're called *Syndicats d'Initiative* or *Offices de Tourisme*. Those designated *Accueil de France* will help you out with your travel and accommodation problems, as well as booking a bed for you for a small fee. The French tourist literature is good and generally free. Always ask for a map. If you're touring a whole region in depth and require further information, look up the address and phone number of the Comité Régional de Tourisme, and contact them.

ISIC BONUSES Up to 40% reduction on long-distance coach journeys. Discounts on OTU car rental. 50% off all state museums galleries, and theatres. 50–70F off Crous University accommodation between 1 June and 30 Sept.

MONEY MATTERS 1 franc (F) = 100 centimes.

Banking hours are 9.30 a.m.–12 noon, 2 p.m.–4 p.m. weekdays. Closed Sat. (main towns) or Mon., and closed early on day before Bank Holiday. Shop around before exchanging currency, as banks vary with their commission charges. Not every bank now changes currency, so if you're arriving on a Sunday night you won't be able to get any anywhere except the main station in the larger cities, where commission charges average 10F and credit cards and some traveller's cheques are not accepted. French traveller's cheques are much more useful than those in sterling or dollars. Also, if relying on Eurocheques, note that not all banks take them.

POST OFFICES Open 9 a.m.–12 noon, 2 p.m.–5 p.m. weekdays and 8 a.m.–12 noon on Sat. The larger railway stations have post offices which keep these, or longer, hours. Stamps can also be purchased from any café or shop with a red *Tabac* sign.

CHANGE TO TELEPHONE SYSTEM The whole country has now been re-coded. In essence it means that 10-figure numbers have replaced the old 8-digit numbers. It means you simply add a prefix of 01 for Paris, 02 for NW, 03 for NE, 04 for SE and 05 for SW France. To dial abroad 19 has been replaced by 00, so to phone the UK, dial 00 44.

SHOPS Tend to shut around 12 noon–2 p.m. and even longer in the south. They generally stay open till 7.30 p.m. Some food shops, especially bakeries, are open Sun. mornings.

MUSEUMS Follow the same pattern as shops; you'll find many of the state-owned ones closed Tues., with municipal ones shutting Mon.

TIPPING France is a tipping nation. Everywhere you go, people are seen leaving various quantities of centimes and francs in dishes and sweaty palms. In restaurants watch out for the *service compris* or *sc* on your bill, this means your tip is included. If you have a coffee or beer on the pavement, always leave some change for the waiter, though this is not necessary if you stand at the bar or counter.

SLEEPING

HOSTELS Your best bet is to use the facilities offered in the various Foyers des Jeunes Travailleurs which are in all major centres. These student hostels are usually more central and less strictly run than youth hostels (they don't make a fuss about unmarried couples, etc.). The Accueil des Jeunes en France (AJF) has numerous hostels throughout France (5,000 beds in Paris alone).

Another organization, Union des Centres de Rencontres Internationales de France (UCRIF), operates several hostels throughout France, with 16 in Paris.

France is well supplied with official youth hostels (*auberges de jeunesse*) which charge 40–80F per person, with an optional 18F breakfast. They can also sometimes sting you for extra 'residence' tax and bedlinen hire, but all in all it shouldn't amount to too much. They do ask for IYHF cards, so membership is obligatory. You can join up in France either at the head office at 10 rue Notre Dame de Lorette, Paris, or at major hostels.

HOTELS Hotels run on a 1- to 4-star system with the government fixing prices; these are posted on the back of hotel room doors. So always check you've been quoted the right price. One-stars start at about 90F and are perfectly adequate so long as you don't expect the luxury of a bath. In France a shower or bath (and often breakfast, too) will almost always cost extra. Try to reduce your costs if you're travelling in a group by getting a third bed put in the room – this'll cost an extra 30% or so and is cheaper than another room.

CAMPING Camping should present no problems in France as nearly every major town has at least 1 site. They also operate on a star system. The International Camping Carnet is advisable at most sites – you can buy it at site offices on the spot.

EATING AND NIGHTLIFE

Eating and drinking are about the only things in France not centred on Paris. Each region has its own specialities based on the local produce. There's no such thing as a hurried snack – the midday lunch break is at least a 12-till-2 affair. The French take their food very seriously and like to think themselves connoisseurs. Cafés are for sitting and watching the world go by, not for cheap eating. If you're desperate for a coffee, check the price and size of cup first, make it last and drink in the atmosphere as long as possible. Also try the chain self-service restaurants, often cheap and cheerful, but do not expect the best in French dining. Vegetarians be warned, some chain restaurants (e.g. Quick) will often refuse to serve beer if you do not order a meat main course! It's far better, though, to get a baguette under your arm and head for the corner charcuterie and crémerie, where you can choose from a huge selection of cheeses (watch out: *chèvre* is goat). Fortunately, supermarkets are reasonable and still maintain a high standard. Look out for branches of Prisunic,

Monoprix, Uniprix, or Codec.

The wines are cheap and the parks free. Unless you're really broke, it's well worth eating out in the evenings with the fixed-price menus always a safe bet. Try where possible to sample the local dishes, as they give an added interest to touring.

Calais

Calais does not have much going for it, but you may find yourself stuck here waiting for a ferry or train. It is some walk into the town and inconveniently the bus stops running late at night and a taxi is expensive. There is a brand new youth hostel, the Centre Européen de Séjour, on av. Maréchal de Lattre de Tassigny (Tel. 21 34 70 20). It's set on the beach within walking distance of place d'Arme. Alternatively, try the cheap hotels in town, the Hôtel du Beffroi, 8 rue André Gersche (Tel. 21 34 47 51), doubles for 220F. Or Hôtel de Signe behind the Hôtel de Ville is another cheap alternative (Tel. 21 34 5 18).

The Tourist Office and accommodation service is at 12 bd Clemenceau (Tel. 21 96 62 40).

Rouen

It is a pity that many Inter-Railers *en route* to Paris pass through the fascinating and historic region of Normandy without stopping. Situated on the Seine, Rouen is the capital of Normandy and is perhaps best known for its links with Joan of Arc.

TOURIST INFORMATION
At 25 place de la Cathédrale (Tel. 35 71 41 77); during summer open Mon.–Sat.: 9 a.m.–7 p.m., Sun.: 9.30 a.m.–12.30 p.m., 2.30 p.m.–6 p.m.; winter, shut Sundays. They will hand out useful leaflets and help you find a cheap room.

SEEING
The OLD TOWN dates from the 12th century and boasts a fine collection of beautiful half-timbered houses. A circular walking tour enables you to appreciate the main sites. Unmissable is the RUE DU GROS-HORLOGE, as it connects the OLD MARKET PLACE to the CATHEDRAL (and is adjacent to Tourist Information). The Old Market Place was where

Joan of Arc was burnt at the stake in 1431 and now contains the STE JEANNE D'ARC national monument, a church and a small covered market, all designed by Arretche.

NOTRE DAME CATHEDRAL dates from the 12th century and is a fine example of Gothic architecture. Rouen has many fine churches; perhaps the most notable is ST MACLOU for its large five-panelled porch. The nearby ST MACLOU CLOISTER at 184–186 rue Martainville should also not be missed. This tranquil cloister is one of the last examples of a medieval plague cemetery and was used as a charnel-house until the 18th century.

SLEEPING

Cheap rooms are plentiful and many are in the heart of the old city. Tourist Information will assist.

HOSTEL Centre de Séjour at 118 boulevard de l'Europe (Tel. 35 72 06 45), which costs 70F including breakfast. Take bus 12, direction Diderot, from the railway station. Alternatively cross over the river, turn left and walk along the river bank.

EATING AND NIGHTLIFE

All the Normandy culinary specialities can be found. The seafood, pâté, Rouen duck, calvados and cider are all recommended. Most restaurants are good value and offer fixed menus. The many small bars offer cheaper snacks or just a single course and the universal burgers are also available. A cheap meal can be had at the Maison des Jeunes, 114 av. de Bretagne, close to the Centre de Séjour, and you'll find the greatest concentration of eating establishments in Place de Vieux-Marché and the area immediately north of there.

Bayeux

An impressive town, Bayeux deserves at least a few hours' sightseeing. It is most notable for its connections with William the Conqueror and the world-famous Bayeux Tapestry, graphically telling the story of the Norman Conquest of Britain.

Tourist Information is in the centre of town on the corner of rue St Martin and rue des Cuisiniers (Tel. 31 92 16 26), and will provide the usual assistance and information. Open 9 a.m.–6.30 p.m., shutting for lunch, and Sundays off season.

SEEING

QUEEN MATILDA'S TAPESTRY, also known as the BAYEUX TAPESTRY, is now magnificently displayed in the Cultural Centre on rue de Nesmond. Open May–mid-Sept. 9 a.m.–7 p.m., otherwise closed over lunchtime and slightly shorter hours; last admission 1 hour before closure. The BARON-GÉRARD MUSEUM has fine displays of old paintings, lace, porcelain and tapestries. A combined ticket for 4 museums can be obtained. The CATHEDRAL was originally completed in 1077 and is now an impressive mixture of Norman and Gothic architecture. Also worth a look is the MUSEUM OF THE BATTLE OF NORMANDY 1944 in boulevard Fabian Ware. Open 9 a.m.–7 p.m. in the summer, the museum recounts the Allied invasion of France June–Aug. 1944 and is near a British military cemetery.

SLEEPING

HOSTELS Should you feel inclined to stay, there is no IYHF affiliated hostel, but you could try the Centre d'Accueil Municipal, 21 rue des Marettes (Tel. 31 92 08 19), situated about 2.5 km from the station, ask at Tourist Information.

The Family Home Hostel on rue Général de Dais 39 (Tel. 31 92 15 20) is good value. Follow the signs from the station. Reservations recommended.

CAMPING There is also a campsite at blvd d'Eindhoven (Tel. 31 92 08 43), open March–Oct.

Mont St-Michel

Although not on a direct railway line, the extra difficulties are well worth it to see the 'marvel of the Western world'. Mont St-Michel is a solitary village and abbey dramatically perched on a small island linked to the mainland by a causeway which occasionally floods completely at high tide. A tide table is available from the local Tourist Office, located at the entrance to the Mont. Open Mon.–Sat.: 9 a.m.–7 p.m.

GETTING THERE

Mont St-Michel is actually on the boundary between Normandy and Brittany. Take the train from Caen to Rennes and get off at Pontorson. Mont St-Michel is about 16 km away and reached by STN bus, from opposite the station – about 7 buses a day during summer. A further disadvantage is the hordes of tourists, but if you make the trip, you will be rewarded by an unforgettable sight and experience.

SEEING

The splendid ABBEY dominates the island and is open 9.30 a.m.–11.45 a.m. and 1.45 p.m.–4.15 p.m. (to 6 p.m. May–Sept., all day during high season), closed on holidays. The guided tour lasts around 45 minutes, at about 1-hour intervals. The MERVEILLE or 'marvel' is the group of superb early 13th-century buildings and is aptly named. The VILLAGE is a steep labyrinth surrounding the abbey and is itself encased in RAMPARTS which have good views of the bay.

SLEEPING

The nearest hostel is at the Centre Duguesclin, rue Patten, Pontorson (Tel. 33 60 18 65), open June–Sept., 0.8 km from Pontorson station. Camping sites are better situated but do not be tempted to sleep rough on the causeway or beach as the tides are very unpredictable and dangerous. The nearest is Camping du Mont St-Michel (Tel. 33 60 09 33), with 350 places.

Brittany

You'll curse the rail network if you want to visit this region in depth. Local trains all connect up to the main Paris–Brest line rather than other nearby towns. On the new TGV line from Paris it now only takes just over 2 hours to Nantes and around 2 hours to Rennes. For accommodation and general information on the area, visit the Tourist Office on the Pont de Nemours Mon.–2 p.m.-6 p.m., Tues.–Sat.: 9 a.m.–6 p.m. (Tel. 99 79 01 98). There is a campsite (Tel. 99 36 91 22), open April–Oct., and a youth hostel at 10–12 Canal St-Martin (Tel. 99 33 22 33).

From RENNES it's possible to make a day trip to the impressive walled port of ST MALO, formerly a pirates' stronghold, and preserved almost intact. Pushing south, NANTES has a majestic 15th-century ducal palace, as well as a very good museum devoted to Breton folk-lore. There are two youth hostels in Nantes one at 2 place de la Manu (Tel. 40 20 57 25), open July and August only; and the other at 1 rue Porte-Neuve (Tel. 40 20 00 80). There is also a campsite (Tel. 40 74 47 94), open all year.

Also consider a trip to CONCARNEAU. Take the train to Rosporden and then a railway bus (free on Eurail) to Concarneau. Check your timetable first, because the bus doesn't connect with every train.

The Loire Valley

This pastoral region contains many of France's most elegant and impressive buildings. To do justice to the area would take at least a week. Fortunately for the eurorailer, most of the châteaux and palaces lie between Angers and Blois, a distance of about 129 km. Where to base yourself depends on your style. Perhaps the most impressive châteaux are CHAMBORD and CHENONCEAU. There are camp-sites everywhere, and youth hostels at Saumur, Tours and Blois.

BLOIS A town typical of the Loire so see the BISHOPS' PALACE, the CHÂTEAU, the OLD QUARTER – all set in a picturesque location among fine churches and gardens. The campsite at Blois is good. About 5 km out of town, by bus or taxi from the station (about 0.40F and 35F respectively) or take the métro to Port Maillot and then the campsite bus. The last bus from Blois leaves at 6.15 p.m.

TOURS For those who prefer a cheap hotel, it's best to base yourself at Tours, where rooms are plentiful around the station. Try Mon Hôtel at 40 rue de la Préfecture (Tel. 02 47 05 67 53), The Olympic opposite the station at 74 rue Bernard-Palissy (Tel. 47 05 10 17), or Hôtel Comté behind the station, at 51 rue Auguste Comté (Tel. 47 05 53 16). If you're out of luck, the Tourist Office is just in front of the station at place Maréchal Leclerc (Tel. 47 70 37 37) (open Mon.–Sat.: 9 a.m.–12.30 p.m., 2 p.m.–9 p.m., Sun.: 10 a.m.–12.30 p.m., 4 p.m.–9 p.m.). For a small fee they will fix you up with a room and give free advice on bus tours, etc., to the châteaux. If you can't afford the bus, don't worry as they rent out bikes at the station for around 70F a day plus a hefty deposit. Most of the châteaux are easily accessible, all shut-ting around 6 p.m. The town itself, like Blois, has a charming OLD QUARTER and a former BISHOPS' PALACE which now hosts the MUSÉE DES BEAUX ARTS.

Further down the line, SAUMUR and ANGERS both have very impres-sive castles perched on high, overlooking the Loire and Maine respectively. If you prefer to stay at this end of château country, the *Syndicat d'Initiative*, opposite the station at Angers, will find you a room for a small charge.

Wherever you end up, it's a good idea to go along to any train information desk in the area and pick up one of the local timetables giving all the smaller stops.

Paris

Everyone has his or her own impressions and expectations of Paris –
so much has been said and written about it, and it all seems a cliché,
yet Paris is everything you've probably ever heard, and more. It's a
fabulous city and you can't help but enjoy a few days there.

First let's get your geography sorted out. Paris has 20 *arrondisse-
ments* (districts) with the Louvre as no. 1. The city is divided into the
Left Bank (*Rive Gauche*) and Right Bank (*Rive Droite*), with the River
Seine dividing them. Generally speaking, the Left Bank is the trendy,
studenty and less expensive area, and the Right Bank is more classy.
Both have style.

STATION FACILITIES

There are 5 international stations in the city: Austerlitz serves south-
ern France, Spain and Portugal; Est serves Germany, Switzerland and
Austria; Lyon serves the south-east of France, Italy and Switzerland.
Nord serves Belgium, Holland, Scandinavia, Germany, the north of
France, and Britain's ferry entry ports of Calais and Boulogne. St
Lazare serves Britain's entry ports of Dieppe and Le Havre.

THE STATIONS All stations have a degree of left-luggage lockers,
bars, cafés, shops, toilets, washing facilities and waiting rooms which
are normally open from early morning well into the evening. Use
your judgement, though – if you arrive on a train after midnight,
you will get a left-luggage locker and a vending machine, but don't
expect a bureau de change or Tourist Office to be open.

Austerlitz station has train information daily 7 a.m.–10 p.m. (Tel.
45 82 50 50) and reservations 8 a.m.–7 p.m. (Tel. 45 65 60 60). Use
both these numbers for all stations, it's a central telephone line. The
station closes 0.30 a.m.–5.30 a.m.

Est's train information and reservations are open the same hours as
Austerlitz (same telephone numbers) though the station is shut for
the slightly shorter time of 1.15 a.m.–5.45 a.m. There are post office
facilities at both these stations (8 a.m.–7 p.m., half day Sat.). SNCF
run buses which connect most of the stations, or métro line 5
connects Paris Est and Paris Nord and Austerlitz. Paris Lyon is reached
by buses 61 and 65 from Austerlitz and bus 65 from Est.

Paris Lyon and Paris Nord, the 2 big stations in the north of the
city, close 1 a.m.–4 a.m. and 2 a.m.–5.45 a.m. respectively and there
are post office facilities at both stations, Mon.–Fri.: 8 a.m.–7 p.m.,

Sat.: 8 a.m.–12 noon (rue Diderot for Paris Lyon). SNCF buses will get you from one station to another, or from Paris Lyon you can get to all the other stations by métro line 1 to Bastille then change to line 5. From Paris Nord, line 5 takes you to Austerlitz, Est and Lyon (change on to line 1 at Bastille). An additional route from Nord to Lyon is to take RER line B to Châtelet Les Halles, then RER line A to Lyon (much faster). With 6 stations in Paris it's important to get the right one.

Plan well ahead, and wherever possible use your timetables, as train information queues can be up to 2 hours long in the summer. At Gare du Nord reservations for the TGV to Lyons are now made at an automated machine.

The other 2 stations are in the south of the city, Gare St Lazare and Gare Montparnasse. Again, use the central train information number and reservations number.

TOURIST INFORMATION
The main office of the Paris Convention and Visitors' Bureau is at 127 av. des Champs Élysées (Tel. 49 52 53 54) (métro to Charles de Gaulle-Étoile). Open daily (during the summer): 9 a.m.–8 p.m. The English-speaking staff will give you information on Paris and the Île de France. They also run a wide-ranging accommodation-finding service on a commission basis. For recorded Tourist Information in English, phone 44 29 12 12. There are also tourist bureaux at all the main railway terminals and the Eiffel Tower.

ACCUEIL DES JEUNES EN FRANCE (AJF) This non-profit-making office for the young is at 119 rue St Martin (Tel. 42 77 87 80), across from the Pompidou Centre (Beaubourg) (métro Les Halles or Rambuteau). Open Mon.–Sat.: 9 a.m.–6 p.m. They'll find you a bed or a place in a Foyer for 1,000F and upwards. They also have offices at Gare du Nord, 139 boulevard St-Michel (Tel. 43 54 95 86), open June and July only (HER Port Royal) and 16 rue du Pont Louis-Philippe (Tel. 42 78 04 82) near métro Hôtel de Ville. The policy these days seems to be to pay the full accommodation price over to AJF when booking, so remember to change money before joining the queue. To get the best rooms be in the queue by 8 a.m.

UNION DES CENTRES DE RENCONTRES INTERNATIONALES DE FRANCE (UCRIF) This centre for young tourists is at 104 rue de Vaugirad, near their hostel (Tel. 45 48 58 80). It can arrange reservations and gives advice on travel.

USIT VOYAGES 6 rue Vaugirard (Tel. 43 29 85 00), Mon.–Fri.: 9.30 a.m.–6 p.m., Sat.: 1 p.m.–4.30 pm. They will help you out with all travel requirements, and fix you up with an ISIC (métro: Odéon or Luxembourg).

FÉDÉRATION UNIE DES AUBERGES DE JEUNESSE (FUAJ) The central booking facility for IYHF hostels in Paris, France and also for some European destinations. Operates from the hostel at 8 blvd Jules Ferry (Tel. 43 57 55 60, métro: République). They can also arrange sight-seeing coaches and various other services.

ADDRESSES

POSTE OFFICE AND POSTE RESTANTE 52 rue du Louvre (Tel. 40 28 20 00), open 24 hours a day (métro: Louvre)

AMEX 11 ru de Scribe, Mon.–Fri.: 9 a.m.–5.30 p.m., Sat.: 9.30 a.m.–5 p.m. (Tel. 47 77 77 07) (métro: Opéra)

UK EMBASSY 35 rue du Faubourg St Honoré (Tel. 42 66 91 42). The British Consulate is at 16 rue d'Anjou (Tel. 42 66 38 10) (métro: Concorde or Madeleine), Mon.–Fri.: 9.30 a.m.–12.30 and 2.30 p.m.–5 p.m.

IRISH EMBASSY 12 av. Foch, 16e (Tel. 45 00 20 87) (métro: Charles de Gaulle-Étoile)

US EMBASSY 2 av. Gabriel (Tel. 42 96 12 02), Mon.–Fri.: 9 a.m.–4 p.m. (métro: Concorde), visa section open 8.45 a.m.–11 a.m.

CANADIAN EMBASSY 35 av. Montaigne (Tel. 44 43 29 86) (métro: Franklin-Roosevelt)

AUSTRALIAN EMBASSY 4 rue Jean Rey (Tel. 40 59 33 00) (métro: Bir-Hakeim)

NEW ZEALAND EMBASSY 7 rue Léonard de Vinci (Tel 45 00 24 11) (métro: Victor Hugo)

24-HOUR CHEMIST Pharmacie Dhéry, 84 av. des Champs Élysées (Tel. 45 62 02 41) (métro: Georges V)

EMERGENCY SERVICES Ambulance dial 15; Police 17; Fire 18

SOS HELPLINE English speakers to help you with personal problems, etc. 3 p.m.–11 p.m. (Tel. 47 23 80 80)

GETTING ABOUT

The métro in Paris is one of the world's best underground systems and you're bound to use it at some point to get you quickly round this incredibly large and sprawling city. The system is open from 5 a.m. to 12.45 a.m. The lines are designated by the terminal station. It's a cheap as well as efficient way of getting about. Buy tickets in *carnets* of 10 for 46F and hold on to them till the end of your journey. The same tickets can also be used on the buses – validate them in the machine on the bus, using 2 if crossing a zone – and central Paris RER trains.

Tourist passes, known as Paris Visite, valid on both métro and buses, are available for 3 or 5 days, over 3 or 4 zones. Available from Tourist Offices, in main métro and RER stations, SNCF stations and at Paris airports, the 1-day pass costs 50F, the 3-day 110F, the 5-day 170F, for 3 zones (not including airports).

Recently there has been an increasing number of reports of crime on the métro, including drug users and dealers causing problems for the authorities. Be especially careful of trouble late at night. Also beware of buying a ticket at anywhere other than an official booth – you are only asking to be ripped off.

SEEING

THE CHAMPS ELYSÉES The ÉTOILE is the great circle at the western end of the Champs Elysées with 12 avenues radiating out from it, literally a 'star'. In its centre is the massive ARC DE TRIOMPHE, Napoleon's thank you to his army; note the sculpture of the Marseillaise by Rude. At the other end of the long and elegant Champs Elysées is the PLACE DE LA CONCORDE, regarded as the most beautiful square in the world. This is where Louis XVI, Marie-Antoinette and some 1,300 others met their death in the French Revolution.

THE LEFT BANK ST GERMAIN-DES-PRÈS, the oldest church in Paris, is surrounded by open-air restaurants and cafés and quiet little streets like PLACE FURSTEMBERG which make a pleasant stroll.

BOULEVARD ST-MICHEL, the centre of Bohemian student life of the 1960s, still makes an interesting excursion! Sitting in one of the cafés along the Boul' Mich' in the Latin Quarter (so called because the Sorbonne students were lectured to in Latin in the Middle Ages), you're bound to make new friends.

The TOUR MAINE-MONTPARNASSE (207m) gives you a great view over the city. (The lift up is advertised as the fastest in Europe.)

Also on the Rive Gauche is the beautiful church of LES INVALIDES with its golden dome and the mortal remains of Napoleon. A good view of NOTRE DAME CATHEDRAL can be seen from SQUARE RENÉE VIVIANI.

THE RIGHT BANK Opposite the LOUVRE is Richelieu's PALAIS ROYAL where the Comédie Française is based, and not far from there is the oldest square in Paris, PLACE DES VOSGES, the beautiful Renaissance square built by Henri IV early in the 17th century; VICTOR HUGO'S HOUSE at no. 6 is now a museum.

The GEORGES POMPIDOU CENTRE (known as the 'Beaubourg') is a good place to meet trendy young Parisians and see interesting exhibitions. Closed Tues., it's open 12 noon–12 midnight; holidays: 10 a.m.–10 p.m.

The SACRÉ-COEUR is the white dome that dominates all of Paris, built on the hill at MONTMARTRE, the artists' quarter that flourished in the late 19th century when many of the Impressionist painters lived and worked there. The artists' quarter is more than the touristy PLACE DU TERTRE. Stroll along rue Norvins into rue des Saules and check out the LAPIN AGILE, a meeting point for writers and artists and very atmospheric. A climb to the dome of the Sacré-Coeur gives you an 80 km view over Paris, and is cheaper than climbing the Eiffel Tower. This is a great place to be in the evening, but watch out for pickpockets in this area. Even someone asking the time might be after your watch.

ÎLE DE LA CITÉ AND ÎLE ST-LOUIS: The tiny island when Paris began in pre-Roman times is the Île de la Cité. The oldest bridge in Paris, the PONT NEUF, leads you to the statue of Henri IV and on to the PALAIS DE JUSTICE (law courts). The SAINTE-CHAPELLE is a Gothic church built to house holy relics, dating from 1248. The relics have now been moved to Notre-Dame, but the stained-glass windows here can be viewed.

NOTRE DAME is only a short walk from here; this 13th-century cathedral is the first church of Paris, where Napoleon was crowned and all national celebrations are staged.

The other main sights are the OPÉRA GARNIER, 1875 (the new opera built in 1989 is located at place de la Bastille) and, of course, the EIFFEL TOWER, which looks its best floodlit at night. A 5-year renovation scheme costing millions of francs has made great improvements, but it is still expensive to ride to the top. There are 3 stages of lifts, getting progressively more expensive the higher you go. It is possible to walk up the first 2 stages to save on the cost (12F), but if you use the lifts all the way there is a 56F charge. The queues can be long, even with all lifts in action, also check you're in the right queue. The view from Sacré-Coeur is just as impressive. If you are visiting it on 14 July (National Day), make sure you go at night and catch the spectacular hour-long fireworks display.

If you want to tour the famous PARIS SEWERS, call in at place de la Résistance 7e.

TOURS There are various city tours: Parisvision buses with prerecorded commentary, and Cityrama tours, or the famous *bateaux-mouches* which sail down the Seine (go for the evening one when the illuminations are on). Shop about, as they vary from reasonably priced to extortionate. Still, if you've only a day or two, the 3-hour Parisvision tour gives you a pretty comprehensive idea of the city.

By far the best value way to see the city is on a *bateaux-mouche* trip. Leaving from Pont de l'Alma on the Right Bank, 30F will buy you a 1½-hr cruise with recorded commentary. (Don't take one of the over-priced lunch/dinner cruises – they're 300F and decidedly not worth it!)

MUSEUMS All state-owned museums in Paris are shut on Tues. and those owned by the city close on Mon. An ISIC will get you into most places for half price. There are over 100 interesting museums in the city; pick up a leaflet on them from Tourist Information.

The MUSEUM AND MONUMENT CARD, available from métro stations, Tourist Office and major museums, permits direct entry to 63 museums and monuments in the Paris region. Valid for 1 day (cost 70F), 3 consecutive days (cost 140F) or 5 consecutive days (cost 200F); unlimited visits are permitted and access is immediate, avoiding the often lengthy queues. The card can be bought in advance, but your name and the date must be written on it on your first visit in order to validate it.

THE LOUVRE, métro: Pyramide, Cour Napoléon. Treasures include the Venus de Milo and the *Mona Lisa*. Open 9 a.m.–6 p.m., except Mon. and Wed., 9 a.m.–10 p.m. On Mon. only certain rooms are open, and many departments close at 5 p.m. or 5.30 p.m. every day. Closed Tues. Entry is 45F, or 26F after 3 p.m. Under-26s are entitled to a reduction and it is half price to everyone on Sun. Remember, you must leave your hand luggage at the entrance. Queues are very long on Sat. and Sun. As it now houses the underground entrance, it is impossible to miss the controversial 21m-high GLASS PYRAMID in the courtyard of the Louvre. Designed by Pei, it not only houses the reception area, including a complex of restaurants and shops, but has greatly expanded gallery and exhibition space.

The Jeu de Paume collection is now included in the wonderful new MUSÉE D'ORSAY, which has also absorbed the contents of a few other museums. It is situated on the Left Bank, near the Tuileries. Closed Mon. Admission 36F, open 10 a.m.–6 p.m., from 9 a.m. on Sun. Reduced entry for 18–24-year-olds and ISIC holders. You can spend all day in the Louvre or Musée d'Orsay.

POMPIDOU CENTRE: A modern multi-cultural art centre conceived by Georges Pompidou and opened in 1977, this eccentric building is home to just about every modern artform you can think of. It also includes an excellent library with hundreds of daily newspapers, including most English and American ones. Although entrance is free, special exhibitions and the cinema usually incur a charge of anything up to 35F. A special 1-day pass is available at 75F. There's usually plenty of free entertainment in the form of fire-eaters and street artists outside.

For button-pushers, the CITÉ DES SCIENCES ET DE L'INDUSTRIE, at 30 av. Corentin-Cariou, will keep you occupied all day. A combination of science exhibitions, computer games, practical demonstrations and videos are all included in the 45F admission, or 35F with an ISIC card. The Planetarium is included, but entry to the giant movie theatre is extra. Take buses 150, 152 or 250a.

MUSÉE NATIONAL DU MOYEN-ÂGE, THÉMES DE CLUNY: 6 place Paul-Painléve (corner of blvd St Michel and blvd St Germain). Open 9.15 a.m.–5.45 p.m., closed Tues. Medieval art housed in a 15th-century mansion next to the Roman baths of Paris.

MUSÉE DE L'HOMME: Palais de Chaillot, place du Trocadéro. Open 9.45 a.m.–5.15 p.m. Very good anthropological museum – documentary films are shown daily.

PARKS There is no shortage of attractive parks and gardens in Paris, and they make good picnic venues.

The BOIS DE BOULOGNE is the wood at the western edge of the city with 7 lakes, a waterfall, various sports facilities and a campsite.

The BOIS DE VINCENNES is the wood on the south-eastern edge. There's a zoo, a racetrack and a couple of museums out here too.

The 2 most central picnic parks are the JARDIN DES TUILERIES and the JARDIN DES CHAMPS ELYSÉES; the LUXEMBOURG, off blvd St Michel, is a very picturesque, formally laid-out garden in French style.

SLEEPING

Campsites are not central, and with so much to see in Paris the commuting may be a waste of valuable time. Private accommodation is hardly heard of in Paris, so your choice is between a cheap hotel, a student hostel or a Foyer. Your choice will be dictated not just by your pocket but also by how many you are. Paris really is a city for lovers – it's often virtually the same price for a single or a double bed so couples are on to a good deal, but singles are better off in a Foyer.

The average night in a hotel double room is anything upwards from 1,200F, for 1 star, and a single Foyer stay will be about 100F. Always ask hoteliers if there's nothing cheaper and get as many as possible into a room to bring the cost down. If you have any problems, try the UCRIF/AJF information office at Gare du Nord, but don't try sleeping there or you'll be ejected about 1 a.m. or mugged. Also try the UCRIF/AJF and FUAJ offices listed under Tourist Information.

IYHF HOSTELS The main youth hostel is at 8 blvd Jules Ferry, near place de la République (Tel. 43 57 55 60). Take the métro to République. Cost is 110F and they'll help you find an alternative if they're full.

A 411-bed hostel called Auberge de Jeunesse d'Artagnan is at 80 rue Vitruve (Tel. 43 61 08 75). The nearest métro is Porte de Bagnolet. Open 24 hours.

There is also a temporary hostel, open July–15 Sept.; book through the Jules Ferry hostel.

HOTELS The number after the street name (e.g. 7e) refers to the *arrondissement* (district) of the city. Hotels in the 10e *arrondissement* are always within easy walking distance of Gare du Nord and Gare de l'Est. The best districts to concentrate your attention on for cheap hotels and basic B&B-type accommodation are around the Marais (4e), Le Quartier Latin (5e), tThe Louvre and Les Halles (1e and 2e) and Gare de Lyon (10e).

Try: Sibour Hôtel, 4 rue Sibour, 10e (Tel. 46 07 20 74); Adix Hôtel, 30 rue Lucien-Sampaix, 10e (Tel. 42 08 19 74); Hôtel du Commerce, rue de la Montagne-St-Geneviève, 5e (Tel. 143 54 89 69); Le Centrale, 6 rue Descartes, 5e (Tel. 46 33 57 93); also Jeanne d'Arc, 3 rue de Jarente, 4e (Tel. 48 87 62 11) and Hôtel des Alliés, 20 rue Berthollet, 5e (Tel. 43 31 47 52).

Also worth a try are Hôtel St Michel, 17 rue Git-le-Coeur, 6e (Tel. 43 26 04 89); Hôtel Henri IV at 25 place Dauphine (1e) (Tel. 43 54 44 53). The Hôtel de France, 11 rue Marie-Stuart, 2e (Tel. 42 36 35 33, is also worth checking out, as is Sainte Marie, rue de la Ville Neuve 6, 2e (Tel. 42 33 21 61). Near the Eiffel Tower, you could try the Hôtel Eiffel Rive Gauche, 6 rue du Gros Caillou 7e (Tel. 45 51 24 56).

FOYERS AND STUDENT HOSTELS CIS Léo Lagrange, 107 rue Martre Clichy (Tel. 41 27 26 90), métro: Mairie de Clichy. Maison des Clubs UNESCO, 43 rue de la Glacière (Tel. 43 36 00 63, métro: Glacière).

Hôtels des Jeunes (AJF), at 4 locations in the city: 11 rue du Fauconnier, 6 rue de Fourcy 4e (both Tel. 42 74 23 45, métro: St-Paul), 12 rue des Barres 4e (Tel. 42 72 72 09, métro: Pont Marie), and 151 av. Lédri Rollin 1e (Tel. 43 79 53 86, métro: Voltaire).

Centres Internationaux de Paris (BVJ), also with 4 locations, 20 rue Jean-Jacques Rousseau 1e (Tel. 42 36 88 18, métro: Châtelet or Louvre), 44 rue des Bernardins 5e (Tel. 43 29 34 80, métro:

Maubert), 5 rue du Pélican 1e (Tel. 40 26 92 45, métro: Louvre or Châtelet). BVJ International at 11 rue Thérèse 1e (Tel. 42 60 77 23, métro: Pyramides or Opéra) is excellent. Open all day but with a 2 a.m. curfew.

Other independent hostels to try: Foyer International d'Accueil de Paris, 30 rue Cabanis (Tel. 45 89 89 15, métro: Glacière), the newly refurbished Auberge International des Jeunes, 10 rue Trousseau 4e (Tel. 47 00 62 00), 91F breakfast included; a Maison International des Jeunes, charging 110F for basic B&B, is at 4 rue Titon, métro: Faidherbe-Chaligny or Nation 11e (Tel. 43 71 99 21); catering for 18–30-year-olds only, it is open 8 a.m.–2 a.m.

The two CISP (Centre International de Séjour de Paris) hostels may also be worth a try, but do not get good reports. They are at 6 av. M. Ravel (Tel. 43 43 19 01, métro: Porte de Vincennes) and at 17 blvd Hellerman (Tel. 45 80 70 76, métro: Porte d'Italie).

Two Foyers normally for women only: 234 rue de Tolbiac (Tel. 45 89 06 42), short stays only allowed during July and Aug., otherwise 1 month minimum (métro: Tolbiac); 93 blvd St Michel (Tel. 43 54 49 63), normally women only, but allows men July–Sept. (métro: Luxembourg).

CAMPING Camping du Bois de Boulogne, allée du Bord de l'Eau (Tel. 45 24 30 00). Take the métro to Porte Maillot, then bus 244, then a short walk. Shower facilities are limited and it costs around 65F per night; get there early in summer.

Also, outside Paris, try Parc de la Colline, route de Lagny (Tel. 60 05 42 32), RER Torcy then bus 421. Choisy-le-Roi (Tel. 48 90 92 30), some way out or Parc Étang, Base de Loisirs (Tel. 30 58 56 20).

STUCK IN PARIS WITH NO MONEY FOR A BED? There are good overnight trains to Salzburg (from Est), Venice (from Lyon) and Copenhagen (from Nord).

EATING AND NIGHTLIFE

Both are a great pleasure in Paris and can be afforded, in one category or another, by everyone. The French seem to have invented the picnic and it's dead easy to knock up a delicious picnic of baguette, pâté, cheese, fruit and of course, wine. There are several open-air markets and *boulangeries* (bakers) in every district while the *épiceries* (grocers) stay open till 7.30 p.m.

If you want a change from French food, there are plenty of alternatives provided by the numerous immigrants from France's ex-colonies. The centre of the North African (Algerian, Tunisian,

Moroccan, etc.) restaurant area is between rue St Jacques and blvd St Michel; there are also many Greek and Italian restaurants here.

There are fast-food chains and self-service cafés too in Paris, usually though it's often just as cheap to look for a French restaurant which offers a *menu du jour*, and eat real French cuisine – for once at a price you can afford. The areas round rue de la Huchette and rue Mouffetard in the Latin Quarter will prove fruitful for reasonably priced restaurants. Around the La Huchette area watch out for the plate throwing, it gets excessive at times. For good cheap French restaurants try the street Grégoire de Tours.

Often the best value set menus are in Chinese restaurants. Try the Palais de Chine for especially good value. It's at 31 rue St Jacques, off the blvd St-Germain.

For those wanting to eat at student restaurants on their ISIC, call at CROUS, 39 av. Georges Bernano (métro: Port Royal), open Mon.–Fri.: 9 a.m.–5 p.m. for a list of all the places you can eat for under 20F in this scheme. CROUS is shut during June and July.

A few suggestions: Crêperie St Germain, 27 rue St André des Arts; Chartier, 7 rue du Faubourg-Montmartre – about 60F for 3 courses and a drink – very traditional restaurant; Restaurant des Beaux Arts, 11 rue Bonaparte – good cheap set menus – expect a really good set meal with wine from 65F; Country Life vegetarian restaurant, 6 rue Daumou, Mon.–Fri.: 11.30 a.m.–2.30 p.m.; Crêperie de la Houff, 9 rue Mouffetard; Au Grain Folic, 24 rue de la Vieuville, Montmartre, 7 p.m.–10 p.m., small but good vegetarian.

For current events in Paris, buy *Pariscope*, or contact Tourist Information. If you were thinking of the stereotyped trip to the Moulin Rouge or Lido, you might as well forget the rest of your European itinerary, as a night out in one of these places will cost you about 500F minimum. It's actually more of a spectacle walking round the Blanche and Pigalle areas, just down from Montmartre, or Montparnasse, but watch out for drug-pushers and pickpockets around here. For the serious red-light seekers, the place is rue St Denis.

Slightly more sedate a time can be had watching the fountains at the Trocadéro and admiring the view of the Eiffel Tower, or wandering down by the Seine; often there are buskers in the area round place du Vert Galant. On a fine evening, wandering around the place de Tertre, Montmartre, is also a great experience.

There's an active theatre and cinema scene in Paris – for details of what's on, see *Pariscope*. The area along the Seine on the Left Bank is best for affordable jazz and rock clubs. Le Caveau de la Huchette, 5 rue de la Huchette, is known to all Parisian students as their informal club, but they ask 60F (70F Friday and Saturday) on nights when there's jazz or dancing. For clubs try Le Palace on rue du Faubourg-Montmartre. Closed Mon. and Tues. Entrance 120F or free if you eat in the restaurant (130F minimum). Les Bains on rue du Bourg-l'Abbé, is the ultimate rowdy club in an old Turkish bathhouse. Live music is good at Gilbus, 18 rue du Faubourg (métro: République). Another good jazz club worth trying is New Morning, 10 rue des Petites Écuries (10e).

The most important thing to do is look around and read the local listings. This works well in larger cities like Paris as there will always be a few English speaking publications. The cafés at Montparnasse remain a typically Parisian vantage point from which to watch life go by, but watch out for the prices. In August, when many French restaurants are closed, these are often the only places open.

EXCURSIONS VERSAILLES, the elaborate palace of Louis XIV, is the main attraction near to Paris. Entrance to the palace costs 45F (35F if you're under 25), with an optional, but worthwhile, 25F guided tour of the opera and chapel. Get there early, or you'll be queueing all day instead of viewing. The gardens cost 17F, but go there after seeing inside, as the fountains usually aren't switched on until after 3.30 p.m. Take RER C5 from St Lazare or Invalides out to Versailles RG. The palace is open Tues.–Sun.: 9.45 a.m.–5 p.m. (free to under-18s, half price on ISIC, half price Sun.).

Also within striking distance is the palace of FONTAINEBLEAU with its beautiful park-forest. Take the train from Gare de Lyon. Open 10 a.m.–12.30 p.m., 2 p.m.–6 p.m., except Tues. Fill in your Inter-Rail and take it to the ticket office: you'll be given a free ticket for Fontainebleau or Versailles on the suburban railway.

CHANTILLY is an attractive small château, reached by train from Gare du Nord, but it's open only on Sun. and holidays.

CHARTRES, home of the world's most famous Gothic cathedral, is an hour away from Gare Montparnasse.

If you really want to make a day of it, take the hour-long train ride to EPERNAY where Moët et Chandon, on av. de Champagne, play hosts for another enjoyable tour with free samples.

Of course, the most publicized excursion from the French capital now is to see Mickey and his pals at DISNEYLAND. Fans of theme parks will love the place, though it is appreciably more expensive than its Florida counterpart. Officially, you're not allowed to take in your own food (as Disney makes as much profit on its food outlets as on entrances). Several readers have, however, written in with tales of successfully smuggled-in sandwiches. Be discreet and you may save money. You can get there on the RER. Take Route A from Charles de

Gaulle-Étoile to Marne la Vallée/Chessy. Journey time, around 45 mins.

Cheaper and more popular with the French themselves is PARC ASTERIX, featuring the indomitable Gaulish village from the series of cartoon books. A day pass costs 160F. A special bus service runs from the Roissy Charles de Gaulle airport RER and bus station 1.

Alsace and Lorraine

After many years of occupation, the German influence is strongly felt in this region, especially in the cuisine: *choucroute* (sauerkraut with ham and sausage) and *backaoffe* (casserole with lamb, pork, beef and potatoes) are our favourites; swallowed down with some *pression* (local draught lager), they make a meal you won't forget.

Strasbourg

Apart from being the seat of the European parliament and the capital of Alsace, it is one of France's most attractive cities. The Tourist Office is opposite the station when you arrive. They will supply you with a map (small charge) and information on the city, as well as provide a room-finding service. The main Tourist Office is at 17 place de la Cathédrale (Tel. 88 52 28 22). Both youth hostels are quite far away, so it's best to try somewhere more central like Hôtel de l'Ill, 8 rue des Bateliers (Tel. 88 36 20 01), or the Hôtel Suisse, 2–4 rue de la Râpe (Tel. 88 32 34 28). There are several hotels near the station, and the Tourist Office by the station puts up a board with suggestions when closed.

STATION FACILITIES
Train information is available daily 7.30 a.m.–9 p.m. (Tel. 88 22 50 50) and there's also a Tourist Information office outside the station arrival hall. The reservations desk is open Mon.–Sat.: 8 a.m.–8 p.m. and Sun.: 8 a.m.–7 p.m. There is also a foreign exchange, left-luggage lockers, left-luggage store, showers, cafeteria, restaurant ,waiting room and post office. Daily trains to: Luxembourg (2 hours), Brussels (4 hours), Munich, Stuttgart (2.5 hours), Basle (1.5 hours), Zürich (2.5 hours), Milan, Lyon, Paris (4 hours).

From the station, walk down to LITTLE FRANCE (well-preserved old houses bordering the canal) and wind your way through the coveted bridges and narrow medieval streets to the Gothic CATHEDRAL. Try and arrive for 12.30 p.m. when the astronomical clock comes into action or see the sound and light show in the evenings. You can also climb to the top for an additional few francs. South of the cathedral, the CHÂTEAU DES ROHAN contains a fine museum of archaeology, ceramics and paintings. Closed Tues. Boat trips are available around the city; try the early evening, it's too busy during the day. For eating, try the areas around place du Marché aux Cochons de Lait and place du Corbeau. If you like to eat in a crowd, try Au Pont St Martin at 13–15 rue des Moulins (Tel. 88 32 45 13) overlooking the river. In early June there is an International Music Festival.

HOSTELS The youth hostel, René Cassin, at 9 rue de l'Auberge de Jeunesse, Montagne Verte (Tel. 88 30 26 46) about 2½ km from the station on bus 3, 13, 23 from Marché Ste Marguerite to Auberge de Jeunesse. Although IYHF membership is obligatory, it is a good investment as card-holders go free to the city's museums. The hostel is good, with friendly staff, cost 69F for B&B; the campsite costs 40F per person.

The CIARUS hostel is at 7 rue Finkmatt (Tel. 88 32 12 12), a well looked after establishment.

There is another hostel at rue des Cavaliers, Parc du Rhin (Tel. 88 60 10 20), but this is further out. Take bus 21 from central station to Parc du Rhin; the nearest station is, however, KEHL in Germany, a kilometre away. Alternatively, stay at the hostel at Kehl.

Another suggestion, if you arrive when it's very busy, is to travel to COLMAR, where there are 2 hostels.

The Alps

In our opinion, CHAMONIX is one of the best places to visit in the Alps by train. The mountain railway which winds its way through picture-book villages is an unforgettable experience; sit on the right-hand side for the best view. Another unforgettable experience is the cable car to the Aiguille du Midi. The Chamonix Tourist Office at place du Triangle de l'Armite (Tel. 50 53 23 33) is open till 7.30 p.m. in summer, they will help you seek out accommodation, etc. (prices are expensive), or you could try camping; the Tourist Office can supply a list of 18 sites in the area. Four are 15 minutes' walk from the centre.

Check out the price of Le Chamoniard chalets or other gîte accommoadation with the Tourist Office. The youth hostel is at Les Pélerins, west of Chamonix (Tel. 50 53 14 52). It does dinners and packed lunches, and you can also get discounts on cable cars here. It is about a 40-minute walk from town and only a few hundred metres from the nearest station. Also try the private hostel, Chamoniard Volant (Tel. 50 53 14 09), friendly and clean; ask for details at the Tourist Office.

If you have only a day and want to head for the hills, ask Tourist Information for the list of *promenades à pied* (walking tours), state how long you want to walk and ask what their suggestions are, as the possibilities are endless. If you take your walking seriously, contact the Club Alpin Français on av. Michel Croz (Tel. 50 53 16 03) for information on mountain refuges and conditions. Even if you don't make it up the mountains, go and rub shoulders with the climbing set and have a beer with them in the Nationale, rue Paccard. Local alpine food specialities include smoked sausage, various cheeses and, of course, fondue.

Two other very beautiful spots are Aix-les-Bains and Annecy. AIX-LES-BAINS is a pretty spa town on a lake, with good walks in the surrounding hills and around the lakeside which afford panoramas of the deep blue lake and of the town. The hostel at Promenade du Sierroz (Tel. 79 88 32 88) is very good. Take bus 2 towards Plage-Piscine and the Grand Port if you don't fancy the walk of about 3 km.

ANNECY is another picturesque lakeside town. The old town with its narrow streets and fortress is well worth seeing. The campsite, Le Belvédère, is good value and gives a great view of the lake (Tel. 50 45 48 30). The hostel is La Grande Jeanne at 16 route du Semnoz (Tel. 50 45 33 19). Take bus 1 towards Paradis!

Burgundy

If wine is what takes you to Burgundy, be sure to visit the MUSÉE DU VIN in the Hôtel des Ducs de Bourgogne at BEAUNE and take the tour at MAISON PATRIARCHE, rue du Collège, where they even give you a little bottle for the train!

Apart from wine, Burgundy possesses some of the finest abbeys in France, the most spectacular one being at VÉZELAY, and though this isn't on the rail, there's a bus from AVALLON which is. From Paris or Dijon, change at Laroche-Migennes. You could also visit the ornate monastery and other historic buildings of CLUNY, which is on the SNCF bus route between Mâcon and Chalon-sur-Saône.

Dijon

Capital of Burgundy and an important centre in the 14th and 15th centuries, Dijon went into a decline for about 400 years until the railway brought commerce and industry back in the 1850s. Now it is known for its edible specialities such as mustard, *cassis* (blackcurrant liqueur), spiced bread (*pain d'épices*) and snails, and is a thriving commercial and industrial centre.

STATION FACILITIES

Train information is available Mon.–Sat: 8 a.m.–7.30 p.m and Sun.: 9 a.m.–12 noon, 2 p.m.–6.30 p.m. (Tel. 80 41 50 50). The reservations desk has the same hours. The station also has all the usual buffets, left-luggage lockers and stores as well as a foreign exchange. The station is shut 1 a.m.–4 a.m.

Daily trains to: Paris (2½ hours, 1 hour 40 min by TGV), Strasbourg (4 hours), Venice, Genoa, Lyon (1½ hours) and Marseille–Nice.

TOURIST INFORMATION AND ADDRESSES

The main Tourist Office is in place Darcy (Tel. 80 43 42 12) and open daily 9 a.m.–12 noon, 2 p.m.–9 p.m. (until 7 p.m. in winter). Room-finding service available.

POST OFFICE Place Grangier, Mon.–Fri.: 8 a.m.–7 p.m., Sat. and Sun.: 8 a.m.–12 noon

24-HOUR CHEMIST Tel. 80 41 28 28

CENTRE INFORMATION JEUNESSE DE BOURGOGNE 22 rue Audra (Tel. 80 30 35 56)

SEEING AND SLEEPING

The best way to see Dijon's well-preserved past is on foot; the Tourist Office gives out a free brochure on walking tours. Recorded commentaries for Walkmans can also be hired here. The former DUCAL PALACE, which houses an art museum, deserves a visit, as do the streets of the OLD TOWN surrounding it. The ARCHAEOLOGICAL MUSEUM has artefacts dating back to the 9th century BC (closed Tues.).

The youth hostel at 1 blvd Champollion (Tel. 80 72 95 20) is good but a long way from the station. Bus 6 from station to place de la République, change to bus 5, to Épirey. The Foyer International d'Étudiants at av. Maréchal Leclerc (Tel. 80 71 51 01) requires an ISIC and is also quite far out of town. Hôtel Confort Lamartine, 12 rue Jules Mercier (Tel. 80 30 37 47) has cheapish rooms, or try the Hôtel du Théâtre, 3 rue des Bons Enfants (Tel. 80 67 15 41).

The campsite is at av. Albertler (Tel. 80 43 54 72), overlooking the lake. It's clean, and in the summer it fills up early, so phone first. Bus 12, direction Fountain d'Ouche.

Restaurants can be an expensive luxury in Dijon, so buy from the market stalls not far from rue de la Liberté. One of the least expensive restaurants is Moulin à Vent at 8 place Françoise-Rude.

For a jar of the famous mustard, go to Maille on rue de la Liberté.

Lyon

This red-roofed city enjoys a spectacular location where the Saône and Rhône rivers meet, with impressive Roman ruins and a gastronomic reputation.

STATION FACILITIES
There are 2 stations of importance: Part-Dieu on the TGV line, and Perrache, for other trains. Both stations have the usual facilities: Part-Dieu has no Tourist Office; Perrache's office is towards the métro interchange. Both stations are open long hours, from around 5 a.m. to 12 midnight.

Daily trains to Paris (2 hours by TGV), Marseille (3 hours by TGV), Turin (4 hours) and Geneva (2 hours).

TOURIST INFORMATION AND ADDRESSES
Central Tourist Office at place Bellecour (Tel. 78 42 25 75), with a smaller branch at the Perrache station. Open Mon.–Fri.: 9 a.m.–7 p.m., Sat.: 9 a.m.–6 p.m., Sun.: 10 a.m.–6 p.m., shorter hours off-season. Also at av. Adolphe Max in the Old Town, during high season.

POST OFFICE Place Antonin-Poncet, close to the Tourist Office and medical emergency service

SOS MÉDECINS Tel. 78 83 51 51

SEEING
The city is split neatly into 3 sections: Vieux Lyon the Saône side (west); the Presqu'Île, which is the tongue of land between the Saône and Rhône; and the Modern City, on the Rhône side (east).

To the west of the old town is the FOURVIÈRE HILL, the site of important Gallo-Roman remains. The hill is reached by the steep streets
and steps known as the MONTÉES. The PARC ARCHÉOLOGIQUE DE FOURVIÈRE
contains an impressive ROMAN AMPHITHEATRE, a smaller ODÈON and other
Roman remains. There is also a museum of finds from the site.

The Old Town itself is a protected area, with well-preserved Renaissance houses. Between and under these run little alleyways called
TRABOULES, originally used for carrying silk around, but exploited by
the Resistance in the war. The Gothic ST JEAN CATHEDRAL, on rue St Jean,
has an astronomical clock and a treasury, which are worth a visit.

The CROIX ROUSSE district, to the north of the Presqu'Île, is where
the silk and weaving trade was based. Today the traditional methods have been revived at the MAISON DES CANUTS, 10–12 rue d'Ivry.
The TERREAUX quarter, with its lead fountain, and the HÔTEL DE VILLE
complex are also worth a visit.

Museums of note include the FINE ARTS MUSEUM, housed in the
17th/18th-century PALAIS ST PIERRE, once a Benedictine abbey. The
MUSEUM OF PRINTING AND BANKING is also worthwhile, looking at the
influence these trades had on Lyon. Probably the most important is
the MUSÉE HISTORIQUE DES TISSUS, with fabrics and silks from around the
world.

SLEEPING

The youth hostel is at 51 rue Roger Salengro (Tel. 78 76 39 23),
about 5 km from the city centre. From Perrache station bus 53 or 80
or 36 from Part-Dieu to États-Unis Viviani or Viviani Joliot-Curie.

The campsites are all about 10 km from the centre; try Dardilly.
At Porte de Lyon (Tel. 78 35 64 55), bus 19 from Hôtel de Ville to
Parc d'Affaires.

Cheap hotels worth trying: Alexandra, 49 rue Victor-Hugo (Tel. 78
37 75 79); Croix-Pâquet, 1 place Croix-Pâquet (Tel. 78 28 51 49);
Hôtel Vaubecour, 28 rue Vaubecour (Tel. 78 37 44 91).

EATING

Whilst there are many gastronomic delights well beyond the price
of the budget traveller, there should be no trouble in picking up a
reasonable meal. Vegetarians can try Le Pâtisson, 17 rue Pont du
Temple. Le Vivarais, at 1 place Gailleton, serves local specialities.

The Riviera (Côte d'Azur)

EXCURSIONS

In the past you would have had to be crazy to try and base yourself anywhere but Nice on the Côte d'Azur, but that doesn't apply any more should you want to visit the swanky resorts such as Cannes, Monte Carlo, Juan-les-Pins and St Tropez. A day's sunbathing will cost you nothing and you'll find prices only slightly more expensive. The beautiful people of St Trop have not permitted such vulgar inventions as public trains to spoil their paradise, so you'll have to bus it from St Raphael to get there. Still, if you want an all-over-tan – or to scrutinize other people's – it's the only place to be.

If you hit a cloudy day, go through to MONACO, put on your best bib and tucker and brave it out in the famous casino at MONTE CARLO: you must be able to prove you're 21 or over. The cheapest slot machine is 1F, and minimum bet at roulette 20F. The palace is also worth seeing, but is expensive. The Oceanographic Museum, where Jacques Cousteau was director for many years, has all things aquatic, including 450 species of fish. Open all year 9.30 a.m.–7 p.m., except during the Monaco Grand Prix when it like everything else in Monaco gives way to the thundering Formula 1 cars.

Those staying overnight should try to get into the Relais International de Jeunesse in Cap d'Ail (Tel. 93 78 18 58) just outside Monte Carlo. The excellent Princess Stephanie Youth Centre (Tel. 93 50 83 20) is at 24 av. Prince Pierre, and has an age limit of 26. No advance reservations allowed here, registrations start at 10.30 a.m., 60 places in mixed rooms.

Another good place to base yourself is at the Saint Michel Ment (Tel. 93 35 81 23) campsite at MENTON near the Italian border. A tent for 2 people a night costs from 36F, depending on season. Look out for bogus lifts from the station to the campsites as we've had reports of drivers taking money and leaving people at the site entrance, knowing it to be full.

The Menton youth hostel offers fabulous views over the bay, as well as what is reputed to be the best youth hostel evening meal in France.

For windsurfing, sailing and other water sports, make for ST RAPHAEL, as prices are cheaper here and there's more likely to be wind than further up the coast.

A reasonably cheap place to base yourself is BIOT. Look hard for the station between Nice and Cannes, as it's easy to miss. Biot has a particularly good campsite opposite the station. Le Logis de la Brague is cheap and close to the beach.

In CANNES itself there is a new 16-bed private youth hostel, Le Chalit, opened in 1994 at 27 av. Gallioni (Tel. 93 99 22 11). Try also the Hostel at 35 av. de Vallauris (Tel. 9399 2679), 70/80F.

Another good spot is VILLENEUVE-LOUBET-SUR-MER, between Antibes and NICE. It is a small pleasant town with several campsites. A friendly and cheap one is the Savoy (Tel. 93 20 16 06) which is right on the beach. Easy access to other resorts by train which runs frequently along the coast.

A good campsite just outside TOULON is Camping Beauregard (Tel. 94 20 56 35), which is reached by bus 27 or 9.

The island of CORSICA can be reached from either Nice or Marseille. The cheapest fare is on a night ferry travelling fourth class (sleeping on deck) from Nice, Marseille or Toulon, one way. Corsica is very beautiful. Bonifacio, Ajaccio (Napoleon's hometown) and Bastia are the 3 most attractive centres on the island. To make a trip to Corsica worthwhile, though, you'll need to be really keen as rail fares are expensive and rail passes aren't valid, although Inter-Railers do get a reduction. Eurotrain have reduced fares from Nice to Corsica, available from USIT.

Nice

This is without doubt your best base for a spell on the Riviera; it's cheaper than the more pretentious resorts along the Côte d'Azur and has more facilities suited to the eurorailer's lifestyle. It gets very busy, especially in August, and you might have to fight hard for your space on the pebbly beach, but at least you're only a few minutes by train from other small Riviera resorts with less crowded beaches like Villefranche, Beaulieu and Menton. Do take care at the station, as professional luggage thieves are on the look-out for tourists.

STATION FACILITIES

Nice Gare de Ville has an information office open daily 8 a.m.–8 p.m. (Tel. 04 93 87 50). Reservations can be made Mon.–Sat.: 8 a.m.–6.45 p.m. and Sun.: 8 a.m.–12 noon, 2 p.m.–6.45 p.m. There is also a Tourist Information office, foreign exchange bureau, cafés, left-luggage lockers and stores, and showers. The station is shut 0.30 a.m.–5.30 a.m.

Daily trains to: Paris, Strasbourg, Genoa, Milan, Rome, Marseille.

TOURIST INFORMATION AND ADDRESSES

The main office is to your left, coming out of the station, at av. Thiers (Tel. 04 93 87 07 07). Youth Information CIJ, 19 rue Gioffrêdo (Tel. 93 80 93 93).

POST OFFICE 23 av. Thiers. Daily 8 a.m.–7 p.m.

POSTE RESTANTE rue des Postes

AMEX 11 Promenade des Anglais, Mon.–Fri.: 9 a.m.–12 noon, 2 p.m.–6 p.m., Sat.: 9 a.m.–12 noon.

NIGHT CHEMIST 7 rue Masséna (Tel. 93 87 78 94). 7.30 p.m.– 8.30 a.m.

SOS MÉDECINS Tel. 93 83 01 01

SNCM 3 av. Gustave V (Tel. 93 13 66 66), for boats to Corsica

USIT VOYAGES 10 rue des Belgiques, 06000 Nice (Tel. 87 33 34 96); also Eurotrain office

SEEING

The old town of Nice with its street markets and Italian atmosphere has some typically Mediterranean walks through narrow winding alleys, which come as a sharp contrast to the commercial, touristy feeling on the main streets of Nice. To get a view over Nice and the Mediterranean, climb the 90m up to the CHÂTEAU. If you've only an hour or two, spend it walking the length of the Promenade des Anglais. Eating in the cafés is prohibitive but the people-watching is great. Among the main things to see are: the PALAIS LASCARIS at 15 rue Droite (former residence of the Count of Ventimiglia), the RUSSIAN ORTHODOX CATHEDRAL, the old PORT of Nice where the beautiful people keep their beautiful yachts, the MATISSE MUSEUM at av. des Arènes with some of the artist's works and personal possessions, and the MUSÉE NATIONAL MARC CHAGALL, av. du Dr Ménard.

SLEEPING

During the Jazz Parade each July beds become very scarce and at any other time beds are still hard to find, so come early and phone around. Most of the cheap hotels are located around the station area.

HOSTELS The IYHF youth hostel is 4 km away at route Forestière du Mont Alban (Tel. 93 89 23 64), bus 14. Use les Collinettes, the university accommodation, at 3 av. de Robert Schumann (Tel. 93 97 10 33) bus 17, girls only. The Relais International de Jeunesse (Tel. 93 81 27 63), av. Scudéry, is OK, but could mean a long wait to be checked in. There is a Foyer, with a good cafeteria, two minutes from the beach at Espace Magnan, rue Louis de Coppet (Tel. 93 86 28 75). Varied reports.

HOTELS Hotels in the following streets are central, clean(ish), and affordable: Les Orangers, 10 bis av. Durante (Tel. 93 87 51 41); d'Orsay, 18 rue Alsace Lorraine (Tel. 93 88 45 02); The Hôtel Antares, 5 Av. Thiers (opp. the station) is reputedly good or try Madame Garstandt, 55b rue Gambetta close by. Meublé Let's Go, 26 blvd Raimbaldi, 2nd floor (Tel. 93 80 98 00), 5 minutes from station. 60F a night in dorms including shower. Hôtel Centrale (Tel. 93 88 85 08) in rue de la Suisse offers good, cheap accommodation and has friendly staff, but go early to get a room overlooking the courtyard.

CAMPING In summer you'll find people camping on the beach, but since it's the only stretch on the Côte d'Azur where it is tolerated it is a bit of a bear pit.There are lots of campsites at Villeneuve-Loubet, 8 km from Nice and on the line from Nice to Cannes. Although expensive, facilities are good. A map of the sites is available from the Tourist Information Centre at Nice Station. If stuck, go to the hostel in Menton.

EATING AND NIGHTLIFE

Food in Nice is among the best in France; the proximity of Italy (30 minutes away) is clear in the cuisine, so the pizzas in Nice are better than many you'll find in Italy, and there's plenty of fresh seafood from the Mediterranean. Sitting in an outside restaurant on one of the pedestrianized streets watching life go by is one of life's great pleasures, and Nice abounds with good set menus at prices under 100F.

Try Le Félix Fauvre, 12 av. Félix Fauvre; Chez Davis, 1/1b rue Grimaldi; Chez Nino, 50 rue Trachel (100 beers).

For self-service try the Café de Paris at one of 3 locations: 42 rue Pastorelli, rue Masséna or in the Old Town. Try the Café Casino, almost opposite the station. For those cutting corners there are some good supermarkets in the centre.

Discos and clubs are expensive, and anyway a walk down the Promenade des Anglais is just as entertaining.

Marseille

Marseille lacks the charm and finesse of the Riviera resorts but it does have character. It's France's oldest city (dating back to 600 BC) and one of the world's major ports, but it does tend to cater more for businessmen than tourists.

STATION FACILITIES

Marseille St Charles has train information Mon.–Sat.: 9 a.m.–7 p.m. but is closed Sun. and holidays. Their telephone number is 91 08 50 50. The reservations desk has the same hours. Tourist Information hours are winter: Mon.–Fri.: 10 a.m.–1 p.m., 1.30 p.m.– 6 p.m; summer: 8 a.m.–8 p.m. The station has all the usual amenities you would expect from a busy international station and it closes down 1.30 a.m.–4.30 a.m.

Daily trains to: Paris, Strasbourg, Lyon (4 hours), Nice (2.5 hours), Milan, Bordeaux, Nantes, Amsterdam, Brussels, Rome, Barcelona.

TOURIST INFORMATION AND ADDRESSES

To be found at the station, otherwise at 4 La Canebière (near the Old Port) (Tel. 91 54 91 11), open 9 a.m.–7.15 p.m., 8.30 a.m.–8 p.m. during high season. They have an accommodation-finding service.

YOUTH INFORMATION rue de la Visitation (Tel. 91 49 91 55)

POST OFFICE Place de l'Hôtel-des-Postes (métro: Colbert)

24-HOUR CHEMIST AND DOCTOR Tel. 91 52 84 85. SOS Médecins Tel. 91 52 91 52

SEEING

Marseille's most famous street is the Canebière ('can-o-beer' to generations of British and American sailors) which leads up from the Old Port to the RÉFORMIES CHURCH. This gets quite lively at night, but you're safer walking round here than in the slums of the North African quarter. Having said that, there is a lot to see of interest. The MUSÉE DES BEAUX ARTS in the Palais de Longchamps is the city's art gallery. The MUSÉE DES DOCKS ROMAINS (Roman docks), 12 place Vivaux, was the unexpected result of a 1943 German bomb, which revealed the ancient storage depots, with giant storage jars. ST VICTOR'S ABBEY, a fortified church, built between the 11th and 14th centuries, has a CRYPTÉ and CATACOMBS. The CATHÉDRALE ST MAIRIE MAJEURE, is a 19th-century, neo-Byzantine building. Off the coast, served by a regular boat shuttle service from the Old Port, is the CHÂTEAU D'IF. This old fortress, once also a prison, is associated with Alexandre Dumas's THE COUNT OF MONTE CRISTO. Slightly further from the centre is the park and CHÂTEAU BORLEY, built in the 18th century. The BASILICA OF NOTRE DAME DE LA GARDE, in Romano-Byzantine style, was built in the 19th century and is surmounted with a gilded statue of Mary. It has a great view over the city and is open 7 a.m.–7.30 p.m., bus 60 from Cours Jean Ballard. By complete contrast visit Le Corbusier's 17-storey CITÉ RADIEUSE, a study in concrete.

SLEEPING

The 2 youth hostels are a long way from the centre but are all right once you get there: Marseille-Bois Luzy (FUAJ), at av. de Bois-Luzy (Tel. 91 49 06 18) bus 8 from Bourse (near Canebière), and Auberge de Bonneveine (FUAJ), at 47 av. J. Vidal (Tel. 91 73 21 81), métro to St Marguerite Dromel, then bus 47. Beware when looking round for a cheap hotel, especially near the docks – many of them are 'multi-purpose' establishments. Two you might try are, Carvelle, 5 rue Guy-Mocquet (Tel. 91 48 44 99) and Piole, 9 rue du Théâtre-Français (Tel. 91 33 11 15).

Try Camping de Bonneveine, on the beach and cheap (Tel. 91 73 26 99).

EATING AND NIGHTLIFE

Bouillabaisse, the famous French fish stew, comes from Marseille, and is at its best here. There's no shortage of restaurants-cafés and fixed-price menus can be found. The Tunisian and Moroccan restaurants are cheap, though not always good, but it's not wise for unaccompanied girls to head into the North African quarter at night. Chez Papa down by the port does a spectacular ice-cream sundae.

Nightlife more or less finds you in Marseille: there are plenty of discos around. Just watch out you don't go into too low a dive as, if things get nasty, we've heard the police don't lose too much sleep over the odd mugged eurorailer. For tips on locations ask at the Tourist Office for their guide *Nocturnes*.

Provence

Renowned for its cloudless skies and Roman remains, Provence's rich countryside has acted like a magnet to artists and eurorailers alike for years. The best time to go is May or Sept. as Aix-en-Provence and Avignon have arts festivals in July and Aug., and rooms are hard to find.

If you're going to or from the south or west and have plenty of time, consider breaking your journey at VALENCE. Valence is a pretty, peaceful town with a good youth hostel/campsite called Centre l'Épèmière. The centre is good value, particularly with its swimming pool and bar/restaurant, though it is quite a walk from the station.

Avignon

If you're coming from Lyon, consider getting off the train half an hour before Avignon at ORANGE to see one of the finest Roman theatres in the world. After a fracas between the Vatican and Philip the Fair of France, Clement V moved to Avignon. The inner walled city is still dominated by his palace, the PALAIS DES PAPES, which is most impressive from the outside; they are progressing with restoration and English tours are available. Be sure to visit the park above the palace for a superb view of the River Rhône.

The Tourist Information office is at 41 Cours Jean-Jaurès (Tel. 90 82 65 11), open 9 a.m.–l p.m., 2 p.m.–6 p.m., Sat. 9 a.m.–1 p.m., 2 p.m.–5 p.m., closed Sun. During the festival in July the Tourist Office is open Mon.–Sat.: 9 a.m.–6 p.m.

Sleeping will be your greatest problem in Avignon, but there are accommodation services at Place de l'Horloge and at the Tourist Office, which you're advised to use to save yourself hassle.

If you don't mind large dormitories, try the youth hostel at Camping Bagatelle (Tel. 90 86 30 39), located on the Île de la Barthélasse in the middle of the Rhône. Prices are good and there is a superb view of the palace.

Centre Pierre Louis Loisil, on the av. Pierre Sémard (Tel. 90 25 07 92) has campsites and dorms.

Also try the YMCA Foyer, 7 chemin de la Justice (Tel. 90 25 46 20), 90F.

Finally, there's a hostel, called the Squash Club, at 32 blvd Limbert (Tel. 90 85 27 78). From the station, walk around the city walls to the right.

If you're camping, Avignon has several sites near each other on the Île de Barthélasse, Camping Municipal (Tel. 90 82 6 3 50), Camping Bagatelle (Tel. 90 86 30 39), Parc des Libertés (Tel. 90 85 17 73) and Camping des Deux Rhônes (Tel. 90 85 49 70). Although they are all within walking distance of the station, the no. 10 bus from by the post office will take you there. Last bus runs about 7 p.m., 5 p.m. Sun.

Arles

An important centre in Roman and medieval times with an impressive AMPHITHEATRE which today has reverted to its function as a blood bath, imported Spanish bulls having replaced the gladiators. The MUSEUM OF CHRISTIAN ART is well worth a visit, as is the ROMAN THEATRE and the ROMAN CEMETERY.

Tourist Information is on blvd des Lices (Tel. 90 18 41 20): they'll supply a ticket for entry to all the museums and monuments as well as help you out with accommodation if necessary.

The youth hostel is on av. Maréchal-Foch (Tel. 90 96 18 25), a block behind the Tourist Office. If you want to venture into the Camargue, Arles is about the nearest you'll get by rail (they rent out bikes at the station, the going is flat).

Nîmes

Some of the best Roman remains in France are here, with the MAISON CARRÉE and the AMPHITHEATRE stealing the show. Tourist Information is at 6 rue Auguste (Tel. 66 67 29 11), open Mon.–Fri.: 8 a.m.–7 p.m., Sat... 9a.m.–noon and 2 p.m.–5p.m., Sun., 10 a.m.–noon, and they run a similar system to Arles: ticket for the monuments, ISIC reduction. They'll also give you the best route to the PONT DU GARD, the 2,000-year-old Roman aqueduct which is almost intact, and the old Crusaders' port of AIGUES-MORTES, now well inland through silting up. Both are well worth visiting.

There are also several castles in the area; the best is at UZÈS, open all year; ask again at Nîmes Tourist Office for the route.

The hostel is about 3 km out at Chemin de la Cigale (Tel. 66 23 25 04). Camping is also a possibility here. Take either bus 6 or 20 – note the last bus is at 8 p.m.

Aix-en-Provence

Birthplace of Cézanne and intellectual and cultural centre of the region, Aix fancies itself somewhat and gives off an air of sophistication that is lacking elsewhere. Sit in any café and you'll feel a strange air of self-importance. The MUSEUM OF TAPESTRIES in the former Arch-bishop's Palace is particularly interesting. Avoid their festival, as prices and crowds increase dramatically. Tourist Information is at 2 place du Général de Gaulle (Tel. 42 16 11 61). Try Hôtel du Casino, 38 rue Victor-Leydet (Tel. 42 26 06 88) or Hôtel Paul, 10 av. Pasteur (Tel. 42 23 23 89), good value and has rooms for up to 4 people. The youth hostel is at 3 av. Marcel Pagnol (Tel. 42 20 15 99). Take bus 8 to Estienne d'Orves or 12 to Vasarely from the pPlace de Gaulle, as it's 2 km from the station. Look out for the Vasarely building.

Central / South-West France

The Auvergne, Dordogne and Languedoc regions are sparsely popu-lated and consequently trains are few and far between; however, if you have the time and patience for the local trains, the rewards are great.

CARCASSONNE, the medieval gem of the Languedoc region, is on the main line and services are good. This is arguably Europe's best-preserved relic of the Middle Ages, and certainly the most interesting walled city in France. After centuries of building and fortifying the town, it was left to rot in the 16th century and it wasn't till the 19th that restoration began. The Tourist Office is on blvd Camille Pelleton; they find rooms and are generally helpful. Arrive early as Carcassonne is not a well-kept secret and in summer rooms get scarce.

CLERMONT-FERRAND and PÉRIGUEUX are not particularly interesting towns in themselves but they make excellent bases tor touring the Auvergne and Dordogne. The tourist board at Clermont is at 69 blvd Gergovia, and Périgueux's is in av. de l'Aquitaine. They'll provide you with details on the surrounding area and how best to reach the places of interest. Accommodation should be no problem in either town: most of the cheap hotels surround the stations.

LES EYZIES-DE-TAYAC (the prehistoric capital of Europe) is about 40 minutes south-east of Périgueux by train and its cave paintings are within easy walking distance of the station, as is the Tourist Informa-tion office (Tel. 53 06 97 05). There are plenty of hotels to choose from in the village and there's camping on the other side of the river.

Bordeaux

Famed for the many quality wines it produces, Bordeaux is a good place to head for if your money's running out and you fancy a week or two working on the grape harvest which is picked in Sept. A short stay here will give you a totally different perspective on French life from your few days in Paris: whilst Paris is very Parisian, Bordeaux is terribly French.

STATION FACILITIES
Train information can be got at Gare St Jean 8 a.m.–9 p.m. (Tel. 56 92 50 50) and the reservations desk has similar hours but shuts earlier and has a limited service at weekends. The station is shut midnight–5 a.m. and has all the usual facilities including a post office and shower. Daily trains to: Paris, Lyon, Nantes, Toulouse, Marseille, Nice, Biarritz, Madrid and Lisbon.

TOURIST INFORMATION AND ADDRESSES
TOURIST INFORMATION 12 cours du 30 Juillet (Tel. 56 44 28 41), just off the Esplanade des Quinconces
POST OFFICE 52 rue Georges Bonnac
24-HOUR CHEMIST OR DOCTOR Tel. 56 90 92 75
CENTRE INFORMATION JEUNESSE AQUITAINE 5 rue Duffour-Dubergier (Tel. 56 56 00 56). They will help with accommodation. The walk into town takes about 30 minutes.

SEEING
Explore Bordeaux on foot, starting your tour at the GRAND THÉÂTRE on the place de la Comédie. From here you can work out the best route on the map to take you to the other sights: the ESPLANADE DES QUIN-CONÉS, the largest square in France, the PLACE DE LA BOURSE with its 18th-century façades, the CATHÉDRALE ST ANDRÉE, the MUSÉE DES BEAUX ARTS, the MUSÉE DES ARTS DÉCORATIFS and the smart shopping streets round RUE BOUFFARD. Also worth a visit is the interesting MUSEUM OF THE RESISTANCE and MUSEUM OF AQUITAINE. In the ESPLANADE DES QUINCONCES see the Monument aux Girondins, erected to commemorate the Deputies of the Revolution. To get the feel of things, take a 'wine tour'; the Tourist Office arranges these daily. The cost is around 150F per person, high season, Sat. only during low season.

SLEEPING

A bed is no problem in Bordeaux, even though many places close down in Aug. The basic FUAJ youth hostel is close to the station at 22 Cours Barbey (Tel. 56 91 59 51). Head down Cours de la Marne, fifth turning on left. There are 247 beds, a bar, kitchen and a great atmosphere. Only open 7 a.m.–10 a.m. and 6 p.m.–11 p.m., but rucksacks can be left at reception.

There are several cheap hotels in the area (ask at the Tourist Office on arrival); these include the Hôtel Blayais, 17 rue Mautrec (Tel. 56 48 17 87) and the Dauphin (Tel. 56 52 24 62).

For camping, check out the site at Courréjan, a half-hour bus ride on route B, leaving from the bus station at Quai Richelieu, down by the river. The site is a few minutes' walk from the terminus.

EATING AND NIGHTLIFE

Predictably enough, the local cuisine makes good use of the regional wines and there are all sorts of dishes using the delicious *bordelaise* sauce. Set menus at affordable prices can be found in restaurants on rue des Augustins, place Général Sarrail, and rue du Maréchal-Joffre.

The main shopping street is rue Ste Catherine, where there are plenty of good supermarkets and eating places. Ask Tourist Information for a *What's On* and try sampling the regional wines at bistros.

Cerbère

If you are heading for Spain along the Mediterranean coast and decide to break your journey for the night at the border, give the station and the beach a body swerve. Instead walk back along the main road towards France for a few hundred metres and take the footpath up the cliff. Both the scenery and sleeping potential here are much better.

NOTES
....

....

....

....

....

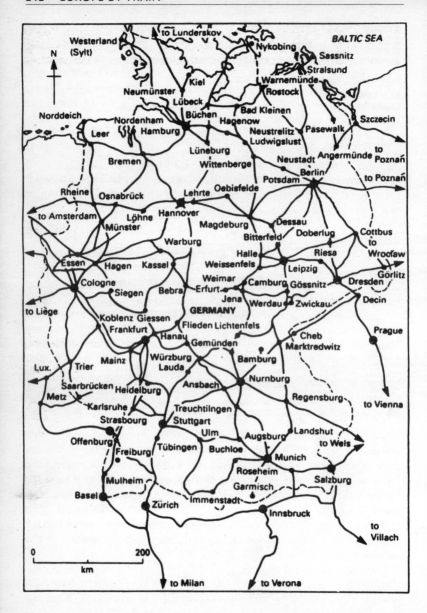

N

Westerland
(Sylt)

to Lunderskov

BALTIC SEA

Nykobing

Sassnitz

Stralsund

Kiel

Warnemünde

Neumünster

Lübeck

Rostock

Büchen

Bad Kleinen

Norddeich

Nordenham

Hagenow

Szczecin

Leer

Hamburg

Neustrelitz

Pasewalk

Bremen

Lüneburg

Ludwigslust

to
Poznań

Wittenberge

Neustadt

Angermünde

Rheine

Oebisfelde

Berlin

to Poznań

Osnabrück

Lehrte

Potsdam

to Amsterdam

Löhne

Hannover

Magdeburg

Dessau

Cottbus
to
Wrocław

Münster

Warburg

Bitterfeld

Doberlug

Essen

Hagen

Kassel

Halle

Riesa

Görlitz

Cologne

Weissenfels

Leipzig

Dresden

Siegen

Weimar

Camburg

Gössnitz

Bebra

Erfurt

Decin

Koblenz Giessen

Jena

Werdau

Zwickau

Frankfurt

GERMANY

Prague

Flieden Lichtenfels

Hanau

Gemünden

Cheb
Marktredwitz

Lux.

Trier

Mainz

Würzburg
Lauda

Bamburg

Saarbrücken

Heidelburg

Ansbach

Nurnburg

Metz

Karlsruhe

Regensburg

to Vienna

Strasbourg

Treuchtilngen

Stuttgart

Landshut

Offenburg

Ulm

Augsburg

to Wels

Freiburg

Tübingen

Buchloe

Munich

Roseheim

Salzburg

Mulheim

Garmisch

Basel

Zürich

Immenstadt

Innsbruck

to
Villach

0   200
km

to Milan

to Verona

GERMANY

Entry requirements	Passport
Population	78,000,000
Capital	Berlin (pop.: 2,.960,000)
Currency	Deutschmark
	£1 = approx. 2.78DM
Political system	Federal Republic
Religions	Protestant and Catholic
Language	German (English spoken in major cities)
Public holidays	New Year's Day, Epiphany (Bavaria and Baden-Württemberg only), Good Friday, Easter Sun./Mon., Labour Day, Ascension Day, Whit Monday, Corpus Christi Day, Ascension of the Virgin Mary (15 Aug.), Day of Unity (3 Oct.), Day of Reformation, All Saints' Day, Day of Prayer and Repentance, Christmas Day and Boxing Day. NB Corpus Christi, Virgin Mary and All Saints' Days are not celebrated in all of the country, mainly Catholic areas only.
International dialling codes:	To Germany: int'l code 49 number
	From Germany: 00 + country code number

The new united Germany has emerged from a nightmare stretching back through partition to the 1930s. The immediate future may be rocky as the backward east is incorporated into the west, but the result may well be a new economic superpower. The east is now accessible and well worth the visit to see not only the effects of the last 45 years but also to see its history, exemplified by the beautifully restored city of Dresden.

The Germans are a restless lot. Wherever you go in Europe, there they are. It's always been like this from the days of the Franks and Saxons. Most people have heard of the Holy Roman Empire, revived by Otto I in 962, which survived till 1806, but few realize that the local German regimes were often much more powerful. The Hanseatic League of merchants, associated with the towns of Lübeck and Hamburg, controlled much of northern Europe's wealth in the medieval period.

Long after the rest of Europe had formed itself into single nation states, 'Germany' was still divided, a fact not helped by the incredible number of feuding princedoms and the country's lack of natural boundaries. These divisions came to a head in the Thirty Years' War of 1618–48 when the Catholic south defending the Habsburg emperors and Protestant north, inspired by men such as Luther and the Reformation movement, fought it out between themselves. In

1871 Bismarck was the force bringing the German nation into being. The autocratic rule, attempts to conquer an empire, and rapid industrialization led to discontent, this topped with Kaiser Bill's blunderings, led to the First World War. After the failure of the liberal Weimar Republic, Hitler started stirring things up again, and we all know what Nazism led to.

The end of the Second World War saw Germany occupied by the Allies. Cold War tensions caused the division into 2 states. Germany has survived all these trials. The Wall is down and, despite the chaos, Germany is united again.

GERMAN RAIL
(DEUTSCHE BAHN, DB)

DB offer one of the best deals in Europe. They're fast, clean and efficiently run. Unlike Britain and France, where all the main lines radiate out from the capital, the Germans have an excellent series of interconnecting cross-country lines which serve all the principal cities and the smaller towns throughout the country. Various timetables are produced for the different regional areas. Trains range from the fast and flashy Inter City Expresses (ICE) which offer 175 mph travel with an hourly service between Hamburg and Munich, to the less speedy Inter City trains (IC) which require a 6DM supplement (supplements for journeys across a frontier vary). The InterRegio (IR) trains are nearly as fast and connect smaller cities to the IC network (they require a 3DM supplement). *Schnellzüge* (D) and the *Eilzüge* (E) serve the regional areas and in the cities *Bahnen* or *Nahverkehrszüge*, are slow local trains.

Apart from the speed on the ICEs, other facilities include built-in radios and coat cabinets; the ultimate in comfort for a bit extra. These trains are excellent but charge a supplement.

PASSES AVAILABLE The German Rail Pass has now been replaced by Euro Domino Germany, allowing 3, 5 or 10 days' unlimited travel within a month, for the whole of Germany (see page 41). As well as the railways the ticket is also valid on KD day ships (not hydrofoils) between Cologne and Mainz. The ticket includes all supplements, but not reservations. However, whilst ICE supplements are included, charges for extra services on these trains are not included. Reservations cost 3DM and are available up to 15 minutes before departure. Adult second-class tickets cost: 3 days £139, 5 days £159 or 10 days £209. Those under 26 can purchase a 3-day pass for £109, 5-day for £119 and 10-day pass for £159. Cards are available from appointed travel agents, continental booking offices or DER, 18 Conduit Street.

London W1 (Tel. 0171 290 1111). In the United States write to German Rail, DER Travel Service for further information at 11933 Wilshire Blvd, Los Angeles, LA 90025 (Tel. 310 479 4140).

If you plan on spending a long time in Germany, look out for the DB Bahn Card. It's valid for a year and gets you 50% reduction on all rail tickets, although you still have to pay EurocCity and IC supplements. Prices start at £51 for those under 22 and £102 for those over 22. Bahn Cards can be purchased from Wasteels, Adjacent Platform 2, Victoria Station, London SW1V 1JT (Tel. 0171 834 7066).

DB also have Regional Rail passes which are available in 15 regions and are valid for unlimited second-class travel for 5 or 10 days out of 21. A 5-day single ticket costs £59, a ticket for 2 is £94 and a family ticket (including any number of children under 16) is £111. First-class tickets are also available. Supplements for IC and EC are included, but supplements for ICE are not, nor are reservations or couchette charges.

For people travelling together throughout Germany a mini-group ticket can be purchased. The first adult pays full fare, additional adults pay half price and children quarter price. The maximum group size is 5.5 (each child counts as half). Another special deal is the Schönes-Wochenende Ticket, which allows up to 5 people to make any round trip of up to 1,000 km between midnight Friday and midnight Saturday for 15DM.

Both Eurail and Inter-Rail passes are valid. Germany is in Inter-Rail Zone C, along with Switzerland, Austria and Denmark. For details of the 8 Inter-Rail zones, see the Inter-Rail section in Part One of this guide. For further information about German Rail contact German Rail Passenger Services, Suite 4, The Sanctuary, 23 Oakhill Grove, Surbiton KT6 6DU (Tel. 0891 88 77 55; Fax. 0181 399 4700).

INTER-RAIL BONUSES NB Inter-Rail tickets are now valid on the Berliner S-Bahn as well as in other German cities, but not on the U-Bahn. For further Inter-Rail reductions, see Appendix I.

EURAIL BONUSES
FREE SERVICES

Ferry crossings from Puttgarden and Rødby Faerge (Denmark) between Sassnitz and Trelleborg (Sweden) as well as Warnemünde and Gedser.

Ships operated by the KD German Rhine Line making regular day trips on the Rhine between Cologne and Mainz and the Moselle between Koblenz and Cochem (but not ships making cruises of several days between Basel and Rotterdam or vice versa, or between Trier and Koblenz or vice versa). An extra charge will have to be paid for the use of hydrofoils.

Europabus line 189 – Burgenstrasse (Castle Road) from Mannheim–Heidelberg–Heilbronn–Rothenburg or der Tauber–Ansbach– Nürnberg-am-Main.

Europabus line 190 – *Romantische Strasse* (Romantic Road): Frankfurt/M-Rothenburg orb der Tauber–Augsburg–Munich/Filssen.

REDUCED FARES

50% reduction on normal fares for TT Line's Travemünde–Trelleborg. Student rate for Finnjet's Travemünde–Helsinki.

50% reductions on some regular Lake Constance steamer services or on Worm and Kock's Passau–Linz line.

25% reduction on the Freiburg–Schauinsland rack railway.

40% reduction to Eurail Youthpass holders on the roundtrip bus fare Braunschweig–Berlin and 25% reduction on the mountain railroad Garmisch Partenkirchen–Grainau–Zugspitzplatt and on some cable cars in the summit area.

TRAIN INFORMATION

In 1994 Deutsche Bahn started a customer-care programme with intensive cleaning programmes and recruiting of security and service staff to improve station standards. One of the main results has been the 'service points' in stations all over Germany. These service points are located in the middle of the station hall and are often open 24 hours a day to answer all sorts of queries. So if you need any help, contact them first for advice.

Left-luggage lockers take 1DM and 50 Pfennig pieces.

RESERVATIONS Can be made up to 15 minutes before departing, but not after 10 p.m. They are not included in the price of the supplement: there is a charge of 3DM for reservations purchased at the same time as the ticket and 9DM for those made separately. A supplement for IC/EC will cost 6DM, or 8DM if you buy it on the train.

NIGHT TRAVEL Some German compartments have pull-down seats which make excellent free beds. Couchettes have 6 berths whilst tourist-class sleepers (4-berth) cost about 50% more. Three-berth compartments are also available and it's often possible to get 1 between 2 out of season, as they're usually underbooked. DB has extended the special couchette service between Dortmund and Munich known as the *Twen-Nachttramper* (Night Tramper); services last year ran between Aachen to Copenhagen via Hamburg, Hamburg to Munich and Dortmund to Munich. It allows you to have a couchette for only a small fee and all you need is a sleeping bag or blankets. If you don't have either, you can buy a paper blanket on board for around 6DM from the conductor. You don't have to worry about reservations either as you can pay the fee on board, although the number of places is limited and the service has proved to be very popular. Look out for extra services being laid on and check with DB before booking couchettes for an overnight journey in case your route has come into the scheme. Some robberies have been reported on the Poland–Germany night trains. Take extra care.

WOMEN-ONLY SLEEPERS *Damen Couchettes* are available on all sleeper trains in Germany, and on 3 international night trains to and from Austria, Belgium and Holland. Prices are the same as for ordinary couchettes, but berths must be reserved at least 2 days in advance.

EATING ON TRAINS Prices are lower than on British trains, while the quality is higher. So if you've the money, it's worth considering a meal on the ICs. Other trains (except E-trains) have mini-bars, which are pricey.

SCENIC ROUTES The Rhine valley, Black Forest, Romantic and Castle roads, as well as the Alps, all provide scenic routes within Germany. If you've always wanted to go cruising down the Rhine, it's best to do it between Koblenz and Rüdesheim or Mainz as this gives you magnificent views of both sides of the valley. If you're coming from the opposite direction and want to stay with rivers, then head to Giessen from Koblenz. To see the Black Forest, there are a variety of options. The Romantic and Castle roads are arguably best seen by Europabus, which are nearly always busy and require advance reservations. The Munich–Nürnberg, Heilbronn–Heidelberg train follows more or less the same route as the bus at no extra cost. For the Alps, try the line to Salzburg or Innsbruck from Munich – both are equally attractive. If you're going to Switzerland, try Freiburg–Basel or Würzburg–Zürich.

BIKES Can be hired from around 370 stations throughout Germany from 7DM upwards to anyone with a valid ticket or rail pass. You can either do a circular tour of the region or merely cycle from A to B and return the bike to another station.

TOURIST INFORMATION

Tourist Offices are usually called *Verkehrsamt* or *Verkehrsverein*. Many towns in eastern Germany have an office, simply described as an 'information office'. Also expect most east German *Reisebüros* to be open. Many cities have free pamphlets specially prepared for the under-26s.

ISIC BONUSES Museum discount, with varying reductions at some sports centres. For further information, contact Europa Sprach Club, Amalienstrasse 67, Munich 40. There are branches in all main cities. In Berlin also try the JugendTourist Office at Alexanderplatz 5, 1026 Berlin.

MONEY MATTERS 1 Deutschmark (DM) = 100 Pfennige.
Banking hours vary, but generally are Mon.–Fri.: 8.30 a.m.–12.30 p.m., 1.30 p.m.–6.30 p.m.; Thurs.: until 5.30 p.m. Closed Sat. It's also possible to change money at some post offices; they often give a better rate, because they make mistakes.

POST OFFICES Open Mon.–Fri.: 8 a.m.–6 p.m., Sat.: 8 a.m.–12 noon.

SHOPS Open Mon.–Fri.: 9 a.m.–6.30 p.m. Thurs. until 8.30 p.m. In smaller towns they shut for lunch, 12 noon–3 p.m. On Sat. they only open till 2 p.m., and until 4 p.m. on the first Sat. of each month.

MUSEUMS Hours vary depending on locality. Generally in West Tues.–Sun.: 9 a.m.–5 p.m., East 10 a.m.–5 p.m. Check with Tourist Information, as many museums are closed on Mondays. Many offer free admission on Sundays.

TIPPING Usually included in restaurants but it is still polite to leave some loose change up to a maximum of 5%. Always tip lavatory attendants, especially if you plan to return!

SLEEPING

Youth hostels cost 16–25DM a night and there are over 600 scattered throughout Germany. Tourist Information will have a free map and brochure showing their locations. In Bavaria there is an age limit of 27 in hostels. Youth guest houses (*Jugendgasthäuser*) are in nearly all the large towns, but they tend to be stuffed with groups, so always phone first. There's no uniform system of classification for Germany's hostels and hotels, so you'll find they vary dramatically.

The accommodation side of Tourist Information, however, is usually very obliging and you need never feel really stuck as in the end they'll fix you up with something in your price range.

As in many other countries, the towns are ideally laid out for euro-railers and many of the cheap hotels are near the stations. In smaller places, look out for signs hanging up saying *Zimmer frei* (room to let) or *Gasthof* (inn), and for private accommodation turn to Tourist Information for lists.

With over 2,000 campsites in Germany, you shouldn't find any problems. Again, Tourist Information will have a free map and brochure showing where they are. Facilities are generally very good and prices usually fair.

There is still a problem in eastern Germany, due to the demand and lack of infrastructure. This is despite the fact that private citizens are now able to offer B&B, and formerly East Germans-only establishments are now available. Inter hotel prices have now risen beyond the budget traveller's range – upwards from £80. This effectively leaves the former Jugendtourist hostels and campsites, but even here the demand will mean overcrowding. Ask at local Tourist Information offices and *Reisebüro* for suggestions, including Verband Christlicher Hospize, which has hostels in Berlin, Leipzig and Weimar.

EATING AND NIGHTLIFE

German cuisine is as varied as French – the only difference is that the former like to eat more of it. There are countless types of beer and *Würste* (sausages), but it's unfair to think that's all there is, as so many do. The food halls of the large department stores (e.g. Hertie, Kaufhof) are real showpieces, and the quality and quantity of the produce means there's no excuse for not living off picnics and saving your Marks that way. Fast food's also available in the major cities, and *Schnell-Imbiss* stalls with *Würste* and beer also crop up. Note that if you drink at one of the beer gardens, it is not unusual to be charged a deposit for your glass – remember to claim it back. Alcoholic drinks can be very expensive in Germany.

As far as regional specialities go, try some of the following: *Grünkohl mit Pinkel* (green cabbage with bacon sausage) from the north, *Sauerbraten* (braised beef in sour sauce) from the west, and for your picnics sample Westphalian *Pumpernickel* (black bread) or *Vollkornbrot* (bread made of whole unground grains of wheat). Many of the *Würste* look revolting, but don't let that put you off. Vegetarians tend not to be well catered for here.

The Germans are keen on large-scale celebrations: some of their festivals resemble Wagnerian opera sets and no expense is spared. If you get a chance to join in, do. As far as music goes, the classics are always well represented and there's an active jazz and disco scene in all the major cities.

Berlin city phone code: 030, occasionally '9' in front of eastern Berlin numbers

There is literally no other city in Europe, or elsewhere, like Berlin. It was once as beautiful and cosmopolitan as Paris or London, but was reduced to rubble in the Second World War. Then in August 1961 the city was cut in 2 by the notorious Wall which split life on either side between the 2 political polarities. Recent events are obvious, and very little of the Wall remains. Now the capital of the united Germany, Berlin is undoubtedly one of the great cities of the world. With a background as dramatic as this, it's only to be expected that it is a city of extremes and contradictions. This was the city at the heart of the Cold War of the mid-20th century and that alone makes it significant enough for a visit – it's not so much the sights that are worth coming for, as the atmosphere, the world-famous *Berliner Luft*. The tremendous changes have made Berlin, once again, a vibrant and exciting city. Even so the 2 halves still have their obvious differences.

STATION FACILITIES

The 3 main stations are Bahnhof Zoo (Zoologischer Garten), Hauptbahnhof (formerly Ostbahnhof) and Lichtenberg. Bahnhof Zoo and Hauptbahnhof currently serve international destinations, and Lichtenberg domestic and eastbound trains, but check timetable carefully. Hauptbahnhof has been undergoing massive rebuilding of its platforms, so watch your feet. The formerly important border station, Friedrichstrasse, has lost its importance, and its steel dividing wall. When arriving, use Bahnhof Zoo.

Train information is available on a central number – 030 19419 – and all stations are open 24 hours. Lichtenberg doesn't have a foreign exchange bureau but other than that all 3 stations have post offices, 24-hour left-luggage lockers, shops, toilets and restaurants. There are also Tourist Offices at all 3 stations.

Luggage lockers also available at Alexanderplatz and Friedrichstrasse S-Bahn stations. Daily trains from Hauptbahnhof to Munich (8 hours direct, 7 with changes), Frankfurt (Oder) (1 hour), from Lichtenberg to Warsaw (6 hours), Dresden (2 hours); from Bahnhof Zoo to Cologne (5½ hours), Hamburg (3 hours), Frankfurt am Main (5 hours), Würzberg (4½ hours) and Hannover (3 hours).

GETTING AROUND

A variety of tickets covering different parts of the transport network are available, so consider the options carefully. A single ticket covering the whole BVG network for 2 hours costs 3.70DM (multiple tickets, *Sammelkanen*, allow 4 journeys for 12DM). A day ticket valid for 24 hours costs 15DM. A 'Welcome Card' (29DM) gives unlimited travel on all public transport for 3 days, plus reductions on entry to many museums, theatres and tours. If you're staying for longer, then the 7-day or -month *Umweltkarte* costs 40DM or 88DM. All multiple tickets must be obtained from the machines at S-Bahn and U-Bahn stations or from the BVG office in front of Bahnhof Zoo. Individual and multiple tickets must be validated before use.

Now the BVG controls all of the system, tickets purchased on the western side are valid everywhere, but only eastern citizens can use their tickets in the west. So if heading to the eastern side, take sufficient tickets to get back. When the subsidy is removed this restriction will not apply.

TOURIST INFORMATION AND ADDRESSES

TOURIST OFFICE On the Budapesterstrasse side of the Europa Centre, open Mon.–Sat.: 8 a.m.–10.30 p.m.; Sun. 9 a.m.–9 p.m. (Tel. 262 6031). Accommodation service for 5DM. The free book *Berlin for Young People* is excellent. Among other bits of interesting information, it lists 20 or so cheap pensions. Tourist Office at Hauptbahnhof, on upper level. Open daily 8 a.m.–8 p.m. (Tel. 279 5209) Also at the Berlin Bahnhof Zoo (Tel. 313 9063), open 8 a.m.–11 p.m., and in the Tegel Airport Main Hall, open 8 a.m.–11 p.m. (Tel. 4101 3145).

POST OFFICE Bahnhof Zoo. Open Mon.–Fri.: 6 a.m.–midnight, Sat.–Sun.: 8 a.m.-midnight. Also *poste restante* here. Most offices are open 8 a.m.–6 p.m. weekdays.

AMEX Uhlandstrasse. 173 (Tel. 884 58 80) and Kurfürstendamm 11 (2nd floor) (Tel. 882 7575), Mon.–Fri.: 9 a.m.–5.30 p.m., Sat.: 9 a.m.–12 noon.

CURRENCY EXCHANGE Alexanderplatz, Bahnhof Zoo, Friedrichstrasse, Hauptbahnhof, also major hotels.

ARTU REISEBÜRO Hardenbergstrasse 9. Student Travel office selling BIJ tickets and IUS card. Open Mon., Tue., Thur., Fri.: 10 a.m.–6 p.m., Wed.: 11 a.m.–6 p.m., Sat.: 10 a.m.–1 p.m.

UK EMBASSY Unter den Linden 32–34 (Tel. 201840)

IRISH CONSULATE Ernst-Reuter-Platz 10 (Tel. 34 80 08 22)
US CONSULATE Clayallee 170 (Tel. 832 92 33)
CANADIAN CONSULATE Friedrichstrasse 95 (Tel. 261 1161)
AUSTRALIAN CONSULATE Uhlandstrasse 181–3 (Tel. 880 0880).
NEW ZEALAND NATIONALS Contact New Zealand embassy in Bonn.

SEEING

The scant remains of the WALL (*Die Mauer*) where so many people died not so long ago, are the tourist attraction of today. You should cross through the site of the old Checkpoint Charlie to compare the development of the 2 sides of the city separated for so long. The actual hut is now in the facsinating MUSEUM OF THE WALL near the checkpoint on Friedrichstrasse which tells its story. Not far outside the main exit of the Hauptbahnhof is the EAST-SIDE GALLERY – a kilometre of wall has been transformed into an open-air art gallery celebrating freedom.

KURFÜRSTENDAMM (Ku'damm) pulsates with life late into the night and is the city's preferred promenade and thoroughfare. The famous Berlin institution CAFÉ KRANZLER is found on the junction with Joachimstalerstrasse, but eat elsewhere, as it is expensive.

The ruined KAISERWILHELM GEDÄCHTNISKIRCHE is unmissable and the focal point of the Ku'damm and a popular meeting place. The church itself reflects the city's story – it has been built, bombed, partly rebuilt and preserved, and mirrors Berlin's present mixture of old and new. A few metres away beyond an elaborate fountain complex stands the massive EUROPA CENTRE, 4 floors of pubs, shops, discos, boutiques and a cinema which shows a useful introductory film on Berlin's history.

Berlin's premier department store, KaDeWe at Tauenzienstrasse, is well worth a look, especially for its food halls. The SIEGESSÄULE, celebrating Prussian victories in the 1860s and 1870s, can be climbed for an impressive view towards the 18th-century BRANDENBURG GATE.

The TIERGARTEN is a beautiful park, next to the city zoo, which has more species than any other in the world. Next to the zoo is the world's most extensive collection of fish and reptiles in the AQUARIUM on Budapesterstrasse. The OLYMPIC STADIUM conjures up images of Jesse Owens and Hitler and is worth the 1DM entrance fee. Take U-Bahn 1.

SCHLOSS CHARLOTTENBURG lies a few km north-west of Berlin, bus 145 or 204. This 17th-century palace houses several galleries and museums and is the best example of Prussian architecture you'll find around Berlin (closed Mon., students half price). The EGYPTIAN MUSEUM opposite has a fine collection, including the fabulous bust of Queen Nefertiti. The DAHLEM MUSEUM, near U-Bahn Dahlem-Dorf, is a complex of 7 museums (closed Mon.), so you're bound to find something to interest you. The BAUHAUS MUSEUM, with exhibits of the school's designs (closed Tues.), is at Klingelhöferstrasse. The photographic story of German 19th- and 20th-century history at the REICHSTAG BUILDING also makes an interesting visit. Another chilling reminder of the past are the crosses to those shot trying to go over the wall close by.

For a good view over the city, climb the Berlin Radio Mast, FUNK-TÜRM, or the FERNSEHTÜRM (TV Tower) at Alexanderplatz (8 DM). Also see the TEUFELBERG not far away in the GRÜNEWALD. At 114m high, it is the highest hill between Warsaw and the Netherlands. It is made of an enormous mound of rubble from the ruins of Berlin after the Second World War. It now has a ski and toboggan run, whilst at the very peak is an American radar station.

The 1,390m long UNTER DEN LINDEN is the most impressive street of eastern Berlin and is at its very centre. From here you can see the Brandenburg Gate, refurbished during summer 1990, and the east's city centre. The BERLINER DOM (cathedral), closed for many years, is close to the east's old parliament building, now without a function. Not far from here is MUSEUM ISLAND, where the main eastern Berlin museums are located. Avoid Mon., when most are shut. General hours 10 a.m.–5 p.m., but various exhibits only certain days.

On Museum Island are: the PERGAMON (stunning collections of Eastern and Roman artefacts), the BODEMUSEUM with its Egyptian works; the 20th-century art gallery, the ALTES MUSEUM and the NATIONAL GALERIE of 19th-century art. Another museum, undergoing reconstruction, on Museum Island is the NEVNES MUSEUM. The work on this is disrupting the whole area. The MUSEUM FÜR DEUTSCHE GESCHICHTE in the Arsenal (*Zeughaus*), the oldest building on Unter den Linden, has German history from prehistory onwards. The MÄRKISCHES MUSEUM traces Berlin's history, at Am Kölnischen Park, closed Mon./Tues. MARIENKIRCHE is Berlin's oldest church, dating from the 13th century, just off Alexanderplatz.

Old Berlin lives again in the NIKOLAIVIERTEL quarter, a veritable cat's cradle of narrow streets and alleys around the ST NICHOLAS CHURCH. It is interesting for the reconstructed half-timbered buildings, mullioned windows and the odd quaint corner.

For signs of the past, try a walk to the SYNAGOGUE on Oranienburgerstrasse. This was burnt on the infamous Kristallnacht 1938, and in recent years has been undergoing restoration. The MONUMENT TO THE VICTIMS OF FASCISM AND MILITARISM on Unter den Linden and the SOVIET WAR MEMORIAL in Treptower Park, which is reached on the S-Bahn, will set you thinking.

More forward looking travellers can gauge just how ambitious Berlin is by visiting the museum and exhibition box on Strasse des 17. Juni,. near the Brandenburg Gate. A huge red box straddles the construction area and with the help of modern gadgets and gizmos gives a powerful insight into Berlin's history and plans for future development including the rebuilding of the Reichstag.

The Spree River flows through the city and it's possible to take a boat ride on one of the white excursion boats (*Weisse Flotte*) from April to Sept. You can get off at various points: the best is the MECKLENBURGER DORF, a reconstruction of a 19th-century German village. Boats leave 8 times a day from Treptower Park S-Bahn station. (The commentary is usually given in German only.) An alternative is 'Bus 100', which takes in many sights, from the zoo or Alexanderplatz.

A good way to see Berlin is on a walking tour. The Yellow Walking Tour Company meet each morning at 10 a.m. outside Banhof Zoo. For 10DM you'll get an up-beat, 3-hour historical and cultural insider's guide to the city.

SLEEPING

Finding a bed isn't easy and this is one city where you would be really wise to book ahead; write about 2–3 weeks in advance to the Verkehrsamt Berlin at the Europa Centre, 10787 Berlin 30 stating how much you can pay. Try booking flats through Zeitraum, who charge from 30DM per day, discounts for students. Open Mon.–Fri.: 10 a.m.–1 p.m. and 3 p.m.–7 p.m. at Horstweg 7, 1000 Berlin 19 (Tel. 030 325 6181). Mitwohnzentralen's room- finding service comes highly recommended. Contact them at least a week in advance at Ku'damm Eck, Kurfürstendamm 227–228, Berlin (Tel. 88 30 51) and they could find you a room for as little as 40DM. They take a 3DM service fee.

During peak periods, Berlin's budget accommodation becomes scarce. If you aren't organized enough to plan ahead, don't worry; ask at Tourist Information for their map of Berlin with all the hotel and hostel listings. For hotels look at the board at Bahnhof Zoo, though they tend to be expensive. You will probably have better luck in the old West Berlin, due to lack of established facilities on the eastern side. But you could try your luck at desk 13 of *Reisebüro* on Alexanderplatz or Jugendtourist, which is also situated there.

HOSTELS Ernst Reuter (IYHA) at Hermsdorfer Damm 48–50, 13467 Berlin (Tel. 404 1610) is good, though well out of the town centre, in a leafy suburb, by a lake; 26DM per night including breakfast, U-Bahn 6 to Tegel then bus 125 (ISIC reductions).

Jugendgästehaus Berlin (IYHA) at Kluckstrasse 3, 10785 Berlin (Tel. 261 1097) is the most central, 32DM including breakfast. It is 10 minutes from Ku'damm by bus 129 or U-Bahn to Kurfürstenstrasse. Being central, it gets very busy, so don't count on getting in.

Although it is 20 minutes on the S-Bahn to Nikolassee, try also at Jugendgastehaus am Wannsee (IYHA), Badeweg 1, Ecke Kronprinzess-Innenweg 14129 Berlin (Tel. 803 2034). It is clean, cheap and very modern (32DM per night). Each room has its own shower, breakfast included. To book these hostels contact DJH Central Booking Service, Kluckstrasse 3, 10785 Berlin (Tel. 26 23 024).

The Studentenhotel is at Meiningerstrasse 10, Berlin 62 (Tel. 784 6720), a way out at Schöneberg. Take bus 146 or U-Bahn 4 to Rathaus Schöneberg; cost for 2-bed room 36DM. You can't check in until 2 p.m. but it is possible to leave luggage there. No curfew.

PENSIONS The area round Fasanenstrasse and Uhlandstrasse is your best bet. Also on Carmerstrasse, Grolmannstrasse and Knesebeckstrasse.

Try Pension Savoy (Tel. 881 3700) at Meinekestrasse 4; just next door are Pension Zeinert (Tel. 881 3319) at no. 5 and Pension Witzleben (Tel. 881 6395) at no. 6. Also ask at Tourist Information for B&B, now opening up on the eastern side of the city.

CAMPING Camping Haselhorst, Pulvermuhlenweg (Tel. 334 5955), is very good and easily accessible. Take bus 204 from U-Bahn Paulsternstrasse or get to U-Bahn Haslehorst and walk.

Try the friendly Camping Kladow 1 and 11, Krampnitzer Weg 111/117, bus 135, then 135e (Tel. 365 2797).

Or Zeltplatz Dreilinden, Kremnik-Ufer (Tel. 805 1201), bus 118. Kohlhasenbrücke, Neue Kreisstrasse, U-Bahn Oskar-Helene-Heim, bus 18 (Tel. 805 1737).

Also try the former Intercamping Krossinsee site – tram 86 to end, then walk across bridge, and take the third turning on the right.

In response to the huge demand for low-budget accommodation in Berlin, city authorities have established 'The Tent' Übernachtung im Zelt, another option for backpackers. Ask at the tourist centres. If you're desperate, the Bahnhofmission in the station will help out.

EATING AND NIGHTLIFE

Berlin's a big cultural centre and there's always plenty happening in the evenings. Festival follows festival and the student community is large and active. Head off to the area round Konstanzerstrasse, Düsseldorferstrasse, Joachimstalerstrasse and Lietzenburgerstrasse.

With literally thousands of pubs, clubs and discos you should find something to occupy you. Many of the bars in the former East Berlin are north of the river from Friedrichstrasse station. Try the Kleine Melodic, Friedrichstrasse 127, for a disco.

For a taste of the 1930s' Berlin atmosphere try Zum Trichler on Schiffbauerdamm, only a stone's throw from the Brecht Ensemble Theatre. A very atmospheric place to have a drink as the walls are lined with old photos of Brechtian productions, murals and clocks. There is even a small stage for cabaret performances.

In the Irish Pub on Eisenacherstrasse (and also in the Europa Centre) you're guaranteed to meet a fellow Brit, most of the staff speak English and in Leierkasten on Zossenerstrasse you'll bump into the local students.

Tip, the bi-weekly listing of what's on, and *Zitty* are worth buying if you're staying a while. Nollendorfplatz and Winterfeldtplatz are the areas for hardcore clubbers. Check out E-Werk (Wilhelmstrasse 43) and Quasimodo (Kantstrasse 12). Techno freaks should not miss Berlin's *Love Parade* usually on the second weekend in July. Last year's techno bonanza attracted some 750,000 ravers. For Happy House go to Tacheles (Orienburgerstrasse 53). Groove, Acid Jazz and Soul seekers head for Delicious Doughnuts (Rosethalerstrasse. 9).

If you miss a hostel curfew don't despair, as many bars begin to serve breakfast at 2 a.m. and Berlin is literally open all night. The cafés here are an institution. Try Schlander on Olivaer Platz. The department stores have good cafeterias and there are fast-food chains and sausage stands. There are many good authentic Turkish restaurants on Oranienstrasse in Kreuzberg.

GAY AND LESBIAN BERLIN As one of Europe's leading gay and lesbian cities, there's no shortage of clubs, bars and other facilities. First the practicalities: the German word for 'gay' is *Schwul* and 'lesbian' is *Lesben*. Men can get information from the gay info centre Mann-o-Meter, Motzstrasse 5 (Tel. 216 80 08) and lesbians can try the Spinnboden-Lesbenarchiv, Anklamerstrasse 38 (Tel. 448 58 48). There's also the Schwules Museum at Mehringdamm 61.

For entertainment try Hafen on Motzstrasse, or the area around the Nollendorfplatz. Don't miss Christopher Street Day Parade in the last weekend of June.

Potsdam city phone code: 0331

In 1744, Frederick the Great chose this town as his permanent seat and from then on Potsdam flourished to become one of the main imperial centres of Europe. As Potsdam is less than an hour from the centre of Berlin (take S-Bahn line S3), it can be treated as a day trip, but, be warned, there is a lot to see.

The impressive SANS SOUCI PARK and surroundings contain baroque palaces and elaborate pavilions. The SANS SOUCI SCHLOSS, the large NEUES PALAIS, SCHLOSS CHARLOTTENHOF, the ORANGERIE and gold-plated CHINESE TEAHOUSE are all here. Nearby is the SICILIAN GARDEN. Another large park, the NEUERGARTEN, on the shores of a lake, includes the SCHLOSS CECILIENHOF, scene of the Three Powers' agreement to divide Germany. Part of this complex is now an expensive hotel. Most palaces are open 9 a.m.–5 p.m., closing at lunchtime; some also close Mon. and out of season. The city centre has been extensively rebuilt, but the Dutch quarter retains its charm and elegance. Just outside the town is the incredible EINSTEIN OBSERVATORY TOWER. Make the effort to see it if you can.

The Tourist Office is at Friedrich-Ebert-Strasse 5 (Tel. 21100). Take one of several trams to the city centre from the Potsdam-Stadt station. Ask at Tourist Information for the usual leaflets, maps and accommodation suggestions. At present the only hostel is shut, with no plans to reopen it. There are several campsites, but some distance away. With its proximity to Berlin, it might be better to commute. While in Potsdam eat out at Altes Jagdschloss, Am Jagdschloss Stern and have a beer at the Froschkasten on Kiezstrasse.

Dresden city phone code: 0351

Two hours from Berlin, Dresden is the cultural centre of eastern Germany and, though the old city was devastated by saturation bombing in February 1945, what was left was carefully restored. The new city is green and well laid out.

STATION FACILITIES

The train information desk and travel centre is open Mon.–Fri.: 6.15 a.m.–9 p.m., weekends 7 a.m.–9 p.m. Reservations can be made 5 a.m.–10 p.m.; 6 p.m. on Sat. and Sun. There's all the usual shops, left-luggage facilities and cafés and the station is open 24 hours. There is a post office near Hauptbahnhof (on Pragerstrasse).

Through trains use the elevated platforms on each side, terminating ones the central platforms.

Daily departures to Berlin (Lichtenberg) (1½ hours), Leipzig, Munich (6 hours), Cologne (7½ hours), Hamburg (5½ hours), Hannover (4½ hours), Frankfurt (6 hours), Warsaw.

There is another main station, Bahnhof-Neustadt, and many trains call at both with eastbound ones tending to use Neustadt only. The facilities here are similar to those at Hauptbahnhof.

TOURIST INFORMATION

Dresden information centre is at Pragerstrasse 10/11 (Tel. 491920) (5 minutes from station). Open Mar.–Oct.: Mon.–Sat.: 9 a.m.–8 p.m.; Sun.: 9 a.m.–12 noon.; Nov.–Feb.: Mon.–Sat.: 9 a.m.–6 p.m. You can change money here (Mon.–Fri. only). The what's on leaflet, *Dresden-Information*, is also available. Bus and tram tickets have to be bought in advance. Most of the worthwhile sites are walkable from Hauptbahnhof, along pedestrianized Pragerstrasse. There is also a Tourist Information office at Neustädter Markt (Tel. 53539) which is open Mon.–Fri.: 9 a.m.–6 p.m.; Sat.: 9 a.m.–4 p.m.; Sun. 11 a.m.–4 p.m.

SEEING

Head down Pragerstrasse, then bear left towards the river where most of the sights are located. Near to Pragerstrasse is the KREUZKIRCHE, which houses a cross made of nails taken from the ruins of Coventry cathedral. At the ALBERTINUM, one of Dresden's great museum complexes, you will find included the GRÜNES GEWOLBE (Green Vault), containing a fabulous collection of the treasures of the Saxon dukes. Opens 10 a.m., closed Thurs. Walk further down the Brühlschen Terrasse above the River Elbe, where you will pass down the Munzgasse. Down here are the remains of the devastated FRAUENKIRCHE, which is surrounded by rubble, but is now being rebuilt. Further along the river is the Catholic CATHEDRAL and the immense RESIDENZSCHLOSS, the palace of the Saxon electors and dukes. It is being rebuilt from the ruins and is hoped to be finished by 2006 for the city's 800th anniversary. Next comes the magnificent OPERA HOUSE. Close by is the old Augustinerbrücke, leading to the New Town across the river, which holds little of interest except a statue of the GOLDEN RIDER, Augustus the Strong, so-named because he fathered 300 children.

Back on this side of the river, close to the opera, is the unmissable ZWINGER PALACE, an incredible piece of baroque architecture containing half of Dresden's impressive museums: the magnificent GEMÄLDEGA-LERIE ALTER MEISTER (closed Mon.); the HISTORIC MUSEUM OF WEAPONS (closed Mon.); the MATHEMATISCH-PHYSIKALISCHER SALON (maths and physics, closed Thurs.); and both the ZINNSAMMLUNG and the PORZEL-LANSAMMLUNG display the famous Dresden porcelain (closed Fri.).

SLEEPING

The youth hostel at Hübnerstrasse 11 (Tel. 4710667), a few blocks from the station, down Winckelmannstrasse, then into Schnorr-strasse, which leads into Hubnerstrasse, is one possibility at 22DM including breakfast.

The other hostel is the Oberloschwitz at Sierksstrasse 33 (Tel. 36672). Take tram 5 to Nürnbergerplatz, change to bus 61 or 93, get off 2 stops after crossing the Elbe. Then it is only a short walk away. Again 22DM.

The campsites are far flung; ask at the Tourist Information Centre for full details. A series of sites are located to the north, in a wooded area; take bus 81 to the terminus, then a 15-minute walk. The Tourist Office will also find rooms in private houses.

EATING

Restaurants in the Am Zwinger complex on Wilsdufferstrasse are worth trying for cheap meals. Places in the Neustadt away from the touristy areas offer better value. Also try Am Thor on Hauptstrasse for a drink. The cafés on the cobbled Munzgasse are worth a try.

Leipzig city phone code: 41

The second city in eastern Germany is only 1½ hours from Dresden, and though it is more a commercial and industrial centre, there are still enough points of interest to make it worth a stop-off. It makes a fascinating contrast to some of the more opulent western towns: bullet holes in walls, crumbling façades of buildings, the old-fash-ioned feel of the tram service. The atmosphere of Second World War damage and post-1945 neglect is still tangible. The Hauptbahnhof is reputedly Europe's largest terminus, with 26 platforms. Tourist Infor-mation is at Sachsenplatz 1 (Tel. 71040/710 4322), open weekdays: 9 a.m.–6 p.m., Sat.: 9 a.m.–12 noon.

STATION FACILITIES

Leipzig Hauptbahnhof has a train information desk open 6 a.m.–10 p.m. (Tel. 0341 70211), with reservations being possible during the same hours. The foreign exchange is open Mon.–Fri.: 7 a.m.–7.30 p.m., Sat.: 10 a.m.–4 p.m, and there are all the usual shops, left-luggage lockers and cafés. The station shuts 11.15 p.m.–4.30 a.m. This is Europe's largest terminus and many facilities are duplicated, so if one is shut, look around. Leipzig's small S-Bahn system departures are also from here (platforms 6 and 7).

Daily departures to Berlin (Lichtenberg) (2 hours), Cologne (6 hours), Dresden (1½ hours), Hannover (3½ hours), Frankfurt am Main (4½ hours), Munich (6 hours) and Warsaw.

SEEING

The main part of Leipzig that is worth seeing is within the RING promenade, a partly pedestrianized area, starting opposite the station. Bach spent his last 27 creative years working as the *Kantor* (Choirmaster) in ST THOMAS'S CHURCH and is buried here. The boys' choir, once conducted by Bach, can be heard on most Fri. evenings and Sat. afternoons. Dating from 1212 and 1496, St Thomas's was recently being restored. The old, 16th-century ALTES RATHAUS (town hall) now houses the city history museum. The NIKOLAIKIRCHE, located nearby, and a focal point of opposition in autumn 1989, is also worth a visit.

As well as having associations with Bach, Leipzig has other musical connections, with Mendelssohn, for example, who conducted the Gewandhaus Orchestra, Europe's oldest, and financed a monument to Bach. The city also has strong literary connections, with large numbers of bookshops and libraries. Goethe set the scene between Faust and the devil in the AUERBACH'S KELLER in Madlerpassage, the decorations of which are now based on the book.

EXCURSION Near Leipzig is the small town of COLDITZ, location of the famous castle which was used as an officers' POW camp in the Second World War, the story of which was made into a film and later a TV series. Much of the castle is inaccessible to the public, but the trip is worthwhile, and the beer brewed here is excellent. A plan to turn the castle into a tourist attraction will lead to a certain amount of disruption in the next few years. Ask at the Tourist Information Centre for details, particularly important if you wish to see the cellars and church escape sections, as this must be arranged with the appropriate museum authorities.

SLEEPING AND EATING

As with the rest of what was East Germany, hotels formerly in the budget pocket are now well outside it. The Jugendherberge hostel is at Käthe-Kollwitz Strasse 64/66 (Tel. 470530). Take tram 2 to just before the Klingebrücke (bridge).

A second hostel, Am Auensee, is at Gustav-Esche-Strasse 4 (Tel. 4611114). Take the S-Bahn to Wahren, or tram 10, 11 or 28 from the Hauptbahnhof. Trams 10 and 28 terminate at Wahren, then walk down Linkelstrasse, continue into Strasse der Jungen Pioniere. There are also some signs to the nearby Auensee campsite, at Gustav-Esche-Strasse 5 (Tel. 4611977).

Ask the Tourist Offices about private accommodation.

There are plenty of reasonably priced restaurants and pubs, but expect the costs to be approaching western German levels. The best places to eat are near the Markt. There are also cheap self-service restaurants on Grimmäischestrasse. There is a well stocked supermarket opposite the station's Wintergartenstrasse exit and in the Horfeu department store.

Weimar

Homeland of Cranach, Bach, Liszt, Schiller, Goethe and Nietzsche and the Buchenwald concentration camp, this town was also the site of the first German Republic (the Weimar Republic) which fell in the 1930s, just before Nazism rose to power. It is only an hour from Leipzig and makes a good day trip from there if you're in a rush and can't spare the time to stay.

TOURIST INFORMATION

Weimar-Information, Marktstrasse 4 (Tel. 202 173), open Mon.–Fri.: 9 a.m.–7 p.m.; Sat.: 9 a.m.–4 p.m. Take bus 1, 4, 6 or 7 from the station to Goetheplatz and walk to Theaterplatz, then along Schillerstrasse to the Marktplatz. Tourist Information is off the square, to the right of the Rathaus. They can arrange the usual bus tickets, accommodation and a museum pass.

SEEING

The LUCAS-CRANACH HAUS is the richly decorated Renaissance building in the Marktplatz. Close by is the SCHLOSSMUSEUM, with its collection of German Renaissance works, and the Gothic church, HERDERKIRCHE. The KIRMS-KRACKHOW HAUS has displays on the philosopher Herder and poets Schiller and Goethe, among others.

There are museums devoted to Schiller and Goethe, also within walking distance. Another famous son of Weimar, Liszt, also has a museum here.

EXCURSIONS The rococo SCHLOSS BELVEDERE, a former royal summer palace, can be reached by bus from Goetheplatz – ask at the information office for details. The Nazi concentration camp of BUCHENWALD can also be reached by bus, leaving from stop no. 31, near the Hauptbahnhof. Now it is a grim memorial to the more than 56,000 Jews, communists and others killed between 1937 and 1945. An excellent English guidebook is available from the memorial bookshop.

SLEEPING AND EATING

The Am Poseckschen Garten hostel, at Humboldtstrasse 17 (Tel. 64021), charges 22DM per person for B&B, including linen. It's around 2½ km from the station.

The Germania Youth Hostel, at Carl-August-Allee 13 (Tel. 850491), has 121 beds, 22DM. Ask at Tourist Information for details of private B&B.

There is no convenient campsite – the nearest is listed under Erfurt, and is some distance from here.

People eat early in Weimar and you'll find places closing from 8 p.m., and all weekend, so get some supplies in. Try All Weimar, Steubenstrasse 27, or the Elephantkeller on the Markt.

Erfurt

This is the capital of the forested and mountainous region of Thuringia, a short journey from Weimar. The very well-preserved medieval centre of the City of Flowers makes the trip well worthwhile. The Tourist Information Centre is on the road to the railway station, at Bahnhofstrasse 37 (Tel. 562 6267) and near the City Hall at Krämerbrücke 3 (Tel. 562 34346). Open at Bahnhofstrasse Mon.–Fri.: 9 a.m.–6 p.m., Sat.: 10 a.m.–3 p.m., at Krämerbrücke Mon.–Fri.: 10 a.m.–6 p.m., Sat.–Sun.: 10 a.m.–4 p.m.

The twin towers of the Gothic CATHEDRAL and the 13th-century ST SERVERUS CHURCH, on the Domberg, dominate Erfurt's skyline. The unusual bridge, KRÄMERBRÜCKE, is lined with a collection of restored 14th-century houses. Not far away is the ANGER, a restored street of

Renaissance and Art Nouveau buildings. Erfurt boasts several monastic buildings, including the Gothic AUGUSTINERKLOSTER, a 13th-century complex, restored after war damage. Martin Luther, who was briefly a monk in Erfurt, has an exhibition here.

The youth hostel is at Hochheimerstrasse 12, about 5 km from the centre. Take line 5 from Hofbahnhof to Hochheimerstrasse (Tel. 526705). Cost per person: 24DM per night. Otherwise ask at the Tourist Office for private accommodation or for the scarce cheap hotels. If stuck, try commuting from Weimar, 20 minutes away by train.

Northern Germany

Northern Germany – the area between Schleswig and Bremen – is comparatively unspoilt by tourism. The main centres of interest are Bremen, Hamburg and Lübeck, and also you could take in the little towns of HAMELN (of Pied Piper fame) and CELLE, if you've enough time left.

Bremen city phone code: 0421

Bremen, with its port, Bremerhaven, is the oldest seaport in Germany. The Tourist Information office is right in front of the station, open Mon.–Wed., Fri.: 9.30 a.m.–6.30 p.m.; Thurs.: 9.30 a.m.–8.30 p.m.; Sat.: 9.30 a.m.–6.30 p.m.; Sun.: 9.30 a.m.–3.30 p.m. (Tel. 30800)

Tackle Bremen on foot and take in the old medieval section round the MARKTPLATZ, the RATHAUS, the STATUE OF ROLAND and ST PETER'S 11th-century CATHEDRAL with its cellar full of mummified bodies. The old section of the town called the SCHNOOVIERTEL is particularly attractive, with its narrow winding streets dating back to the 1500s and its half-timbered houses. Take a stroll down the WALLANLAGEN (Rampart Walk) with its windmill. Have a look in the craft shops in Böttcherstrasse, a narrow pedestrian street.

The youth hostel is at Kalkstrasse 6 (Tel. 171102), about 20 minutes' walk from the station, or bus 26 or tram 6 from the station to Brill.

The campsite at Am Stadtwaldsee 1 is excellent. Take bus 26 outside station. At Hemmstrasse, change to bus 28, which stops at the campsite. Clean, friendly, with a good cheap restaurant, it's only open Apr.–Oct. and costs 7DM per person and 4–8DM per tent.

Hamburg city phone code: 040

Germany's second largest city, after Berlin, and largest seaport. Unlike many of Germany's cities, Hamburg does not lack character or things to see.

STATION FACILITIES
The train information is open daily, 6 a.m.–11 p.m. (Tel. 30051201) and reservations desk daily, 5.30 a.m.–11 p.m. There's 24-hour a service point and during normal hours there are all the usual facilites including a post office.

Daily trains to: Copenhagen (5 hours), Hannover (1½ hours), Frankfurt (3½ hours), Vienna, Munich (5½ hours), Basel (6½ hours), Zürich, Milan, Bremen (1 hour), Düsseldorf (3¾ hours), Cologne (4 hours), Brussels, Paris.

The Hamburg metro, particularly around the Hauptbahnhof, is unsavoury at night, so be careful.

TOURIST INFORMATION AND ADDRESSES
There is a Tourist Information office inside the station (open daily all year round, 7 a.m.–11 p.m.), and the head office is just around the corner on HachmarmpPlatz, open Mon.–Fri.: 9 a.m.–6 p.m.; Sat.: 9 a.m.–3 p.m. They'll supply you with maps, a fortnightly programme of local events, *Where to Go in Hamburg*, and *The Hamburg Guide*. Ask for Muzikszene, Tango or Oxmox for entertainment.

A cheap suggestion for those wishing to see several of the sights: try the Hamburg Card. Available from any Tourist Office, it covers the city transport systems, as well as 11 museums. Current prices are 10.80DM for a 1-day ticket and 21DM for a 3-day ticket.

There's a separate information office (*Hotelnachweis*) also at the station and they'll find you a bed for a fee. Rail pass holders go free on Hamburg's S-Bahn.

US CONSULATE Alsterufer 27 (Tel. 411710).
BRITISH CONSULATE Harvesthuder Weg 8a (Tel. 448 0320)
IRISH CONSULATE Feldbrunnenstrasse 43 (Tel. 4418 6213)
NEW ZEALAND CONSULATE Heinthuderstrasse 56 (Tel. 4425 550)
Other nationals should contact Bonn or Berlin.

POST OFFICE Munzstrasse 1, is near the station. *Poste restante* and 24-hour telephone service are here also.
AMEX Rathausmarkt 5 (Tel. 331 141)
STUDENT TRAVEL OFFICE Rothenbaumchaussee 61 (Tel. 410 2081) is worth a visit.
24-HOUR CHEMIST Tel. 228 02

SEEING

The PORT dominates the city and is difficult to ignore. It's also quite interesting to watch what goes on and there are tours of it available. The best leave from Landungsbrücken. ST MICHAEL'S, the 18th-century baroque brick church, affords a good view from its tower, currently under renovation. If there at 10 a.m. or 9 p.m., listen out for the tower herald playing his trumpet. Lift up the tower costs 3.50DM. Of the many museums in Hamburg the best are: the HAMBURG ART GALLERY; the DECORATIVE ARTS AND CRAFTS MUSEUM; the MILLERS' VETERAN CAR MUSEUM; and the HAMBURG HISTORY MUSEUM. Take a day trip to the nearby open-air museums: the VIERLANDE MUSEUM (S-Bahn to Berge-dorf) and the MUSEUM VILLAGE in Volksdorf (U-Bahn). All museums are closed Mon.

SLEEPING

There are plenty of cheap pensions north of the station along Stein-damm and Bremer Reihe so you shouldn't have any problems. Consider spending 1DM for the Hotelführer list available from the Tourist Office. Try Pension Nord at 22 Bremer Reihe (Tel. 244 693).

At 24DM the Jugendherberge auf dem Stintfang Hostel overlooking the harbour is excellent, though the evening meal is poor value. It is at Alfred-Wegener-Weg 5 (Tel. 313 488). Always use the lockers provided, as security has been a problem in recent years. Nearby Landungs-brücken station is on both S-Bahn (free to Inter-Rail) and U-Bahn.

Less central is the Horner-Rennbahn hostel at Rennbahnstrasse 100 (Tel. 6511671). Take the U-Bahn to Horner-Rennbahn.

Also try Pension Terminus, Steindamm 5 (Tel. 2803 144), 50–70DM for a twin room, including breakfast and shower, and with helpful English-speaking staff. Pension Sternschanze (Tel. 433389), Schanzenstrasse 101, located close to the Congress Centre and the student area, is good value.

The best of the campsites, Buchholz, is at Kielerstrasse 374 (Tel. 540 4532), open summer.

For cheap hotels – and there are plenty – head for the commercial area or, if you don't mind the noise of squeaking bedsprings, the red-light district.

EATING AND NIGHTLIFE

The university Mensa is at Schlüterstrasse 7 and represents your best bet. Being a port, seafood and fish restaurants are plentiful and good in Hamburg. Try the ones along Landungsbrücken or the Fischerhaus at the St Pauli fish market. Landüngsbrücken however, has recently become more expensive. Also try near the station. One thing Hamburg's not short of is nightlife. The famous Reeperbahn and St Pauli area is one of the liveliest in Europe with the trendiest clubs, discos and bars in the town. The sex shops and porn movie-houses, which made the area's name, are also obvious, but this should not put you off. Use your judgement to avoid falling into the tourist rip-off traps: also do not look for beds in the Palais d'Amour as it offers more than beds for the night.

Before leaving Hamburg be sure to visit DIE FABRIK on Barnerstrasse, one of Germany's first and best-known youth centres for music and student hangouts. Also try the laid-back Templehof (Hamburger Berg 12), Mojo-Club at 1 Reeperbahn or Hamburg's oldest jazz venue, The Cotton Club at Alter Steinweg 10.

Lübeck city phone code: 0451

Only 40 minutes away from Hamburg is the attractive old town of Lübeck, former headquarters of the medieval trading group the Hanseatic League. Since 1987 Lübeck has been a UNESCO World Heritage Site. You'll see as many Scandinavians as Germans here as this is one of their favourite holiday destinations.

Tourist Information is in the station. Open Mon.–Sat.: 10 a.m.–6.30 p.m., Sun.: closed. The office on the Markt is open Mon.–Fri.: 9.30 a.m.–6 p.m., Sat.–Sun.: 10 a.m.–2 p.m. There is also an office at Beckergrube 95, closed weekends.

Lübeck is known as the 'City of Seven Spires' because the skyline is dominated by the spires of 5 imposing churches, including the cathedral. Extensively bombed during the war, you can see the shattered bells at the foot of the former belfry in the MARIENKIRCHE where they have lain undisturbed since being blasted free of their fastenings in 1942. For a good view of the city the lift up the tower of the PETRIKIRCHE is good value at 2.50DM (reductions for students).

Lübeck is renowned for its brickwork, so take a close look at the gabled houses, particularly BUDDENBROOKHAUS, the house Thomas Mann (a Lübecker) used as the background to his novel *Buddenbrooks*. The actual city centre is quite small and it's possible to walk round all the sights there: the 13th-century RATHAUS with its original black glazed tiles, the Romanesque ST MARIEN DOM, the HOLSTEN GATE and the old city walls and MUSEUM.

One of the youth hostels, the Folke-Bernadotte-Heim, is at Am Gertrudenkirchhof 4 (Tel. 451 33433). A second more expensive hostel is at Mengstrasse 33 (Tel. 451 70399). A good campsite at Steinrader Damm 12 (Tel. 893090) is reached by bus 7 or 8 from the station towards Dornbreite. The buses stop near the site entrance. Tourist Information will find other rooms for you.

Hannover city phone code: 0511

Primarily known as a centre for trade fairs, Hannover is nevertheless deserving of a visit. Hannover will host the world exhibition Expo' 2000.

The Tourist Information office is next to the main station at Ernst-August-Platz 2 (Tel. 0511 301421). Open 8.30 a.m.–6 p.m., until 2 p.m. on Sat. Ask for the booklet *The Red Thread* which takes you around the main sights of the city by following a red line painted on the pavements.

Sights worthy of special mention are the 300-year-old ROYAL GARDENS, BAROQUE GARDEN, BERGGARTEN and GEORGE GARDEN. The gardens are linked to the city by the 1½ km Herrenhausen Avenue lined by 1,300 lime trees. The gardens are often the venue for music and theatre, and Festivals of Light are often held. Check with Tourist Information for details.

Look out for the Marksmen Festival and Lake Maschsee Festival during the summer. The flea market on Hohes Ufer every Sat. is an interesting diversion. The KESTNER MUSEUM, the MUSEUM OF HISTORY and LOWER SAXONY REGIONAL MUSEUM are also worth a look.

The hostel is at Ferdinand-Wilhelm-Fricke-Weg 1 (Tel. 0511 1317674), 20 minutes from the station on tram 7 or 3 to Fischerhof. A more expensive youth guest house operates at the same address.

There is also the Naturfreundehaus at Hermann-Bahlsen-Allee 8 (Tel. 051 691493), 30 minutes from the station by tram 3 or 7 to Spannhagenstrasse.

Eurotrain has an office at Karl-Wiechert-Allee 23 (Tel. 0511 5670). The German ICE links Hannover to the southern part of Germany, with Munich 5½ hours away, Frankfurt 2½ hours.

The Central Belt and the Harz Mountains

Frankfurt, Düsseldorf and Bonn are all fairly modern industrial centres which offer little worth breaking your journey for. You would do far better to head for centres like MARBURG, GÖTTINGEN, HANNOVERSCH-MÜNDEN, KARLSHAFEN, GOSLAR or the resorts round Münster: ATTENDORN, ALT-ASTENBURG and BERLEBURG. These have far more of the aspects of German life you're probably looking for.

Baden-Württemberg – the Black Forest

The south-western region of Germany from Karlsruhe to Basel is considered by many travellers its most enchanting. The pace of life is slower and the villages and towns dotted round the forests really are as attractive as the tourist brochures make them look. The main towns of this region are Heidelberg, Freiburg, Tübingen, Baden-Baden and Stuttgart. The first 3 are picturesque old university towns and worth a day or two; unless you've time, forget Baden-Baden as it's very expensive; Stuttgart is an interesting industrial city. A day trip from Heidelberg to Freiburg, Donaueschingen and Offenburg is a good 'pushed for time' introduction to this area.

Heidelberg

Famous for its university and magnificent castle, most of Heidelberg's sights can be seen in a day, and are well worth the trip. Start your tour (get a bus or taxi as it's a 40-minute walk into town) at the MARKTPLATZ and take in the HEILIG-GEIST KIRCHE and HAUS ZUM RITTER, a Renaissance mansion house, now a hotel and restaurant. The OLD UNIVERSITY has an interesting students' jail, *Studentenkarzer*, which proves that graffiti isn't a 20th-century invention. From here cross the Karl-Theodor Bridge or Old Bridge over the River Neckar and take the hour-long PHILOSOPHER'S WALK to the 429m HEILIGENBERG. Apart from a good view of the town, there are reconstructed Roman ruins and the 12th-century ST STEPHEN'S CLOISTER. Back across the river, inside the amazing SCHLOSS is the GERMAN APOTHECARY MUSEUM with interesting reconstructions of laboratories of the 17th century. You can get up to it by funicular railway from Kornmarkt if you don't fancy the climb.

The Tourist Information office, just outside the station, is open Mon.–Sat.: 9 a.m.–7 p.m., Sun. 10 a.m.–6 p.m.: Mar.–Dec., closed Sun. Jan. and Feb. They run an accommodation-finding service for a small fee and supply you with leaflets and maps. Ask for *All Around Heidelberg*, *Heidelberg This Week* and the official town map, which includes a picture map and a walking tour of the main sights.

AMEX is at Friedrich-Ebert Anlage 16. *HS Reisebüro*, who do student travel deals, are at Bismarckplatz (Tel. 06221 27151). Try to get around town by bus and tram. There is a special Tourist Ticket available, 36 hours at 7DM or 11DM depending on the areas travelled; ask at the Tourist Office.

Hotels tend to be expensive, as Heidelberg gets its fair share of middle-class, middle-aged tourists, so they don't cater for eurorailers in a big way. Still, there's a youth hostel at Tiergartenstrasse (Tel. 06221 412066), on bus routes 33 or 330 with connecting tram at night.

The Neckertal campsite is in Schlierbach (Tel. 06221 802506). You are not allowed to leave the campsite before 8 a.m., so don't pitch your tent there if you have an early start the next morning. Your passport is kept as security. There is a train station nearby, but services are limited to 2 trains at night, and 1 in the morning. The Haide campsite is between Heidelberg, Ziegelhausen and Kleinge-mund. Take bus 35 to Orthopädische Klinik, then across the bridge and 10 minutes further along the river (Tel. 062232111).

Use the Mensa restaurants for meals – there's one off Universitäts-platz and another in Marstallhof – or an historic student inn. These are dotted all round the city, the most famous including Roter Ochsen, Hauptstrasse 217 and Schnookeloch, Haspelgasse 8. The station restaurant is reasonably priced, providing you pick carefully from the menu. A filling meal with beer can be had for around 15DM.

Freiburg-im-Breisgau city phone code: 0761

An attractive city of over 189,000 people which has fully recovered from its heavy wartime destruction and is restored and as picturesque as ever. Though the university is the source of most young Freiburgers' social life, the summer schools based there make sure things don't grind to a halt outside term-time.

Two blocks down Eisenbahnstrasse from the station is the Tourist Information at Rotteckring 14 (Tel. 368 90 90). They can arrange accommodation for you, or if you're staying more than 2 days, you can get into private accommodation (*Privatzimmer*). Also ask for details of the 24-hour, 48-hour and 72-hour passes. These will save you money if you find yourself staying out of the centre.

The Altstadt (Old Town) has at its centre the MÜNSTER, the beautiful medieval cathedral with its intricate carvings and gargoyles. Climbing the Münster spire is a rewarding and exhilarating experience (cost 1.50DM). Opposite the cathedral to the south is the 16th-century KAUFHAUS (merchants' hall), and nearby is the RATHAUS (town hall) made out of 2 old patrician houses. Medieval and baroque art of the Upper Rhine can be seen in the AUGUSTINER MUSEUM.

There's a youth hostel and a campsite in Kartäuserstrasse at 151 and 99 respectively (Tel. 0761 67656 and 0761 35054). Take tram 1 from the station to Römerhof. With woods and forests all around, you shouldn't be stuck for a place to pitch your tent, but if things are desperate, see the Bahnhofmission at the station.

The last week of June sees the Wine Festival; Baden white wine is well worth trying, and Freiburg has many wine bars and cheap (by German standards) eating places. Concentrate on the university area: Augustinerplatz and Escholzstrasse (where cheap pasta dishes can be found 6–7.30 p.m.).

Tübingen

The University of Tübingen, founded in 1477, still makes use of the town's Renaissance castle (SCHLOSS HOHENTÜBINGEN) and you can only visit it at weekends Apr.–Oct. There is a good view over the old town and the Neckar from its gardens. In the centre there are old gabled houses and a 15th-century church, STIFTSKIRCHE. In the Neckar on a man-made island is the PLATANENALLEE, an avenue of plane trees which makes a good walk. Reach it via the Eberhard bridge.

The youth hostel is at Gartenstrasse 22/2 (Tel. 07071 23002), 10 minutes from the station, and there's a campsite on the banks of the Neckar (Tel. 07071 43145). The university Mensa restaurant is on the corner of Wilhelmstrasse and Keplerstrasse and is open for lunches and dinners.

Stuttgart city phone code: 0711

Described as 'one of the most interesting cities in Europe' by one reader, Stuttgart has got to be worth visiting. Stuttgart is the capital of Baden-Württemberg and, despite being an industrial centre (home to the Porsche factory and Bosch electronics), boasts that over 50% of the city is woods, vineyards and parks. It is also the largest wine-growing city in Germany.

TOURIST INFORMATION

Tourist centre: *i-Punkt*, Königstrasse 1a, near the station (Tel. 0711 2228 240/241), open 9.30 a.m.–8 p.m. (Sat. 9.30 a.m.–6 p.m., Sun. and holidays 11 a.m.–6 p.m., Sun. Nov.–Apr. 1 p.m.–6 p.m.). In addition to providing details of walking tours and maps, they will also provide details of budget accommodation.

Also try JIZ (*Jugend-Informationszentrum*) at Hohestrasse 9 (Tel. 0711 293058), specifically for forthcoming events and where the action is.

SEEING

As the centre of Stuttgart is largely pedestrianized, it is best seen on foot.

SCHLOSSPLATZ and SCHILLERPLATZ are typical of Stuttgart and are surrounded by most of the major sights. The SCHLOSSGARTEN stretches northwards to the River Neckar and here you can enjoy landscaped woods, lakes and a zoo. Stuttgart boasts the most abundant mineral water springs in western Europe, and the mineral baths make an interesting diversion from the Schlossgarten. Alternatively take U14 to Mineralbäder, where LEUZE mineral baths have both an outdoor swimming pool and a heated indoor pool.

Museums especially worth a visit include the imposing extension of the STAATSGALERIE (built by a British architect) on Konrad-Adenauer Strasse and the MERCEDES BENZ AUTOMOBILE MUSEUM just outside the main city, open Tues.–Sun.: 9 a.m.–5 p.m. Take S-Bahn 1 to Neckarstadion or bus 56. All city-owned museums are free of charge.

SLEEPING

Should be no problem as *i-Punkt* will help.

The DJH Hostel at Haussmannstrasse 27 (entrance on the corner of Werastrasse and Kernerstrasse) is central and modern and is only 10 minutes from the station. Take S-Bahn 15 to Eugensplatz (Tel. 0711 241583).

The campsite at Cannstatter Wasen (Tel. 0711 556696 or 561503) is less central, on the banks of the river Neckar. The unofficial *Jugend- actimheim* in Richard- Wagner-Strasse (Tel: 0711 241132) has expensive but comfortable single or double rooms.

EATING AND NIGHTLIFE

It should be easy to find a decent place to eat. Follow the locals to a nearby *Kneipe* for a popular meeting place and refreshment. They normally fill up very quickly and become quite lively. Wine is varied and excellent, whilst local culinary specialities include *Maultaschen* – lentils – with Wiener sausages, and hand-made noodles or roast beef with sauerkraut.

Stuttgart has a lively youth scene and the many jazz clubs are popular. Ask at *i-Punkt*, JIZ or any young resident for the latest details. Not to be missed in summer/early autumn are the variety of street fairs and 'happenings'. Equally, the WINE FESTIVAL in late Aug.–Sept. at Schillerplatz and Marktplatz is lively, whilst the CANSTATT VOLKSFEST in late Sept.–Oct. should not be missed as it is only equalled in scale by the Munich Oktoberfest.

The Harz Mountains

QUEDLINGBURG has some 1,600 protected buildings which provide a unique opportunity to see the development of half-timber construction through the centuries. The historical value of the town has been recognized by UNESCO. Tourist Information is at Markt 2 (Tel. 03946 905622). WERNIGERODE has half-timbered houses, a fine town hall and a hilltop castle, as well as being the starting point of the Ham narrow-gauge steam railway. There are youth hostels at Leninstrasse 53 and Am Grossen Block 27.

To reach either of these small towns, take a train from Halberstadt. Services connect Halberstadt to Magdeburg and Halle. A few buses a day cross the old border to Bad Harzburg, which has train connections to Hannover and Braunschweig.

A short distance from Bad Harzburg is the old imperial town of GOSLAR, with numerous half-timbered buildings, the IMPERIAL PALACE and the frescoed HALL OF HOMAGE in the town hall. Tourist Information is at Marktplatz 7. The youth hostel is at Rammelsbergerstrasse 25 (Tel. 05 321 22240), just outside the old town, 20DM.

The Rhine Valley

The section of the Rhine that flows through Germany is considered the most scenic, and the popular image of sailing down the Rhine is a pleasure cruiser passing vineyards, castles and cliffs. This is founded on truth but is somewhat idealistic as the Rhine today is still Europe's main commercial waterway and as such takes its fair share of barges and freight loads. Köln–Düsseldorfer lines run boats from Frankfurt to Cologne which give a 50% discount to Inter-Railers and are free to Eurail card holders. The most attractive segment of the journey is from Rüdesheim to Koblenz, or vice versa. OBERWESEL is a lovely place, but almost closes down on Mon. The youth hostel is fantastic, complete with swimming pool. It's at Auf dem Schönberg (Tel. 06744 93330) and costs 26.80DM, including breakfast. Phone to book in after 8 a.m. Stop off here on your way from Cologne to Bingen – it's about 3 hours down the line – and finish your journey by boat.

Cologne (Köln) city phone code: 0221

The main reason for stopping off at Cologne is undoubtedly the cathedral (KÖLNER DOM) which took from 1248 to 1880 to complete; see the 14th-century stained-glass windows, altarpiece and the Shrine of the Magi. In the Second World War, 90% of Cologne was razed to the ground, but amazingly the cathedral escaped almost intact. Open 7 a.m.–7 p.m. For an impressive view of the city, climb the 509 steps up the tower (half price with ISIC), tower open 9 a.m.–4, 5 or 6.00 p.m. daily depending on the season.

From Cologne, you can take an hour-long round-trip on the Rhine for around 10DM. It makes 2 stops to allow break of journey, so if you wish to visit the zoo or take the cable-car across the river, this is a relatively cheap and pleasant way to do it. You also get a great view of the *Dom* from the river.

Other things of interest are the ROMAN-GERMANIC MUSEUM exhibiting Cologne's Roman remains and the WALLRAFF-RICHARTZ-MUSEUM/MUSEUM LUDWIG with its impressive collection of German works. The MUSEUM OF ARTS AND CRAFTS at An der Rechtsschule includes vast collections of arts and crafts from the Middle Ages to the present day. Open Tues.–Sun.: 10 a.m.–5 p.m., until 10 p.m. first Thurs. each month. Admission 5DM. Even if you can only afford a few hours you should have no problems, as everything is near the station. Museums are closed on Mon.

EXCURSION If you are based in Cologne, AACHEN is well worth a half-day visit, being 40 minutes away by train. The Rathaus and cathedral are of great interest in this ex-capital of the Holy Roman Empire.

STATION FACILITIES
The HAUPTBAHNHOF has an information desk open from dawn till dusk and a 24-hour service point. It has all the usual amenities and is shut 1 a.m.–4 a.m.

Daily trains to: Düsseldorf (30 mins), Hamburg (4 hours), Copenhagen (9 hours), Hannover (3 hours), Mainz (16¾ hours), Frankfurt -am-Main (2½ hours), Würzburg (3½ hours), Nürnberg (4½ hours), Stuttgart (3 hours), Vienna (10 hours), Munich (5½ hours), Innsbruck, Zürich (6 hours), Basel (4½ hours), Paris (5½ hours), Brussels (2½ hours), Rotterdam (3 hours), The Hague (3 hours), Amsterdam (2½ hours).

SLEEPING
HOSTELS There are 2 hostels in Cologne which are very good but suffer from the same problem – they fill up fast. The nearest to the main station, and reputedly the best, is at Siegesstrasse 5a (Tel. 814711). It's a 20-minute walk across the Rhine, but is only 2 minutes' walk from the Deutz station and is well signposted. 30DM for a bed, breakfast included.

You can also try the other youth hostel at An der Schanze 14 (Tel. 767081), which is more luxurious, but further out and more expensive; 37DM. You cannot book by phone, so get there as soon as possible after reception opens at 11 a.m. Take U-Bahn lines 5, 15, 16 or 18 to Boltensternstrasse and then a 5-minute walk.

CAMPING There are 2 campsites at the end of the Rodenkirchen Bridge. Campingplatz der Stadt Köln is at Weidenweg (Tel. 831966). Although facilities are limited, there is a good bar across the road. Cost is 6DM per person and 4DM per tent. Tourist Information, just opposite the cathedral, will also find rooms from about 35DM upwards.

EATING AND NIGHTLIFE
Salzgasse in the Old Town is where to go for eats, and in the city centre are all the usual excellent department stores with food halls for buying groceries. The square immediately in front of the Cathedral is lively and interesting, often with street musicians performing, and a 'peace wall' to which you can contribute messages.

The Moselle Valley

Less commercial, and some say less scenic, is the Mosel in German region where wine-making is the main regional industry, apart from tourism. Boats run between Cochem and Koblenz (KD lines with the same reductions as on the Rhine). The hostel at Koblenz is very good and overlooks the confluence of the Rhine and Mosel. It's at Koblenz-Ehrenbreitstein on the right bank, bus 7, 8, 9, 10 from the station (Tel. 0261 73737). The towns to get off at are: BERNKASTELKUES, TRABEN-TRARBACH and COCHEM. You can hire bikes at Cochem. This is the region for wine tasting – ask at the Tourist Information offices for tours of the local cellars.

Frankfurt-am-Main city phone code: 069

Frankfurt is Germany's most important finance and trading centre, a city of large skyscrapers with an important international airport and what is claimed to be Europe's largest railway station.

STATION FACILITIES
FRANKFURT (MAIN) HAUPTBAHNHOF is massive. It simply has everything and the only thing to note is that it shuts 1 a.m.–4 a.m., though left-luggage lockers are always available and there's a 24-hour service point.

Daily trains to: Hamburg (3½ hours), Hannover (2½ hours), Munich (3½ hours), Cologne (2½ hours), Berlin (5½ hours), Brussels (5 hours), Amsterdam (5 hours).

TOURIST INFORMATION AND ADDRESSES
TOURIST OFFICE The main Tourist Information Centre, opposite platform 23, is open Mon.–Fri.: 8 a.m.–9 p.m.; Sat.: 8 a.m.–8 p.m.; Sun.: 9.30 a.m.–8 p.m. (Tel. 2123 8849).Another office is at the Römerberg, open Mon.–Fri.: 9 a.m.–6 p.m.; Sat.–Sun.: 9.30 a.m.–5 p.m. (Tel. 2123 8708).
POST OFFICE On the second floor of the station, open 24 hours. The main branch is at Zeil 110; open Mon.–Fri.: 8 a.m.–6 p.m., Sat.: 8 a.m.–noon.
AMEX Kaiserstrasse 8; open Mon.–Fri.: 9.30 a.m.–5.30 p.m., Sat.: 9 a.m.–12 noon

UK CONSULATE Bockenheimer Landstrasse 42 (Tel. 170 0020)
IRISH NATIONALS See Berlin.
US CONSULATE Siesmayerstrasse 21 (Tel. 75350/75352441)
CANADIAN NATIONALS See Berlin.
AUSTRALIAN CONSULATE Gutleutstrasse 85 (Tel. 273 9090)
NEW ZEALAND NATIONALS See Bonn.
24-HOUR DOCTOR Tel. 7950 2200
24-HOUR PHARMACY Tel. 11500

SEEING

An area worth visiting is around THE RÖMERBERG, with the rebuilt 15th-century RÖMER, or city hall, beautiful timber-worked houses and ST NIKOLAIKIRCHE. Nearby is the DOM (Cathedral), built between the 13th and 15th centuries. The coronation of German Emperors look place here between 1562 and 1792. Amongst the museums that are worth a visit are the HISTORICAL MUSEUM, collections from the Middle Ages to the present day, and the GERMAN FILM MUSEUM, about the history and origins of the film industry. The JEWISH MUSEUM, NATURAL HISTORY MUSEUM and various art museums are also worth a look. Museums generally open Tues.–Sun.: 10 a.m.–5 p.m., Wed.: 10 a.m.–8 p.m.

SLEEPING AND EATING

The youth hostel is pleasantly situated across the River Main and on the edge of the city's liveliest area for entertainment and reasonable eating places (with their copious cheap *Apfelwein*), Sachsenhausen. The hostel is at Deutschherrnufer 12 (Tel. 619058). Take tram 16 to Textorstrasse.

The fruit stalls and shops in the underground mall in front of the station are quite good for stocking up on picnic items. Frankfurters are not a Frankfurt speciality (they are known locally as *Wieners*!)

Trier

Germany's oldest city and one-time capital of the western Roman Empire (with Roman baths, arches and amphitheatre remains to prove it), Trier has many interesting churches and museums, as well as the house where Karl Marx was born. Tourist Information is next to the Porta Nigra, the (IYHF) youth hostel is at An der Jugendherberge 4 (Tel. 0651 146620) and the campsites are at Monaiserstrasse (Tel. 0651 86210) and Luxemburgerstrasse 81 (Tel. 0651 86921). Between April and October you could test your sea legs and stay on the good ship Uranus moored in the Mosel (Tel. 0651 35730). A dorm bed will cost 20DM.

For cheap eats try either of the 2 university Mensas at Universität Schneidershof or at the Tarforst campus. The Greek restaurant next to the youth hostel serves good, filling and reasonably-priced meals. For cheap beer and good food, head for the Löwenbrau Brauerei, near the amphitheatre. It is off the Gartenfeldstrasse, 100m after the railway bridge. The tree-shaded patio, where food and drink are served, is across the road from the main entrance. There is also a good market next to the cathedral and while you are there take a look at the impressive interior decor. For a good view of the city itself, follow the Römerstrasse up from the north bank of the Mosel to the Madonna statue.

Munich (München) city phone code: 089

Munich is the capital of Bavaria and is regarded by some as the ultimate German city. It is beautifully landscaped, tastefully decorated, carefully laid out and has a glut of things to do and see.

Ruled for over 650 years by the Wittelsbach family who brought the world-famous art collections and rich architectural heritage to the city, Munich seems to have continual festivals all the year round: Fasching with its masked carnivals from February, ending on Shrove Tuesday; the beer inaugurations in March; the summer season of concerts and operas from May to August; the famous Oktoberfest beer festival lasting from end Sept. to early Oct., followed not long after by the Christmas markets. And this doesn't even take into account the countless student-based activities going on round SCHWABING, Munich's lively Latin quarter.

STATION FACILITIES

München Hhauptbahnhof's train information is open daily 6 a.m.–11 p.m. (Tel. 19419), travel centre 6 a.m.–10.30 p.m. and reservations Mon.–Fri.: 5.20 a.m.–11 p.m., Sat.: 5.10 a.m.–10.40 p.m., Sun.: 6 a.m.–10.40 p.m. There's also a Tourist Information (Mon.–Sat.: 8 a.m.–10 p.m., Sun.: 11 a.m.–7 p.m.) on site and a foreign exchange desk which is open daily 6 a.m.–11 p.m. There's all the usual other things, including a 24-hour café and waiting room, though the station shuts 1.30 a.m.–4.30 a.m.

Daily trains to: Paris (8½ hours), Brussels (8 hours), Zürich (4¼ hours), Milan (7½ hours), Vienna (4½–5½ hours).

TOURIST INFORMATION

The *Fremdenverkehrsamt* (Tourist Office) (Tel. 239 1256/57) is at the front of the Hauptbahnhof, opposite platform 11, and is open daily 8 a.m.–10 p.m. The staff are helpful, fluent in English and will supply you with maps, details of walking tours and pamphlets and find you a room for 5DM. Get the monthly programme of events and the *Young People's Guide to Munich*, which is excellent.

Munich's city transport system is one of the best in Europe, and also one of the most complicated. There are buses, trams, the U-Bahn and the S-Bahn. Note: Rail pass holders get free travel on the S-Bahn only. You need only 1 ticket, even if your journey takes in the tram, bus and underground systems. For further information, pick up leaflets at the underground at Hauptbahnhof, or S-Bahn stations. Weekly passes (Mon.–Mon. 12.40DM), day passes aand multiple journey tickets are available. Day tickets cost 10DM for all city zones, 20DM for city and S-Bahn region. Blue striptickets cost 14DM for 12 strips, stamp 2 strips for every city zone crossed.

Whilst it is tempting and apparently easy to travel free on public transport, you take the risk of an on-the-spot fine of 60DM if a squad of police operates a random check (which are frequent). Ignorance is no excuse – the police reason that anyone who can work out how to get to their destination can operate the idiot-proof ticket dispensers or obtain a pass! Offenders or those unable to pay are taken to the police station for a statement. It obviously makes sense to have a valid ticket.

ADDRESSES

POST OFFICE Bahnhofplatz 1 (opposite station). Mon.–Fri.: 6 a.m.–10 p.m.; Sat.-Sun.: 7 a.m.–10 p.m. Also *poste restante* here.
AMEX Promenadeplatz 6, Mon.–Fri.: 9 a.m.–5.30 p.m., Sat.: 9 a.m.–12 noon (Tel. 21990)
UK CONSULATE Bürkleinstrasse 10 (Tel. 211090)
IRISH CONSULATE Mauerkircherstrasse 1a (Tel. 985723)
US CONSULATE Königinstrasse 5 (Tel. 28880)
CANADIAN CONSULATE Tal 29 (Tel. 22266l)
AUSTRALIAN NATIONALS Contact the embassy in Berlin.
NEW ZEALAND NATIONALS Contact the embassy in Bonn.
MEDICAL HELP Try the university clinic at Ismaningerstrasse (Tel. 41401)
STUDIOSUS-REISEN (STUDENT TRAVEL) Amalienstrasse 73 (Tel. 500 60540)

SEEING

MARIENPLATZ, the attractive pedestrian zone, is at the centre of Munich. The neo-Gothic TOWN HALL is located here (look out for the Glockenspiel show at 11 a.m., noon, 5 p.m. and 9 p.m. May–Oct.; 11 a.m. Nov.–Apr.), as is the old town hall (ALTES RATHAUS). On Sunday mornings in summer, a brass band in full Bavarian uniform plays in front of the town hall. Just off Marienplatz is the 12th-century church of ST PETER. If a white disc is out on the platform, climb its tower for a view extending to the Alps (a red disc means you'll just see over Munich). Also near here is the FRAUENKIRCHE, with its green onion-topped twin towers; it is the symbol of the city and houses various works of art, tombs and relics as well as the mausoleum of Emperor Ludwig IV (presently closed). ST MICHAEL'S CHURCH and the baroque THEATINER CHURCH are also worth a look. Eight blocks west of Marienplatz is KARLSPLATZ, the main square of Munich. All the city transport starts from here and SONNENSTRASSE, a major shopping street, begins. For yet more exciting retail opportunities, check out NEUHAUSENSTRASSE and KAUFINGERSTRASSE. The palace of the Bavarian rulers (the RESIDENZ) houses a spectacular array of riches. Open Tues.–Sat.: 10 a.m.–4.30 p.m., Sun. till 1 p.m. 4DM.

North of the Residenz is the university area (Schwabing) with Leopoldstrasse at its centre. Nothing much goes on in daytime here, but it's a lively place at night. To the east of Schwabing lies the ENGLISH GARDEN, ideal for sunbathing (nude!) and a picnic.

MUSEUMS The ALTE PINAKOTHEK is one of Europe's finest art galleries. The DEUTSCHES MUSEUM is a fascinating museum located on an island in the Isar River; it is the largest technical museum in the world (with lots of buttons to push), and has exhibits such as U-boats, a Messerschmitt jet fighter, a planetarium and old locomotives. Entrance 8DM (ISIC 3DM) Open 9 a.-m.–5 p.m. The BAVARIAN NATIONAL MUSEUM gives a good introduction to what makes Bavaria different from the rest of Germany and has the most extensive collection of arts and crafts in the world (closed Mon. but open till 5 p.m. even on Sat.; if you turn up after 3.30 they sometimes let you off without paying the admission fee).

The BMW MUSEUM (part of the factory) is well worth a visit if you have had enough of trains for a while. You can't get guided tours of the factory itself, but the museum is superb and includes a spectacular audio-visual show. It's the last stop on U-Bahn 2 and 3. While there, visit the park itself, scene of the 1972 Olympic Games and marvel at the impressive architecture either from ground level or from the top of the Olympia Tower. Entrance to the park is free, 5DM for the lift up the tower, which is well worth it for the stupendous view, unless the weather is lousy. Don't eat in the restaurant at the top as the prices are exorbitant. An equally good panorama can be obtained free by walking up one of the hills in the Olympic Park. A break from sightseeing is offered by the rowing boats on the lake (7DM for half an hour) or a visit to FC Bayern, one of Europe's most successful football clubs. Tickets can be bought from Tourist Offices or try your luck with the touts at the ground.

SLEEPING

Munich is busy all year, particularly during the Oktoberfest, when beds are very scarce. Still, there are plenty of places if you know where to look. Expect to pay about 25–40DM for student accommodation, 17–36DM at youth hostels and up to 70DM in pensions. Try to arrange hostel accommodation ahead of time or turn up early! Ask at Tourist Information for the *Accommodation Guide to Munich*.

The cheapest sleep to be had is at the Youth Camp (Jugendlager am Kapuzinerhölzl, known as the 'Big Tent') at Frank-Schrank Strasse 8 (Tel. 1414300); open end June–early Sept., 5 p.m.–9 a.m. For a few marks you get an air mattress, blankets and a place in the circus tent, not to mention tea (free) in the mornings and evenings. You won't get turned away, and there is a great 'international' atmosphere, maximum stay is 3 days only. Take U-Bahn1 to Rotkreuzplatz, then tram 12 to Botanischer Garten. Take your passport for ID to avoid paying a 50DM deposit for blankets; ask for plenty of these if it is late in the season as it can get chilly.

YOUTH HOSTELS You must be under 27 or accompanying a child to use Bavarian youth hostels. Wendl-Dietrich Strasse 20 (Tel. 131156) is fairly central but large, impersonal, fills up early and is usually full of noisy adolescent school groups. It could be cleaner, and the lockers are dodgy. Security is a bit suspect too. Costs 23.00– 25.50DM including breakfast. Take U-Bahn 1 to Rotkreuzplatz. The one at Burgweg 4–6, Pullach (Tel. 7930643 and 7930644), is more fun, but this renovated castle is a half-hour journey and also fills up early. There are no lockers and it has an infuriating token system for showers. The staff, however, are very helpful and it costs 15.50–17.50DM including shower and breakfast in a small dormitory. Take S-Bahn 7 (free on Inter-Rail) to Pullach, signposted from station. Last train from Munich is 10.40 p.m. and curfew is at 11.30 p.m.

Haus International, Elizabethstrasse 87 (Tel. 120060) is good but more expensive with prices from 39DM for a shared room, to 81DM for a single, so share in a large room to cut down costs. No IYHF card required. There is a disco in the basement and no curfew.

Also Jugendgasthaus Thalkirchen (IYHF) at Miesingstrasse 4 (Tel. 7236550), where couples need to produce a marriage certificate to share a room. Take U-Bahn 1 or 2 to Sendlinger-Tor-Platz, change to U-Bahn 3 to Thalkirchen (Tierpark).

Try CVJM Jugendgasthaus, Landwehrstrasse 13 (Tel. 5521 410) near to Hauptbahnhof', dorm beds at 32DM. If you're stuck for a place to stay try the Augsburg Youth Hostel, at Beim Pfaffenkeller 3 (Tel. 0821 33909), about 40 minutes away by DB train.

PENSIONS Some of the cheapest are located in Schillerstrasse and Landwehrstrasse. Try Pension Schiller (Tel. 592435) at Schillerstrasse 11; further down the street at no. 32 there's Lugano (Tel. 591005). Westfalia at Mozartstrasse 23 (Tel. 530377) is also worth a try.

For a reasonable hotel try the Helvetia in Schillerstrasse (Tel. 554745) or Haberstock next door is a good-value pension.

One well-equipped campsite is at Zenterlandstrasse 49 (Tel. 7231707), open mid-March–Oct. Take U-Bahn 3 to Thalkirchen (Tierpark), then bus 57 to Campingplatz Thalkirchen (or a 20-minute walk). Although central and convenient for the Oktoberfest, it can get very crowded and noisy, with cleanliness suffering as a result (5DM per person, up to 5DM per tent).

You could try sleeping in the Hauptbahnhof, although it is draughty, busy and you will get woken up and moved on by the police around 5 a.m.

EATING AND NIGHTLIFE

Bavarian cooking is tasty, filling and not for the weight-conscious. Munich's speciality is *Weisswurst*, a sausage made of veal and parsley. You can buy it at any number of stalls and eat it as a quick snack with a beer to keep you going. The VIKTUALIENMARKT is an attractive sight, but it's invariably cheaper to buy your supplies from one of the superb food halls of the department stores, Kaufhof, Hertie, Deutscher Supermarkt or the cheaper Pennymarkt and Aldi. The displays and high standards in these places really open your eyes if you've been weaned on dull supermarkets at home.

The student canteens (*Mensas*) have cheap lunches at Arcisstrasse 17 or Leopoldstrasse 15, open 11 a.m.–2 p.m., and all over Schwabing you'll find reasonably priced eating places. If you're desperate there's also a Wendy self-service outside the station.

A quarter of the world's beer comes from Bavaria and Munich is at the heart of this, with its social life revolving round the beer halls and gardens. These are good places to eat, drink and make new friends. Avoid the touristy Hofbräuhaus as you're unlikely to meet the locals there; try instead the beer gardens in the English Gardens below Chinesischer Turm or the studenty Max Emanuel brewery (Adalbertstrasse 33). For an excellent taste of real Munich nightlife Augustinerkeller at Arnulfstrasse 52, Donisl at Marienplatz, and Hundskugel (Munich's oldest pub) at Hotterstrasse 18 are the most representative. For cheap and delicious doughnuts and so on, try Strüdel Stube in Orlandostrasse (near the Hofbräuhaus).

For nightlife, Schwabing is the area to head for. Studiosus Reisen, Amalienstrasse 73, have tickets for concerts, theatres, etc., with reductions. There's music and dancing at The Drugstore, Feilitzschstrasse 12, and the university has occasional 'events' such as open-air discos outside term-time which you can go along to if you can pass yourself off as a German student. You could also check out one of Munich's increasing number of Irish pubs.

EXCURSIONS

Just 22 km north-west of Munich is the concentration camp of DACHAU, built in 1933. A visit here will put into perspective the atrocities that were committed and will leave an impression with you that all the opulence of Munich can't take away. The old administration block is now a museum, and a film in English is shown twice a day, check times at Tourist Information. Get there on the S-Bahn line 2, direction Peterhausen (free to Inter-Railers) to Dachau, then buses 720 or 722 to the camp (closed Mon.). Buses are infrequent on Sundays and the alternative is a 45-minute walk.

NYMPHENBURG PALACE AND PARK is Munich's Versailles. Home of the Bavarian kings, situated in a 495-acre park, the palace makes a pleasant day trip. Closed Mon. The surrounding park is free, but entry to the palace is not. If visiting in winter, don't forget to pack your skates because the lake freezes to form a spectacular open-air ice rink.

Other ideas for trips are Europe's largest zoo, HELLABRUNN, 6 km south of the city and the Benedictine monastery at ANDECHS (buses 951 or 956), whose beer hall serves some of the strongest home brew in Munich.

A good day trip from Munich is to the fairy-tale castle of NEUSCHWANSTEIN, which featured in the famous film *Chitty Chitty Bang Bang*, and was built by 'mad' King Ludwig II. Take the train to Fussen and bus Bf 971 (half-price on Inter-Rail) the 5 km to Hohenschwangau. It is then a steep 1 km walk up to the entrance. The entrance fee includes a rather hurried guided tour.

While on the subject of films you may wish to spend some time at the Bavarian Film Studios, which are near Pullach. Although quite expensive, with the tour only in German, you can walk through the U-boat used for the film *The Boat* and see other sights.

Augsburg

Just over half an hour up the main line from Munich is the ancient city of Augsburg, which is well worth visiting. Founded by the Roman Emperor Augustus in 15 BC, the city developed into a very important medieval trading centre. Today Augsburg is the capital of the region known as Bavarian Swabia and it is Bavaria's third city.

ADDRESSES
TOURIST INFORMATION Bahnhofstrasse 7; open Mon.–Fri.: 9 a.m.–6 p.m.; Sat.: 9 a.m.–1 p.m. (Tel. 0821 502 070)
POST OFFICE Karlstrasse or Viklofiastrasse 3, next to main station.

SEEING
Don't be put off by the view from the main station, which is not situated among the city's best attractions. Augsburg's sights are close together and best seen on foot. Organized walking tours in German and English start from the city hall.

A walk along Maximilianstrasse is a good start to a stop-off in Augsburg. Its southern end is dominated by the 93m high tower and onion dome of the church of ST ULRICH AND AFRA. This dates from the 15th century. Further along, at no. 46, is the SCHAEZLER-PALAIS, the finest example of rococo architecture on offer in Augsburg. It houses the best of the city's art collection. Particularly of interest is the finely decorated banqueting hall on the top floor. This is 23m long, the walls are lined with mirrors and it has an impressive ceiling fresco. There are no entrance fees for this and the other museums in the city at weekends and public holidays.

Augsburg is famous for its fountains and the 3 most attractive of these are to be seen on Maximilianstrasse: HERKULESBRUNNEN, MERKUR-BRUNNEN and AUGUSTUSBRUNNEN. The latter personifies the 4 rivers of Augsburg and when you reach it you will be standing in front of the RATHAUS. This looks impressive from the outside, and once inside proceed to the top floor for the newly refurbished GOLDENER SAAL (golden hall), which had been destroyed in the last war. The adjoining PERLACHTÜRM offers – for a mere 2DM – a good view of the entire city from a height of over 70m. From here the DOM (cathedral) can be seen. This stands at the northern end of Augsburg's main street. The oldest part of it, the crypt, is said to date back to AD 823. Since then the cathedral has been greatly expanded. Aside from its appealing architecture it also holds some Romanesque and Gothic frescoes. On Saturday evenings at 6 p.m. organ recitals are performed in the cathedral.

Augsburg's main attraction, for which it is world famous, is the FUGGEREI, the world's oldest social housing scheme. The main entrance is in the Jakoberstrasse, a short walk eastwards from the city hall. It was begun in 1516 by Jakob Fugger, whose family was at the time very rich and influential in Augsburg. Residence in the Fuggerei has always been reserved for Catholics, poor but hard-working and free of sins. Their annual rent amounts to a mere 1.72DM. One of the houses has been restored as a museum in order to depict life as it was there when the Fuggerei was founded.

A good tip for seeing the rest of Augsburg is to follow the coloured signs which will lead you on a leisurely tour of the old town. Augsburg has a large network of canals and is said to have more bridges than Venice. Parts of the city wall are still intact and are of great historical interest. A plan of the various routes is available at the Tourist Office.

SLEEPING

The youth hostel is at Beim Pfaffenkeller 3 (Tel. 0821 33909), near the cathedral, and is reached from the main station by tram 2 to Stadtwerke.

EATING AND NIGHTLIFE

The cheapest meals in the city are to be found in the traditional Bavarian *Gasthaus*, of which there are many. If you're willing to pay a bit more, a good meal at a reasonable price can be had at John Bentons, Maximilianstrasse, just beyond the Perlachtürm.

The best pubs are in the old town. Try Die Kneipe (The Pub), or the Irish pub, Fuchsbau, both on Mittlerer Lech. When the weather is good a visit to a Biergarten is a must. The best are Thing, on Vorderer Lech, and Zeughaus, on Zeugplatz.

The Alps and the Romantic Road

The *Romantische Strasse* is the name for the undeniably scenic stretch from Füssen to the vineyards of Franconia. The towns *en route* are very picturesque, and this is the route to take for fairytale castles and medieval churches set among rolling green hills.

To get to those hidden little corners of Bavaria, the train is not the best way: use the Europabus 'Romantische Strasse'. They offer two alternative routes: Füssen to Würzburg, and Munich to Füssen (free to Eurail, Euro Domino and German Rail card holders). Make further enquiries at the Starnberger Bahnhof part of Munich station.

Places of note *en route* are: NÖRDLINGEN, with its perfectly preserved circular medieval fortifications and 15th-century St George's church; DINKELSBÜHL, also with a St George's church which is a Gothic master-piece, *Deutsches Haus* and Old Town Hall; ROTHENBURG: visit the Rathaus, St Jakob's church and the Folterkammer (torture chamber); and WÜRZBURG.

Würzburg

In the heart of wine country, Würzburg is the baroque city in western Germany. The Franconian RESIDENZ is the magnificent palace of the prince-bishops and is the main sight of Würzburg.

Open April–Sept.: Tues.–Sun.: 9 a.m.–5 p.m.; Oct.–Mar.: 10 a.m.–4 p.m. (4.50DM, 3DM on ISIC). The MARIENBERG FORTRESS, another of the princes' homes, is on the other side of the river Main, which intersects the town. Near the fortress is the KÄPPELE, an ornate baroque church which allows you an excellent view from the top. The MAINFRÄNKISCHES MUSEUM houses sculptures and carvings and is located in the Marienberg Fortress.

STATION FACILITIES
The Hauptbahnhof has train information 7 a.m.–9.30 p.m. and a 24-hour service point and luggage lockers. The station itself shuts down after midnight and opens at dawn. All the usual facilities are at hand.

Daily trains to: Nürnberg (1 hour), Vienna (6½ hours), Munich (2½ hours), Stuttgart (2½ hours), Mainz (2 hours), Paris, Cologne (3½ hours), Frankfurt-am-Main (1½ hours).

TOURIST INFORMATION
Located just in front of the station (open Mon.–Sat.: 8 a.m.–8 p.m.) and in the centre at the Haus zum Falken, by the Marktplatz (Mon.–Fri.: 9 a.m.–6 p.m., Sat.: 9 a.m.–2 p.m.). They'll find you a room for 3DM (Tel. 0931 37398).
STUDENT TRAVEL OFFICE SRID Reisen, Zwinger 6 (Tel. 0931 52176).
EUROPABUSES Buses down the Romantic Road from Würzburg to Rothenburg and Munich depart daily at 10 a.m. and to Frankfurt at 6.45 p.m.

SLEEPING AND EATING

The IYHF youth hostel is at Burkarderstrasse 44 (Tel. 0931 42590), under 26 only, and costs 25–29DM. The campsite is at Mergent-heimerstrasse 13b (Tel. 0931 72536). Trams 3 and 5 get you there. The campsite is not signposted, but follow directions to the Würzburg Canoe Club and register in the club restaurant, whence you will be directed to your pitch. For cheap hotels and pensions ask at the Tourist Office for suggestions. Recommended are Siegel, Reisgrubengasse 7 (Tel. 0931 52941) or Spehnkuch, Röntgenring 7 (Tel. 0931 54752).

Eat at the university Mensa in the Studentenhaus at the corner of Mänzstrasse and Jahnstrasse. Open for lunch and dinner on weekdays, during term times only. There are several cheap fast-food places around the centre, and if you have time, try the local white wines.

NOTES

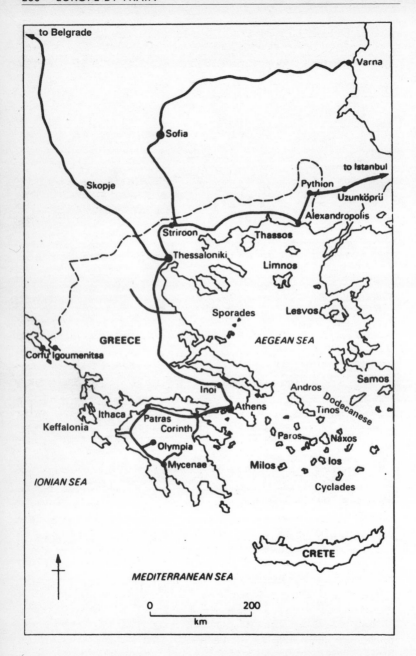

GREECE

Entry requirements	Passport
Population	10, 264, 156
Capital	Athens (pop.: 3, 500, 000)
Currency	Drachma (GDR)
	£1 = approx. 457GDR
Political system	Parliamentary Democracy
Religion	97.6% Greek Orthodox
Language	Greek (English is the second language)
Public holidays	1, 6 Jan.; Ash Monday, 25 Mar., Good Friday,
	Easter Monday, 12, 15 Apr., 1 May, Whit
	Monday, 15 Aug., 28 Oct., 25, 26 Dec.
International dialling codes	To Greece: 00 (international access code) + 30
	(country code)
	From Greece: 00 + country code number
Railway office	1 Karolou St, Athens (Tel. 5224563) or 3 Filelli-
	non St, Athens (Tel. 324 1884)
Time	GMT + 2 (+3 in summer)
Emergency telephone	166

Every year, Greece acts like a magnet to thousands of eurorailers from the north, causing the summertime population to increase by up to 50%. The islands offer the best under-30 social scene you're likely to find. Ironically, it's much easier to get to know Germans and Swedes here than Greeks, and you get to know them very well indeed if you share the same nudist beach, although it is technically only legal at 3 beaches in Greece. It's difficult to have a bad holiday in Greece, the birthplace of Western civilization and a haven not only for lovers of sunshine, but also for those interested in history, archaeology and the arts.

Greek history begins about 2,500 BC with the Minoan civilization on Crete, 1,000 years before the Mycenaeans got it together on the mainland. The classical period reached its peak in 5th-century BC Athens. As independent city-states, the Greeks shared the same culture, but were always at each other's throats, until Alexander the Great of Macedon sorted them out and conquered an empire. Greece became part of the Byzantine Empire and was eventually conquered by the Ottomans.

The War of Independence in 1821 started the formation of the modern Greek state, a process which ended in 1947 with the return of the Dodecanese. They still play cricket on Corfu, which was under British rule till 1864. After the Germans pulled out in 1944, civil war broke out and continued for 5 years until the communists lost. Relations with Turkey remain as strained as ever, particularly after the Turkish invasion of Cyprus in 1974, and political tensions are growing with Macedonia.

Greece is one of the poorest countries in the EC. But despite that about 200,000 Albanians have sought refuge here, allegedly raising the crime rate.

GETTING THERE

Travelling by train is still the cheapest way of getting to Greece, especially since the introduction of a new airport tax. Charter flights offer little in the way of flexibility, although 'bucket shops' in Athens offer cheap flights to those with ISIC cards. There are problems in going by train, not least of which is deciding on your route, especially considering recent events in the former Yugoslavia. Note that it is now illegal to take into Greece any substance containing codeine. Whilst guards rarely check you can technically be prosecuted.

THE BELGRADE–ATHENS RUN Before the troubles in the former Yugoslavia, this journey was a good alternative route into Greece. Of course, it is now more or less impossible to make this trip and the intrepid few who have overlanded do not tell a pleasant tale. Our advice is to stick to the Brindisi–Patras ferry. If you do decide to risk it, heed this good advice:

1. Travel out of season, or at least try to avoid mid-July/August.
2. Go for the fastest train possible – it's worth the supplement. Try and get on the through-train from Munich or Vienna, or travel overnight in a couchette/sleeper. (It's advisable here to book in advance.) Sleepers are expensive but couchettes are cheaper.
3. Take along plenty to eat and drink. The trains aren't air-conditioned and you don't know how long a train may stop *en route*.
4. If you get on a train, try to pay for a couchette or sleeper. Have plenty of 'hard' currency on you as dinars are usually refused. Always keep a receipt in case you are asked for extra payment.
5. Look out for Greek or 'Yugoslav' guards trying to extract unwarranted supplements. Simply waving a Thomas Cook timetable can sometimes scare them off. Otherwise argue and kick up as much of a fuss as possible.

THE ITALIAN RUN Trains are crowded and the toilets dirty, but your real problems start at Brindisi, beginning with the 1½ km walk down to the docks. Avoid the rip-off reservation agencies at all costs.

It can be windy on the Brindisi–Patras ferry, but don't let the cooling breeze kid you into not taking precautions against the sun. Putting a rucksack on sunburnt shoulders rather takes the edge off your holiday enjoyment.

If you are going to Corfu, seriously consider flying from Athens, rather than taking the boat from Brindisi. It can cost as little as £40 and only takes 50 minutes.

GREEK RAILWAYS
(ORGANISMOS SIDIRODROMON ELLADOS, OSE)

Greece is a mountainous country and therefore many towns are not connected by rail, although OSE uses a large number of connecting buses and the few local trains there are will seem slow except by Eastern European standards. The international long-distance trains are flatteringly called 'expresses', although some new trains on the Athens–Thessaloniki route have cut the travel time to 6½ hours. Some of these require a small supplement. There are some Inter-Rail bonuses in Greece, but always ask for student discounts.

Recently a lot of money has been invested in OSE, particularly in northern Greece. Speed, service and efficiency are expected to improve no end. The Patras–Athens run is earmarked for major investment – and that should come as a relief to many inter-railers.

EURAIL BONUSES

FREE SERVICES Eurail Pass and Eurail Youthpass travellers can use steamers operated by Hellenic Mediterranean and Adriatica di Navigazione between Patras and Brindisi and vice versa. If you have the choice, opt for the latter. However, between 10 June and 30 Sept., you must pay a high-season surcharge. During July and Aug., advance reservation is recommended. Special accommodation (airline-type seats or cabins) and port taxes are extra. Before boarding, all passengers must check in at the Shipping Line Office. Passengers who wish to break their voyage at Corfu must declare their intention of 'stop over' upon delivery of the ticket. Euro Domino tickets are available (see p. 41).

REDUCED FARES 30% reduction on the published full fares of the Adriatica Line between Piraeus–Candia–Venice or Alexandria and vice versa on the M.S. *Egitto Express*, except between Candia and Piraeus. Contact the local Adriatica offices. Check your dates carefully when taking this run as it can work out substantially cheaper to travel outside the high summer season which usually starts towards the end of July. If you do find yourself with time on your hands waiting for a ferry, the companies will usually let you leave your luggage in their offices while you go to the beach.

TRAIN INFORMATION

English is spoken by information officers at all major stations. Phone 145 or 147 for up-to-date schedules and prices.

RESERVATIONS Wherever else you may decide against reserving, it's well worth thinking about it here. Go to an OSE office rather than the station – the staff are more helpful and it's generally less hassle. Book a seat as far in advance as possible for international trains. On some expresses (ask at station), reservations are obligatory. You can reserve up to a month in advance. It pays to be organized here. It's possible to reserve on internal routes in Greece, but you have to do it by post in advance and it's really not worth the hassle. Reservations for the Intercity between Athens and Patras can only be made within the hour prior to departure. Beware – there are no tickets placed on reserved seats so chaos often ensues!

NIGHT TRAVEL Couchettes and sleepers are both cheap by northern European standards. If you can get one, go for it.

ROVER TICKETS The Greek Tourist Card covers second-class travel only and offers 10, 20 or 30 days' unlimited travel for 1–5 people. Prices for 10 days range from 6,000GDR for 1 person to 17, 000GDR for a group of 5; 20 days costs 9,000–27,000GDR; and 30 days costs 10,000–37,000GDR. For information on the Freedom Pass (Euro Domino), see p. 41.

The Inter-Rail pass has been broken down into zones, therefore you pay only for the places you want to visit. For £159 you can travel for 22 days in one zone. Greece, along with Italy, Turkey and Slovenia, is in Zone G. The pass also covers the ADN/HML ferry service. For details of the 7 Inter-Rail zones, refer to the Inter-Rail section in Part One of this guide.

FERRIES The only way to get to the islands. Tour agencies in Greece do not always advertise rival lines so it is worthwhile to tour all the agencies. In Piraeus, most of the agencies on the waterfront block offer a comprehensive chart of everything sailing that week, and some will also recommend cheap hotels in the area.

On the islands, check and re-check: Greek ferry timetables change without notice from day to day, depending on the season and weather conditions. Note that the majority of islands are connected to Piraeus (Athens).

TOURIST INFORMATION

For information about the country, accommodation and the main sights, see the National Tourist Organization of Greece, known as EOT in Greece. For any other information, see the Tourist Police. Don't be put off by their name – their role is to help you sort out your problems.

ISIC BONUSES Up to 50% off internal flights and ferries, up to 80% reductions on theatres and museums. Olympic will grant reduction only if the internal flight is part of an international journey charged at a standard fare, and not Apex. Consult the nearest Olympic offices or USIT Student Travel Service, 3 Fillellinon St, Athens (Tel. 01 322 5974 or 324 1884).

MONEY MATTERS Banking hours are generally Mon.–Fri.: 8 a.m.–1 p.m. All banks give more or less the same rate.

You can also change money at the Post Office (ELTA). Trying to change money at weekends other than in large resort hotels can be a non-starter.

POST OFFICES Open Mon.–Fri.: 8 a.m.–2 p.m. Stamps can also be bought from kiosks. The price is the same everywhere; it is illegal for anyone to sell stamps for more than their face value.

SHOPS Hours can vary wildly. Supermarkets are open Mon.–Fri.: 8 a.m.–8 p.m., Sat.: 8 a.m.–3.30 p.m. Food shops: Mon.–Fri.: 9 a.m.–2 p.m. and 5 p.m.–8 p.m., Sat.: 9 a.m.–3.30 p.m.

MUSEUMS Usually open in winter 9 a.m.–3.30 p.m.; summer 8 a.m.–5 p.m. They tend to close on Mon. or Tues. EU students get in free, other students get a 50% reduction.

SLEEPING

HOTELS Hotels are graded L, A, B, C, D and E (L is deluxe; D and E are equal fourth class – usually pre-war hotels with very basic facilities). For a C-class hotel, expect to pay at least 4,000GDR each.

HOSTELS The youth hostels are nothing to get excited about. Many hostels have an annoying habit of imposing a curfew on guests (sometimes this can be as early as 10 p.m.). As usual, you need an International Youth Hostel Federation (IYHF) card. It's possible to get one in Athens if you haven't already got one: IYHF Athens International Hostel, 16 Victor Hugo Street, Athens (Tel. (01) 523 4170).

Some pensions and hotels charge 10% extra for short stays during high summer and charge extra for showers. Off season, the boot's on the other foot and it's worth bargaining to get the price down. All hotel prices are fixed and should be posted at the reception. Expect to pay an extra 20% in high season.

CAMPING The National Tourist Board (2 Amerikis Street, Athens) and the Tourist Guide of Greece (137 Patission Street, Athens) issue a list with all the official campsites and facilities, giving an approximate price. Expect to pay at least 900GDR. It is illegal to camp outside the official campsites, since the country is increasingly concerned about campers leaving litter, causing fires and destroying the environment. The EOT will provide you with a comprehensive list of campsites.

THE ISLANDS On the islands, accommodation is inadequate. Privately let rooms (*dhomatia*) are divided into 3 classes (A down to C); they are usually slightly cheaper than hotels and are, in general, spotlessly clean. There's usually a choice of rooms on offer (the most expensive room tends to be shown first). Price is not necessarily an indicator of quality, so always ask to see the room before agreeing to take it at the price quoted.

Camping is illegal on many islands but nearly everyone is forced to do it at some stage as during July and August all the hotels and private rooms are full. There is some `legal' camping on licensed campsites. The police are stepping up action (they can confiscate your passport) and the official policy of EOT now is that you can't come to Greece by charter flight without having prebooked accommodation. If you have to camp illegally, keep the place clean.

EATING AND NIGHTLIFE

Don't expect to eat as cheaply as you would have done a few years ago, as high inflation continues to push up prices. Always check the prices first in small shops and bakeries and make sure you know what you're paying for. On the islands it's easy to live off bread, cheese and watermelon (*karpouzi)* during the day, and eat out at night. If you need that added luxury of a cup of coffee for breakfast to see you through the day, be sure what you're ordering or you'll end up with sweet Greek coffee instead. An alternative is *café frappé* (iced coffee), which is much more refreshing.

When eating out, you'll often be ushered into the kitchen. Take your time, as this is the local custom of choosing. *Arni* is lamb;

moschari, veal; *chirino*, pork; *kotopoulo*, chicken. Avoid the fish unless you've got plenty of money or are on the islands, where it's fresh. *Moussaka* is a combination of meat with potato or aubergine, in béchamel sauce. *Dolmades* are minced meat and rice wrapped in vine leaves and are delicious hot or cold. If you're down on your luck, there's always a *souvlaki* stand (meat kebab wrapped in bread) not far away. For drinks, don't overdo it with *ouzo* (the local aniseed spirit), or you'll know all about it the next morning. Give Greek beer a try – if only for a change. For the evening meal, try at least one bottle of the local *retsina* (wine with pine resin) before returning to the *aretsinato* wine. A service charge is usually included in the bill, but it is polite to leave some small change.

There are numerous local festivals celebrating everything from Easter to wine. The Greeks use any excuse to have one, as they love to let their hair down and dance. Once a bouzouki gets going, anything can happen. Nightclubs are dull and expensive by comparison. Films are shown in their original language, and are always cheaper in the suburbs.

Northern Greece

Northern Greece is real 'spaghetti western' country. The mountains are rugged and the scenery wild and untamed. The 2 provinces of this area are Macedonia and Thrace.

If you're entering Greece from Macedonia or Bulgaria, your first main centre will be THESSALONIKI. This is Greece's second city, founded in 316 BC. Although the station is unattractive, the people are very friendly and hospitable. Take a stroll through the old Turkish KASTRA QUARTER, visit the ARCHAEOLOGICAL MUSEUM and the churches of ST GEORGE and ST DEMETRIUS (the city's patron saint). The Byzantine walls around the city can be an afternoon's walk. The Roman palace of Galerius is in Navarino Square. Tourist Information can be obtained from the office at 34 Mitropoleos St (Tel. 031 271888), open Mon.–Fri.: 8 a.m.–8 p.m.; Sat.: 8.30 a.m.–2 p.m. The tourist police at 4 Dodekanissou Street (5th Floor) (Tel. 544162 or 554871) or at the airport (Tel. 425011) can also help you.

Thessaloniki is cooled by sea breezes and the wide streets have many attractive shops. There is also an excellent copper market and several good beaches near the city with frequent buses and boats to them.

The youth hostel at 44 Alex. Svolou Street (Tel. 225946) is noisy, basic and quite expensive. An IYHF card is required for the privilege.The XAN (YWCA) at 11 Agias Sofia Street (Tel. 276144) is a much better hostel, located opposite the cathedral. Good hotels include the Argo, at 11 Egnatia Street (Tel. 51 97 70), Continental (Tel. 277553) and Lido. Camping grounds include Epanomis (Tel. 0392 413789) and Retzika Beach, Epanomi (Tel. 0392 41090)

EXCURSIONS For an impressive day trip from Thessaloniki, head east by bus (nearest train station is Droma) to the port of KAVALA. This prosperous town has an amazing OLD QUARTER and a huge medieval AQUEDUCT leading from Mount Simbolon. The Tourist Office is at the corner of Eleftherias (Tel. 222425 or 23 653). Open Mon.–Fri.: 7 a.m.–2.30 p.m. It helps with accommodation and gives out a useful town map.

Hourly ferry crossings are possible from here to the popular resort island of THASSOS, mythical home of the Sirens. Here you'll find many rooms for rent and the campsite Irini (Tel. 051 229785).

There are many good beaches on the mainland but the best are on SITHONIA, the central prong of the HALKIDIKI peninsula. All are well connected to Thessaloniki by bus. South-east of Thessaloniki is the self-governing monastic commune of MOUNT ATHOS (no female has been allowed in for 900 years). If you want to visit, contact the Ministry of Northern Greece in Thessaloniki and be able to give a sound reason for your visit (Room 221, Pl. Dikitirou, Thessaloniki. Tel. 257010). A letter of recommendation (e.g. from a University) is usually required and this should cite proven religious or scientific interests.

To see some early Christian art and visit 9 Byzantine monasteries and nunneries at METEORA is much easier (closed Tues.). The sight is breathtaking: 24 perpendicular rocks upon which, 600 years ago, the Byzantine monks chose to worship God and built their monasteries. Situated 21 km north of Kalambaka, it takes 4 hours to reach by train from Thessaloniki; change at Larissa. If you are planning to stay in the region, your best bet would be to camp at Vrachos Kastraki (Tel. 0432 22293), 800m from Kalambaka station.

LARISSA is a picturesque town with a medieval fortress and an ancient theatre. The Tourist Office is at 18 Koumoundorou Str (Tel. 041 250919). If you are travelling to Athens from Larissa, stop at Thebes (Thiva), the birthplace of Hercules, whose wondrous feats feature in Greek mythology. Nearby is the spring of Agios Theodoras, better known as the Fountain of Oedipus.

North-east from Thessaloniki is ALGAIA ELENI, near Langadas. The best thing to happen here is the ritual of the fire-walkers which takes place annually 21–23 May. The police station (Tel. 0321 63333) can give you more details and help find accommodation.

The Peloponnese

This most southerly part of Greece's mainland is separated from the central belt by the Isthmus of Corinth, through which runs the spectacular CORINTH CANAL. The Peloponnese has remnants of ancient Greeks, Turks, Franks and Venetians, and is becoming increasingly popular with tourists. On the main circular line from Patras to Athens lie Kalamata, Tripolis, Argos and Corinth. KALAMATA is a sprawling town which was devastated by an earthquake in 1986 but it makes a good base. The Kástro, built by the Franks, survived the quake and is one of the most pleasant parts of the town. There is a tourist police post at the station (Tel. 01721 23187), and a campsite, Patista (Tel. 29525) to the east of the city.

Near Argos lies the unspoilt town of NAUPLION with a picturesque Venetian fort in the middle of the neighbouring bay. There are frequent bus connections (the bus station is on Odhos Singrou) to surrounding towns. There is a good youth hostel, which requires an IYHF card, at 15 Argonafton Street (Tel. 0752 27754). A 15-minute walk from the bus stop, it charges about 900GDR per person per night and a further 800GDR for huge home-cooked dinners.

You can rent bicycles from Riki and Pete, Navarino St (Tel. 24547 or 21407) for 1,000GDR per day. The Tourist Office can be found at 25 Martiou but you are better off trying the Tourist Police (Tel. 0752 28131) which are to the right at the top of Syngrou.

The new town of CORINTH has nothing much to recommend it but the old town has a lot hidden away in its quiet corners. The station is in the new town, but buses leave for 'Arhea Korinthos' where you can see columns from the Temple of Apollo and the rostrum from which St Paul preached Christianity to the Corinthians. To catch these sights at their best visit them around 9 a.m., as by lunchtime the coach tours arrive and they become besieged by tourists. For tourist information Tel. 0741 23282. If you are staying overnight in New Corinth, try Hotel Acti, 3 Ethnikis Anistasis St (Tel. 0741 23337) down by the sea, or camp at Corinth Beach (Tel. 27967), 3 km west of town for 900GDR per night. A regular train and bus service connects it to the city station.

Just down the line is MYCENAE (Mikines) which dates back to 3000 BC and was founded by Perseus, the mythical slayer of Medusa. Many of the treasures found here are now in Athens, but you can still see the Gate of the Lions, royal tombs and the Treasury of Atreus. The small youth hostel is at Iphigeneia Street 20 (Tel. 0751 76285), which offers beds for 850GDR but again requires an IYHF card. Take the bus to Ancient Corinth and get off at the bottom of the hill.

Mycenae is served by 2 campsites. Camping Mycenae (Tel. 66247) lies in the middle of the town and charges 500GDR per person, 400GDR per tent, and offers a tent rental facility. Camping Atreus (Tel. 66221) is a little further out.

Further south is EPIDAVROS whose main attraction is the 4th-century BC amphitheatre in which classical Greek dramas are staged on Fri. and Sat. nights from June through till the last weekend in Aug. Plays are performed in Greek, but by the end of the performance the language ceases to be a barrier. For information about performances contact the Festival Office, 4 Stadion Str Syntagma, Athens (Tel. 322 1459). Tickets can also be purchased before the show at the theatre (Tel. 0753 22026) and cost around 2,000GDR.

SPARTA was the seat of a mighty empire in ancient Greece, but the modern town is a big disappointment. But MYSTRA, a 200GDR bus ride away, has an impressive display of Byzantine churches, palaces and a castle.

PATRAS is the main town of the Peloponnese, the ferry landing from Brindisi in Italy. There's not much to see, but if you're killing time look round the VENETIAN CASTLE, ARCHAEOLOGICAL MUSEUM, MUNICIPAL THEATRE and PSILA ALONIA SQUARE. The busiest and most spectacular time to visit is in July–September, when the summer festival takes place, and drama, dance and music are abundant. The carnival in Feb./March is one of the biggest in the country, with a grand parade through the city centre. The police station (Tel. 061 220902) can help with enquiries, and a good camping site can be found May–Oct. at Patro EOT camping ground (Tel. 061 42413), 5 km outside Patras (take bus no. 1 from the waterfront). The youth hostel is at 68 Iroon Polytechniou St (just over a kilometre's walk from the ferry terminal); it has no curfew (Tel. 65 21 52). There is a port tax of 1,500GDR in Patras.

About 5 trains a day make the worthwhile 7-hour trip to OLYMPIA, site of the first Olympic Games in Ancient Greece. There are many archaeological sites and museums in the city and its surrounding area, not surprisingly since the Temple of Zeus used to hold Pheidias' gold and ivory statue of the God, one of the Seven Wonders of the Ancient World. The youth hostel is at 18 Kondhili Street (Tel. 0624 22580); it's cheap but has an 11.30 p.m. curfew. Camping Diana (Tel. 0624 22314) is a shaded site 200m uphill from Praxitelous

Kondilia Avenue where you'll find the Tourist Office (Tel. 0624 23100). Open: 9 a.m.–10 p.m. daily in the summer. The campsite offers students a 10% discount. There is another campsite 2 km out on the road to Pirgos (Tel. 0624 22745).

Athens (Athinai) city phone code: 01

Athens, 'the cradle of Western civilization', generally considered to be the high spot of a European tour. It can also offer you dirty, squalid accommodation, unbearable heat and street after street of ugly concrete blocks. Modern Athens has nothing much to offer, but it's all worthwhile when you climb up to see the classical beauty of the white-stoned Parthenon, Temple of Athena and the beginnings of Western drama, the Theatre of Dionysus.

If you're going island-hopping, Athens – or rather Piraeus, its port – is your starting point. Ferries leave from here for the islands (there are 1,500 to choose from in the Aegean and Ionian seas), and the average fare for a deck passenger on a 5-hour voyage is about 2,500GDR.

STATION FACILITIES

ATHINAI-LARISSA There is a full range of facilities here including a Tourist Police office. Left luggage is also available in the daytime only. There are daily trains to Thessaloniki and Istanbul.

ATHINAI-PELEPPONESE If you're travelling to the Peloponnese or Patras (for the ferry to Italy) use the Athinai-Peloponnese station, adjacent to the Larissa station (6 Patras trains daily).

TOURIST INFORMATION

The Tourist Police are at 77 Dimitrakopoulou St (open 24 hours) and there's an information desk in the National Bank of Greece on Syntagma Square (Tel. 32 22545), open Mon.–Fri.: 8 a.m.–6.30 p.m., Sat.: 9 a.m.–2 p.m.

The main EOT office is at 2 Amerikis St (Tel. 32 23111). Pick up the free map and leaflets on campsites, hostels, etc., and *This Week in Athens,* which provides information on clubs and sights. They don't operate an accommodation-finding service, but try the Hotel Chamber desk in the National Bank of Greece. A good source for information is the Athenian newspaper which is published in English every month.

ADDRESSES

POST OFFICE 100 Aiolou St, near Omonia Square. Also Syntagma Square. Open Mon.–Fri.: 7.30 a.m.–8 p.m., Sat.: 7.30 a.m.–2 p.m., Sun.: 9 a.m.–1 p.m.

OTE OFFICE (MAIN TELEPHONE OFFICE) 15 Stadhiou Street; open 24 hours

AMEX 2 Ermou Street, Syntagma Square, weekdays: 8.30 a.m.–4.30 p.m., Sat.: 8.30 a.m.–1 p.m. (Tel. 32 44975)

UK EMBASSY 1 Ploutarehou (Tel. 72 36211); open: Mon.–Fri.: 8 a.m.–1 p.m.

US EMBASSY 91 Vassilissis Soas (Tel. 72 12951); open: Mon.–Fri.: 8.30 a.m.–5 p.m.

CANADIAN EMBASSY 4 Ioannou Gennadiou St (Tel. 72 54011)

AUSTRALIAN EMBASSY 37 D. Soutsou St (Tel. 64 47303); open: Mon.–Fri.: 8.30 a.m.–12.30 p.m.

ISIC/USIT 3 Filellinon Street (Tel. 32 41884)

EUROTRAIN 11 Nikis Street (Tel. 32 21267)

LATE-NIGHT CHEMIST Tel. 107 or 102

RED CROSS FIRST AID CENTRE 21, 3 Septemvriou St (Tel. 150 or 552 5555)

TOURIST POLICE Tel. 171; English spoken

GETTING ABOUT

Looking at the taxis' tariffs, they seem a huge bargain, but by the time you've been ripped off they don't work out as such a hot idea (each person pays what's on the clock so it doesn't help travelling in groups). Make sure the meter is switched on and that the display reads zero when you first get in – attempts at overcharging tourists are all too common. Make a note of the cab number and if in doubt ask for a receipt. Having said that, Greek taxis can be the bargain of Europe.

The buses and trolley-buses are usually packed (run 5 a.m.–12.30 a.m.). You can take a bus out to the nearby beaches from the bus station in the centre of town. City buses are blue with 3 digit numbers, the flat fare is 75GDR. Tickets are purchased in advance from kiosks or newsagents': look out for the sign *Isitiria Edho* ('Tickets here'). After midnight, there is only an hourly service.

There is now an Electric Railway which runs every five minutes between Piraeus and central Athens from 5 a.m. till 12.15 a.m.

SEEING

Athens reached its zenith around 400 BC when Plato, Socrates and Aristotle were strolling around the Acropolis which today is the heart of the city. What's worth seeing in Athens – the antiquities – are all clustered round the old town, or PLAKA district. The ACROPOLIS should be seen as soon as it opens at 8 a.m., before the hordes swarm up and destroy its atmosphere. The PARTHENON, the temple dedicated to the goddess Athena, is held up as the epitome of architectural perfection. See also the ERECHTHEION, TEMPLE OF ATHENA NIKE and the PROPYLAEA, the gates to the sacred site. The ACROPOLIS MUSEUM contains some of the finds: statues, friezes, etc. The summer opening hours for sites and museums given below are included with some trepidation as the authorities are notorious for changing the times without notice. To be sure of admission, visit between 9 a.m. and noon. Don't count on getting in anywhere on a Monday.

The Acropolis is open Mon.–Fri.: 8 a.m.–6.30 p.m., weekends: 8.30 a.m.–2.30 p.m.; there are discounts for students, and everyone gets in free on Sun. and public holidays (normal admission is 2,000GDR). PNYX HILL offers a beautiful view of the Acropolis, and there's a *son et lumière* show here at 9 p.m. each night, which costs 1,000GDR.

The ancient AGORA, north of the Acropolis, was the marketplace and still has the remains of the old administrative centre. THE TEMPLE OF HEPHAISTOS is considered the best preserved in Greece. This site is open 8.30 a.m.–2.45 p.m. Tues.–Sun. It is well worth a visit (800 dr admission, 400GDR for students).

The NATIONAL ARCHAEOLOGICAL MUSEUM at 28 Patission St has the best collection of ancient Greek artefacts in the world: gold death-masks, vessels, jewellery, statues and frescoes. Open Mon.: 12.30 p.m.–6.45 p.m., Tues.–Fri.: 8 a.m.–6.45 p.m., weekends: 8.30 a.m.–2.45 p.m. Admission 2,000GDR, student reductions available.

SYNTAGMA (Constitution) Square, is the centre of modern Athens. Avoid the cafés, which are very expensive. Constitution Square is flanked on one side by the Greek Parliament where you can watch the bizarre changing of the guard ceremony. From here take Amalias Avenue to the attractive NATIONAL GARDENS and HADRIAN'S ARCH. Also in this direction lie the PRESIDENTIAL PALACE and the OLYMPIC STADIUM.

The famous FLEA MARKET on Ifestou St, adjacent to Monastiraki Square, makes a colourful walk and can produce some good bargains in equipment and leather goods. Beware of pickpockets and bum-pinchers. Closes 2 p.m. Sun.

For a fantastic view over Athens, an uphill climb to the summit of Likavitos is well worth the effort.

A word of warning: Athens can become oppressively hot and polluted in the summer, so beware of heat exhaustion and breathing difficulties, especially if you are an asthma sufferer. In an attempt to control the pollution, city-centre traffic bans may be put into effect when the air quality deteriorates below a certain level in hot weather. Public transport can get very crowded at such times; check local weather forecasts or contact tourist information for day-to-day details.

SLEEPING

There are literally hundreds of places to stay in Athens and unless you're arriving very late on an August night you should be OK. That's not to say that all places are clean, friendly or have the bare essentials, but most are cheap. Always try to book in advance. Head for the Plaka as it's not only an attractive central place to stay (right underneath the Acropolis) but also one of the cheapest districts. Basically, the nearer to Syntagma Square, the more you can expect to pay. You may find young English-speakers from various hostels (some of which are fairly grotty) joining the trains just before Athens extolling the virtues of their establishments and handing out leaflets. This is a good way of earning bed and board for those who plan on spending some time in Athens. Take what they say with a pinch of salt, but go and see for yourself nonetheless. Security regarding belongings and valuables is sometimes suspect.

HOSTELS Try Student Hostel No. 5, 75 Damareos St, Pangrati (Tel. 7519530). A bit out of town, but worth the trouble of travelling to. Very clean, well organized and extremely friendly. Trolley-buses 2 and 12. Dorm bed 1,500GDR, single room 3,500GDR.

Also try Mystra-5, 26 Kerameon Street (Tel. 52 27737) or Diana, 70 Patission St (Tel. 82 23179).

Directly opposite the station there's Olympos (Tel. 52 23433).

Cheap, friendly and 3 minutes from Larissis Station, Hotel Phaedra (Herefondos 16) in the Plaka is clean and reasonable (5,000GDR for a double).

Thisseus Inn on Thisseus 10 (Tel. 32 45960) is centrally located, 3 blocks west of Syntagma; it's cheap but clean.

There's a hostel at 1 Agiou Meletiou and the YWCA is at 11 Amerikis St (Tel. 362 4291) (women only).

The Annabel youth hostel, 28 Koumoundourou (Tel. 52 45834) has a pleasant ambience.

Athens Connection, 20 Ioulianou Street (Tel. 82 24592) has a bar, a safe and free showers.

Finally, Athens International Youth Hostel is at 16 Victor Hugo Street and is (at time of writing) the only officially IYHF-affiliated hostel in the whole of Greece! (Tel. 523 4170; Fax 523 4015).

CAMPING The nearest campsite is quite far out: 198 Athinon Avenue, Peristeri (Tel. 58 14114); take buses 822 or 823 from Eleftherias Square (Thission underground station).

There is another, better, campsite: Voula Camping, 3 Alkionidon (Tel. 89 52712). Take bus 118, 122 or 153 from Vass. Olgas Avenue. It's 15 km from Syntagma, but offers a pool, bar, restaurant and beaches.

If you're still stuck for a bed, drop into the ISYTS student centre at 11 Nikis St (Tel. 32 21267) and they'll help you.

EATING AND NIGHTLIFE

There are lots of restaurants, bars and discos in the Plaka district. The hippest of a crop of discos around the Voula suburb is Aerodhromio with its open-air dance floor (so you can watch the planes passing over until 4 a.m.). Piraeus is also lively at night, particularly Zea Marina nearby, and in the National Park people gather on summer evenings to see performing artists. For the Athens gay scene, check the listing magazine *Athinorama*.

For cheap eats, fill up on shish kebabs (*souvlaki*) and *dolmades* (vine leaves stuffed with meat). There are plenty of cheap supermarkets. Avoid fruit from stalls as it's over-priced and the quality suspect.

For great food at good prices in a friendly atmosphere, try Kouklis at Tripidon 14 which is an excellent, reasonably priced Greek restaurant. Vegetarians are catered for at Eden,12 Lissiou St, Plaka, which is open every day until midnight and is housed in an historic neoclassical building.

If you choose to eat out in Athens and if the signs are in English, then more often than not the food is more expensive and touristy.

The Athens festival takes place during the summer. This includes open-air performances in the Herodus Atticus Odeon. For details contact the box office at 4 Stadhiou Street (Tel. 32 21459).

EXCURSIONS Sixty-nine km away is the amazing TEMPLE OF POSEIDON at Cape Sounion. It dates back to 440 BC and is dedicated to the God of the Sea. Like the Acropolis, get there as early as possible; buses leave from Mavromateon St every half hour, until 9.30 p.m. Byron carved his name on to the temple, but the Greek tourist board do not recommend current visitors, famous or otherwise, to do the same.

For DELPHI, 178 km north-west from Athens, take the local train to Livadhia and take the bus direct from there (700GDR). Alternatively, take a KTEL bus from 260 Liossion Street: approximately 8 buses run a day (2,600GDR). This is the site of the Delphic Oracle and was the holiest place in Ancient Greece. Little is left of the Temple of Apollo but there's still a fascinating museum (which houses the famous bronze charioteer), a 400 BC theatre and the stadium where the Pythian Games were held. The Tourist Office is at 44 Pavlou St, close to the bus station (Tel. 0265 82000). Open: Mon.–Sat. 8 a.m.–8.30 p.m.; or at 40 Apollonos St, on the left and up the hill from the bus station lies the Tourist Police office (Tel. 82220), open 8 a.m.–2 p.m.

At the top of the hill at 29 Apollonos is a youth hostel (Tel. 0265 82268), open March–Nov. Other cheap hostels are in Vassileos Pavlou. The campsite Apollon (Tel. 0265 82750) is 1½ km west of Delphi on the Amfissa road. The cheapest place to eat in town is Taverna Vakhos, next door to the youth hostel. Buses for Patras depart from Kifissoo St.

The Islands

For many people, Greece *is* the islands. Each year quiet fishing villages are becoming both touristy and cosmopolitan, and while some remote islands probably still have a decade or so to go before they're turned into mini Majorcas, many have only a year or two, and some are there already. For a remote haven, choose an island which has only a weekly sailing from Piraeus – the fewer the ferries, the fewer the crowds, although the less reliable the service. Another way to find a 'goodie' is to ask backpackers. Here are 6 things to bear in mind:

1. Buy your ticket from one of the agencies in Piraeus, not on the boat – they often charge 20% surcharge. Some of the Athenian hostels offer what appear to be bargain tickets – beware of hidden port taxes and surcharges. Daily departures include: Chios, Eyina, Crete, Paros, Naxos, Ios, Samos, Kos, Lesvos, Milos, Andros and Tinos in the summer. Many agents act for specific boats and will tell you that theirs is the only service; don't accept them at their word. Ask around and compare prices. Take into account that routes taken and the speed of the boats can vary considerably. Before buying a ticket, establish how many stops there will be *en route* to your island and the estimated time of arrival.
2. Avoid the southern Aegean islands in August because they can receive the incredibly strong *meltemi* (northern wind) which can ruin your sunbathing and sightseeing.
3. If you plan on going far afield, go for an overnight boat as it costs

no extra to sleep on deck and saves you the price of a night's accommodation.

4. The Port Police at Piraeus are contactable on Tel. 42 26000 if there are any problems, and the Directorate of Tourism of Mainland Greece and the Islands is situated in Zeas Marina (Tel. 41 35716 or 45 93145).

5. Whichever ferry you disembark from, you will find touts peddling their accommodation. Much of it is cheap, but ensure that you know exactly where it is before you agree to anything – it is not uncommon for a 'within walking distance' site to be, in reality, a half-hour bus trip away.

6. Always check departure times for your next visit as soon as you arrive on an island. Ferries out here are notoriously unreliable, so work out alternatives and plan for the worst. Keep some spare cash for port taxes.

The Saronic Gulf Islands

These islands are within 4 hours of Athens and consequently are among the most crowded.

EYINA (Aegina) is the closest to Athens and sailings are from the central harbour at Piraeus (Tel. 45 11311). (For the other islands sailings are from Zea Marina, close to Piraeus, Tel. 45 2 7107.) Take the hydrofoils which supplement the steamer services and take only half an hour. The tourist police are on Leonardov Lada St (Tel. 0297 23243). Look for bed and food around the port in Eyina town and admire the well-preserved Doric TEMPLE OF ARIA and the view from the TEMPLE OF APOLLO. The bay of Agia Marina has the best beaches but is packed with Athenians at weekends.

Eyina is very much a family tourist area, so accommodation is not cheap and fills up quickly. Try the Sklavenas Hostel at 19 Kapodhistrias (Tel. 0297 22327), which offers roof space as an option.

POROS is packed out in summer and heavily commercialized. It has some good beaches and lush pinewoods. The Tourist Information in the town of Poros will help you find a bed. See the MONASTERY OF ZOODHOHOS PIYI. The Tourist Police are situated on Agiou Nikolaou Street (Tel. 0298 22256), open 24 hours. Try to get out to the village of Trizina, close to Poros on the mainland. It lies close to the ancient city of the same name and is the legendary birthplace of Theseus.

HYDRA (Idra) is 3½ hours from Piraeus and is one of the beautiful people's islands, consequently the prices, especially along the harbour, are crippling. Best avoided in peak season. For a truly memorable view, climb up to the hilltop monastery of AGIA TRIADA. Hydra is all you expect a Greek island to be: narrow winding streets, donkeys (no cars allowed), beaches, blue sea and sky. The Tourist Police at Navarhou N. Votsi St (Tel. 0298 52205) will find you rooms, which are cheaper on the other side of the town. Alternatively, ask around the fishermen's quarter of Karmini, a kilometre to the west of town.

SPETSES is a small wooded island of great charm with AGII ANARGYRI as its best beach. The harbour town of Spetses has 2 cheap hotels (the Acropole and the Saronicos) and the Tourist Police on Botsari St (Tel. 0298 73744) will fill you in with any other information you may need.

The Cyclades

These are the most visited of the Aegean islands and the hub of the Greek ferry system. There are 211 of them in all, but it's still possible to find a few of the inhabited ones that will offer you relative 'splendid isolation'.

Visit the 'dry islands': SIFNOS with its estimated 365 churches and chapels, and a gastronomic delicacy of roast kid and olives; SIKINOS, which has a very good beach; SERIFOS, with iron ore mines and annual August fiesta; and MILOS. All are relatively quiet, but their landscape is rather arid. Milos (Plaka) the capital is the discovery site of the Venus de Milo, and houses an archaeological folklore museum.

ANDROS and TINOS are very attractive and large enough to allow the tourists to spread themselves out. Tinos becomes a sacred island on 15 August, and pilgrims attend celebrations in honour of the Virgin Mary. Her icon at the Church of Evangelistria is said to have miraculous properties. The Tourist Office, by the harbour, is open Mon.–Fri.: 7.30 a.m.–2 p.m. and Tinos Camping (Tel. 0283 22502) is a 10-minute walk from the port.

NAXOS: in Greek mythology this is the place where Dionysus sprang from the thigh of Zeus. It is large and fertile with a mountainous interior. The Tourist Office can be found across the boat dock on the waterfront (Tel. 24525/24358), open daily 8 a.m.–midnight. The Panorama Hotel on Afitritis (Tel. 0285 22330) in the old town is reasonably priced. Much cheaper is Naxos Camping (Tel. 0285 235 00) off Agios Giorgios Beach. You can rent mopeds from Theoharis (Tel. 23900), left of the Tourist Office and open daily 8 a.m.–2 p.m.,

5 p.m.–9 p.m. The Tourist Police (Tel. 22100/23280) are again left of the Tourist Office, take another right and a left to get there. The bus service for the islands is very good. Try and get to the town of Apiranthos: the folk art and Michael Bardini (Cycladic Art) museums are free in the mornings. Apollon and Ayia Anna have the best beaches.

If you do not want to leave the mainland for too long, take a ferry from the port of Lavrio (south-east of Athens) to KEA, a journey of only 90 minutes. It is a quiet picturesque island, and its most famous asset is a colossal lion carved into the solid rock during the 6th century BC at the port of Korissa.

MYKONOS is the Greek island to experience tourism, not Greece. It's very beautiful, very touristy, very expensive and very gay. There are nude beaches (the Paradise beach and Super Paradise, mostly gay) and countless bars, clubs and restaurants. There's also stunning scenery, magnificent beaches, whitewashed houses and windmills. There are a few reasonably priced hotels: the Philippi at Kaloyera 32 (Tel. 0289 22294) and the Apollon on Mavroyenous (Tel. 0289 22223). Tourist information is available from both the Tourist Office (Tel. 22 699), open 9 a.m.–9 p.m., and the Tourist Police (Tel. 22482), on the waterfront. Paradise Beach Camping is the only officially listed site on the island and a van arrives to meet all boats as they arrive. It is inexpensive and well-appointed. Mykonos is very well connected by ferry – there is at least 1 ferry a day travelling to Tinos, Paros, Santorini, Ios, Naxos, Andros and Piraeus. If you're travelling to the latter, less than half the time (though twice the price) are the Supercats Marine Co.'s hovercrafts (Tel. 01 3609911) which travel Wed.–Mon.: 9 a.m.–4 p.m. and cost 6,142GDR.

There are also boat trips from Mykonos to DELOS, the ancient religious centre of the Greek world, where you can see the ruins of the Sanctuary of Apollo, the Terrace of Lions and the Sacred Harbour.

PAROS is a beautiful and very clean island, but very touristy, and all that makes it worth the trip is its beautiful old church, Panagia Ekatondapiliani (open 9 a.m.–1 p.m. and 5 p.m.–9 p.m.). Boats depart, several times a day, to all the major nearby islands. A complete schedule is posted at the Tourist Office in the windmill by the dock (Tel. 24528), open daily 8 a.m.–midnight. You'll find most of the hotels and rooms just off the waterfront and into the old town of Parikia. Camping Koula (Tel. 0284 22081) is 400m north of the town, while Camping Koulous is further out.

ANDIPAROS, the virtually undeveloped, smaller island opposite Paros, has a very frequent ferry service and you can find more secluded accommodation here. Camping Andiparos (Tel. 61221) lies 800m north-west of the town on Agios Yiannis beach and Hotel Mandalena (Tel. 0284 61206) is inexpensive. Buses go directly to the stalactite caves on the south side every hour from 10.30 a.m. to 2.30 p.m. A return trip costs about 1,000GDR (plus 400GDR for entrance to the caves).

IOS is a popular destination for those with lots of energy and little money. If you don't want to join the crowds sleeping on the beach, try Camping Stars (Tel. 0286 91302) or Far Out Camping at Milopatas (Tel. 0286 91468). The beaches to the south of Ios at Manganari are secluded and beautiful. The main village is packed full of bars, but during the day try getting your water bottle filled up with locally produced wine from the greengrocers!

Santorini (Thira/Fira)

A massive volcanic explosion 4,000 years ago formed Santorini. From the harbour, get to the town of FIRA (ferries dock at Athinios now) where you can find rooms at reasonable prices. Beware of the hotel touts at Athinios: they will hustle you into a mini van and take you somewhere miles out of town. The best beaches are Kamari, Monolithos and Perissa with its black sand. There are ruins from the Minoans, Romans and Venetians. The boat trip out to the little island of NEA KAMENI, where the volcano started and still smoulders, is worth it.

The monastery of PROFITIS ILIAS on the island's summit houses a great religious celebration each year on 20 July. Visitors are invited to join the islanders in a meal of traditional dry pea soup followed by energetic folk dancing. Guest houses are operated by the GNTO at the small village of 01A on the north-west coast of the island, site of a spectacular sunset. Alternatively the Kontohori youth hostel on Agios Eleftherios (Tel. 0286 22722 or 22577) offers a very good deal, but avoid the offer of roof accommodation: it's cold and mosquito-infested. Perissa Camping (Tel. 0286 81343) is situated near the beach of the same name, and there is a new campsite, Santorini Camping, at Fira (Tel. 0286 22944/23203). Beware of some hoteliers' habit of charging for 2 nights if you book in before noon. It may be unethical but it's technically legal.

The Sporades

These archetypal holiday islands offer fine sandy beaches, translucent waters and dense pine forests. Once the quietest islands in Greece, they have in recent years succumbed to commercialization and now tend to be very busy in season. You approach them by boat from Kimi (port authority: Tel. 0222 22606), Ayios Konstandinos (port authority: Tel. 0235 31920), or Volos (port authority: Tel. 0421 38 888) which you reach by bus or train from Athens. To get to Volos, change at Larissa (almost hourly). You can book accommodation on the mainland before leaving for the islands at the Hotel Chamber of Greece, 2 Karageorgi Servias St, Athens (Tel. 323 7193).

SKIATHOS is the most touristy, but that's because it's very beautiful. It's also lively, and one of the best Greek islands for nightlife. For a night's rest try one of the pensions on Evangelistras St in Skiathos town. KOUKOUNARIES is a superb beach surrounded by pine groves. Many homes advertise rooms to let (*dhomatia*) in the summer months and their prices are reasonable. Try Hadula Tsourou, 17 Mitrop Ananiou St (Tel. 0427 22364) and Maria Papagiorgiou just off Grigoriou before Christina's Bar (Tel. 0427 21574). There is a good selection of rooms on offer at 14 Kapodhistriou. Of the 4 official campsites, Aselinos, Xanemos and Koukounaries (Tel. 0427 49290) are recommended.

On first impression, ALONISSOS may appear soulless and unattractive. It is, however, one of the more traditional and friendly Greek islands. From the port of Patitiri, head for Marpounda or Kokkinokastro where there's a good pebble beach and archaeological remains such as the sunken Byzantine ship at AYIOS PETRAS. The sea around this island has been declared a Marine Conservation Park, so do not leave rubbish lying around. The local room-owners' association (Tel. 0424 65577), located on the waterfront, will help you find accommodation. The official campsite is Ikaros Camping (Tel. 0424 65258) on Steni Vala Beach.

SKOPELOS has cheap rooms in its town and good beaches at STAFILOS and AGONTAS. Inland lie the ruins of the medieval bishops' palace, and many churches and monasteries. If you intend to stay in SKOPELOS TOWN, try and get a room up the hill, as the town sewage discharges into the harbour and can smell awful on a hot day. The Tourist Office (Tel. 0424 23220) is situated on the waterfront. There is a fabulous but very remote campsite at Iluminasis Beach Velanio (by boat from Agnontas).

SKYROS is the most beautiful and unspoilt island of the Sporades. Flat-topped white houses stand on the cliffs and folk crafts still flourish. The long dark sand beach is wonderful, and there are countless little coves for swimming and sub-aqua diving. Try the campsite (take bus from ferry to Magazia), or use one of the restaurants for a room. The Tourist Office in Hora, Skyros Travel, Main Street (Tel. 0222 91123 or 91600), operates all the information services you'll need, including help with accommodation, boat trips and buses.

North-East Aegean

If you don't mind going a bit further out of your way, the islands of the north-eastern Aegean have their rewards: Samos, Lesvos and Hios are the 3 most popular, and all are linked by boat services to the islands of the Dodecanese, Cyclades and Crete.

SAMOS, the birthplace of the goddess Hera (Juno) and Pythagoras, is heavily wooded with a rocky coastline and a good beach resort, Kokari. The capital, SAMOS TOWN (Vathi) has a good archaeological museum (open Tues.–Sun.: 8.30 a.m.–3 p.m.; 500GDR). When you arrive, go to Samos Tours at the end of the ferry dock (Tel. 0273 27715) or the Tourist Office further down the waterfront, by Pythagoras Sq. (Tel. 0273 28530) for all the information you want. The municipal tourist board (Tel. 28582) also sell ferry tickets. Accommodation is scarce in the summer months, but try the Pension Ionia on Manoli Kalmoiris (Tel. 0273 28782) or the Pension Avliat Areos 2 (Tel. 0273 22939). The central island area around PIRIGOS and MITILINI are rich in archaeological sites and museums.

LESVOS, also known as Mitilini after its principal city, homeland to Aesop of the fables, is a mass of olive trees and has some incredible, traditionally designed buildings in its port of Mithimna. The coast of Patraon in the northwest is abundant in archaeological finds and there is a petrified forest at Sigri. To get to Lesvos from Piraeus, there is 1 service a day, and from Salonica, one service a week. The Tourist Police in Mitilini situated behind the customs house, open 8.30 a.m.–5.30 p.m., possess a list of lower priced hotels and rooms to let in private houses. Try the Rex on Katsakouli (Tel. 0251 28 523). Expect to pay about 4,000GDR per double room.

CHIOS (Hios), birthplace of Homer, has an interesting Byzantine monastery, the Nea Moni, and a lively bazaar. Because of its literary connections, the village of VRONTADO, 5 km from Chios, holds a 'Homeria' (events of art and literature) every summer. The Tourist

Police, 37 Neorian St, on the north side of the harbour (Tel. 0271 26555), can help you find accommodation and fill you in on the details. The New Zealander-managed Rooms with a View (Tel. 0271 20364), located near the Acropolis, is a good budget option. A ferry connects the island to Turkey and Lesvos once a day, and to Inousses every hour. Contact the port authority (Tel. 22837) or the Tourist Office at 18 Kouari St (Tel. 44 389) for more information.

The Dodecanese

These are the most easterly islands of Greece, a few kilometres from Turkey. The boat trip from Piraeus can take up to 20 hours. Ferries travelling this route have alternately scheduled departures at 1 p.m. every day. These boats stop at Kos *en route*. You're rewarded for your efforts by superb beaches, mountains, medieval buildings and an air of historical importance which you don't find on any other islands.

The 2 main islands are RHODES and KOS, the latter of which is regarded as the birthplace of modern medicine. The Knights of St John captured the islands in the 14th century, and they were occupied by the Italians during the Second World War. If you are travelling by ferry around these islands, expect cancellations due to rough seas, especially out of season.

Kos, Rhodes and Leros all have airports, and with a student discount of 25% on Olympic Airways flights, air travel can become as competitive as unreliable services by sea. Women beware of Rhodes men (*Kanaki*), who are real charmers.

RHODES: the island of eternal summer (300 days of sunshine a year). In Rhodes town, see the old city, the Suleymaniyah Mosque and the Grand Masters' Palace. The Tourist Police and Tourist Information (Tel. 0241 27423) are at Rimini Square near Mandraki (the port area) (Tel. 35945) or the EOT at Archbishop Makarios and Papagou Streets (Tel. 0241 23655/23255) will help you with accommodation, bus and boat schedules (they close at 3 p.m.). The old town has the best cheap places to sleep, such as Pension Andreas, Omirou 28D (Tel. 34156), Pension Apollo, Omirou 28Cc (Tel. 32003), or Pension Massari, 42 Irodotou St (Tel. 22469). Also try Tina's Studios on the corner of Kathoponli and Constantopodos. For eating, check out Artemis Pizza on Dimostheres St 12 (Tel. 34235). If you need hydrofoil, ferry and excursion boat information, look no further than Triton Tours on Plastira St (Tel. 21690/30657). The ferries to Israel stop at Rhodes, but only for a couple of hours. The west coast of Rhodes is incredibly windy and the east coast is where the best beaches are. FALIRAKI BEACH is good, although it's packed for most of the season with a youngish package-holiday clientele. A campsite is situated near here (Tel. 0241 85 358) and there's another one 64 km down the east coast at Lardos (Tel. 0244 44203/44249). Nightclubs are as plentiful as the bars. Most shops stay open until well past 9 p.m., so do your souvenir hunting in the evening. Rhodes is tax-free, so booze is a bargain.

LINDOS has archaeological remains and is an extremely picturesque town, but the package-deal customers flock here in summer and prices become astronomical. It can still be very romantic if you are with the right person!

KOS, the birthplace of Hippocrates, is a fascinating island: great beaches, ancient Roman and medieval monuments, mosques, a Crusader fortress (Tues.–Sun.: 8.30 a.m.–3 p.m. Admission 400GDR), and a wonderful atmosphere. Camping, though not legal, is idyllic. The official campsite: Kos Camping (Tel. 0244 23910) is 2.5 km out of town, towards Cape Psalidhi, and is closed during the off-season. The Tourist Ppolice (Tel. 24444) on the waterfront will be able to tell you the best way of getting there. Opening hours are: Apr.–Oct.: 7.30 a.m.–9.30 p.m. On the south-eastern outskirts are the ruins of Hippocrates' medical school and sanctuary at the Asclepion. Further west, on the coast road, lies the PETALOUDES VALLEY, where millions of butterflies gather each summer. For accommodation try Pension Alexis, at 9 Irodotou and Omirou St (Tel. 28798) or – the rock-bottom option – Kalimnos at Riga Fereou 9 (Tel. 22336) in Kos Town. If it is nightlife you are after, go to Platia Eleftherias. At PARADISE BEACH, 50 km south of the capital, you will find unspoilt sand, peace and quiet – except for a nearby Club Med complex. Kos has good ferry and boat links with the other islands and the mainland, but check with boat operators beforehand, since times are prone to change.

Crete (Kriti) city phone code: 81

Crete is the legendary birthplace of Zeus and home of the minotaur, and is divided into 4 regions with Heraklion, Hania, Rethymnon, and Ayios Nikolaos as their capitals. HERAKLION (Iraklion) is the main port of Crete with connecting ferries to Piraeus. Apart from the amazing ARCHAEOLOGICAL MUSEUM off Eleftherias Square, where you'll find the Hall of the Minoan frescoes, the city has little to recommend it. If staying, try the youth hostel at 5 Vironos St, just off 25 Augustou

Avenue (Tel. 286281) or the new hostel (Tel. 280858) at 24 Handnakos St. From Heraklion, you can visit the Minoan ruins at KNOSSOS, legendary home of the Minotaur. The ruins are open Mon.–Fri.: 8 a.m.–7 p.m., Sat./Sun.: 8.30 a.m.–3 p.m. Admission is 1,500GDR but there is a student discount and they are free on Sunday. To get there take bus 2 which stops along 25 Augoustou Avenue. There are also ruins to visit at PHAESTOS (1,200GDR), or the beach at PLAKIAS. The Tourist Office in Heraklion is opposite the Archaeological Museum at 1 Zanthoudhidhou St (Tel. 228825), open, Mon.–Fri.: 8 a.m.–2.30 p.m. Camping Iraklion (Tel. 286380), west of the city, is strictly run and expensive.

Further west is RETHYMNON with its Venetian and Turkish buildings. There is an excellent and popular youth hostel at 41 Tombazi St (Tel. 0831 22848), and the Tourist Office is on E. L. Venizelou Avenue (Open 8 a.m.–2.30 p.m. Mon.–Fri.: Tel. 0831 29148). Camping Arkadia (Tel. 28825) and Camping Elizabeth (Tel. 28694) are 4 km out of town.

In HANIA (Khania), the elegant ex-capital of Crete, the Venetian architecture makes you feel more in Italy than Greece. The Tourist Office at 40 Kriari Street is open 8.30 a.m.–2 p.m. (Tel. 0821 26246). Try the harbour area for rooms, or the youth hostel at 33 Dhrakonianou St (Tel. 0821 53565). Open Mar.–Nov., Camping Hania is 4 km west of the city (Tel. 31686). For the high spot of your trip, walk along the SAMARIAN GORGE, the largest in Europe and a nature lover's dream, but in the summer a tourist haven. Take the bus to Xyloskalo, through the Omalos mountains, for this 6-hour walk. The walk will end in the small town of Ayia Roumeli, on the southern coast. From here you can get a boat to Loutro or Hora Sfakion, where you can catch a bus back to Hania. Before you set out for this trip, pack refreshments and sensible footwear. You'll need them.

In eastern Crete AYIOS NIKOLAOS, like Malia, is the tourist trap. It's very picturesque but often short of rooms. Enquire at the Tourist Information Office at 20 Akti Koundourou (Tel. 0841 22357). Or try the Pension Marilena at 14 Erithou Stavrou (Tel. 0841 22 681). The harbour nightlife is the best thing about this town, and Club Scorpio plays dance music until the early hours. Fifty-two kilometres west, at the village of PSIHROS, is the path that ascends to the Dhiktan Cave (*Dikteon Andron*), the legendary birthplace of Zeus, and venue of cult worship (open daily 10.30 a.m.–5 p.m.). At the village you can hire a donkey from the locals if you do not wish to ascend to the cave by foot. Admission is 150GDR for students. There are many other caves of archaeological and historical interest; ask at Tourist Information for more details. SITIA, east of the city, is near the fantastic palm beach of VAÏ, as seen in the Bounty Bar adverts, which is swamped with tourists during the day (beware: the authorities are very strict on illegal camping). The youth hostel at 4a Odos Therisou St (Tel. 0843 22693) can usually squeeze you in. The Tourist Office has closed! For more information try the Tourist Police at Mysonos 24, open 7.30 a.m.–2.30 p.m. (Tel. 24200).

There are daily sailings from Piraeus to the ports of both Hania (Tel. 0821 89240) and Heraklion (Tel. 081 226073), both of which take approximately 12 hours. Sailings for Rethymnon leave on Mon., Wed., Fri., Sun. (Tel. 0831 29221).

The Ionian Islands phone code: 66 In Islands

These are the islands off the north-west coast, lusher than most, with Corfu as their main tourist trap. Italian is widely spoken.

Corfu

If you're taking the ferry from or to Italy, you can stop off here. Take the opportunity if you've a day or two to spare, particularly if you can avoid the crush months of July and August. Corfu doesn't look terribly Greek; in some ways it's more like the French Riviera. The Venetians, French and British have all occupied the island and left their colonial marks in the buildings, food and people. If you are travelling from Patras, possession of an Inter-Rail ticket entitles you to travel deck class, not second class, on the ferry, so the trick is to get on early and find a bench to lay out your sleeping bag.

When you disembark, turn left to the Old Port; the road to the right of the Hotel Constantinopolis is where to start your search for a cheap bed. Try the Hotel Europa (Tel. 0661 39304), in Neo Limin, which charges about 6–8,000GDR for a double room, and rents out mopeds for 3,500GDR. You are likely to be met at the port by reps from just about every hotel with spare beds. Another recommendation is Hotel Elpis at 4 Neo Theokoki St (Tel. 30289) in an alleyway opposite 128 Neo Theokoki St near the Old Port. Basic double rooms cost about 2,500GDR, or 2,800GDR for triples. Hot showers are an extra 200GDR. The Tourist Police, 31 Arseniou St (Tel. 30265), will fix you up in a private home if they like the look of you. Follow the street along the waterfront from the new port. Tourist Information is in the Governor's House (Tel. 37520) between Mantzaran and Dessila streets. The youth hostels are far out and invariably full. The IYHF hostel is 4½ km north (Tel. 91292), take bus 7 from Plateia San Rocco to Kondokali. The reception is open 8 a.m.–12 noon, 5 p.m.–8 p.m.

Camping Vatos, on the opposite side of the island to Corfu Town is cheap, friendly and has full facilities including bar and restaurant. You can get free minibuses to and from the nearest beach as well as a free minibus service to the early-morning ferries (Tel.94505).

Pelekas Beach, on the west coast, is a favourite of eurorailers, as is Karousadhes in the north of the island, which offers excellent facilities for 800GDR a night. We don't recommend you hire a moped, but if you must, make sure you get a helmet and haggle for the petrol, which is always a rip-off. Moped hire usually costs around 4,000–5,000GDR.

The lively Pink Palace Hotel is owned by Dr George and his sister (Tel. 531031 4). At Agios Gordhios, it's right on the beach and can be reached by bus from the Old Port. It is a backpacker's heaven and there are many activities designed for even the quietest person to join in the fun, such as the infamous ouzo circle. It charges from 5,000GDR per person, with breakfast, dinner and shower included. Laundry costs an extra 2,500GDR.

For your evening meal, the Old Port area is good. Try Pizza Pete at 19 Arseniou St, which serves brilliant vegetarian and pizza specials for around 1,500GDR. Café Corner at 10 Agais Sofias is a licensed café in the old part of the town. English-speaking service provides organic vegan dishes, and special dietary requirements can be catered for in advance (Tel. 26457). Yisdhakis at Solomou is an authentic Greek restaurant. For picnics, the best place to shop is the produce market on Odhos Dhessila. Beware of some of the cheap food stalls, as food poisoning seems to be a recurring hazard.

The festival of Corfu takes place in Sept. and features ballet, concerts, operatic and theatrical offerings. From June until then the GNTO puts on a season of folk dances and 'sound and light' performances in English, French and Italian at the old fortress to the north-east of the town.

Paleo Kastritsa, on the west coast, has sandy beaches, blue water and stalls selling jewellery. You could even go scuba diving (Tel. 0663 41211, Baracuda Club).

PAXI and its little neighbour ANDIPAXI, 30 minutes away, are becoming more touristy due to their proximity to Corfu, but these small islands still have a lot of charm. Every day a car ferry leaves Corfu for Paxi, which takes about 3 hours. Paxi is covered with grape vines and olive trees, and on 15 Aug. there is a festival at the monastery of

PANAYIA, carrying on into the evening with dancing taking place in the main square in GAIOS. The Tourist Police (Tel. 0662 31222) should be able to help you find rooms to stay in. If you decide to camp illegally on the sandy beach at Mogonissi, be tidy and careful; fire can start particularly easily in summer.

ITHACA, the home of Odysseus, is a small mountainous island with many historical caves associated with the hero. Linked daily by boat from Paxi and Corfu, it has a music and drama festival every July and Aug. The main town of VATHI has many shops and houses in the middle of a horse-shoe-shaped harbour. Try to find rooms to let by walking up around the backstreets of the ferry quay, or enquiring at Polyctor Tours in the main square, or the tourist police (Tel. 0674 32205).

ZAKINTHOS, to the west of the Peloponnese, is a lush, mountainous island with a rich Roman and Venetian history, though much of the capital has been rebuilt following an earthquake in 1953. Visit the huge beach and clubs at Laganas. Reached by ferry (60 minutes) from Killini, near Patras, or by plane (45 minutes) from Athens, Zakinthos is a mostly unspoilt island, deserving of the title 'Flower of the East'. Visit the neo-Byzantine Museum and the Venetian fortress in Zakinthos Town, and stay at the Oasis at Koutozi 58 (Tel. 22287) or the Nea Zakynthos at 7 Filikou.

On Zakinthos, and also the nearby island of KEFALONÍA, the MARINE TURTLE PROJECT is currently taking place. There are free talks and slide shows when arrangements to see the beaches can be made. The project organizers are keen to promote wildlife issues here and to generally educate people as to the importance of protecting nature. Check it out if you are in the area.

These latter islands are much quieter than many of the better known places, and if a quiet time is what you are looking for, this is the area to come to!

NOTES

....

....

....

....

....

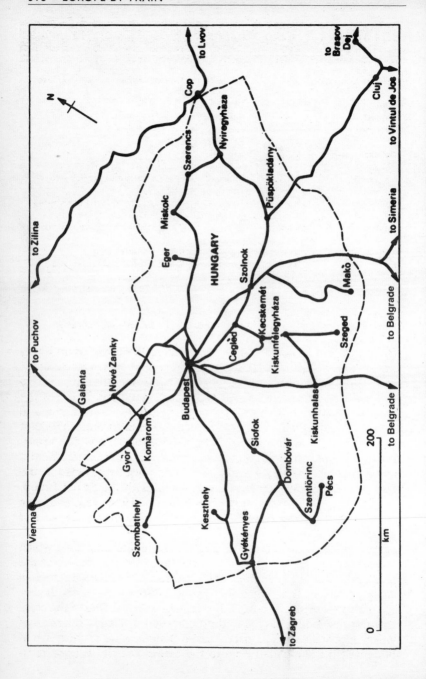

HUNGARY

Entry requirements	Passport. Australians and New Zealnders also require a visa.
Population	10, 275, 000
Capital	Budapest (pop.: 1, 930, 000)
Currency	Forints £1 = approx. 150ft
Political system	Republic
Religions	65% Catholic, 25% Protestant
Language	Hungarian (some German and English understood)
Public holidays	1 Jan.; 15 March; Easter Monday; 1 May; Whit Monday; 20 Aug.; 23 Oct.; 25, 26 Dec.
International dialling codes	From outside Hungary: 00 (international access code) + 36 (country code) From Hungary: 00 + country code For long-distance calls within Hungary: 06 + number
Eurotrain office	Szabadsàg tér 16, H-1395 Budapest 5 (Tel. 01 119898)
Time	GMT + 1 (+2 in summer)
Emergency telephone	Ambulance 04, Fire Brigade 05, Police 07

During the 9th century, mounted Magyars rode westwards until they were stopped by the Holy Roman Empire in what is now Hungary. They settled down and converted to Catholicism. In the 15th century the Turks turned up. A century and a half later, with most of the area's medieval monuments destroyed, the Austrians took over and in 1867 they agreed to grant Hungary equal status under the joint monarchy of the Austro-Hungarian Empire. Things fell apart, however, at the outbreak of the First World War and Hungary went it alone until 1945. Two years later the Communist Party, aided by the Russians, took power. Hungary was linked with the Soviet Union, despite the attempted counter-revolution of 1956. Tensions have risen since then over Hungarian minorities in Romania, Serbia and Slovakia.

Travel within Hungary can be slow, but fortunately the areas which have most to offer are the most accessible. Budapest is one of the most beautiful of the world's cities. Its cuisine is unusual and well worth sampling. The people are friendly and prices are lower than in Austria, for example. Tourism is the growth industry. One of the areas that this new boom has focused on is 'museum villages' or *skanzens* which appear all over Hungary – in the Danube Bend to the north of Budapest, the Hungarian Plain to the east of the city and in Transdanubia, to the west of the capital. Ask at Tourist Information for a special leaflet on them. There is also a specialist leaflet on the various sites of architectural interest throughout the country.

Hungary has led the way in Eastern Europe, preferring to liberalize peacefully, with democratic elections. However, more recently, Wwestern capitalism has not developed into all that it had hoped to become, with many Hungarians proclaiming loudly that they were better off under communism. Hungary, like the rest of the former communist world, is struggling to mix Western commercialism with decades of restrictive politics.

HUNGARIAN STATE RAILWAYS
(MAGYAR-ÁLLAMVASUTAK, MÁV)

Trains are slower than in Western Europe, as well as being crowded in summer. There are often long gaps between services, but with patience it's possible to explore nearly all the larger towns and tourist centres on an Inter-Rail ticket. Inter-City followed by *Sebesvonat* expresses are the fastest services. The ultra-slow *Személyvonat* take an age to get anywhere. Bear in mind that the railway network is very centralized and it's always easier to enter or leave Hungary via Budapest. Whenever possible, make your seat reservations (*fielyjegy*) in advance, at the MÁV booking office at Andràssy út 35, Budapest (Mon.–Fri.: 9 a.m.–6 p.m.). Keep an eye out for any trains with new carriages, especially the new Inter-City trains, as they are a vast improvement on the old rolling stock.

INTER-RAIL BONUSES Free entry to Metró Museum, metro station Deák Ferenc tér, Budapest V; Transport Museum, Városligeti-Körút 11, Budapest XIV; and Horse Carriage Museum, Paràd-fürdö.

PASSES AVAILABLE For information on the Euro Domino and Euro-train Explorer Passes, see pp. 39–40,41.

The Inter-Rail pass has been broken down into zones, so that you don't have to pay for travel to places you've no intention of visiting. Hungary is in Zone D, along with the Czech Republic, Slovakia, Poland, and Croatia, Macedonia and Yugoslavia. For £159 you get 22 days' travel in a single zone.

TRAIN INFORMATION

German has often been the best language to use, but the Germans are not always popular these days. Try English first so as to establish your nationality, rather than letting people think you are German and that you have a lot more money than you actually do have.

RESERVATIONS (FIELYJEGY) To be sure of a seat, it's best to book several days ahead. Booking is obligatory on some international (*nemzetkfözi gyorsvonat*) and other express trains.

EATING ON TRAINS All long-distance trains have either a buffet car or mini-bar, but it is cheaper to stock up beforehand in a supermarket.

TOURIST INFORMATION

All towns have their own local Tourist Information offices (*Idegenforgalmi Hivatal*) in addition to the IBUSZ offices which deal with all aspects of travel and accommodation.

MONEY MATTERS 1 Forint = 100 Fillers.

Banking hours are generally 8 a.m.–3 p.m. Mon.–Thu. and 8 a.m.–1 p.m. Fri. When changing money you should use only the official exchange offices. Do not change it on the street as you may receive counterfeit money and in any case it is illegal. Foreign exchange brought into the country can be taken out when leaving, as can Hungarian currency up to the value of 10,000ft. Make sure you keep receipts for any money changed and for any major purchases you have made. Many offices will accept credit cards, traveller's cheques and Eurocheques.

POST OFFICES Open Mon.–Fri.: 8 a.m.–6 p.m. The quickest service for phone calls, faxes, telexes and telegrams is the main Post Office or the Telecom Information and Service Office (Budapest V, Petöfi S. utca. 17–19. Stamps can also be bought from tobacconists (Mon.–Fri.: 8 a.m.–8 p.m. and Sat.: 10 a.m.–4 p.m.).

SHOPS Most shops are open Mon.–Fri.: 7 a.m.–7 p.m. and Sat.: 10 a.m.–1 p.m. Late-night opening on Thurs. is usually till 8 p.m., with many tobacconists, pastry shops, foodstores and large shopping centres in general also opening on Sun. Growing numbers of round-the-clock foodshops are appearing in Budapest. While the cost of living has increased dramatically for Hungarians, prices are still comparatively low for Western European tourists.

MUSEUMS Most open Tues.–Sun. and are closed on Mon., admission is generally no more than 80ft, and is usually free on either Tues. or Wed. Show your ISIC cards in case there's a reduction. More information available from Tourinform (Tel. 117 9800)

BICYCLES Certain stations rent out bicycles throughout the year and MÁV are now encouraging people to take their bike on the train. Help with routes, maps and other matters can be obtained from the Bicycle Touring Association of Hungary (*Magyar Kerélípáros Tírázok Szahŏv*), 1091 Bp, Kálvín tér, I. em. (Tel. 217 7208). Ask for the *Cycling Tours in Hungary* booklet published by IBUSZ.

HIKING The best areas are in the north, including the woods around Visegrád and Badacsony, north of Budapest; the Matra mountains near Eger; and the Bukk mountains west of Miskolc. There is no network of huts for hikers, and most campsites tend to be located near towns but Youth Hostels are a good option.

MEDICAL CARE First aid is free, but a fee is charged for proper medical treatment, the rate of which depends on the institution concerned. Medical insurance is advised.

TIPPING Leave 10–20% if you have had good service and it is not included on the bill.

SLEEPING

The local Tourist Offices may fix you up in a private house for about 2,000–3,000ft for 2 people per night (plus 30% for the first night). In small towns, look for the sign *Szoba Kiadó* (or *Zimmer frei*) and don't automatically refuse a room if you're approached at a railway station. If you're out of luck, the student travel service Express has several hostels and cheap student hotels. Beds in a hostel/student hotel start at about 700ft. There's no need to be a member of the IYHF, and it's possible for couples to get a room to themselves. Most hotels, especially the budget ones, are booked up and are expensive, but if you are desperate, 1-star hotels both in and out of Budapest can be had for 1,200–1,600ft.

Camping is a realistic possibility. There are over 200 authorized sites, officially graded from 1 to 3, depending on the facilities offered, and many are concentrated along the Danube and Lake Balaton. For more detailed information, contact the Hungarian Camping and Caravanning Club at Ulloi út 6, Budapest (Tel. 01 336536), where you can get copies of their Hungarian camping guides. Camping in the wild is prohibited but undertaken none the less.

EATING AND NIGHTLIFE

Hungarian food is excellent by any standards, and it's cheap. Try *pörkölt* (a stew with paprika), *paprikás csirke galuskával* (chicken with a sour cream paprika sauce), *hogybegy* (meat pancakes) or *goulash*. Vegetarians should try *gombafejek rántva* (mushroom coated with breadcrumbs) with *gnocchi*, and *somlói galuska* (sweet dumplings in rum and chocolate sauce) or *rétes* (strudel) to follow. The cheapest places are the self-service restaurants. Choose and collect your food, then pay the cashier. Look out for the tourist menus as they're normally exceptionally good value; if you're really broke and don't mind standing up, try a *bisztró*. Also try the Hungarian spirit, *pálinka*, a clear brandy made from apricots, cherries or other fruits. Hungary has quite a bit of nightlife, particularly in Budapest. There are student discos and open-air concerts as well as nightclubs.

Budapest phone code: 01

The Danube flows through the heart of the capital, looking far more impressive than in Vienna, and spanned by some fine bridges. Buda, west of the river and set among gentle hills, is a mixture of winding medieval streets, views over the city and neat suburbs; Pest is the centre of commerce and government. The 2 were united, along with Obuda, in 1873, to become Budapest. There's plenty to see and do and because food and transport are still relatively cheap by Western standards it allows your lifestyle to rise above its usual humble level. Budapest is more lively, cosmopolitan and 'Westernized' than any other Eastern European city.

STATION FACILITIES
There are 3 main stations: Déli (south, Tel. 1756 593) which serves the south-west, Keleti (east, Tel. 1136 342) and Nyugati (west, Tel. 1498 503). For rail information within Hungary call MÁV Central Information (Tel. 122 8049, 227860 or 429150) between 6 a.m. and 8 p.m. If you are stuck, remember *pályaudvar* means station. Expect delays, especially left luggage. Give yourself plenty of time, especially in the evenings. Nyugati has a 24-hour mini market.

TOURIST INFORMATION
Of the 6 major tourist agencies operating in Budapest, the best overall source of information is Tourinform at V, Sütö utca 2 (Tel. 117 9800), open daily 8 a.m.–8 p.m. The staff here speak 6 languages and will answer any questions you have. About 50m from the Karoly Korut exit of the Deák tér metro station.

IBUSZ has an office at V Ferenciek tér 10 (Tel. 118 6866) and operates an accommodation service at V, Petöfi tér 3 (Tel. 118 5776). Open round the clock. Express is at Semmelweis utca 4 (Tel. 117 8600) and at Keleti station (Tel. 114 2772); Cooptourist is at Bajcsy-Zsilinsky utca 17 (Tel. 156 9567/111 7034).

ADDRESSES

MAIN POST OFFICE AND INTERNATIONAL TELEPHONE EXCHANGE
Petöfi utca 13 (also *poste restante*), open Mon.–Fri.: 8 a.m.–8 p.m.; Sat.: 8 a.m.–2 p.m. There are 24-hour post offices sited near Keleti and Nyugati stations.
UK EMBASSY V, Harmincad utca 6 (Tel. 266 2888).
US EMBASSY V, Szabadsàg tér 12 (Tel. 112 6450).
CANADIAN EMBASSY XII, Budakeszi utca, 32 (Tel. 1767711).
STUDENT TRAVEL CENTRES EXPRESS, Semmelweiss utca 4 (Tel. 117 6634 or 117 8600). They sell ISIC cards, book student hostels, tours etc. Branch Office at Keleti station. BUDGET TRAVEL EXPRESS, Szabadsàg tér 16 (Tel. 131 7777).

GETTING ABOUT

Public transport is efficient and cheap. A single cósts 35ft. Buy tickets in advance for buses, metro, trolley buses and trams from tobacconists and ticket offices. Validate the tickets on entry. Tram, bus and metro services run 4.30 a.m.–11 p.m., with night services on the busiest routes. The metro has 3 lines, transfer at Deák tér. There is also a 1-day travel pass valid for all public transport in Budapest, for 280ft (or a 3-day pass for 560ft), which is worth buying if you plan to make at least 8 journeys. Do not be tempted to dodge paying because of the ease with which you can avoid paying; fines are up to 2,500ft, and inspectors do not take a day off. Make sure you validate a new ticket when changing lines.

SEEING

The old town of Buda has at its centre VÁRHEGY, CASTLE HILL and the FISHERMEN'S BASTION, Halaszbastya, which is noteworthy for its 7 turrets denoting the 7 tribes of the Magyars and its view of the Buda hills, Margaret Island and the bridges over the Danube. Crowning the hill is the MATTHIAS CHURCH where the Hungarian kings were crowned. The ROYAL PALACE, virtually destroyed in 1944, was rebuilt and houses the HISTORICAL MUSEUM OF BUDAPEST and the NEMZETI NATIONAL GALLERY with its superb collection of Hungarian art. The latter is particularly recommended for its world-class collection of modern works and entry is free for students. The Margaret bridge takes you to MARGARET ISLAND, in the middle of the Danube. The island is a recreation park and often has outdoor concerts and plays on summer evenings.

For the best views over the city, cross the Elizabeth bridge and climb Gellért hill to the Liberation Monument. You can get a bus back if you're shattered. The floodlighting on summer evenings makes a walk by the riverside well worthwhile. You can also get excellent views by taking the cog railway into the Buda hills. Take the metro to Moszkva tér and then tram 56 for 2 stops to the start of the railway, a narrow-gauge system operated almost entirely by children, who do everything but drive the trains on the 11km route through the Buda Forest (Tel. 175 5604). One of the most scenic bus routes is the number 16, which runs between Erzsèbet tér and the castle district, crossing the chain bridge. Tram 2 also has a pretty route, rattling alongside the Danube from the central market to the Parliament building.

ST STEPHEN'S BASILICA is the impressive church in Pest beside the PARLIAMENT. A walk through the courtyards of this complex with the sun setting over the Buda hills can be truly memorable.

The PARLIAMENT LIBRARY is the fifth largest book collection in Europe, with 400,000 volumes. Visitors can go on a guided 40-minute PARLIAMENT TOUR around the CUPOLA HALL, MAIN CHAMBER (unless the National Assembly is in session) and ORNAMENTAL STAIRCASE of this neo-Gothic building. Open Wed.–Sun. from 10 a.m., 400ft. payable at Gate X. Two other museums are the FINE ARTS and the HUNGARIAN NATIONAL. The Fine Arts is in Városliget (the city park) which has rowing boats for hire on the lake, and amusement parks. In the centre of the lake is an island upon which is VAJDAHUNYAD CASTLE. If you want to cleanse your pores from the grime of train travel, try an authentic Turkish bath. Try the old Ottoman baths of Kiràly Fürdö on Föutca 84. Men's sessions take place on Mon., Wed. and Fri., and women's on Tues., Thurs. and Sat., all 6.30 a.m.–6 p.m. Also try the Hotel Gellért. For backpack relief, you just have to get your body in the thermal waters which are kept constant at 38°C.

Pick up a copy of the *Budapest Panorama* which is issued monthly by the Tourist Office and gives details of special exhibitions and has a city map.

SLEEPING

Budapest gets busy in summer, so don't hang about getting organized on the bed front. Head for the student accommodation office for Hostelling International IYHF (which has 18 hostels in the city) at Keleti station or EXPRESS main office at Semmelweis utca 4 (Tel. 117 8600). Often you may meet students advertising this accommodation service on the international trains arriving in Budapest, so you chat to them and find out what's what! These are good places to stay if you want to meet fellow travellers. For private rooms IBUSZ and Budapest Tourist have desks at the main train stations. Generally speaking, it is safer to go here than with private touts. You can also try the Strawberry youth hostel at Raday út 43–45 (Tel. 218 4766), or the Strawberry II Hostel at Kinizsi utca 2–6, which is the student quarter near the university (Tel. 217 3033); the Donati IYHF hostel is close to Battyanyi tér (Tel. 201 1971), or just 5 minutes from Keleti Station and 10 minutes from Deák tér is the Ananda Youth Hostel, XVI Köszeg út 21 1141 (Tel. 220 2413).

If you do not want a youth hostel, try City Centre Apartments Inc. They have a dozen or so apartments either near Keleti station, Deák tér, or 1 of the metro stations in between, which can sleep up to 4 people. Many of the rooms have *en suite* facilities and they all have small kitchens, so you can boil up some water for that badly missed cup of tea! Prices vary slightly from room to room, but average between US$18 for the cheapest single and US$44 for the most expensive quadruple. Note that the prices are per *room*. Ring the day before (if possible) or on arrival in Budapest, and one of the staff will meet you. Tel. 272 3388 (office) or 30422263/30447546 (mobile). (From within Hungary, dial 06;). Szilagyi Andras, the manager, speaks good English, so he can easily advise you in detail about what to do and where to go.

You will probably be approached at the transport terminals or outside city-centre accommodation offices or on the main Inter-City trains arriving in the city by people offering rooms. Discuss terms before accepting and make sure you do not take a room which is not convenient for public transport. Remember that University dorms are available in summer – and cheap.

Also, you can try Universum Hostel Vasarhelyi, Budapest XI, Krusper utca 2–4 (Tel. 463 4326/463 4356/463 1950), which offers 2- and 4-person rooms with showers. The Backpack guest house at 33 Takacs Menyhert (Tel. 185 5089) charges around 800ft.

The 2 official campsites are a good last resort as they're rarely full to capacity: Hárshegyi is at Hárshegyi utca 7 (Tel. 176 1921/115 1482) and Római Camping, Szentendrei utca 189 (Tel. 188 7176/168 6260). Bus 22 from Moszkva terminal (metro line 2) gets you there. Check availability through Budapest Tourist Office. To get to Római Camping take the metro to Batthyány tér, where you change to the suburban railway, HEV. Get off at Római Fürdö, within sight of the campsite. Check at the Tourist Office for other sites.

EATING AND NIGHTLIFE

Hungarian cuisine is one of the best in Europe and in Budapest you can eat well at any price. Fixed menus for lunch are common. Look out for places called *bisztrós*, *büfés*, self-services and grills for even lower prices. Even a tourist trap, with gypsy music, wine and 3 courses, should not be excessive, but exercise your discretion! Try New York Restaurant, VII, Terez Körút. 9–11, which has amazing *fin-de-siècle* decor, gypsy music and dancing. The carp from Lake Balaton are a speciality here. There are no restrictions on dress and it is possible to get a 3-course meal with wine and coffee for a good price.

Another place worth trying is the Apostolok Restaurant, Kigyó utca 4–6 (Tel. 118 3704) or Kisakakukk, XIII, Pozsonyi út 12, which is also very reasonable, as is Corso, off Rakoczi. An Italian restaurant on Museum Kit opposite the National Museum is also very good value. For those seeking an alternative to the aggressively carnivorous menus of most eateries, try the Vegetarium, a reasonably priced vegetarian restaurant at V, Cukor út 3.

The meals on the Danube are good, too. Boats leave from below the Duna Hotel at 5.30 p.m. and 8 p.m. and the cruise lasts 2–3 hours – plenty of time to enjoy the meal knowing it won't break the bank. Wine cellars (*borozó*) often serve good meals and the Hungarian wines, particularly Tokaji and Egri Bikavér (Bull's Blood), are quite something. With food being not so cheap these days consider coffee and cakes or ice-cream on the terrace by the river at the Atrium or Forum hotels.

The other 'must' is a visit to the world-famous pastry shop, Ruszwurm (Szentháromsàg 7, opposite the Matthias church, closed Wed.), which has its own varieties of cakes and strudels plus original furnishings and intricate bread sculptures.

The covered central market at the Pest end of the Szabadsàg bridge buzzes with life and has some of the best food in the city, including wonderful cheeses and cooked meats. Skala Csarnok, just north of Blaha Lujza, is open until 8 p.m., selling fresh produce and a range of tasty snacks upstairs.

The Planetarium (near Népliget station on metro line 3) puts on a different show each night of the week with lasers and special lighting effects set to music. Admission is around 400ft. Angyal, at VII Rakoczi utca 51, east of the Astoria metro station, is Budapest's liveliest and most popular gay bar. Open Thu.–Sun.: 10 p.m.–5 a.m. Less crowded is Lokal, VII. Kertesz utca 31. Open 9 p.m.–4 a.m.

Check out the Express Cocktail Ship, one of the Danube cruisers, which takes you round Margaret Island. There's rock, dancing and boozing. Times vary depending on the time of year, so make sure you get on the right boat. There's traditional folk dancing in Buda Park and a list of events is published in *Coming Events in Budapest*. There are also open-air concerts (rock and classical) on Margaret Island. For up-to-the-minute information, buy a copy of the *Daily News*, a newspaper published in English and German every day except Sun. and Mon. Apart from reporting national and international news, it carries regular listings of English language films in Budapest and other cultural events, and is available from news stands and hotels.

The Danube Bend

This has Hungary's most spectacular scenery and it's possible to see much of it on a day trip from Budapest. The Danube makes a dramatic sweep about 24 km north of Budapest, and the mountain scenery and villages up here are among the best in the country. Boats leave the capital from Vigadó tér dock every day – later boats make it possible for you to stop off and sightsee before continuing your journey. (Further information on boats is available from Duna-tours (Tel. 131 4533), Bajcsy Zsilinszky utca 17, and also from Mahart, Belgrád RKP (Tel. 118 1743). The journey to Esztergom, the heart of medieval Hungary, takes 1½ hours. Consider taking a single (to Szentendre) and return to Budapest by bus and then suburban train.

SZENTENDRE, the 'Town of the Arts', is an old Serbian market town and artists' hangout, with lots of small museums, churches and baroque houses (the Margit Kovács ceramics collection, inspired by Hungarian folk art, is superb; open daily 9 a.m.–5 p.m.).

The main square (Fö tér) is the venue for a summer festival and one of the many OPEN-AIR ETHNOGRAPHIC MUSEUMS (near Angyal utca, about 5 km from the station) has examples of traditional buildings from all over the country. Try the inns and coffee shops for a taste of the culinary overlap of the many cultures in this town. The Tourist Office, Tourinform, is at Dumtsa J.U22, 2000 Szentendre (Tel. 26 317965). The Duna Parti Diakhotel hostel is located at Somogy Bacso part. 12 (Tel. 26 12657), near to the river and a short walk from the square. The campsite is on Pap Sziget (Tel. 26 10697), open May–Sept.

A few kilometres up river, VISEGRAD is right on a bend among the forested mountains. This was a Middle Ages stronghold and has a FORTRESS and ROYAL PALACE. The views over the Danube Bend are out of this world, and there's considerable scope for woodland walks. Tourist information (of a sort) is available from the Folk Art place at Fö utca 46 and a camping site can be found at Mogyoro-hegy (Tel. 398217), open May–Sept. only.

ESZTERGOM has some of the oldest and best-preserved remains in Hungary – including the first cathedral of the Christian religion. This was the residence of the Magyar kings until the 13th century and has the honour of being the oldest royal town in Hungary. Take in the CHRISTIAN MUSEUM and ROYAL PALACE remains, but most of all visit the BASILICA. For around 20ft you can climb the dome/bell tower and walk around it to enjoy superb views over the surrounding country and into Slovakia. Note that Esztergom Kertváros is not the main station. Camping is provided at Gyopár Természetbarát Camping (Tel. 33 311401), open May–Oct., and Gran Camping, Nagy-Duna Setany (Tel. 33 311327).

The Hungarian Plain

East of the Danube lies the dusty central plain which is real Hungarian peasant land. An in-depth exploration of this region will reveal pockets of rural life virtually unchanged for generations. Trains run through the Plain and the Budapest–Bucharest line stops off at the main settlements like Kecskemét and Szeged. KECSKEMÉT, home town of the composer Kodály, has only a small area of old town left. Walk along BÁNK BÁN and János Hoffman streets. The TOWN HALL is another typical building in Kossuth tér where you will also find the regional Tourist Office Puszta Tourist. The campsite is 5 km from the station at Sport utca 5 (Tel. 76 329398).

SZEGED, near the frontier with Serbia and Romania, was completely destroyed by flood in 1879, but the town still has something of its rich past when it was under Turkish and, later, Austrian rule. The DÓM TÉR (Square) was created in 1920 for the VOTIVE CHURCH, and Hungary's best Serbian Orthodox church is on the north side of the huge square. Also worth seeing are the BLACK HOUSE – HEROES' GATE and a performance of the Szeged OPEN-AIR THEATRE FESTIVAL (the town comes alive in late July and Aug. when the festival takes place). The local Tour-inform office is at Victor Hugo utca 1 (Tel. 62 311711).

There are 2 student hostels: Apáthy, Kollegium, Eotvos u. 4. (Tel. 23 155), bookable through EXPRESS at Kigyout 3 (open Mon.-Fri.: 8 a.m.–4 p.m.; Tel. 322 522) and Semmelweiss on the street of the same name (Tel. 11644). Camping is provided at various sites; try

Napfeny at Dorozsmai út 2 (Tel. 421 800), Naturista Camping and Strand (Tel. 62 361488) or Sziksósi Camping (Tel. 62 361029). Both are open May–Sept.

Eger

The historic baroque city of Eger, in the north-east, is Hungary's Bordeaux. This is where the good red wine Egri Bikavér (Bull's Blood) originates. It is not surprising, therefore, that an interesting local tour exists, involving the 'Election of the Wine-General of the Valley of the Beautiful Lady'. The worthiness of any particular candidate for this post is linked to an ability to drink as much wine as possible. For more information, contact Tourinform, Dobo tér 2, Eger 3300 (Tel. 36 321807). The Tourist Motel at Mekcsey utca (Tel. 36310014) is a fairly cheap option. DOBO ISTVAN SQUARE is the town centre; just north of this is the CASTLE and the underground casements.

Eger is a good place to base yourself if you fancy delving into the forests and villages of inner Hungary, and there are various campsites, such as Autós Camping at Rákdóczi út 79 (Tel. 36/410 558).

East of Eger is MISKOLC, east of which in turn lies the world-famous wine-producing town of TOKAJ.

Further south and east of there is the NATIONAL PARK OF HUNGARY, where you can see protected animals and beautiful plants, many of which can only be found in this region. There are the bird reservations, which contain one of the largest water-bird feeding and breeding sites in Central Europe.

North-west of Miskolc is Aggteleki National Park; and the nearby BARADLA CAVES. The caves are cold but fascinating, with stalactites as long as 45m.

Lake Balaton

Lake Balaton is Central Europe's largest lake, measuring 600 sq km, and is known as the 'Hungarian Sea', with rolling hills and vineyards interspersed with picturesque old towns. This is the region you'll pass through if you're coming in from southern Austria, and if you've hit a good spell of weather this is where to break your journey, as there are good beaches and everything you need for a few days' beach-bumming, Hungarian-style. Back in the days of the Iron Curtain, it was one of the few holiday places where West German could meet East German.

SIÓFOK, on the southern shores of the lake, has warm shallow waters and seethes with tourists in the summer. There are 8 camp- sites in this area, the nearest, Aranypart Nyaralótelep (Tel. 84 352 519 or 352 801) being 200m from the train station. Try Ifjúsàg Camping at Siófok-Sosto (Tel. 84 352571). Bicycles can be hired from the train station if you can produce your train ticket.

BALATONFÖLDVÁR is the most scenic of the southern Balaton resorts, with trees coming down close to the lakeside. It's a good centre for watersports and has quite a bit of nightlife. Express office at Jozsef Attila utca 9 will fix you up with a room at the Express International Youth Centre or Hotel Juventus (IYHF) (Tel. 84 340 313). Camping sites are located at Naro Camping, Kismartoni utca 4–8 (Tel. 84 340966). Try walking out, as the lake is not deep near to the shore.

TIHANY and BALATONFÜRED are on the northern shore and are quieter and prettier. Tihany has Celtic and Roman ruins and a beautiful yellow BENEDICTINE ABBEY looking down on the peninsula, where you will find the Club Tihany complex. Organ recitals are held inside the abbey in summer. The OPEN-AIR MUSEUM (Tue.–Sun: 10 a.m.–6 p.m.) gives a good idea of the Balaton folk traditions and the thatched- roof houses set among the hills add to the charm. The Tourist Office is at Balatontourist, Kossuth utca 20 in Tihany village (Tel. 86/348 519. Open Mon.–Sat.: 8 a.m.–6.30 p.m., Sun.: 8 a.m.–1 p.m.).

Balatonfüred is a health spa which tends to attract wealthy Hungarians and Germans. See the MEDICINAL SPRINGS, busy HARBOUR and ROUND CHURCH. The Tourist Office is Balatontourist, 8230 Bala- tonfürd, Blaha Lujza utca 5 (Tel. 87/342 822) open Mon.-Sat.: 8 a.m.–6.30 p.m., Sun.: 8.30 a.m.–12 midday, and camping can be found by the water's edge 600m from the train station at Fured Camping, Széchenyi utca 24 (Tel. 87 342 341 or 87 343 823), open Apr.–Oct. It is the biggest site in the country with a 3,500 capacity. Two hotels offering reasonably cheap rates are the UNI at Széchenyi utca 10 (Tel. 87 341 822 or 87 634 2239) and the Kelén Gyogy hotel at Petöfi utca 38 (Tel. 87 342811).

KESZTHELY is at the western end of the lake. There are various things to see: the first European agricultural college, GEORGIKON; the HELION LIBRARY, with many rare books and antiquities; and the BALATON MUSEUM, which gives an account of the natural history and geology of the lake region. There is a good campsite, Castrum, at Mora Ferenc út 48 (Tel. 83 314 422 or 83 312 120).

Day trips to try in this area are the Lóczy Cave, the Gaspar and Jokai look-out points and wine-tasting at Badacsony.

Western Hungary

Between Budapest and Austria lies TRANSDANUBIA, which can be over-run with bargain-hunting Austrians. GYÖR is a large industrial city 90 minutes from Budapest by train. The old town has been lovingly preserved. See the CARMELITE CHURCH and baroque CATHEDRAL. For enter-tainment sample the gypsy atmosphere of Vaskakas Tavern beneath the castle or the magnificent Kisfaludy Theatre at Czuczor Gergely utca. The bustling open-air market is at Dunakapu tér. Rooms in the area are neither plentiful nor cheap. Express at Bajcsy-Zsilinszky út 41 (Tel. 328 833), open Mon.–Fri.: 8 a.m.–4 p.m., can arrange accommodation during the summer in the KTMF student hotel. The Hotel Szarnyaskerek at Revai Miklos utca 5 (Tel. 96 314629), by the train station, is one of the cheaper hotels.

Only 60 km from Vienna is SOPRON – over 700 years old with over 400 protected buildings. It was the location of the largest Iron Age settlement in Europe and the amber road from the Roman period ran through here. Scores of late Renaissance and baroque structures are found in the inner city, including SZÉCHENYI PALACE, the DOMINICAN CHURCH, FABRICIUS HOUSE, the SYNAGOGUE and the FRANZ LISZT MUSEUM. Look out also for the Firewatch Tower and the Gate of Loyalty. The SOPRON FESTIVAL takes place at the end of June and the start of July. Also worth visiting is a performance in the CAVE THEATRE IN FERTO RAKOS (between Sopron and Lake Ferto). The Festival office is at Széchenyi tér 17. Worthy of a day trip is the ESTERHÁZY PALACE FERTO CASTLE, the 'Hungarian Versailles' where Joseph Haydn spent some years as court musician. One of his compositions, the *Farewell Symphony*, received its first performance at the palace. The MUSIC HOUSE was built as a home for him by the Esterházys, and now serves as the HAYDN MEMO-RIAL MUSEUM.

The Lóvér campsite (Tel: 11715), a couple of kilometres south of town, is accessible by taking bus 12 from a train station. When cross-ing from Sopron to Austria, expect to be surrounded by Austrians returning from shopping expeditions, who can cause delays at customs!

KÖSZEG is a quiet town on the Austrian frontier, which is famous for holding off the huge Turkish siege of 1532. On JURISTIC TÉR, the cobbled main square, is the Gothic ST JAMES CHURCH with its wonder-ful frescoes. JURISTIC CASTLE, where the Turks were beaten back, is now a historical museum (closed Mon.).

South-West Hungary

Southern Transdanubia has a pleasant mild climate and lovely green hills. NAGYKANIZSA is the major town of the Zala hills which lie in the west; it is also home to many horse shows. Much of the architecture is baroque and the town is surrounded by forest parkland and a rowing lake. Apart from the TOMB OF MUSTAFA PASHA and the THURY GYORGY MUSEUM (open Wed.–Sun.: 10 a.m.–6 p.m.), the town is also famous for its beers, especially Dreher. The area is poorly connected by train, so the bus service is the major form of transport to and around neighbouring villages. Information on accommodation can be obtained from Zalatour in Fö utca 13 (Tel. 93 311185) or at the IBUSZ office in Szabadsàg tér 21 (Tel. 93 311126). The nearest camping site is Zaratour Camping, Kemping utca 1 (Tel. 93 319119), open May–Sept. It also rents out bungalows.

SZIGETVÁR, which lies further south, is another place famous for being besieged by the Turks. This story is told in the museum (open 10 a.m.–4 p.m., closed Mon.) in the FORTRESS. Also visit the ALI PASHA MOSQUE, now a church. The Tourist Bureau is located inside the Oroszlán Hotel on Zrinyí tér 2 (Tel. 73 310116), open 8.30 a.m.–4 p.m. and will set up accommodation. You can stay in dormitories in the fortress itself (advance booking is advisable because soldiers and school parties are often billeted there).

MOHÁCS, in the south-east of the region, is situated on the banks of the Danube and plays host to the BUSOJARAS PARADE of monstrous figures wearing traditional carved masks held seven weeks before Easter on the last Sunday of Shrovetide. The great Battle of the Mohács of 1526 made the town famous and a memorial site is open on the battle round.

Pécs phone code: 72

Pécs, situated 4 hours away from Budapest and 30 km from Mohács, is home to many fantastic churches, such as the Romanesque CATHE-DRAL, the former Turkish mosque of GAZI KASIM PASHA, and the enormous SYNAGOGUE, which is open daily (except Sat.) from 9 a.m. One of the city's most famous treasures is the painted burial chamber and CHRISTIAN MAUSOLEUM unearthed in I. Istvan tér. A later ROMAN CRYPT and graves can be found in Apaca utca, open May–Oct., closed Mon.

and 1–3 p.m. although opening times are erratic. A walk down Káptalan utca brings you to the Vasarely Museum, named after the initiator of 'Op Art', and Zsolnay porcelain museum. There is a MINING MUSEUM on Maria utca 9, which is open all day except Mon.: 10 a.m.–6 p.m.

The Mecsek Tourist Office at Széchenyi tér 9 (Tel. 213315), open in the summer months 8 a.m.–5 p.m. Mon.–Thu. and 8 a.m.–2 p.m. Friday, will arrange accommodation for you and can also exchange money, as can the IBUSZ office next door (both closed Sun.). The Express Youth and Students Travel Bureau is situated at Bajcsy-Zsilin-szky utca 6 and can organize accommodation in student hostels. To get there, turn right when leaving the train station.

A good camping site is Familia Camping on Gyöngyösi I utca 6 (Tel. 329938), which is 2 km from the train station and provides catering facilities, a post office and tennis courts.

Mandulás Camping on Angyán Janos utca 2 (Tel. 315981) is much larger. Get there on bus 34. Alternatively, try Hotel Laterum, Hajoczy utca 37–39 (Tel. 254963) or Hotel Kikelet, Karolyi M. utca 1 (Tel. 310777).

The environs of Pécs have much to offer for days out: take bus 35 into the scenic MECSEK HILLS and climb the 194m TELEVISION TOWER, on Misina Peak, for a stunning view, or try ABALIGET, 15 km away, which has a stalactite cave and 2 artificial lakes for rowing and swimming. Less than 2 hours away is the GEMENC FOREST NATIONAL PARK, which is the largest and most beautiful wildlife reserve in the country. A flood plain forest, it contains otter, deer, wild boar, white-tailed eagles, black storks and wildcats. For those wishing to stay in this peaceful area, a camping site is located at Baja: Sugovica Camping on Petőfi-Sziget (Tel. 79 321755) which has swimming, rowing and tennis facilities. Further information from Tolna Tourist in Szekszard (Tel. 312144).

NOTES

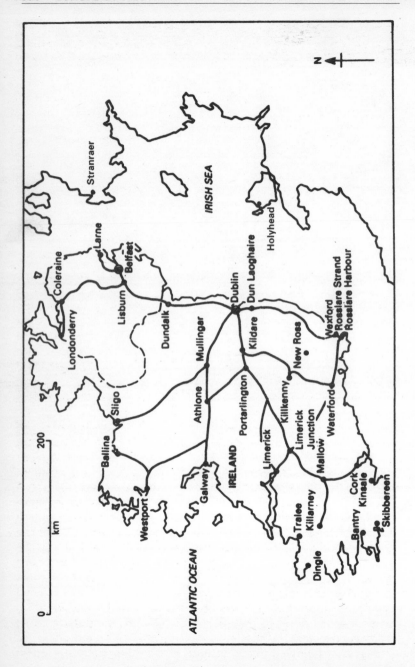

IRELAND

Entry requirements	Passport (not necessary for UK nationals)
Population	3,549,000
Capital	Dublin (pop.: 1,057,000)
Currency	Punt £1 = approx. 1.08 punt (IR£)
Political system	Parliamentary democracy
Religion	94% Roman Catholic, 4% Protestant, 2% Other
Languages	English and Irish (Gaelic)
Public holidays	1 Jan.; 17 March; Easter Monday; 4 May; 1 June; 3 Aug.; 26 Oct.; 25, 26 Dec.
International dialling codes	To Ireland: 00 (international access code) + 353 (country code)
	From Ireland: 00 + country code
Eurotrain office	Compass Travel, 34 Lower Abbey Street, Dublin 1 (Tel. 01741777 or 787028)
Time	GMT (+1 in summer)

The history of Ireland is both turbulent and fascinating, as are its folk-lore and legends. The Romans never conquered Ireland, enabling the Celts to develop a pre-Christian culture free from outside inter-ference, and many examples of their art and civilization still exist today. The dawn of Christianity came with the arrival of St Patrick in the 5th century, when he is said to have banished all snakes from Ireland. While the rest of Europe languished under the 'barbarian' invasion that followed the collapse of the Roman Empire, Ireland became a centre of learning. Their role as the scholars of Europe was brought to an end when the Vikings began their attacks in the 9th century. The Norsemen were finally defeated by the High King of Ireland, Brian Boru, at the Battle of Clontarf. The infighting among the various chiefs that followed Boru's death gave the Normans their opportunity to extend their influence beyond England. Parliament came under the control of a British minority, who gradually began taking land from the Irish Catholics to give to Protestant settlers from Scotland and England, thus ensuring their allegiance to the English Crown. After the 1801 Act of Union, Ireland became part of the United Kingdom, but the Great Famine (1845–48) that followed the repeated failure of the potato harvests and caused a million deaths gave rise to both an increase in Irish nationalism and the mass emigration of a further million people. A number of unsuccessful rebellions occurred, but it was not until the Easter Rising of 1916, when a group of rebels took over most of Dublin and declared an Irish Republic, that the final impetus for independence arrived. In the 7 days that followed fierce fighting gutted the city, until British troops regained control. The execution of the rebel leaders sparked the War of Independence that led to the 1921 treaty removing British forces from all of Ireland, except the 6 counties that today constitute Northern Ireland. A further civil war was embarked upon, between the anti-treaty (Republican) and the pro-treaty (Free State) forces. In 1937 the 26 counties became fully recognized and independent as Eire.

Irrespective of the troubles in Northern Ireland (see under United Kingdom), the South is peaceful and hospitable. Although trains will get you to all the main centres, the best way to get to grips with Ireland is to hire a bike – even if you don't really know where you are going, it should be worth your while when you get there. The Irish are justifiably proud of their hospitality, and although not every Irishman is a William Yeats, most have the 'gift of the gab' and will be only too happy to pass the time of day with you. Head for the local pub, enjoy the beer, and ask around for bed and breakfast.

GETTING THERE

Irish Ferries operate from Le Havre to Cork and from Le Havre, Roscoff and Cherbourg to Rosslare (Tel. +44 990 171717). Brittany Ferries operate from Roscoff and St Malo to Cork. Stena operate regular sailings from Britain to Ireland (Tel. 0990 707070). For a little more money you may like to take their new catamaran service from Holyhead which reduces the crossing time to under two hours. Swansea Cork Ferries also operate on the one route (Tel. +44 (0)1792 456116). Eurail pass holders get to travel free (or gain big reductions) on services to Rosslare, which is a considerable saving as the normal fare is around IR£65 adult single, IR£100 adult return. Interrailers get approx. 50% reduction on most routes. Check with the relevant operator or see USIT, 52 Grosvenor Gardens, London SW1 0AG (Tel. 0171 730 3402) for details. If you're not a student, check the prices. Return air fares from London to Dublin can be had for as little as £70.

IRISH RAILWAYS

(IARNROD EIREANN, IE)
ENQUIRIES: 1850 366222

Travelling on trains is extremely expensive, but ISIC card-holders with a valid travel-save stamp receive up to 50% off. A travel-save stamp costs IR£7, available from USIT in either London or Dublin, and provides substantial discounts on trains and provincial buses, half price on all single or return fares on Northern Ireland Railways and similar discounts on car ferries and boats to the Aran Islands. Buy one.

Trains are reasonably fast around the Dublin area and to major towns, but don't expect speeds similar to those on the continent. In many areas (especially in the west), buses are the main form of transport.

PASSES AVAILABLE Eurail and Inter-Rail Passes are valid in the Republic. The Inter-Rail pass has been broken down into zones, so that by carefully selecting zones you can avoid paying for travel to places you have no intention of visiting. For £159 you get 22 days' travel in a single zone. The Republic of Ireland is in Zone A. (For further details on the 8 Inter-Rail Zones, and the Freedom (Euro Domino) Passes, see Part One of this guide.)

INTER-RAIL BONUSES Discounts of 25–50% are available on all routes to Ireland from the UK and France with Irish Ferries and Stena Line.

EURAIL BONUSES Free ferry crossings on Irish Ferries between Rosslare and Le Havre (21 hours), or Cherbourg (17 hours), and between Cork and Le Havre (22 hours). An extra charge is made for cabin accommodation. Port taxes are extra and payable in Irish punts (IR£). During July and August advance reservation is recommended and is compulsory if cabin accommodation is requested. Always check the sailing schedule.

REDUCED FARES Bus Eireann offers Eurailpass holders a reduction on the price of their 3-day Bus Rambler Ticket (which covers bus services operated by Bus Eireann and Cork, Limerick, Galway and Waterford City buses). The reduced fare is IR£25. The ticket is valid for 3 days' travel within 8 days.

TRAIN INFORMATION

RESERVATIONS Not necessary. If you want to make one, you must do so by 5 p.m. on the preceding day.

NIGHT TRAVEL AND EATING ON TRAINS There are no night services in Ireland. Most long-distance trains have catering facilities ranging from bar service to set meals, but are quite expensive.

ROVER TICKETS
The Irish Explorer ticket offers 5 out of 15 days' travel within the Republic for IR£60. This also includes suburban trains and the Bus Eireann network. Alternatively, for the whole Irish rail network,

including Northern Ireland, there is the Rover Ticket: 5 of 15 days for IR£75.

BIKES Are often the only way to get to the local hostel and see the neighbourhood. Hire costs about IR£7 (deposit IR£40) a day from most towns. The fee for taking your bike on a train or bus is around IR£5. More information from Walking/Cycling Ireland in Limerick (Tel. 061 419477).

TOURIST INFORMATION

There are 86 offices scattered throughout Ireland, 28 of which are open all year round. They are open Mon.–Fri.: 9 a.m.–5 p.m., Sat.: 9 a.m.–1 p.m. They have a good selection of local and national maps and literature; although these will cost you, the staff are always friendly. It is a shame all of Ireland is not run as efficiently as the Tourist Board, so use their offices while you have the chance.

ISIC BONUSES With the ISIC you can get a travel-save stamp ticket. This entitles you to up to 50% off all 1-way journeys, on buses and trains, as well as reductions to some cinemas, theatres and museums.

MONEY MATTERS 1 Irish pound (IR£1) or punt = 100 pence (p.). Banking hours are Mon.–Fri.: 10 a.m.–12.30 p.m., 1.30 p.m.–3 p.m.
   The British pound is nearly equal to the Irish pound but is not interchangeable.

POST OFFICES, SHOPS AND MUSEUMS Mostly open 9 a.m.–5.30 p.m., Mon.–Fri. and 9 a.m.–1 p.m. Sat. Some shops stay open as late as midnight. Museums vary the most, so check with the nearest Tourist Information Office.

SLEEPING

Hotels are very expensive, so if you don't want to camp, stick to approved Irish Tourist Board bed and breakfast (B&B, IR£12–15) or youth hostels (IR£6–8). Most approved premises display the shamrock sign. The overall recommended guide is *Ireland Accommodation Guide* (IR£5), which gives a complete list of all approved bed and breakfast, youth hostel, holiday hostel and caravan and camping accommodation. It is available in all Tourist Information offices, as is the *Irish Farmhouse Association Guide* (IR£3) (Tel. 061 400700) or the *Family Homes of Ireland B&B Guide* (Tel. 091 82634).

HOSTELS For advance information on youth hostels contact An Oige, 61 Mountjoy Street, Dublin 7 (Tel. 01 8304555). There are 37 registered holiday hostels, confined to IYHF members.

There are also over 150 independent hostels of all sizes and with ranges of activities. While some of their listed hostels are good, others are not. The Irish Tourist Board do not approve them. Their information office is at Dooey Hostel, Glencolumbkille, Co. Donegal (Tel. 073 30130). They also allow camping in their grounds for considerably less than the price of a room.

Youth hostels tend to be situated in the most scenic parts of the country, but are not always near a station.

CAMPING Organized campsites charge IR£3–6 a tent. There is usually no problem camping in fields, provided you ask the owner's permission. Most hostels will let you camp on their land for IR£3 per night, which includes the use of kitchen and shower facilities.

EATING AND NIGHTLIFE

Food is also quite expensive in Ireland, particularly in tourist traps, and the only way to survive on a tight budget is to rely on the very good bakeries and 'pub grub' offered in most bars. Some restaurants outside Dublin shut by 9 p.m., so eat early. Junk food addicts are more than adequately catered for in all cities. Ask at Tourist Information for their booklet *Special Value Tourist Menu*, which lists many restaurants that provide decent 3-course meals at fixed prices. Irish food is wholesome but basic and very similar to English fare. Pubs and cafés offer a wide variety of traditional dishes (tripe and drisin (white pudding)) at 'reasonable prices', but other than them, the only time you are likely to get the chance of traditional Irish cooking is in a guesthouse or B&B, where Irish stew or boiled bacon and cabbage may appear on the menu.

Pubs are the focal point of Irish life and you will find great food, good beer (Guinness, Murphy's) and a chance to meet the Irish, who are mostly a lovely, warm lot. Ask about to discover which pubs have folk music and dancing (*ceilidh*). The best way to relax is over a pint of stout while listening to the local characters swapping stories. With a little coaxing, they will be only too happy to let you know the local legends, whether it be fairies, witches, leprechauns or heroes like Prince Cuchulain. And if sport is what grabs you, make tracks for the local Gaelic football pitch, or catch a game of the ancient Irish sport of hurling. The illicit Irish liquor, poteen, is made by many farmers and can be bought if you find the right person.

Dublin city phone code: 01

There's no denying Dublin has character. The contrast of the elegant Georgian quarter with the dingy slums only a mile or two away is typical of the division of Irish history. In Gaelic, the city's name means Blackpool, but it is the very antithesis of that kitsch resort. This is the setting James Joyce used for *Ulysses* – his own home town. It's a rich experience, so don't hurry it.

STATION FACILITIES

Dublin has 2 main stations: Connolly (Tel. 703 1843), with north-bound trains; and Heuston Station (Tel. 783 1842) for trains to the south and west. The Dublin Area Rapid Transit (DART) serves 27 stations in County Dublin and County Wicklow.

There are all the usual facilities at both stations, including left luggage, which is only available during the day.

TOURIST INFORMATION AND ADDRESSES

MAIN OFFICE 14 Upper O'Connell St (Tel. 284 4768); open Mon.–Sat.: 9 a.m.–5.30 p.m. In July and August, opening hours are extended till 8.30 p.m. Mon.–Sat. and 11 a.m.–5.30 p.m. on Sunday. Also on Suffolk Street (Tel. 605 7748). Money exchange facilities are provided; visitor information (Tel: 1550 11 22 33)

GENERAL POST OFFICE O'Connell St, open Mon.–Sat.: 8 a.m.–8 p.m., Sun.: 10 a.m.–6.30 p.m. (Tel. 705 7000).

AMEX 116 Grafton St (Tel. 6772874), open Mon.–Sat: 9 a.m.–5 p.m.

STUDENT TRAVEL AGENCY ISIC/USIT are at 19–21 Aston Quay; open Mon.–Fri.: 9 a.m.–6 p.m., Sat.: 11 a.m.–4 p.m. (Tel. 679 8833). Also a Eurotrain office.

UK EMBASSY 29/31 Merrion Rd (Tel. 269 5211)

US EMBASSY 42 Elgin Rd, Ballsbridge (Tel. 668877)

CANADIAN EMBASSY 65–68 St Stephen's Green (Tel. 478 1988) Emergency telephone 285 1246

YOUTH INFORMATION CENTRE Sackville Place (off O'Connell St) (Tel. 878 6844), open Mon.–Wed.: 9.30 a.m.–6 p.m., Thurs.–Sat.: 9.30 a.m.–5 p.m. Information on organizations, travel and accommodation.

EUROTRAIN Compass Travel, 34 Lower Abbey St (Tel. 741777)

GETTING ABOUT

City buses cost up to IR£1.60 and operate 6 a.m.–11.30 p.m. You won't need them for sightseeing, as it's all easily negotiated by foot ('shanks's mare' as they call it). Tel. 873 4222 or 872 0000 for information on all public transport. Buy a bus/train pass (1-day pass IR£5; 4-day pass IR£12) from Dublin Bus in Upper O'Connell Street. Late-night buses operate until 3 a.m. Thurs.–Sat. Catch them at the Bank of Ireland building, IR£2.50, no passes accepted. DART stops at 11 p.m.

SEEING

Start with O'Connell Street and your visit to the Tourist Office, then, via the GENERAL POST OFFICE, where the Easter uprising of 1916 started, head for TRINITY COLLEGE. The oldest in Ireland, this university has produced such men as Oscar Wilde and Thomas Moore. See the beautiful LIBRARY, which is the home of some of the world's most outstanding manuscripts. Pride of place in the Long Room is reserved for the 8th-century *Book of Kells*. Admission is IR£3 (IR£2.25 for students), and it's open Mon.–Sat.: 9.30 a.m.–5.30 p.m.; Sun.: 12 p.m.–5 p.m.

A recent addition to Dublin's list of tourist attractions is the college's 'Dublin Experience'. Open daily 10 a.m.–5 p.m., this sophisticated multi-media interpretation of the city's history costs IR£2.75 (IR£2.25 for students). At the back of the university, through the grounds, sit the Dáil and Seanad, the seats of the Irish Parliament on Kildare Street. You cannot visit when Parliament is in session. In the same street is the NATIONAL MUSEUM (Free; Mon.: 10 a.m.–9 p.m., Tue.–Wed.: 2 p.m.–9 p.m., Thu.–Fri.: 10 a.m.–5 p.m. and Sat.: 10 a.m.–1 p.m.), which is good for historians and has a comprehensive exhibition on the 1916 uprising. Around the corner, on Merrion Square, is the NATIONAL GALLERY, which has an excellent collection of Rembrandts and several rooms devoted to portraits of Irish literary men such as George Bernard Shaw and Brendan Behan.

DUBLIN CASTLE (IR£1.75 adults, IR£1 for students) is the historic heart of the city. Preceded by a Gaelic ring fort and a Viking fortress, there are significant portions of the original 13th-century Norman castle remaining. The STATE APARTMENTS were built as the residential quarters of the viceregal court and, along with the VIKING UNDERCROFT FORTRESS and the CHAPEL ROYAL, are open to visitors. CHRIST CHURCH (started in 1038) and the 12th-century ST PATRICK'S CATHEDRAL are also worth a look.

The most elegant buildings of Dublin are the CUSTOM HOUSE, on the north bank of the river Liffey, and the BANK OF IRELAND in College Green (formerly Parliament House).

The JOYCE MUSEUM at Martello Tower (near the nudist beach at

Sandycove) focuses on the life and works of the Irish author, James Joyce. Take DART to Sandycove. Back in the city, the DUBLIN WRITERS MUSEUM is at 18 Parnell Square North. For a breath of fresh air, head for ST STEPHEN'S GREEN, an oasis in the middle of the city. Just off the park, at Earsfort Street, is the new NATIONAL CONCERT HALL, which features music to suit all tastes. Or you might like to visit the famous PHOENIX PARK, the largest enclosed park in Europe, which features everything from motor racing to rock concerts. Phoenix Park has the second highest obelisk in the world and one of the world's oldest zoos, famous for breeding lions. Take bus 10 from O'Connell Street. Don't be tempted to pitch your tent here, as the official residence of the President of Ireland is nearby and the police take a dim view of campers in the vicinity. It's also unsafe at night.

Across the river is KILMAINHAM GAOL, a central character of Ireland's passionate history, as the leaders of rebellions from 1799 until 1916 were detained here. A visit to the gaol includes a guided tour; an audio-visual presentation and an exhibition. Opening hours are June–Sept.: 10 a.m.–6 p.m. daily. Off-season admission: adults IR£2, students IR£1.00.

For a few 'free' pints of Guinness, go to their brewery at St James' gate, watch the film about its production, then sup up. Open Mon.–Sat.: 9.30 a.m.–5 p.m., Sun.: 10 a.m.–4.10 p.m. (last admission). Oct.–May: 10 a.m.–3.50 p.m., Mon.–Fri. IR£3, IR£1.50 students.

SLEEPING

You can expect to pay IR£25 upwards in a hotel, so head for the student and youth hostels. Go round to the USIT office, 19 Aston Quay (Tel. 677 8117 or 679 8833).

The Dublin ISAACS Hostel, 15 Finchman's Lane (Tel. 855 6215) is a very central old warehouse and costs IR£7–18 a night. Also try The Young Traveller at St Mary's Place (Tel. 830 5000). It's a lot cleaner and is IR£8.50 for B&B.

YOUTH HOSTELS 61 Mountjoy St (Tel. 830 1766) is very good and costs IR£9 a night.

The YWCA at Radcliffe Hall, St John's Rd (Tel. 269 4521) and Lower Baggot Street are also worth checking out, as are the 2 independent hostels that charge IR£6.50 and IR£8 a night respectively: Cardijin House at 15 Talbot Street (Tel. 788 4841 and 741 720) and Kinlay House at 2–12 Lord Edward Street (Tel. 679 6644).

B&BS Avoid the ones near the station. Instead, try Mrs Gartland at 2

Goldsmith Street (Tel. 830 1857), only 5 minutes or so from O'Connell Street. Be assured of a warm welcome and a full Irish breakfast at IR£10–11 per person. Check out Mrs Ryan at 10 Distillery Road (Tel. 837 4147) at IR£12.50 per person; take bus 51a from near the station with your pack, but, once in residence, it's close enough to the centre to go on foot.

Finally, if you can't find a B&B near the city centre, try Mrs Canavan at 81 Kincora Road, Clontarf (Tel. 833 1007), reached by bus 30 or 44a from the Abbey Street bus station. Clontarf is a pleasant suburb with views out to Dublin Bay, but it's several miles out.

CAMPSITES You can pitch a tent for IR£5 at Donabate, just north of the city. Shankill Caravan and camping park (Tel. 282 0011) is open all year round, 16 km south on the N11. Bus 45/84 or the DART to Shankill and costs about IR£6 for a tent. Also check out the site at Camac Valley, Carhagh Park on Naas Road (Tel. 464 0644).

EATING AND NIGHTLIFE

There are the usual fast-food chains in the centre and also quite a few pubs offering excellent-value lunches. Anywhere around the university is your best bet, as restaurants here cater for the student market. Bewley's have cafés at 78 Grafton St, 13 South Great George St and 12 Westmoreland St, all doing good meals at reasonable prices. Cheaper places to eat include Flanagan's at 61 O'Connell St and the Kylemore Café in O'Connell St (across from the Tourist Information Centre), and Beshoff's in Westmoreland St. Shop for food in Moore St.

The pub is at the centre of Ireland's social life, and the atmosphere in a good Dublin pub takes some beating. The following all have something unique, whether it be folk music, good beer or a great atmosphere; most have all of them, and are the sort of places you'll be looking for to eat, drink and make merry: O'Donoghue's, the Baggot Inn, both in Baggot Street; Mulligan's Pub, Poolbeg Street; Scruffy Murphy's, off Mount Street; An Beal Boacht, Ranelagh Bridge; and The Norseman, Temple Bar.

For an organized *ceilidh* or musical pub-crawl, meet at Oliver St John Gogarty's on the corner of Anglesea Street and Fleet Street at 7.30 p.m. Sat.–Thurs. (IR£6, IR£5 students).

South-East Ireland

Counties Wexford, Carlow, Kilkenny, Tipperary and Waterford are the home of Anglo-Norman castles, race-courses, crystal factories, early Christian relics and tributes to the occasional US president who claimed Irish roots.

The Wicklow mountains lie only 16 km from Dublin, and a day or two exploring this area from the base towns of GLENDALOUGH (with its 7th-century monastery) or Wicklow can be rewarding, before crossing the county border south into Wexford.

ENNISCORTHY is a small town in the Slaney Valley and on the main line south from Dublin. It was a rebel stronghold during the 1798 revolt against the British. The castle is now a folk museum (Tel. 35926) and if you hit it in the first week of July, expect a great atmosphere, as the Strawberry Festival livens things up considerably. The town offers excellent angling. Further west, the port of NEW ROSS contains St Mary's Abbey and the 600-acre forest of the John F. Kennedy Arboretum Park, with nature trails, gardens and panoramic views (May–Aug.: 10 a.m.–8 p.m., April and Sept.: 10 a.m.–6.30 p.m., and Oct.-March: 10 a.m.–5 p.m.; adults IR£2, students IR£1).

In WEXFORD, see the BULL RING and ruins of the SELSKAR ABBEY, which was razed by Oliver Cromwell, and ask for information on the free guided walking tours at Tourist Information on Crescent Quay (Tel. 23111).

FERRYCARRIG, home of the Irish National Heritage Park (open daily: 10 a.m.–7 p.m. March–Nov., admission: IR£3.50, IR£3.00 for students), lies 4 km inland from Wexford. Using full-scale models of settlements, homesteads and burial places from the Stone Age through to Norman times, it charts 9,000 years of social change in Ireland.

Take the road into CARLOW COUNTY from Bunclody and turn off at the Tullow road to see the herbaceous ALTAMONT GARDENS (open Sun. 2 p.m.–6 p.m., till the end of Oct., admission IR£1, Tel. 0503 57128) with its homemade teas.

Nearby, CLONMORE CASTLE was completed in 1180 from the stones of a ruined abbey, but it is for its MEGALITHIC FIELD monuments (dolmen), that Carlow County is best known. Particularly noteworthy are the HAROLDSTOWN PORTAL TOMB (northeast of Tullow) and the BROWNESHILL DOLMEN (reputedly the largest in Europe, and dating from 2000 BC).

TULLOW possesses a museum (open every Sun. afternoon and also on Wed. afternoons in the summer) by the Slaney River Bridge.

Nearby CARLOW TOWN has a museum (May–Sept.: 11 a.m.–5 p.m., admission IR£1) in the town hall, and a castle dating from 1207 (access permission from the mineral water company who own the site). You can still view it through the gates.

LEIGHLINBRIDGE is guarded by the ruins of a 12th-century Anglo-Norman castle.

BAGENALSTOWN was originally modelled on Athens. For walkers, the South Leinster Way is a pleasant section of the proposed round-Ireland walking route, from Wicklow in the north-east, via towpaths along the River Barrow, to GRAIGNAMANAGH in the south. This ancient town, in south-eastern Kilkenny County, contains the massive Norman DUISKE ABBEY, fully restored, with a larger-than-life effigy of a Norman knight inside. Guided tours of both the abbey and town can be arranged via the Kilkenny Tourist Office.

Up the road at THOMASTOWN lies the 12th-century Cistercian JERPOINT ABBEY, well preserved and restored, open mid-June–Sept. (9.30 a.m.–5 p.m., adults IR£2, students IR£1).

The town of KELLS, just west of Thomastown, is noteworthy as the only completely medieval walled town remaining in Ireland, although the eponymous book has been removed to Dublin.

KILKENNY CITY took its name from a monastic settlement established by St Canice. Its peak of some 1,500 years as a centre of civilization came in 1642, when it became a major political capital during Cromwell's reign. ST CANICE'S CATHEDRAL was begun in 1251 (its Round Tower offers a staggering panorama to those who ascend its 167 steps), and this impressive Gothic building has a large collection of sculpted monuments. The city's annual Arts Week takes place in August. Walking tours of the city depart from the Tourist Office at Shee Alms House, Rose Inn St (Tel. 056 51500), 6 times a day March–Oct. and cost IR£2.50. They can also fix you up with accommodation. The city's CASTLE was started in 1172 and was the home of the powerful Anglo-Norman Butler family. The LONG GALLERY of the building has an interesting collection of family portraits, but the building is perhaps most remarkable for its modern art gallery. (Castle opens 10 a.m.–7 p.m. daily; admission IR£3 adults, IR£1.25 students.) Also worth visiting is the ST FRANCIS ABBEY brewery, in the yard of Smithwick's Brewery. Guided tours are available Mon.–Fri. at 3 p.m. for the brewery (June–Sept.). For sporting enthusiasts, a hurling match takes place most summer Sundays, in the city's NOLAN PARK.

Over the border from Kilkenny in County Tipperary, 7 ornate early Christian HIGH CROSSES can be found at Ahenny, Killamery, Kilree and Kilkieran.

CARRICK-ON-SUIR contains a fine Elizabethan MANOR HOUSE residence of 1568, next to the remains of CARRICK CASTLE (open mid-June–Sept.: 9.30 a.m.–6.30 p.m., adults IR£2, students IR£1).

On the way west to the racecourse at CLONMEL (one of many in this equine heartland) is the TIPPERARY CRYSTAL WORKS, a recently established industry that carries on the region's world reputation for hand-cut crystal. Guided tours give visitors the opportunity to view all stages of crystal production. The NORTH MUNSTER WAY can be picked up on the banks of the Suir and followed via Clonmel to the borders of County Cork.

A medieval ecclesiastical centre, CASHEL is the location of ST PATRICK'S ROCK, with the remains of its magnificent cathedral and Round Tower dominating the countryside. A subterranean museum displays items of historical interest; and a full guide service is provided (June–mid-Sept., 9.00 a.m.–7.30 p.m., off-season 9.30 a.m.–4.30 p.m., admission IR£2.50 adults, IR£1 students). The nearby BRU BORU has been developed as a major cultural centre for Irish music, drama and tradition, in the shadow of Cashel's ancient rock.

North-east of Cashel, on the border with Kilkenny, are the SLIE-VEARDAGH HILLS, an area strongly connected with the revolutionary 19th-century Young Irelanders movement and the development of a coal-mining industry. The history and geography of the area are the focus of a study weekend held in July.

Passing through TIPPERARY TOWN and its racecourse will bring you to the town of CAHIR and its CASTLE, built in the middle of the river Suir, and containing an audio-visual unit for the whole south-eastern area, and a full guide service; open June–Sept.: 9 a.m.–7.30 p.m., and for the rest of the year 10 a.m.–6 p.m. (admission IR£2 adults, IR£1 students).

South and west towards the KNOCKMEDOWN MOUNTAINS at the border with County Waterford, the limestone caves of MITCHELSTOWN should be visited (open all year, with guide service 10 a.m.–6 p.m., admission IR£2, students IR£1), before passing on to the PRESIDENT REAGAN CENTRE at BALLYPOREEN, commemorating the birthplace of the former US President's ancestors, and his visit there in 1984 (opened by appointment).

County Waterford is best entered via THE VEE, a switchback route through the Knockmedown mountains, which allows the visitor the best views of the beautiful border area. Nestling in the southern foothills is MOUNT MELLERAY, a Cistercian monastery.

Proceeding south from here to the cathedral town of LISMORE, you can see the majestic CASTLE perched above the river Blackwater. The magnificent castle gardens are open 1.45 p.m.–4.45 p.m.

May–Sept., except Sat., admission IR£2. A visit to the Lismore Heritage Experience exhibition is recommended. Directly east of Lismore is DUNGARVAN, with its substantial Anglo-Norman CASTLE, which was sacked during the Cromwellian Wars. Portions of this castle still overlook the town's harbour.

If, at the end of a hard day, you are seeking a change from medieval castles and early Christian monasteries, you could do worse than follow the N25 north from the coast to BALLINAVOUGH (near LEMY-BRIEN), where the collection of antique dolls and toys of Helen Collendar can be viewed 6 p.m.–9 p.m. daily, June–Sept., at her home (admission IR£2.50).

WATERFORD CITY, only an hour away from the ferry port of Rosslare, was founded by the Danes and grew to be Ireland's fifth largest city. Walking tours of the city leave the Tourist Office (41 The Quay) and end at Reginald's Tower, visiting 10 historic locations *en route*, at 11 a.m. and 3 p.m., Mon.–Sat. (IR£2 per person, information from the Tourist Office (Tel. 051 75788)).

REGINALD'S TOWER is a Viking fortification built from AD 1003. The FRENCH CHURCH was given to Huguenot refugees in the 17th century.

The nearby WATERFORD HERITAGE CENTRE is a well presented exhibition of the Viking and early Norman settlement of Waterford (Mon.–Fri.: 10 a.m.–1 p.m. and 2 p.m.–5 p.m., admission IR£1). Famous for its crystal, the WATERFORD CRYSTAL CENTRE is a logical place to visit at Kilbarry, with regular (free) factory tours and a video presentation (open Mon.–Fri.: 9 a.m.–5 p.m. Tours at 10.15 a.m., 11 a.m., 11.45 a.m., 1.45 p.m. and 2.30 p.m. Tel. 73311).

Cork (Corcaigh) phone code: 21

Three hours away from Dublin on the main line, Cork is more than a stopover on the way to south-west Ireland. Ireland's second largest city, it is bursting with history and charm. Its reputation as the 'Venice of Ireland' comes from its construction on a marsh (*corcaigh*), which has led to a network of bridges being built to span the river Lee and her tributaries.

Starting in Washington Street, see the neo-classical COURTHOUSE, and further along Western Road is University College Cork, as well as the old COUNTY GAOL, where many republican prisoners were held during the Civil War. The gates of the gaol are a replica of those at the Temple of Bacchus in Athens. North of Western Road is Fitzgerald's Park, which houses Cork's PUBLIC MUSEUM (open 10 a.m.–5 p.m.).

The park provides a perfect setting for a picnic, with beautiful scenery on the banks of the Lee. ST ANN'S CHURCH ('Shandon') in John Redman Street is known as the '4-faced liar' and offers the opportunity of a go at ringing the bells. Expect to pay to enter the church and to ring those bells!

In Bishop Street, the large Gothic ST FINBAR'S CATHEDRAL stands on the site of the saint's original monastic settlement, and boasts a golden angel who, legend has it, will blow its horn to signal the end of the world. Near St Finbar's, on Barrack Street, is the ELIZABETH FORT, which dates back to the 16th century. A walk down towards the city's docks brings you to CITY HALL. Enter to see the busts of the 2 Lord Mayors (Tomas McCurtain and Traolach McSuibhne), who died during the Civil War.

Cork boasts 2 breweries: Beamish & Crawford in South Main Street and Murphy's in Lady's Well; it's worth enquiring about brewery tours, as they do happen.

A good day trip is to Dundanion castle in BLACKROCK (take the no. 2 bus) where, in 1669, William Penn sailed for America. Nearby Blackrock castle is a fine setting for a pint and a sandwich.

BLARNEY CASTLE, 10 km down the road from Cork, is worth a visit as long as you don't suffer from vertigo. It is the site of the famous Blarney Stone, where legend says you can gain the 'gift of the gab' once you have paid the IR£3 (students IR£2) for the honour of kissing it. A short (15 km) rail-journey away is COBH (pronounced 'Cov'). Information on guided walking tours can be obtained from the Tourist Office (Tel. 021 813301) on Grand Parade (open 9 a.m.–7 p.m. in the summer, Sun. 11 a.m.–1 p.m.).

SLEEPING

Hotels are unbelievably expensive, so head for Western Road where you will find plenty of bed and breakfasts and the An Oige youth hostel at 1&2 Redclyff (Tel. 543289). Independent hostels can be found at Sheila's Budget Accommodation Centre in Wellington Road (Tel. 505562, IR£6 in dorms) and Campus House at 3 Woodlands View, Western Road (Tel. 343531). You could try the ISAACs Hostel (Tel. 500011) on MacCurtain Street (5 minutes from the train station) or Kinlay House (Tel. 508966) on Infirmary Road (in Shandon, take the no. 3 bus northwards), which costs IR£7, breakfast included.

For B&B, it is hard to beat Mrs Flynn at Kent House, 47 Glanmire Road (Tel. 504260); 5 minutes from the station (turn right on leaving the building), she charges IR£10–15 per person for good facilities and a full Irish breakfast. Moreover, if you ring her in advance, she will usually meet you from the bus station or the port. Go today!

There is a campsite on the Doughcloyne Road (take the no. 14 bus), which charges IR£4 per tent, and another on the Kinsale Road at IR£4 per tent (Tel. 312171).

EATING AND NIGHTLIFE

Eating out can be an expensive business, so examine menus carefully before ordering. The Lon Wah Chinese in Oliver Plunket Street does a good value high tea. There are plenty of fast-food joints in the city centre for burger addicts and Paddy Garaboldi's Pizzas are worth trying (in Carey's Lane). Head for the pubs, where everything is happening, and fill up on pub grub over a good Cork pint of stout. The Western Road also boasts the Western Star, a watering hole for Cork's many international rugby stalwarts. For those who require more after all this, the de Lacy House (Oliver Plunket Street) offers the best in music and socializing. The Grand Parade Hotel (Grand Parade) gives a great choice with its 2 stages and 3 dance floors. The most unusual venue in Cork is Nancy Speirs Backstage in Barrack Street, with its excellent architecture. To sample a local *ceilidh*, enquire at the Aras, Conradh na Gaeilge at Dyke Parade.

South-West Ireland

Known as 'the Garden of Ireland' for its rugged unspoilt landscapes, commanding mountain ranges, breathtakingly beautiful lakes and islands. It is practically impossible to travel through towns and villages here without encountering the myths and legends which haunt the area. Old Celtic crosses, ruined abbeys, castles and ring forts (mystical places where the Celts believed the faerie gods lived) are all here. This is the land of the banshee (a mythical ghost who forewarns a death in your family with her earsplitting scream), leprechauns (spirits who jealously guard the pot of gold at the end of each rainbow), and tree gods (who will curse you should you harm the tree they are assigned to guard).

KINSALE (Cionn-tsaile) lies 27 km from Cork. In 1601, the Spanish landed here to help O'Neill against the English, but suffered defeat a year later. A small, attractive fishing village, Kinsale is Ireland's culinary capital, and there is no shortage of bed and breakfasts here. Dempsey's Hostel (Tel. 021 772124) on Eastern Road costs IR£6. For a great night out with traditional music, head to The Spaniard on the hill.

The town of BANTRY is a peaceful place famous for its summer regatta and beautiful views of Bantry Bay. For B&B head to the Bantry Hostel off Glengariff Road (Tel. 027 51050). For a good meal, reasonably priced, try Pete's Grill, washed down with a pint and some atmosphere in the Anchor Tavern near the bus stop.

For a day trip from Bantry, go to GLENGARIFF, for a walk up to Lady Bantry's View: an excellent view of the countryside and bay for miles around. Alternatively head to the parks and mountains of GOUGHAN BURRA, source of the River Lee, for a perfect picnic site.

A third option for a day trip is to CAPE CLEAR ISLAND. Take the bus to Skibbereen, famous for its international busking festival, and from there travel on to Baltimore, where a ferry (IR£6 return) will take you out (remember to check the times of the boat back!) to an island so peaceful and trouble-free there is no need for a Garda (police) station there. *All Gaeilge* (Irish Gaelic) is still the main language of the island, but everyone can also speak English. See the ring of St Ciaran's church and the Holy Well there, then head to the pub and chat to the locals.

DINGLE is a harbour town where the shops and houses which line the tight knot of streets are painted all the colours of the rainbow. The town has several good fish restaurants and there are reputed to be 52 pubs. Since 1984 the town's most famous resident has been Fungi the bottle-nosed dolphin; you can take a boat trip to see him out in the bay for IR£5, or swim with him for rather more (Tel. 066 51967). Hire a bike in Dingle and enjoy the scenery, but beware of the potholes! Cycle up the hill, if you are fit, to Connor Pass for some impressive views (but only if the weather is good), or take the Slea Head coastal route to the west. Visit the ancient Dunberg Fort and other Stone Age settlements on the coast, where you can enter some of the beehive dwellings.

Limerick phone code: 061

Ireland's third largest city is on the River Shannon, the longest navigable river in Ireland or Britain. A port with Georgian houses and elegant buildings, it has had its ups and downs over the centuries. In recent years it has greatly benefited from the tax-free area around nearby Shannon airport which has brought much employment and economic regeneration. Buildings to see in the city include THE GRANARY, a grain store which was adapted to a warehouse and later a pub and library. The Tourist Office is on Arthur's Quay (Tel. 317522). Also worth checking out are the CUSTOM HOUSE, the 13th-century KING

JOHN'S CASTLE and ST MARY'S CATHEDRAL. The town is famous for its beautiful handmade lace and the Limerick Lace Collection can be seen in the CONVENT OF THE GOOD SHEPHERD in Clare St (open business hours on weekdays only).

The youth hostel is at 1 Pery Square (Tel. 314672) or try Barrington's Lodge at George's Quay (Tel. 415 222).

For B&B try Shannon Grove House, Athlunkard, Killaloe Road (Tel. 345756), run by the friendly Mr and Mrs Marsh. Facilities are excellent for only around IR£15 per person. It is easy to reach by bus: take the Shannon Banks Service from the town centre, which runs approximately every 30 minutes, and the stop is near the house. There is storage space for bikes and the house is only a short distance from the start of the walking trail from Limerick to Galway via Gort.

Thirteen kilometres from Limerick City on the main Galway road stands the fully restored medieval BUNRATTY CASTLE which houses a superb collection of antique furniture and furnishings. It is open to visitors daily (last admission 4.15 p.m.; IR£4), and medieval banquets and entertainments are held twice nightly. The FOLK PARK in the grounds of the castle contains farmhouses and cottages, a forge and other features of life at the turn of the century.

Just around the coast from Galway in the North Shannon region lies the BURREN, a region of stark and unique beauty. Consider a day-trip to visit the Cliffs of Moher (but only if the weather is fine) and the Aillwee Caves at Ballyvaughan.

Galway phone code: 091

Galway is a port and university town which was ruled in the 16th century by Anglo-Norman nobles. It had extensive trade with Spain, particularly in the wine business, and still has some architectural remains such as the Spanish Arch, one of the gateways to the old town.

TOURIST INFORMATION AND ADDRESSES

TOURIST OFFICE East of the station in Victoria Place, off Eyre Sq., open Mon.–Fri.: 9 a.m.–6.45 p.m., Sat.: 9 a.m.–12.45 p.m. (Tel. 563081); also on Seapoint Promenade, Salthill. Open daily June–Aug.: 9 a.m.–8.30 p.m.

POST OFFICE Eglinton St; open Mon.–Sat.: 9 a.m.–5.30 p.m.

STUDENT TRAVEL USIT, Kinlay House, Eyre Square (Tel. 565177)

SEEING

Eyre Square, where the train and bus stations are (and where drunks and hustlers have been known to buttonhole passing tourists), is the city centre. The SPANISH ARCH is a kilometre's walk from Eyre Square down Shop Street, which becomes High Street and finally Quay Street. LYNCH'S CASTLE, down Shop Street, is named after a mayor who hanged his own son. The CHURCH OF ST NICHOLAS, where it is said that Columbus prayed before setting out on one of his voyages of discovery, is also in Shop Street.

Walk by the banks of the River Corrib and see the salmon jump at SALMON WEIR BRIDGE in the spawning season, and in the summer evenings check out the Simsa, a traditional music presentation in the Irish-speaking theatre on Middle Street.

SLEEPING, EATING AND NIGHTLIFE

There is an IYHF Hostel at St Mary's College from late June to August (Tel. 527411). In the centre of town you have no alternative but to use B&Bs, of which there are a great proliferation in Galway, or independent hostels. A number of hostels offer accommodation for upwards of IR£6 a night: these are Wood Quay Hostel (Tel. 62618), The Grand Holiday Hostel in Salthill (Tel. 21150). Try also Stella Maris in Salthill (Tel. 521950). If these are full up, try camping at 151 Upper Salthill or Barna.

There is a selection of eating places in the *Special Value Tourist Menu* booklet, and there's plenty of fish 'n' chip shops to keep you going. An Pucain in Forster Street, Crane's Bar, William Street, and Connor's in Salthill are lively at night and have traditional music. Also worth a try is the King's Head on Shop Street, which serves possibly the smoothest Guinness in Ireland. For Italian and French cuisine, try Brannigan's in Upper Abbeygate Street.

At the end of July, Galway plays host to Ireland's premier horse racing and trading festival, known as 'the crack'. The town is swollen with Irish expatriates back from Britain and drinking reaches Olympic proportions. Pubs stay open late and there is much dancing and card-playing.

EXCURSIONS Ninety minutes from Galway pier (sailings in summer only; contact Aran Ferries on 68903 or Island Ferries on 61767) you can reach the remote and fascinating ARAN ISLANDS: Inishmore, Inishmaan and Inisheen. Inishmore may be visited from Rossaveal all year round, weather permitting (the crossing takes 30 minutes and costs IR£12–15 return; a connecting bus runs from the Galway Tourist Office). Go into the pubs of Kilronan (the main village on the island) to hear the Gaelic-speaking jaunting-car drivers and have a chat with them (they are bilingual). Life out here is a hard one based on fishing. This is where the famous Aran sweaters come from and where tweed trousers and skirts are woven to keep out the Atlantic winds. You'll find peace and solitude among spectacular granite mountains. Visit the prehistoric forts and remains during your hike round these fascinating islands. Inisheen has particularly nice sandy beaches. There are plenty of B&Bs and camping is IR£2 on official sites with water and toilets. The Aran Tourist Office can help you find accommodation (Tel. 099 61263) and there are a couple of good hostels, one at Kilronan (Tel. 099 61255), the other at Mainiseit House Hostel on Inishmore (Tel. 099 61169 or 61322), which charge IR£6.50 a night, breakfast included. They are crowded in the summer.There is also an IYHF hostel at Burtonport on Aranmore Island (Tel. 75 20574).

Neighbouring villages to Galway all have their beauty spots and interesting features. DOOLIN, south of Galway, has great pubs with live music, whilst TUAM has many remains that show it to be the 12th-century seat of the kings of Ireland. The nearby Craggaunowen Centre features excellent reconstructions of ancient houses, and a Bronze Age crannog, *The Brendan*, in which the explorer Tim Severin sailed the Atlantic to prove that Irish missionaries could have made the journey long before Columbus, is also preserved here. For the Tourist Office tel. 093 24465. In the summer a steam railway plies the 20-minute route from Tuam to Athenry and connects up with the main Dublin to Galway intercity line.

One kilometre off the main Galway to Limerick Road (NIB) is THOOR BALLYLEE, the lower home of the poet W. B. Yeats. Visits are available by coach from Easter to October, and admission is IR£3. For further information Tel. 31436.

The best way of exploring the area is by bicycle. These can be hired from Round the Corner bicycle hire, Queen Street, Victoria Place, or at Europa Bicycles, Hunters Building, Earlsland (Tel. 63355).

Connemara

North of Galway is the bleak and rugged mountain region of Connemara. The shoreline is unspoilt and jagged with several interesting traditional villages where Gaelic is the mother tongue. Connemara needs to be explored by bus or bike as there are no trains. If you are coming from Galway, the youth hostel at Indreabhan (Inverin) is probably your best starting-point (Tel. 593154).

The nearby village of CARRAROE holds summer festivals and is worth a visit. The CONNEMARA NATIONAL PARK runs 2-hour accompanied nature trails every Mon., Wed. and Fri. throughout the summer. Connemara ponies are wild, rugged creatures which can be seen in all their glory during August at the Connemara Pony Show in Clifden. ROSS ABBEY, a ruined Franciscan friary near Headford, has fine views from its tower. Accommodation can be found at Spiddal Village Hostel (Tel. 83678) where beds are IR£5 a night, and Lough Corrib Hostel in Camp Street, Oughterard (Tel. 091 82634) which charges IR£5.50, and is open from March onwards.

North-West Ireland

Counties Mayo, Sligo and Donegal may lack the warmer climate of the south, but more than make up for it with their dramatic and beautiful scenery. These counties are full of prehistoric remains and reminders of turbulent clashes with the British. However, they have also seen a number of improvements in recent years and have much to recommend them. In County Mayo, WESTPORT, in Clew Bay, is worth stopping at to see the beautiful estate of the Marquess of Sligo, 3 km from the town. WESTPORT HOUSE is his Georgian mansion, open to the public Apr.–Sept., entry IR£6.00. Westport is a busy place on the last Sunday in July, when thousands of pilgrims climb CROAGH PATRICK, where St Patrick is said to have fasted and prayed. The Tourist Office (Tel. 098 25711) and the post office are in the Mall. Try the Club Atlantic on Altamount Street (Tel. 098 26644) and the Granary Hostel on The Quay (Tel. 098 25903), which charges IR£8.00 a night.

SLIGO, the county of W. B. Yeats, is incredibly rich in archaeological sites and atmosphere. Sligo town, with a population of only 25,000, is the main town of north-west Ireland. The mountains are the area's big attraction – principally Knocknarea and Benbulben. Knocknarea is easy to climb and well worth the effort for the view you get from the summit. There is a 24m cairn, rumoured to be that of Maeve of Connacht, a warrior queen. The imposing hulk of flat-topped Benbulben inspired a number of Yeats' poems. The Tourist Office at Temple St (Tel. 071 61201) will give you help and information, and has guided walks at 11 a.m. every day during the summer. The main sight in the town is the ruined 13th-century Dominican friary, SLIGO ABBEY. Also worth a visit is the COUNTY MUSEUM, which has an extensive collection of first editions of Yeats, and the Yeats Memorial Building on Hyde bridge, open in the summer on weekdays 10.30 a.m.–1 p.m. and 3 p.m.–5 p.m. Just outside the town is CARROWMORE megalithic cemetery which contains an array of tombs dating back to 4000 BC, open in the summer. If it is sea and sand you desire, travel to Rosses Point, a holiday resort 8 km from Sligo.

For accommodation, try the hostel Edenhill on Pearse Road (Tel. 071 43204) or the White House Hostel on Markievicz Road (Tel. 071 45160). A recommended day trip from Sligo is the walk around Lough Gill, a broad lake with luscious woodland covering the surrounding hills. If you have transport, the northern shore is the most interesting.

COUNTY DONEGAL is not served by rail, but if you want to do a bit of hitching, this region will provide you with unspoilt, wild and beautiful terrain. The GLENVEAGH NATIONAL PARK, 22½ km north-west of Letterkenny, covers an area of 10,000 hectares and has various nature paths and a castle in its grounds. From the visitor's centre, take a bus along the banks of Lough Beagh to the crenellated 19th-century castle and gardens. Climb the steep path behind for views over the lake.

LETTERKENNY itself holds an International Folk Festival in August: information is obtainable from the Tourist Office in Derry Road (Tel. 074 21160). DONEGAL TOWN has its own 15th-century castle which is open in the summer months 9.30 a.m.–6.30 p.m.

West of Donegal is the valley of GLENCOLUMBKILLE, where the village, overlooked by dramatic cliffs on either side, is home to a number of craft shops and a folk museum incorporating restored houses from the 18th and 19th centuries (open Mon.–Sat.). The Donegal Tourist Office (Tel. 073 21148) can help with accommodation, though there is a good hostel in the town at Ball Hill (Tel. 073 21174). There is much here for the visitor to admire: Slieve League, for instance, near Carrick, has the highest sea cliffs in Europe, where a 630m mountain seemingly falls into the Atlantic. The tweed industry is alive and thriving here. Magee's of Donegal is the main exponent, though for the major centre of the handknits and weaving industry go to ARDARA, west of Donegal itself. The most breathtaking route to get there is to travel via the Bluestack mountains; once in the village itself you can hire a bicycle from Donal Byrne (Tel. 075 41156) and explore the coastal scenery.

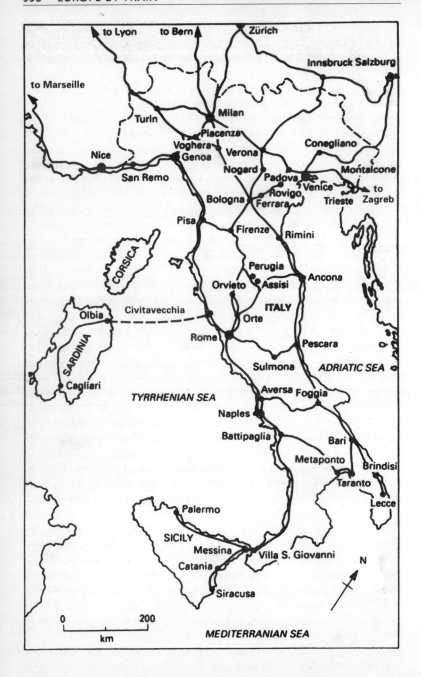

ITALY (Italia)

Entry requirements	Passport
Population	57,426,000
Capital	Rome (pop.: 3,800,000)
Currency	Lire
	£1 = approx. 2,500L
Political system	Republic
Religion	Roman Catholic
Language	Italian (some English spoken in some major cities)
Public holidays	1, 6 Jan.; Easter Sunday; Easter Monday; 25 Apr. (Liberation Day); 1 May; 15 Aug.; 1 Nov.; 25, 26 Dec.
International dialling codes	To Italy: 00 (international access code) + 39 (country code)
	From Italy: 00 + country code number
Eurotrain office	Via Nazionale 66, 1-00184 Rome (Tel. 06 46791)
Time	GMT +1 (+2 in summer)
Emergency telephone	113

Italy is like a spoilt child. You'll be annoyed and frustrated, but your greatest Inter-Railing stories will probably originate in this exciting and beautiful country. If you want to understand Italy, spend some time here and it will grow on you.

Italy's history is dominated by 3 familiar themes: Empire, Church and the Renaissance, all of which have played a major role in the forming of European culture. From the 8th century BC onwards there were Greeks in southern Italy and Sicily, and Etruscans in the north. The Romans conquered an empire which reigned supreme over much of the barbarian world until its downfall in the 5th century AD. As the power of Rome declined it found a new role as the centre of the Christian Church. Italy became disunited and power was left in the hands of local kings and dukes. Even the Pope and the Holy Roman Emperor could not agree as to who ruled what and eventually the Pope moved base to Avignon in 1303. Later the Kingdom of Naples and powerful city-states such as Venice and Florence provided patronage for the arts. Another factor which gave rise to this 15th-century Renaissance was the new humanism which produced men like Leonardo da Vinci and Michelangelo. Disunity and continued rivalry led to outside intervention by Spain, Austria and finally Napoleonic France. This foreign domination created the desire for unity, initially under Garibaldi, leading to the ultimate unification of Italy in 1870. After the First World War, Mussolini and the Fascists rose to power, which eventually brought about an alliance with Hitler just before the Second World War. Since then, industrialization and emigration have characterized the economy, particularly in the south, where poverty continues to be a problem. The wealthy north is a world away.

Italy today, as it has been for centuries, is a beehive of politics. Governments come and go with predictable regularity and just how far are the Mafia involved in politics? Italy, nevertheless, is a must on any European tour, offering an unbeatable combination of the ancient and the modern, spiced with good food (though not always) and excellent wine (frequently), topped off with lots of sunshine. What more could you want?

ITALIAN STATE RAILWAYS
(FERROVIE DELLO STATO, FS)
NATIONAL TRAIN INFORMATION TEL. 147 88 80 88

The Italian rail network can be one of the best in Europe, but you can still have some pretty wild experiences, especially in the south. If you set out prepared for anything you won't be surprised when a grandmother tries to board a busy train through your window and grabs your seat. In peak season second class gets incredibly busy on the main lines, so either move early for a seat or, if it is a long trip, reserve. Beware of dishonest passengers who claim your reserved seat as their own. Ask for proof. If forced to stand in the corridor, try and reach one of the pull-down seats that are often available.

There are various categories of train in Italy. These include the Rapido, Express, Fast (Diretto) and very fast (Direttissimo). Intercity, Eurocity and most definitely the new EUROSTAR all usually require a supplement. Pay beforehand at the station as it's twice the price on board. Check your timetable for precise details. Do not forget to stamp your supplement ticket in one of the gold coloured machines, or your ticket will not be valid. Avoid the 'Diretti' and 'Locali' services for any long-distance travel, as they are agonizingly slow and often prone to delays.

Much of your travel on the FS will be uneventful. However, there are still many stories of crime on certain routes, especially on the Bari/Brindisi run and South to Sicily. Common sense should prevail at all times. Keep your valuables well hidden and be careful who you talk to, and what food or drink you accept from them. If possible, be especially alert overnight.

Finally, when catching a train, cross reference the main automated departure board with the yellow 'partenza' sheets, just in case things have inexplicably been changed. Travel on the FS with a twinkle in your eye and have fun!

PASSES AVAILABLE The Italian Chilometrico ticket (no age restrictions) is valid for up to 20 trips or a maximum of 3,000 km travel and can be used by as many as 5 different people. Each trip is calculated by multiplying the distance travelled by the number of adults. This pass can be bought from every large station in Italy as well as from any Compagnia Italiana Turismo (CIT) office, and costs £88 second-class if bought in London or around 216,000L when bought in Italy. In practice, this pass is only worthwhile if you're travelling in a group.

If you are intending to do a lot of travelling it may be worth considering the Travel-at-Will / Italy Railcard or BTLC ticket (*Biglietto turistico libera circolazione*) which is valid for 8, 15, 21 or 30 days in first and second class. You can buy it in major Italian stations or from CIT or Wasteels in London before you go. It is possible to extend the validity of all but the 8-day ticket. Prices in second class are $122 for 8 days, $150 for 15, $176 for 21 and $210 for 30.

Tourists can also buy circular tickets for journeys of over 1,000 km which start and finish in the same town, or start and finish at any frontier. These work out slightly cheaper than the normal fare but are likely to be of limited appeal, as you are not allowed to go through the same town twice and every break of journey has to be endorsed.

Day return tickets for journeys over 50 km have a 15% discount, as do 3-day return tickets for journeys over 250 km.

For information on Freedom (EuroDomino) passes, see p. 40.

The Inter-Rail pass has been broken down into zones, so that you pay only for travel within the area you want to visit. For £159 you can spend 22 days touring a zone. Italy is in Zone G, along with Greece, Turkey and Slovenia (the Zone G pass also includes the ADN/HML ferry). For details of the 8 Inter-Rail zones, see the Inter-Rail section in Part One of this guide.

EURAIL BONUSES

FREE SERVICES Eurail Pass and Eurail Youthpass travellers can use steamers operated by the Adriatica di Navigazione and Hellenic Mediterranean Lines between Brindisi and Patras and vice versa. Between 10 June and 30 Sept., they must pay a 16,000L high-season surcharge. During July and August, advance reservation, which costs about 5,000L, is recommended. Special accommodation and port taxes are extra. Before boarding, all passengers run check in early at the shipping line office at the pier. Passengers who wish to break their voyage at Corfu must declare their intention of 'stop over' upon delivery of the ticket. Holders of tickets for Corfu (as final port of destination) cannot continue their voyage to Patras. In Brindisi, beware signs announcing 'Inter-Railers Sailing to Greece This Way' – these will take you to agencies which have recently been ripping off innocent Inter-Railers with £25 'reservation' fees. Go straight to the shipping offices in the harbour, where you will be charged a port tax of around £5 (with an extra £2.50 if you stop off at Corfu). Adriatica are less strict about deck passengers staying on deck than Hellenic. You will need your boarding card stamped by the police before embarking.

REDUCED FARES

About 20% reduction on first-class fares for holders of Eurail Pass and on second-class fares for holders of Eurail Youthpass on the Steamship Company Tirrenia between Naples and Palermo, Naples and Malta, Syracuse and Malta and for crossings to Sardinia.

20% reduction on the normal fares of the Steamship Company DFDS between Genoa and Tunis, Genoa–Alicante and Málaga.

30% reduction on the published full fares of Adriatica Line between Venice–Piraeus–Candia or Alexandria and vice versa on the M.S. 'Egitto Express', except between Piraeus and Candia. Contact the local Adriatica offices.

Half-price reductions are granted by Europabus on the following routes: Venice–Florence, Florence–Rome, Rome–Naples–Pompeii–Sorrento–Amalfi, Palermo–Agrigento–Siracusa–Taormina–Palermo.

TRAIN INFORMATION

Information officers generally speak English, but are sometimes less than helpful as they get fed up with the long queues in the summer, so try and use your timetable whenever possible. Many stations have Digiplan machines which issue free computerized print-outs of train times and possible routes to your chosen destination.

RESERVATIONS Are optional on all non-supplement trains. It's a good idea to do this on runs between major cities, as the trains are always crowded. It's possible to reserve a seat for the entire journey from London to Italy.

LEFT LUGGAGE (BAGAGLI) Many Italian stations seem to count a rucksack with bedroll and sleeping bag attached as three items, and charge accordingly. It's approx. 5,000L per item for 12 hours.

NIGHT TRAVEL This is a good move in Italy where prices are low and distances often long. You can get a couchette from Paris to Rome or vice versa for about 24,000L. They are either first-class 4-berth or second-class 6-berth. When reserving, ask for 'Finestrino' or 'Superiore' as these are the top bunks which offer the most room and privacy. If you're asked to give up your passport for the night, don't worry as this is standard practice. Many Italian trains (espressio) also have pull-down seats. Avoid seats next to the corridor as theft is rife, especially in the south. Do not take moneybelts off under any circumstances.

EATING ON TRAINS
There are mini-bars on all major trains, but if you're on a tight budget it would be cheaper to take a picnic as prices can be very high.

SCENIC TIPS The Berne–Brig–Milan and the Zürich–Lugano–Milan runs offer some of Europe's most spectacular alpine scenery. The runs Innsbruck–Bolzano–Verona and Vienna–Venice also offer some fine mountain views. One of the most popular routes is from Nice down to Pisa, as there's a lot more than just the Mediterranean coast to feast your eyes on (the train passes most of the Riviera beaches). Make sure you sit on the coastal side, however! Anywhere around the Bay of Naples has excellent coastal views, particularly along the private narrow-gauge line to Sorrento.

If you're arriving at Brindisi, there are 3 very different routes to choose from: along the southern coast to Catania in Sicily; up the Adriatic coast to Rimini; or over the mountains to Naples. Another beautiful run is Sulmona to Isernia, part of the excellent electrified line from Rome to Pescara.

BIKES Scooters and bikes can sometimes be hired from local Tourist Offices.

TOURIST INFORMATION
The Italian State Tourist Service (in Italy) is in the process of being privatized and hence the situation is in a state of flux. Before you set off to Italy, it's worth writing to their State Tourist Office (ENIT) at 1 Prince's Street, London WIR BAY, or Italian Government Travel Office, 630 Fifth Ave., New York, NY 10111, asking them to send you their excellent free *Travellers' Handbook* which is updated annually and contains the latest information. The most common (and popular) State Tourist Offices were the ATPs which may still exist in some places and, if so, use them. Otherwise, you will have to use the mélange of private agencies that are springing up everywhere. A

word of warning – they operate on a commission basis so don't expect to get impartial or complete information.

ISIC BONUSES 20–50% discounts on sea travel. For further information, contact CTS Viaggi per la Gioventù, Via Nazionale 172, Rome. Discounts on Museum entry.

MONEY MATTERS The only unit of currency is the lira, for which there are notes for everything between 1,000 and 100,000. Banking hours are Mon.–Fri.: 8.30 a.m.–1.15 p.m. and 3 p.m.–4 p.m. Some exchange agencies (*cambio*) give a better rate; you will have to shop around. In general, a bank like Credito Italiano is better. The *gettone* (Italian phone token used as currency) is used as the equivalent of 200L. Cash point machines are widely available, so get your cirrus symbol working for you.

POST OFFICES Open 8.30 a.m.–1.30 p.m. Mon.–Fri., till noon Sat. Stamps are also sold at tobacconists' (*Tabacchi*).

SHOPS Open 9 a.m.–1 p.m. and 4 p.m.–7.30 p.m., except in northern Italy, where the lunch break is shorter and shops close earlier. Most stores take a half day on Mon., generally opening at about 4 p.m. Supermarkets, e.g. CRAI and ESSELUNGA, can be difficult to find in town centres, so if you see one, use it.

MUSEUMS Many museums are shut on Sun. afternoons, Mon. and public holidays. A number of churches shut between 12 noon and 3 p.m. NB. Most churches, especially the major cathedrals, will not admit people wearing shorts or with uncovered shoulders (or girls with short skirts), so dress sensibly and with respect. Museum cards have been discontinued, though a pass is still available for Rome. Any UK citizen under 18 can get into state museums free.

CRIME Small-time crime is prevalent in the major cities and in the south of the country. Crowded streets or markets and packed tourist sights are favourite spots for criminals. Minimize the risk of losing your valuables by being discreet: don't flaunt valuable belongings. Gypsies or hustlers sometimes approach using a piece of cardboard or newspaper to distract your attention while their accomplices relieve you of your possessions: be alert.

NATIONAL DRUGS HELPLINE 167 011 222 (run by the Italian Department of Social Security)

SLEEPING

There is a vast array of hostels, hotels and pensions in Italy to choose from; each has its own fixed charges, mostly 15,000–40,000L, as worked out by the provincial tourist boards. Always check behind the door to see if it includes IVA (Italian VAT), breakfast and a shower, as these are often extra.

There about 50 youth hostels scattered throughout Italy (open for IYHF members only), as well as numerous student hostels in all the main towns (open to everyone). Many Italian hostels do not accept phone reservations. For further information on youth hostels in Italy contact Associazione Italiana Alberghi per la Gioventù (AIG), Via Cavour 44, 00184 Rome (Tel. 06 4871152). Hostels are not automatically your best bet, as many operate a curfew (usually about 11.30 p.m.) and shut during the siesta. We've found inexpensive hotels are more reliable in their cleanliness and flexibility. Look for the signs *Pensione, Albergo, Locanda* and *Soggiorno*. Girls also have the option of staying at the local *Casa Famiglia*, which are run by nuns and offer a bed for about 25,000L. Wherever you stay, don't be afraid to give up your passport when you check in as this is standard practice.

Camping represents another alternative. Prices range from 9,000 to 18,000L.

EATING AND NIGHTLIFE

Finding a supermarket or a public toilet in the town centre can be a problem in Italy. You may be forced into a café – with high prices and an old crone posted outside the toilet demanding money. To avoid this it's best to be organized. In general, breakfast at a hotel or pension isn't worth it, as all you're likely to get is a cup of coffee and a roll (it's normally cheaper at the local bar). If you can do without breakfast, go straight to the nearest supermarket or local market. In the evening *rosticcerie, trattorie, tavole calde* and *osterie* represent the best value. Cheap restaurants can be found and the standard of cooking can be high, even on a fixed-price menu.

Italy represents one of the best deals in Europe for good, cheap meals. The pizza stalls give you a cheap and tasty lunch, and in the evening, especially in Rome, you're spoilt for choice. Some places bump up the bill if you choose to sit outside to eat your meal, so check first. Always check the bill. Watch the *pane e coperto* – the bread and cover charge. It ranges from 1,000 to 3,000L. Also check whether the bill includes service (*servizio compreso*). Snacks and afternoon coffees can be a bad idea: they inevitably end up costing as much as a meal. Expect to pay 17,000–25,000L for a full meal with wine in a trattoria, and 15,000–20,000L for the *menu turistico*. After the evening meal most Italians wander round to a few cafés and bars, soaking up the local colour and chatting to friends and neighbours. Fast food abounds in Burghy Bars, however these are presently being converted into McDonald's outlets.

Even if a service charge is included, it is polite to give an extra tip if service has been good.

Finding vegetarian food should not be too difficult, but just in case, contact the Vegetarian Society in Altrincham before you go.

The disco and nightclub scene is not startling, but there are a few flash – and expensive – places in the main cities. Musical and cultural events are thick on the ground in places like Rome, Florence and Milan and museums are open 10 a.m.–7 p.m. every day except Mon. Pick up the *What's On* from the local Tourist Office of whichever centre you're in, and make good use of your ISIC card.

Northern Italy

The North is where the money's made, and to a large extent stays. Parts of it are industrial, and prices tend to be higher, but there are too many interesting towns in this area simply to head south regardless. Milan and Turin are the industrial powerhouses, while Venice and Florence are the jewels of the North.

Piedmont and Trentino – Alto Adige

TURIN (Torino) is more of a stopping-off place than a tourist centre. It's on the main line to Rome, Florence, Naples and Paris, and is one of Italy's main industrial centres, though there are seemingly hundreds of museums to choose from. The SIXTEENTH-CENTURY QUARTER is attractive enough to merit a visit, as is the former ROYAL PALACE, the PALAZZO MADAMA and the EGYPTIAN MUSEUM and ANCIENT ART MUSEUM in the Palace of the Academy of Sciences, Piazza Castello (open 9 a.m.–2 p.m. Wed., Fri., Sat.; 2.30 p.m.–7.30 p.m. Tues. and Thurs.) recommended for its outstanding collection of Chinese porcelain. Another must is the famous fake in the CHAPEL OF THE HOLY SHROUD, housed in a casket behind the apse of the DUOMO. Admission is free, though the cathedral is closed on Mon. and Sun. afternoons. Climb the 164m MOLE ANTONELLIANA for a panoramic view over the city and on to the distant Alps (daily 9 a.m.–7 p.m., closed Mon. 4000L). The Tourist Office is at Via Roma 226 (Tel. 011 535181) and there is an information office at Portanuova station, open Mon.–Sat.: 9 a.m.–7 p.m. The MEDIEVAL VILLAGE in the Parco del Valentino is free but undergoing restorations.

If you want to stay, try the IYHF Ostello Torino, Via Alba 1 (Tel. 6602939) which is situated across the river from the park: take bus 52 to the third stop over the river.

The campsite is much further out at Campeggio Villa Rey, Strand Val. S. Martino 27 (Tel. 8190117); open March–Nov.

The pink-coloured DOLOMITES and the proximity to Austria and Switzerland make ALTO ADIGE feel like a totally different country. BOLZANO (Bolzen) is on the main line from Munich and feels more Austrian than Italian in character. This is the capital of the Südtirol/Alto Adige area and was part of Austria till 1918. Tourist Information is at Piazza Walther 8 (Tel. 0471 970660 or 975656), where the GOTHIC CATHEDRAL stands. This Tourist Office gives excellent lists of accommodation information and can also direct you upon the best walks and hikes in the area. It is open Mon.–Fri.: 8.30 a.m.–6 p.m.; Sat.: 9 a.m.–12.30 p.m. There is another Tourist Office on Piazza Parrocchia 11 (Tel. 0471 993880), which is open Mon.–Fri.: 9 a.m.–12 p.m.; 2 p.m.–5 p.m.

The MUSEO DELL'ALTO ADIGE has a rare collection of wooden sculptures and paintings and the village of GRIES, across the River Talvera, makes a lovely walk. There is a campsite at Moosbauer, Via San Maurizio 83 (Tel. 918492). Take bus no. 10 A/B from the station (last one is at 8.30 p.m.) and get out at the hospital. Then it's 1 km down San Maurizio.

BRUNICO, half an hour from the Austrian frontier, still feels like a part of Austria. The dominating Tyrolean CASTLE OF BISHOP BRUNO was built in 1251. Walk for half an hour to the PLAN DI COROES for an incredible alpine view.

TRENTO, half an hour from Bolzano on the line to Verona, is another Roman town on the Brenner route. Walk down VIA BELENZANI and look at the Renaissance and Venetian palaces, the church of SAN FRANCESCO SAVERIO and the bishops' house, IL CASTELLO DI BUON CONSIGLIO (the Castle of Good Counsel). Trento's Tourist Office, Azienda Autonoma, is in Via Alfieri 4 (Tel. 0461 983880) and is open Mon.–Fri.: 9 a.m.–12 noon, 3 p.m.–6 p.m.; Sat.: 9 a.m.–12 noon. The hostel is the best place to stay while you're here. It charges 16, 000L per person, including breakfast, and is situated on Via Manzoni 17 (Tel. 461 234567). The mountains near Trento are good for day trips. The Tourist Office in VANEZE, halfway up MONTE BONDONE (Tel. 947128) can help you with accommodation, if you decide to stay here.

Lombardy

This region stretches from the Swiss border to the plains of the Po valley, taking in Como, on Lake Como, Bergamo, Mantua (Mantova) and its main city, Milan.

COMO is an ancient silk-producing city on the southern tip of Lake Como. Half an hour from Milan by train, it attracts masses of tourists. Head for the PIAZZA DEL DUOMO to see the old PRETORIAN PALACE called Il Broletto (1215). Next to this is the PALAZZO DEL COMUNE and the Renaissance Gothic DUOMO. The church of SAN FEDELE is reached by taking Via Vittorio Emanuele. Tourist Information is at Piazza Cavour 16 (Tel. 262091), and at the station in Via Venini. (Tel. 267214). Highly recommended is taking a water bus up the lake which stops at all the small villages *en route* (avoid the set tours as they are expensive and not good value).

The IYHF hostel is the Villa Olmo, on Via Bellinzona 2. Open March–Nov., it is situated 1 km from the station and charges 14,000L for bed and breakfast (Tel. 031 573800). Try and stay at MENAGGIO on the lakeside. The hostel there, 'La Primula', Via Quattro Novembre 38 (Tel. 0344 32356) is open March–Nov., overlooks the lake and offers a superb 3-course evening meal with wine, reasonably priced, with no curfew or restriction on drink.

BERGAMO is divided in 2: the lower city, built under the Fascists in the 1920s; and the upper city (*Città Alta*), a medieval settlement reached by funicular from Viale Vittorio Emanuele II. Apart from the PALAZZO DELL'ACCADEMIA CARRARA, forget the modern city centre. Once you've taken the funicular up, head for the PIAZZA VECCHIA where the PALAZZO DELLA RAGIONE stands. Opposite this is the PALAZZO NUOVO. VIA ROCCA takes you to a park which has a medieval lookout post from where the view over the Bergamasque valleys is excellent. Tourist Information is on Vicolo Aquila Nera 2 (Tel. 232730) and is open 9 a.m.–12.30 p.m. and 2.50 p.m.–7.30 p.m. daily. The IYHF hostel Bergamo has reopened (Tel. 035 217126) and is on Via Galileoterraris 1.

MANTUA (Mantova) was one of the Renaissance courts, ruled for 400 years by the Gonzaga family. Their sumptuous palace (PALAZZO DUCALE) is on Piazza Sordello. There are over 500 rooms, including the miniature suite specially constructed to house the court dwarfs. It's 2000L or free on ISIC, closed Mon. and Sun. afternoons. Opposite the palace is the medieval CATHEDRAL which is impressive enough, but pales into insignificance beside the beautiful CHURCH OF

SANT'ANDREA. The PALAZZO DEL TÈ in the south of the city was the Gonza-gas' summer home (closed Mon.). Tourist information is at Piazza A. Mantegna 6 (Tel. 0376 328253); watch out for their 12–3 p.m. sies-tas.

For cheap beds, try the youth hostel Ostello Sparafucile (Tel. 0376 372465), open Apr.–Oct., on the outskirts. Take bus 2, 6 or 9 from Piazza Cavallotti to get there. Camping is allowed in the grounds in July and August.

Milan (Milano) city phone code: 02

Most eurorailers don't get off at Milan, but while it is not exactly Venice in the sightseeing stakes, the city's got a lot more than most people realize, and as the rich man of Italy it has the perks of a high living standard (and higher standards of cleanliness) and more things going on in the evenings than elsewhere. It's the place to find super-models and where you will *never* feel overdressed.

STATION FACILITIES
There are 5 stations in Milan: Centrale, Genova, Vittoria, Nord and Garibaldi. Unless you are taking local trains, you will only use Centrale. Some consider the Centrale station to be one of the most impressive in Europe, if only for its sheer size. Since a fire in 1983, the whole station has had a facelift, making it even more spectacular. It is a thoroughly modern station with full facilities. There is a particu-larly useful supermarket here, which also has a snackbar attached, downstairs and to the right (with the trains behind you) which is open 5.30a.m. to midnight. Left luggage 5000L for 12 hours. Take care at night and avoid the main entrance area which is often frequented by drug pushers.

TOURIST INFORMATION AND ADDRESSES
PROVINCIAL TOURIST BOARD Via Marconi 1 (Tel. 809662), open Mon.–Fri.: 9.45 a.m.–12.30 p.m. and 1.30 p.m.–5 p.m., Sat.: 9 a.m.–12.30 p.m., 1.30 p.m.–5 p.m. For information on Milan, go to the Duomo then walk to the left side of the square under the arches (opposite the Galleria Vittorio Emanuele). They will supply you with a free map of the city which marks the metro and main train/bus lines. Another useful free map gives locations of all the hotels and pensions within the commune. Get the free guide *Tutta Milano* in English.

POST OFFICE Piazza Cordusio 4 (near the Duomo); also *poste restante*. Open Mon.–Fri.: 8.15 a.m.–7.40 p.m., Sat: 8.15 a.m.–5.40 p.m.
AMEX Via Brera 3, beyond the Piazza della Scala (Tel. 72003693). Mon.–Thu.: 9 a.m.–5.30 p.m. Friday closes at 5 p.m.
UK CONSULATE Via San Paolo 7 (Tel. 723001; after hours Tel. 872490)
US CONSULATE Via P. Amedeo 210 (Tel. 29001841; after hours Tel. 653131)
CANADIAN CONSULATE Via Vittore Pisani 19 (Tel. 67581; after hours Tel. 66980600 or 67583994).
AUSTRALIAN CONSULATE Via Borgogna 2 (Tel. 777041)
24-HOUR CHEMIST Centrale station (Tel. 6690735 or 6690935)
SOS FOR TOURISTS Tel. 5456551. For legal complaints.

SEEING

The CATHEDRAL (*Duomo*) is one of the largest Gothic cathedrals in the world. Ascend to the roof for the view. The building's situated at Piazza del Duomo, though you'd have a job missing it.

The famous opera house, LA SCALA, with its perfect acoustics, has been the scene of many a Verdi premiere, and there's a museum there showing costumes, manuscripts and other operatic memorabilia. It's north of the Duomo, through the gallery, on Piazza della Scala (open 9 a.m.–12 noon, 2 p.m.–6 p.m., entrance 6,000L). At the central crossroads in the Gallerie del Duomo is a little hole in the floor. If you place your heel in it and spin around it is meant to bring you luck for the coming year!

The BRERA PALACE and ART GALLERY on Via Brera is Milan's finest gallery. Housed in a palace is a varied collection of Italian art and a library of books and manuscripts (open 9 a.m.–5.30 p.m., Sun. 9 a.m.–12.30 p.m., closed Mon., entrance costs 8,000L, or is free to EU residents under the age of 18). The POLDI-PEZZOLI MUSEUM is a private collection with some rare sculptures and tapestries (closed Mon., open weekdays until 6 p.m., Sat. until 7.30 p.m., entrance 10, 000L), Via Manzoni 12.

The MUSEUM OF ANTIQUE ART is housed in SFORZA CASTLE (closed Mon., entrance is free). It can be reached by underground from Centrale station. Among its collection is Michelangelo's *Rondanini Pietà*, his last, unfinished work. Enter from Corte Ducale, Piazza Castello. Behind the castle is the SEMPIONE PARK. SANT'AMBROGIO BASILIA houses religious treasures and a few dead saints as well as a jewel-studded altar. If you'd like to see the rapidly decaying masterpiece, Leonardo's *Last Supper*, go to the convent next to SANTA MARIA DELLE GRAZIE, though they charge 12,000L to see it unless you are under 18. The MUSEUM OF SCIENCE AND TECHNOLOGY, Via S. Vittore 21, is worth visiting to see the complete aircraft and ships as well as working models of Leonardo's inventions. Open all day except Mon., entrance costs 10,000L.

For those of you sightseeing for a day, invest in a 1-day tourist ticket costing 5,000L for unlimited travel on buses, trams and the underground. Tickets are available from the Duomo underground station and the Central FS and Cordorna underground stations. Otherwise, single fare tickets cost 1,500L and must be purchased in advance.

SLEEPING

There are plenty of suitable places just north or west of the station, except during an international trade fair. The Tourist Office will help you out if you've hit a fluke blackspot.

The Piero Rotta youth hostel, Via Martino Bassi 2 (Tel. 39267095), open 7 a.m.–9 a.m., 4 p.m.–12.30 a.m., is half an hour away by metro (Line 1, direction Molino Dorino, get off at QT8) and allows 3 days' stay maximum. Bed and breakfast costs 23, 000L including sheets and shower. IYHF card-holders only. You can only check in between 4 p.m. and 11 p.m. and you must leave by 9 a.m. the following morning. It is clean, efficient but unfriendly.

For pensions in the 55,000–65,000L range, try Pensione Paganini, Via Paganini 6 (Tel. 278 443) or Pensione Trentina, Via Lippi 50 (Tel. 2361208), which are close to the station and cheap. There are a few pensions in Via Dante at 35,000L per double or try the Pensione Dante (Tel. 866471) they charge 60,000L for a double with free showers. Also try Hotel Rivoli at Via Giovanni Lulli 11 (Tel. 204681 5).

Another cheap hotel is the Ballarin, Via Soncino 3 (Tel. 800 822), which offers single rooms for 24, 000L and doubles for 35, 000L.

Milan's main campsite, San Donato, is not to be recommended – it is dirty and unsafe. Try Campeggio Autodromo di Monza (Tel. 039 387771) instead: open Apr.–Sept.; take a train to Monza (11 minutes) from Centrale station and catch a bus. It's full of motor-racing buffs due to the nearby track.

EATING AND NIGHTLIFE

The speciality of Milanese cooking is that they use butter, not olive oil, as they do elsewhere in Italy. With the amount of money knocking about Milan, the Milanese tend to eat out a lot, so restaurants are more expensive here than elsewhere. Street markets are scattered throughout the city and generally open Tuesday, Thursday and Saturday, providing all the ingredients for picnics. For a cheap meal near the centre, try the Spizzico Pizza Bars. There are plenty of cheap places in the Via Marghera area. If you want to go up-market without paying up-market prices, try Pane e Farina at Via Pantano 6 (Tel. 803274). Flash in Via Bergamini (near the Duomo) serves good-value sandwiches and pizzas. Students at the Università degli Studi di Milano, like Pierluigi, tell you to go to the pizza place opposite their University main entrance on Piazza Sant'Alessandro. Good pizza at good prices, nearest metro stop is Missori. The station area is not good for restaurants, so take the metro to the centre. Ice-cream lovers should head for Milan's most famous *gelateria*: Viel Gelati on Via Lucia Beltrami, open Thurs.–Tues. until 2 a.m. A cheaper alternative is Viel on Via Marconi 3E next to the Tourist Office.

For a good night out in the Navigli district take the metro (Green line) to Sant'Ambrogio. This area is full of pubs, bars and jazz music. For an interesting evening and a closer look at Milan's transvestite community, try Scimmie, a jazz fusion club, at Via Ascanio Sforza 49. Elefante is one of Milan's gay clubs. For pubs try Giamaica at Via Brera and for rock/disco try Rainbow and Grandi Magazzini featuring live music.

Emilia-Romagna

This is the region from the lower Po valley to the Apennine mountains north of Tuscany. It has the richest cuisine in Italy, is where tortellini, tagliatelle and Bolognese sauce originated, and from Parma have come Parma ham and Parmesan cheese.

PARMA is known for its architectural and gastronomic delights. PIAZZA GARIBALDI is the old town centre with the TOWN HALL, CLOCK TOWER and GOVERNOR'S PALACE. The DUOMO is Romanesque and on its cupola is Correggio's *Assumption of the Virgin Mary*. Also noteworthy in Piazza Duomo is the striking red marble BAPTISTRY. The HISTORICAL PHARMACY OF ST JOHN (in Piazza di San Giovanni) features some early decorative work of Parmigianino. In contrast, the MADONNA DELLA STECCATA (just off Piazza Garibaldi) marks the painter's last work for his home town, as he was imprisoned twice for failing to meet the deadline for completion of the frescoes.

The PALAZZO DELLA PILOTTA has been restored since its Second World War bombing to become the city's museum and the NATIONAL GALLERY reviews the school established by Correggio as well as the medieval-Renaissance Italian works.

Tourist Information (*Azienda Promozione Turistica*) is available at Piazza Duomo 5 (Tel. 234 735) and a youth hostel at 5 Parco Cittadella (Tel. 0521 581546: it's advisable to phone in advance). This hostel is also the only campsite near Parma. Like the hostel, it allows only 3 days' maximum stay and is open Apr.–Oct.

FERRARA today is an agricultural and industrial centre, but it was once an independent duchy ruled by the dukes of Este, and in their courts flowered some of the most gifted philosophers, artists and writers of the Renaissance period. The CASTELLO ESTENSE fortress, surrounded by a moat and complete with dungeons and a chapel, is open to the public. The town's CATHEDRAL stands opposite the PALAZZO COMUNALE. The PALAZZO SCHIFANOLA, in Via Scandiana, is where the dukes went for amusement; it's now a museum; the archaeological museum is in the Renaissance PALAZZO DI LUDOVICO IL MORO, currently undergoing restoration.

Camp at Campeggio Comunale Estense in Via Gramicia (Tel. 75 23 96), open Easter–Oct. Take bus 11.

RAVENNA was the 5th-century western capital of the Byzantine Empire and the birthplace of Christian iconography. The Tourist Office at Via Salara 8 (Tel. 354 04) will supply maps, information and help with accommodation. There is also video information round the corner on Via S Vitale. SAN VITALE BASILICA, the octagonal church, contains some mosaics, but the TOMB OF GALLA PLACIDIA has the best mosaics in Ravenna. Dante is buried in the grounds of the CHURCH OF SAN FRANCESCO. The high spot of Ravenna is a visit to the CHURCH OF SANT'APOLLINARE IN CLASSE (bus 4 or 44 from the station). Ravenna is a well-heeled town with a higher calibre of tourist!

There's a youth hostel, Dante, on Via Aurelio Nicolodi 12 (Tel. 0544 420405), open April–Oct. It's good, cheap at 16,000L for bed and breakfast, and reached by bus 1-11. For camping, head to Marina di Ravenna in Via delle Nazioni, or further along the coast to Camping Classe out at the Lido di Dante, which is extremely friendly and serves cheap food. Be warned, the campsites are not cheap (though most include tennis courts and swimming facilities) and access to and from the town is difficult because bus services are poor. Also, beware of mosquitoes – pack the repellent now!

For a hostel try Albergo Minerva, Via Maroncelli 1 (Tel. 0544

34543), just to the right of the station, or Albergo Al Giaciglio at Via Rocco Brancaleone 42 (Tel. 0544 39403). There's a student refectory at 8 Via Oberdan but arrive as early as 11.45 a.m.

Bologna city phone code: 051

One of the oldest university towns in Europe, one of the gastronomic centres of Europe, a Renaissance city of culture and learning, and today as red as Moscow was. This is where some eurorailers met a tragic death in 1980 when the station was bombed. Things are back to normal now, and a rebuilt station stands on the northern edge of Bologna. Trains run to Florence, Venice, Rome, Vienna, Sicily and other destinations.

TOURIST INFORMATION AND ADDRESSES
Apart from the one at the station, there are offices at Piazza Maggiore 6 and Via Marconi 45 (Tel. 237413 or 239660). General siesta-time is 12.30 p.m.–3.30 p.m. They'll help out on accommodation (they book rooms for free) as well as providing the usual services.
POST OFFICE Piazza Minghetti, Mon.–Fri.: 8.15 a.m.–6.30 p.m., Sat.: 8.15 a.m.–12.20 p.m. Tel. 223598.
STUDENT TRAVEL OFFICE CTS, Largo Respighi 21F (Tel. 237307 or 261802)
24-HOUR CHEMIST Tel. 192. Late- night chemists are also at the train station (Tel. 246603) and at Piazza Maggiore 6 (Tel. 238509).

SEEING
The main street is the VIA RIZZOLI with at one end the pedestrianized PIAZZA RAVESNANA, where the Garisenda and Asinelli towers can be admired, or climbed. At the other end is the PIAZZA MAGGIORE, which on Sun. becomes the site of puppet theatre shows. The Basilica of St Petronius is huge. Seven churches join into another conglomeration at the BASILICA SANTO STEFANO; the courtyard behind one of the churches has the BASIN OF PILATE where Pontius Pilate is said to have washed his hands when symbolically absolving himself of responsibility for Christ's death. It is actually worth coming here just to enjoy the porticoes which line all the main streets of the city.

SLEEPING, EATING AND NIGHTLIFE
The scope isn't huge in Bologna for budget beds, especially since

the youth hostel is about 6 km from the city at San Sisto, Via Viadagola 14 (Tel. 519202). To get there take bus 20 or 93 from Via de' Mille or Via Irnerio (the main road running parallel to the train station on the right). This hostel charges 17,000L for bed and breakfast, as does the second IYHF hostel further up the road, Le Torri San Sisto 2, at number 5 (Tel. 501810); both are open late Jan.–mid Dec.

Try Apollo, Via Drapperie 5 (off Via Rizzoli) where single rooms cost 46,000L and doubles 75,000L; Garisenda, Galleria del Leone 1 (Tel. 224369); or Ideale, Via Sirani 5 (Tel. 358270).

If you are arriving late, check outside the station's Tourist Office, for they post up-to-the-minute accommodation vacancies here after hours.

Eating's a totally different proposition: the cooking is terrific and cheap, and it's almost unheard of to have a bad meal. Vegetarians should head for Centro Naturista Bolognese in Via degli Albani 6, and though there is a university refectory, this is one place it'd be a shame to use it as there are so many family-run *trattorie*. For a variety of restaurants near the station, bear left across the main road and enter the courtyard there.

In the evening the young crowd hang out around Piazza Maggiore. For information on what's happening, look out for posters advertising events, especially around the university quarter. Bologna's city council encourages open-air raves, where entrance is either free or very cheap. The summer arts festival, Bologna Sogna, involves everyone taking to the hills for all-night revelry. To reach the Piazza Maggiore from the station take the bus if you are short of time as it is about a mile to walk.

Liguria (The Italian Riviera)

East of the French Côte d'Azur lies the less flashy but cheaper Italian Riviera. Genoa is the main town of this region, though it's hardly a resort. There's a comprehensive and picturesque rail line serving the Riviera which starts at Marseille in France, passes through the border at Ventimiglia and serves Bordighera, San Remo, Albenga and Genoa. Rather than staying on the Côte d'Azur, you may wish to stop off on the border here at VENTIMIGLIA. Worth checking out are the Hotel XX Settembre, Via Roma 16 (Tel. 351 222) or the Hotel Regina, Corso Genova 39.

BORDIGHERA was a favourite among European royals in the 19th century. The oldest part of the town is on the hill, and below is the new town. Bordighera is an attractive resort which prides itself on its abundant palm trees (they supply the Vatican for Palm Sunday). Prices tend to be high here, so try sleeping on the beach (although the police aren't keen on this practice) and avoid restaurants without fixed menus. In late July and August, the town presents the Salone Internazionale Umorismo, a comedy festival, with performances in the Palazzo del Parco. Ask at the Tourist Office on Via Roberto 1 for more information (Tel. 26 23 23).

SAN REMO is the Riviera's largest resort, but unless you've money to waste in the casino, stick to the beach. There are plenty of pizzerias and cafés, but this resort is one of the most commercialized and is not recommended too highly. If you do decide to stay, the Tourist Office at Largo Nuvoloni 1 (Tel. 571571) can help you find accommodation. At the end of February there is a song festival and recent guests have included David Bowie and the Spice Girls!

ALASSIO has a good long beach. The old town used to be a haunt of the wealthy British, and there's tennis, golf and skiing on offer. Check out the wall which has been signed by a host of celebrities. Off this stretch of the coast you'll find the island of Gallinara, which was once a haven to monks. For further information, the Tourist Office is on Viale Gibbi 26 (Tel. 640346).

At ALBENGA you can visit the ROMAN NAVAL MUSEUM and see the remains of a Roman ship sunk in the 1st century BC. Today Albenga is a market town and is more down to earth than many of the surrounding resorts. This city has a wealth of cathedrals and churches which outline its artistic, architectural and historical development over the centuries.

Two campsites lie to the west of Albenga: Camping Delfino (Tel. 0182 51998), which is open all year round, and Camping Sant'Anna (Tel. 0182 640702), closed Nov.–March.

Genoa (Genova) city phone code: 010

The largest port of northern Italy with a medieval harbour-quarter, Renaissance upper town of merchants' palaces and, above all this, modern Genoa. Crowning this is the CIRCONVALLAZIONE A MONTE, a boulevard which winds its way in and out of the hills.

Genoa became an artistic centre in the 16th and 17th centuries when Flemish masters, including Rubens and Van Dyck, came to paint the wealthy merchants' portraits. It is also the birthplace of Christopher Columbus and the city where Marco Polo was kept as a prisoner of war in 1298.

STATION FACILITIES

Information Tel. 284 081 from 7 a.m.–11 p.m.

Genoa has 2 stations: the Porta Principe (main station) and Brignole. Trains bound for the north use Principe, trains heading south use Brignole. Through-trains stop at both, except for those going north-west (Milan–Nice) – they use only Principe. There are interstation connecting trains regularly.

Daily trains to Frankfurt, Milan (1½ hours), Venice (4½ hours), Turin (2 hours), Bologna (3 hours), Florence (4½ hours), Rome (5½ hours), Naples and Nice (3 hours). Left-luggage 6 a.m.–10 p.m., 5,000L for 12 hours.

TOURIST INFORMATION AND ADDRESSES

Tourist Information is at Principe station (Tel. 2462633) and the main office at Via Roma II (Tel. 576 791); open Mon.–Fri.: 8 a.m.–1.15 p.m. and 2 p.m.–6.30 p.m., Sat.: 8 a.m.–1.30 p.m.

POST OFFICE Piazza Dante 4, Via Rela 8

UK CONSULATE Via XII Ottobre 2, 13th floor (Tel. 564833)

24-HOUR CHEMIST Piazza Acquaverde (Principe station) or Via Balbi 185 (Tel. 26 26 97) or dial 192

SEEING

Get hold of a map (from Informegiovanni in Palazzo Ducale 7), as it's a confusing city. There are 17 museums and galleries, but PALAZZO BIANCO and PALAZZO ROSSO are the cream of the crop. The former contains a Flemish collection and the latter displays works by many famous masters such as Tintoretto, Caravaggio and Van Dyck. Other cultural sites worth a visit are the gallery and frescoes of PALAZZO CATALDI and the antiquities in PALAZZO DORIA TURSI. The CHRISSONE MUSEUM houses a wonderful collection of Japanese and Chinese paintings and artefacts, including 1,000 engraved Japanese sabres (Tel. 54 22 85).

Via Balbi, running east from the main station, is a fine example of Old Genoa and is also the site of the PALAZZO REALE FINE ART GALLERY. In the historical centre of the city, visit the DUOMO SAN LORENZO, off Piazza Matteot. Near the port, the AQUARIUM is the biggest in Europe.

Around the east of the harbour, the Via San Lorenzo leads past the cathedral of the same name into Piazza de' Ferrari. Beyond this square Via Dante leads past the main post office to Piazza Dante and the site of Christopher Columbus's childhood home. Further north, along Via Antonio Gramsci, is the poverty-stricken district of Pré, which is worth a visit – but not after dark!

SLEEPING, EATING AND NIGHTLIFE

If you want an adequate room then Hotel Alicia, Via Balbi 15/5, charges about 50, 000L for its doubles. The International Youth Hostel Genova in Via Costanzi 120n (Tel. 242 2457) charges 19,000L per night for bed and breakfast and is situated 3 km from the station.

Women can use the clean and safe Casa della Giovane hostel at Piazza Santa Sabina 4, near Via Fontane (Tel. 206632) for around 18,000L.

The campsites are unpleasant; you're better off heading down the coast to the towns of Riviera di Levante.

There are scores of pizzerias and restaurants, and the prices all seem very much on a level, but we recommend Emma's Trattoria in Piazza de Serraglio. Try the regional specialities of *cima genovese* (stuffed cold veal) and *pandolce* (orange-flavoured cake).

Veneto

Veneto encompasses the north-eastern Po valley from the Dolomites to the coastal resorts. This is the region around what many consider to be the most beautiful city in the world, Venice. The art towns of Padua, Verona and Treviso are close by, while Lake Garda is a stretch of azure water in the foothills of the Alps. Trains from Verona stop at Peschiera and Desenzano, and there are numerous campsites in both towns.

Venice (Venezia) city phone code: 041

Venice is a 'must' on any European tour, and it's worth all the crowds and hugely inflated prices, because you'll never forget it. The town consists of 118 islets connected by 400 bridges with 150 canals winding their way through the maze. There are no cars, only boats.

The history of Venice is long and colourful. Her buildings reflect her glorious past when, as an independent city-state, she ruled over most of the Mediterranean. During the Renaissance, Venice was the trading port with the Middle East, and became the centre of European commerce. The doges (the city rulers) had enough money not only to build sumptuous palaces and churches, but also to commission large-scale works of art from the Venetian school (Titian, Tintoretto, etc.) and patronize the sciences too. Their 1,000-year independence came to an end in 1797 when Napoleon gave Venice to the Austrians. When Italy was united, Venice joined, and its popularity as a tourist trap of the 20th century has brought it new wealth, much of which is used to prevent the entire city sinking and being lost for ever.

STATION FACILITIES

The main station is called Santa Lucia. It is a very busy station with full amenities including showers and left luggage, though allow extra time to queue!

Some trains stop only at Venezia-Mestre on the mainland, so check. To reach Venezia-Santa Lucia from Mestre, there are both trains and buses. The station is situated at the west end of the town right on the Grand Canal. It's possible to go everywhere by foot, but it's more fun to take the *vaporetti* (waterbuses) from outside the station. Nos 1 and 34 take you down the Grand Canal to San Marco Square. No. 2, which is the faster, limited-stop service, takes you to San Marco and Lido following the Giudecca canal route.

TOURIST INFORMATION

The Tourist Office in the station (Tel. 719078) handles accommodation and gives out maps. Your best bet is to head for the central Tourist Office near San Marco Square at Palazzetto Selva (Tel. 522 6356), but they will not help you with accommodation.

The student Tourist Office (CTS) is at Dorsoduro 3252 (Tel. 520 5660); they'll help you out with accommodation and student travel.

Tourist Offices are always busy, so try and fix up accommodation beforehand. All APT offices are outlets for the useful youth discount passes (*carta giovane*).

ADDRESSES

POST OFFICE Fondaco dei Tedeschi, near the eastern side of the Rialto Bridge. Telephone office here also. Mon.–Sat.: 8.15 a.m. –6.45 p.m. Also at San Marco Square.

AMEX Salizzado San Moise, 1471 San Marco. Mon.–Fri.: 9 a.m.–5.30 p.m., Sat.: 9 a.m.–12.30 p.m.

UK CONSULATE Dorsoduro 1051 (Tel. 5227207)

FIRST AID Tel. 192 or 113

GETTING ABOUT

The waterbuses cover all Venice. A trip on bus 1 or 82 is good, as it takes in quite a few sights down the Grand Canal. They run frequently and fares are around the 4,000L mark. A 24-hour pass (*biglietto turistico 24 ore*) costs 15,000L. A 3-day pass is also available at 30,000L. There are also a few buses, but their routes are restricted. The gondolas look beautiful, but at 80,000L plus an hour it's not surprising few eurorailers use them.

SEEING

There are so many little winding back-streets and alleys, unexpected quiet squares and little hump-back bridges making Venice the easiest place in Europe to get lost in (no wonder Venice's famous son Marco Polo was so good at exploring). Venice is divided into 6 main districts, and each district (or *sestiere*) can have duplicate street names, so be sure to *which* district your required street belongs. Streets do not possess individual numbers, but a *sestiere* number, which can go up to 6,000, but not in any obvious logical pattern. Highly recommended tools for getting about in Venice include the red storti-Edizioni Foligrat *Mestre-Venezia* map and the English–Italian magazine *Un Ospite di Venezia (A Guest in Venice)*, which gives up-to-date information on exhibitions, special events and *vaporetto* timetables. The following are some of the most unmissable sights:

1. ST MARK'S SQUARE (*Piazza San Marco*): The city revolves round this incredible piazza. ST MARK'S BASILICA and the DOGES' PALACE are here, as are the LAW COURTS, the beautiful MOORS' CLOCK TOWER and the OLD LIBRARY, now an archaeological museum. Follow the sign posts to walk here from the station.
2. ST MARK'S BASILICA: This amazing Byzantine church is a riot of gold, marble and mosaic. It was originally the chapel for the doges, and became the city cathedral in 1807. Do not miss the Bronze Horses or the Scala d'Oro. (Women: bring a shawl to cover your shoulders and arms; men: wear long trousers to be let in.) Climb up the basilica for 4,000L and a grand view.
3. DOGES' PALACE (*Palazzo Ducale*): This pink-and-white fairytale palace was the home of the Venetian government and the rulers of the republic. The connecting bridge between the palace and the prison is known as the BRIDGE OF SIGHS, 8,000L for a reduced price tour.
4. THE ACADEMY OF FINE ART (*Galleria dell'Accademia*) has the best of the Venetian school's work: Canaletto, Tintoretto, Bellini, Veronese, etc. Closed Mon. Entrance costs 13,000L and there are no ISIC reductions. Tel. 522 2247
5. CHIESA DEI FRARI: After St Mark's, this is Venice's most prized church. It houses 2 Titians and a Bellini. Next to it is the SCUOLA DI SAN ROCCO, with a collection of 56 Tintorettos on biblical themes.

Entrance costs 8,000L (6,000L for reductions).

6. SCHOOL OF ST GEORGE: Beyond St Mark's Square at Calle dei Furlani, this offers a frieze of paintings by Carpaccio, is beautiful, and usually much quieter than the other museums. Entrance costs 5,000L (3,000L for reductions). Closed Monday.

7. GUGGENHEIM GALLERY: A modern art gallery with an excellent, extensive choice of Surrealist works. Open Sun.–Mon. and Wed.–Fri.: 11 a.m.–6 p.m.; Sat.: 6–9 p.m.; closed Tues. Admission 10,000L, Sat. free.

8. Take the lift up the Campanile (6,000L) for a view you'll never forget. Remember your map and you can study the city and islands laid out below you.

A few streets away from the 'sights' is the quieter, less touristy western side of Venice. It's a great place to go to escape the hordes and just sit in a square or by a canal watching a gondola go by.

FESTIVALS The Masked Carnival takes place in the first 2 weeks of Feb. and the *Festa del Redentore* (including an hour-long firework show) on the third Sat. of July. If you are in Venice in the last week of Aug. and the first week of Sept., partake of the International Film Festival and stay around for the *Regata Storica* – a pageant of beautiful boats down the Grand Canal on the first Sun. in Sept.

EXCURSIONS Just east of Venice lies the LIDO, the beach resort of the rich and famous. Also worth a trip is the island of MURANO (ferry 12 from Fondamente Nove) where Venetian glass is blown (but buy it in Venice itself as prices on Murano are even more inflated); BURANO, a colourful little fishing island; and TORCELLO with its Byzantine cathedral.

SLEEPING

Accommodation in Venice is not as troublesome as it used to be. Recently prices have levelled out, and it's no more expensive here now than in Rome or Paris. Watch out for hotel guides offering 'cheap' rooms at the station: some are not as good a bargain as they seem. The area near the station is as good as anywhere to look. If all else fails, take the train to Mestre, 8 minutes away, and base yourself there where bed and food are cheaper. It is illegal to sleep in railway stations in Italy and you are likely to have a hose trained on you and end up soaked.

You should also seriously consider travelling to Padua for accommodation in high summer. It's only 30 minutes by train from Santa

Lucia station and there is a regular service. Accommodation is much cheaper, even in the summer, but you are strongly advised to book (and arrive) well in advance, as there can be an unwillingness to hold cheap rooms until your time of arrival if demand is high.

HOSTELS The youth hostel is on the island of Giudecca at Fondamenta Zitelle 86 (Tel. 523 8211); take the waterbuses 5 and 84 from the landing stage along from the Piazza San Marco. Open Feb.–Dec., no phone bookings. Reception is closed between 9.30 a.m. and 1 p.m. (11 p.m. curfew). Expect to pay 21,000L for bed and breakfast.

Also out here are a few pensions and a religious hostel (women only), Istituto Canossiane, Ponte Piccolo 428 (Tel. 5222157); curfew 10.30 p.m. To get there take waterbus 5 to Sant'Eufemia, and walk to your left when you get off. Reception opens at 4 p.m. and it's 20, 000L each.

More expensive is the Istituto Ciliota at San Marco 2976 (Tel. 52 04888), which caters for women and married couples only. To get there take *vaporetto* 2 to San Samuele. A double room costs in the region of 65,000L.

CAMPSITES Head for the Jesolo Peninsula. Take *vaporetto* 14 from near San Marco to Punta Sabbioni. Camping Miramare (Tel. 966150), open Feb.–Nov., is neat and clean and offers 4-person cabins for 47,000L to those without tents.

There is also an extremely expensive year-round site at Fusina in Via Moranzani (Tel. 5470055), which you can get to by waterbus or road bus no.13 from the railway bridge near Mestre station, though reports differ as to cleanliness. It costs 9,500L per person (and 28, 000L per tent)! Don't forget mosquito repellent.

Camping Rialto at Via Orlanda, Mestre, is open May–Sept. Expect to pay 4,500L per person plus 2,500L per tent. Further out, on the island of Lido, the very basic campsite San Nicolò, Ballarin Giancarlo (Tel. 767 415), charges more (reduction with a camping carnet [the international camping card]). Bus A from Lido ferry will get you there.

HOTELS AND PENSIONS A single room will cripple you financially. If you are travelling alone, find a partner quick, or head for a hostel. There are many cheap pensions in the Lista di Spagna near the station. Locanda Stefania, Fondamenta Tolentini 181a (Tel. 5203757), is across the bridge at the station. Doubles cost around 65 ,000L.

Archie's House, Cannaregio 1814/b, San Leonardo (Tel. 720884) is only 10 minutes from the station.

Locanda Ca' Foscari, Dorsoduro 3887 1B (Tel. 710817) is clean and reasonably priced on Calle della Frescarda.

Near the Mestre station, at Via Parini 4, you should be able to get a double for about 40,000L.

A friendly welcome and attractive rooms (double around 40,000L) are offered at Col di Lana (signposted from just outside Mestre station).

EATING AND NIGHTLIFE

Do not buy food and drink from stalls outside the station – items are half the price 2 minutes further on. There are quite a few fixed-price menus floating about and the food markets provide all you need for picnics. The main market is at the foot of the Rialto bridge and is open until early afternoon. There is a lot of choice if you wander around. The fewer tourists there are, the cheaper it will be. For example, while on the walk from the station to St Mark's Square, we paid 6,000L for a coffee. The same in the great square itself cost 20,000L!

Verona phone code: 045

It's not surprising Shakespeare chose Verona as his setting for *Romeo and Juliet,* as it is a romantic city of palaces, churches, gardens and vineyards. Midway on the line from Milan to Venice, it is a popular destination with eurorailers who make their base here and travel to Padua and Venice for day trips. From the station, it's a 15-minute walk to the centre of Verona, or take bus 1, 11, 12, 13 or 72 to the PIAZZA BRA, where the incredibly preserved ROMAN ARENA is. Tourist information is at Via Leoncino 61 (Tel. 592828). The VERONESE MERCHANTS' PALACES are located in the same square, and the adjoining PIAZZA DELI SIGNORI contains the TOMBS OF THE SCALIGERI, Verona's medieval enemies. Their house was the CASTEL VECCHIO, and this fine medieval building is now a showpiece painting and sculpture museum, open Tues.–Sun.: 8 a.m.–6 p.m. Admission is 5,000L. The Romanesque church of SAN ZENO MAGGIORE is well worth seeing. Visit Juliet's house, *Casa di Giulietta* (5,000L or 1,500L students) or see the infamous balcony there for free. If you rub the breast of Juliet's statue it is meant to bring you luck! You can visit her tomb in the church of San Francesco al Corso.

For a bed, try the Casa della Giovane (for women), Via Pigna 7 (Tel. 596880), who charge about 18,000–25,000L. Advance bookings taken. Open 8 a.m.–10.30 p.m. The Ostello Verona hostel at Salita Fontana del Ferro 15 (Tel. 590360) is 3 km from the station, just across the Ponte Pietra, behind the Teatro Romano; it's inexpensive and well run. The Al Castello Hotel, Corso Cavour 43 (Tel. 8004403), offers singles for 30,000L and doubles for 50,000–60,000L, with bathrooms.

Camping is available at Campeggio Castel San Pietro, Via Castel San Pietro 1 (Tel. 592037). Take bus 3 to Via Marsala. They charge 6,000L per person and 4,000L per tent and are only open mid-June–mid-Sept. Camping Romeo e Giulietta (Tel. 8510243) on Strada Bresciana 54 is open all year round. It is situated 5 km from the centre of Verona, so take the blue AFT bus to Peschiera from the train station and tell the driver you want the *campeggio*.

Try Trattoria alla Canna at Via Scrimiari 5, Osteria al Cristo at Piazzetta Pescheria 6, or Trattoria da Mario, at Stradone Porta Palio, for cheap set menus. Wash the meal down with the local Soave or Valpolicella wine.

During the summer there are performances of opera in the 22,000-capacity Roman arena. Seats start at about 25,000L, but it's an experience you won't easily forget A daytime visit costs 6,000L or 1,500L for students. Closes mid-afternoon on performance days.

Padua (Padova) phone code: 049

About 30 minutes from Venice lies Padua, the famous 13th-century university town. It's not as attractive as it once was, due to heavy industry, so a 1-day visit should suffice. Tourist Information (Tel. 875 2077) is at the station. Pick up maps here and make use of the accommodation service, which is free (open Mon.–Sat.: 9 a.m.–7.30 p.m., Sun.: 8.30 a.m.–12.30 p.m.). You can also exchange money. There is normally only 1 person working here, so don't be surprised if it shuts at odd times. There is another office at Riviera Mugnai 8, which shuts at 6 p.m. and another at the entrance of the MUSEO CIVICO EREMITANI (same entrance for the Scrovegni chapel) where you can get maps, hotels and change (open Tues.–Sun.: 9 a.m.–7 p.m.).

The CAPPELLA SCROVEGNI is *the* sight of Padua: Giotto's masterpiece of medieval art shook the theories of the time. Open 9 a.m.–7 p.m. in the summer (until 6 p.m. in the winter); admission to the chapel is 10,000L, or there is a combined 15,000L ticket which will get you into most other museums as well. Next door is the CHIESA DEGLI EREMITANI, where frescoes by the young Mantegna hang. Entrance is free, and the building is open 8.15 a.m.–12 noon, daily.

Further up Corso Garibaldi, on the Via Roma is the university. If you visit nothing else in the building of BOPALACE, visit the anatomy theatre; this breathtaking construction is the oldest in the world. The PALAZZO DELLA RAGIONE, next door, keeps a magnificent 14th-century wooden horse and some beautiful frescoes. Entrance is 8,000L (students 3,000L) and it is open Tues.–Sun.: 9 a.m.–7 p.m. If from here you walk up Piazza Antenore and turn right up Via del Santo, you'll come to IL SANTO on the Piazza. This church, dedicated to St Anthony (patron saint of the lost), holds his remains and has thus become a site of pilgrimage. The SCUOLA SANT'ANTONIO contains 4 Titians also dedicated to this saint, the patron of Padua.

A useful item to invest in if you're on a cultural mission in the city is the *Padua biglietto unico*, a collective ticket for Padua's museums and monuments. They cost in the region of 15,000L (students 10,000L) and are valid for a whole year. Buy them from the entrance of individual monuments and museums or at the ITA offices.

Accommodation shouldn't be a problem. The youth hostel is a renovated medieval castle. It's at Porta Legnano in Montagnana (Tel. 0429 810762). Take a local train to Monselice and change for Montagnana. Buy your tickets from the booth here, or at any tobacconist's instead of on the bus.

In town, try the busy, clean and friendly IYHF Ostello della Città di Padova at Via Aleardi 30 (Tel. 875 2219).

The nearest campsite is in Montegrotto Terme, Strada Romana Aponese 104 (Tel.793400), an upmarket site which offers a swimming pool and thermal baths. Take bus M.

For food, go to the excellent market, the Salone, near the university, or try one of the 3 Mensas: at Via San Francesco 122 (closed Aug.), Via Padovanino or Via Leopardi. La Mappe, Via Matteotti 17, serves decent self-service fare.

San Marino state telephone code: 00 378

On the slopes of Monte Titano, 23 km south-west of Rimini, you enter foreign territory. San Marino is the world's smallest republic. It's also the oldest and has preserved its independence since the 4th century, despite scheming princes and popes. Its democratic constitution so impressed Napoleon he offered to enlarge the Republic. The offer was turned down – San Marino has never sought to expand but has been regarded as a place of sanctuary ever since it was founded (according to legend) by St Marinus, a Dalmatian stone-cutter fleeing religious persecution. Garibaldi once sought sanctuary there.

This unaccountably famous 'toy town' is tacky, full of tourist rip-offs and milks its unique position for all it's worth. You no longer have to wave your passport on the border but you'll probably send postcards with the specially issued San Marino postage stamps (valued by collectors). Beware of getting too much San Marinese currency in your change – it has only souvenir value in the rest of Italy and the lira is valid here anyway.

GETTING THERE

There are no direct trains, so take the train to Rimini and bus the remaining 24 km. Take the cable car from Borgo Maggiore at the foot of Monte Titano to San Marino (the capital).

TOURIST INFORMATION

There is a Tourist Office in the city of San Marino on the Contrada Omagnano 20 (Tel. 882400 or 882 998).

SLEEPING AND EATING

It's probably better to do a day trip rather than an overnight stay because the cheapest hotels are in the region of 70,000L. There are lots of good restaurants, though you may find yourself paying over the odds. Duty-free drink makes this a good place to stock up on your favourite tipple.

SIGHTS

The PALAZZO DEL GOVERNO in San Marino city is a splendid neo-Gothic affair. In front of it is the FREEDOM STATUE of San Marino. The palace is on the old town's main square – Piazza della Libertà. Just off the square is the neo-classical BASILICA SAN MARINO. From the Basilica take the road south-east to the 3 peaks of Monte Titano with their 3 (rebuilt) medieval tower fortresses. Try the Garibaldi museum, the stamp and coin museum, the Museum of Weaponry or the intriguingly named Museum of the Incredible but True. The National Day of the Republic is celebrated on 3 Sept. with a crossbow competition.

Outside the city, on the border, the medieval village of VERUCCHIO has a fortress (once the stronghold of Rimini tyrants), the Rocca Malatesta and a small Archaeology Museum with ceramics dating from 1400 BC. SAN LEO, also a border town, has a particularly fine castle built by the Dukes of Urbino and containing a small picture gallery.

Tuscany

Italy's wealthiest region in every way. This was the birthplace of the Renaissance and, apart from the mountains and coastal beaches, it offers some of the finest old cities in the world: Siena, Pisa and the Renaissance city, Florence. The countryside is beautiful, without the south's poverty or the north's heavy industry, and trains serve even the smallest towns.

Florence (Firenze) city phone code: 055

The Medici family made Florence the central point of the Renaissance, and her citizens included Leonardo, Botticelli, Michelangelo, Galileo and Machiavelli. The legacy lives on in today's Florence and even the occasional gypsy beggar preying on tourists in summer can't take away from the centuries of elegance that make this a pilgrimage for artists the world over. There are enough churches, galleries, palaces and museums to interest everyone, but there aren't enough beds, so come early to Florence, and avoid joining the throngs of August station-sleepers who wake up to find they've lost more than a good night's sleep, if they haven't been arrested first.

STATION FACILITIES
Florence Santa Maria Novella station is well-equipped. However beware of pickpockets and the rates in the foreign exchange office. Left-luggage 5,000L for your rucksack for up to 12 hours. Closed 1.30 a.m.–4.15 a.m.

Daily trains within Italy to Venice, Pisa, Rome, Naples, Turin, Bologna and Milan. Daily trains internationally to Geneva, Zürich, Munich, Vienna and Paris.

TOURIST INFORMATION
There are two Tourist Offices at the station. The best is ITA (Tel. 28 28 93 or 21 95 37) which is at the end of the bus station to the left as you leave the train station. It also deals with accommodation (*commission*) and is very helpful. The other is Turistica (Tel. 21 22 45 or 23 81 226). Expect long queues. The city Tourist Office (Tel. 290832) is at Via Cavour 1r, north of the Duomo. They give out maps of the city and a useful 1/3/5-day guide. Open Mon.–Sat.: 8.15

a.m.–7.15 p.m., Sun.: 8.15 a.m.–1.45 p.m. They do not book rooms. If you are desperate you can get a town map from McDonald's in the station.

ADDRESSES

POST OFFICE Via Pellicceria in a very impressive building. Also poste restante. Open Mon.–Fri.: 8.15 a.m.–7 p.m.; Sat.: 8.15 a.m.–12.30 p.m.

PUBLIC TELEPHONE OFFICE has moved to 21/red Via Cavour (from Piazzadel Duomo towards Piazza San Marco). Here you can telephone and pay a cashier after your call.

BANK San Paulo (inside station). Open Mon.–Fri.: 8.25 a.m.–1.25 p.m. and 2.40 p.m.–4.10 p.m., Sat.: 8.25 a.m.–11.55 a.m.

AMEX Via Dante Alighieri 20 (Tel. 50981), Mon.–Fri.: 9 a.m.–5.30 p.m., Sat.: 9 a.m.–12.30 p.m.

UK CONSULATE Palazzo Castelbarco, Lungarno Corsini 2 (Tel. 284133)

US CONSULATE Lungarno Vespucci 38 (Tel. 2398276)

STUDENT TRAVEL CTS, Via Ginori 25 (Tel. 289570)

24-HOUR CHEMIST At the station by track 16, Comunale no. 13 or Via Calzaiuoli 7r (Tel. 289490)

TOURIST MEDICAL OFFICE Tel. 475411

POLICE Via Zara 2 (Tel. 49771) or Emergency 113

SEEING

Once you have found a place to stay, soak up the atmosphere – it is as important in this city as rushing around the never-ending historic sites. Aim to visit museums and galleries first thing in the morning to avoid the crowds. Cars are banned from the city centre in the day.

The DUOMO is the amazing multicolour cathedral with the huge dome which gives merciful shade in summer. The dome was hailed as the wonder of the 15th century, but the façade of the cathedral is only 19th-century. Climb the 414 steps for an unrivalled view over Florence (8,000L; open 9 a.m.–6.50 p.m.). The CAMPANILE (8,000L; open 9 a.m.–5.30 p.m.) was Giotto's idea and the BAPTISTRY is beautiful (free; open Mon.–Sat.: 1.30 p.m.–6 p.m. and Sun.: 9 a.m.–12.30 p.m.).

The UFFIZI is one of the world's largest art galleries and where there was a bomb in 1993. There's a glut of sheer genius here, including Leonardo and, best of all, *The Birth of Venus* by Botticelli; visit it more than once and try to avoid the crowds. It's closed on Mondays and Sundays. Entrance is currently 12,000L.

Across the River Arno from the Uffizi is the PALAZZO PITTI (admission

8,000L), which the Medici used during the 16th century. You can wander round it today and see Raphaels, Rubens and Titians in the Palatine Gallery, and on its ground floor the ROYAL APARTMENTS and MUSEUM OF GEMS. All are open 9 a.m.–2 p.m. and closed on Mon. The GIARDINO DI BOBOLINI (palace gardens) are as rewarding as the museum and are open 9 a.m.–7.30 p.m. Photographers, you can get that famous skyline view of the city from here, scaffolding excepted! The medieval BARGELLO PALACE holds the NATIONAL MUSEUM, an important sculpture collection (open 9 a.m.–2 p.m., closed Mon. 8,000L). If, like thousands of others, you came to Florence to see Michelangelo's *David*, you'll find him in the GALLERIA DELL'ACCADEMIA on Via Ricasoli (admission 12,000L). The massive PALAZZO VECCHIO was once a Medici residence and contains the sumptuous Hall of the Five Hundred. It's at PIAZZA DELLA SIGNORIA (open Mon.–Wed. and Fri.–Sat.: 9 a.m.–7 p.m. Sun: 8 a.m.–1 p.m.). The other palace you ought to see is the MEDICI-RICCARDI on Via Cavour (open 9 a.m.–12.45 p.m., 3 p.m.–6.45 p.m., closed some Wednesdays and Sunday afternoons). The tiny chapel on the first floor contains Gozzoli's frescoes *The Procession of the Magi* and the Medici Museum downstairs is open 9 a.m.–1 p.m. on Sun.

Take in the Medici's Renaissance parish church, SAN LORENZO. Most of them are buried here in the MEDICI CHAPELS (closed Mon. and Sun.), and the LAURENTIAN LIBRARY is considered to be Michelangelo's architectural masterpiece. SAN MARCO (admission 8,000L) is worth seeing for the monks' cells which Fra Angelico painted his unique shade of blue as an aid to monastic contemplation. The BRANCACCI CHAPEL of Santa Maria del Carmine has some beautiful Masaccio frescoes. Giotto has some work in SANTA CROCE and next door is that harmonious architectural gem, the CAPPELLA DEI PAZZI, designed by Brunelleschi.

The PONTE VECCHIO was the only bridge to survive the war intact, when the Germans blew up all the others but were rushed by New Zealand troops before they could destroy it. It dates back to 1345 and now is the preserve of upmarket jewellers and goldsmiths.

Pollution levels can be high in the summer heat, so if you are an asthma sufferer, take precautions. Check at the Tourist Office for details and advice.

SLEEPING

Florence is more expensive than average, so be prepared to spend more wherever you stay. Breakfast is rarely included. Postal booking is recommended for all accommodation and is essential during peak season.

HOSTELS The highly recommended youth hostel is at 2/4 Viale Augusto Righi (Tel. 601451) with 322 beds, but it's for IYHF members only. Rock-bottom price (20,000L a night), amiable staff, no reservations. Take bus 17b from the station. Pio X-Artigianelli is another hostel at Via dei Serragli 106 (Tel. 225044). It's near the Pitti Palace, but try to get there early. Ostello Santa Monaca, Via Santa Monaca 6 (Tel. 268338), 21, 000L including sheets and shower, is a private hostel near the centre, bus 11 or a 15-minute walk from the station. It is shut 1 p.m.–3 p.m., but you can reserve a place and leave your luggage at other times and register properly 4 p.m.–11.30 p.m. The Istituto Gould, Via dei Serragli 49 (Tel. 212576), is an excellent hostel, very popular (advance postal booking recommended). Women and families can try the convent Suore Oblate dello Spirito Santo, Via Nazionale 8 (Tel. 2398202), open July–mid-Oct.

PENSIONS There is a glut of suitable places within 5 minutes of the station. If you come up with nothing in this area, drop off your pack as the other pensions are a good walk away. From the station, turn left then try places along Via Nazionale, Via Fiume, Via Faenza, Via 28 Aprile, Via Guelfa and Via Cavour. Albergo Mia Cara at Via Fuenza 58 (Tel. 216053) and Hotel Soa, Via Cavour (Tel. 283930) are OK.

Pensione Mary is clean, bright and you can get a bed in a four-bed room for 30,000L. It's at Piazza Indipendenza 5 (top floor) – turn left down Via Nazionale from station. Show this book to get a free breakfast (normally 5,000L) or 10% reduction on a double room! There's no curfew. Tel. and Fax. 496310.

CAMPSITES Italiani e Stranieri at Viale Michelangelo 80 (Tel. 681 1977) is a site open Apr.–Oct. but get in early or the best pitches will have gone. It has good views of Florence and kitchen facilities, and charges 10,000L per person and 10,000L per tent. Take bus 13 from the station.

Camping Camerata is next to the youth hostel (Tel. 610 300) on the 17b bus route. They charge 9,000L per person and 10,000L per tent.

There is a municipal site at Villa Farvard, 6 km out of town, which provides free shelter and showers. Take buses 14a, b or c from the station and stop at Rocco Teddabla. Open 7 p.m.–10 a.m. The Panoramico, Via Peramound, outside Fiesole (Tel. 599069), is another recommended campsite north of the city. Take bus 7 from the station to Fiesole then walk up the hill to the campsite.

EATING AND NIGHTLIFE

The self-service restaurant at Piazza della Stazione 25 does a really cheap meal; another favourite is Trattoria ZaZa at Piazza Mercato Centrale 26. A busy but good place is Trattoria il Constadino, Via Palazzuolo 69/71. If you've really reached rock bottom, Casa San Francesco on Piazza Sant'Annunziata (diagonally opposite Chiesa di Sant'Annunziata), run by monks, does a full lunch for a good price. The university Mensas are on Via dei Servi 52 and 66–68. For picnic food, the Mercato Centrale, near San Lorenzo, is your best bet; open Mon.–Sat.: 7 a.m.–2 p.m.

For a taste of simple Florentine food, try Ottavino, a small bar that is the established meeting place of the market workers: it's at Via dell'Ariento and is open until 1.30 p.m.

Florence has by far the best *gelati* (ice cream) in Italy. Vivoli, on Via dell'Isola delle Stinche, is held by many to produce the world's best. You can sample a tiny pot for 2,500L.

The Maggio Musicale Fiorentino festival is held in May at the Teatro Comunale. On 24 June there are fireworks on Piazzale Michelangelo after the parade in 16th-century costume and the *calcio* (football) match of the afternoon. On balmy summer nights groups of students and travellers congregate at the Duomo and Piazzale Michelangelo.

Siena

While Florence is Renaissance, Siena is medieval. It's 1½ hours from Florence, and there are trains daily passing through Empoli and Poggibonsi. (Trains from Rome go via Chiusi, and you have to change at these stops unless you're taking a direct train.) The heart of the city is the PIAZZA DEL CAMPO, where the Palio (an inter-district horse-race) is held as part of the 2 July and 16 Aug. celebrations, with costume parades and all-night dances following on.

The closest you'll get to the centre by bus from the station is Piazza Gramsci; walk the rest. The Gothic TOWN HALL (*Palazzo Comunale*) and the bell tower in the piazza are well worth a visit. Entrance is 6,000L.

In the PIAZZA DEL DUOMO (bus 1: tickets at station or a 45-minute walk) is ST CATHERINE'S CATHEDRAL. The CHIGI SARACINI PALACE is a music academy, but on request they'll show you round the Renaissance apartments and gallery of Tuscan paintings. Further along is PIAZZA SALIMBENI with its 4 palaces. The MUSEO CIVICO in the Palazzo Comunale houses an exhibition of Sienese art, including frescoes by Pietro and Ambrogio Lorenzetti: *Allegories of Good and Bad Government and their Effect on Town and Country*. Admission to the museum is 6,000L.

The busiest and most colourful time to visit the city is on 2 July or 16 August when *Il Palio* takes place, a night-long celebration and torchlit procession in medieval costume. The central event is a traditional horse-race around Piazza del Campo at 7 p.m. Standing room for the race is free, but arrive early, and remember to book accommodation in advance for this period.

Cheap rooms are a bit of a problem here, but try Locanda Garibaldi, Via G. Dupre 18 (Tel. 0577 284204). Tourist Information is at Piazza del Campo 56 (Tel. 0572 280551), open Mon.–Sat.: 8.50 a.m.–7 p.m.; reduced hours in winter.

There's no shortage of good *trattorie* and the Mensa Universitaria is on Via Sant'Agata.

There is a hostel at Via Fiorentina 89 (Tel. 0577 52212), a 20-minute bus ride on no. 15 from the station. Beds from about 25, 000L, including breakfast. Casa del Pellegrino (Tel. 44177) is at Via Camporegio, behind San Domenico.

The nearest camping ground is at Siena Colleverde, Strada di Scacciapensieri 47 (Tel. 280044). To get there take bus 8 or 10 from Piazza Gramsci. The site is well maintained and secure, and is open March–Nov. It costs 13,000L per person, including tent.

Pisa city phone code: 050

Head straight for the PIAZZA DEL DUOMO with its famous Leaning Tower (*Torre Pendente*) which Galileo used in his experiments (bus 1 from the station). There is a Tourist Office in this square, though you are better off using the one to the left of the station as you leave. Beside the tower is the CATHEDRAL (open Mon.–Sat.: 10 a.m.–7.45 p.m. Sun.: 1 p.m.–7.45 p.m.) and the BAPTISTRY. Nearby is CAMPO SANTO, a beautiful cemetery built by the Crusaders. The MUSEOD NAZIONALE DI SAN MATTEO, near Piazza Mazzini, houses important works by many 15th-century artists. Admission is 8,000L and it is open Tues.–Sat.: 9 a.m.–7 pm., Sun.: 9 a.m.–1 p.m. The city's big traditional event is the GIOTO DEL PONTE, held on 27 June, when there are festivities in medieval costumes. Other celebrations, regattas and art events occur during the summer.

Lodgings are difficult if you arrive late. Try Locanda Galileo, Via Santa Maria 12 (Tel. 050 40621), down Via San Lorenzo, or the women's hostel, Casa della Giovane, Via F. Corridoni (Tel. 43061). The latter is a 10-minute walk (turn right from the station) and offers women bed and breakfast for around 23, 000L.

The campsite Torre Pendente is at Viale delle Cascine 86 (Tel. 050 560665). Take the number 4 bus from Stazione Centrale or follow the signs from Pl. Manin – go past the cathedral and baptistry and out through the old walls. then turn right, then left. Prices are about 9,000L per person and 3,500L per tent. Next to the site is a super-market where you can stock up on food and drink at reasonable prices.

The Mensa Universitaria on Via Martiri offers good food at cheap prices and is open 12–2.30 p.m. daily, and on weekdays for evening meals 7–9 p.m.

Umbria

PERUGIA The capital of Umbria is a medieval hill town about 1½ hours from Florence. It's fairly industrialized nowadays and can feel claustrophobic, however there are some big attractions including the CATHEDRAL, NATIONAL GALLERY OF UMBRIA, NATIONAL ARCHAEOLOGICAL MUSEUM and the ARCH OF AUGUSTUS. The GALLERIA NATIONALE DELL'UMBRIA at the Palazzo dei Priori has a rich collection of paintings. It is open 9 a.m.–7 p.m., and entrance is 8,000L. Next door is the COLLEGIO DEL CAMBIO where there are frescoes painted by Raphael and his teacher, Perugino. The opening hours are Mon.–Sat.: 9 a.m.–12.30 p.m. and 2.30 p.m.–5.30 p.m. Sun: 9 a.m.–12.30 p.m. Entry is 5,000L. The annual jazz festival takes place from late June to early July. Contact the Tourist Office on 075 572 5341.

The youth hostel is 2 minutes from the CATHEDRAL on Via Bontempi 13 (Tel. 075 5722880) and the price per person is about 15,000L. There are many cheap pensions and guest houses in the city which charge between 30,000 and 45,000L for a single room and between 50,000 and 65,000L for a double. Try the Cassadel Sacro Cuore, Via del Brozzo 12 (Tel. 33141) which has a restaurant and bar. Tourist Offices can be found at Via Mazzini 21 (Tel. 5725341) or at Corso Vannucci 2 (Tel. 572 6061) or at Pl. IV Novembre.

The campsite at 11 Rocolo, Colle della Trinità, is open in the summer months only. Expect to pay about 6,000L per person, plus 5,000L per tent.

If it's sun and swimming that you're after, Perugia is well linked by rail and bus to LAKE TRASIMENO (where you will find superior campsites).

ASSISI Famed for its saint, is very near. The city and its environs are encrusted with history and monasteries. Despite the crowds and the commercialism, Assisi still manages to retain some medieval hill town charm – worth a day's excursion. Make sure you visit the fort/castle for superb views over to Perugia. At the basilica of ST FRANCIS AND SACRO CONVENTO 2 churches have been built 1 above the other, with a crypt that houses St Francis's tomb. The upper basilica is adorned by Giotto's frescoes illustrating the life of the saint (but they could be the work of an imitator). Open daily, except for Sun. mornings. Also worth a visit are the CATHEDRAL OF ST RUFINO and the BASILICA OF ST CHIARA, where the body of St Claire is preserved in the crypt. Outside the city walls is a Franciscan shrine in SAN DAMIANO, built on the spot where St Francis heard the voice of Christ and wrote his *Canticle of the Creatures*.

In the centre of the city is the 1,000-year-old TEMPLE OF MINERVA, behind which is the Roman Forum. The Tourist Office is opposite the temple on the Piazza del Comune (Tel. 075 812534) which is open 9 a.m.–1 p.m., 3.30 p.m.–6.30 p.m. Ask here for addresses of private homes and religious institutions that offer accommodation.

A hostel and campground is situated 1 km from Assisi at Fontemaggio (Tel. 075 813636). It charges 24,000L for a bed and is only a short bus journey from the station to Piazza Matteotti.

The IYHF Ostello della Pace in Via di Valecchi is 1.5 km away from the train station (a 10-minute walk from Piazza San Pietro). Open Mar.–Dec., it charges 21,000L for bed and breakfast (Tel. 075 816767).

On the northern outskirts is the cathedral ROCCA MAGGIORE where you can climb up for a superb view over the town and valley.

On the opposite side of the town is the basilica of SANTA MARIA DEGLI ANGELI , in a suburb 5 km away, which contains the Porziuncula: the nucleus of the first Franciscan monastery and the Cappella del Transito where St Francis died.

Rome (Roma) city phone code: 06

There are really 3 Romes: the world centre of the Catholic Church, the incredible ruins of the capital of the Roman Empire, and the modern, dirty, bustling metropolis. All seem incongruous, yet they live inside and beside each other with great ease. Everything is on a massive scale, solid and 'eternal'. You'll find the Romans proud, arrogant and conceited, but you'll look back with affection on the overwhelming beauty and dimensions of St Peter's, the atmosphere in the Colosseum, and the Trevi Fountain when it's floodlit and buzzing with people. Keep a close eye on purses and wallets, even if in handbags or waist pouches, as pickpockets are very good at their job.

The main station is Roma Termini, which has comprehensive facilities. There are daily trains within Italy to Pisa, Genoa, Milan, Venice, Florence, Bologna, Ancona, Naples, Brindisi and Sicily. Daily international trains to Nice, Innsbruck, Munich, Brussels, Vienna, Basle and Paris. Trains running from the north of Italy to the south and vice versa stop at Tributina station so you don't have to come into the centre.

TOURIST INFORMATION

Opening times telephone hotline: 23267695 (24 hours) run by Rome City Council Department of Social Relations. Also offers information for persons with disabilities. In Italian and English.

Before leaving the station, go to the Tourist Office at the end of platform 3 and pick up a map of the city. Apart from the office at the station (Tel. 4824070), there's one at Via Parigi 5 (Tel. 488 991), open Mon.–Sat.: 8.15 a.m.–7 p.m., which is very near the station, and queues are shorter. To get there leave the station by the main doors and head towards the large fountain in Piazza della Repubblica. Once past this, take the small road which is the first turning on the right.

There is another information centre called Enjoy Rome (Tel. 445 1843), which is on Via Varese 39 just past the junction with Via Milazzo. It is a great meeting point for backpackers, can give you all the information you may need about Rome, provides a free map and free luggage storage for customers. It has information about short-term apartments and other types of accommodation, walking and bus tours and emergency aid. Enjoy Rome information centre is open Mon.–Fri.: 8.30 a.m.–1 p.m., 3.30 p.m.–6 p.m., and Sat.: 8.30 a.m.–1 p.m.

Let's Go Italy 2000 is a new Tourist Information Service on Via Calatafimi 15 which is open everyday from 9.30 a.m. to 6 p.m. Come out the station and turn left along Via Marsala, Via Calatafimi is fourth right. The staff speak seven languages and they can provide you with free maps of Florence, Rome and Venice as well as information on night life, trains, accommodation, city tours, theatres, museums, restaurants and trips out of town. They can save you money and time; show this book to get a 10-20% discount on accommodation!

Generally, shops and churches are open 9 a.m.–1 p.m., 4 p.m.–8 p.m. Museums generally close about 1 p.m. or 2 p.m. and all day Mon. In August, Romans take their holidays and you'll find many restaurants shut.

ADDRESSES

POST OFFICE Piazza San Silvestro 19, open Mon.–Fri.: 9 a.m.–6 p.m. for *poste restante*, Sat.: 7 a.m.–2 p.m., telephones 8 a.m.–12 midnight

AMEX Piazza di Spagna 38; open Mon.–Fri.: 9 a.m.–5.30 p.m., Sat.: 9 a.m.–3 p.m. (Tel. 72282)

UK EMBASSY Via XX Settembre 80a (Tel. 482 5441)

US EMBASSY Via Vittorio Veneto 121 (Tel. 46741)

CANADIAN EMBASSY Via Zara 30 (Tel. 4459 8421)

YOUTH TRAVEL SERVICE CTS, Via Genova 16 (Tel. 46791). They help out on accommodation, issue ISICs, etc. Also a Eurotrain office.

LATE CHEMIST near station; Piazza della Repubblica (Tel. 488 04 70)

AMERICAN HOSPITAL (ENGLISH SPOKEN) (Tel. 225 3333)

CITY POLICE Tel. 46861

GETTING ABOUT

The buses are cheap and the underground continues to expand yearly. Bus tickets (1,500L) are valid for an hour and a quarter, and you may use the bus or tramway with the same ticket provided you do not exceed the time limit. On boarding the bus, you should cancel the ticket in the machine. Buy tickets from Tabac shops or the stations (look out for the ATAC sign). The machines sell 3 kinds of tickets: BIT – normal ticket; BIG – 1-day ticket (6,000L) and BIS – 1-week ticket (24,000L). Buses run 5.30 a.m.–12 midnight. You can buy a route map from the bus kiosk at the station (9,000L), which shows all major sites and streets. Avoid the taxis which are expensive. There are many stands throughout the city which rent out bicycles, especially along the Via del Corso. The rates are generally 15,000L a day. Drive in Rome at your own risk!

SEEING

Though the 3 sides of Rome are virtually inseparable, we've tried to separate the sights into the 3 categories. Ideally, you need 4–5 days here, but the prices and the pace of the city may put you off. Be on your guard constantly for pickpockets, including young children begging to distract your attention and particularly the motorized ones who cruise about on mopeds and whip handbags off shoulders and wallets from pockets. Avoid children or hustlers who approach holding cardboard: they will try to distract your attention by thrusting the cardboard in your face while an accomplice swiftly lifts your valuables.

ANCIENT ROME The sites of ancient Rome are clustered south of the Piazza Venezia, the modern city centre. THE COLOSSEUM is the biggest site of ancient Rome (free for lower levels, 8,000L for upper). Check the opening times when you arrive, as they can vary greatly from day to day. This huge arena sat 55,000 Romans who passed many an afternoon watching Christians being eaten by lions, or gladiators fighting it out to the bitter end. The PALATINE HILL (Monte Palatino) is where Nero, Mark Antony and other famous historical figures were based. The PALAZZO FARNESE incorporated many ancient structures into it when it was built in the 16th century. See the frescoes on the HOUSE OF AUGUSTUS and the remains of the PALACE OF THE FLAVIANS and the PALACE OF SEPTIMIUS SEVERUS.

The ROMAN FORUM was the commercial, religious and civic centre of ancient Rome. Look out for the 3 TRIUMPHAL ARCHES, HOUSE OF THE VESTAL VIRGINS and the 6 temples. Enter by Via dei Fori Imperiali (closed Sun. and afternoon, costs 12,000L). Opposite is the IMPERIAL FORUM, including TRAJAN'S FORUM with its famous column, and the BASILICA OF ST MAXENTIUS, the ancient law court and exchange. The MAMERTINE PRISON, just off Via dei Fori Imperiali, is where Nero kept St Peter.

THE PANTHEON is the best preserved of all the sites of ancient Rome. It was started in 27 BC and, having been a temple to the gods for over 600 years, became a Christian church in the 7th century. The kings of Italy and the artist Raphael are buried here. It's at Piazza della Rotonda. Entrance is free, and opening times are 9 a.m.–6.30 p.m. Mon.–Sat. and 9 a.m.–1 p.m. Sunday. Mass on Sunday is 9.45 a.m.–11.15 a.m.

On the APPIAN WAY, the ancient Roman road to Brindisi, you'll find the BATHS OF CARACALLA (near Piazzale Numa Pompilio), and the CATACOMBS OF ST SEBASTIAN. There are 5 tiers of burial chambers and many Christian saints and martyrs here, at 110 Via Appia Antica (admission 8,000L). Remember to buy 2 tickets, if travelling by bus, as there is nowhere to buy them at the catacombs. Bus 218 from Piazza San Giovanni.

The NATIONAL MUSEUM OF ROME has the best collection of artefacts from the Roman Empire. It's opposite Termini station, (open 9 a.m.–2 p.m., Sun. closes at 1 p.m. and closed Mon.). CASTEL SANT'ANGELO (Hadrian's Mausoleum) was the Pope's fortress to flee to in times of danger. Now it's a museum of weapons, art and relics (Lungotevere Castello), open 9 a.m.–7 p.m., closed Tue. (admission 8,000L). That leaves only the THEATRE OF MARCELLUS, the PYRAMID OF CAIUS CESTIUS on Piazza San Paolo and the remains of 4 ancient ROMAN TEMPLES in Largo Argentina. All the Roman remains that don't close on Monday tend to close on Tuesday.

PAPAL ROME The independent state of the VATICAN CITY is the spiritual centre for 630 million Roman Catholics. The Vatican has its own stamps, printing press, currency, radio station, newspaper and railway, all within 1 sq. mile. The Pope's in charge here and the Swiss Guards keep order.

ST PETER'S SQUARE is a 17th-century masterpiece which leads up to ST PETER'S BASILICA, the church whose incredible dome can be seen all over Rome. Inside are works by Raphael, Michelangelo, Bernini and Bramante. (Cover your legs and shoulders if you want to get in.) For the full emotion of this church to hit you come at 8 a.m. and climb the stairs to the top of the dome for a breathtaking view (5,000L on foot, 6,000L if you take the lift). The basilica itself is open 7 a.m.–7 p.m. in summer.

The VATICAN MUSEUMS, which include such treasures as Michelangelo's SISTINE CHAPEL, the RAPHAEL ROOMS, the GRAECO-ROMAN MUSEUMS and the VATICAN LIBRARY are located north of St Peter's on Viale Vaticano. It costs about 10,000L on ISIC, 16,000L without, but it's well worth it. They are open 8.45 a.m.–1 p.m. (last entry 45 minutes before closing) Mon.–Sat. and the last Sun. of every month, when admission is free for everyone. Note that only an ISIC card is accepted as proof of student status. Not even your passport will do!

Outside the Vatican, the most important churches are ST JOHN LATERAN, with the HOLY STAIRS and SANTA MARIA MAGGIORE. The former is the church of the popes; the stairs are believed to be those from the palace of Pontius Pilate which Christ ascended during his Passion. You can only climb them if you're officially worshipping, and then only on your knees. The church is south-east of the Colosseum at Piazza San Giovanni in Laterno. The latter has a 5th-century church, the *campanile* is the tallest in Rome and there are some interesting mosaics (Via Liberiana). It's four blocks to the left of Termini.

MODERN ROME The PIAZZA DEL CAMPIDOGLIO, designed by Michelangelo, is considered to be the political city centre. Of the 3 palaces around it, one is the Senatorial Office, one is the CAPITOLINE MUSEUM of antique sculptures, and the other is the CONSERVATORIO, which has large chunks of hands, toes and heads from Roman statues. The Capitoline Museum offers free access on the last Sun. of each month, otherwise it charges 10,000L or 5,000L with ISIC. It's open Tues.–Sat.: 9 a.m.–5 p.m., Sun.: 9 a.m.–1.30 p.m. The PIAZZA NAVONA is another Bernini work, as is PIAZZA BARBERINI.

The famous SPANISH STEPS (*Piazza di Spagna*) and the Barcaccia fountain at the bottom attracts a young crowd, but the fountain of Rome has got to be the TREVI, off Via del Corso. This baroque work was recently renovated and floodlit. Legend has it that if you toss a coin into the water you will return to Rome. Next to it is the BASILICA SANTA MARIA, which is as beautiful as the more renowned tourist attractions and far less crowded.

The MONUMENT TO VITTORIO EMANULÉ II, in the Piazza Venezia, is the huge white marble 'wedding cake' at the southern end of Via del Corso. It was built in 1911 to celebrate Italy's unification.

The VILLA BORGHESE, in the north, is the most splendid of Rome's parks. The zoo (open 8 a.m.–6 p.m., late night Thurs.–Sat. Admission 8,000L) and 3 art galleries are out here. The NATIONAL GALLERY OF MODERN ART on the Viale delle Belle Arti houses the biggest collection of Italian art from the 19th century to the present day. Entrance is around 8,000L and opening times are 9 a.m.–7 p.m. Tues.–Sat., 9 a.m.–1 p.m. Sunday.

There are many street markets for those who wish to browse for material items. Via Sannio plays host to a new and secondhand clothing market, whilst that of the Porta Portese is a curio heaven every Sunday morning. Arrive about 8.30 a.m. for the best viewing and remember to watch your wallet.

SLEEPING

Though Rome gets packed in July and August, beds are never really a problem as there are literally hundreds of pensions, *locande* and *alloggi*. There are plenty of cheap places beside the station and the prices are the cheapest in town. To help you find a place, use either CTS (see addresses), the student help office or the Tourist Offices.

HALLS OF RESIDENCE There are 3 university halls of residence, which are opened from the end of July to the end of September by the IYHF. They are at Via Cesare de Lollis 20 (take bus 492 from the Termini station); CIVIS, 7 km from the station at Viale del Ministero degli Affari Esteri 6 (take subway A to Ottaviano, then bus 32); and at Via D. De Dominicis 13 (subway A to Colli Albani, then bus 409). All charge around 25,000L for bed and breakfast. Bookings for these hostels are handled by a single office (Tel. 3242571 or 3242573).

STUDENT HOSTELS The IYHF youth hostel is at Viale delle Olimpiadi 61 (Tel. 3236267); it is 6 km out and reports on it are good (costs 20,000L per night). To get there take the subway to Ottaviano and then bus 32.

There's the Centro dei Giovane at Via degli Apuli 40 (Tel. 4953151); it's cheap and convenient but tends to fill up quickly. At 25,000L but far more crowded are the dorms at the Pensione Ottaviano 4 (Tel. 383956) near Piazza del Risorgimento. Another recommended place is Pensione Lachea, Via San Martino della Battaglia 11 (Tel. 4957256). Here singles cost 25,000L, doubles 45,000L and triples 60,000L a night. Advance reservations and deposits are necessary.

PENSIONS NEAR THE STATION The nearest is Soggiorno Simona run by 'Mr Carlo', Via Marsala 90 on the first floor (Tel. 494 1296). It has 1 double, 2 triples and 2 quadruples at 55,000L, 80,000L, L100, 000 per room respectively and 2 dormitories at 23,000L per bed. Aug.–March (10% discount if you show this book!) No curfew, 11 a.m. checkout. Very clean and friendly with a backpacker crowd. At 9 Via Palestro is Pensione Lella, which charges around 60,000L per double, and at no. 35 is Pensione Katty (Tel. 4441216), which has singles for 34,000L and Hotel Home Michele (Tel. 444 1204). At no. 15 is Hotel Bolognese, which has clean rooms and showers and costs about 50,000L for a double, 65,000L if you want a shower (Tel. 490045). Also try M&J Place at Via Solferino 9 (Tel. 44 62 802). It's on the the third floor, so take the lift. Television, radio, fridge and pub available!

To the left of the station is a very Roman working-class neighbourhood, full of colour and life. Via Principe Amedeo has a collection of good pensions; all ask about 36,000L a person. They include Cotorillo, Contilia, Govoni and di Rienzo (Tel. 446 7131), which are all very acceptable.

If things are desperate and you're sleeping out, avoid flaking out in the park outside the station or at Villa Borghese. Each summer the muggings get more numerous and the gypsies that hang out there should be watched like hawks. Don't do it, or be prepared for the consequences.

CAMPSITES There are several sites around Rome, but none are near the centre. One of the nearest is Flaminio, at Via Flaminia (Tel. 333 1431 or 3332604), open Mar.–Oct. To get there take the underground from Piazza Flaminio and request the stop for the camping site called Due Ponti, or take the 225 tram (from Station Termini take bus 910) to the endstation Piazza Mancini, followed by bus 200 to the site. Or Metro A to Flaminio then bus 202/3/45. The cost is 11, 000L per person, 8,000L per tent and the campsite has free pool and shower facilities. Single and double tents are available for hire the campsite, and there is a bar, shop and restaurant on site.

Try also Camping Roma on Via Aurelia 8B1 (Tel. 662 3018). Take bus 38 from the train station to Piazza Fiume, then bus 490 to Piazza Irnerio, where you change to bus 246.

For Camping Nomentano, Via della Cesarina, take bus 36 from outside Termini station to Piazza Sempione, then bus 330 to Via Nomentana.

Salaria Camping, Via Salaria 2141, is a new campsite 16 km north of the city centre (Tel. 888 7642).

EATING AND NIGHTLIFE

For about 18,000L you can eat a good, filling meal in Rome. Go for the *menu turistico* and spoil yourself on the delicious pasta and pizza dishes, which are good value. If you are buying food for picnics, head for the main market in Piazza Vittorio Emanuele, about 5 minutes east of Termini. In Piazzale Flaminio, near the campsite of the same name, is a *rosticcerie* which sells cheap chicken and pizza. Palmerie, Via Cimarra 41 5, is where the trendy Roman crowd hang out. The fixed-price menus are reasonable. La 'Reatina' trattoria and pizzeria offers good value traditional Italian food at Via San Martino della Battaglia 17 (Tel. 490314). Try the house red!

The area on the right-hand side of the station as you leave is good for tourist menus. The Osteria da Salvatore at Via Castelfidardo 39c is good value at 16, 000L for an all-in meal. Trattoria da Bruno e Romana offers good, traditional, wholesome food at Via Varese 29 (Tel. 490403). For a self-service restaurant, try the one at Piazza Cinquecento 47 near the station and others in this area. For vegetarian dishes, try L'Albero del Pane, Dei Bianchi Vecchi 39, a health food store selling organic foods. Open 9 a.m.–1.30 p.m., 5 p.m.–8 p.m.

Giolitti's are reputed to have the best ice-cream in Rome. They're near the Pantheon at Via Ufficio del Vicario 40. If opera is your cup of tea, try and make it along to the outdoor performances in the Roman Baths of Caracalla. Buy tickets from the Teatro dell'Opera.

Avoid the discos – they are extravagantly expensive – but Piper is reputed to be the biggest and best in Rome. Saint Louis, Via del Cardello 13a (Tel. 474 5076) is a modern club, known for its serious quality jazz. Try the Julius Caesar Pub at Via Castelfidardo 49 (Tel. 446 5845) which has a good mix of locals and US/British.

EXCURSIONS East of Rome is the Renaissance cardinals' palace, VILLA D'ESTE at Tivoli. The gardens are the main attraction here. Take Metro line B to Rebbiba and then the blue Cotral bus (6,000L return). If you bus it, you could also take in the sumptuous VILLA ADRIAN (admission 8,000L; closed Mon.).

Mussolini's 1940s quarter of Rome – the EUR – has an amusement park (LUNA PARK) and the MUSEUM OF ROMAN CIVILIZATION, which reconstructs ancient Rome as it was under Constantine. The nearest beach is OSTIA LIDO. It's not one of Italy's best (the sea is very dirty) but it's only 29 km away (metro Line B to Magliana then train to Ostia).

The ancient ruined city of OSTIA ANTICA is only a further 5 km away and can be reached by the same train or by bus no. 4, which leaves Ostia-Lido every 15 minutes. The excavated ruins are accessible 9 a.m.–7 p.m., admission 8,000L. During the summer classic plays are staged in the Roman theatre.

A good campsite is situated 3 km from the ruins at Capitol Campground, Via dei Castelfusono (Tel. 565 7344). It costs 13,000L per person with an extra 10,000L per tent, but there is a free swimming pool and tennis court facilities. To get there take bus 5 from Ostia-Lido central.

Southern Italy

Using the old geographical 'boot' analogy of Italy, CAMPANIA is the ankle, BASILICATA the arch, PUGLIA the heel (the departure point for the Brindisi ferry to Greece) and CALABRIA the toe.

There's a lot to see in CAMPANIA. Apart from the colourful chaos of Naples, there's the smouldering volcano of Vesuvius, the archaeological remains of Pompeii, Herculaneum and Paestum, the romantic towns of Sorrento, Amalfi and Positano and the islands off the coast of Naples: Capri, Ischia and Procida. The Italians head for Agropoli, Catellabate and San Marco, all south of Naples, for their holidays, so these are places to avoid in August.

Naples (Napoli) city phone code: 081

Naples is a crazy city: overcrowded, dirty, smelly and alive. It has the worst traffic you can imagine, with pollution to match, but no tour of Italy is complete without a stop here. If you've come down from the north, you'll feel you're in a different country. The main streets are bustling with car horns and lunatic Vespa riders, while the back-streets are right out of the Middle Ages – tiny, cobbled alleys where children kick footballs. Watch your belongings in this city; it has more crime than any other city in Italy. Naples has its own way of getting things done (much of it involving corruption, for the power of the local mafia – the Camorra – is legendary), which the visitor will find unfathomable. You may also find that many of the sights are wholly or partly under restoration or have strange opening times. Change your money prior to arrival in Naples because banks here have a very high commission. Do not expect northern standards of hygiene; until 1973 Naples had no sewers. Despite all this it is a vibrant and exciting city. There is more than one face to Naples. Once away from the choking medieval centre you have a chance to explore both the countryside and seaside delights of the area.

Napoli Centrale is the main station. It has full facilities (including digiplan machines), but the mass of concrete is hard on the eyes if you have just arrived on an overnight service! Beware of pickpockets!

There are daily trains to Rome, Florence, Bologna, Genoa, Milan, Sicily, Venice and Brindisi.

Trains from Rome, and those going on to Sicily, invariably use the central station. The Rome–Bari trains stop at both stations, Piazza Garibaldi and Centrale. There's a connecting elevator between them. Trains to Sorrento on the privately run Circumvesuviana railway leave from Napoli Piazza Garibaldi. Napoli Centrale is the station most used by Eurorailers.

TOURIST INFORMATION AND ADDRESSES

Apart from the one at the station (Tel. 268779), there's an office of Ente Turismo at Piazza del Gesfi (Tel. 552 3328) and the main office at Via Partenope 10a (Tel. 418988).

POST OFFICE Piazza Matteotti, open Mon.–Fri.: 8.15 a.m.–7.30 p.m, Sat: 8.35 a.m.–12 noon (Tel. 5511456)

AMEX Tel. Sorrento 081 807 30 80

UK CONSULATE Via Francesco Crispi 122 (Tel. 663511), open Mon.–Fri.: 8.30 a.m.–1 p.m.

US CONSULATE Piazza della Repubblica (Tel. 793284, 24-hour phone line)
24-HOUR CHEMIST At the Station Centrale (Tel. 268881)

SEEING

Naples has none of the famous sights of Rome, Florence or Venice, but still has much to offer. If you visited Pompeii or Herculaneum and are disappointed to find none of the artefacts – or bodies – there, visit the NATIONAL ARCHAEOLOGICAL MUSEUM on Piazza del Museo (close to the Piazza Cavour metro station). Here you'll find one of the best Graeco–Roman collections in the world, as well as the frescoes and jewellery from Herculaneum and the Borgia collection of Etruscan art. It is open Wed.–Sat.: 9 a.m.–2 p.m., Sun.: 9 a.m.–1 p.m., 12,000L admission.

In nearby Via Duomo, tucked away from the main street, is the SAN GENNARO CATHEDRAL, where every year St Gennaro's blood apparently turns to liquid. You can tour the crypt every day 9 a.m.–12 p.m. and 4.30 p.m.–7 p.m.

The church of GESÙ NUOVO in Piazza Gesù Nuovo (opposite the Tourist Office) may look like a prison on the outside, but inside is a feast of the baroque. Not far away is the medieval church of SANTA CHIARA and SAN DOMENICO MAGGIORE. The latter contains a painting that spoke to St Thomas Aquinas. Off a small side street to the east is the chapel of SAN SEVERO, which charges a small admission fee (6000L or L2,000 students). It's open Mon. and Wed.–Sat.: 10 a.m.–5 p.m.; Tues. and Sun.: 10 a.m.–1.30 p.m.) Inside are some brilliant sculptures, including a veiled Christ hewn out of a single block of marble, so realistic you feel you are looking at the body through a veil.

The museums are no less breathtaking. The CAPODIMONTE MUSEUM which overlooks the city from its highest hill at VOLMERO is unfortunately closed at time of writing. Check if it's open now by telephoning 744 1307. It was the view from here that inspired the saying 'See Naples and die'. The opera house, TEATRO SAN CARLO (a source of much Neapolitan pride), and the GALLERIA UMBERTO I, a 19th-century shopping arcade, are near the CASTEL NUOVO on Piazza Municipio. The castle was built in the late 13th century for Charles I of Anjou; it is open daily.

The city's transport system has some useful offers for the tourist. You can buy 1½ hour passes for 1,200L and they are valid on all buses, trams and funiculars, but not on the subway. A whole day pass costs 4,000L. The flat fare is 1,200L for each single journey and all tickets are available from convenience stores.

SLEEPING

Hotels have a reputation for unreliability as regards changing their rates once you are in. Get a clear agreement before you move into your room, but if there are still problems, phone EPT (Tel. 405311). One suggestion is Hotel Eden, Corso Novara 9, near the station (Tel. 285344). Hotel Imperia (Tel. 459347) is a friendly hotel located in the heart of old Naples at Piazza Luigi Maraglia 386; it's inexpensive, too. Or try the Albergo Ginevra at Via Genova 116, near the station (Tel. 283 210) which gives 10% off to holders of this guide!

The Mergellina youth hostel is excellent and is at Salita della Grotta a Piedigrotta 23 (Tel. 761 2346); it imposes a 3-day maximum stay policy during July and August. Go to the Mergellina stop on the underground.

You can camp on the edge of the volcano crater at Camping Solfatara (Tel. 526 7413), open Apr.–Oct. Take bus 152 directly there or a local train from Piazza Garibaldi station to Pozzuoli and then walk 850m, mostly uphill. The municipal Città di Napoli campsite is within the Mostra d'Oltremare complex. Take the train to Campi Flegrei and walk. Fees are 8,000L each but you are better off going to the nearby small coastal towns.

EATING AND NIGHTLIFE

Pizza was born in Naples, so this is the place to find out just how far from the original the fast food variety really is. There are hundreds of cheap pizza places, but the best is Trianon, Via Pietro Colletta 46 (off Via Tribunali). If you're flush, try one of the seafood restaurants down by the port in the Santa Lucia district. Renzo e Lucia on Via Tito Angelini 31133 do good baked fish and Caffè Osteria at Via Miroballo 14 gives good value for money. The university Mensa is on Via Mezzocanone. Try the vegetarian-Indian Restaurant Campania, Gapala-Corso Vittorio Emanuele, open 8 p.m.–12 midnight daily except Monday. Trattoria Avellinese, Via Silvio Spaventa 31–35 (off Piazza Garibaldi), does great seafood at reasonable prices. Wherever you go, try the Neapolitan coffee (caffè lungo) with plenty of sugar and a cake. Sfogliatelle is the speciality cake of the region. Try Pintauro at 275 Via Ranoy Toledo. The more familiar chips and sandwiches are readily available around the Piazza Garibaldi.

There are plenty of shady bars and rip-off joints down by the port. You'll find your evening strolls being interrupted by people trying to sell you anything from cabbage-leaf Marlboros to watches made from bottle lids. Nightlife doesn't take off until around midnight, after the public transport systems shut, although taxis are affordable. The popular area is around Piazza Amedeo, where there are plenty of bars and restaurants. Nightclubs are expensive and cost around 20,000L with a free drink thrown in.

EXCURSIONS The PHLEGRIAN FIELDS (*campi flegri*), on the peninsula west of Naples, have some active volcanoes you can visit.

Further east, MOUNT VESUVIUS hasn't erupted since 1944, but it could go at any time so take the chair lift to the crater at your peril! If you do, make sure it's a clear day, and go early. The private Circumvesuviana Line, from Stazione Vesuviana – it is 1 floor underground at Central station – serves this area, including Herculaneum and Pompeii, and runs on to Sorrento, but it does not take the Inter-Rail ticket as payment. It takes approximately 15 minutes from Naples to Herculaneum (descend at the Ercolano stop) and 45 minutes to Pompeii (make sure you get off the train at the Pompeii Scavi stop). You can also get to Pompeii on the main Naples–Salerno line from Napoli Piazza Garibaldi (free with Inter-Rail ticket).

Both HERCULANEUM and POMPEII have entrance charges of around 16,000L from 9 a.m. until an hour before sunset. These 2 towns fell foul of a Vesuvian eruption in ad 79. Pompeii was covered with ashes, Herculaneum with mud. Both offer a unique insight into Roman Imperial life since you can see houses and baths preserved from that age.

If you wish to stay in Pompeii, there is a good campsite by the Villa dei Misteri station. Camping Zeus (Tel. 861 5320 or 863 5320) is convenient, cheap, friendly and open all year round, and no tent is necessary (7,000L per person).

It is also possible to take a ferry over to the islands in the Gulf. Take the ferry from the port, or the hydrofoil from Mergellina.

CAPRI, home to the mythical Sirens, is the most touristy of the islands and very expensive, but the beach at Marina Piccola is the best in the area and the Blue Grotto is unmissable.

The Italians favour ISCHIA, a volcanic island famed for its thermal springs and mud baths.

The town of CASERTA, 45 minutes by train from Naples, has a superb Bourbon palace, PALAZZO REALE, known as *petit Versailles*.

South of Naples lies the beautiful AMALFI COAST. It is an area of mountains, limestone rock and beaches. There are many small towns dotted along the coast, so the best way to take it all in is by hiring a scooter. AMALFI is a pleasant seaside town with a magnificent Moorish-style cathedral. The Tourist Office is at Corso delle Repubbliche Marinare 27 (Tel. 87 11 07). Since Amalfi can become quite crowded, it's better to stay at other small towns, like ATRANI, about a 10-minute walk away. Here you can stay by the beach at A

Scalinetta, Piazza Umberto 12 (Tel. 089 871930) for 30,000L per night including a course at a local restaurant.

Make sure you visit the spectacular cliffside town of RAVELLO and the EMERALD GROTTO, about 4 km from Amalfi, in the bay of Corica dei Marini. If you're heading for Sicily, you can stop off at Salerno and catch a bus (it takes about an hour) to PAESTUM, where you'll find ancient Greek temples better than many in Greece, and some impressive tomb paintings. There are a number of campsites and hotels strewn along the sandy shoreline.

Puglia

BARI and BRINDISI are stopping-off places for those on their way to Greece. Neither offers much in the way of culture but you may need to use their facilities before you depart to nicer scenery. Both have received immigrants due to the recent troubles across the Adriatic Sea in Albania.

BARI In an attempt to attract the young tourist, Bari has introduced a 'Stopover in Bari' scheme whereby people under the age of 30 can enjoy free camping, buses throughout the town, free information centres, free museums, cheap meals, free luggage storage and free bikes. To get to the campsite take bus 5 to Pineta San Francesco park. The offer lasts from the end of June until September. Staff at the campsite are friendly and helpful, and if you get there early you can borrow a tent. All the information you'll need about the stopover is available from the booth near the station. Another part of the scheme they can help you with is the package that puts you up in a private home for 2 nights for 35,000L. For more information, contact the main office at Via Dante Alighieri 111 (Tel. 5214538, open 8.30 a.m.–8.30 p.m. daily). There is also a 24-hour telephone hotline (Tel. 577 2349 or 441186).

If you're staying in town out of season, then try the International Youth Hostel, Ostello del Levante at Via Nicola Massaro 33, 8 km from the rail station (Tel. 080 5300282). Take no. 1 bus from Piazza Aldo Moro.

From Bari ferries depart for Corfu and Patras, but it's best to book your voyage in advance and to get to the station at least 2 hours early so that you can pay your tax.

BRINDISI This is worse than Bari, so arrive in the afternoon in time for the regular evening ferry service to Corfu and Patras. Make sure you have both currencies before boarding, but avoid changing money here. Most of the ferry lines offer discounts to the under-27s and ISIC card holders. Eurail and Inter-Rail pass holders are given free passage on deck on Adriatica Lines (preferable option) and Hellenic Mediterranean Lines, but in the summer months you must pay a tax of around 29,000L.

Check the schedules carefully if travelling in winter, as not all the boats operate. The boat offices are as follows: Adriatica Lines, Via Marlines le Regina Margherita 13 (Tel. 590 471); Hellenic Mediterranean Lines, Corso Garibaldi 8 (Tel. 528 531).

The Tourist Office is EPT, Lungomare Regina Margherita 5, at the dock to the left of the station Marittima (Tel. 521944). Opening hours are Mon.–Fri.: 9 a.m.–1.30 p.m. and Tues.: 3 p.m.–6.30 p.m.

Pizzeria L'Angoletto, Via Pergola 3, near the fishing port, does great traditional pizzas and pasta.

Sicily

The journey from Naples to Sicily takes about 8 hours. Sicily is an interesting place to visit despite, or perhaps because of, its reputation as the home of the Cosa Nostra. Because of its strategic position it has been in the hands of just about every empire there ever was.

GETTING THERE
The standard crossing is from VILLA SAN GIOVANNI to MESSINA on the train-ferry. In summer the Rome–Sicily run gets crowded, so reserve a seat if you can. Once you're there you'll have to use the railway as your main sightseeing medium. The buses are reasonably punctual and usually air-conditioned. Ignore the ferries from Naples to Catania, Siracusa and Palermo. If you're on Inter-Rail you have to pay to get over.

THE EAST COAST The port of MESSINA, founded by the Greeks, has been rebuilt twice this century, once after the 1908 earthquake and again after the bombing of the Second World War, consequently there's not much to see, but if you've time to kill waiting for a ferry, take in the following sights: the largest ASTRONOMICAL MECHANICAL CLOCK in the world in the Norman cathedral and the church of the ANNUNCIATION OF THE CATALANS. The Tourist Office is on Via Calabria Isolato 301 (Tel. 64022).

Half an hour from Messina is TAORMINA, a resort popular with middle-aged Italians and famous for the outstanding remains of its classical theatre. The GREEK THEATRE looks out over the live volcano Mount Etna, which makes this setting for Greek drama suitably dramatic. The PALAZZO CORVAJA, the Sicilian parliament house, is in Piazza Vittorio Emanuele and the beach of MAZZARO can be reached by funicular. CATANIA hasn't been swamped by Mount Etna since 1693, but in 1992 the mountain engulfed nearby villages and the countryside with lava.

SIRACUSA was once as important as Rome or Athens and there are plenty of archaeological sites to back this up. The ARCHAEOLOGICAL MUSEUM is at Piazza del Duomo and the remains are on Ortigia Island. The GREEK THEATRE is considered the best of its kind in the world. Opposite is an altar that was used for public sacrifices; a short walk takes you to the ROMAN AMPHITHEATRE built into the rock.

The cuisine in Catania is highly praised and fresh fish is a particular speciality. The youth hostel is at 45 Via Epipoli (Tel. 0931 711118). For pensions, try Gran Bretagna, Via Savoia 21 (Tel. 0931 68765). There is a campsite, Agriturist, at Loc Rinaura 115 (Tel. 721224).

AGRIGENTO has frequent train services to other parts of Sicily. The main town is 8 km from the sea, where there is a beach resort called San Leone. This hillside town is the site of the VALLEY OF TEMPLES, a collection of captivating ancient columns and temples. The Tourist Office is at Viale della Vittoria 255 (Tel. 401352) and at Via Atenea 123 (Tel. 20454).

PALERMO The capital of Sicily is notable for the mixture of Arabic and Western influences, as can be seen in THE PALACE OF THE NORMANS (especially the PALATINE CHAPEL MOSAICS). Admission is free; open Mon.–Fri.: 9 a.m.–12 noon and 3 p.m.–5 p.m. Sat.: 9 a.m.–12 noon and Sun.: 9 a.m.–10 a.m. and 12 noon–1 p.m., unless the Sicilian Parliament is in session.

Tourist Information is available at Piazza Castelnuova 34 (Tel. 605 8351) open Mon.–Fri.: 8 a.m.–8 p.m., Sat. 8 a.m.–2 p.m. For a guide to what's on, pick up a copy of *Un Mese a Palermo*, the arts and entertainment guide. A late-night pharmacy, Lo Casio, can be found in Via Roma 1 near the train station (Tel. 616 2117). Try round the harbour for cheap rooms, or near the station. Pensione Sud, Via Maqueda 8 (Tel. 6175700) single, for 21,000L, doubles for 30,000L, or Albergo Rosalia Conca d'Oro, Via Santa Rosalia 7 (Tel. 6164543), singles for 22,000L, doubles for 35,000L. Or if you prefer to camp, take bus 628 from the Politeama Theatre to Sferracavallo, 13 km north-west of town, where there are 2 campsites: Trinacria on Via Barcarello (Tel. 530590) and the cheaper Ulivo, Via Pegaso (Tel. 533021).

Palermo's nightlife is at Mondello (which also has a fine beach), but for good eating the Da Pino, Via dello Spezio 6, on Piazza Sturzo, open Mon.–Sat.: 12 noon–3.30 p.m. and 8 p.m.–11 p.m., is highly recommended.

Eight kilometres away in Monreale is the NORMAN CATHEDRAL with its extraordinary medieval mosaics (admission free; open 8 a.m.–12 p.m. and 3.30 p.m.–6 p.m.) and next door the BENEDICTINE CLOISTER.

Sardinia (Sardegna)

The mountainous, untamed island of Sardinia is halfway between Italy and North Africa. The Sardinians have a strong independent streak; the region has been granted autonomous status. The west is mainly cultivated; the east is wild and almost completely untouched. There are few large towns and only a few real roads, so be prepared to rough it a bit if you're camping, though camping is still by far the best form of accommodation on the island and the scenery is beautiful.

GETTING THERE
From Italy there are ferries to Cagliari (the capital), Arbatax and Olbia (on the east coast), and Porto Torres (the northern tip). The best overnight crossing is with the Tirrenia Line from Civitavecchia (an hour north of Rome) to Olbia. It costs about 40,000L for deck class and reservations are advisable. The Tirrenia office in Rome is at Via Bissolati 41. Genoa to Olbia and Porto Torres is also a good choice.

For a daytime crossing, the state railways one from Civitavecchia to Golfo Aranci is the cheapest. A second-class reclining seat costs 20,000L plus. The crossing takes about 9 hours and there are 4 crossings a day. Golfo Aranci is a short train ride from Olbia.

GENERAL INFORMATION
The rail network connects up the northern and western coasts, but is limited elsewhere. Services are slow and a bit unpredictable, but it's better than hitching. Good cheap pensions are thin on the ground and hotels are expensive. In the north, youth hostels are your best bet. They're cheap and usually on the beach. But you can't beat camping. There are several official sites, but the true joy comes with setting up on your own.

Avoid the restaurants and go for *pizzerie*, *tavole calde* or *rosticcerie*. Fish and seafood are cheap on the coast (cook them yourself), and the markets provide ample picnic food. The local wine is Vernaccia.

THE EAST COAST South from Olbia is the most unspoilt region of Sardinia. There are miles of beautiful quiet beaches. NUORO and ARBATAX are the sites of archaeological remains. To get to this area, you'll need to take the train from Macomer or Cagliari. The coast around SANTA MARIA NAVARRESE is good for beaches.

North of Olbia is COSTA SMERALDA, the 'millionaires' playground'. This is the most commercialized part of the island. PORTO CERVO has some of the most expensive land in Italy. The Golfo di Orosei is one hour away from Olbia and there is a campsite Cala Ginepro with the best beach in Sardinia!

ARAZACHENA has some very good beaches. The Tourist Office is at Via Risorgimento (Tel. 82624).

It's also worth taking a scenic bus ride from Olbia along the dramatic rocky coastline with its many picturesque bays to SANTA TERESA DI GALLURA on the northernmost tip of Sardinia. This little fishing village has a ferry link to Bonifacio in southern Corsica. The Tourist Office can be found at Piazza Vittorio Emanuele 24 (Tel. 754127).

THE WEST COAST SASSARI, Sardinia's second city, has an interesting old town which centres on the CATHEDRAL. The SARDINIAN NATIONAL MUSEUM is here and Tourist Information is at Viale Caprera 36 (Tel. 079 299544). This is your best base for exploring north-west Sardinia, and you'll find cheap rooms and meals along Corso Vittorio Emanuele.

An hour from here is one of the prettiest towns on the island, ALGHERO. It's more Spanish than Italian, as for many years it was a Catalan colony. There is an IYHF Hostel at Via Zara 1, open all year round (Tel. 079 930 353 or 93 00 15 From here take a boat out to CAPO CACCIA and the Neptune Grotto, a series of underground caves. The Tourist Office can be found at Piazza Portaterra 9 (Tel. 979054).

CAGLIARI is the capital of Sardinia. Concentrate on the medieval centre, the CASTELLO, near the harbour. The cathedral is here and not far away is the ROMAN AMPHITHEATRE. The NATIONAL ARCHAEOLOGICAL MUSEUM is famous for its collection of bronzes from the prehistoric Nuraghe civilization. Tourist Information is at Piazza Deffenu 9 (Tel. 070 651698). Open Mon.–Sat.: 9 a.m.–2 p.m. and 4 p.m.–7 p.m. For cheap beds and meals try the streets between Corso Vittorio Emanuele and Via Roma. The nearest campsite is at Quartu Sant' Elena (Tel. 070 803107), a 45-minute bus journey east along the coast; bungalows are also available.

Don't miss the flea market at Bastione di San Remy on Sun. mornings and try to coincide your visit with the July–Sept. arts festival when plays are put on in the amphitheatre.

NOTES

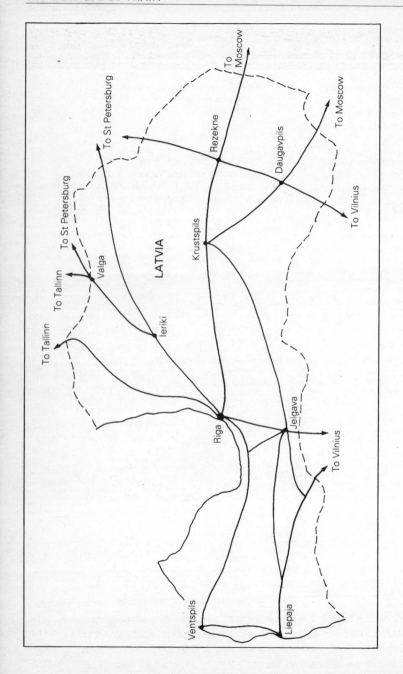

LATVIA (Latvija)

Entry requirements	Passport. Canadians, Australians and New Zealanders require visas.
Population	2,700,000
Capital	Riga
Currency	Lats, santims
	£1 = approx. 0.95Ls
Political system	Parliamentary democracy
Religion	Lutheran, Russian Orthodox and Catholic
Language	Latvian, Russian widely spoken (see note on languages), some English and German
Public holidays	1 Jan., Good Friday, 1 May, 23, 24 June, 18 Nov., 25, 26 Dec.
International dialling codes	To Latvia: 00 (international access code) + 371 (country code)
	From Latvia: 007 to book an int'l call
Time	GMT +3 (+4 in summer)

The idea of an independent Latvia didn't really come about until the start of the 20th century. It is believed that the region was settled by various tribes as early as 2000 BC, though the only existing historical records commence with German conquest of the region in the 12th century. Unlike its northern neighbour Estonia, Latvia was often a battlefield and the country was regularly divided between warring parties. Latvian nationalism did not begin to surface until the dawn of this century, but the First World War turned the country into a combat arena once more. Although Latvian nationalists declared independence in 1918, the Germans and Russians continued to do battle in Latvia until 1920, when the Latvian parliament signed a treaty with the Soviets which led to the country becoming independent. The war, coupled with emigration (or, rather, forced relocation by the Soviets), meant that the population was virtually halved. The Second World War saw the Russians reoccupy Latvia under the Nazi–Soviet Pact. Then the Germans occupied Latvia from 1941 to 1944 and many thousands of Jews died in the Latvian death camp of Salaspils near Riga. After Germany's surrender, the USSR moved in to retake Latvia and continued the policy of forcefully relocating Latvians elsewhere.

A variety of protests sprang up during 1987–88 on everything from politics to the environment and an independence movement started to take shape. The reformists won a majority of seats in the Supreme Soviet and immediately repealed the communist constitution. In an attempt to stem the drive for independence, the central government in Moscow sent in Soviet commandos to wreak havoc in the Latvian parliament. However, the attempted coup in August 1991 indirectly helped the Latvians, who used the confusion to declare independence on 21 August. Recognition from the West was swift and on 6 September even the Soviets granted their 'approval'.

TRAIN INFORMATION

Information on train schedules Tel. 075 or 232 134.

There should be someone at the Riga station who speaks English, though outside the capital you will probably have to depend on your ingenuity. As with the other Baltics, decades of Russian occupation means most people speak Russian, but you should ask first to avoid offending anyone. Information signs are rapidly being changed from Russian to Latvian, though you will probably see both.

PASSES AVAILABLE Inter-Rail and Eurail passes are not valid in Latvia. The 'Baltic Rail Explorer Pass' is available to anyone under 26, ISIC-holders and to academic staff. For a period of 7, 14, or 21 days the prices are £15, £19 and £27 respectively. However, as trains are so cheap, you would really have to do a lot of travel to make one of these passes cost-effective.

RESERVATIONS Mandatory on international trains and highly advisable on all other routes, as most trains are packed. The price difference between first and second class is not too great and it's worth the extra money.

NIGHT TRAVEL The country is too small to have any internal overnight services and the facilities offered on international trains are not conducive to getting a good night's sleep.

INTERNAL TRAVEL Buses are the best way to explore the country, being more reliable and faster than trains.

TOURIST INFORMATION

Information offices are not numerous. However, there is one at Riga airport and also an office in the city at 4 Pils Laukums (Tel. 232 75 48). There is also one in the city of Valmiera.

ISIC BONUSES As with most Eastern European countries, your ISIC card will usually get you discounts, but it's hard to say where. Always show your card whenever you buy a ticket for *anything*.

TELEPHONING Old telephones still require tokens. The new telephones take cards which can be bought from kiosks.

MONEY MATTERS Banking hours are generally 10 a.m.–4 p.m. Mon.–Fri. At present, traveller's cheques and credit cards are limited in use, so bring cash – ideally US dollars and Deutschmarks in low-denomination notes. Try to change money in Riga; the Bank of the Republic of Latvia tends to offer the best rates. It is at 2 a.k. Valdemara iela. There is also a 24-hour exchange facility at the Central Station.

SHOPS Generally open 10 a.m.–6 p.m. (often shut for lunch 2 p.m.-3 p.m.). Prices for tourists remain fairly cheap, despite recent increases. Establishments within the service industry are still known to charge foreigners 2 or 3 times the local price.

MUSEUMS Generally open 10 a.m.–6 p.m., though there's a great deal of variation.

WEATHER Best time to visit is in June or July, when the wind drops and the sea is warm.

LANGUAGE Latvian is the national language, but only half the population are native Latvians who regard it as their mother tongue. This has sparked fierce nationalist sentiments and your efforts to master a few phrases will endear you to the locals. Here are some useful ones to help out a little:

Hello	*Sveiki*	Thank you	*Paldies*
Goodbye	*Ata*	Excuse me	*Atvainojiet*
Yes	*Ja*	Do you speak	*Vas jus runajet*
No	*Ne*	English?	*anliski?*
Please	*Ludzu*	Russian?	*krievski?*

TIPPING Leave up to 10% if you think you have had good service.

SLEEPING AND EATING

The universities open their dormitories for travellers in the summer, with prices ranging from £4 per person. For the Riga Technical University Hostel ring 201 491 and for information on Youth Hostels ring 225 307. Fish and dairy products are the staples here and there are some cheap cafés and restaurants around if you look for them. One of the best local fish dishes is *Riga Tel'noe*, deep-fried fish fillets stuffed with a mushroom and anchovy filling. The soups (*zupa*) tend to be a meal in themselves. Bakeries are usually fairly well stocked and there are decent vegetable markets, so you should be able to put together good picnics.

Riga phone code: 2 (except tel. nos with 7 digits)

The city was damaged badly in both World Wars and most of what you see today is an industrial and technological showpiece of the ex-Soviet empire. Some of the old remains, however, are notable reminders of the pre-war days when Riga was known as the 'Paris of the Baltic'. The main train station lies at the southern end of Raina bulvaris. Information is available from the travel desk in the Latvija Hotel.

TOURIST INFORMATION AND ADDRESSES
The Tourist Office is at 4 Pils Laukums (Tel. (371) 232 7548); for further assistance, try your own embassy:
UK EMBASSY 5 Alunana iela (Tel. 7338126-31)
US EMBASSY Raina bulvaris 7 (Tel. 721 0005 or 722 0367)
CANADIAN EMBASSY Doma Laukums 4 (Tel. 783 0141 or 782 1161)
POST OFFICE Central PO, 21 Brivibas bulvaris. Open 24 hours.
CITY CLINICAL HOSPITAL Bruninieku iela 8.
PHARMACY 21a Elisabetes iela

SEEING
The old town stretches along the Daugava river and the east side is full of well-preserved 17th-century German houses. Much of this area is pedestrianized and the streets twist and turn. Keep a look out for the 2 big cathedrals that dominate the skyline: the DOME and ST PETER'S. The Dome cathedral is a magnificent building which took over 500 years to complete; the result is a mixture of styles which remain pleasingly simple. It contains beautiful wood-carvings and the world's fourth largest organ. The large Gothic church of St Peter offers a breathtaking panorama over the rooftops of Vecriga.

Other notable sights include the POWDER TOWER, the SWEDISH GATE and the churches of ST JEKAB'S and ST JOHN'S. Look out too for RIGA CASTLE, which contains the museums of literature, history and art. The MUSEUM OF APPLIED ART lies across from St Peter's at Skarnu iela 10/20 in a 13th-century church; it contains an excellent collection of Latvian arts and crafts. Open Tue.–Sun.: 10 a.m.–6 p.m.

The new town doesn't have much to recommend it other than the large parks, with the old town moat winding through them, which are excellent for picnics.

See also the contemporary FREEDOM MONUMENT, a focus for political activity which is situated near the southern end of Brivibus iela.

SLEEPING, EATING AND NIGHTLIFE

There is a YMCA-run hostel in the new town at 10–12 Kalnciema iela (Tel. 33 21 31), situated on the west bank. It is only open 1 July–15 Aug., however. The Turists, Slokas iela 1 (Tel. 61 54 55), is a big Soviet-style hotel on the west bank; it's clean and reasonably priced. The Saulite Hotel, near the station at Merkela 12 (Tel. 22 45 46), is drab but clean, and charges a similar price to the Turists.

Alternatively, there are several hotels to the north-west of the station near the old town. Ring the Tourist Club of Latvia (Tel. 22 17 31) for information on private rooms.

There are quite a few cafés and other eateries in the old town. If you don't care for the price of the restaurants, shop for bread and cheese and head for one of the parks just west of the river in the new town. There are also fast-food outlets in the city.

The Esplanade near the Latvija and the Mezaparks offer open-air music, from classical performances to traditional folk.

If you need an all-night chemist go to 21a Elizabetes iela.

EXCURSIONS JELGAVA, 40 km south-west of Riga, is the setting of the magnificent 18th-century Rundale Palace. The grounds are extensive and worth exploring.

SALASPILS was the site of one of Hitler's concentration camps and virtually all Latvia's 50,000 Jews died here. Take the train to Darzini and from there you can walk to the monument.

The GAUJA NATIONAL PARK is situated at SIGULDA, 48 km north-east of Riga, in the breathtaking Gauja valley. Within the designated area are woods, caves, lakes and several castles. For accommodation, try the reasonably cheap Sigulda Hotel at Pilsiela iela 6 (Tel. 972 263).

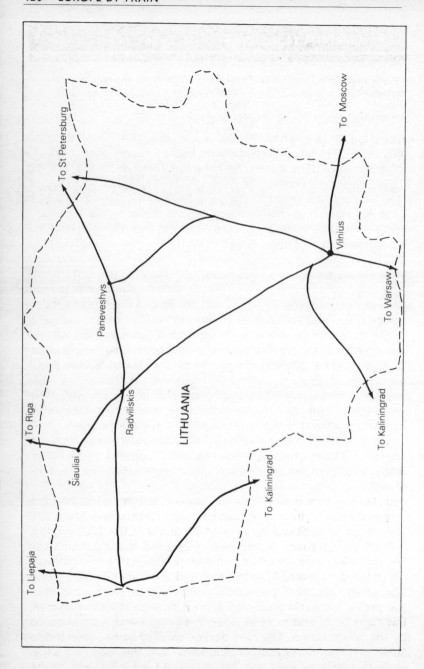

LITHUANIA (Lietuva)

Entry requirements	Passport. New Zealanders also require a visa.
Population	3,715,499
Capital	Vilnius (pop.: 574 423)
Currency	Litas, cent (ct)
	£1 = approx. 6Lt
Political system	Parliamentary democracy
Religion	Catholic
Language	Lithuanian, Russian widely spoken (see note on languages), some English and German
Public holidays	1 Jan.; 13 Jan., 16 Feb., 11 March, Easter, 1 May, 14 June, 6 July, 23 Aug., 8 Sep., 25 Oct., 2 Nov., 25, 26 Dec.
International dialling codes	To Lithuania: 00 (international access code) + 370 (country code)
	From Lithuania: 00 + country code
Time	GMT + 2 (+3 in summer)
Emergency telephone	Fire 01, Police 02, Ambulance 03

Lithuania's history differs significantly from that of its fellow Baltic neighbours in that it has not been so downtrodden over the centuries. When the Teutonic Knights swept through the area, the dense forests of the country allowed the Lithuanians to harangue the Germans and limit their conquest to a strip of coastal land. Indeed, the decline of Russia in the 14th century saw the Lithuanians push eastward, conquering land in their own right, and by the end of the century they managed to take everything between the Lithuanian border and Kiev. In 1386, a marriage between the Lithuanian heir and the Queen of Poland formed an alliance which was to last for 4 centuries, during which time the Lithuanian upper classes amalgamated with the Poles, while the peasants were reduced to the level of serfs.

In 1410 a great victory over the Teutonic Knights eliminated the threat of invasion from that quarter, so that Lithuania enjoyed 200 years of peace until war broke out with Russia in the 17th century. Poland and Lithuania combined forces and managed to seize Moscow – albeit for a short time. Russia quickly retaliated and Lithuania all but disappeared from the map until the end of the First World War, when nationalists pressed for independence. During the inter-war period, Lithuania prospered as an independent state. However, this came to an end in 1939 when the Baltic States were annexed by the Soviet Union. The next decade saw Lithuania subjected to Soviet and Nazi occupation in turn. Firstly 200,000 Jews were killed in death camps by the Nazis, but things did not improve with the return of the Red Army, who supervised the deportation of a further 250,000 Lithuanians.

Lithuania's recent history parallels that of Latvia and Estonia: in the late 1980s Lithuania was the first country to recognize parties other than the communists. Independence was declared in March 1990, though it seemed doomed to failure due to the country's dependence on the USSR. The coup against Gorbachev brought the central government tumbling down, thus giving the independence movement a chance. Today Lithuania is rapidly progressing in every way and has a strong cultural identity.

TRAIN INFORMATION

RESERVATIONS Trains are often crowded and reservations are a must on all routes (and mandatory on international ones). The Reservation Bureau at Sopeno 3 (Tel. 62 69 47) is open Mon.–Sat.: 8 a.m.–8 p.m., Sun.: 8. a.m.–5 p.m. and sells tickets for all destinations within the former Soviet Union, although not for departure the same day. For tickets to Poland and other destinations, contact the Travel Bureau, Lietuva Hotel, Ukmerges 20 (Tel. 72 62 25).

It is usually worth the extra money to upgrade to first class, which tends to be only 20–30% full. *Coupe* compartments (which seat 4) or the expensive *SV-deluxe* compartments are more comfortable.

PASSES AVAILABLE Inter-Rail and Eurail passes are not valid in Lithuania. The 'Baltic Rail Explorer Pass' is available to anyone under 26, ISIC-holders and to academic staff. For a period of 7, 14, or 21 days the prices are £15, £19 and £27 respectively. However, as trains are so cheap, you would really have to do a lot of travel to make one of these passes cost-effective.

NIGHT TRAVEL The only night trains are the international ones and these are not good for sleeping on, or worth the money.

EATING ON TRAINS On trains from Poland you may find a trolley service offering decent food, otherwise it's 'cash and carry'.

BUS INFORMATION Travelling by bus is quite popular in Lithuania as many towns and villages are not covered by the rail network. For distant destinations, choose an express bus. The Vilnius bus station is at Sodu 22, next to the railway station (Tel. 26 24 82).

TOURIST INFORMATION
The Lithuanian Tourist Board is at Ukmerges 20 (Tel. 622 610).

VISAS Many visitors, including those from Britain, the USA, Italy and Australia, no longer need visas. Check at the Lithuanian embassy in your country of origin for up-to-date details. In the UK the address is: 84 Gloucester Place, London W1H 3HN.

ISIC BONUSES Always show your card whenever you buy a ticket for *anything* – you never know where a discount will show up.

MONEY MATTERS Banking hours are generally Mon.–Fri.:9 a.m.–5 p.m., and Sat.: 9 a.m.–1 p.m. Traveller's cheques and credit cards are limited in usefulness (although steadily gaining acceptance), so bring cash. US dollars and Deutschmarks are the most widely accepted currencies. It is recommended that you change money because paying in foreign currencies generally involves a rip-off and is illegal! You can change money at the station, but beware of pickpockets.

SHOPS Generally open 9 a.m.–8 p.m. Mon.–Fri. with lunch break 2 p.m.–3 p.m. Weekend 10 a.m.–4 p.m.

MUSEUMS Most open 11 a.m.–4 p.m. but vary considerably.

LANGUAGE In Vilnius, you should find someone who can speak English. Unfortunately, this will not be the case outside the capital and you will have to depend on your ingenuity. Decades of Russian occupation and strong Polish ties mean that many people speak Russian and/or Polish. Lithuanian is the national language, but it's in danger of disappearing, even though 81% of the population are Lithuanian. Here are some phrases that may help:

Hello	Labas	Thank you	Ačiú
Goodbye	Viso gero	Excuse me	Atsiprašau
Yes	Taip	Do you speak	Ar kalbate
No	Ne	English?	angliškai?
Please	Prašau	Russian?	rusiškai?

TIPPING Leave up to 10% if you think that you have had good service. It is expected at hotels, restaurants, in cloakrooms and in taxis.

SLEEPING AND EATING
Lithuania is not easy for accommodation. There are some campsites advice is to check out the situation when you arrive or contact the

embassy in your home country for advice.

As regards eating out, there are cheap cafés and restaurants if you look hard enough. Check the bakeries and local farmers' markets for picnic ingredients. National dishes include *cepelinai* (meat-stuffed potato dumplings), *kugelis* (a rich potato pie), and a range of dishes made with wild mushrooms.

Vilnius phone code: 2

The bulk of the city lies south of the river and the train station is located on the southern outskirts. Luckily, most of the sights are in the 3 km between the station and the river. *Vilnius in your Pocket*, the official city guide, is an excellent companion for seeing the city. Alternatively, for further help and advice, try your own embassy: the British embassy is at Antakalnio gatvė 2 (Tel. 22 20 70), the American embassy is at Akmenu gatvė 6 (Tel. 223 031) and the Canadian embassy is at Ciurltonio gatvé 84 (Tel. 661 731).

STATION FACILITIES
Money can be changed in the railway station at the currency exchange office situated in the waiting hall on the left. Open 6 a.m.–10.30 a.m. 11 a.m.–3.30 p.m. and 4 p.m.–11 p.m. A left-luggage office, open 24 hours, operates from the wagon on the left side of quai 1.

TRANSPORT Take the bus. Tickets have to be purchased at a news stand. Avoid the taxis which are expensive. Take trolley bus 2, 5 or 7 to the city centre from the stop to the right as you exit the train station.

PHARMACY Apotheke Didzioji 13, Vilnius (Tel. 22 42 32). German/Lithuanian Pharmacy with Western medicines.

SEEING
Vilnius has many churches, monasteries and convents. Unfortunately, many of the buildings have suffered the ravages of wars, fires and general neglect. The strikingly squat and cumbersome Catholic cathedral, ARKIKATEDRA BAZILIKA dates originally from 1387 and was later reconstructed in 1777 in the neoclassical style. From the cathedral a path leads from the square up to CASTLE HILL. All that remains is the GOTHIC TOWER, which affords an excellent view of the mosaic of

steeples and rooftops of the city. Following the road east round the foot of the hill, there is the MUSEUM OF APPLIED ARTS (*Taikqmosios Dailes Muzéjus*) which houses collections of Lithuanian tapestries, jewellery and ceramics.

The graceful PETER AND PAUL'S CHURCH is probably the finest example of late baroque architecture in Lithuania; its simple white façade contrasts with the breathtaking interior.

Near the top of Pilies gatvé (one of the key streets in the old city) a narrow little street leads east to the stunning 16th-century Gothic ST ANN'S CHURCH.

Ausros Vartu is an attractive street running south-east to the MEDININKAI GATE, the only city gate to have survived intact.

VILNIUS UNIVERSITY is one of the oldest in Eastern Europe, dating back 400 years. It retains its charming courtyards and arcades. Visit the state JEWISH MUSEUM at Pamienkalnio gatvé 12 (Tel. 62 07 30). Open 9 a.m.è5 p.m., Fri. till 4 p.m.

South along the river, Vingio Parkas is the city's main park, a very pleasant place to stroll, with a huge open-air theatre where festivals are held. In North old town, by the river, is the LITHUANIAN STATE MUSEUM (*Lietuvos Valstybes Muzéjus*), whose exhibits relate the history of the people of Lithuania from the Stone Age to 1940 (the display on the history and achievements of the Lithuanian Republic during the inter-war period is particularly worth seeing). Open Wed.–Sun. : 11 a.m.–5 p.m. (Tel. 62 94 26).

SLEEPING AND EATING

Vilnius in your Pocket, the city travel guide, lists a range of accommodation possibilities and gives helpful recommendations. The Litinterp Pension, Bernardinu 7–2 (Tel. 22 38 50 or 22 32 91), has 30 rooms and offers B&B in the heart of the old town. A single costs about 60Lt and a double is 125Lt. Try also the YHA, which can be booked at Kauno 1A 407 (Tel. 26 26 60) near the station.

Youth Hostel 'Filaretai' is at Filaretai gatvé 17 and on the International Booking Network (IBN) so you can reserve it from any other IYHF Hostel in the world. Tel. (3702) 69 66 27 or 69 69 46. $7–$9 per night.

There are a variety of little cafés on the walk into town from the station and you are bound to find one that suits both your standards of cleanliness and your budget if you look hard enough. Almost everything here is located between the train station and Castle Hill.

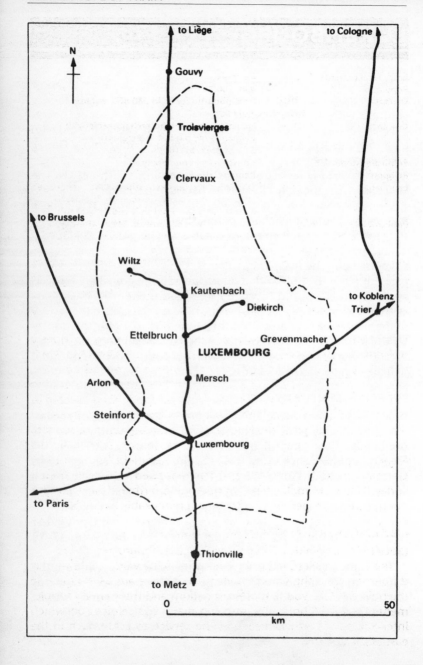

LUXEMBOURG

Entry requirements	Passport
Population	400, 900
Capital	Luxembourg City (pop.: 80 000, agglom. 120,000)
Currency	Luxembourg Franc (interchangeable with Belgian Franc but not in Belgium) £1 = approx. 51LUF
Political system	Constitutional monarchy
Religion	Roman Catholic
Language	Officially Letzeburgesch (the people's language), although French and German are spoken by almost everyone. English is widely spoken.
Public holidays	1 Jan., 25, 26 Feb. Carnival, Easter Monday; 1 May; Ascension, Whitsun, 24 June, 15 Aug., 2 Sept., 1 Nov., 25, 26 Dec.
International dialling codes	To Luxembourg: 00 (international access code) + 352 (country code) From Luxembourg: 00 + country code
Time	GMT +1 (+2 in summer)
Emergency telephone	112

Described as the 'green heart of Europe', Luxembourg provides a welcome break from travelling. The greater part of its 2,587 sq. km is heavily wooded and makes ideal camping and hiking country. During the medieval period it was 3 times the size, encompassing much of southern Belgium, and 4 of its royal family were elected as Holy Roman Emperors. In 1443 Philip the Good of Burgundy seized the city and added it to the Netherlands. It subsequently passed into the hands of the Spanish and Austrian Habsburgs, and finally the French. Independence came in 1815 and despite being overrun by Germany in both World Wars, it has managed to survive intact. Today its low unemployment and declining birthrate make Luxembourg a very prosperous country with a remarkably high GNP.

LUXEMBOURG NATIONAL RAILWAYS
(Société Nationale des Chemins de Fer Luxembourgeois, CFL)

This is the smallest national rail network in the world – it takes only 2 hours to cross the whole country – but there are 64 stations, so the train can take you to most destinations and there are no supplements to worry about. CFL also run many bus services on which Inter-Rail passes are valid such as the service to Echternach in the east of the country.

TRAIN INFORMATION

For information on international trains, go to the Railway Information Office in Gare Centrale, where English is spoken. If there's a queue, or it's a simple question, look for the information officers wearing yellow capbands.

PASSES AVAILABLE Network tickets are available for an unlimited number of journeys for second-class travel on all lines of the Luxembourg railway and bus system. As soon as you stamp them they are valid for the rest of the day (until 8 a.m. the following morning). If you are taking a bicycle, 40LUF has to be paid to carry it on the train. All train and bus stations sell *Billets Réseaux*. These are good for unlimited second-class train and bus travel. They are not valid on buses running within the capital. A 1-day ticket costs 140LUF.

Another type of ticket which is inexpensive for the non-Inter-Rail traveller is the Benelux Pass. This ticket entitles the holder to 5 days' unlimited travel in 1 month in Belgium, the Netherlands and Luxembourg. It costs only 3,200LUF (4,300LUF for over-26s).

The Inter-Rail pass has been broken down into zones, so that a careful selection of zones means you don't have to pay for travel to areas you have no intention of visiting. For £159 you can spend 22 days in a single zone. Luxembourg is in Zone E, along with France, Belgium and the Netherlands. (For further details of the 8 Inter-Rail zones, refer to the Inter-Rail section in Part One of this guide.)

For information on the Freedom Pass (Euro Domino) and Eurail, see pp.41 and 45.

RESERVATIONS It's not possible to reserve on internal trains and on internationals it's optional, but must be done 24 hours in advance as the train will invariably be starting in another country.

TOURIST INFORMATION

The National Tourist Office is now in the main station and open 9 a.m.–12 noon and 2 p.m.–6.30 p.m. daily. From July till 15 Sept., opening hours are extended to 9 a.m–7 p.m. Otherwise, there are local offices (*Syndicats d'Initiative*) scattered throughout the country. Most open at 9 a.m. and shut at 6 p.m. with an hour-long lunch break but this varies greatly.

ISIC BONUSES Some museums and galleries are half price but ISIC and U26 are not widely recognized. Your IYHF membership card will get you reduced entrance to the Casemates in Luxembourg City.

MONEY MATTERS 1 Luxembourg Franc (LUF) = 100 centimes.

Banking hours are Mon.–Fri.: 9 a.m.–12 noon and 1.30 p.m.–4 p.m., though some banks are open earlier, longer or do not close for lunch; some are open on Sat. mornings. The Luxembourg Franc is interchangeable with the Belgian Franc, but you're best to change them before leaving the country.

POST OFFICES Open Mon.–Fri.: 8 a.m.–12 noon and 2 p.m.–5 p.m. Station branch opens 6 a.m.–8 p.m. It's possible to cash and pay by Eurocheques in all offices.

SHOPS AND MUSEUMS These vary in their times of opening. Tues.–Fri.: 9 a.m.–12 noon and 2 p.m.–6 p.m. seems to be the general rule. All shops are closed on Mon. mornings, and some museums are shut all day.

TIPPING Tipping is relaxed here as in much of Europe. Leave around 10%, or perhaps only your change, but only if you have had good service.

SLEEPING

Pick up the tourist board's excellent free guide on accommodation at the main office next to the station. This lists prices and facilities for all Luxembourg's hotels and pensions. If you're thinking about camping, ask for the free folder giving all the campsites and prices. There are 13 youth hostels, charging between 345 LUF and 780LUF per night with breakfast included. There are a large number of campsites all over the country. Expect to pay from 110LUF per tent plus a further 120–130LUF per person.

EATING AND NIGHTLIFE

Dishes have a strong French flavour and specialities include Ardennes ham which you can pick up at supermarkets and butchers' in towns. Check up with the Tourist Offices for what's happening in the week ahead.

Luxembourg City

The oldest part of this 1,000-year-old city is on a high plateau over-looking cliffs and the valleys of the Petrusse and Alzette rivers. Around the edge of the plateau is the CHEMIN DE LA CORNICHE and BLD ROOSEVELT, which offers spectacular views over the city. Just below the promenade are the CASEMATES, 21 km of underground passages, hewn from solid rock, from the times when this area was a fortress (Tel. 22 67 53). To explore them, enter from Place de la Constitution or from the Beck fortress, but check the opening times and remember to show your IYHF membership card for reduced admission.

Also in the old town is the CATHEDRAL OF NOTRE DAME and the NATIONAL MUSEUM (closed Mon., Sat. mornings and Sun. lunchtimes), with a selection of historical, natural and artistic artefacts. Next door is the Folklore Museum, which is rarely open. From the National Museum take the glass LIFT down the wall of the gorge for spectacular views (see page 432).

The main annual event in the city is the *Schoberfouer*, an amusement fair and market which arrives on the penultimate Sunday in August and lasts into the first week in September. The Catholic Octave Festival is held in late April and early May.

For those with a little bit of cash to spare and a head for heights, the Compagnie Aéronautique in Junglinster offer an original way to see the city by hot air balloon. Tel. 78 90 75 for further details.

See also the EUROPEAN CENTRE, located in the western suburbs and home to a number of European agencies, including the Supreme Court of the EU and the General Secretariat of the European Parliament. Luxembourg is one of the most 'European' of European cities.

At the other end of the scale there is a *bric-à-brac* market on the PLACE D'ARMES on the second and fourth Saturday of each month.

STATION FACILITIES

Luxembourg City Gare Centrale has all the facilities you would expect from a modern and wealthy capital. Look out for the little conveyor belts to assist you with your baggage up the stairs! Tourist Information is now in the station and there are electronic information boards all over the city.

TOURIST INFORMATION AND ADDRESSES

The City Information centre is in the City Hall at place d'Armes (Tel. 22 28 09), open Apr.–Oct., Mon.–Sat.: 9 a.m.–7 p.m., Sun.: 10

a.m.–6 p.m. Pick up an *Agenda Touristique* which lists everything that's going on. Also get a leaflet on the self-guided City Walks (Wenzelwalks) which come with a free map and are designed to take you around the principal attractions in 100 minutes.

POST OFFICE Place de la Gare 38, Mon.–Sat.: 6 a.m.–8 p.m. Poste restante till 8 p.m. Also at rue Aldringen 25, open 7 a.m.–8 p.m.

STUDENT TRAVEL TEJ, Voyage Sotour, place du Théâtre 15 on the corner of Rue Beaumont (Tel. 46 15 14), open Mon.–Fri.: 9 a.m.–6 p.m., Sat.: 9 a.m.–12 p.m.

CHEMIST Pharmacie du Mortier, avenue de la Gare, open Mon.–Fri. 8 a.m.–6.15 p.m. but there is a little LCD display outside which lists others or Tel. 112 in an emergency

UK EMBASSY boulevard Roosevelt 14 (Tel. 22 98 64)

US EMBASSY boulevard Emmanuel Servais 22 (Tel. 46 01 23)

AMEX 34 avenue de la Porte-Neuve (Tel: 22 85 55)

BUS INFORMATION A 1-trip ticket costs 40LUF, all-day tickets cost 160LUF; they are available from the driver, as are the better value 5-trip tickets which several people can use.

SLEEPING

Stay close to the station for cheap hotels. Directly opposite the station, rue Joseph Junck is a safe bet, as is rue de la Liberté. Doubles average about 2,200LUF in this area.

The youth hostel is good, located right in the historic part of the city. The scenery on the bus ride is worth the 10-minute trip. It is sometimes full of adolescent groups and there is a 9 a.m. eviction. Take bus 9 from the station. The fare is about 40LUF and it will cost the same again for your rucksack. You can walk through town to it in half an hour. The address is rue du Fort Olizy 2 (Tel. 22 68 89 or 22 19 20) and single beds cost 415LUF per night, including breakfast (500LUF if you are over 26).

Kockelscheuer Camping, route de Bettembourg 22 (Tel. 47 18 15), is quite a way from the station so it is better to take bus 2. Open from Easter till October, it costs 150LUF per tent and 150LUF per person.

EATING AND NIGHTLIFE

The city is small-scale cosmopolitan and food isn't terribly cheap, so use the supermarkets and bakeries near the station. The latter offer good sandwiches, but also try the delicious *pâté au Riesling*. Always look out for the restaurants which offer a *menu du jour*. These meals are the best buy of the day and prices range between 300 and 450LUF.

Place d'Armes is where to head to in the evenings. People generally congregate here and there are often free concerts in the square. There are also fast-food restaurants in this part of town. Pizza Hut has 2 outlets at place d'Armes and at rue Origer; both are open until midnight every day. Generally, the Italian and Chinese restaurants are the cheapest in town.

La Semaine à Luxembourg events guide is available from Tourist Information as is Vade-Mecum, the cultural diary. It lists all theatres, concerts, films, galleries and museums. Nightlife is low-key. However, young people tend to congregate in GRUND down in the gorge below the city centre, a trendy area full of bars and cafés. There is a spectacular glass LIFT which makes the descent and it is big enough to take bikes and it operates till 3 a.m. so you can stay out late and return safely to the city centre above. Get further information and a special leaflet from the Tourist Office.

Provincial Luxembourg

On the banks of the river Sauer (Sûre) lies the medieval town of ECHTERNACH. Though badly damaged in the Second World War (Germany is across the river), it has been well restored and the TOWN HALL is as good as ever. Echternach has a big International Music Festival in May and June (student tickets cost 300LUF and are available from the Tourist Office) and the dancing procession of St Willibrod takes place on Whit Tuesday. The Tourist Office at Porte St Willibrod is contactable by telephoning 72 02 30, and is open 9 a.m.–12 noon and 2 p.m.–5 p.m.

The BENEDICTINE BASILICA has some impressive frescoes and stained-glass windows, and the buried remains of St Benedict.

There's a youth hostel at rue André Duchscher 9 (Tel. 720158) or try Hotel Le Petit Poète, place du Marché 13 (Tel. 720072): doubles from about 1,500LUF.

The cheapest of the town's 2 campsites, Camp Officiel, is 500m from the bus station in rue de Diekirch (Tel. 720272). It charges 120LUF per person, 120LUF per site and is open March–Oct.

Buses are the easiest method of getting from Luxembourg City to Echternach (every ½ hour between 8 a.m and 6 p.m.) and they are free to Inter-Rail pass holders. There are 12 daily, taking just over an hour to travel the distance. Just a few minutes north of Echternach is a small wedge of hiker's paradise: LITTLE SWITZERLAND. This is a beautiful section of the Ardennes, and a walk through the steep gorges and forests makes an exhilarating hour or so. Luxembourg has the densest network of marked paths in the world. National routes are marked by yellow signs. The YHA maintains the walking routes and maps are available from the YHA at place d'Armes 18 (Tel. 22 55 88) and cost 180LUF. In the northernmost part of the Ardennes is TROIS VIERGES, the heart of hiking country. There is an IYHF Hostel at 24–26 rue de la Gare (Tel. 9 80 18).

The Clerve Valley leads to CLERVAUX, about an hour north of Luxembourg City. The 11th-century castles of BOURSCHEID and CLERVAUX are set in fairytale surroundings. There are permanent exhibitions in Clervaux Castle, including Edward Steichen's *Family of Man* collection. The Tourist Office at Clervaux (open 9.45 a.m.–11.45 a.m.; 2 p.m.–6 p.m. on Sundays) is next to the castle (Tel. 920072). The official campsite at 33 Klatzewe costs 140LUF per person (Tel. 920042).

VIANDEN is worth a visit. It is not directly linked to Luxembourg City by rail or bus; so travel via Echternach. Here you'll find cobbled streets and a magnificent castle, admission 120LUF (open daily 10 a.m.–6 p.m.). This was the cradle of the Grand-Ducal dynasty and dates back to the 9th century. Try the chairlift (*télésiège*) which operates from rue du Sanatorium and costs 160LUF (Easter–Oct., daily 10 a.m.–6 p.m.), and also the open-air swimming pool with impressive views over the castle. Less scenic, but no less historic is the DOLL AND TOY MUSEUM (Tel. 84591), which is open Easter–Oct. and features a display of over 500 dolls dating from 1860. Admission is 100LUF.

The youth hostel is situated over the bridge from the train station at montée du Château 3 (Tel. 8 41 77). You'll also be able to find cheap hotels along this road. The Tourist Office is in Victor Hugo's former house (Tel. 84257, closed 12 noon–2 p.m.).

Three campsites are situated on the edge of the river Oúr: Op dem Deich, Du Moulin and De l'Oúr, costing 130LUF, 130LUF and 120LUF, per person and per site, respectively.

Just north of Luxembourg City, at the entrance to the Valley of the Seven Castles, lies MERSCH with its prehistoric caves and the remains of a Roman villa and a feudal castle. Maps and information are available from the Tourist Office at the town hall (Tel. 32 50 23), closed 11.30 a.m.–1.30 p.m.

Further north lies DIEKIRCH, home of a festival on the third Sunday of July, and 3 camping grounds. Bicycles can be rented at Camping de la Sûre (Tel. 80 94 25) where maps and information are also available. The Tourist Office is contactable on 80 30 23 at 1, Esplanade.

WILTZ, like Clervaux, borders on a valley, and is divided into 2 parts with a castle situated in the High Town. An international open-air festival in July takes place in the amphitheatre in the castle yard and a Battle of the Bulge museum is housed in the castle. A walk through the town leads along a path of stone crosses which remember the plague. The youth hostel is at 6 rue de la Montagne (Tel. 95 80 39) and has kitchen facilities.

Travelling back along the western side of the country is the village of BASCHARAGE on the main line from Luxembourg to Paris. Here you can get guided visits to the Bofferding Brewery, with a free drink of beer (admission 80LUF; Tel. 50 90 11-21), or to gem-cutting workshops (Tel. 50 90 32). Telephone in advance to book.

If your destination is France, stop off at ESCH-SUR-ALZETTE on the French border, Luxembourg's second city, only 20 km away from Luxembourg City with a direct rail link. It is a good place for shopping at reasonable prices and houses the National Museum of the Resistance. The Tourist Office can be found at the town hall, office 8 (Tel. 54 73 83-246, open Mon.–Fri.: 7.30 a.m.–12 noon, 1.30 p.m.–5 p.m.), and camping is available at the Gaalgebierg site (Tel. 54 10 69) for 130LUF.

NOTES

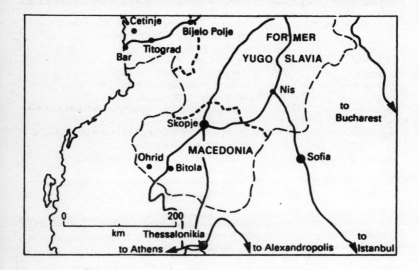

REPUBLIC OF MACEDONIA

Entry requirements	Passport (UK only). USA, Canada, Australia and New Zealand nationals require a visa.
Population	2,100,000
Capital	Skopje (pop.: 600,000)
Currency	Denar
Political system	Parliamentary democracy
Religion	Orthodox
Language	Macedonian (some French, English and German spoken)
Public holidays	1, 2 Jan. 7 Jan; 1, 2 May 24 May 4 July 2 Aug. 8 Sept. 11 Oct. 29, 30 Nov.
International dialling codes	To Macedonia: 00 (international access code) + 389 (country code) From Macedonia: 99 + country code number or 00 + country code

The Slavs settled here in the 7th century and enjoyed 200 years of peace. Later they fell under alternating periods of rule by the Byzantine and Bulgarian Empires. At the end of the 10th and the beginning of the 11th century (969–1018), a vast empire of the Macedonian Slavs emerged – the Empire of Tsar Samuil – with its capital in Ohrid. When that empire was defeated by Byzantium in the 11th century, Macedonia became a pawn to be passed between Bulgaria, Byzantium and Serbia. This unsettled period came to an end in the 14th century when the Balkan peninsula was added to the Ottoman Turk empire. It remained under Turkish rule for 500 years until the end of the 19th century when Russia defeated Turkey. Macedonia briefly reverted to Bulgarian control, but the Western powers forced Bulgaria to give it back to Turkey.

The struggle for control of Macedonia has continued throughout this century, and the present state is half the size it once was, Greece, Albania and Bulgaria each having seized territory along the way. A referendum was held on 8 September 1991 and approximately 95% of those who took part voted for independence. For once, Belgrade permitted a former republic to withdraw from the federation without bloodshed. However, when EU recognition finally came in June 1992 it was granted on condition that the country temporarily use an appellation. This proviso was added at the insistence of the Greeks, on the grounds that there is a region of that name in northern Greece. For the sake of convenience we use 'Macedonia' throughout this section. This does not imply that we either agree or disagree with any interested parties over disputed territory in either Greece or the former Yugoslavia.

Macedonia is a poor country which suffered a great deal because of sanctions imposed by Serbia and Montenegro. Since it is on the main line between western Europe and Greece you might want to consider a brief stop – but be sure to make your outbound train reservations before arriving!

The political situation in this part of Europe continues to be potentially unstable. Check on current local conditions before travelling. Politically speaking, the Balkans are a really interesting place!

TRAIN INFORMATION

Obtaining information on the trains here can be nigh on impossible. In Skopje, you should find an information officer who speaks English, but elsewhere you will have to rely on your ingenuity.

RESERVATIONS Required on all international trains passing through Macedonia.

PASSES AVAILABLE For information on the Euro Domino and Eurotrain Explorer Passes, see 'Eurorailing: the options'.

The Inter-Rail pass has been broken down into zones, so that you don't have to pay for travel to places you've no intention of visiting. Macedonia is in Zone H, along with Bulgaria, Romania, Bosnia Hercegouinia and Macedonia. For £159 you get 22 days' travel in a single zone.

NIGHT TRAVEL There are usually both couchettes and sleepers on the international trains passing through Macedonia, and there are ex-Yugoslavian sleepers on the Bitola–Belgrade run.

EATING ON TRAINS On international trains you can expect the normal range of services. When travelling on local trains you would be well advised to bring your own supplies of food and drink.

BUSES These are frequently the only way to get around in Macedonia and are relatively cheap.

SCENIC ROUTES The only route here worthy of note is the line down to Bitola, which places you within striking distance of Lake Ohrid.

TOURIST INFORMATION
The bigger cities will have travel agents and Tourist Offices. Before travelling to Macedonia we strongly recommend you write to the National Tourist Office at 10 Harcourt House, 19a Cavendish Square, London W1M 9AD (Tel. 0171 499 5152) to check on any recent developments.

ISIC BONUSES Discounts are given on admission to some museums and sights (most admission fees are reasonable). Your best bet is to show your ISIC card whenever buying tickets.

MONEY 1 denar (dn) = 100 deni
Although the currency is the Macedonian denar, we recommend that you carry a supply of Deutschmarks as an extra safeguard. Credit cards are not widely accepted. Banking hours can be anytime between 9 a.m. and 7 p.m.

POST OFFICES Generally open Mon.–Sat.: 7 a.m.–3 p.m. Stamps can also be purchased at the various newsagents and hotels, though be sure to get an airmail sticker or your post may take months to reach its destination.

STREET NAMES Warning: Names of streets have been changed but the old signs may remain.

TIPPING Tipping is not expected, but loose change may be given away.

SLEEPING
Hotels here are very expensive, but there are many cheap pensions. The only hostels are in Ohrid (open summer only) and Skopje. There are student dorms (*Studentski Dom*) and campsites in both these cities and other major towns scattered across the country. You can pick up lists at Tourist Offices. The cheapest option is usually to try and find a private room. Write to the Macedonian Youth Hostel Association for up-to-date information on hostels in Macedonia: PO Box 499, Prolet 25, 91000 Skopje. Tel. (389) (91) 23 99 47: Fax. (389) (91) 23 50 29.

EATING
The food here shows a mixture of oriental and European influences with the local speciality being *bezbequed* meat. There are also bland, self-service worker cafeterias in the cities. In Ohrid they have innu-

merable ways of cooking trout from the lake and it is worth the effort to try some. Macedonia is big on agriculture, so you should be able to piece together good picnics at local markets.

Skopje phone code : 091

Skopje has been beset by floods, fires and earthquakes (the last, in 1963, levelled part of the city). As a result, the capital now has 2 distinct personalities: the old town and the modern new town. The modern sector is garish and already falling apart from lack of repair: avoid it. The old town, however, has much to recommend it.

SEEING

From the railway station, make your way north-west until you come to Koco Racin, then cross the river. When you come to Bulevar Goce Delcev, turn left and you will pass the 15th-century TURKISH BATHS on your right just before the Tourist Information centre. A left turn here takes you to the stone KAMENI BRIDGE and over into the new city and the huge, recently refurbished shopping centre.

To the right of the Tourist Centre is the CHURCH OF SVETI SPAS with some excellent 18th- and 19th-century icons, and the MUSTAFA PASHA MOSQUE where you can climb the minaret for a good view of the old city.

Across the street is a park with the ruins of FORT KALE (10th–12th centuries).

There are several museums in town; the best of these are the CITY ART GALLERY near the Turkish Bridge and the MUSEUM OF MACEDONIA, which is past the mosque behind an old inn. Nearby is the local vegetable market.

SLEEPING AND EATING

There is an IYHF Associate Hostel at Prolet 25 (Tel. 11 55 19 or 11 48 49: Fax. 23 50 29) which costs 18–26DM per person including breakfast and it is 500m. from the station. From April to October you can camp at Autocamp (Tel. 22 82 46) for around 450dn per person. Alternatively, for around 700dn the Tourist Office will fix you up with a private room.

Foodwise, your best bet is to wander round the old town. There are a variety of dingy-looking restaurants here which are quite good and frequented by the locals. If you have a weak stomach, head for the self-service restaurant in the new town just south of the Turkish bridge.

Western Macedonia

OHRID Though worth a visit, Ohrid is heavily touristed and not on the rail lines, so you'll have to take the train to Bitola and catch a bus from there. From spring to early autumn, there is always one festival or another going on, courtesy of the Tourist Office, to keep the visitors pouring in. The city is still surrounded by a medieval wall and near the north entrance are 2 churches worth seeing: SVETI KILMENT and SVETI SOFIJA. From the churches, walk west until you come to the old ROMAN AMPHITHEATRE then continue on to the CITADEL. Follow the walls of the citadel for beautiful views of the area, and then head south to the nearby basilica and check out the mosaics in its ruins. Keep walking south and you will pass the ruins of another church and come to a cliff overlooking the lake. At the bottom there are some nice beaches.

There is a hostel about 1½ km to the west of town (Tel. 21671) which costs around 850dn per person. Alternatively, have the Tourist Office set you up in a private room.

BITOLA This town has been underrated by most guides and as such it is a good place to unwind during the summer. Many visitors simply pass through on their way to Ohrid and miss out on an interesting little town with a definite Turkish feel to it. If nothing else, try to do some exploring while waiting for the connection on to Ohrid.

On the south side of town are the pre-Christian ruins of HERACLEA. The Roman ruins are still being excavated and there is also an early Christian palace and a small museum on the site. On Marshal Tito Square is a 16th-century BEZISTAN BAZAAR, the MOSA PIJADE ART GALLERY (in an old mosque) and the CLOCK TOWER. Near the Bezistan is the STARA CARSILJA, or bazaar district, and the city's market.

Other than hotels, your only chance of a place to sleep is to ask at the Tourist Office for a private room. Although officially they can't fix you up, they should be able to point you in the right direction.

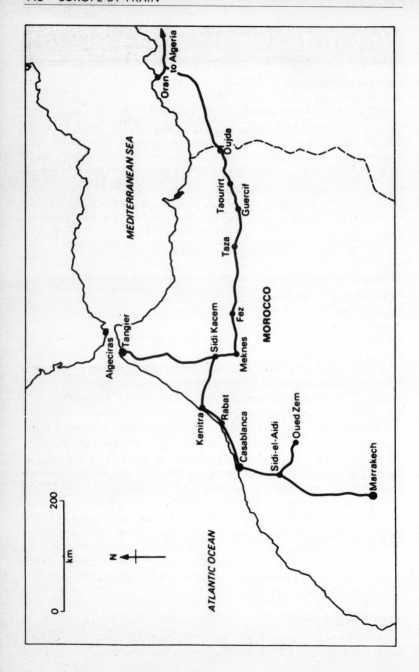

MOROCCO

Entry requirements	Passport
Population	27,800,000
Capital	Rabat-Sale (pop.: 950,000)
Currency	Dirham (dh) = 100 centimes
	£1 = approx. 13.9dh
Political system	Constitutional monarchy
Religion	Islam
Language	Arabic, French and Spanish (in tourist towns)
Public holidays	1, 11 Jan., 3 March, 1, 23 May, 9 July, 14 Aug., 6, 18 Nov.
	There are 4 movable religious festivals: Aid El-Fitr in early March, Aid Al-Adha in mid-May, Muslim New Year in late May and Prophet's Birthday in mid-August. Note: Ramadan, the Muslim fasting month, is not a public holiday and takes place for 4 weeks in January/February.
International dialling codes	To Morocco: 00 (international access code) + 212 (country code) + area code
	From Morocco: 00 + country code
Eurotrain office	112 avenue d'Espagne, Tangier (Tel. 0993 5540)
Time	GMT (GMT +1 in summer)
Emergency telephone	Police 19, Fire/Ambulance 15

Morocco comes as a bit of a culture shock: everything appears alien, exotic and exciting, and if this is what you're after, you'll enjoy it. The further south you travel, the more 'foreign' things will appear. In Marrakech you can sample the vibrant colours, smells, tastes and baking hot sun of this Arab land. The rail network has been vastly improved and travelling around the country is relatively trouble-free. Morocco is a Muslim country, therefore women should cover up when travelling in more remote areas. It is a country which makes a tremendous impression on you, and is a place which everyone 'doing Europe' should make an effort to get to.

Most of Morocco was a French protectorate between 1912 and 1956, except for the north, which was Spanish. Morocco also claims the Western Sahara, where the United Nations are currently holding a referendum. Morocco is largely unaffected by the dangerous political events in neighbouring Algeria, where it is definitely not recommended you go!

GETTING THERE
There are various ferries from Spain to Tangier (2½) and Ceuta (1½), with the Algeciras–Ceuta crossing being the shortest and cheapest,

but as it's not on the railway it might be easier to use the Algeciras–Tangier route. It costs about 3,200 pesetas. Make sure to get your passport stamped by the passport control below deck. The Ceuta ferry is cheaper (2,000ptas). Avoid dealing in drugs and be careful not to be used as a courier. Border guards do not look kindly on anyone caught in possession.

To get from Ceuta to Tetouan or Tangier, walk from Ceuta port to town centre, then catch a bus (40ptas) to the border. Then take another bus (or share a *petit-taxi*) to Tetouan or Tangier. Buses (CTM) are very cheap and quite comfortable. Tetouan–Sidi Lyam-ani by bus is a beautiful run and you can connect from there to trains to Casablanca.

MOROCCAN RAILWAYS
(OFFICE NATIONAL DES CHEMINS DE FER, ONCF)

Recently there has been a big improvement in Moroccan trains, although they still do not run as frequently as you might wish. There are 3 classes on the trains: first, second and *économique*. It is well worth paying the supplement of around £2 to travel in an air-conditioned carriage. The rail network runs north from Marrakech to Casablanca and Rabat, then splits at Sidi Kacem, one line going north to Tangier, the other to Fez and on to Algeria.

The Trans-Maghreb Express, which travels from Casablanca through Meknes, Fez and the fringes of the Atlas mountains to terminate in Algeria, is a laid-back, but beautiful route to travel on, if you are intending to pass through, rather than stay in, Morocco. Remember it is definitely *not* recommended to visit Algeria.

PASSES AVAILABLE The Inter-Rail card is valid here (Eurail is not) and the railway runs to the main tourist towns. Your Inter-Rail or BIJ ticket entitles you to use the second-class facilities. The Inter-Rail pass has been broken down into zones, so that a careful selection of zones means you do not have to pay for travel to areas you have no intention of visiting. For £159 you can tour a single zone for 22 days. Morocco is in Zone F, along with Spain and Portugal. (For further details of the 8 Inter-Rail zones, refer to the Inter-Rail section in Part One of this guide.)

For information on the Freedom Pass (Euro Domino), see p. 41.

The *carte d'abonnement* is valid for unlimited travel for a month on all trains but the fast TNR services. It costs 1,146dh for first class and 767dh for second (which works out at about £5 return per 100 km).

TRAIN INFORMATION

You'll find the odd official who speaks pidgin English, but generally you'll have to resort to French, which is the official second language, or Spanish.

RESERVATIONS Not compulsory, but a good idea if you're on a long haul in peak season.

NIGHT TRAVEL Sleeping cars are first class only and come in singles or doubles. They're fairly expensive, so unless you're feeling particularly delicate, try and schedule your travelling for daytime. Second-class cars are often crowded at night.

TOURIST INFORMATION

Most towns have both a Tourist Office and a *Syndicat d'Initiative*. The Tourist Office should be your first port of call, as they have information and will help find a bed if necessary. When you're organized, make your way back to the *Syndicat d'Initiative,* which will have leaflets on local sights, etc.

A word of warning – unofficial guides (mostly young boys) will pester you with their dubious services. Fool them into thinking you're Finnish – that usually puts them off. Hustlers are another problem – they'll approach you in the medina and kasbah, being incredibly friendly and conversant in a dozen languages. Ignore and avoid them. Finally, when you're at the sights, don't feel obliged to accept the custodian's offer of a guided tour or feel it necessary to give him a tip, as he is already paid by the government. If you do want an official guide, head for the nearest Tourist Office where you can expect to pay about 100dh for half a day of the guide's time.

If you wear contact lenses, bear in mind that it can be very dusty, and you may be more comfortable wearing glasses.

MONEY MATTERS 1 dirham (dh) = 100 centimes.

Banking hours are Mon.–Thurs.: 8.15 a.m.–11.30 a.m., 2.15 p.m.–4.30 p.m. (during Ramadan 9.30 a.m.–2 p.m.). Banks charge no commission and have the same rate of exchange everywhere. Buy dirhams in advance if arriving outside banking hours. Keep your receipts, as you will probably be asked to produce them when changing dirhams back, and remember to use banks – the rate on the boat back to Spain is a rip-off. Note that it is forbidden to import or export dirhams.

POST OFFICES Open Mon.–Fri.: 8.30 a.m.–12 noon, 2.30 p.m.–6 p.m.

SHOPS Open Mon.–Sat.: 8.30 a.m.–12 noon, 2 p.m.–6.30 p.m. Haggle like mad wherever you go in the markets (*souks*), even when you see the *prix fixe* sign. Haggling is a way of life here and unless you manage to get the price down by at least 50%, you are a failure. As a general rule, a fair price is about 25% of the first price suggested. Remember, never make any kind of offer, however low, unless you are seriously interested in buying. Decide in your mind what you are genuinely willing to pay and do not exceed that figure just to relieve the pressure.

Check with the *Syndicats d'Initiative* for opening times of museums and other sights.

BUSES More frequent and cheaper than trains, though less comfortable. If you are trying to board a bus at an intermediate stop between its point of departure and its destination, be warned – you will find it difficult to get a space and you could be waiting at your stop for longer than you bargained for.

TIPPING Waiters in restaurants will appreciate tips, up to 10%, if not already included in the bill. More unusual situations may occur when you are out and about, however, but it can be difficult to know when. Consider tipping a tour guide or someone who has put themselves out for you 5–10dh. Do not allow yourself to be pressurized into parting with your money if they have not really done anything for you – for example, showing you where a hotel is when it is only a few metres away!

SLEEPING

Morocco is a country where it pays to be tough. You can live off next to nothing if you don't mind roughing it a bit. Camping and youth hostelling (*Auberges de Jeunesse*) are very cheap, as little as 15dh a night under canvas or 15–30dh in a hostel dormitory, but you're not guaranteed central locations or first-class conditions. The medina hotels/pensions offer the most central and colourful locations and are usually cheaper than the places in the new areas of town. Hotels are graded from 1 to 5 stars and there are fixed maximum prices for each category. You usually pay by the room, so doubling up with friends can bring the unit cost of a room down. The cheapest hotel rooms cost somewhere between 89 and 160dh for a double room, with extra for shower and breakfast. If you find the water is hot at any time, seize the chance for a shower while you can, as the plumbing here is decidedly erratic. Always carry your own loo paper.

EATING AND NIGHTLIFE

If you've an iron stomach, take full advantage of it in Morocco by eating in the kasbahs and from shish kebab stands. Most decent restaurants offer a good selection of Moroccan dishes. Try *harira*, a rich soup of chicken, macaroni and spices, followed by *touajen* (lamb or chicken stew) or *couscous*, Morocco's most famous dish (semolina topped with lamb, fish or chicken). Try the *djaja maamra* – steamed and stuffed chicken with couscous, almonds and raisins. If you like something sweet to end with, ask for *kab el ghzal* (almond pastries) and mint tea. Often it is difficult in the more remote places to find meals during the day, so eat well at night.

Don't take chances with tap water; drink only mineral water, which you have to ask for by brand name. You can trust Sidi Ali or Sidi Harazem brands. There is little alcohol in this country, although it is not illegal.

The local *Syndicat d'Initiative* will let you know where the nearest belly-dancer performs and what's happening on the disco scene. Smoking *kif* (hashish) is widespread, but any tourists making a purchase risk unpleasant hassle and demands of fines/bribes at the hands of police – real or bogus.

Tangier phone code: 09

This isn't the best Morocco has to offer, but if you're on a day trip from Spain, it'll show you some of the exotic differences between Europe and Africa. Be on your guard for hustlers and pickpockets. Many readers feel the best advice is to head straight for the station and take the first train out. This is primarily because of the excessive amount of hassle one experiences here.

The MOUNTAIN is occupied by villas of the rich and famous and makes a pleasant walk. The main market place, GRAND SOCCO, connects the medina and the new town. Tourist Information (Tel. 93 82 39 or 93 29 96) is at 29 boulevard Pasteur (open Mon.–Fri.: 8 a.m.–2 p.m. in summer). The post office is at blvd Mohammed V. Visit the 17th-century SULTAN'S PALACE, which is now a museum containing a fine collection of Moroccan art, carpets, jewellery and weapons. Climb the Kasbah, to the highest point, for views over the city and across to the Straits of Gibraltar. Catch a glimpse of mosaic courtyards and fountains at mosque entrances – but it is illegal for non-Muslims to enter a mosque.

In the medina, the av. Mokhtar Ahardan is where to look for cheap hotels and restaurants. Accommodation may be a problem during July and August, with some of the unclassified places doubling their prices. So for cheap accommodation in high season, use only officially classified establishments. The Pension Palace (Tel. 93 6128) is at 2 av. Mokhtar Ahardan and costs about 80dh per person. Other budget accommodation possibilities are the new youth hostel at 8 rue El-Antaki (Tel. (09) 94 61 27), or the Magellan, 16 rue Magellan (Tel: 93 87 26).

Ten kilometres out of town and in sight of the Rock of Gibraltar lies the camping site Tingis. It is situated east of the city on the Malabata Rd near Camping Miramonte Mar-Bel. To get there take bus 15 from the Grand Socco, then walk along the Doubonah Rd and turn right, or along the rue de la Vieille Montagne.

The beaches and nightlife are both good, though single girls are in for a hard time from the locals.

If you are leaving the country from here, remember to turn up early for the boat as you will end up having to queue for passport control, customs and – finally – the boat itself. To buy a discounted ferry ticket to Algeciras you must produce a photocopy of your Inter-Rail/Eurail Pass (the Café Terminal across from the main station will do one cheaply). The Eurotrain office is at 112 av. d'Espagne (Tel. 935540).

A useful point of information that will save you unnecessary trekking: the train station (GARE DU PORT) is right below the ferry terminal in the city. Most trains leave from this stop, as well as from the GARE DE VILLE, which is 300m beyond the port gate.

Rabat city phone code: 07

From Tangier to the capital of Morocco – Rabat – is about 5 hours on the main line. This is a clean, organized and structured city. It has numerous parks and gardens, and most of the town is new and affluent by Moroccan standards. There is a kasbah in the old town but the medina lacks atmosphere and you feel you're back in Europe a lot of the time. Rabat's *souks* have a good reputation for beautiful rugs and embroidery.

TOURIST INFORMATION AND ADDRESSES

TOURIST INFORMATION Tourist Office is at Angle av. Al Abtal, rue Oued Fes. (Tel. 77 51 71) or Tourist Centre (*Syndicat d'Initiative*) is at rue Patrice Lumumba (Tel. 723272), which is nearer the station and is open 8.30 a.m.–6.30 p.m. every day in season.

POST OFFICE Av. Mohammed V; open Mon.–Fri.: 8 a.m.–12 noon; 2 p.m.–6.45 p.m., Sat.: 8.30 a.m.–12 noon

BANK Banque Al Maghrib, av. Mohammed V (Tel.763009)

AMEX In Rabat Hilton (Tel. 772151). Take bus for Agdal.

UK EMBASSY 17 boulevard de Tour Hassan (Tel. 731403)

US EMBASSY 2 avenue de Marrakech (Tel. 762265)

CANADIAN EMBASSY 13 rue Jaafar Essodik, Agdal (Tel. 672880)

POLICE Rue Seekamo (Tel. 19)

SEEING

The TOUR HASSAN minaret in the 12th-century mosque and the MAUSOLEUM OF MOHAMMED V are close to each other, and a 1 km walk away is the CHELLAH, an Arab necropolis built in the Old Roman section of Rabat called SALA COLONIA (admission 10dh). There are gardens here that are ideal for a picnic. The KASBAH OF THE OUDAIA FORTRESS has another beautiful garden, a Moorish café and the MUSEUM OF MOROCCAN ARTS: carpets, musical instruments, furniture, etc. The ROYAL PALACE is on the other side of the city, though it only dates back to the 1950s.

SLEEPING, EATING AND NIGHTLIFE

Try to book your rooms in advance, especially in July, since it can become vastly overcrowded. The youth hostel on 43 rue Marassa, Bah El Had (Tel. 725769), is conveniently sited and standards have recently improved. Stick to the area around the train station where you will find many hotels in the surrounding roads.

For camping, try Camping la Palmeraie Temara on Temara Beach or Camping Gambusias on Casablanca Road-Chiahna Tel. 74 91 42.

For cheap hotels, try Hotel Splendid at 24 rue Ghazza (Tel. 72 32 83) with its nice interior courtyard, or Hotel Central on 2 rue el Basra (Tel. 706 73 56 or 72 21 31).

The medina is the place for cheap eats. There are plenty of stalls and restaurants, with the Restaurant Bahia on blvd Hassan II offering good food at budget prices. It's located to your right as you approach the medina from av. Mohammed V. If you want to brave a nightclub, investigate the Sahat Melilya and Temara Beach areas.

Casablanca (Dar Beida) phone code: 02

Despite its 'Play it again, Sam' image, this is the least attractive of Morocco's towns. With 2½ million inhabitants and a busy port, Casablanca is a crowded, modern and somewhat squalid city. Take the train to the port station for the medina and beaches, but be careful taking photographs, as this is a sensitive military area.

Casablanca has some character and among its sights are the neo-Moorish public buildings round the PLACE DES NATIONS UNIES and the MAKHAMA (regional courts). A must to visit is the brand new HASSAN II MOSQUE, the world's largest, which has room for 80,000 worshippers and a 200m minaret. Try the friendly, well-maintained and nicely sited youth hostel at 6 place Admiral Philbert (Tel. 0222 0551), which charges 32dh per person including breakfast. To get there, turn right from the station, turning up the first small flight of steps on the left.

The Tourist Offices at ONCF, 98 boulevard Mohammed V (Tel. 22 15 24 or 27 95 33), and at 55 rue Omar Slaoui (Tel. 27 11 77), can provide good maps and listings for the party animals.

The 55-minute journey south to Casablanca from Rabat involves the best trains in Morocco, but if you're going further south, make sure you have supplies with you as the buffets are awful. If you can afford it, pay the supplement from second to first class (if you're travelling in peak season). On a branch line a few kilometres north of Casablanca is the beach resort of Mohammedia.

Marrakech city phone code: 04

This ochre city on the edge of the Sahara desert is what you expect Morocco to be like: vibrant markets with snake-charmers, fortune-tellers and acrobats; palm trees; remains from ancient dynasties and incredible midday temperatures of around 40°C (August maximum). On arrival get hold of a *petit-taxi* (regular ones cost double) and haggle to fix a price for a ride to the Jamaa el Fna. Or you can save 15dh and take a 3 or 6 bus from outside the station. You'll be dropped off in the city's main square and from there it's no problem finding a cheap hotel bed. The walk takes about 25 minutes.

TOURIST INFORMATION AND ADDRESSES

TOURIST OFFICE Place Abdelmoumen Ben Ali (Tel. 43 10 88 or 44 88 89). English spoken. Ask for a map and a list of accommodation (it doesn't list the real cheapies). Open Mon.–Sat.: 8.30 a.m.–12 noon, 2.30 p.m.–6.30 p.m. Don't bother making the 1½ km trek here unless you're desperate for them to book a hotel for you. Also, there is a Tourist Centre at 176 av. Mohammed V (Tel. 432097 or 43 47 97).

POST OFFICE Place du 16 Novembre, off av. Mohammed V; open Mon.–Fri.: 8.30 a.m.–12.15 p.m. and 2.30 p.m.–6.45 p.m.

AMEX c/o Voyages Schwartz, 1 rue Mauritania, 2nd floor (Tel. 43 66 00); open Mon.–Fri.: 8.30 a.m.–12 noon, 3 p.m.–6.30 p.m.

CHEMIST Place de la Liberté. Open till 10 p.m. There is an all-night chemist at rue Khalid Ben Oualid (Tel. 43 04 15).

BUS STATION Bab Doukkala (Tel. 43 39 33). Buses to the beach leave from here, but travel at a relaxed pace.

EMERGENCY TELEPHONE NO. 19

SEEING

The JAMAA EL FNA (Assembly of the Dead) is the showpiece of Marrakech and the hub of life of the city. In daytime it's a busy colourful market and at night the street artists arrive. Be particularly careful of your valuables here. The medina is particularly lively and there are various photogenic markets like the ones for musical instruments or dyed wool. The old theological school, MEDERSA BEN YOUSSEF, has some fine marble, mosaics and wood-carvings, and the pale green minaret of the KOUTOUBIA MOSQUE is Morocco's best example. The BAHIA PALACE is 19th-century and the PALACE EL BADII is 16th-century. The SAADI TOMBS contain the remains of various sultans (admission 10dh; open daily from around 9 a.m. till noon and 2.30–6 p.m. – go in the late afternoon if possible).

If it is spectacle you are after, visit during the annual National Festival of Popular Art held in the Badii palace during June. Evening shows (tickets cost about 100dh) of authentic, visual performance span the whole spectrum of Moroccan music. Also go and see the camel *souk* (traditional trading station) which takes place every Thursday. Hire mountain bikes from Lune Car, III rue de Yugoslavie (Tel. 44 77 43 or 43 43 69).

SLEEPING, EATING AND NIGHTLIFE

Head for the Dejemaa el Fna area for cheap hotels and restaurants. Hotel Farouk, 66 av. Hassan (Tel. 44 59 13) has been recently modernized and is convenient for the station. Or try CTM Hostel (Tel.

442325); they have doubles for about 95dh and singles for 80dh.

The youth hostel (Tel. 432831 or 44 47 13) is good by Moroccan standards and is 5 minutes' walk from the station. (IYHF cards are compulsory.) Located near the station on rue el Jahed, Quartier Industriel, the hostel closes 9 a.m.–2 p.m. and after 10 p.m.

The area around the station is the best place to find the cheapest hotels. This area is also abundant in French-style restaurants and also contains the majority of the city's bars. Café Restaurant Oriental at 33 rue Bah Agnaou (off the Jamaa el Fna) does good menus at reasonable prices. The Hotel de la Jeunesse at 56 Derb Sidi Banloukate (Tel. 43631) is one of the best budget hostels on this street, charging 45dh for a double room and 55dh for a triple, including cold showers. Try the Café Restaurant Marocain at place Jamaa el Fna nearby, open 8 a.m.–11 p.m. Rue Bani Marin, just off from here, houses good food venues like Mik Mak on place Foucauld which has an excellent *pâtisserie*. Make sure you sample mint tea at least once!

Meknes phone code: 5

On the line to Fez and the Algerian border, 4½ hours from Tangier, lies the imperial city of Meknes. From the station, turn left for the medina, hotels and the old town. Tourist Information is at place Administrative (Tel. 0552 44 26) and is open Mon.–Fri.: 8 a.m.–2 p.m.; Sat.: 8.30 a.m.–12 noon, 3 p.m.–6 p.m. English is spoken, and some literature is available. Another Tourist Centre can be found at Esplanade de la Foire (Tel. 0552 0191).

MANSOUR, the pavilion where the Merinid Sultan Moulay Ismail received ambassadors, is up here. There are UNDERGROUND CAVES where the Sultan's slaves were kept, which can be viewed if you ask the guards nicely. The elaborate tomb of MOULAY ISMAIL is further up on the right. The mosque in which the tomb is located is the only one in the country to admit non-Muslims. Dress appropriately so as not to cause offence.

The 19th-century DAR JAMI PALACE, at the back of place el Hedim, is now a museum which houses an excellent display of Middle Atlas carpets, particularly the bold geometric designs of the Beni Mguild tribe. The DAR EL-KEBIRA (Great Palace) was once the largest in the world. The theological school MEDERSA BOU INANIA is the elaborate building in the medina. Entry is 10dh and there is a good view from here.

SLEEPING, EATING AND NIGHTLIFE

Around place el Hedim there are quite a few cheap hotels, but if you don't fancy these the best alternative is camping. One of the best sites is Camping Agdal.

The youth hostel at bBoulevard Okba Ben Nafii (Tel. 0552 1743) is well-maintained but out of the way.

For food, rue Dar Smen and av. de Roumazine are the best ideas. Free-Time Fast Food is at 27 av. Hassan II (Tel. 52 25 62). Moroccan-style nightlife is not hard to find in Meknes.

Fez (Fes) city phone code: 05

The oldest imperial city in Morocco is today considered her cultural and intellectual centre. The huge medina here is unmatched elsewhere in North Africa. You could easily spend days in it; the colours, smells, filth and constant arguments are as endless as the memories you will keep.

TOURIST INFORMATION AND ADDRESSES

TOURIST INFORMATION Place de la Résistance, Immeuble Benani (at the end of av. Hassan II) (Tel. 62 34 60 or 62 02 97); open Mon.–Fri.: 8.30 a.m.–12 noon, 2.30 p.m.–6.30 p.m. Also at place Mohammed V (Tel. 62 47 69).

POST OFFICE av. Mohammed V (corner of av. Hassan); open Mon.–Fri.: 8.30 a.m.–12 noon, 2.30 p.m.–6.30 p.m.

BUS STATION CTM, LN, Av. Mohammed V (Tel. 62 20 41) with buses to Rabat, Casablanca, Marrakech, Meknes and Tangier. Private buses from Gare Routière in Bah Bou Jeloud.

24-HOUR CHEMIST Av. Abdelkrim El Khattabi (Tel. 62 33 80).

SEEING

Expect to get lost in Fez: the MEDINA is so sprawling and unstructured it's inevitable. There is a map to help you out, but it is not well detailed. You will inevitably be pestered by unofficial guides, but be careful. The majority of them hang out in Bah Bou Jeloud (the location of the Tourist Office), so watch out (also for pickpockets), and if you accept an offer, haggle him down to about 10dh and emphasize that you wish to go sightseeing, not shopping (he will receive a commission on any goods you buy, and you will end up paying more). Official guides are available at the hotels or Tourist Offices for 100dh per half day and are identified by their traditional costume and badge.

There are countless *souks* in the medina to look at, but only ferret out the tannery one if you've got an iron stomach: the vast vats of coloured dyes are intriguing, but the smell is not.

Before entering the medina, check out the DAR BATHA PALACE, which houses the MUSEUM OF MOROCCAN ARTS at place du Batha (Tel. 63 41 16) (open 9a.m.–12 noon and 3p.m.–6 p.m., closed Tues.; admission 10dh) and features local artisan traditions; the pottery rooms are outstanding. The medina is the site of the EL QARAOUIYIN MOSQUE, built in the ninth century and the KORANIC UNIVERSITY, which claims to be the oldest in the world, along with the theological schools of ATTARINE and BOU INANIA.

Climb uphill out of the city centre where you will still find working pit ponies. If you come at dusk, you can have a wonderful view and soak up the atmosphere as you hear the calls to prayer.

SLEEPING, EATING AND NIGHTLIFE

Round Bah Bou Jeloud you'll find a few cheap (and fairly basic) hotels with doubles for 90dh. Other cheap non-classified hotels are found in the new town, around the area of av. Mohammed V. The youth hostel on 18 rue Abdesslam Serghrini (Tel. 62 40 85) is good value and, by Fez standards, very clean and comfortable, with space on the roof if the dormitory is full. Reach it by walking 6 blocks down from the Tourist Office along boulevard Chefchaouni, turn left to the street below and look for signs. It is about 5 km from the station.

For camping, try Camping Moulay Slimane (Tel. 62 24 38) or out at Sefran (Tel. 66 00 01).

The Hotel Renaissance at 47 rue Abdelkrim el-Khattabi (Tel. 622193), near the av. Mohammed V, charges 70dh for a single room, but has no showers.

The Hôtel du Commerce in place des Alaouites in Fes-el-Jdid is very clean and charges 65dh for a single room and an extra 10dh for showers.

Bah Bou Jeloud and the medina are the cheap eating districts. The place Mohammed V also boasts plentiful eating places, but is more expensive. The youth hostel has a kitchen, so you could buy food and cook it yourself (watch the meat). Sample the local delicacy of *bisteela* (pigeon, vegetables and nuts, covered in sweet pastry).

An evening stroll in the old Jewish quarter is more rewarding than the formal entertainments you'll find. In late May, Fez hosts a Festival of World Sacred Music

Off-the-Track Places

Many of Morocco's best places are not on the railway, so buses are the only answer.

TETOUAN, 1½ hours away from Tangier (cost about 35dh), is a relatively unspoilt town with a fascinating medina – eat there and try round place Hassan II and av. Mohammed V for rooms. The Tourist Office (Tel. 96 44 07) is situated on the latter at no. 30; open Mon.–Fri.: 8 a.m.–2 p.m. and 3p.m.–6 p.m., weekends 8 a.m.–2 p.m. There is a municipal camp-site at Martil Beach (Tel. 97 94 35).

ASNI is 48 km from Marrakech and buses leave each morning from Bab Doukkala (Tel. (04) 43 39 33) and Bab Errob coach stations. It's more fun to share a taxi with several others and a full load should mean your share of the fare comes to about 15dh. This is in the RIF mountain region.

ESSAOUIRA is a Berber town on the south-west coast. If you're tired out with travelling and need a break before the long haul back home, sleep here free on the beaches and take advantage of this opportunity to share in a very un-European culture and lifestyle. Excellent windsurfing and surfing conditions. Take a leisurely walk up to the 18th-century Moorish fortress (the SKALA) at sunset. The Tourist Office is on Porte Portugaise.

AGADIR was rebuilt after an earthquake in 1960 and is now a modern beach resort populated by package holiday tourists. The Tourist Office is at 'A' Building, place du Prince Heoitier Si di Mohamed (Tel. 84 28 94 or 84 13 67) and can help you with accommodation. There is also an office at av. Mohammed V (Tel. 84 03 07). The Railway Terminus is at route des Orangers (Tel. 82 42 07) and the bus station is on blvd. Mohammed Cheikh Saadi. There is an International Campsite at blvd. Mohammed V (Tel. 84 09 21 or 84 03 74).

Way out at MESUGA you are definitely in the Sahara and can experience the mountains of sand that were the setting for *Lawrence of Arabia*.

NOTES
....

....

....

....

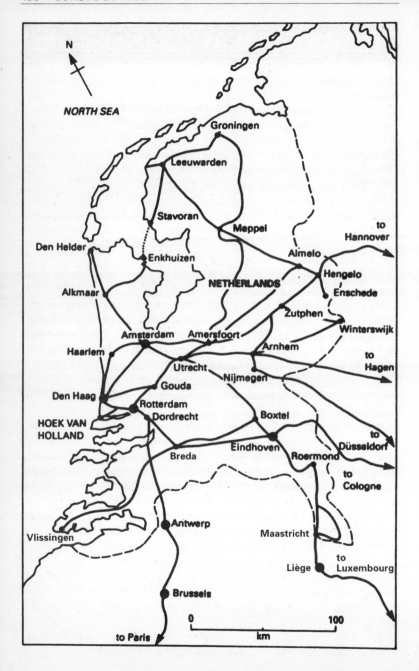

THE NETHERLANDS (Nederland)

Entry requirements	Passport
Population	15,500,000
Capital	Amsterdam is the capital; the seat of government is The Hague (pop.: 500,000)
Currency	Guilder (Florin) (NGL) £1 = approx. f2.45
Political system	Constitutional monarchy
Religion	Protestant and Roman Catholic
Language	Dutch (English widely spoken in cities)
Public holidays	1 Jan., Good Friday, Easter Monday, 30 Apr., 5, 8, 18, 19 May, 25, 26 Dec.
International dialling codes	To Netherlands: 00 (international access code) + 31 (country code) From Netherlands: 00 + country code
Eurotrain office	Schipholweg 101, NL2316XC Leiden (Tel. 071253 333)
Time	GMT +1 (+2 in summer)
Emergency telephone	112

Most of the Netherlands' major cities are concentrated in the flat, mainly Protestant west (Holland) where one has visions of windmills and clogs. But not all of the Netherlands is like this; the south is very different: the land is not as flat, and many of the people are Catholic and more like the French in many respects.

Under the Burgundians and the Habsburgs, Holland was politically linked to Belgium to form the Netherlands (lowlands). Then the Spanish rulers started to levy heavy taxes to pay for their army, fighting for the Catholic cause. The northern Netherlands had mostly become Protestant by this time, so this didn't go down too well. King Philip tried to intervene by sending in Spanish governors, but this was the last straw for the Dutch, who fought the Eighty Years' War and emerged as an independent country in 1648.

The Dutch got it together for the remainder of the 17th century and showed the rest of Europe a thing or two about seafaring and commerce. At the same time, Rembrandt *et al.* were hard at work creating the Dutch Golden Age of arts and science. The Netherlands was eclipsed by Britain in the 18th century when William III moved to England to share the throne with Mary. After the Napoleonic Wars and French domination, life gradually developed into parliamentary democracy.

The Netherlands is the ultimate civilized country in Europe, combining history with culture, making it a joy to visit.

NETHERLANDS RAILWAYS
(NEDERLANDSE SPOORWEGEN, NS)

Netherlands Railways are as trouble-free and efficient as you're likely to find anywhere in Europe. So efficient and successful are they that they hope to double the number of passengers they transport by 2005. There are frequent intercity services between all parts of the Netherlands, at least once an hour. The short distances involved mean you can see most of the country while based in a single city. Be careful not to end up on the 'stop-trains' which do just that, before connecting up to the main intercity network. Supplements are only necessary on Euro-City trains. Electric trains often consist of portions for 2 different destinations. Apart from a serious accident at Hoofd-dorp in 1992, NS has a superb safety record.

EURAIL BONUSES Free passage on ships of BV Rederij NACO between Enkhuizen and Stavoren or vice versa between 15 May and the first week in September. 30% reduction with Stena Line between Harwich and Hook of Holland.

TRAIN INFORMATION

There should be no problem with language as nearly everyone speaks English. Ask at the information desk for the *Travelling by Rail in Holland* booklet, which has a useful map with frequency times.

RESERVATIONS Because trains are so frequent it is not possible to make seat reservations, except on international services outside the Benelux countries. This must be done at a Dutch station.

NIGHT TRAVEL There are couchettes and sleepers on international routes only. There is an hourly all-night service between Utrecht, Amsterdam, The Hague and Rotterdam.

EATING ON TRAINS All intercities have the usual trolley refreshments but only Euro-City trains have restaurant cars.

SCENIC TIPS If you're fortunate enough to be travelling at any time from March to May through the bulb fields (*bollenvelden*) region (on any runs between Amsterdam and Leiden via Haarlem) the sight is astonishing.

TAXIS *Treintaxis* are available at most stations, but not in Amsterdam, The Hague or Rotterdam, as these cities are already served by comprehensive public transport systems of their own. Pay f6NGL at the station ticket office and the taxi will take you anywhere in the region covered by the station. You can also order them to come and pick you up.

BIKES Most stations hire out bikes and give reduced rates if you show your ticket. It usually costs only about f8 per day, but you must leave a deposit and return the bike to the same station. As about 20% of all Dutch bikes are stolen, be sure to lock yours up securely.

PASSES AVAILABLE For information on the Freedom Pass (Euro Domino), see p. 41.

The Inter-Rail pass has been broken down into zones, so a careful selection of zones means you do not have to pay for travel to areas you have no intention of visiting. For £159 you can tour a single zone for 22 days. The Netherlands is in Zone E, along with France, Belgium and Luxembourg. (For further details of the 8 Inter-Rail zones, refer to the Inter-Rail section in Part One of this guide.)

The Rail Rover is a 1-day pass costing f88 for second class for two persons. A Holland Rail Pass can be bought with either 3, 5 or 10 days' validity for $68, $104 and $184 respectively. Youth fares are cheaper. In addition you can buy a Public Transport Link which extends the ticket for use on all public transport, including Amsterdam and Rotterdam metros, but excluding airport buses. The price is an additional $13, $21 or $33 respectively. For more information, telephone Holland Rail in the UK on 01962 773546.

If you are travelling as a group, consider the Multi Rover ticket, which gives 2–6 passengers a day's unlimited rail travel Mon.–Fri. It costs £40 for 2 passengers and £68.50 for 6.

A Benelux Tourail Card is also available any 5 days in a month: adults £80, under 26 (junior) £54.

TOURIST INFORMATION (VVV)

The local offices can be found in every town and village in the Netherlands. They find you accommodation if required and supply you with all the information about the area. If you plan to cycle, ask for a cycle map. Unfortunately it's not always free. Cycle maps are also available from the Netherlands Board of Tourism in London (Tel. 0891 200277 premium charge line).

ISIC BONUSES Up to 50% reduction on museums. You can get into all state museums free once you've bought your museum card (f15 for those under 19, f45 for those over) from any state museum or VVV office.

MONEY MATTERS 1 guilder (NGL) (florin) (f) = 100 cents (c).

Banking hours are Mon.–Fri.: 9 a.m.–4.15 p.m.; there are also exchange offices in 35 railway stations, some of which are open in the evenings and at weekends. GWK exchange offices provide the best rates and service. Some VVV Tourist Offices also exchange money. Steer clear of 'store front' style exchange shops which charge as much as 9% commission

POST OFFICES Open Mon.–Fri.: 9 a.m.–5 p.m. and, in major towns, 9 a.m.–4 p.m. on Sat.

SHOPS In general, Mon.–Fri.: 9 a.m.–6 p.m. and on Sat.: 9 a.m.–5 p.m. Late night opening till 9 p.m. on Thu./Fri.

MUSEUMS Opening times are fairly uniform: Tues.–Sat.: 10 a.m.–5 p.m., Sun.: 1 or 2 p.m.–5 p.m. Most state museums are closed on Mon.

TIPPING Leave up to 10% if you think that you have had good service.

SLEEPING

Netherlands Reservation Centre Tel. 070 317 54 54
Ask at a VVV office for the *Youngster* brochure which lists all youth hostels and sleep-ins. No special documents are necessary on any of Holland's 2,000 or so campsites. Expect to pay up to f30 per night. For the 52 youth hostels, you have to be an IYHF member; charges vary from f20 to f40, depending on whether breakfast and an evening meal are included. Student hostels are open in summer and are fairly lax if you look like a student. Hotels are graded on a star basis with breakfast usually included in the price. Expect to pay f55 minimum for a 1-star single room.

Fortunately, the Netherlands has plenty of boarding houses and private houses, most of which are very relaxed. The local Tourist Offices keep a list and charge a small commission. Things get busy from May to August, especially in Amsterdam, so try and get along early. Expect seasonal price increases, especially in busy places.

EATING AND NIGHTLIFE

Most of the Dutch go in for a *koffietafel* (sandwich lunch and coffee) which is just as well, as evening meals have a tendency to be very high in carbohydrates. The best advice is to follow their example at lunchtime. There are over 26 types of cheese, so there's no excuse for sticking to Edam or Gouda. There are numerous regional specialities to sample; one of the best is *nieuwe haring* (salted herring), which is surprisingly tender and savoury. Eat it from the street stalls. It's at its best during the first few weeks in May and makes a welcome change from hamburgers. For your main meal, keep your eyes skinned for one of the 600 restaurants which serve the tourist menu. This is filling and cheap and is the same price everywhere, so if you like what's on it, don't waste your time looking elsewhere. If you prefer something a little more exotic, try *rijsttafel* from one of the numerous Indonesian restaurants in most cities.

In the larger cities there are plenty of nightclubs and bars, but expect to pay out quite a bit. Cinemas show films in the original language with Dutch subtitles. Prices usually start at about f25.

The Northern Netherlands

This region encompasses Friesland and Groningen. The province of North Holland includes Alkmaar, Hoorn and Amsterdam. Much of the northern Netherlands has been reclaimed from the sea and is naturally flat.

FRIESLAND is known for its lakes, its wildlife and bird sanctuaries, and is more like a separate country (with its own language and separate history). The Frisian capital, LEEUWARDEN, is not only the birthplace of the spy Mata Hari but also a birdwatchers' paradise. See the FRIES MUSEUM, OLDHOVE TOWER and PRINCESSEHOF MUSEUM OF CERAMICS.

On the other side of the Zuider Zee are ZAANDAM, the 'living museum': a reconstructed village of mills and old houses; ALKMAAR (40 minutes from Amsterdam) with its cheese market on Friday mornings from mid-April to mid-September; and HOORN, which puts on a crafts and folklore market.

Amsterdam city phone code: 020

There are 2 distinct faces to Amsterdam: the quiet graceful old town of endless canals, narrow houses and tiny winding streets and the harsh reality of 20th-century capitalist consumerism – fast food, fast sex, loud kinky music and drugs. The 2 sides live incongruously together and have made Amsterdammers famous for their tolerance of different standards and opinions. There are so many things to experience in this city that it is pretty well essential to see it during any comprehensive European tour.

TOURIST INFORMATION

The VVV Amsterdam Tourist Office is opposite the station at Stationsplein 10 and is open 9 a.m.–5 p.m. Others at Leidsestraat 106, open Mon.–Fri.: 9 a.m.–7 p.m. and Sat./Sun.: 9 a.m.–5 p.m.; Stadionplein, open Mon.–Sat.: 9 a.m.–5 p.m. and in the Central Station, open Mon.–Sat.: 8 a.m.–7.30 p.m., Sun.: 9 a.m.–4.30 p.m.

Ask for *Use It*, a student-orientated magazine on what's where and how much. *What's On in Amsterdam* lists current events. Tickets for public transport and excursions, low-priced maps and guides are also available here.

ADDRESSES

POST OFFICE Singel 250, Mon.–Fri.: 9 a.m.–6 p.m., Sat.: 10 a.m.–3 p.m.

AMEX Damrak 66 (Tel. 520 7777), Mon.–Fri.: 9 a.m.–5 p.m., Sat.: 9 a.m.–12 noon

MONEY EXCHANGE Bank at end of Nieumarkt, open 9 a.m.–5 p.m. and Thomas Cook in Stationsplein.

UK CONSULATE 44 Koningslaan (Tel. 676 4343)

US CONSULATE 19 Museumplein (Tel. 575 5309)

MEDICAL HELP Tel. 695 5638

24-HOUR CHEMIST Tel. 694 8709

GAY AND LESBIAN SERVICES COC Rozenstraat 14 (Tel. 623 4079); open Wed.–Sat.:, 1 p.m.–5 p.m. or telephone the Gay switchboard on 623 6565.

CRISIS CENTRE Tel 612 7576

NBBS Rokin 38, near Dam Square. Sells Eurotrain tickets.

POLICE 622 2222 or emergency 112

GETTING ABOUT

Telephone information 7 a.m.–midnight: 06 92 92

Information and a map of the city's buses, trams and underground are available from the GVB pavilion in front of the station. Ask for their *Tourist Guide*. Open Mon.–Fri.: 7 a.m.–7 p.m., Sat./Sun.: 8 a.m.–7 p.m. If you're going to make more than 3 journeys, invest in a 24-hour pass which costs f11.50, or if you are staying longer, the 2-day or 3-day passes are good value, costing f13.60 and f16.80 respectively. You can also buy a *Strippenkart* (a book of tickets). Try and buy your tickets at the station as buying them on the bus or tram is more expensive. To buy tickets on the bus, board from the front (otherwise always board from rear) and stamp the ticket on your first journey, since unstamped ones are invalid. Bus inspectors are extremely vigilant, especially in Amsterdam in the summer, and it is not uncommon for up to 6 inspectors to board a single vehicle at each exit. Anyone caught without a ticket is liable to a f60 on-the-spot fine plus the cost of the ticket.

The new CIRCLE TRAM (no. 20) passes the most important attractions and operates every day 9 a.m.–6 p.m. Buy a ticket for this, validate it early on in the day and it will be valid on all public transport within the city for the rest of the day. Well worth the NGL10 cost (NGL23 for 4 days) and available from VVV Offices.

STATION FACILITIES

There is a comprehensive range of facilities here at AMSTERDAM CENTRAAL STATION, which never shuts. There is a 24-hr waiting room available for passengers awaiting overnight trains.

There are daily trains to Hamburg (6 hours), Düsseldorf (2½ hours), The Hague (55 minutes), Brussels (3 hours), Paris (6 hours) and London (either via Brussels and Eurostar (6 hours) or Hook of Holland boat train). Internal trains run approximately every 15 minutes.

SEEING

The 4 main canals (Singel, Herengracht, Keizersgracht and Prinsengracht) wind their way past the main sights, and the canal boats give you the best introduction to the city. Make sure you take a museum boat; these are open-topped in fine weather and have guides as opposed to video recordings. NGL15 for a complete circular tour. Information at Stationsplein 8 (Tel. 622 2181) They may make you feel like a tourist, but they're cheap during the day. At night they can cost up to 4 times as much, due to exploitation of candlelit cruises.

HERENGRACHT passes the 17th-century merchants' houses; at MUNT on the SINGEL is a colourful flower market.

DAM SQUARE is the heart of the city. It lies at the end of the main shopping thoroughfare, the DAMRAK, which has recently been tidied up and refurbished. This area is always lively, and you can often find buskers and street artists performing. To the east of the Dam lies the old city centre, known as WALLETJES. Parts of it (Oudezijds Achterburgwal, Oude Zijds Voorburgwal and their surroundings) turn into the sex streets of Europe at night (and even during the day).

JORDAAN is another district worth a wander. This is a Bohemian working-class quarter bordered by Prinsengracht, Brouwersgracht, Marnixstraat and Elandsgracht. There's a good market at Lindemarkt, open on Fridays and Saturdays 9 a.m.–5 p.m.

Just west of the Dam is the WESTERKERK, which has a good view from its tower. Round the back is ANNE FRANK'S HOUSE where she wrote her famous diary while in hiding from the Nazis. See the Anti-Semitic Exhibition downstairs. It's at Prinsengracht 263, open Mon.–Sat.: 9 a.m.–5 p.m. and Sun.: 10 a.m.–5 p.m.; June–Aug., open till 7 p.m. Entrance NLG10.

The RIJKSMUSEUM at Stadhouderskade 42 (Tel. 673 2121, open 10 a.m.–5 p.m. every day) is one of the world's great art museums and comes top of the list of Amsterdam's 71 museums. It's big on Rembrandts and the other Dutch masters. Open daily 10 a.m.–5 p.m. Entrance f12.50 for adults.

The ROYAL PALACE on Dam Square is held up by 13,659 bits of wood; this led it to be known as the 'Eighth Wonder of the World'. Open every day 12.30 p.m.–4.45 p.m. in summer, costs NLG5. There's nothing new about the Gothic NIEUWE KERK, which dates from around 1500. Entrance costs f8. Just behind it is a 'tasting house', THE THREE BOTTLES (*De Drie Fleschjes*), which dates from 1650. Try the Bols and Hoppe liqueurs. On the subject of booze, the HEINEKEN BREWERY at Stadhouderskade 78 has daily tours at 9.30 a.m. and 11 a.m. (with extra tours June–Aug. at 1 p.m. and 2.30 p.m., Mon.–Fri. only and Sat. in July and August).

A museum card gives you unrestricted entry to most collections in the country. After visiting 5 or 6 museums it has paid for itself, and can be purchased at any museum ticket office. A similar *Culture and Leisure Pass* costs NLG30 for NLG140 worth of entry, available from VVV Offices. The favourites are the AMSTELKRING at Oude Zijds Voorburgwal 40, a preserved 17th-century house where repressed Catholics used to hide; REMBRANDT'S HOUSE at Jodenbreestraat 4–6 (admission f7.50), which contains virtually a complete collection of the artist's etchings and drawings; the STEDELIJK MUSEUM at Paulus Potterstraat 13 (admission NLG11; open daily, 11 a.m.–7 p.m.), which has a diverse modern art collection (including a lot of paintings by the Russian artist Malevich); and the VAN GOGH MUSEUM, just along the street at no. 7 (admission NLG12.50). The MARITIME MUSEUM, although a bit pricey at f12.50, is very interesting and has very few tourists. In Vondelpark a 19th-century pavilion is the home of a permanent exhibition on cinema history; the FILM MUSEUM is open Mon.–Fri.: 10 a.m.–9.30 p.m. with filmshows at 8 p.m.

The FLEA MARKET at Waterlooplein (near the Muziek-Theater, open Mon.–Sat.) is also worth a visit.

Amsterdam is also the diamond centre of the world. Information about tours of cutting rooms is available from VVV, Amsterdam Tourist Office who will supply you with the leaflet *City of Diamonds*.

The Dutch go in for cycling in a big way. You can rent a bike at several places in the city, although the most convenient is Rent-a-Bike at Pieter Jacobszdwarfsstraat 11: f7 a day, plus a deposit of about f100. You can extend this to the canals as well by hiring a canal bike from 4 moorings in the city centre. The cost is NLG18 per hour for a 2-seater, with a returnable deposit when you 'park' the bike at any of the mooring points. Open from 10 a.m. to 10 p.m. in summer and till 4 p.m. in autumn. You can also pick up bikes at Utrechtsedwarsstraat 105, Sint Nicolaasstraat 16 and Keizersgracht 181. Yellow Bike at Nieuwezijds Kolk 29 organizes bike tours throughout Amsterdam from 30 March until 31 Oct. For further details call 620 6940. Watch out for bike-thieves and people who throw bikes into the canals!

FESTIVALS In June, the HOLLAND FESTIVAL has a quality programme of dance, opera, theatre, film, art exhibitions and music, along with traditional events. Tickets are available through the Netherlands Reservation Centre (Tel. 070 317 5454) or AUB Ticket Shop at Leidseplein 26 (Tel. 621 1211) open seven days a week 10 a.m.–6 p.m. or VVV Offices.

The DRUM RHYTHM FESTIVAL in July features music from the world of rock and jazz (Tel. 070 350 2034), and in July and August the ROBECO SUMMER CONCERTS at Concertgebouw feature international vocal groups, ensembles and orchestras.

DRUGS SCENE Possession of any amount of drugs is technically a criminal offence, although in practice the police are only interested in prosecuting street pushers. If you want to partake in some 'wacky backy', stick to the coffee shops, where you can eat 'special cake' and drink 'special tea' with little fear of prosecution. Avoid hard drugs at all costs. The law is tightening up.

SLEEPING

As Amsterdam is the fourth most popular European city (after London, Paris and Rome), it's busy in summer, and hotels are often full. You'll always find a bed in one of the hostels or campsites. Be prepared for problems from hoteliers, as well as drug pushers at Amsterdam Centraal, trying to fill up their rooms out of season. It is possible to book accommodation via the Netherlands Reservation Centre in The Hague (Tel. 070 317 5454) or AUB Ticket Shop at Leidseplein 26 (Tel. 621 1211), open seven days a week 10 a.m.–6 p.m. or VVV Offices.

HOTELS Try the Frisco Inn at Beursstraat 5 (Tel. 620 1610), 5 minutes' stroll from Centraal station. Centrally located with good security. Singles, doubles and dormitory accommodation, dorms from around f35, many with private showers. Very helpful and friendly staff with a lively bar. Even if you're not staying there it's worth checking out for its daily happy hour, weekly half price night, regular live music and no curfew.

Other recommendations are (prices do not include breakfast):

La Bohème, Marnixstraat 415 (Tel. 624 2828). This has recently changed management. It is only 2 minutes' walk from Leidseplein (one of the main centres for nightlife) which is connected to the central station by several tram routes. Singles are f60, doubles f105 and triples f135, all with *en suite* facilities.

Van Ostade Bicycle Hotel, Van Ostadestraat 123 (Tel. 679 3452).

Hotel Acro, Jan Luykenstraat 44 (Tel. 662 5538). Clean, comfortable and quiet.

PRIVATE ACCOMMODATION The average is f50 per person; VVV will fix you up for a f5 fee.

HOSTELS You should find a bed in one of the following:

Arena Sleepinn, Gravesandestraat 51 (Tel. 694 7444) open all year.

Vondelpark IYHF hostel, Zandpad 5 (Tel. 683 1744). In July and August you'll need proof of membership. Around f25 in dorms. Tram 1, 2 or 5 from station to Leidseplein, then a 5-minute walk. Written reservations only.

Stadsdoelen IYHF hostel, Kloveniersburgwal 97 (Tel. 624 6832). NLG25. This is more central. Good value food served in restaurant. Take tram 4, 9, 16, 24 or 25 to Muntplein or U to Nieuwmarkt.

Hotel Kabul (Student Hostel), Warmoesstraat 42 (Tel. 623 7158). Dormitory accommodation from NLG30. Near station (and red-light district). Very noisy – the bar closes at 4 a.m. Double rooms from f92.

Flying Pig Travellers' Hostel, Nieuwendjik 100 (Tel. 420 6822). First right to the end after Victoria Hotel on Damrak. Is very convenient for the station, no curfew and free lockers but a very stingy breakfast.

There are 2 Christian hostels charging NLG25 for bed and breakfast. The Shelter is the more central at Barndesteeg 21 (Tel. 625 3230), but is in the red-light area – approach the hostel from the Damrak side rather than from Nieuwmarkt. The Eben Haezer is at Bloemstraat 179 (Tel: 627 6137) and is reached by taking tram 13 or 17 to Marnixstraat.

CAMPSITES Try the brilliantly cheap Zeeburg at Zuiderzeeweg 29

(Tel. 694 4430), which costs about NLG9 per person per night and NLG5 for a tent. It's aimed at young travellers and has regular live music. Take bus 22 or 37 from the Centraal station.

Gaasper at Loosrechtdreef 7 (Tel. 696 7326) costs NLG7 per person. Sleeping out is risky and best avoided.

EATING AND NIGHTLIFE

There's a glut of cafés and restaurants near Dam Square, round the red-light district and Leidseplein: Dutch, Chinese, Italian and Indonesian. Go for the day's menu and fill the gap with deep-fried *poffertjes* (mini-doughnuts) from street stalls. For Indonesian *rijsttafel* avoid the more expensive restaurants around Damrak and head for Binnen Bantammerstraat, south-east of Centraal station or Sukasari on Damstraat. Also try the Azie or the Ling Nam. For pastries, visit BLOM on Nieuwendijk 117–119.

A lively Irish pub is Mulligan's on the Amstel, no. 100, about 200m from Mint Square on the right. It opens at 2 p.m. and serves Guinness and Irish stew.

Vegetarian restaurants are plentiful; try Bolhoed at Prinsengracht 60–62 near Anne Frank's House, Harvest in Govert Flinkstraat 251 (which is open 5.30 p.m.–9.30 p.m. Tues. to Sat. and caters for special dietary requirements if ordered in advance), and Bent Hamazan Kosher restaurant at Anteliersstraat 57/2 (open 5 p.m.–10 p.m.).

The further out of the town centre you go, the cheaper the beer gets; Heineken costs around f8 around Rembrandtsplein, f7 in and around the red- light district and in Happy Hours only f5. There are several good street markets to buy picnic supplies from, and if you want to go out for a drink, head for Hoppe at Spui 18.

If you want to see 'sin city' and wander through the notorious red-light district of Zeedijk, go east of the Damrak to the area bordered by Warmoesstraat and Damstraat. Don't take photographs, as some of the locals don't like it and your camera may end up in a canal.

Recommendations for restaurants are: De Keuken Van 1870 at Spuistraat 4; and Egg Cream at Sint Jacobsstraat 19, open 11 a.m.–8 p.m. Also worth checking out is the Great Rijsttafel at Mandarin Rokin 26, and Haesje Claes at Voorburgwal 320. For dancing try Melkweg at Lijnbaansgracht 234a (general admission f5, closed Mon. and Tues.), or Maloe Melo at Lijnbaansgracht 60. The nicest old cafés are off Jordaan. Good for a laugh is the Café Chris at Bloemstraat 42, whose toilet can be flushed only from the bar!

For free pop concerts head for the Vondelpark (not Tues.).

There is a host of nightclubs in the city. De Kroeg at Lijnbaansgracht 16 is worth a look in, whilst Paradiso at Weteringschans 6 and Roxy at Singel 465 are two of the trendiest clubs and cost NLG10 entrance. Or try Mazzo at Rozengracht 114 or Homolulu at Kerkstraat 23 for an alternative night out.

Most cinemas are located around the Leidseplein and Rembrandtsplein areas. Try Desmet at Plantage Middenlaan 4a for art films.

Outside Amsterdam

LEIDEN This town lies half an hour south-west of Amsterdam and makes a pleasant day trip. It is where Descartes first published his *Discourses* and the university is still considered the Netherlands' finest. Tourist Information is at Stationsplein 210 (Tel. 071 514 6846).

See THE OLD TOWN, BOTANICAL MUSEUM (one of the oldest in Europe, founded in 1587), the RIJKSMUSEUM VAN OUDHEDEN (National Antiquities). Both these are on Rapenburg. To clamber up a windmill and nose about, go to the MUSEUM DE VALK (Falcon), Binnenvestgracht 1, open Tues.–Sat:. 10 a.m.–5 p.m., Sun.: 1 p.m.–5 p.m. NLG5 entrance.

Try sleeping at Hotel Witte, Witte Singel 80, and eating at Augustinus at Rapenburg 24. Check out LaBota on Herensteeg 9. The Eurotrain office is at Schipholweg 101 (Tel. 071 253 333).

The world-famous KEUKENHOF flower garden is 10 km north of Leiden (bus 54) and is open from mid-March to mid-May (costs NLG16; or NLG22 including the bus).

WASSENAAR This lies on the coast 10 km from Leiden. It houses a campsite and amusement park, whilst a nice beach lies further down at Scheveningen.

The Hague (Den Haag) city phone code: 070

As a major political centre, The Hague has more than its fair share of elegant buildings and smart people. There are 2 royal palaces, over 20 excellent museums and 2 government bodies based in Den Haag: the Dutch government located in the attractive BINNENHOF and the International Court of Justice housed in the PEACE PALACE.

STATION FACILITIES

There are 2 stations in The Hague: Hollandsspoor handles all international trains and Amsterdam trains, while Centraal station handles trains to the east (Utrecht), south (Rotterdam) and short intercity and suburban lines.

As in Amsterdam, both of these stations have everything a traveller would wish for. There is a particularly useful supermarket at Centraal station quite close to the Tourist Office.

Daily trains to Amsterdam (55 minutes), Rotterdam (30 minutes), Antwerp (1½ hours), Brussels (2½ hours), Paris (6 hours) and Cologne (3½ hours).

Tram 12 connects the 2 stations – or take a train!

TOURIST INFORMATION

The Tourist Office is outside Centraal station at Koningin Julianaplein 30 (turn right) (oOpen Mon.–Sat.: 9 a.m–5.30 p.m. Tel. 6-340 35051). There is another office situated at Gevers Deynootweg 1134, Scheveningen, which is open Mon.–Sat.: 9 a.m.–5.30 p.m. (till 8 p.m. in high season). Pick up the city map and guide (NLG3.50).

ADDRESSES

POST OFFICE Kerkplein; open Mon.–Fri.: 8.30 a.m.–6.30 p.m., Thurs.: till 8.30 p.m., Sat.: 9 a.m.–4 p.m.
UK EMBASSY Lange Voorhout 10 (Tel. 364 5800)
US EMBASSY Lange Voorhort (Tel. 310 9209)
CANADIAN EMBASSY Sophialaan 7 (Tel. 361 4111)
AUSTRALIAN EMBASSY Carnegielaan 4 (Tel. 310 8200)
MEDICAL HELP Tel. 346 9669 (night)
NBBS EUROTRAIN Schoolstraat 24 (Tel. 346 5819)
POLICE Tel. 310 3274

SEEING

The BINNENHOF – the Dutch Westminster – is a complex of buildings with the RIDDERZAAL, or Knight's Hall, at its centre. This is open Mon.–Sat.: 10 a.m.–4 p.m., admission f5.50. On Thursdays the imposing Lange Voorhout turns into an open-air antique market.

Other attractions are the MAURITSHUIS GALLERY, Korle Vijverberg 8, with its superb collection of Dutch art, including 16 Rembrandts, open Tues.–Sat.: 10 a.m.–5 p.m., Sun.: 11 a.m.–5 p.m., admission f10; the GEMEENTE MUSEUM (Hague Municipal Museum), Stadhouderslaan 41, which houses a collection of musical instruments and Mondrian's major works, open Tues.–Sun.: 11 a.m.–5 p.m., admission f7; and the GEVANGENPOORT (Prison Gate) MUSEUM, Buitenhof 33, a morbid torture chamber stuffed with medieval instruments to set your nerves on edge, open Mon.–Fri.: 10 a.m.–5 p.m., Sun.: 1 p.m.–5 p.m. admission f5.

Another interesting find is the PUPPET MUSEUM at Nassau Dillen-burgstraat 8, which houses puppets collected from all over the world from the last 200 years. Admission is only f1 on Sun. between 12 noon and 2 p.m. A performance is given for adults on Fri. evenings. The MESDAG PANORAMA is a popular place to visit, with one of the world's largest circular paintings. Open Mon.–Sat: 10 a.m.–5 p.m. Sun.: 12 noon–5 p.m. At Zeestraat 65, entrance f5.

One of the main attractions is the miniature city at MADURODAM, open Apr.–Sept.: 9 a.m.–10 p.m. Tram 1 or 9, or bus 22 will take you out to Holland's Disneyland. It's expensive (f19.50). Built to a 1/25th scale, it has everything from trains to houses and street lamps – and everything works.

The Hague is Holland's 'greenest city', there are plenty of picnic places to be had. Try the HAAGSE BOS, WESTBROEKPARK or CLINGENDAEL PARK. The latter plays host to a Japanese Garden, entrance is by Wasse-naarseweg and is open mid-May–mid-June. A no. 18 bus will take you there from the station.

If you fancy beach-bumming it, SCHEVENINGEN is your nearest place (it's also good to sleep out in).

Ten minutes from The Hague is the town of DELFT, famous for its pottery. You can see it being made at the Porceleyne Fles, Rotter-damseweg 196.

Bicycles can be rented at various venues, though most outlets will want f100 deposit. The Garage du Nord at Keijerstraat 27, Scheveningen (Tel. 355 4060) charges f10 a day and wants an iden-tity card as deposit.

SLEEPING

Hotels aren't cheap, so try the alternatives. Try Hotel Hage (Tel. 351 4696), with doubles at 90f.

For camping try Ockenburgh at Wijndaelerweg 25 (Tel. 325 2364) near the beach (tram 3 from Centraal station).

The youth hostel at Monsterseweg 4 (Tel. 397 0011) is very good and costs about NLG25. Take ZWN buses 122 or 123 from the station to Ockenbergh YH.

Try the Marion Hostel at Havenkade 3 (Tel. 354 3501); rooms NLG30–50.

EATING AND NIGHTLIFE
SCHEVENINGEN is lively at night and your best bet for cheap eats and bars, or try the streets of Denneweg. For groceries, try the market at Markthof, near Binnenhof, or the V&D supermarket on Grote Markt Straat. The city has plenty of the usual fast-food outlets like McDonald's and Burger King, but far more filling is the inexpensive Italian fare served at Broodjeszaak Panini at Gortstraat 16. For vegetarians, try De Dageraad at Hooikade 4. 'T Goude Hooft at Groenmarkt 13 has an old Dutch interior and does 3-course meals cheaply.

In mid-July The Hague plays host to the North Sea Jazz Festival. Swinging Scheveningen takes place from mid to late July and involves street parades and music.

Rotterdam phone code: 10

The largest port in Europe, Rotterdam is Holland's second city after Amsterdam and, were it not for a Nazi air raid in 1940, would still be her architectural rival. The rebuilt Rotterdam is an attractive, modern city, best seen from the 180m Euromast.

TOURIST INFORMATION AND ADDRESSES
MAIN TOURIST OFFICE VVV, Coolsingel 67, on the corner of Stadhuisplein (Tel. 4023 200). Open Mon.–Sat.: 9 a.m.–7 p.m., Sun.: 10 a.m.–5 p.m.
DOCTOR AND 24-HOUR CHEMIST Tel. 4362244

SEEING
You can tour round the massive port by boat for f12, or wander round some of its 48 km on foot. The BOYMANS VAN BEUNINGEN MUSEUM on Mathenesserlaan (entry f6) is a superb modern art museum, and the SCHIEL ANDSHUIS MUSEUM at Korte Hoogstraat 31 has an exhibition on the Blitz (admission f6). The MARITIME MUSEUM at Leuvehaven is also worth a look (entry f6).

One part of Rotterdam which wasn't wiped out was DELFSHAVEN, from where the Pilgrim Fathers left in 1620 for America. In Delfshaven they are restoring the 110 buildings left and turning the area into a craft centre.

Rotterdam's youth hostel is at Rochussenstraat 107–9 (Tel. 436 5763); take tram 4 to Saftleuenstraat or Uto, B&B around NLG27.50. For camping, try Kanaalweg 84 (Tel. 415 9772), bus 33, NLG10.

A good hotel near the station is the Bagatelle (Tel. 467 6348) Provenierssingel 26. Leave Centraal station by the rear exit, turn right, and it is about 5 minutes' walk. Prices range from f39 for singles to f68 for doubles. From mid-June to mid-August check out the Sleep-inn at Mauritsweg 29b (Tel. 414 3256).

Across the square from the main station exit is a large food plaza selling groceries and meals at good prices. Stock up here! If you are staying in Rotterdam, try Ristorante Michelangelo (main square) for a good night out.

EXCURSIONS Not far from Rotterdam is the only remaining area with lots of windmills: KINDERDIJK. Go on Saturday afternoons in July and August to see all 19 at work.

The cheese town of GOUDA is 25 minutes by train from Rotterdam. See its colourful cheese and old craft market in the central market on Thursday mornings (10 a.m.–12 p.m.) late June–mid-August.

Southern, Central and Eastern Netherlands

The southern part of the Netherlands, bordered by Belgium, has as its main stopping-off places the beautiful historic town of BREDA and the reconstructed medieval town of MIDDELBURG, with its miniature town on a 1/20th scale, 'Walcheren'.

LIMBURG, the south-eastern province between Germany and Belgium, boasts MAASTRICHT with its 9 castles, 193 km network of man-made tunnels and site of historic EU Treaty. Sadly, this town has gained a reputation as a drugs mecca and many addicts hang around the station. If coming from Belgium, take care not to get off the train too soon at the first of Maastricht's stations.

UTRECHT has a medieval city centre and a 13th-century cathedral, but also the largest shopping mall in the country, Hoogcatharijne. There's a railway museum in the old station here, housing steam locomotives. See also the MUSIC BOX MUSEUM and the RELIGIOUS HISTORY MUSEUM in Het Catharine convent.

ARNHEM suffered great damage in 1944 (as seen in *A Bridge Too Far*), but the 12th-century DOORWERTH CASTLE outside the town has survived. The main reason to stay in Arnhem is for its proximity to the HOGE VELUWE NATIONAL PARK, an isolated wilderness (open daily 8 a.m.–sunset; f7.50 admission includes entry into open-air museum) only an hour from the bustle of Amsterdam. Also worth visiting is the KROLLER-MULLER MUSEUM, which has 278 Van Gogh works as well as some by Picasso. Open Tues.–Sat.: 10 a.m.–4.30 p.m.: free admission for those visiting the Hoge Veluwe Park.

Haarlem phone code: 023

Fifteen minutes west of Amsterdam is Haarlem, one of Holland's most historic and well-preserved towns, and the nearby resort of Zandvoort. Pick up a copy of *Zandvoort Haarlem*, a multi-lingual guide to the city, at the Tourist Office at Stationsplein 1 (Tel. 531 9059 or 571 2262).

SEEING
The GROTE MARKET is the historic centre where the RENAISSANCE MEAT MARKET, ST BAVO'S CATHEDRAL, which houses the grave of Frans Hals, and the TOWN HALL are located.

See also the FRANS HALS MUSEUM at GrootHeiligland 62, which displays not only a fine collection of the painter's own work, but also that of other Dutch and Flemish masters, and a comprehensive modern art collection. The museum is open Mon.–Sat.: 11 a.m.–5 p.m., Sun.: 1 p.m.–5 p.m.

The TYLERS MUSEUM at 16 Spaarne is the oldest museum in the country, with a collection of drawings by Michelangelo and Raphael, open Tues.–Sat.: 10 a.m.–5 p.m., Sun.: 1 p.m.–5 p.m., and the CORRIE TEN BOOM MUSEUM, at 19 Barteljorisstraat, which is devoted to the life and works of a family who in the Second World War saved the lives of many people in hiding from the Nazis. It is open Mon.–Sat.: 10 a.m.–4.30 p.m.

SLEEPING AND EATING
The youth hostel (*Jeugdherberg*) is at Jan Gijzenpad 3 (Tel. 537 3793). To get there, take bus 2 from the station; it's a 10-minute journey. Open Mar.–Oct.; around f22 per bed.

The nearest camping site is De Liede at Liewegje 17 (Tel. 332360). It is open all year round and provides excellent facilities: a canteen, showers and laundry for f4.50. The VVV can put you up in a private home if you do not have any success here.

The fast-food freak can find haven at McDonald's in Grote Houtstraat 75, whilst the vegetarian is well catered for at the Eko Eel Café in Zijlstraat 39 which is open until 9.30 p.m. For cheap meals try the Italian Piccolo Restaurant at Rivier Vismarkt 1 and the Chinese restaurant New China at Prinses Beatrixplein 5, both open until 10 p.m.

ZANDVOORT The town has miles of sandy beaches and dunes, and was awarded the coveted Blue Flag by the European Environmental Organization for its safe and hygienic beaches and clean water. Zandvoort has its own VVV at Schoolplein 1 (Tel. 571 7947). For accommodation ask at the Tourist Office.

NOTES

NORWAY (Norge)

Entry requirements	Passport
Population	4,200,000
Capital	Oslo (pop.: 465,000)
Currency	Krone
	1 = approx. 9.75kr
Political system	Constitutional monarchy
Religion	Lutheran
Language	Norwegian (English widely spoken)
Public holidays	1 Jan.; 4, 8, 9, 11, 12 April; 1, 17, 20, 30 May; 30 June; 25, 26 Dec.
International dialling codes	To Norway: intl code 47 number
	From Norway: 095 + country code number

Norway has the lowest population density in Europe – even her cities are small by Western standards (Bergen 213,000, Stavanger 87,500) – a fact which is not surprising when one realizes that about a quarter of Norway's land is above the Arctic Circle. Don't listen to the preconceptions – it doesn't always rain here. But it is one of Europe's most spectacular countries: 80% of the land is taken up by forests and mountains. The Sognefjord, one of Norway's best-known fjords, runs for over 160 km inland with 1,200m walls in places. It was from fjords like this that Harald Fairhair's longboats sailed westward, after his unification of Norway in 885, a process which continued until the death of Harald Hardrada, at Stamford Bridge in 1066, while trying to conquer England. During the medieval period, the plague knocked off most of the Norwegian population and left the German Hansa merchants in control of the country's trade. This was followed by 400 years of Danish rule, to be succeeded by rule by Sweden after the Napoleonic Wars. Independence came in 1905 when Haakon VII was elected king, succeeded by his son Olav (1957–91), whose heir was his son Harold.

Today, Norway has one of the highest standards of living in Europe, thanks to cheap hydro-electric power and the discovery of oil. Politically, they are always prepared to explain their opinion, especially, it seems, over their tradition of whale hunting, which makes the headlines periodically. Norway's well worth the inconvenience of getting there – even if you can only afford a quick train through.

NORWEGIAN STATE RAILWAYS
(NORGES STATSBANER, NSB)

The Norwegians have one of the cleanest and most efficient railway systems in Europe and even though a majority of the trains are pretty slow, they pass through some of the most spectacular scenery. There are no supplements in Norway so Inter-Rails are valid on all trains. The fastest and most comfortable trains are the *Ekspresstog* (Et, expresses). They run between all the major cities and stop only at main stations, while the *Regionaltog* (Rt, IC) run to and from Oslo and the towns in the surrounding area, and the local trains (Lt) stop at every station. High-speed trains (ICE) run to Göteborg and Skien – supplements are payable.

NSB have an office in London at 21–24 Cockspur Street, SW1 (Tel. 0171 930 6666). They are also agents for Swedish railways.

PASSES AVAILABLE The Inter-Rail pass has been broken down into zones, so that a careful selection of zones means you do not have to pay for travel to areas you have no intention of visiting. For £159 you can tour a single zone for 22 days. Norway is in Zone B, along with Sweden and Finland. (For further details of the 8 Inter-Rail zones, refer to the Inter-Rail section in Part One of this guide.)

For information on the Freedom Pass (Euro Domino), see p. 41.

The ScanRail pass is valid for travel by train (and a few ferries) in Norway, Denmark, Sweden and Finland. Available in North America (Rail Europe Inc.), Australia (Bentours), Singapore, New Zealand, Hong Kong and UK (NSR Travel). The different types of ticket are as follows:

ONE MONTH

Class	2nd
Adult	£260
Youth (12–25 years)	£195

21 DAYS

Class	2nd
Adult	£198
Youth (12–25 years)	£149

ScanRail Flexi tickets are available at the following prices:

	5 days within 15 days	10 days within 1 month
Class	2nd	2nd
Adult	£132	£180
Youth (12–25 years)	£99	£135

INTER-RAIL BONUSES

Hirtshals–Kristiansand	50%
Narvik–Frederikshavn	50%
Flåm–Bergen and other services by Eexpress steamers and	50%
Fjord steamers run by Fylkesbaatane i Sogn og Fjordane	
Buses in north Norway (Nordland, Tromsø and Finnmark)	50%

EURAIL BONUSES

Hirtshals–Kristiansand	30%
Flåm–Bergen and other services by Eexpress steamers and	
Fjord steamers run by Fylkesbaatane i Sogn og Fjordane	50%

SCANRAIL AND SCANRAIL FLEXI PRINCIPAL BONUSES

Free travel on NSB Trondheim–Storlien v.v. bus service	
Flåm–Bergen and other services by Express steamers and	50%
Fjord steamers run by Fylkesbaatane i Sogn og Fjordane	
Moss/Oslo–Frederikshavn (Stena)	50%
Kristiansvand–Hirtshals (Color Line)	50%
Oslo–Copenhagen (DFDS)	50%
Narvik–Frederikshavn (Narvik Line)	50%
Bodø–Fauske–Narvik–Tromsø–Alta–Kirkenes (Finnmark	
Fylkesrederi og Ruteselskab)	
Narvik/Fauske–Sortland–Solvaer (Nordtraffik)	50%
Stavanger–Bergen (Flaggruten)	25%
Boat runs in the Hardangerfjord (Snoggbatane)	25%
Malmö–Copenhagen (DSO Hydrofoil)	25%

TRAIN INFORMATION

No problems here as everyone speaks good English. NSB also publish an excellent free series of leaflets giving maps and descriptions of their main tourist routes.

RESERVATIONS Domestic reservations (25kr) are compulsory on all major routes, so check first. They should be made in advance. You may get a discount for more than 1 domestic reservation at a time. If you're travelling to Copenhagen, you're advised to reserve 36 hours in advance and 48 hours at weekends. International seat reservations cost 20kr. Reserved seats are not always marked, so don't be surprised if you get moved on, just when you thought it was safe to get comfortable. On the other hand, don't be too surprised to find someone already sitting in a seat you have reserved in advance. Be polite, and remember: if you reserved the seat, you have the right to it.

NIGHT TRAVEL Second-class sleepers with 3 berths costs about 100kr; with 2 berths 265kr. Prices are per person. Standards are high – video and snacks are available – and 100kr buys you an excellent hearty breakfast.

EATING ON TRAINS Expresses between Oslo and Bergen have dining cars, and if you have a lot of money to blow the food is excellent, as is the scenery. All other express trains have buffets which serve hot meals as well as snacks, while *Regionaltogs* have a trolley service.

SCENIC TIPS There are more scenic routes in Norway than anywhere else in Scandinavia, and possibly even Europe. The jewel of them all is the Bergen–Oslo run. Two other excellent ones are Flåm–Sognefjord and Dombås–Åndalsnes. Be sure to get hold of the free NSB leaflets which give good descriptions of the various lines.

TOURIST INFORMATION

There's a Tourist Office (*turistinformason*) at every major town and in most villages in Norway. They help to find accommodation if necessary and have a good supply of local information leaflets. Extended hours always operate from the beginning of June to end Aug. Norway's one of the most health-conscious of all European countries, and at weekends you'll find, depending on the season, the ski slopes, forest tracks and waterways well used by the 'great outdoors' fanatics. For detailed information on hiking and mountaineering, contact DNT, Stortingsgata 28, PO Box 1963 Vika, 01 25 Oslo.

ISIC BONUSES 50% discounts on museums, theatres and some coastal steamers. Also 30% reductions on some bus services. For further information, contact UR Universitetssentret, Blindern, Oslo (Tel. 2246 6880).

MONEY MATTERS 1 Norwegian krone (kr) = 100 øre.
   Banking hours are Mon.–Fri.: 8.30 a.m.–3 p.m. (3.30 p.m. in winter). Some stay open till 5 p.m. on Thurs.

POST OFFICES AND SHOPS Mon.–Fri.: 8/9 a.m.–4/5 p.m., late-night opening Thurs. till 7 p.m.; closed Sat. p.m.

MUSEUMS Vary throughout Norway, but the general pattern is 10 a.m. opening and early closing at 3 p.m. or 4 p.m.

EATING AND NIGHTLIFE

Norway is one country you're bound to lose weight in; it's not that the food is bad, or that you'll be press-ganged into spending all day out hiking in the fjords – it's just that food is so expensive here that you'll rarely be able to afford the luxury of a full stomach. This is the problem in Norway; it's quite easy to spend 200kr a day just feeding yourself with average-quality meals. (That said, it is now much on a par with places like Venice or Florence, and at least the quality is excellent here.) Avoid expensive meat dishes and turn instead to fish, and try and copy the locals: eat a full breakfast of *smørbrødbord* (a huge open sandwich, heaped with a variety of garnishes), have a snack at lunch (bought from a market/shop) and aim for a *koldtbord* (cold table) meal in the evening, where you can eat as much as you like, or a fixed-price menu. If you're planning on self-catering a lot in Norway (and you should), bring some basic supplies with you from home. Vegetarians are in for a hard time, but for vegans the problem is even greater: when Norwegians are not consuming meat and fish, they are attacking the fantastic selection of dairy products on offer.

The Norwegians have a reputation for being quite a serious lot, and to an extent that's fair comment – though catch them after a few drinks at night and you'd never believe it. They're very culture-conscious, and much effort is made to preserve the folk songs and dances of their forebears – the displays of these you may encounter are not put on purely as commercial stunts for the tourists.

TIPPING

Leave up to 10% if you feel the service has been good, but not if it has already been included in the bill.

SLEEPING

Norwegian law allows you to camp for free anywhere you want for 2 nights, provided you keep 150m from all buildings and fences, and do not litter or vandalize the area. If you are camping while you are in this country, remember to bring your own supply of camping gas since it is not freely available in Norway. There are hundreds of official sites, most of which are listed by the Norges Automobil-Forbund (NAF) (Tel. 2234 1400) whose Oslo office is at Storgaten.

Check out Den Norske Turistforening (DNT, the Norwegian Mountain Touring Association) for unusual accommodation. They sell maps and keep many attractive mountain huts (*hytter*) all over the country. Expect to pay about 40–125kr per night, with a 45kr surcharge to non-members. Huts are open from the end of June to the beginning of September. The best place to contact them is at

Roald Amundsengate 28 in Oslo.

There are just under 90 youth hostels in the country and standards vary, as do prices (75–150kr). Only a few are open all of the year round. It is strongly advised that you ring ahead to reserve a hostel bed, as demand is high.

Alternatively, try booking a private room through the Tourist Office; it is reasonable to pay from 150kr for a single to 200kr for a double room. There is a surcharge for non-members.

Those looking for some real luxury and who have a little more money can buy a Scandinavian BonusPass for £17. This entitles you to a 15–50% discount off room rates (including a very good break-fast) in, usually, 3/4-star hotels. Even with the reduction, it will be expensive, but it may be that you have more funds available than the average traveller and want to see Scandinavia in some style! Ring NSR Travel on 0171 930 6666 for details.

Southern Norway

If you've arrived in Norway at Stavanger, it'll take you about 8 hours to get to Oslo by train or around 7 to Bergen by ferry.

Stavanger

Norway's fourth largest city, and the hub of North Sea oil explo-ration, Stavanger has some interesting sights to see. The information office (Tel. 5189 6200) is in the central Kulturhus, Soluberggate 2 (open Mon.–Fri.: 9 a.m.–5 p.m., Sat. 9 a.m.–2 p.m.).

The cobbled streets of the GAMLE STAVANGER (Old Stavanger) are lined with gas lamps and the whole area is full of 18th-century wooden houses said to be the best preserved in Europe. The medieval cathedral, STAVANGER DOMKIRKE, is located in the colourful MARKETPLACE, which will give you a feel for what Norway was once like. At the inner harbour, see the FISH MARKET and pick up a free Stavanger Card from the nearby information kiosk (open in summer only) which is good for 50% off museums and city buses. Both the MARITIME and CANNING MUSEUMS (open daily, 11 a.m.–3 p.m.) are worth a look if you're into boats or fishing.

For a cheap tour of Stavanger, take yellow bus no. 10 on its circu-lar route round the city. Make sure to get off at Gosen and climb the

ULLANDHAUG TOWER for a good view of the city (free).

PULPIT ROCK is a 600m cliff rising above the Lyse Fjord. Skip the sightseeing boats and take the cheaper local ferry to Lysebotn. During the summer you can hike up the backside of the cliff in about 2 hours. Take the ferry to Tau, where a connecting bus will drop you at the trail. If you want to spend the night here, the Mosvangen youth hostel (Tel. 5187 2900) and Mosvangen Camping are both about 3 km south of town, or you can catch the indispensable no. 97 or 130 bus from Musegate behind the train station. The cheapest place in town is the YMCA hostel (Tel. 5153 2888), open July and the first week of August.

For eating, try the youth hostel, which offers 3 meals a day, the Thai restaurant on Nedre Strandgate near the harbour, which does cheap lunches, or fill up on a pizza buffet at the Dickens pub on the harbour.

Kristiansand

Located between Oslo and Stavanger is Kristiansand. The surrounding countryside is beautiful and there are some good beaches nearby too. There are ferries to Hirtshals in Denmark and this is the only glimpse of Norway many ferry passengers will get.

CHRISTIANSHOLM FORTRESS dates back to the 17th century and offers a great view of the sea. On your way back to the train station, take in the TOWN SQUARE and CATHEDRAL. About a 20-minute walk north of the station is the massive RAVNEDALEN PARK and there is a ZOO to the northeast of town.

The Tourist Office is at Kapt Bodtkersgata 19 (Tel. 3802 6065). The youth hostel (Tel. 3802 8310) is on Badminton Senteret (open only in summer) and a campsite near the beach is about 3 km east of town.

Oslo

On Norway's south-eastern coast at the head of a 97 km fjord lies Oslo, the oldest of the Scandinavian capitals. Outside the city limits are acres of forests, hills and unspoilt countryside which the Osloites use at every opportunity to pursue their many outdoor activities. The town itself has no distinctive style and you have to look below the surface for its real attractions: the museums and parks.

STATION FACILITIES

There is a full range of station facilities at Oslo (Central). Luggage may be left free at the Inter-Rail Centre, otherwise you can use the 24-hour storage lockers for 10–20kr. The centre is open 7 a.m.–11 p.m. mid-June until August. It also offers showers, telephones and information, including maps. All eurorailers welcome.

TOURIST INFORMATION

Pick up maps, guides and what's on information from the Tourist Office in the Central station. (Tel. 2283 0050). They are extremely helpful and will give you maps, the *Oslo Guide*, *Oslo This Week* and ferry and bus timetables.

ADDRESSES

POST OFFICE Dronningensgate 15; open Mon.–Fri.: 8 a.m.–5 p.m., Sat.: 9 a.m.–1 p.m.

AMEX c/o Winge Travel, Karl Johansgate 33 (Tel. 2286 1334), open Mon.–Fri.: 8.30 a.m.–5 p.m., Sat.: 8.30 a.m.–1 p.m. No traveller's cheques exchange, but there is an Amex money dispenser outside.

STUDENT TRAVEL AND NORWEGIAN YOUTH HOSTEL ASSOCIATION Terra Nova Travel, Dronningensgate 26 (Tel. 2242 1410), open Mon.–Fri.: 8.15 a.m.–3.15 p.m.

USE IT Mollergate 3 (Tel. 2241 5132), is now open all year round and offers information on student activities.

DEN NORSKE TURISTFORENING (NORWEGIAN MOUNTAIN TOURING ASSOCIATION) Stortingsgaten 28 (Tel. 2283 2550). If you've come to Norway to climb or camp, call in for leaflets on mountain huts, etc. Open weekdays: 10 a.m.–4 p.m., Thurs. till 6 p.m.

UK EMBASSY Thomas Heftyesgate 8 (Tel. 2255 2400)

US EMBASSY Drammensveien 18 (Tel. 2244 8550)

CANADIAN EMBASSY Oscarsgate 20 (Tel. 2246 6955)

AUSTRALIAN GOVERNMENT INFORMATION OFFICE Contact Canadian embassy.

24-HOUR CHEMIST Jernbanstorget Apotek, opposite Central station.

GETTING ABOUT

City transport includes buses, trams, undergrounds, ferries and local trains (free on Inter-Rail). Pick up the transit map at the station or Tourist Information. The Oslo Card (120kr for 1 day, 190kr for 2 and 240kr for 3) is good value and gives free transport and entry to most of the sights; a student card gets reductions on most things too.

SEEING

The RÅDHUS (town hall) is down by the harbour. This *avant-garde* 1950s structure was decorated by contemporary Norwegian artists and can be visited free. From the Rådhus Gate you can enter AKERSHUS CASTLE, built by King Haakon V around 1300, then rebuilt in Renaissance style by Christian IV. It's open weekdays 10 a.m.–4 p.m. (May–Sept.); and in the grounds of the castle is the NORWEGIAN RESISTANCE MUSEUM describing the Nazi occupation of Norway. The ferry from the Rådhus over to the peninsula of BYGDØY takes you to 5 very interesting places:

1. The incredible NORSK FOLKEMUSEUM, with 150 wooden buildings filled with material artefacts recreating Norway's past. These include Ibsen's study, houses from Lapland and museums of domestic furniture, clothes and implements.
2. THE VIKING SHIP HOUSE: 3 preserved Viking longboats from AD 800–900.
3. KON-TIKI MUSEUM, showing the balsa-wood rafts used by the explorer Thor Heyerdahl on his voyages.
4. THE NORWEGIAN MARITIME MUSEUM.
5. THE FRÅM MUSEUM: the ship used in the polar expeditions of the 19th and early 20th centuries.

All these museums are within walking distance of one another. Opening times vary.

The VIGELAND SCULPTURE PARK and VIGELAND MUSEUM (admission free) show the work and the background of the Norwegian artist Gustav Vigeland. This park is one of Norway's finest and 1,750 sculptures dotted round it have been termed everything from 'obscene' to 'serene'. To get there take the 20 bus from National Theatret.

The other famous Norwegian artist, EDVARD MUNCH, has his MUSEUM in the east of the city at Tøyengata 53. It's a particularly fine gallery, housing literally thousands of his Expressionist works. Both these museums tend to close on Mon., except in high season, but for more time-efficient sightseeing, note that these museums both stay open until 6 p.m. for the rest of the week. Check first with Tourist Information.

The NATIONAL GALLERY is at Universitetsgata 13 and has Norway's principal art collection.

EXCURSIONS Skiers should find the world's oldest SKI MUSEUM interesting. It's located inside the take-off point of the huge Holmenkollen ski jump. Exhibits here trace the history of the sport and produce evidence that it dates as far back as about 500 B C. Take the Holmenkollen railway from its underground station and walk about 10 minutes from the station.

EKEBERG PARK gives a great view over Oslo from its hills, where Stone Age carvings from 1000 BC have been found.

SLEEPING

Oslo's not easy on eurorailers. Forget hotels completely and concentrate on the few hostels and campsites, or settle for private accommodation. You can get a room in a private house for 150kr single, 250kr double, and you must stay at least 2 nights. The accommodation centre at Oslo 5 (Tel. 2241 6221) is open 8 a.m.–11 p.m. and can provide lists of accommodation; there is a 20kr booking fee per person.

HOSTELS Both youth hostels are very good, clean, efficient, and with plenty of facilities, but they could hardly be called central. Haraldsheim is at Haraldsheimveien 4 (Tel. 2222 2965). It charges average prices. Reservations cost 13kr and are recommended. It's open all year and is at the bottom of the hill from Sinsen tram terminus (trams 10 or 11). Price is 145kr, including breakfast, per night. The other Oslo youth hostel is at Sognsvn 218 (Tel. 2223 7640) and costs 148kr including breakfast for members. It is open from the beginning of June to late August. Take the underground to Kringsja station.

The Seamen's Hostel, *Oslo Sjømannshjemmet*, Fred Olsengate 2 (Tel. 2271 2005), has fair rooms. Reception is open 24 hours.

The cheapest place in town is to be found at KFUM in Mollergate (Tel. 0272 1066). For 80kr a night, in July and August, it provides sleeping accommodation and kitchen facilities. Reception is open 7.30 a.m.–11 a.m. and 5 p.m.–12 midnight, though it is advisable to book in advance.

If you don't mind an institutional atmosphere, Holtekilen Summer Hotel at Micheletsvei 55 (Tel. 6753 3853) is good value. You can choose between the 10-bed classroom accommodation (it's a school except in summer) or, if you're keen to escape the classroom, the hotel side does doubles for a bit more.

Head 50 minutes up the line to Moss for a YH sleep-in for around 80kr.

CAMPING The campsites are Bogstad Camping at Ankerveien 117 (Tel. 2250 7680) (bus 41) and the Ekeberg site at Ekebergveien 65 (Tel. 2219 8568) which is more central but only open late June to late August (bus 24 from in front of Central station). Showers are hot and free, but shared with the adjacent football pitches.

The cheapest camping you will find in Oslo is around 65kr per tent, although you are allowed to camp free in any of the wooded areas north of the city provided you stay away from public areas.

EATING AND NIGHTLIFE

Here more than anywhere else in Europe, youll find prices sky-high. Don't attempt restaurants or stopping off for a coffee and cake. Eat like the Norwegians: a hearty breakfast and big dinner and expect to average 100kr for a full meal. There are fast-food chains – Wimpy and Kaffistovas – which can help eke out the finances, and Kveldsmat on Universitetsgata, off Karl Johansgate, is cheap. Vegetarians should venture to Vegeta Vertshus at Munkedamsveien 3b, which has a self-service buffet. Small main meals cost about 60kr but go for the 98kr meals which include dessert, a drink and coffee.

For entertainment listings, check out *Natt & Dag*, available free from cafés, bars and shops.

Central Norway: The Sognefjord

The rail run from Oslo to Bergen is one you should go out of your way to take. The scenery is incredible and during the course of this 6-hour journey, youll pass through fjords, glaciers, tundra, mountains, lakes, plateaux and gorges. Should you choose to break this journey and savour its delights slowly, stop off at MYRDAL and take the other line for the 19 km and 900m journey down to FÅLM. Please note that a charge of 50kr is now payable on board the train by all travellers with any form of rail pass.

Should you decide to stay at Flåm, the Solhammer Pension, across the river from the station, is reasonable, and there's camping next door (Tel. 5763 2121) (though if you don't camp independently here, you never will). The campsite has good facilities, but showers are extra. Expect to pay around 60kr per tent. The Tourist Office in Flåm is right next to the train station (Tel. 5763 2106) and is open from June to mid-August 8.15a.m.–8.30 p.m.

From Flåm you can tackle the fjords. A favourite trip of mine (and it won't take you out of your way from Bergen) is to take the ferry from Flåm to GUDVANGEN. This 2-hour trip takes you past the spectacular scenery of the Nørøyfjord and calls at some isolated settlements *en route* whose sole means of communication is the ferry. From Gudvangen take the bus to Voss, where you're back on the Bergen line again.

Another trip worth taking is from Flåm to Voss, which is 70 minutes east of Bergen on the Oslo rail line. It costs around 80kr with Inter-Rail and includes bus and ferry connections. There is a commentary in English on both the train section (from Flåm to Myrdal) and the ferry. The bus ride is particularly spectacular as you cross the roof of Norway via the steep road and many hairpin bends. If you stop off in voss there is a very good folk museum including a restored farm which dates back to the 17th century. The Tourist Office can be found in Tinghose (Tel. 5651 0051), about 5 minutes from the station. For the youth hostel, turn right at the station and walk along the lakeside (Tel. 5651 2017).

Bergen city phone code: 55

During the 13th century Bergen was the first capital of Norway. Now, the colourful harbour, red-roofed houses and spruce trees nestling under imposing Mount Fløyen give Bergen the reputation of being Norway's most attractive city. This was the northernmost city in the Hanseatic League and the HANSEATIC MUSEUM – a reconstruction of a 16th-century merchant's house – makes an interesting visit. This is in the quarter called BRYGGEN, and in the old timber houses today weavers and craftsmen carry on their trade. Take a guided tour when visiting ROSENKRANTZ TOWER and KING HAAKON'S HALL; it makes the visit all the more interesting. Also take the funicular up Mount Fløyen and see the view: a return ticket costs 30kr and the cable car operates every half hour from the early morning to 11 p.m.

On the edge of the LILLE LUNGENGARDSVATNET park is the RASMUS MEYER, an art gallery with many works by native artist Edvard Munch (admission 35kr for adults). The GAMLE BERGEN (old town) with its traditional timbered buildings makes a pleasant walk. The Romanesque church of ST MARY'S is considered Norway's most beautiful church. Tourist Information has details on the May–June INTERNATIONAL FESTIVAL held here and also about the trips to the fjords that start from Bergen.

Consider investing in a Bergen Card which gives free bus travel and either reduced price or free entry to museums. The 24-hour pass costs 110kr for adults.

TOURIST INFORMATION AND ADDRESSES

Tourist information is on Bryggen (by the old town) (Tel. 32 1480), open 8.30 a.m.–9 p.m. in the summer. They change money, book you into private houses and supply maps and the *Bergen Guide*.

POST OFFICE Smästrandgate; open 8 a.m.–5 p.m., Thurs.: till 7 p.m., Sat.: 9 a.m.–1 p.m.

24-HOUR CHEMIST Accident Clinic, Lars Hillesgale, no.30 (Tel. 32 1120. (A chemist at the bus station stays open until midnight.)

STUDENT TRAVEL Universreiser a/s Parkveien 1 (Tel. 54 5000). 25% reductions on fare to Newcastle.

BUSES A quick journey, which combines historical interest with beautiful countryside, is to Troldhaugen, Nordas Lake, the home and burial place of composer Edvard Grieg. Get there by taking any bus to Hop; they depart about every 15 minutes. It is open in the summer 9.30 a.m.–5.30 p.m. During the festival period recitals take place on Wednesday and Sunday evenings. Tickets can be obtained from the Tourist Office.

SLEEPING, EATING AND NIGHTLIFE

If you are dumping rucksacks, note that left luggage may be cheaper than the lockers. For accommodation the tourist pavilion charges 15–20kr commission per person. Private homes are expensive and charge around 145–170kr for single rooms and 235–295kr for doubles. A deposit is also required.

The youth hostel Montana is nearly always full (Bergen is very touristy), so call first. It's in a good position, halfway up Mount Ulriken. It costs 150kr, including breakfast. It's on bus route 4 at Ravneberget (Tel. 29 2900), but apply at IYHA office at Strandgaten 4.

There's a YMCA Interpoint hostel at Nedre Korskirkealm open from mid-June to early September, costing 90kr, 10 minutes' walk from the station.

Bergen's main camping site, Bergenshallens Camping (Tel. 27 0180), is a 10-minute journey from the city centre at 24 Vilh, Bjerknesvei; take bus 3. It is only open in the summer and is very busy, so if you want the fresh outdoors, check with the information centre first to find out if room is available.

Another campsite to try is Bergen Camping Park at Haukås i Åsane on road no. 1 (Tel. 24 8808). You can either bring a tent or use one of the camping huts.

The Polar Bear Bar in Ole Bulls Plass 9–11, just around the corner from the taxi central, offers the cheapest menu outside the fast-food chains. At night there is music until the small hours. Café Opera, at

24 Engen, is a little more expensive for food, but its atmosphere is more conducive, with live bands and art exhibitions making up the surroundings. Foreign newspapers and board games are available on request from the counter. Open 11 a.m.–1 a.m., Fri. and Sat. until 3 a.m.

Vegetarians are catered for at the Spisestedet Kornelia, at Fosswinklegate 18. Open 11 a.m.–8 p.m., it serves organic vegetarian and Italian lunches, herbal teas and home-made ice-creams.

On the whole, though, the food and nightlife news is not too good. All you'll be able to afford are picnics and some of the fairly boring café-type places. Try Peppe's Pizza in Bryggen's, Finne-gården 2a – all-you-can-eat pizza and salad for 70kr on Mon. (no wine though!) The restaurant in the Fantoft Sommerhotel is decent and offers a 20% student discount (bus 14 or 15) and Hulen is a club run by the town's university students in an old air-raid shelter beneath Nygaardsparken. Location is at 47 Olav Ryesvei, and opening times are Wed./Thurs.: 8 p.m.–1 a.m., Fri./Sat.: 9 p.m.–3 a.m. Gays should go to Café Fincken.

If all this travelling is making you want to crash out at the movies, there is no problem with language, as all films are shown in their original language with Norwegian subtitles.

Trondheim city phone code: 73

Trondheim is the historical capital of Norway, founded in 997 by the Viking king, and now saint, Olav Tryggvason. Now, in the 1990s, it boasts the second largest university in the country and has become a centre for technology, research and business enterprises. Pick up a map and the *Trondheim Guide* at the station.

TOURIST INFORMATION AND ADDRESSES
The Tourist Office is over the bridge along Søndregate – turn right into Kongensgate and walk along to the market place. The office is on the corner (open 8.30 a.m.–late in the summer) and they rent bikes (Tel. 92 9400).

In July and August there is an Inter-Rail Centre at Elgesetergate 1 (Tel. 89 9538) which offers basic bed and breakfast accommodation, cooking facilities, seat reservations and all the usual Inter-Rail facilities, with a frequent day and night service to Bodø, Oslo, and Stockholm.

POST OFFICE Dronningens gate 10; open Mon.–Fri.: 8 a.m.–5 p.m., Sat.: 9.30 a.m.–1 p.m.
CHEMIST St Olav Vaklapotek, Kjopmanrlsgate 65 (Tel. 52 3122); open 8.30 a.m.–12 midnight all week

SEEING

The sights of the city are the medieval NIDAROS CATHEDRAL, erected over the grave of St Olav and host to the Norwegian Crown Jewels, now on public display, the 12th-century ARCHBISHOPS' PALACE and the interesting RINGVE MUSEUM OF MUSIC HISTORY, the KRISTIANSTEN FORTRESS and the old town bridge, from where the view of the wharf row is excellent.

The recently opened TYHOLT TOWER is worth visiting. From this rotating 80m tower you can view all Trondheim and the Trondheimsfjord.

SLEEPING, EATING AND NIGHTLIFE

The youth hostel is at Weidemannsvei 41 (Tel. 53 0490). If you are wanting to camp, the nearest campsite is 10 km out at Sandmoen Camping (Tel. 7388 6135). A 44 bus will take you there from the bus station and tents are charged at 90kr each. With a Eurail ticket you can travel for free on the NSB buses in the direction of Stjordal or Storlien. This is excellent if you want to stay at the Vikhammer Camping, 15 km north of Trondheim (Tel. 97 6164) or Storsand Camping, 17 km north of Trondheim (Tel. 97 6360).

The majority of restaurants in Trondheim are situated around the area of Kjopmannsgate, and fast-food venues gather around Olav Tryggvasons gate. Pizzakjelleren at Fjordgt 7 challenges the famished traveller to eat as much as possible for 49kr, and is open until 4 a.m.

Bodø

It's 11½ hours from Trondheim to Bodø, but the scenery and the comfortable trains make it feel a lot less. The bus ride from Bodø to Narvik joins up the northern part of the Norwegian railway system and is a fabulous experience. 50% discount on fare with Inter-Rail and Nordturist card. From 2 June to 10 July, the sun never sets here. If you hit a particularly good spell of weather, walk up MOUNT RONVIK, taking your camera with you. This is the coastal area that you should be in if you want to see the Northern Lights (Aurora Borealis) between November and February, although this does depend upon meteorological conditions.

The 1956 CATHEDRAL is about the only noteworthy building in the town, but you don't come here for the towns. Head instead for SALSTRAUMEN, where every 6 hours millions of gallons of water squeeze through a tiny passage between 2 fjords, making a spectacular sight. Buses sometimes run to coincide with the tides – ask for the timetable at Tourist Information. There is a reductiion with Inter-Rail.

MO-I-RANA, 3½ hours before Bodø, is located on a magnificent fjord. The youth hostel (Tel. 7515 0963) is open May–Sept. and costs 110kr.

SLEEPING

Bodø's Tourist Office is at Sjogata 21, open Mon.–Fri.: 9 a.m.–9 p.m. in season. (Tel. 7552 6000). They can book private accommodation for you.

There is a youth hostel above the station on the third floor which costs about 125kr a night. For camping, try Lundhogda Camping (Tel. 7564 3966), which is 3 km from Fauske and costs 45kr per tent.

Northern Norway: Nordland

If you are wanting to visit the LOFOTEN ISLANDS, travel from Bodø by Nordland Express and change at Narvik. The journey is expensive, and does not include an overnight stay in Svolvacr. Narvik also has a separate rail link – the Ofoten Line – which runs the 43 km to the border and on to Sweden. It is a particularly scenic journey. For many years it was the world's must northerly border and today it is still the most northerly electrified line and carries about half the total goods transported by Norwegian Railways, mainly about 20 million tons of Swedish iron ore.

When in NARVIK, Tourist Information can be found in the main street in Kongensgate 66 (Tel. 7694 3309, Mon.–Sat.: 9 a.m.–9 p.m. ,Sun.: 12 p.m.–9 p.m.). Note that the exchange rate offered here is not that good, but you can book private rooms from here for a fee, single rooms being about 150kr and doubles 210kr.

The youth hostel (Tel. 7694 2598) is situated beside the harbour at Havnegate 3 (turn left from the Tourist Office and walk down Kongensgate for 10 minutes). Reservations are recommended.

The campsite is crowded and uneven and doesn't have showers, but you can get cheap showers and sauna in town at the Seamen's Mission, near the harbour. It is open 4 p.m.–10 p.m. and has a pool table, as well as cheap coffee and snacks.

From June to August you can take a 15-minute cable car ride in the *Gondolbaner* for magnificent views of the area and, at night, the midnight sun. The service runs from 10 a.m. to midnight or later, depending on weather conditions, and costs 50kr. If you are intending to take the early morning train out of Narvik, bear in mind that the station closes from 10.30 p.m. to 5 a.m.

North Cape (Nordkapp)

A worthwhile detour off the rail system is the superbly scenic bus journey from Narvik to North Cape – the land of the midnight sun and the most northerly point of Europe. This trip necessitates at least 2 overnight stops, but the reward is breathtaking scenery over all of its 739 km length. The most popular expedition starts with the midday bus from Narvik, arriving at Alta 11¼ hours later. The feeling of complete isolation is quickly apparent – apart from the abundant wildlife, that is: from June-Oct., Nordkapp is the pastureland for around 5,000 reindeer.

There is a convenient youth hostel in Alta at Midtbakken 52 (Tel. 7843 4409), but in common with most hostels this far north, it does not open until mid-June.

There are also 4 campsites with cabins to rent. Alta Strand Camping and Apartments is the best-equipped site, or try Alta River Camping at Øvre Alta (Tel. 7843 4353) about 5 km out of town. On current timings, the North Cape bus continues on its way the following morning at 7.35 a.m., arriving at Europe's northernmost point at 1 p.m. The North Cape Hall is worth a visit, even if just to sip a coffee overlooking the Arctic Ocean. For those wanting to stay longer, there is a youth hostel (Tel. 7847 3377) at Honningsvag and cabins to rent (expensive).

The adventurous might consider joining up with the coastal voyage or continuing to Kirkenes on the Russian border. Otherwise, the return bus to Alta departs at 2.55 p.m., arriving back in Alta at 7.55 p.m., for an overnight stop. The journey continues to Narvik at 9 a.m. the following morning. Check your *Thomas Cook European Timetable* for the current schedule.

NB: There is a reduction over this route with Inter-Rail or Nordturist. This does not apply to the Honningsvag to North Cape section or to the ferry crossings.

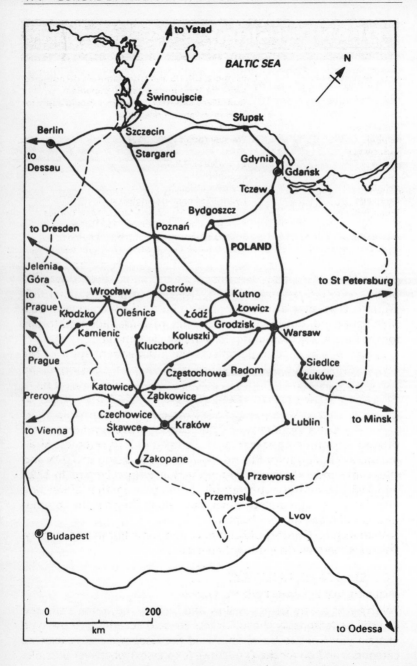

POLAND (Polska)

Entry requirements	Passport. UK, US and Irish nationals do not need a visa for stays up to 90 days. Canadians, Australians and New Zealanders should apply for visas in advance, price $40.
Population	38,600,000
Capital	Warsaw (pop.: 1,700,000)
Currency	Złoty
	£1 = approx 4.8zl
Political system	Republic
Religion	Roman Catholic
Language	Polish (German and English spoken)
Public holidays	1 Jan., Easter Monday, 1 May, 3 May, Corpus Christi, 15 Aug., 1, 11 Nov., 25, 26 Dec.
International dialling	To Poland: international code 48 number
	From Poland: 00 + country code number

After a long struggle by the Solidarity trade union, Poland was the first country in Eastern Europe to throw off communism in 1985. With the election of a Solidarity prime minister the seemingly impossible happened, but the harsh economic measures adopted to pay for the failures of communism have made life difficult.

Solidarity's long struggle reflects the independent spirit of the Poles, who resent outside pressure from anyone. Looking at the history of Poland this is understandable, as the country has had more than its fair share of invasion and occupation. The process began in the 10th century with the eastward expansion of Germanic tribes and continued long afterwards; the country has been conquered, divided up and had its boundaries changed dozens of times. As an independent kingdom, Poland first came into being in 1025 and later came under the protection of the Holy Roman Empire. In 1795 and 1939 Poland disappeared off the map altogether under first Napoleon and subsequently Hitler, but neither they nor the communists could break the Polish spirit.

With its mix of history old and new, and some fine inland scenery, Poland is more worth visiting than ever.

POLISH STATE RAILWAYS
(POLSKIE KOLEJE PAŃSTWOWE, PKP)
Polish trains are no longer as slow and busy as they once were, but can still be reasonably cheap. Tickets are sold according to the type of train you want to travel on. Avoid the *Osobowe* and *Pośpieszne* categories and go for the *Ekspresowe* (expresses) whenever possible.

It is worth paying the small additional fare for an upgrade to first class to ensure a seat. All the large cities have their own commuter trains, called *pociâgi elektryczne,* which are more crowded than normal.

Watch out for the change to a winter schedule at the end of September: if you are in Poland your Thomas Cook timetable will not correspond.

A growing problem in Eastern Europe is the emergence of organized gangs of thieves on trains (Warsaw station is a particular black-spot). The tactic seems to be that one member of the group distracts the tourist while accomplices make off with any accessible luggage.

PASSES AVAILABLE The Inter-Rail pass is broken down into zones, so that you pay only for travel within the area you want to visit. Poland is in Zone D, along with the Czech Republic, Hungary, Slovakia and Croatia. For details of the 8 Inter-Rail zones, see the Inter-Rail section in Part One of this guide.

Euro Domino tickets are also available (see p. 41).

Don't be talked into buying a Polrail Pass unless you plan on spending a lot of time going around in circles, as fares are cheap enough that you won't save any money. If you do acquire a pass it is valid on all trains where reservations are obligatory and entitles the holder to free seat reservations (which can be booked at the station of departure, any railbooking office, or on the train itself). The pass for under-26s costs $46 (or $70 for first class) for 8 days, $52 ($76) for 15 days, $57 ($86) for 21 days and $64 ($96) for 1 month. Over-26s pay a few pounds more.

TRAIN INFORMATION

Few officials speak much English, so if you want to make a reservation write down the name of your destination and the time your train leaves. Most people speak a little English, but if stuck try German in the south and west, or French in the north. If really stuck, try:
Z' którego peronu odjezdza pociâg do...? (From which platform does the train to... leave?)

RESERVATIONS If you want to guarantee a seat, you'll have to make a reservation, as trains are regularly crowded to capacity. Go to the station at least a day in advance (several days for the Warsaw–Cracow–Zakopane run). For international trains you'll have to use the Orbis agency or brave the queues at the international windows (marked *Polres*) as they deal with seat reservations (*miejscówka*) which are compulsory on express and international trains.

NIGHT TRAVEL Don't expect high standards unless you're willing to travel first class, which is worth the extra as the seats recline right back. Reserve well ahead of time at Orbis, Polres and travel agents, particularly for couchettes, which are always cheaper than paying for a night's accommodation. You may have no alternative but to reserve a couchette if you are going to the Czech Republic or Slovakia, as you will probably be told they are the only seats available. International journeys are still cheap to some former Eastern Bloc countries. Try and get into a carriage supplied by a western country such as Austria. Some couchettes can only be booked shortly before departure.

EATING ON TRAINS There's either a WARS restaurant or buffet car on all long hauls in Poland, but some international trains have only minimal facilities.

TOURIST INFORMATION

There are local *Informacja Turystyczna* (IT) offices in every major town. If you plan to stay for a while, it's worth buying *A Guide for Young Tourists* from any Ruch kiosks in Poland.

VISAS The visa situation is being liberalized all the time. Since September 1994 no visa has been required for UK, Irish or US nationals. Australian, New Zealand, Canadian and South African nationals do need visas at present and should apply in advance. Check with your local Polish consulate for an update on the situation before you travel.

ISIC BONUSES For an IUS Card you have to go to Almatur in Warsaw; this gives you 25% reductions on international trains within the former Eastern Bloc. New ISIC cards in Poland are combined with the IUS card.

MONEY MATTERS 1 złoty (zl) = 100 groszy (g)
A new currency was introduced in 1995 and old notes have ceased to be legal. Banking hours are Mon.–Fri.: 8 a.m.–1 p.m., some banks Sat.: 8 a.m.–10.45 a.m. It's also possible to exchange money at Orbis, at travel agents and post offices, hotels, and hundreds of Kantor kiosks (*bureaux de change*), which may give slightly better rates. Currency exchange has been opened to the free market, thus

eliminating the need for a black market at a stroke. You now get the same rate everywhere and so living here for foreigners can be very cheap. You should still keep your exchange receipts, as they may be checked when you leave. You aren't allowed to take złotys out of the country, but foreigners can change back unused money.

POST OFFICES Open Mon.–Fri.: 8 a.m.–6 p.m. Getting mail sent on is more trouble than it's worth (allow at least 3 weeks). Most embassies will keep your letters for at least 2 weeks.

SHOPS For food, 8 a.m.–7 p.m., others 11 a.m.–6 p.m. For opening times of museums, etc., check with the local IT office.

TIPPING 10–15% is standard in restaurants. Taxi drivers usually include a mark up in the fare they charge.

SLEEPING

It can be difficult to find a room in Poland without having fixed it up beforehand. To do this contact Polorbis (see Appendix V for address), who will issue you with student accommodation vouchers (around $7 for students). These vouchers allow you to stay at any of the ISHs (international student hostels) (open July, Aug. and Sept.) in Poland if you're a student or under 25. If you haven't already done this, then your best plan is to arrive as early as possible in the day, and even this does not ensure you a bed at an ISH.

Vouchers are a prerequisite in Warsaw, so don't waste time going along unless you have them. If you've no luck with the ISHs, try the Polish Youth Hostel Federation (PTSM). Officially, most require an IYHF card, but it's not always essential. The good news is that they're very cheap; the bad news is that some can be like overcrowded prisons. There are a huge number of hostels (*schroniska młodzieżowe*) in Poland, all of which are spartan even by Western YH standards.

The more money you have, the fewer your problems are likely to be. PTTK is an organization which runs cheap hotels called *Domy Turysty*; you can find out about these from the local IT office, but don't build your hopes up as they are nearly always full. Standard Polish hotels are not too expensive.

Another organization, Biuro Zakwaterowania, arranges for you to stay with private families. Be careful about accepting offers of private rooms on the street, as the room in question might well be a long way out of town.

If you're under 26 and travelling during the summer months, Almatur, the student travel organization, can help find inexpensive university dorm beds.

Finally, if you're really desperate, try the long queue at the Orbis office; they might have a spare bed in one of their hotels, if you're prepared to pay the high prices asked.

With almost 70 well-equipped sites, camping is another budget option in Poland. Prices are likely to be around 10zl. per person, but are rising fast. Some sites have bungalows available for hire, a bed here will be around 25zl. Ask for details and location at the local Tourist Information.

EATING AND NIGHTLIFE

The austere economic measures have affected tourists as well as the Poles, but things are improving and new restaurants appear almost daily. Things are not as bad as the media make out, and it's still possible to eat very well if you know where to look. Pork, fish or poultry will normally be the best bet. You can get a good meal (but not a gastronomic delight) at the top hotels and restaurants. Expect to pay around 25zl. for a 3-course meal. Avoid station restaurants completely, except in Warsaw, and only go there if you are stuck.

Nightlife is developing with the freeing up of society. It revolves around *kawiarnie* (cafés) and *winiarnie* (bars) and in some places student clubs. Polish vodka is, of course, internationally known.

Poland is still a strongly Catholic country and morals can be strict – it is not always the best place to advertise open homosexuality.

THINGS TO BRING AND BUY

Food is relatively cheap and plentiful here so there's no need to stock up on consumables before arriving, unless there is something you can't live without. In fact, due to Poland's status as a 'developing country', special concessions from Western manufacturers mean alcohol (but not spirits) and cigarettes are cheaper here than in most European cities. Photographic film is readily available here, though it's not very cheap and often past its expiry date.

Poland is rich in handicrafts and if you travel about the countryside you will no doubt find bargains – from tapestries and rugs to pottery and woodwork. For the most part, you can take any goods up to a total of US$200 out of the country duty-free. Some notable exceptions are crystal (80% duty!) and any pre-Second World War books or artwork. If you think these restrictions will not apply to you as a budget traveller, think again: after experiencing rampant inflation, many Poles are willing to sell their prized family possessions for hard currency. However, beware of street sellers peddling Russian military paraphernalia! If you are travelling on to other Eastern European countries you may not only have your purchases confiscated, but it could also cause you some very real problems with border officials. If you must have that furry hat or grey trench coat, post it home.

Some things that can be had cheaply here are lace, hand-painted silks, wooden toys and handmade utensils. Amber necklaces are cheap. If you can't make it out to the countryside, there are outlets in the major cities: the Cepelia shops sell arts and crafts; Desa sells artwork by professional Polish artists; and Jubiler stores sell jewellery. Imports and flashy souvenirs can be purchased at the Baltona and Pewex shops, which only take hard currency, and though more expensive, are still relatively cheap by Western standards.

Warsaw (Warszawa) city phone code: 022

The beautiful city of Warsaw could have looked very different today had the patriotic Poles decided to replace the bombed buildings of 1944 with concrete blocks, instead of rebuilding replicas of the original 19th-century structures. Ignore the few Stalinesque buildings that have crept in, and judge the city instead on her elegant palaces and parks. Her past is bloody and tragic, and you only have to look back to 1943 when Hitler ordered that no stone of Warsaw should be left standing, for evidence of this. The HISTORICAL MUSEUM OF THE CITY, on the old town Market Square, has film captured from the Nazis which shows the systematic destruction of this city, and there are reminders of the holocaust dotted all round the centre.

TOURIST INFORMATION
The Warsaw information office is located at pl. Zamkowy 1/13 (Tel. 6351881 or 8310464). The main Orbis office is at ulica Bracka 16 (Tel. 8274516), open Mon.–Fri.: 8 a.m.–7 p.m., Sat.: 8 a.m.–5 p.m. The Orbis branch at Marszałkowska 142 sells international train tickets and changes traveller's cheques.

ADDRESSES
MAIN POST OFFICE Świâtokrzyska
AMEX Orbis, Marszałkowska 142
ALMATUR (POLISH STUDENT TRAVEL) At the university on ulica Kopernika 23 (Tel. 263512); open Mon.–Fri.: 8.30 a.m.–8 p.m (4.30 p.m. Sept.–June), Sat.: 10 a.m.–6 p.m., Sun.: 10 a.m.–4 p.m. in season.
OUR ROOTS (JEWISH INFORMATION AND TOURIST BUREAU)

Grzybowski Sq 12/16 (Tel. 6200556); open 9 a.m.–5 p.m. Sells publi-
cation. in English, describing walks of particular historical interest.
UK EMBASSY ulica W. E. Plater 28, 00-688 Warsawa (Tel. 6253030)
IRISH EMBASSY ulica Humansica 10, 00-789 Warsawa (Tel. 496633)
US EMBASSY ulica Ujazdowskie 29/31 (Tel. 6283041)
CANADIAN CONSULAR OFFICE ulica Matejki 1/5 (Tel. 6298051)
AUSTRALIAN EMBASSY uical Estońska 35 (Tel. 6176081/85)
NEW ZEALAND Citizens should contact the UK embassy.
FIRST AID Hoza 56 (Tel. 999)

STATION FACILITIES

There are 3 stations in Warsaw, but the only one you're likely to use
consistently is the new Centralna. For train information: Tel.
6200361. The Wasteels office is also at Centralna station. Be on
guard for pickpockets.

GETTING ABOUT

Buy your tram and bus tickets at the kiosks marked Ruch (*bilety
tramwajowe* and *bilety autobusowe*). Buy as many as you think you'll
use in one go to avoid queues. Show your ISIC card for discount on
fares. Kiosks also sell 1-day and 1-week passes. Buses marked with
letters are expresses and cost twice as much as normal buses. After
11 p.m. all fares are doubled. Don't forget to get your ticket
punched by the machine at both ends of the bus or tram, or you
risk a fine if you're caught; as the standard fare is only 0.1zl. it is
hardly worth the risk. However, note that you have to pay an extra
1zl for your baggage. Poland is known for its plain-clothed ticket
inspectors.

SEEING

Between the STARE MIASTO (old town) and the LAZIENKI PARK lie the main
sights of Warsaw. The centre of the old town is the beautiful RYNEK
STAREGO MIASTA (market square). Rebuilt baroque houses line the
square and a block to the south lies ST JOHN'S CATHEDRAL, the main
church for Warsaw's deeply religious Catholics. In Zamkowy Square
stands Warsaw's oldest monument, the SIGISMUND III COLUMN (1644),
and this adjoins the ROYAL CASTLE, which dates back to the 14th
century and is still being worked on to repair its 1940s damage. The
tin-roofed baroque PALACE is close by.

The Jewish population of Warsaw was wiped out under Nazism
and the PAWIAK PRISON where 35,000 were executed and 65,000
detained is now a museum. The JEWISH HISTORICAL INSTITUTE at
Tliomackie ulica 5 looks at what happened in the famous Warsaw

ghetto, and the MAUSOLEUM TO STRUGGLE AND MARTYRDOM on the al Amoni is housed in the former Gestapo HQ and prison. The OUR ROOTS bureau can give more information on what to see.

AZIENKI PALACE AND PARK were built for the last Polish king in the 18th century. The palace has been restored and there are many other buildings and monuments in this graceful park. On the southern edge of the park is the monument to Chopin and on Sunday afternoons there are often Chopin recitals.

The WILANÓW PALACE AND PARK was one of the 17th-century kings' summer houses. The restored palace can be visited, along with the MUSEUM OF THE POLISH POSTER in the palace grounds. The palace is closed Tues., the museum shuts Mon. and you reach them by bus 8 from ulica Marszałkowska.

Markets remain a good way to see ordinary life. The daily market on ulica Targowa, Bazar Rózokiego, can be dangerous for tourists, but the Sunday flea market in Stadion Moczytlo, ulica Goczewska (bus 109) is worth a look. The Saturday bazaar in the PRAGA district (Stadion 10-lecia) is also interesting.

SLEEPING

Finding a bed in Warsaw can be a depressing and soul-destroying experience. Your best course of action is to go to the Almatur office (see above) and ask them for the addresses of their current YHs (they change locations annually). These are open July–Aug. and are cheaper if you are a student. Almatur also have lists of the campsites. If you're an IYHF member, go along to PTSM at ulica Chocimska 28 for a list of Polish hostels. There are 6 hostels in Warsaw; they are cheap, rule-ridden and fairly depressing. Their locations are: Karolkowa 53a (Tel. 6328829), tram 20; Smolna 30 (Tel. 278952), tram 25; Lokalna 51; Kłopotowskigo 36; Solidarnosci 61; and Reytana 6. Plan on arriving before 9 a.m. to be in with a chance at any of the above hostels. PTTK at ulica Marszałkowska 124 will give you a list of their *Domy Turysty*.

The best place to stay from May to Sept. is the campsite Gromada on ulica Żwirki i Wigury 32 (Tel. 254391). There are bungalows here as well as tent sites, and they offer one of the best deals going: about 8zl. per person in a 4-person bungalow (bus 512, 188, 136 or 175 from Centralna, direction airport).

Hotels are likely to be too expensive to be a serious option, though one just slightly more expensive than a *Domy Turysty* is Hotel Harctur at ulica Niemcewicza 17 (Tel. 6590011), tram 25 towards placa Narutowicza.

A few agencies have recently sprung up which find private rooms.

Try Syrena, ulica Krucza 17 (Tel. 6287540). Alternatively, Informaia Nuclegowa is a telephone service which directs people to hotels according to their budget: call them on 6415366 or 8310464.

EATING AND NIGHTLIFE

Make up for all the hardships you've had to endure by eating out in style. Food here is cheap enough to let you eat in all the best restaurants and still think you had a bargain. If you're cutting back on food too, eat in the milk bars (*bar mleczny*), but only if you're prepared to risk salmonella, or at the university cafeteria on the campus at ulica Krakowskie Przedmieście. On the other hand, allegedly the best cake shop in Europe – A Blikle – is on Nowy Swiât 35, close to the hostel at Smolna 30. For food, try the Fukier, Rynek Starego Miasta 27, or the Krokodyl, Rynek Starego Miasta 21, (old town market square) Rycerska, ulica Szeroki Dunaj 911, Mekong (for oriental food) Wspólna 35, or Pizzeria Bambola at ulica Putawska and ulica Wspolna. There are also plenty of fast-food outlets and Pizza Huts.

The *kawiarnie* and *winiarnie* are the hub of social life in Warsaw, as elsewhere in Poland. It's not difficult to find good ones, but the Fukierowska wine-cellar at Rynek Starego Miasta 27 (old town market square) is Poland's best and dates back to 1590. Also look up Pod Herbami on ulica Piwna.

For dancing, Hybrydy, ulica Kniewski ego 7/9, is a lively student disco. The cinema is cheap, and Bajka, ulica Marszałkowska 136/138, shows Polish films with English or French subtitles. For opera, concert or theatre tickets, go to ZASP on ulica Jerozolimskie (Tel. 6219454).

Warsaw is a pretty conservative city and the gay scene is decidedly limited. The Paradise disco/bar at the 'Skra' centre on the corner of ulica Wawelska and Zwirki i Wigury is supposed to be a good general place for Saturday nights.

If you need to get rid of some złotys, try the Centrum shopping centre on ulica Marszałkowska near the central station. Above all, keep your eyes and ears open, as new bars and restaurants are opening all the time and the in place changes on a frequent basis.

Cracow (Kraków) city phone code: 012

A visit to Cracow in the south is a must, as it is the ancient city of Polish kings and culture. Gothic, Renaissance and baroque architecture reflects this long history. It is the only city in Poland to survive the war and has retained its medieval air.

TOURIST INFORMATION

The competing local Tourist Offices are linked to local hostels and hotels, so beware of rushing into signing up for the first accommodation they offer. However, they do usually speak good English. Two possibilities are the Hotel Warszawski near Główny station at ulica Pawia 6/8 (Tel. 220471, open Mon.–Fri.: 8 a.m.–7 p.m.), and Dexter, Rynek Główny 1/3 (Tel. 217706 or 213051, open Mon.–Fri.: 9 a.m.–6 p.m). Pick up *What, When and Where in Cracow*. There is an English speaking gay/lesbian information line, Tel. 6285222, but it only operates between 6 p.m. and 9 p.m. on Wed. (for women) and Fri. (for men).

ADDRESSES

POST OFFICE Corner of Westerplatte and Wielopole.
ORBIS In the main square at Rynek Główny 41.
AMEX At Orbis.
ALMATUR Rynek Główny 7/8 (Tel. 226123)
US CONSULATE ulica Slolarska 9 (Tel. 221400)
PHARMACY Komorowskiego 11 (Tel. 223027). Open 24 hours.

STATION FACILITIES

Make sure you get off at Kraków Główny, the recently modernized main station a 10-minute walk from the centre, and not one of the suburban stations. Train Information: Tel. 222248. The bus station is adjacent.

SEEING

To see the sights, wander around the old town (STARE MIASTO), which is surrounded by a park where the old walls once stood. At the centre is the huge central market square, RYNEK GŁÓWNY, which is the largest medieval market square in Europe. Also here are the Renaissance mercantile CLOTH HALL (museum upstairs) and the CATHEDRAL, from whose spire the bugler plays an unfinished daily warning, a reminder of the days when Mongol hordes surrounded the city.

WAWEL CASTLE dominates the river Vistula and encloses a CATHEDRAL, overseen for many years by Karol Wojtyla (now Pope John Paul II). The 15th-century COLLEGIUM MAIUS on SW Anny is the oldest building of the famous JAGIELLONIAN UNIVERSITY and is well worth a visit. The old Jewish quarter of KAZIMIERZ has Poland's oldest synagogue, the STARA SYNAGOGA at Szeroka 40. Also try listening to the first independent commercial radio station in Eastern Europe on Radio Marpolska, a far cry from the 7 minutes of illegal radio from Solidarity during the 1980s. Trams are cheap – as elsewhere in Poland, make sure you punch your ticket rather than risk a heavy fine.

SLEEPING

Finding somewhere can be a problem as Cracow is a popular destination for schools and coach parties. The Biuro Zakwaterowan, ulica Pawia 8 (Tel. 221921) will arrange accommodation.

There are 3 official youth hostels: ulica Oleandry 4 (Tel. 338822), tram 15 (well recommended by previous travellers); Kościuszki 88 (Tel. 221951); and ulica Załotej Kielni 1 (Tel. 372441).

Reputedly the cheapest beds are those in the *Dom Turysty* at Westerplatte 1516 (Tel. 229566), which is on the edge of the old town.

For camping try Camping Krak on ulica Radzikowskiego 99 (Tel. 372122), bus 208, open mid-May to mid-September.

Hotel Pollera is only 5 minutes from the station and old city at ulica Szpitalna 30 (Tel. 221044) and has been highly recommended.

EATING AND NIGHTLIFE

Street stalls are often the best place to eat, but few restaurants will stretch your budget either. Try Staropolska, ulica Sienna 4; Balaton, ulica Grodszka for Hungarian food or Jadlodajnia Stanisław at ulica Mikolajska 16 for a haunt popular with the locals.

Cracow has better nightlife than much of Poland because of the university. Try the student club Pod Jaszczurami at Rynek Główny 8 or the disco Rotunda, ulica Oleandry 1.

EXCURSIONS Less than 2 hours away is the town of OSWIECIM, better known as AUSCHWITZ, site of the largest concentration camp in Hitler's Final Solution. There are actually 2 camps, AUSCHWITZ itself and the huge BIRKENAU about 20 mins away. A shuttle bus runs between them. The Auschwitz camp, now a museum providing a harrowing impression of life and death in the camps, is a 3 km walk from the station, but is poorly signposted. You may prefer to take a bus from Cracow; it won't stretch your budget. Entry to the museum is free. Watch the spine-chilling film showing the camp just after liberation (admission 3zl). An all-inclusive coach trip from Cracow costs around £6.

The salt mine at WIELICZKA is an amazing complex of underground chambers, including the CHAPEL OF THE BLESSED KINGS, intricately carved from salt. The guided tour lasts 2 hours. Try and go early to be finished by lunchtime. Open Tues.–Sun., 8 a.m.–6 p.m.

CZÊSTOCHOWA is the most important religious site in deeply Catholic Poland. Pilgrims come from around the world to the JASNAGORA MONASTERY to see the BLACK MADONNA, an icon which is said to have cried during a 17th-century Swedish siege.

The Tourist Office is at Aleje NMP 63 (Tel. 41360). The youth hostel, at ulica Waclawy Marek 12 (Tel. 033131296), is on the other side of town. The campsite is basic, but cheap, and is at ulica Oleńki 3 (Tel. 47495).

South of Cracow is the beautiful TATRA NATIONAL PARK with lofty 1,800m mountains of granite and limestone.

ZAKOPANE This is the largest town in the Tatra area and is a good place to base yourself to explore the surrounding area. You may choose to take the bus from Cracow to Zakopane: it is quicker, more scenic and only costs a couple of dollars.

A funicular railway runs to the top of MOUNT GUBALOWKA (1,116m) and a cable car up MOUNT KASPROWY WIERCH (1,953m). There is a great hike to the top of MOUNT GIEWONT (1,878m) which takes about 6 hours. You will have a magnificent view from each peak.

MORSKIE OKO is a beautiful mountain lake about 40 minutes from Zakopane by bus and well worth the trip. The Tourist Office is at ulica Kosciuszki 7 and the PTTK at ulica Krupówki 37 will give you information on mountain shelters. The youth hostel is at ulica Nowotarska 45 (Tel. 0165 4203). For camping, try Pod Krokiwa, ulica Zeromskiego (Tel. 2256) opposite the foot of the ski jump.

Gdańsk city phone code: 058

The port of Gdańsk in north-eastern Poland is famous as the birth-place of Solidarity and has a lot to offer the eurorailer. Its historic old town dates from the time of the medieval Hanseatic League, when the city was known as Danzig.

TOURIST INFORMATION AND ADDRESSES
TOURIST OFFICE ulica Heweliusza 27 (Tel. 314355); open Mon.–Fri.: 9 a.m.–3 p.m., Sat.: 8 a.m.–4 p.m., Sun.: 8 a.m.–3 p.m.
ORBIS Hotel Hevelius, ulica Heweliusza 22 (Tel. 314777); open Mon.–Fri.: 10 a.m.–5 p.m.
POST OFFICE ulica Pocztowa and ulica Dluga
AMEX At Orbis in Monopol Orbis, placa Gorkiego (Tel. 311466)
ALMATUR Dlugi Targ 11 (Tel. 317801); open Mon.–Tues. and Thurs.–Fri.: 9 a.m.–3 p.m.
TRAINS Gdańsk Główny is 10 minutes from the centre. Train infor-mation: Tel. 310051

SEEING
Around the market square, DLUGI TARG, is the headquarters of the old

Hanseatic League and the imposing TOWN HALL which contains a very interesting HISTORICAL MUSEUM (closed Mon.). There is a great view from the tower. Walk along ulica Mariacka to see the grand façades of 17th-century burghers' houses.

North of the old town is the home of Solidarity, the former Lenin Shipyards, now STOCZNIA GDAŃSKA (Gdańsk Shipyards); an open-topped boat tour starts at the Moltawa canal, and there's a monument to workers killed during the rising of 1970.

During the summer Gdańsk is packed with beachgoers; try STOGI BEACH (tram 9); although heavily polluted, windsurfing is popular. East of Gdańsk is the beautiful Mazurian lakeland. Take the train via Olsztyn.

SLEEPING

There are many hostels in the area, but the most central is at ulica Walowa 21 (Tel. 312313), 5 minutes from the station; closed 10 a.m. –5 p.m. Be aware of the fact that dormitories are mixed.

Use the Biuro Zakwaterowan at ulica Elźbietańska 1011 (Tel. 312634) to help you find a room.

For camping try Gdańsk-Jelitkowo, ulica Jelitkowska (Tel. 532731). Tram 5 or 8 from the Oliwa train station to the last stop, then a short walk.

For a hotel, try Hotel Jantar on Dlugi Targ 19 (Tel. 319532) for a good location from around 10zl.

A short train ride away at the seaside town of Gdynia is a YMCA, 10 minutes' walk from the station at ulica Zeromskiego 26 (Tel. 48/58 203115), open 15 June–31 August.

EATING AND NIGHTLIFE

Milk bars are probably your best bet, but if you want to splash out, try Pod Łososiem, ulica Szeroka 54, which serves excellent fresh fish. Flisak, ulica Chlebnicka and Kameralna, ulica Dluga 57, are popular student clubs, or the Gedania Restaurant, ulica Dluga 75, has live music in the evenings.

EXCURSIONS The castle by the River Vistula (Wisla) in MALBORK is one of the most awesome military fortifications in Europe. The sheer scale of the project is best appreciated from the opposite bank of the Wisla (best photographs as well). The construction of the MARIENBURG was begun by the Teutonic Knights in 1274 after they were driven out of Palestine. In 1309, the Marienburg became their European head-quarters and powerbase, and remained so until 1457 when the Grand Master was forced to flee to Königsberg (though the power of the Teutonic Knights had been on the wane since their defeat at the battle of Grünwald in 1410). During May–Sept. the castle is open Tues.–Sun.: 9 a.m.–4.30 p.m.; at other times of the year, Tues.–Sun.: 9 a.m.–3 p.m. The price of admission doubles if you want a tour in English. Malbork is about 45 minutes south of Gdańsk on the main line to Warsaw.

Toruń

Toruń is best known nowadays as the birthplace of Nicolaus Copernicus, but in its heyday during the late medieval period Toruń was one of the most important Hanseatic trading cities, evidence of which remains today in its host of Gothic ecclesiastical and secular buildings. The town's economy went into a sharp decline after the Polish Partitions. Toruń (or Thorn, as it was then called) remained under Prussian and German control until 1919 when the Treaty of Versailles handed it over to the recently formed Polish state as part of the 'Polish corrido'r.

TOURIST INFORMATION
A good source of information on the town is the PTTK office at placa Rapackiego 2 (Tel. 24926/28228, open Mon.–Fri.: 8 a.m.–4.30 p.m., weekends: 10 a.m.–1 p.m). The official Tourist Office is in the town hall, across the square from the PTTK (Tel. 10931).

Orbis is just off Rynek Staromiejski at ulica Zeglarska 31 (Tel. 22553, open Mon.–Fri.: 9 a.m.–5 p.m., Sat.: 9 a.m.–2 p.m.) and Almatur is at ulica Gagarina 21 (Tel. 20470), near the university.

STATION FACILITIES:
Most trains stop at Toruń Główny (main station), about 3 km from the centre, across the River Vistula (Wisla). Buses 12 and 22 maintain a frequent service between the station and placa Rapackiego. Toruń Miasto is much closer to the centre.

SEEING
As well as the TOWN HALL, be sure to take in the MEDIEVAL WALLS and some of the several excellent red-brick churches around, including ST MARY'S CHURCH on the north-west corner of the town square and ST JOHN'S CHURCH on ulica Zeglarska. Near St John's on ulica Kopernika is the house where Copernicus was born, now a museum. There are no less than 6 museums in the city and the opening times are posted

at the town hall, which itself contains the HISTORICAL MUSEUM.

SLEEPING

There are several decent, affordable hotels in the town centre. The Pod Orlem at ulica Mostowa 15 (Tel. 25024) and the Polonia at placa Teatralny 5 (Tel. 23028) are both within 5 minutes' walk of Rynek Staromiejski. Private rooms can be arranged through the office at Rynek Staromiejski 20. The PTTK *Dom Turysty* at ulica Legionów 24 (Tel. 23855) is quite far from the centre, as are the IYHF hostel at ulica Rudacka 15 (Tel. 27242) and Camping Tramp at ulica Kujawska 14 (open May–Sept.), both of which are in the area around Toruń Główny. In summer, student residences at the university are converted into temporary hostels.

EATING

The local speciality is gingerbread, which is widely available in the old town. There is a good selection of cafés with seats outside, especially along ulica Szeroka. The restaurants of the Polonia hotel (see above) and the Kosmos on Ks J. Popiełuszki provide reasonably priced meals, but better quality food at much the same price is available at the restaurant of the Zajazd Staropolski hotel on ulica Zeglarska.

Poznań city phone code: 061

Due to its position at the crossroads of several important trade routes, Pozań flourished in the 15th and 16th centuries, though the following 200 years saw a marked decline in the city's fortunes. The Industrial Revolution brought about its revival, but by then Poznań was the Prussian city of Posen. Following German unification in 1871 an attempt was made to Germanize the city. Resistance to this policy established Poznań as a centre of Polish nationalism. A successful uprising by the local Polish population in late 1918 ensured the city's incorporation in the reconstituted Polish state.

TOURIST INFORMATION

Office at Stary Rynek 77 (Tel. 8526156); open Mon.–Sat.: 8 a.m.–4 p.m. Good range of material on the city and surrounding area. Helpful, well informed staff. Orbis have offices at placa Wolności 3 (Tel. 8524011) (sells international train tickets), al Karola Marcinkowskiego 21 and ulica Święty Wojciech 33.

ADDRESSES
POST OFFICE The main office is on al Marcinkowskiego.
ALMATUR al Aleksandra Fredry 7 (Tel. 8523645)

STATION FACILITIES
Poznań Główny is about 15–20 minutes' walk from the Stary Rynek at the heart of the old town. Trams 5 and 21 connect the station to the city centre.

SEEING
The impressive MAIN SQUARE (*Stary Rynek*) is lined by gabled houses. The most important public buildings are located in the centre of the square. Pride of place goes to the TOWN HALL (now containing the MUSEUM OF THE HISTORY OF POZNAŃ). At noon the figure-play on the Town Hall clock re-enacts the local legend of the 2 rams which saved the city from burning down. To the rear of the town hall is the WEIGH-ING HOUSE. The red-brick buildings of the old ecclesiastical quarter are a 15-minute walk across the River Warta. The imposing castles of ROGALIN and KÓRNIK (11 and 23 km from Poznań respectively) are easily reached by bus.

SLEEPING
Hotels are expensive by Polish standards because of the town's status as host to many international trade fairs, but private rooms are available from the Biuro Zakwaterowania at ulica Glogowska 16 (Tel. 8660313) across from Poznań Główny, or from Glob-Tour (Tel. 8660667) at the station. As regards location, you cannot better the PTTK *Dom Turysty* at Stary Rynek 91 (Tel. 8528893).

Of the 3 IYHF hostels, the most convenient is at ulica Berwińskiego 2/3 (Tel. 8663680).

Both the campsites are far from the centre; the Streszynek at ulica Koszalińska 15 (Tel. 8483129) is easier to reach (bus 95), as well as having a pleasant lakeside setting.

EATING AND NIGHTLIFE
The food at the U Dylla bistro, Stary Rynek 37, has a good name amongst the locals and serves imported beers and spirits. Alternatively try Przyneta at ulica Święty Wojciech, noted for its fish specialities. One of the better milk bars is the Mewa on placa Wolnosci. Poznań produces 2 good-quality beers, Lech and Ratusz, which make a pleasant change from the ubiquitous Tatra Pils. If the Tourist Office cannot help you find the type of pub or club you are looking for, the most obvious place to ask around is the Odnowa,

the largest of the student clubs, at ul Świêty Wojciech 80/82.

Wrocław city phone code: 071

After Prussia seized Breslau from Austria in 1763 it developed into Prussia's second most important city (after Berlin). By the early 20th century, Breslau was one of the leading cities of the new German state. At that time, Poles constituted only around 5% of the population. So important was the city to Germany, that Polish leaders never envisaged it would become part of Poland in the aftermath of the Second World War – which is exactly what occurred. The German population fled, or were forced out, leaving the depopulated city to be filled with Poles from Lwów (Lvov), which Poland lost to the USSR. Breslau was then re-named Wrocław, though many Silesians still use the Germanic name (as they do for other towns in Silesia). Today, Wrocław is a university town and cultural centre, famous for its 100 bridges spanning the river Oder (Odra), its canals, parks and gardens.

TOURIST INFORMATION AND ADDRESSES

TOURIST INFORMATION Rynek 14 (Tel. 443111); open Mon.–Sat: 9 a.m.–5 p.m.
ORBIS Rynek 29 (Tel. 3439605/434780); open Apr.–Sept., Mon.–Sat.: 8 a.m.–5 p.m.; Oct.–Mar., Mon.–Fri.: 8 a.m.–5 p.m.
POST OFFICE The main office is at ulica Zygmunta Krasinskiego 1. Smaller offices operate in front of Wrocław Główny and at Rynek 32.

STATION FACILITIES

Your most likely point of arrival is the main station Wrocław Główny, about 10–15 minutes' walk from the Rynek. Wrocław Nadodrze receives trains from Łodz. Tram 0 or 1 to the centre.

SEEING

The MARKET SQUARE (Rynek) is dominated by the 14th-century TOWN HALL with its astronomical clock, one of the most impressive public buildings in Poland. The building now houses the TOWN MUSEUM, which is worth visiting, if only to see the interior of the town hall. Around here are many medieval houses which have benefited from the town's conservation programme.

The university area is a short walk from the Rynek, with the ecclesiastical quarter further on, across the River Oder on Ostrów Tumski.

Walking along the Oder affords particularly fine views of the ecclesi-astical district. By the river is the NATIONAL MUSEUM, best known for its collection of medieval stone sculptures and Silesian wood carvings. Close by is Wrocław's major tourist attraction, the RACŁAWICE PANORAMA (open daily 9 a.m.–6 p.m., 9zl). The panoramic painting (120m long and 15m high) depicts the defeat of the Russians in 1794 by the people's militia led by the national hero Tadeusz Kościuszko. The Prussian King Frederick the Great had a residence at the Spaetgens Palace down near the river, which is worth a look.

The Sudeten mountains can be reached from Wrocław by heading south towards the Czech border.

SLEEPING

There are several affordable hotels along ulica Pilsudskiego, right opposite Wrocław Główny: the Piast, no. 98 (Tel. 3430033); the Polonia, no. 66 (Tel. 447310); the Grand, no.100 (Tel. 3436071); and at no. 88 the Europejski (Tel. 443433).

Private rooms can be booked at the Biuro Uslug Turystycznych at ulica Pilsudskiego 98. Of the 2 IYHF hostels, one is in the area behind Wrocław Główny at ulica Kołłataja 20 (Tel. 343856).

The campsite near the Olympic Stadium at al Ignacego Paderewskiego 35 (Tel. 484651) is good. Trams 16 and 17 run along ulica Adama Mickiewicza: the stadium is off to the left.

EATING AND NIGHTLIFE

A good milk bar is the Miś, close to the university at Kuźnicza 48. For cheap but substantial meals try the Academia Brasserie at Kuźnicza 65. The Pod Chmielem beer hall at ulica Odrzańska 17 (between the Rynek and the Oder) offers surprisingly good-quality meals in lively surroundings. The main student club, the Pałacyk, is at ulica Tadeusza Kościuszki 34, on a street between the main train station and the Rynek. The Rura at ulica Lazienna 4 offers live music nightly (blues and, especially, jazz).

NOTES

....

....

....

....

....

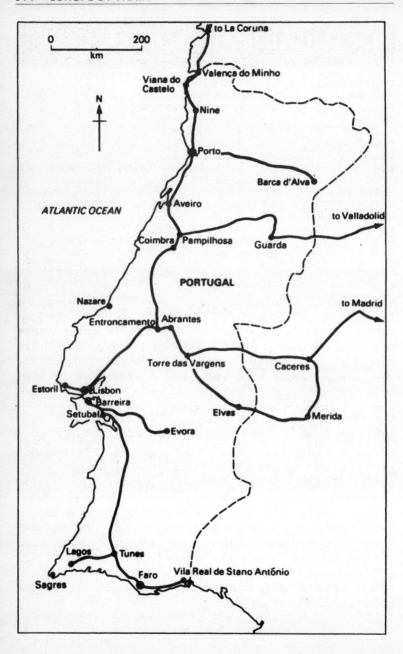

to La Coruna

Valença do Minho

Viana do Castelo

Nine

Porto

Barca d'Alva

ATLANTIC OCEAN

Aveiro

to Valladolid

Coimbra Pampilhosa

Guarda

PORTUGAL

Nazare

to Madrid

Entroncamento Abrantes

Torre das Vargens

Caceres

Estoril Lisbon

Barreira

Setubal

Elvas

Merida

Evora

Lagos Tunes

Sagres Faro Vila Real de Stano António

0 200
km

N

PORTUGAL

Entry requirements	Passport
Population	10,300,000
Capital	Lisbon (pop.: 1,500,000)
Currency	Escudo ($)
	£1 = approx 290$
Political system	Republic
Religion	Roman Catholic
Language	Portuguese (some English, French and Spanish spoken)
Public holidays	1 Jan., Shrove Tuesday., Good Friday, 25 April, 1 May, Corpus Christi, 10 June, 15 Aug., 5 Oct., 1 Nov., 1, 8, 25 Dec.
International dialling	To Portugal: int'l code 351 number
	From Portugal: 07 + country code number

Portugal's early history is shared with the rest of the Iberian peninsula, with the Phoenicians, Greeks and Romans all leaving their mark. Portugal was recognized as a separate nation in 1143 although the Moors weren't pushed out until 1249. Throughout the 15th century, explorers such as Vasco da Gama helped Portugal's overseas empire to grow quickly through the discovery and exploration of the African coast, India, China and finally Brazil. Before long, Portugal had the world's largest empire. But her glory was to be short-lived, as conflict with Spain and rivalry with other European powers gradually brought about her decline. Eventually, even the royal family packed their bags and set off to Brazil during the Napoleonic Wars.

Portugal is Britain's 'oldest ally' and the 2 nations share a special relationship going back more than 600 years. The 1974 revolution gave Portugal a liberal constitution after a spell as a military dictatorship and since 1986 Portugal has been a member of the European Community.

There's a lot of rubbish talked about Portugal, not least about it being a place where inviting a girl out can still be misinterpreted as a proposal of marriage. Today, certainly in the main tourist areas, attitudes of young people are likely to be the same as those of their contemporaries anywhere else in Europe. Portugal remains one of Europe's most affordable countries, where it's possible to cultivate a good tan and eat well while doing it.

PORTUGUESE RAILWAYS
(CAMINHOS DE FERRO PORTUGUÊSES, CP)
The British originally built the Portuguese network with a wide gauge for extra comfort. Much of the 3,600 km network is electrified, but you will also find some of the more remote inland lines are narrow-gauge and steam-hauled. Seat reservations are essential on all international and *rápido* trains. The fastest of the non-supplement trains are the expresses (*directos*). Next down the list are the *semi directos*, which stop nearly as often as the slow *regionals*. Away from the Lisbon area, services can be very slow, so you might feel justified in paying the extra supplements for the intercity *rápidos*; this works out at about 25% above the normal tariff. The standard has improved in recent years, though.

PASSES AVAILABLE Portugal is in Inter-Rail Zone F, along with Spain and Morocco. (For further details of the 8 Inter-Rail zones, refer to the Inter-Rail section in Part One of this guide.)

Eurail passes and the Euro Domino ticket (Freedom Pass) are also valid in Portugal (but see Supplements, below).

CP issue a more expensive Tourist Pass which entitles the holder to 1, 2 or 3 weeks of unlimited travel for 17,000$, 27,000$ or 38,000$ respectively.

TRAIN INFORMATION
English is spoken by most information staff. Always check the timetabling of trains with the posters on station walls, as printed timetables cannot always be relied upon to be accurate.

RESERVATIONS Are optional on inland trains and are quite cheap. For international and express trains, reservations are free of charge providing they are made the day before departure. In general trains are crowded, so it's best to reserve seats in advance.

SUPPLEMENTS Eurail Pass holders need to pay a supplement to travel on express trains. Some *rápido* trains carry a saloon observation car which requires a supplement to travel in it. Don't buy tickets on the train, as you face a whopping surcharge. It's far better to queue at the station if you possibly can. Ask first about the train you are taking. It is worth paying the small supplement on the Lisbon–Porto line.

NIGHT TRAVEL There are couchettes on the Sud Expresso (Lisbon–Paris) and the Lusitania Expresso (Lisbon–Madrid).

Sleepers run from Lisbon to Hendaye and on the Lusitania Expresso.

EATING ON TRAINS All trains except the *regionals* have bars or mini-bars, and some of the *rápidos* have dining cars.

SCENIC TIPS As with Spain, you may have enough problems getting where you want to go without worrying about scenic routes; however, the run from Valença in the north down to Lisbon is one of the best Portugal has to offer. Also try the line from Porto along the Douro valley and its branch lines, such as the one to Braganza.

TIME DIFFERENCE Portugal is on GMT, which means it is 1 hour *behind* Spain.

TOURIST INFORMATION
Is provided by the government-run Postos do Turismo. They have offices all over the country and stalls at major stations.

ISIC BONUSES The main perk here is admission to the cheap student restaurants on your ISIC. In addition about 1,200 places – discos, theatres and so on – also offer discounts. For further information, contact Turismo Social e Juvenil, Turicoop (1st floor), Rua Pascual do Melo, Lisbon.

MONEY MATTERS 1 escudo ($) = 100 centavos.
 1,000 escudos is known as a *conto*. Banking hours are Mon.–Fri.: 8.30 a.m.–2.45 p.m. There are late-night exchange facilities at major tourist resorts.

POST OFFICES AND SHOPS Open Mon.–Sat: 9 a.m.–1 p.m., 3 p.m.–5 or 7 p.m. (closed Sat. p.m.).

MUSEUMS Open 10 a.m.–5 p.m., although some close for lunch and most are closed all day Mon.

TIPPING High tips are not common. Round up your bill to the next highest unit in restaurants and give porters a small note. Add 10% to the meter fare for taxis.

SLEEPING
The government-run tourist board controls all the accommodation within Portugal and will book you a room if required. Hotels are

graded from 2 stars to 5, boarding houses (*estalagem*, *albergaria*, *pensão*), 1–4. By law, prices should be shown at reception and behind the door of each room. A double room in a 3-star hotel costs about 4,500$ a night.

A student hostel tends to be more expensive than a cheap *pensão*. There are 20 youth hostels (*pousadas de juventude*) in Portugal; all require IYHF cards, most impose a midnight curfew, and prices range from 1,000 to 2,000$.

Camping is another possibility: sites are generally close to towns; cheap, but may be quite basic except in the Algarve, where you have to have a Camping Carnet and things are quite plush.

I recommend cheap hotels and boarding houses. They're normally near the stations, and as prices are unaffected by location, it's not really worth shopping around.

EATING AND NIGHTLIFE

Food is cheap in Portugal and eating out is a relatively inexpensive affair (1,000–1,500$), except in the Algarve, where prices are marked up for the tourists. In most restaurants the locals will often eat standing at the counter rather than sitting down. Go for fish dishes, especially chowders if you get the chance: they're invariably cheaper and tastier than meat dishes. National specialities include *linguado delícia* (sole cooked with banana). If you don't like fish, pork represents the best value among the meat dishes. Vegetarians will have to cope largely with omelettes and salads. A bottle of wine is often thrown in for the price of the meal; if not, ask for the local plonk (*vinho da casa*). The port is excellent, especially the fruity white port, but, rather surprisingly, it's not drunk a lot in Portugal. The other wines are excellent too.

If you're living on the beaches and need a meat 'booster', keep your eyes skinned for the mobile shops which serve cheap steak sandwiches (*pregos*). Taverns tend to be very basic, but go down well with the local lads.

Bull fighting in Portugal is not as gory as it is in Spain – they're not allowed to kill the bull – but it's still a national obsession. Of the 2 types of Portuguese bullfight, the *tourada à antiga* is perhaps the more spectacular. Here the bullfighter is dressed in 18th-century costume and fights from a horse.

Discos and bars are at their best in Lisbon, though by northern European standards many of the discos are pretty tame and you'll do better heading for a bar which has *fados* (melancholic Portuguese ballads) on the bill. There are no licensing hours in Portugal, so things can often drag right through the night till dawn.

Lisbon (Lisboa) city phone code: 01

This westernmost capital of Europe escaped many of the influences that shaped the rest of the continent: among them the Reformation, the Industrial Revolution and the Second World War. It has developed out on a limb at a different pace and in a different way, and if any one force can be said to have affected its development, it was – and is – the sea. Lisbon was rebuilt after the 1755 earthquake; only the old Moorish quarter of Alfama escaped destruction. Essentially, it's a pleasant city to visit: beds and meals are cheap and plentiful, the nightlife's lively and there are several places of great interest to visit. In 1998 a major redevelopment is planned for the international Expo, so catch the unmodernized city while you can.

STATION FACILITIES

International trains and northern and eastern trains use Santa Apolónia station. Trains to the south and south-east leave from Barreiro station (linked to Santa Apolónia by a ferry across the Tagus (free on Inter-Rail)); trains to Sintra and the west use Rossio (on bus routes 9, 39 and 46 from Santa Apolónia), and trains for Estoril and Cascais use Cais do Sodre Station (bus 28).

There are daily trains to Porto, Madrid, Irún, Paris.

TOURIST INFORMATION

The Portuguese National Tourist Office (Tel. 346 3314 or 342 5231) is in Palácio da Foz on Praça dos Restauradores, open Mon.–Sat.: 9 a.m.–8 p.m., Sun.: 10 a.m.–6 p.m. The municipal Tourist Office is at Rua Jardim do Regedor; and the national Tourist Office headquarters is at Avenida Augusto de Aguiar 86 (Tel. 357 5086), open Mon.–Fri.: 9.30 a.m.–5.30 p.m.

ADDRESSES

POST OFFICE (CORREIOS DE PORTUGAL) Praça do Comércio, open Mon.–Fri.: 8.30 a.m.–6.30 p.m., or Praça dos Restauradores 58, open Mon.–Fri.: 8 a.m.–10 p.m; Sat., Sun. and national holidays: 9 a.m.–6 p.m.

AMEX Top Tours, Avenida Dunque de Loulé 108 (Tel. 315 5885)

UK EMBASSY Rua de S. Bernardo 33 (Tel. 392 4000)

IRISH EMBASSY Imprensa a Estrekka 14 (Tel. 604 519)

US EMBASSY Avenida dôs Forças Armada 5 (Tel. 726 6600)

CANADIAN EMBASSY Avenida da Liberdade 144, 4th floor (Tel. 347 4892)

AUSTRALIAN CONSULATE Rua Marques S. da Bandeira 8r/c (Tel. 353 0750)
NEW ZEALAND CONSULATE Avenida Antonio Augusto Aguiar 122, 9th floor (Tel. 350 9696).
BRITISH HOSPITAL 49 Rua Saraiva de Carvalho (Tel. 602020)
EUROTRAIN Rua C. C. Branco 20 (Tel. 525709)
24-HOUR CHEMIST British Hospital, Rua Saraiva de Carvalho 49 (Tel. 602020).

GETTING ABOUT

It's best to get your tram or bus ticket from a Carris kiosk rather than on the vehicle, where it costs about 150$. There are passes valid on buses, trams and funiculars for from between 1 day only, at 430$, up to 7 days at 2,265$. Buy them from Carris booths in the main stations, open 8 a.m.–8 p.m. The metro system is limited, but a fast way of getting around and only costs around 70$. If you're travelling in a group, taxis can work out cheaper than in other European capitals. The Lisboa Card, available from the municipal Tourist Office on Rua Regedor, gives free and unrestricted access to buses, trams and the metro, as well as free entry to 25 museums and places of interest. It costs 1,500$ for 24 hours, 2,500$ for 48 hours or 3,250$ for 72 hours.

SEEING

It's pointless our suggesting a route round the ALFAMA district as it's so sprawling you're bound to get lost, so just wander through at your own pace, and if you happen to pass the church of SÃO MIGUEL or LARGO DO SALVADOR 22 (16th-century mansion house), look in. This is one of Europe's most colourful districts, especially in the morning when the fish market's on, or on Fridays (washday) when the narrow streets are hung with locals' shirts and undies. The area is enclosed roughly by the banks of the Tagus, the castle, the church of St Vincent-outside-the-Walls and the cathedral.

ST GEORGE'S CASTLE, the fortress on the hill, has dominated Lisbon in one form or another for 1,500 years. Its gardens of peacocks and flamingos make a good vantage point to look over the city. Near the centre is the SÉ (cathedral), worth a look for its ambulatory and burial chapel. A good view of Lisbon is obtained by taking the ASCENSOR DE SANTA JUSTA up the ornate tower created by Eiffel (admission 150$).

On the outskirts of the city are quite a few sights worth visiting. Go to the BELÉM quarter (tram 15 or buses 14 or 43 from Figueira Square), get off at the Museu Nacional dos Coches, and head for the HIERONYMITE MONASTERY (Mosteiro dos Jerónimos, closed Mon.). Here

Vasco da Gama is buried, as are various Portuguese kings. The affluent merchants in the spice trade put up most of the money for this
beautiful place which was built in the early 16th century. Opposite is
the MONUMENT TO THE DISCOVERIES (free). Take the lift (320$) for a view
of the city. Also in this district is the TOWER OF BELÉM (400$, free with
ISIC), one of Lisbon's landmarks, an elegant mixture of Gothic and
Renaissance architecture.

As far as museums go, the GULBENKIAN ARTS AND CULTURE CENTRE, Av.
de Berna 45 (closed Mon.), the MUSEU NACIONAL DE ARTE ANTIGA, Rua
das Janelas Verdes 95, and the FOLK ART MUSEUM, Av. Marginal, Belém,
are the best.

EXCURSIONS

SINTRA 30 km north-west of Lisbon, Sintra is one of Portugal's
oldest towns and was part of the famed Grand Tour in the 19th
century; it was favoured by Byron. The summer residence of the
royal family was here and the PENA PALACE and PARK, originally set up
by a mad Bavarian prince, are well worth the day trip (closed
Mondays). The MOORISH CASTLE is a must with its fantastic views. The
park has more than 400 kinds of trees and many rare plants. Also
out here is the 16th-century monastery of SANTA CRUZ DE CAPUCHOS
and MONSERRATE PARK. From June to September the Sintra Festival
attracts large numbers of music, opera and ballet enthusiasts and
the piano concerts are incredibly popular. Tourist information is
at Praça da República (Tel. 9231157 or 9233919).

From Sintra you can catch a bus to CABO DA ROCA, the most west-
erly point in Europe, with a memorable view from the lighthouse.
No. 403 departs to Cascais every 90 minutes and stops at Cabo da
Roca. Get off at the Azoia turn-off and walk the last couple of kilometres.

ESTORIL If you want a day on the beach, head here, a jet-set resort
26 km west of the city, or to CASCAIS, 3 km further on. The journey to
Cabo da Roca is shorter from here than from Sintra. If you want to
stop off but can't afford the hotel prices, head a few kilometres back
towards Lisbon and get off the train at OEIRAS. Here you can enjoy a
fine beach and an excellent modern, cheap and friendly IYHF hostel
just a stone's throw away. It is at Catalazete, Estrada Marginal (Tel.
4430638). It's quite small (100 beds) and fills up quickly, so don't
lose time in booking your place.

QUELUZ Another idea is to visit this town 13 km north-west of Lisbon, where the rococo palace used to entertain VIPs of the Portuguese government. It's stuffed full of antiques and can be reached by train from Rossio station (palace is closed Tues.).

SLEEPING

An average double in a pension is about 4,000$ per person (singles cost about 5,000–6,000$). There are plenty of cheap places in Lisbon – not everywhere is clean and quiet, but the ones listed are about as close as you'll get. If these don't come up lucky, try yourself round Rua da Alegria, Rua dos Correiros, Rua Augusta and Praça da Figueira. Lisbon's youth hostel is at Rua Andrade Corvo 46 (Tel. 353 2696); it's cheap and a 20-minute walk from the centre, but next to Picoas metro.

As far as camping goes, there are plenty of sites – and free beach camping close by – but the recommended sites are the Parque Municipal de Campismo (Tel. 760 2061) (bus 43 from Praça da Figueira) or Parque Nacional de Turismo e Campismo (Tel. 370 4413) (bus to Parque Florestal, Monsanto).

As regards budget hotels, Pensão do Sul, Avenida da Liberdade 53 (Tel. 365647) has cheap rooms, as does Pensão Pembra at Avenida da Liberdade 11 (Tel. 325010,) Pensão Ninho de Aguias, Costa do Castelo 74 (Tel. 860391), is of very high quality. Doubles start at 4,500$ including breakfast. The cheapest place in town at the time of going to press is the Pensão Madeireuse, Rua da Glória 22–1 (Tel. 3961992). It lies in the pension-filled area at the town-centre end of venida da Liberdade.

EATING AND NIGHTLIFE

Between the port and the Praça da Figueira is the best district. Lisbon is no longer as cheap as in the '80s, so choose your district carefully. Try Rua dos Correiros (near Terreiro do Pão). Use the Mercado da Ribeira outside the Cais do Sodré for picnic food, and watch out you don't get stuck on Sundays, especially in July, when many places close. Fish is generally good value, but don't eat the bread and savouries put out on the tables unless you're prepared to pay the extortionate prices that are often asked for them. Restaurante Trevo da Madalena and Restaurante Central on Rua da Madalena are both inexpensive. Alternatively, try Glória on Rua da Glória 39a. The area near the youth hostel is quite good for eating places, and the cheapest part of town is around the Barrio Alto and in the sidestreets off the rua Misericórdia.

Nightlife starts late and can get pretty lively. The authentic

Portuguese folk music, the *fado*, is performed in several restaurants and cafés. Don't go till around midnight, unless you're happy to share your evenings with coach parties from package tours. Senhor Vinho, Rua do Meio à Lapa 18 (Tel. 397 2681), and the São Cactano, Rua São Cactano 27 (Tel. 397 4792) , offer authentic *fados*, but not for under 3,000$. Taxi drivers can be a good source of information on the location of an authentic *fado*. Lively nightlife can be found in the Barrio Alto especially around Rua Diário das Notícias. The gay nightlife centres around here, with several good mixed gay/straight bars and dance spots – try Frágil on Rua da Atalaia or Harry's Bar on Rua São Pedro de Alcantara.

Port, the national drink, can be sampled at the PORT WINE INSTITUTE, Rua São Pedro de Alcantara 45, Mon.–Fri.: 10 a.m.–11.30 p.m; Sat.: 11 a.m.–10.30 p.m. In the summer the LISBON AMUSEMENT PARK gives you somewhere to spend time before heading for the bars or cafés later on. The fair goes on till 1 a.m. and can be reached by the underground (station: Entre-Campos).

Porto and the Costa Verde

If you're approaching Portugal from the north, the places worth stopping for are Viana do Castelo and Porto.

VIANA DO CASTELO This pretty little fishing resort, 1½ hours north of Porto, has a vantage point for views over the whole region including the BASILICA OF SANTA LUZIA. You can take the funicular up or, better still, walk up the twisting road past the pine and eucalyptus trees till you reach the top. Back down in the town, look out for reminders of the Renaissance in the buildings of the PRAÇA DA REPÚBLICA and the church of SÃO DOMINGOS. If you're here in the third week of August, you'll catch the festival: bullfights, processions, fireworks, dancing, etc. The MUNICIPAL MUSEUM has a collection of the ceramics Portugal is famous for. Rooms aren't a problem: try the streets off Avenida dos Combatentes, or camp at Cabedelo beach.

PORTO This is an industrial town, very much a mixture of old and new. Tourist Information is at Rua Clube dos Fenianos 25 (Tel. 312740). Climb the IGREJADOS CLERIGOS church tower, then visit one of the 20 or so PORT HOUSES for a free tour and tasting, but avoid buying any in the port houses' own shops as you will probably find it cheaper in town. Much of this region is unspoilt, as most eurorailers head for either Lisbon or the overrated Algarve.

The youth hostel is at Rua Rodrigues Lobo 98 (Tel. 60655 35). Take bus 19 or 20 from Praça da Liberdade, but arrive early, as it is often full. The campsite is at Rua Monte dos Burgos (Tel. 81 2616); bus 6 from Praça da Liberdade.

A day trip to REGUA in the Douro valley is possible from Porto. This is one of Europe's most scenic routes.

The Costa Prata

Moving further south, the next region of Portugal is the Costa Prata (Silver Coast). ÓBIDOS is a little medieval village, 11 km from the sea. It is worth seeing for its preserved CASTLE, old TOWN WALLS and the 2 churches of SANTA MARIA and the MISERICÓRDIA. Tourist Information is on Rua Direita (Tel. 959231).

COIMBRA This university town is second only to Lisbon in terms of historical and cultural importance. It is set among the beautiful forests and woods of the Beira Litoral region, and is less than 2½ hours from the capital. Get off at Coimbra-A station, walk 2 blocks east for the *turismo* in Largo da Portagem. It's open Mon.–Fri.: 9 a.m.–7 p.m., Sat and Sun.: 1 p.m.–5.30 p.m (Tel. 23886 or 33028).

The UNIVERSITY is the best sight of the town. The OLD LIBRARY (*Biblioteca*), the CHAPEL and the MUSEUM are all impressive (knock on the door to be let in) and the CEREMONIAL HALL is decorated with some fine *azulejos* (ceramic tiles). The MACHADO MUSEUM nearby is a former episcopal palace, and today houses many of Portugal's artistic treasures.

The town's CATHEDRAL is 12th-century, as is the Cistercian convent, MOSTEIRO DE CELAS. On the other side of the bridge is a reconstructed village of all the famous buildings in Portugal, miniature-size: PORTUGAL DOS PEQUENINOS.

For cheap beds, look out for *dormidas* round the station: Rua da Sota and the streets around should produce something. The youth hostel at Rua Henriques Sêco 14 (Tel. 39 22955) is recommended. Take bus 7, 29 or 46 from Coimbra-A to Liceu José Falcão. The campsite at Praça 25 de Abril (Tel. 712997) costs 250$ per person plus 350$ per tent.

For eats, try Zé Manel, Beco do Forno 12, just off Rua da Sota. Apart from good cheap food, this place has character. Open 12 noon–3 p.m., 5 p.m.–10 p.m. and closed Mon. Much cheaper food than in Lisbon. *Fado* can be found, along with several bars, on Travessa da Rua Nova–the Diligência Bar is recommended.

NAZARE 5 km away, is an unspoilt resort where traditional Portugal survives alongside tourism (take the bus from Valado on the Lisbon –Coimbra line). There is a nice beach and a funicular (150$) to the old town.

The Plains (Plâncies) and Mountains (Montanhas)

The hinterland of Portugal, between Spain and the Tagus, lies off the beaten track – a good place for avoiding your fellow tourists.

EVORA This is the main town, 3 hours from Lisbon. See the ROMAN TEMPLE OF DIANA, the CAPELA DE OSSOS (chapel) containing the bones of 5,000 monks, the SÉ (cathedral) and the MUSEU D'EVORA (free on ISIC). Look for the pensions off the Praça do Giraldo. Camping is on the Alcáçovas Road (500–1,200$ per person), outside town. Food is cheaper than in Lisbon. Good regional specialities can be found at Restaurante Fasca on Rua da Raimundo.

The Algarve

Portugal's famous southern region used to be one of the best-kept secrets in continental Europe: mile after mile of white sand interspersed with picturesque fishing villages. Sadly that is no longer the case, as the package holiday industry has really taken off in a big way in the Algarve since the early 1970s. Many of the small villages have been turned into overgrown building sites, crowded with British package holidaymakers and overpriced accordingly. The Algarve has practically no evidence left of its historical past.

Most of the small villages were flattened by a major earthquake in 1755, and only FARO, LAGOS and SAGRES (home of Prince Henry the Navigator) have any traces worth visiting. The region as a whole retains some appeal, if you can manage to avoid all the busy package resorts, including QUARTEIRA, VILAMOURA, MONTE GORDO and (especially) ALBUFEIRA. These over-commercialized villages really have nothing to offer other than superb beaches. If you're lucky, you might find a few empty feet of sand all to yourself among the package tourists.

One advantage of the huge package trade is that English is practically the second language of the region. The local cuisine is worth investigating – plenty of fish and seafood delicacies – and regional wines are really cheap. House wines are normally less than a pound (about 240$) even in some of the better cafés and restaurants. The region is a paradise for those interested in sport, assuming they're not short of a few quid, and there are many exclusive golf and sports clubs tagged on to the bigger hotels.

The Algarve is well connected by rail from Lisbon and the north, and the region's main line runs across from Lagos, through Faro, to Vila Real de Santo António in the east.

SLEEPING

Finding an inexpensive base in the Algarve is next to impossible during the peak summer months from June to August. Look out for *casas particulares* (private accommodation) or else consider sleeping on the beach. If you're around Lagos, an alternative for Inter-Railers is Novastar (Tel. 082 342049) which offers beds from 1,200$. They have a mixture of dorms, 6-, 4- and 2-bedded rooms and camping. Call them at Silves and they'll pick you up.

If you've really set your heart on spending a few days in the Algarve then you ought to consider arriving out of season. March and April are good months, when the weather is mild with temperatures occasionally straying into the low twenties (C). Cheap accommodation is also relatively plentiful in towns like Faro and Lagos. The weather can become quite windy after September, so bear this in mind before packing too much suntan lotion later on in the year.

LAGOA This small town, between Albufeira and Lagos, is one good place to base yourself. There is a complex specially designed for young travellers, which offers the major service of sending transport to meet all local trains in the small towns. It is open from the end of May to the beginning of October. It is a self-contained unit with a choice of 3 restaurants/snack bars, and a disco with parties most nights. Accommodation is in dormitories or tents. Also there is a shuttle bus all day to its own beach which gives access to other, more secluded beaches. It is very popular among eurorailers because of the cosmopolitan atmosphere. For further information contact Astor Hostels, Thurloe St, London SW7.

LAGOS This is the region's westernmost town of any size and has a colourful past dating back to the time of the Celts. There's still quite a bit to see, including the scattered remains of the MEDIEVAL WALLS and the magnificent church of SANTO ANTÓNIO, on Rua Silva Lopes, which contains some of Portugal's finest gilt carvings. The REGIONAL MUSEUM next door has an interesting, if rather disjointed, collection of artefacts telling the town's history.

The Tourist Office is on Largo Marquês de Pombal (Tel. 763031). Accommodation is more expensive than elsewhere but there is a wide choice, and many private rooms. The youth hostel is at Rua Lancerote de Freitas 50 (Tel 761970).

FARO The Algarve's capital, this is well worth at least a day trip. Its jumbled streets spread out from a small MARINA just along from the railway station. Faro has an empty old CATHEDRAL just opposite the BISHOP'S PALACE. Nearby is an ARCHAEOLOGICAL MUSEUM, the better of a couple of modest museums in town. Try and get to the CARMELITE CHURCH at Largo do Carmo, near the main post office, as the church has a spectacular gilt interior, and a bizarre CHAPEL OF BONES behind it. The chapel was built by an over-zealous bishop in the last century using the skulls and bones of over l,200 monks.

Faro is your best bet for accommodation in the Algarve if you insist on arriving mid-summer. Room prices are over-inflated but you may find something away from the smart shopping centre part of town – aimed very much at the British tourist with lots of cash. Try the 3-star Pensão Residêncial Marim on Rua Gonçalo Barreto (Tel. 089 24063). The Tourist Office, open daily 9 a.m.–8 p.m. in the summer, is on Rua da Misericórdia (Tel. 803604), but don't expect much help in finding cheap accommodation. There is a youth hostel on Rua da PSP (Tel. 801970).

SAGRES This has some excellent beaches, is off the package tour track and popular with backpackers. It is best reached by the frequent buses from Lagos. Private rooms are widely advertised; expect to pay 2,000$. The youth hostel is in the FORTRESS (Tel. 82 64129). The main street, Praça da República, is the centre of nightlife and has good cheap restaurants.

For a total contrast, head inland for a day. The contrast with the heaving coastal resorts in many of the isolated rural villages is amazing, although you'll need to take the bus or cycle since the railway sticks rigidly to the coast! If you're heading east into Spain, VILA REAL DE SANTO ANTÓNIO sits right on the border and is a pleasant little town for a few hours, stop. Even if you're not heading onward through

Spain, day trips from Vila Real across to AYAMONTE take 15 minutes by ferry (every half-hour, cost 200$) and customs formalities are minimal. Once in Ayamonte, you can catch a bus to Huelva, where you join up with the Spanish rail network again.

NOTES

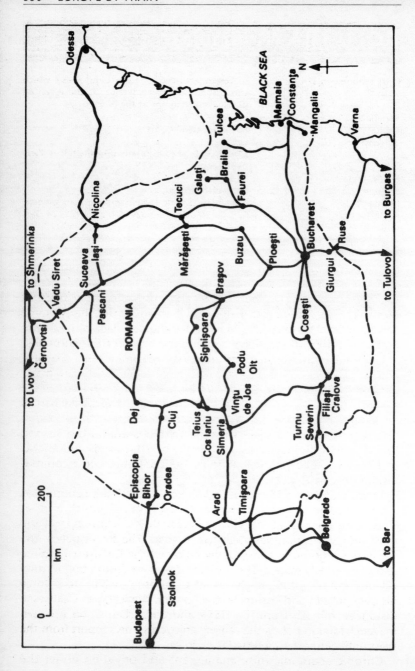

ROMANIA (România)

Entry requirements	All foreigners need a passport and a visa, which should be bought in advance, as there can be problems buying one at the border.
Population	23,200,000
Capital	Bucharest (2,300,000)
Currency	Leu
	£1 = 12,000 lei (but inflation means this is likely to increase)
Political system	Republic
Religion	Romanian Orthodox
Language	Romanian (a little French and German spoken)
Public holidays	1, 2 Jan., Easter Monday, 1 May, 1, 25, 26 Dec.
International dialling	To Romania: international code 40 number
	From Romania: 00 + country code number

Romania is keen on encouraging and developing tourism, especially after the extremely violent revolution which overthrew the Stalinist Ceauşescu regime in December 1989 and which affected all facets of Romanian life. Although the new government under the National Salvation Front has yet fully to convince the populace of its democratic intentions, things have become more lax for the eurorailer.

Once a Roman province, the area was overrun by Asian, Slavonic and Turkish tribes, giving a real mixture of peoples, including many gypsies. Moldavia in the east and Wallachia in the south were united to form Romania in 1859. Transylvania, the area in the central part, is full of forests, its beauty and diversity overshadowed by the legend of Count Dracula. Initially allied to the Germans during the Second World War, the Romanian leadership was overthrown by anti-fascists in 1944 and, following liberation by the USSR, became a communist republic in 1946.

From 1965 to the December revolution of 1989 the country was led by Nicolae Ceauşescu and remained firmly Stalinist, and, as Ceauşescu established his cult of personality, became one of the most repressive countries in Eastern Europe. The secret police, the *Securitate*, vigorously and brutally enforced the Ceauşescu regime and were widely feared. There was widespread destruction of rural villages and of historic Bucharest at Ceauşescu's whim, to enforce his own policies and ensure central control. Ironically, as Ceauşescu distanced himself from the USSR and embarked upon his own maverick foreign policy, the regime enjoyed some support from the West until *glasnost* established itself in the USSR.

Chronic economic mismanagement and privation under the

Ceauşescu regime have made Romania one of the poorest countries in Europe. The new government has taken steps to begin the mammoth task of reconstruction. However, food and general shortages may continue and the potential of the market economy has yet to be fully realized.

Although the democratic sentiments of the National Salvation Front have been questioned by many Romanians, the tourist infrastructure is rapidly being expanded and the warmth of the people is entirely genuine. Romania is on the threshold of a new era and remains one of the last European countries where you are less a tourist and more a genuine traveller.

ROMANIAN RAILWAYS
(CĂILE FERATE ROMÂNE, CFR)

In recent years Romania has improved its services considerably in response to increased demand. Most trains are still dirty and overcrowded by Western standards, so imagine what they were like before. To travel at reasonable speed and comfort on any of the *rapide* (fast) and *accelerate* (semi-fast) trains you will have to pay a supplement. To avoid this, you have to travel on the local *tren de persoane* trains – a fate worse than death. In other words: pay the supplement. Never rely on split-second connections – there are often delays, sometimes running into hours. The Budapest–Bucharest run is a notorious example.

PASSES AVAILABLE Romania is in Inter-Rail Zone H, along with Bosnia Hercegovia, Yughoslavia and Macedonia. For information on the Freedom Pass (Euro Domino), see p. 41.

TRAIN INFORMATION

English is not widely spoken, so be prepared with a French back-up (German can also be useful, especially in the north of the country). If all else fails, try: *De la ce peron pleaca trenul spre?...* (From which platform does the train to ... leave?)

Romania has train connections to most neighbouring Eastern European countries, via Budapest, Vienna, Prague and Munich.

RESERVATIONS Compulsory on all trains except the *tren de persoane*. The best strategy is to reserve your place out as soon as you arrive, especially on crowded routes, such as BucharestConstanţa. Reserve your exit seat before entering the country – queues are horrendous.

NIGHT TRAVEL Couchettes and sleepers hardly come up to Western standards and need to be booked well in advance, particularly on the Bucharest–Budapest run. Kick up a fuss if officials demand additional 'reservations' once you're aboard. Rates vary according to distance.

EATING ON TRAINS There are restaurants on many long-distance fast trains and buffets on shorter-distance fast trains.

TOURIST INFORMATION

ONT is the national tourist organization. They have offices in all large towns which give out information and help in finding a room.

ISIC BONUSES Reductions for all international rail travel in Eastern Europe. Also museum entrances reduced with an IUS card. For further information, contact CTT, Strada Oneşti 4–6, Bucharest 1.

Inter-Rail bonuses on offer include free entry to the railway museum at Gara de Nord, Bucharest.

MONEY MATTERS 1 leu (plural, lei) = 100 bani (not used).

Banking hours are Mon.Sat:, 9 a.m.–12 noon, 1 p.m.–3 p.m. (closed Sat. p.m.). The leu has undergone high inflation recently and there is a black market paying over the official rate. Although the risks are also greater because of informers, there is now probably more chance of being duped by a fraudster than being jailed. Cigarettes, especially Kent or Marlboro, are an alternative informal means of exchange and are useful for tipping. There is also a good black market for coffee. Extra hard currency is useful.

POST OFFICES, SHOPS AND MUSEUMS All vary their times of opening, depending on the district. Most keep to the 9–5 routine 6 days a week. In Bucharest, some shops open on Sun. mornings.

TIPPING It is really up to you how much you want to give. Restaurant prices often include a 10% service charge, but waiters will often rush to help Westerners on the assumption that you have hard currency and will leave them a hefty tip as well. Bring a few packs of cigarettes for tipping (Kent, or BT from Bulgaria).

SLEEPING

Choices are limited in Romania by the absence of cheap class-3 hotels, but rooms in private homes may now fill this gap; expect to pay in hard currency. Hostels (*căminul de studenţi*) are run by the student travel service, CTF, and give preference to large groups when they open during July and August. If you're lucky and make the effort to get to the hostel direct, you will find it inexpensive, although prices have recently shot up. Most eurorailers camp and accept the poor facilities, or pay for a class-2 hotel, which can be anything up to $30 for a double room. All hotel bills/campsites must be paid for in hard currency and receipts must often be produced from where you changed your money: you may have great difficulty if you have changed unofficially.

EATING AND NIGHTLIFE

Eating is more expensive than elsewhere in Eastern Europe and the food is generally of low quality, as is the beer. Supermarkets usually have reasonably full shelves but with little choice or variety. You will do well if you happen to like jam, which is colossally oversupplied – unfortunately, this isn't always true of bread to spread it on. Romania's nightlife is not up to Hungary's standards, but after a few glasses of ţuică, the local plum spirit, you'll never know the difference. Almost all restaurants take lei, so if the waiter claims only dollars are accepted he's most likely out to rip you off. Avoid restaurants without menus, since prices will fluctuate wildly.

THINGS TO BRING AND BUY

Luxury items are scarce or expensive in Romania, so try to bring whatever you may need. If you must have your morning coffee, bring a jar of instant with you, as coffee is almost a myth here and is sold only in the hard currency shops of luxury hotels. In fact, bring 2 jars and use 1 to barter with other eurorailers at campsites or hotels. For those planning on camping or hiking, bring in as much pre-prepared and tinned food as you can carry. Chocolate is almost non-existent and expensive when you can find it, and film is in short supply and of poor quality.

The people here are generally very poor and this is reflected in what you will find for sale. Colourfully embroidered women's blouses are plentiful and cheap in the countryside, as are the small carved wooden flutes which you will see everywhere. There is also a wide variety of woodcrafts, ranging from toys to bowls and kitchen stuffs. Romarta shops carry pottery, glassware and clothing at reasonable prices, and accept lei.

Bucharest (Bucureşti) city phone code: 0

The journey here on the dismal trains is not one of Europe's best and you'll probably wish you hadn't bothered halfway through the night, but take heart: Bucharest is known as the 'Paris of Eastern Europe', though considering the lack of nightlife and scarcity of actual 'sights', this is a bit over the top. Much of historic Bucharest disappeared under Ceauşescu's bulldozers and you have to work hard to find the character remaining.

STATION FACILITIES

There are 4 train stations, Gara de Nord, Băneasa, Obor and Basarab. Gara de Nord is the biggest and most depressing station and is used most by Eurorailers. Left luggage is only for Romanians – foreigners have to use the 'Hand Luggage' office near Platform 13. Beware of beggars and conmen here: you can expect to be hassled both by them and by the station police.

There are daily trains to Athens, Cluj, Belgrade, Berlin, Basle, Budapest, Munich, Paris, London, Prague, Sofia, Warsaw, Vienna and Zürich.

TOURIST INFORMATION

There is a Tourist Office in the station which is open 7 a.m.–9 p.m. weekdays, 7 a.m.–3 p.m. weekends. The main Tourist Office is at Blvd Magheru 7 (take tram 87 from the station to Piaţa Romana), open Mon.–Sat.: 8 am.–8 p.m., Sun.: 8 a.m.–2 p.m., info. only 8 a.m.–4.30 p.m. Mon.–Fri. Don't be surprised if there are no street maps available – if not, the main Tourist Office has one on its wall which you can consult, or take yourself off to Hotel Griviţei on Calea Griviţei 130 near the station for maps. You can change money at all offices.

CTT, the youth tourist service that deals with groups (the whole of Romanian tourism centres on groups), is at Strada Oneşti 4–6. The CFR offices are at Brezoianu Street 10, in the Tarom Building, and on Calea Grivţei, open Mon.–Fri.: 7.30 a.m.–6 p.m., Sat.: 7.30 a.m.–12 noon.

ADDRESSES

POST OFFICE Strada Malei Millo 10, off Calea Victoriei, open 7.30 a.m.–8 p.m. Mon. Fri., 7 a.m.–2.30 p.m. Sat.

UK EMBASSY Strada Jules Michelet 24 (Tel. 31203035 or 6153571)

US EMBASSY Strada. T Arghezi 7 (Tel. 3124040 or 3124042)
CANADIAN EMBASSY Strada Nicolae Iorga 36 (Tel. 3120365 or 6506140)
AUSTRALIAN CONSUL Liviu Buzula, Strada Dr E. Racota 1618, ap. 1 (Tel. 666 6923)
IRISH AND NZ CITIZENS Try the UK embassy.
EMERGENCY MEDICAL TREATMENT Spital Clinic de Urgenta, Calea Floreasca 8 (Tel 6794310)
24-HOUR CHEMIST Blvd Magheru 18. Also at Gara de Nord.

GETTING ABOUT

Buses, trolley-buses and trams are cheap, and tickets can be bought from all kiosks. Taxis too are a bargain. A metro system is still being built in Bucharest, with 3 lines having been completed. This merely adds to the chaos, as some roads have been closed and many tram routes have been cancelled. There is a flat fare of two 50 lei coins – kiosks at the stations give change. Beware of pickpockets, especially on buses which are chronically overcrowded.

SEEING

Modern Bucharest is hard on the eye, so ignore the new and concentrate on the old. The name Bucharest was given to this town in 1459 by none other than Dracula, a local lad, known here as Vlad the Impaler. By far the most pleasant day's sightseeing is spent out on the HERĂSTRĂU PARK where the VILLAGE MUSEUM is, along with many bars. This collection of peasant houses gathered from all over the country is open 9 a.m.–6 p.m. (5 p.m. Mon.).

Parks and museums are Bucharest's main assets. LIBERTY PARK, the STUDENT PARK on Lacul Tei, or the central CIȘMIGIU PARK are great meeting places and the places to head for to meet young Romanians. Go to Piața Unirii for the bustling market where Romania's gypsies sell their wares.

As far as museums go, out of the 40 or so to choose from, I'd recommend the HISTORY MUSEUM; the former royal palace, today the NATIONAL ART MUSEUM; and the GEORGE ENESCO MUSEUM.

For an insight into turbulent recent history, visit the TV station (bus 131 from Piața Aviatoriler) and observe the bullet-ridden buildings where the opposing factions of the 1989 revolution battled for control of the media. Also view the Victory of Socialism Boulevard and the monumental HOUSE OF THE REPUBLIC constructed by Ceaușescu for his own purposes and bear in mind that over one-fifth of Bucharest was destroyed in their construction. Take the metro to the Piața Uniiri stop.

SLEEPING

The ONT office (see above) will arrange rooms in private homes for about US$15, or you may be approached directly at the station, which will usually be cheaper. For a bed in a student hostel, go to ONT or CTT and ask them for addresses as these change yearly.

Camping is out at Camping Băneasa (Tel. 794525) and while not very appealing it is relatively cheap (about US$7 per person) and is next to the zoo. It is reached by taking bus 205 from Gara de Nord to its terminus at Plaţa Presei Libere, then bus 148. The site is hidden in the trees.

Grade-2 hotels are your best bet in Bucharest. Get a list from ONT and if you're told they're all full, ignore it and go along to the hotels regardless and ask at reception. There are quite a few near the Gara de Nord, charging about US$13–15 single, and US$20–24 for a double. Try Hotel Dunărea, Calea Grivilei 140 (Tel. 173220); Hotel Bucegi, Strada Witing 2 (Tel. 159350); Hotel Cişmigiu, Blvd M. Kogălniceanu 18 (Tel. 147410).

EATING AND NIGHTLIFE

The 24-hour stand-up *Buffet Expres* are the cheapest form of eats, but a lot of the food is fairly revolting and high in stodge content. For quick self-service snacks you could also try the self-service restaurants at the Dorobanţi or Lido Hotels. For a pizza joint, Salon Spaniol at Calea Vitorei 116 is favoured by students but closes at 6 p.m. Traditional Romanian cuisine can be found at Hanul Manuc at Strada Iuliu Maniu 62, a bar/restaurant in an attractive setting. Good food and authentic gypsy music can be found at La Doi Coçosi at Şoseaua Străuleşti 6. Next to the History Museum at Strada Stavropoleos 5 is Caru cu Bere, which does some fine meals and has a good selection of beers.

As far as nightlife goes, don't build your hopes up as it's a bit of a non-event. ONT will tell you what's on in town, but usually the choice is between the circus at Aleea Circului, the cinema or the theatre. The university student club is an alternative on Saturdays where you can meet young Romanians, an impressive number of whom speak English. It's on Calea Plevnei 61 (metro: Eroiler) and you need your ISIC/IUS. If you are a student and have the advance approval of the Institute of Architecture, you can gain entrance to the architects' club on Strada Academiei 2–4 (near the Interconti-nental Hotel). The club is popular with the locals and the entertainment varies from disco and jazz to theatre and film. The Institute is near the club.

EXCURSIONS SNAGOV, 40 km to the north, is well worth a day trip. The lake here is a great place for swimming and boating during the summer. Take a boat to the island in the middle of the lake, to visit the 16th-century monastery where the infamous Vlad the Impaler (Dracula to some) has his final resting place. No women are permitted to enter the monastery.

Transylvania

This picturesque region, home of the notorious Count Dracula, is Romania's most scenic. The Transylvanian Alps and the small peasant villages with their rich, active folklore make travelling here interesting and rewarding. The best towns to base yourself in are Braşov or Sighişoara.

BRAŞOV
This town is about 2½ hours from Bucharest, on the edge of the Carpathian mountains, set among the Transylvanian Alps. In its old town are the BLACK CHURCH and the TOWN HALL, both 14th century, but the main attractions are outside the town.

A visit to the summer residence of King Carl at SIRIA CASTLE is a must for its wonderful interior decoration and furnishings.

The Disneyesque CASTLE OF BRAN, apocryphally Dracula's summer house, is reached by bus 12 to the bus station, then bus 23 (runs Mon.–Sat. only) to the castle, and is open 9 a.m.–6 p.m. (closed Mon.). Postăvarul, 9 Eroilor Blvd (Tel. 42840), will give you details of the best excursions. It is about 2 km from the train station and reached on bus 4.

CTT in Strasma Armata Roşie will hand you this year's list of student hostels (bus 4 from station). Just past the Hotel Carpati is the Braşov University Rector's Office. Ask for Simone Dobresan, the rector's secretary, who may find you a cheap room in a private house (open Mon.–Fri.: 10 a.m.–5 p.m.).

Camping Zimbrul is on the road to the mountain resort of Volna–Braşov. Take bus 4 to Parc Central, then bus 20.

Braşov saw heavy fighting in the revolution of December 1989 and many buildings, especially on Piaţa Teatrului, are pock-marked by bullets, save the Communist Party building, which remained oddly unscathed.

THE FAGĂRAS MOUNTAINS of the Carpathian range make a great place for hiking amongst the 1,800m peaks and 70 lakes. GARA SEREŞ OLT on the main line from Braşov is a good place to start. There are mountain huts (*cabanas*) spread throughout the region high up on the slopes. Get a map ahead of time in Braşov and reserve *cabana* beds through the Tourist Office there. Make sure to bring a lot of food and a good pair of shoes.

SIGHIŞOARA

A 2½ hour journey from Braşov this beautiful medieval town is as yet unspoilt by tourism. This is an ideal spot to break the long haul from Bucharest to Budapest (nearly 14 hours) and it offers more in the way of sights than Braşov.

The OLD WALLED TOWN is well preserved and among its sights are the CLOCK TOWER, the TOWN MUSEUM (closed Mon.), the GUILD TOWERS and the BERGKIRCHE, a church with good views over the town. The CHURCH OF THE MONASTERY off the clock tower square is the town's oldest building and not far from here is Dracula's father's house.

ONT (Tel. 77 1022) is across from the main thoroughfare of Strada Ch. Gheorghiu-Dej. It's open Mon.–Sat.: 8 a.m.–1 p.m., 2 p.m.–8 p.m., Sun.: 8 a.m.–11 a.m. Get your map here.

You've a choice of camping at Campground Hula Danes (bus direction Medias) about 4 km from town, or paying up for Hotel Steaua, Strada Ch. Gheorghiu-Dej (Tel. 771930). To meet the locals and have a drink, try the beer hall at 34 Piaţa Lenin.

Moldavia

This region of Europe is known for beautiful painted mountain monasteries of northern Bucovina, small rural villages and its completely unspoilt lifestyle, where locals still wear national costume and not a word of English seems to be spoken. The trains are pitifully slow and you can't afford to be in a rush. Ask at Bucharest for times and routes – mostly you have to change to the smaller lines at Cluj.

SUCEAVA

This is the capital of Moldavia and the best starting-point for a tour of the monasteries. The FOLK ART MUSEUM is a worthwhile visit. It's in the 16th-century Princely Inn at Strada Ciprian Porumbescu 5 and in an hour or so fills you in on the culture of the people that surround you.

The ONT office is at Nicolae Bălcescu 2 (open Mon.–Sat.: 8 a.m.–8 p.m., Sun.: 9 a.m.–12 noon.), and they'll supply you with bus schedules and details of the monasteries.

THE MONASTERIES VORONET is the most famous and ancient of the monasteries, dating back to 1488. It's known as the 'Sistine Chapel of the East', owing to its amazing frescoes and unique shade of blue. *The Last Judgement* is the most amazing fresco in Moldavia, showing a whole panoply of figures and scenes from the Bible.

HUMOR, a nearby village, has a monastery obviously built by misogynists (the devil is portrayed as a woman in the frescoes). and from here you can set off for SUCEVIȚA MONASTERY. This one is absolutely covered in fascinating frescoes inside and out, from portraits of Plato to the *Arabian Nights*. There is also a small museum here. The actual village of Sucevița has got to be the most charming in Romania. There is a wonderful view over the monastery from the hill opposite and you can camp at the bottom of the hill.

To experience religious life visit the PUTNA MONASTERY, where you will rub shoulders with chanting monks. There is no shortage of accommodation here with a large hotel, campsite and bungalows.

The Black Sea Coast

Romania's coastline starts at the Danube delta on the Russian frontier and stretches south for 246 km to the Bulgarian border. The area is dominated by resorts and huge hotels.

CONSTANȚA A curious mixture of Roman, Greek and Eastern Byzantine (there's even a mosque and minaret here). See the remains of the ROMAN DOCKS with its huge piece of preserved mosaic, the ARCHAEOLOGICAL MUSEUM and the ROMANIAN NAVAL MUSEUM. Outside the Archaeological Museum is a statue of the city's most famous resident, the poet OVID.

Part of the beach is sheltered by a tree-and-hedge wind-break; however, you may find that Constanța gets busier than the other resorts in summer, so use your rail ticket to the full and head off for somewhere smaller down the line.

ONT, Blvd Tomis 66 (Tel. 614800), can arrange private accommodation. For hotels, try the Continental, further up Blvd Tomis. Camping is at Constanța is at Mamaia. Take trolley-bus 150 from the station, and it is a 2-minute walk to the site, situated by the sea and usually very crowded in summer.

The resorts of Mamaia, Efone Nord, Efone Sud, Neptun, Saturn and Mangalia are all good places to soak up the sun in more isolated surroundings.

TULCEA This is the gateway to the Danube delta. Nature lovers should take a boat trip to see the wildlife in this unique delta; over 300 species of birds, 60 species of fish and well over 1,000 species of plants are to be found in the shelter of this protected area. Excursions are organized by ONT in the Hotel Delta, 10 minutes' walk down the quay from the station at Strada Isaccea 2 (Tel. 14720).

Hotel Egreta is the cheaper hotel at Strada Păcii (Tel. 17103). For the ultimate in budget-balancing, the Three Star Hotel, Strada Carpal 1300, charges around US$2 for a single room.

The nearest campsite is at Maliuc (2 hours by ferry) and is infested with mosquitoes.

Western Romania

All trains east to Romania from Hungary and Yugoslavia pass through this area, once known as THE BANAT when it formed part of the great Habsburg Empire. The land is mostly flat and is dominated by the 3 cities of Timişoara, Oradea and Arad.

TIMIŞOARA The city which played such an important role in the revolution of 1989 is an interesting one whose architecture reflects its population of Hungarians and Serbs (now deported). The Hungarian people of western Romania led the fight against Ceauşescu and so it is no surprise that the December 1989 revolution started here and made the city world famous. The impressive DICASTERIAL PALACE on strada Ceahlău is an indication of the great opulence of the old Habsburg rulers. Two trains a day go to Belgrade, and there is a Yugoslav consulate here if you need a visa (Strada Remus 4, Mon.–Thurs., 9 a.m. till noon).

Around the picturesque square PIAŢA UNRII is a baroque CATHOLIC CATHEDRAL and a SERBIAN CATHEDRAL, as well as the MUSEUM OF FINE ARTS. The ETHNOGRAPHIC MUSEUM at Sir. Popa Şapcă is in the remains of the old Magyar fort around which the city grew.

Take a walk along the BEGA CANAL through a whole series of parks and visit the THERMAL BATHS on Blvd Vasile Parvan. For a bit of fun go to the PUPPET THEATRE at Piaţa Furtuna.

The Tourist Office and CFR international booking office are both at 6 Blvd Republicii.

The cheapest place to stay is the campground in the Padurea Forest (tram 1), where there are also bungalows. You could also try to get a place in the dormitories from CTF, but these are often full with groups.

ARAD This is dominated by a huge star-shaped 18th-century CITADEL, around which the river Mureş flows through a park. The HISTORY MUSEUM (closed Mon.) is housed in the PALACE OF CULTURE on Piaţa George Ionescu and has displays on the complex history of the whole area. The Philharmonic Orchestra is also located here.

Bulevard Republicii is the main street and here you will find the Tourist Office at no. 72, just across from the neoclassical TOWN HALL. There is also a Tourist Office geared towards foreigners next door in the Hotel Astoria at no. 89 (Tel. 16650).

For accommodation the youth hostel organization CTT is at 16 Piaţa Avram Iancu. To get to the Subcetate campsite, follow the river south of the citadel about a kilometre from the bridge near the Park Hotel.

There are a whole series of fairs and gatherings in the villages around Arad well worth day visits, especially the Kiss Fair in HĂLMAGIU in March, as well as festivals in PINCOTA (February), BIRSA (April), SINTANA (May) and AVRAM IANCU (June). Ask at the Tourist Office for exact dates.

ORADEA This is a common stopping-off point on journeys from Budapest to Bucharest, although probably does not warrant any more than a day's visit. Oradea has its own CITADEL and the largest baroque CATHOLIC CATHEDRAL in Romania. Nearby is the grand BISHOP'S PALACE, which was based on the Belvedere Palace in Vienna and is now a large MUSEUM (open Tues.–Sun.: 10 a.m.–6 p.m.) which has displays on the history and people of the Crişana region.

Tourist Information is on the main shopping street at 4 Piaţa Republicii and the CFR Railway office is at number 2.

Cheap places to stay are hard to come by, so you should try the campground 8 km south-east of Oradea at Băile Felix (tram 4 or 5), near the famous thermal baths, or else contact CTT at 9 Stada Vulcan.

There are many fascinating caves in the area; try to visit the VADU CRISULUI CAVE (take a slow train east from Oradea), which has tours 9 a.m.–6 p.m. each day.

NOTES

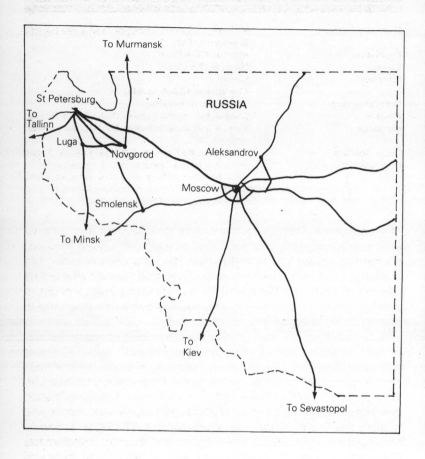

RUSSIA and BELARUS

Entry requirements	All foreigners need a passport and a visa bought in advance ($40).
Population	Approx. 150 million
Capital	Moscow (9 million)
Currency	Rouble
	£1 = approx 10,000 roubles
Political system	Federation of Republics
Religion	Several, but mostly Russian Orthodox in Europe.
Language	Russian and dialects (some English and German spoken)
Public holidays	1, 2, 7 Jan., 8 March, 1, 2, 9 May, 12 June, 7 Nov.
International dialling	To Russia: international code + 7 + number
	From Moscow: 810 country code number. International calls may be easiest made through a post office or (more expensively) a hotel.

The emergence of Russia as a major tourist destination was unthinkable only a few years ago; even now, as you walk around Moscow, it's hard to believe you're really there. This is a country facing big challenges and as a traveller you may well find yourself affected by some of its problems. But it is also a country with a huge amount to offer the visitor, and if nothing else, you can guarantee that a trip to Russia will be an experience.

Russia's history is a book in itself, but most people still remember it as the centre of communism. The Revolution in 1917 was proclaimed as the triumph of the working classes, but the new regime soon turned out to be even more repressive than the old. That didn't stop Lenin, Stalin and their successors exporting Russian domination to the neighbouring states, putting men into space and making the Soviet Union into a superpower. The USSR began to come apart at the seams in 1991, but its transition to capitalism has not been easy, nor is it complete. Accounts of political instability and rampant crime continue to challenge travellers to face the fact that this is not an ordinary tourist destination.

Under communism, the Russian tourist administration, Intourist, controlled every aspect of the visitor's stay, right down to the choice of hotel and the itinerary. Intourist has now fragmented into many different parts which may or may not be on speaking terms with each other, but no alternative system of tourism has yet developed. In the past, visitors to the USSR had to be fairly wealthy to cope with Intourist's demands, which made life difficult for the budget traveller. Russia's floundering economy means that things are now slightly easier and Westerners can find things incredibly cheap, but because in the absence of a regulatory body to manage the tourist industry people can charge what they like, or what they think you can pay, travelling on a budget is still far from simple. This should not deter you; budget travel is still possible – and the feeling of accomplishment which rewards the successful traveller is immense.

The situation is magnified even more in the smaller, landlocked republic of Belarus, formerly called Belorussia or White Russia, which lies on the direct route between Russia and Poland. If you feel Russia doesn't offer you enough of a challenge, then a stop here could be for you!

GETTING THERE

It's possible to enter Russia from Poland, Estonia, Latvia or Finland. Warsaw to St Petersburg, a 31-hour odyssey, will cost around £30 one-way (student rate), and any journey involving a border crossing will be at an inflated price. It is important to remember that Belarus, though lacking in charm as a tourist destination, is *en route* to many of the places you will want to visit and a Belorussian visa *may* therefore be required. The situation is unclear: you might not need a visa for Belarus if the train only passes through *en route* to Russia, but if you are stopping off in the Baltics – so that your destination is not, immediately, Russia itself – then you will need one, and many people have been hauled off trains in the small hours for precisely this reason. Check before leaving home whether a full Russian visa will be sufficient to get you through.

Full visa services, including invitation and registration, are operated by the American-run Traveller's Guest House in Moscow (Bolshaya Pereyaslavskaya ulitsa 50, floor 10; Tel. and Fax 095 971 4059, e-mail tgh@glas.apc.org) and the St Petersburg International Hostel (3rd Sovetskaya ulitsa 28, St Petersburg, Tel. 812 329 8018, Fax 812 329 8019, e-mail ryh@ryh.spb.su): a month's visa costs from $30. (Increasingly, reputable hotels and other agencies are now contactable by e-mail as it's often the most reliable method of communication.)

RUSSIAN STATE RAILWAYS

Travelling east across Europe, standards drop markedly (Germany to Poland being a particular culture shock) and you could be forgiven for expecting Russian trains to be worse still. For the most part, this isn't the case, especially since as a foreign tourist you will only be given a choice of the best types of train accommodation. The distances involved make overnight trains particularly viable as a mode of transport, the more so since they save you the ordeal of attempting to find a hotel that night.

You'll get a sense of the magnitude of the Russian train system if you travel between St Petersburg and Moscow. Every night, at least 8 trains make the journey each way, most of them consisting of around 20 carriages – all of them full. Russia's railways carry more people than any other country's and the first rule of Russian train travel is to buy your ticket in advance. (Russia is not in Inter-Rail or any other international rail scheme.)

Foreign tourists are usually put on a *skoryy poezd* (fast train, although frankly it isn't), or an *express* (which is faster). You have the choice between soft (*myagkiy*) or hard (*zhyostkiy*) class accommodation, with soft (2 upholstered berths in a compartment) being equivalent to first class, and hard (4 plastic berths) equivalent to second class. It's worth remembering that on overnight trains you may be obliged to pay a small supplement for your bedding, so don't spend all of your currency before boarding a train west. On many services you will be provided free of charge with tea or coffee by the attendant, called a *provodnik* (male) or *provodnitsa* (female), and hot and cold water is usually available.

Russians and non-Russians both use roubles to buy train tickets, but prices asked of non-Russians are about 20% higher. Asking in Russian will help, though in any case you're supposed to ask at a separate Intourist window and you have to show your passport. The regulations can seem arbitrary – and you're hardly in a position to argue. The hostels in St Petersburg and Moscow will order tickets for you for a $5 handling charge, which saves a lot of wasted energy and at least guarantees you the end product.

Bear in mind that you are unlikely to be allowed to purchase a ticket out of any former Soviet Republic (not counting the Baltics) using local currency and be prepared for the fact that the cost of leaving Russia will not be in line with the cost of living in the country. Stories abound of eurorailers being charged extortionate sums of money to go home, and in this respect the hostel services represent something of a lifeline. They're still not cheap: Moscow to Warsaw will set you back around $63. The moral is, don't leave yourself short: getting money wired to you in Russia is no easy task.

One final word of warning: crossing your legs in the 'American' manner (one foot balanced on the other leg) is considered the height of bad manners. You could find yourself emptying a compartment of sensitive Russians by forgetting this peculiar fact.

PASSES AVAILABLE Russia is not yet linked into any international schemes. For cheap rail travel, contact the Traveller's Guest House in Moscow or the Sindbad Travel Agency at the International Hostel in St Petersburg (addresses as above).

TRAIN INFORMATION Some officials speak English and some German, although they may be loth to do so.

RESERVATIONS When buying a ticket you will be given a reservation as a matter of course. It's advisable to buy your ticket well in advance. You won't be allowed to buy one on the train or to board without one. The tried and tested method of slipping an attendant a few dollars has been known to work, but unless you're in trouble it's not advisable. 'Scalpers' are often to be seen in stations selling train tickets at an inflated rate: if you've been too late to get a place on a train you need to catch, it may be worthwhile taking them up.

NIGHT TRAVEL Most journeys you are likely to take in Russia are long enough to justify an overnight trip and all long-haul trains are designed with this in mind. Compartments have 2 or 4 berths which convert into beds. Sleeping compartments are mixed sex, and when women want to get changed, men are expected to go and loiter in the corridor.

EATING ON TRAINS: All long-distance trains have (usually crowded) buffet cars.

SCENIC TIPS If you're travelling by day, the journey from St Petersburg to northern towns like Petrozavodsk across the Kola peninsula passes through beautiful tundra scenery.

TOURIST INFORMATION

Russian tourism has yet to gear itself towards the independent traveller, and in St Petersburg and Moscow you may find that the maps provided by the hostels are the best tourist information you're likely to find in English. For an intensive guide to the whole country, the *Lonely Planet Guide to Russia* is recommended.

VISAS The Russian visa system is notorious as an example of rampant red tape. While visa requirements are dropping all over the world, Russia's remain intact, and any ideas of attempting to enter the country without one should be forgotten.

If you're prebooking a holiday through Intourist, then they'll handle most of the visa application process for you, but it's also possible to do it yourself. In England, this can be done by contacting the Russian Embassy, 5 Kensington Palace Gardens, London W8 (Tel. 0171 229 3215). (Some overseas Russian embassies – those in Poland and the Baltics, for example – are less strict in their requirements.) You will need a passport valid for at least a month beyond your return date, 3 passport photos, a completed application form including your entry and exit dates and your itinerary, proof of accommodation and a fee, varying upwards from a base of £40 (depending on where you get your visa and how quickly you need it). The system is speeding up, but you should still allow at least a month.

Officially, you cannot visit a town which is not on your visa, but these days the Russian police tend to have more important things to worry about and almost certainly the worst that can happen is that you will be sent back to a town which is on your visa.

If you know somebody in Russia who can invite you and is prepared to put up with the mindblowingly obstructive bureaucracy, ask your nearest Russian embassy for invitation application forms and send one to your friend, who must fill it out and take it to the local OVIR (Russian visa) office for approval. A confirmation of approval will be sent to you, making you eligible for a visa.

Alternatively, the Traveller's Guest House in Moscow and the International Hostel in St Petersburg operate a speedy visa service which can help you obtain a visa in as little as 24 hours (for a fee). Fax them on 095 971 4059 or 812 329 8019 respectively, giving all personal details (including passport information) and the dates you want to stay there, and they will sort out the red tape for you. Moreover, they won't necessarily hold you to stay for all the nights you have 'booked', leaving you free to move around Russia and choose your own accommodation.

Those who only want a brief taste of Russia can take the trip offered by the Finnish IYHF in Helsinki, which visits St Petersburg but is not subject to such stringent restrictions.

MONEY MATTERS 1 rouble = 100 kopecks.

The only time you're likely to need kopecks is to make a local phone call from a public telephone. These use 15 kopeck pieces, which have become so rare that people sell them on the street for about 40 times their face value.

There are officially 3 exchange rates in Russia:

1. The *bank rate* is what you will get when exchanging hard currency or traveller's cheques in a bank, and is by far the best. There are exchange facilities in most cities. You may have to show your passport, visa and customs declaration form when changing money.
2. The *commercial rate* is used to calculate the price of hard-currency goods (an increasing number of Russian shops sell desirable goods for hard currency only, souvenirs, for example) and credit card purchases. It's increasingly possible to buy for roubles with a credit card in Russia, but it's hard even to calculate how much you'll lose on the transaction.
3. The *official rate* is the extremely poor one Intourist uses to calculate the cost of accommodation and so on: hence the fact that, booked through them, a double room in Moscow will cost about £40.

There's no longer any need to change money on the black market: it's illegal, unprofitable and potentially unsafe. If you're still tempted, bear in mind that Russians are likely to have notes from the old USSR, from the various styles of currency issued by the Russian Republic and possibly from other ex-Soviet republics as well. They come in all colours and sizes and are written in Cyrillic script. If you don't feel confident you can tell which are legal, you shouldn't feel confident that you can change money on the street without being cheated. Keep exchange receipts: you may be asked to show them when you leave the country and in any case without them you will be unable to reconvert roubles to hard currency.

POST OFFICES Main post offices are open Mon.–Fri.: 8 a.m.–8 p.m. Outward post usually takes 3 weeks or so to reach its destination. It helps to start the address of international mail with the country name in Cyrillic: England is **Англиа** . All postal services are charged in roubles. Poste restante facilities exist but are something of a national joke: see individual cities for details.

SHOPS Shopping in Russia, particularly for food, is an experience you may well be glad to leave behind. The idea is that you find the product that you want and its price, then go to a till and pay for it, at which point you will be given a ticket to take to another counter where it can be exchanged for the goods. You will truly learn the value of body language in Russia. Shops don't openly advertise themselves and it takes a bit of investigation to find them. There are shortages, certainly, but goods are available: half the problem is knowing where to look for things. *Beryozkas*, or hard currency shops, are dependable for life's little necessities like toiletries (and, indeed, food) if you despair of finding them anywhere else.

LANGUAGE Russian is written in the Cyrillic alphabet and it will help to familiarize yourself with it; that way you can at least make an educated guess as to what words mean (the word for 'restaurant', for example, reads like *pectopah* – in fact its pronounced *restoran*). It was invented by a monk (named Cyril) who used a printing set from Greece and then represented some additional sounds by re-using some of the letters backwards. It will also be invaluable on Russia's metro systems.

(The Cyrillic alphabet is reproduced in the **Bulgaria** chapter, see p. 128.)

TIPPING It is really up to you how much you want to give, if anything. Restaurant prices often include a 10% service charge and more shouldn't be needed, but staff will expect a further tip as well.

SLEEPING
The problem with travelling anywhere adventurous is that you leave home comforts behind. In Russia, this is particularly true of regulated accommodation. Intourist will happily book you into a hotel, but the absolute *minimum* you will pay is £30 for a single. They offer campsite chalets at lower prices, but these tend to be inaccessible and, in St Petersburg's case, reputedly dangerous. Thus youth hostels have been nothing short of a godsend to budget travellers, charging between $10 and $16: well worth it for the security they provide in a very unfamiliar world. Unfortunately, beyond that, your options are anything but clear. Russia is a very poor country, and many hotel owners, upon realizing your nationality, will request a hugely inflated sum in hard currency. Remember, they're accustomed to think of Western travellers as being extremely wealthy. The price you pay will depend on your haggling skills and obviously it helps immeasurably to be able to speak Russian. The same is true in university dorms, where room is often available if you can talk your way in. It would be unethical to advocate bribery, but Russia is a country in which the barter system is alive and well, so slipping somebody a few dollars (Marlboro cigarettes, the old 'unofficial currency' of Russia, are so freely available now as to be almost worthless for opening doors) isn't quite so illicit as it might seem.

In some stations or hotel lobbies you may see a woman at a desk with a stack of postcards with addresses on them. If so, chances are you've found a private accommodation network. For a (negotiable) fee you can stay in the home of Russian citizens supplementing their income. The service isn't aimed at foreigners – few are even aware of it – so if you don't speak Russian, get ready to use body language.

EATING AND NIGHTLIFE

Purchasing everyday food involves undergoing the Russian shopping experience (see above). In cities you may well find yourself snacking your way through the day on a diet of pastry creations (perfectly safe, provided they have no meat in) sold on the street by people trying, like every other Russian, to supplement their inadequate income. Food is available, but be prepared to queue, and go equipped with at least a little vocabulary. Similarly, Russian restaurants are an experience: suffice to say that the 'customer is always right 'ethic has yet to work its way this far east. Don't expect to be able to eat a meal in a hurry, as staff obviously feel that diners need time for digestion between courses – about 2 hours seems to be just enough. If you want fast food, go to McDonald's. Hard currency restaurants are more likely to have English-speaking staff, and consequently they cost more.

Nightlife of the pub and club variety is somewhat limited, most young Russians being more inclined to sit at home with a few friends and a good supply of black market *pivo* (beer). The Russians have worked hard to get their reputation as a nation of alcoholics – there are reports of them taking beer supplies home in fully filled condoms when they can't find anything else. Should you find yourself knocking back the vodka in Russian company, remember the all-important phrase *Droozh-bal* (spoken with gusto). It means 'Cheers!'

What discos there are usually take place in hotels. A better option is to visit the ballet or opera: at the Bolshoi or Kirov you may have to haggle with touts for tickets, but at smaller venues you can pay a minimal amount for a uniquely rewarding experience and if you're lucky you may find a free buffet included in the price. Try not to look too scruffy.

Russia can be a dodgy place for open displays of homosexuality, which only recently became legal and is still frowned on by many citizens.

Moscow (МОСКВА) city phone code: 095

There's a feeling of other-worldliness when visiting Moscow, so long portrayed in American blockbusters as the enemy's den, that can be rivalled almost nowhere else on earth. Here you can wander around the Kremlin, watch the goosestepping soldiers change the guard and visit Lenin's mausoleum: not necessarily the most beautiful of sights, but certainly things that a few years ago most people would never have expected to see.

Though it lacks the buzz you would expect of such a huge city, Moscow has more than enough to keep the traveller occupied and fascinated for weeks. Most of the sights are central. The Kremlin is the heart of the city, flanked by Red Square and the Moscow river, and it makes the best starting point for explorations elsewhere.

STATION FACILITIES

Moscow has 8 main stations with rail links to every part of the USSR. Coming from Warsaw and the west you will arrive at Belorussia station (*Belorussky Vokzal*); from St Petersburg, Leningrad Station (*Leningradsky Vokzal*). Going to Kiev, depart from Kiev station (*Kievsky Vokzal*). Pavelets and Kursk stations serve other parts of the Ukraine. Most of these stations have lockers, left-luggage facilities, cafeterias and national rail information.

St Petersburg, Kiev and the Baltics are all comfortable overnight trips. Direct trains run to Warsaw, Berlin, Prague, Vienna, Budapest, Belgrade, Bucharest, Sofia and even Paris and London (50 hours).

BUYING TICKETS Foreigners are supposed to buy their tickets not at the station but at the Central Railroad Agency, Ulitsa Griboeda 6 (metro: Chistie Prudy), or, for international trains, at Intourtrains, Petrovtrason 15 (metro: Okhotny Ryad).

GETTING AROUND

All of Moscow's stations are linked by the metro, a stunningly efficient and frequently bewildering creation spanning 130 stations. Cards or tickets for use on the metro can be purchased at the stations. Unless you speak Russian, be prepared for a confusing time, as signs are in Cyrillic letters only. The *Let's Go* guide to Russia includes an English map. A recorded voice on the train will tell you which station you are approaching, but it probably won't sound like you imagined it. Furthermore, stations where lines cross can have as many as 4 names. And as if all that wasn't enough, many of the station names have changed completely due to post-communist name-purging. A map is therefore very useful; use it constantly and count the number of stations you pass. You'll get the hang of it eventually and in the meantime you can admire the architecture of Moscow's metro stations: it's worth traversing the Koltsevaya (Circle) line just to see the elaborate archways and chandeliers.

TOURIST INFORMATION AND ADDRESSES

Intourist's information desk is at Tverskaya Ulitsa 1 (Tel. 203 1497), but the only thing they're liable to be able to help you with is entertainment information or an expensive bed. Intourist also has an information line (203 6962) which operates 9 a.m.–6 p.m., but their limited English prevents them from being as helpful as they might. Your best bet is to start at the Travellers' Guest House, where information, maps, etc. are forthcoming, even if you choose to look elsewhere later.

POST OFFICE Mezhdunarodnyy Glavpochtamt (main international post office) at Varshavskoe shosse 37a; metro: Nagatinskaya. Poste restante mail should be addressed: USSR, 103600, Moscow, Tverskaya Ulitsa 3–5, Hotel Intourist, Poste Restante, surname, given name. Don't place much faith in it, though.

AMEX Sadovaya-Kudrinskaya Ulitsa 21a (Tel. 254 2111). Open Mon.–Fri.: 9 a.m.–5 p.m.

CURRENCY EXCHANGE Facilities at all banks and major hotels; the Vneshekonombank on Tverskaya Ulitsa is recommended.

UK EMBASSY Naberzhnaya Sofiskaya 14 (Tel. 230 6333)

IRISH EMBASSY Grokholsky Pereulok 5 (Tel. 288 4101)

US EMBASSY Novinsky Bulvar 19–23 (Tel. 252 24519)

CANADIAN EMBASSY Starokonyushenny Pereulok 15–17 (Tel. 241 5013)

AUSTRALIAN EMBASSY Kropotkinsky Pereulok 13 (Tel. 246 5012)

SEEING

The KREMLIN, probably the most famous building or group of buildings in Russia, is in the middle of Moscow (metro: Okhotny Ryad, connected by an underpass). Tourists enter through the Kutafia Tower Gate, on the side nearest to the metro. Certain parts of the Kremlin are very much off-limits, but there's a lot to be seen: tourists are shepherded around CATHEDRAL SQUARE and other very Russian oddities by soldiers with whistles. The cost is minimal; with student ID you may get in for nothing.

Next to the Kremlin, on the eastern side, is RED SQUARE (*Krasnaya*

Ploshchad, which actually means 'Beautiful Square'). The square is dominated by the fairy-tale ST BASIL'S CATHEDRAL, once described as 'a box of crystallized fruits'. You can look around its labyrinthine interior for a few roubles.

Set back against the walls of the Kremlin is the LENIN MAUSOLEUM, where you may undergo the surreal experience of seeing Lenin's embalmed body. It looks remarkably like a waxwork. Behind the mausoleum are the ashes of dozens of communist heroes, most of them now in disgrace: Stalin, Brezhnev and Yuri Gagarin, to name a few. It was outside the Lenin Mausoleum that the famous goose-stepping soldiers used to appear and the party leaders assemble to watch May Day parades.

Opposite the mausoleum is the GUM store, a symbol of capitalism's rise in Russia. It can be a depressing place, though big Western names like YSL and Benetton are now moving in. The cafés on the top floor have cheap food in exchange for roubles.

Interesting historically is the LENIN MUSEUM (free admission) at Ploshchad Revolyutsii 2, a little way north-east of Red Square. It houses a vast collection of memorabilia about the man himself, and after a visit you can begin to gauge the scale of the impact Lenin had on Russia and the world. The excellent and diverse PUSHKIN MUSEUM is at Ulitsa Volkhona 12, 2 blocks from metro Krouotkinskaya; admission 25 roubles. Across the street is the Moskva outdoor swimming pool, where Russians are to be seen bathing at almost any time of year, regardless of the weather conditions.

Though its future is uncertain, the ARBAT (metro: Arbat) remains a hive of industry in Moscow. It is a pedestrianized precinct which has long been a haven for free expression, but recently the street artists who populated it disappeared (supposedly temporarily).

GORKY PARK, south and upriver from the Kremlin, is a pleasant spot. Further upstream is the LENIN STADIUM, where the 1980 Olympics took place.

Watch out for entrance fees: a dual pricing policy is now in operation in Russia whereby foreign visitors are charged substantially more than natives for admission. For example, each church inside the Kremlin charges foreigners 25 times more than Russians!

SLEEPING

Intourist will offer you a range of expensive accommodation: currently their cheapest double is £41, without breakfast. They also offer campsite accommodation, starting at £9 for a tent site.

The first budget accommodation run on Western lines opened in 1993 at the Travellers' Guest House, ulitsa Bolshaya Pereyaslavskaya

50, floor 10 (Tel. and Fax 971 4059). It's not easy to find: take the metro to Prospekt Mira, turn left, and take a right turn after about 400m: if you're heading towards 4 chimney stacks, you're going in the right direction. Turn left on Pereyaslavskaya, and the building – which hardly advertises itself – is on your right. Rates are $15 per night in dormitories, $40 for a double room. The Prakash Guesthouse, ulitsa Profsoyznaya 83 (Tel. 334 2598), is another option. It's near the Belyaova metro stop.

Independent Russian hotels, upon realizing your nationality, may charge as much as Intourist would, but by all means try your luck. It's impossible to recommend specific places since so much depends upon luck and timing.

In the lobby of the Gostinitsa Centralnaya, next door to Pizza Hut on Ulitsa Tverskaya, there is usually a woman with a pile of postcards offering private accommodation with Moscow residents. A knowledge of the Russian language will help you considerably, but for a few dollars a night you could find yourself enjoying a unique experience with a Russian family or pensioner, within easy reach of the city centre.

Alternatively, Russian Bear Travel Services, on Prospekt Andropov 35 (Tel. 114 4223), arrange dorm-style accommodation in apartments around the city from $6 upwards.

EATING

Whatever you may have heard to the contrary, Moscow has a wide variety of eateries catering for almost every taste and representing a surprising diversity of nationalities. As in any Russian city, it is quite possible to get by on a diet of pastry, popcorn and ice-cream, sold cheaply for roubles all over Moscow. Cheaper still, the cafeterias on the top floor of the GUM store are acceptable. Avoid the steaming heaps of (whole) fish that go for about 7p a pile unless you are extremely strong of stomach. Some hotels reputedly still offer all-you-can-eat buffets for roubles: a bargain beyond belief. Try your luck at the Hotel Intourist (opposite the Kremlin) or the Hotel Moskva (between Teatralnaya and Manezhnaya squares). Finally, Pushkinskaya Ploshchad, a lively and youthful part of town, is the home of Moscow's first and most famous McDonald's. Much as you might scorn the endless queues of people anxious for a Big Mac, you'll be surprised how good one tastes after a week or so of trying to buy Russian food. Pizza Hut is round the corner. Expect to pay $10–20 for a meal.

For nightlife there are a now a lot of clubs and discos, but none that we can particularly recommend. The Chance club in Dom Kultury Serp I Molot (metro 7: Ploshchad Ilicha) is supposed to have a mixed gay and straight clientèle. Remember also that Moscow has excellent theatres, orchestras, ballets, operas, and so on, with tickets often priced very reasonably.

St Petersburg (САНКТ-ПЕТЕРСБЧРГ)
city phone code: 812

St Petersburg, formerly Leningrad, is often said to be Russia's most European city. Certainly, its beautiful buildings and canals aren't the sort of images Westerners tended to associate with a city of the former Soviet bloc. In every way, St Petersburg is one of the best introductions to Russia, with the most Westernized accommodation systems and probably the most cosmopolitan citizens in the country.

Warning: Don't drink the water in St Petersburg. It is infested with the giardia parasite which causes diarrhoea. Even brushing your teeth in the tap water may infect you. Always use bottled water.

STATION FACILITIES

St Petersburg has 4 main stations. Moscow station (*Moskovsky Vokzal*) at Ploshchad Vosstaniya, just off Nevsky Prospekt, at Naberezhnaya Kanala Griboedova, handles trains to Moscow and most of Russia; Warsaw station (*Varshavsky Vokzal*) at Naberezhnaya Obvodnogo Kanal 118, handles trains to and from Eastern Europe and the Baltics; and Vitebsk station (*Vitebsky Vokzal*) at Zagordnoy Prospekt 52, covers Belarus and most of the Ukraine. These 3 are all south of the Neva river. Finland station (*Findlandsky Vokzal*) on Ploshchad Lenina, handles trains to and from Scandinavia.

Direct international services to and from St Petersburg include the Baltic capitals, Helsinki (2 trains a day, journey time 7 hours), Warsaw and Berlin. Domestic lines cover much of European Russia and the Ukraine.

Moscow station has the best facilities, including a full range of restaurants, shops, a left-luggage store and lockers. The others all have lockers and travel information.

BUYING TICKETS Foreigners are supposed to buy their tickets at the central ticket office on Nevsky Prospekt, but Moscow station has an Intourist window on the second floor which should be able to help. The International Youth Hostel will buy tickets on your behalf for a $5 fee.

GETTING AROUND

St Petersburg's metro is less extensive than Moscow's, but equally efficient and no less confusing. Many trains have outer doors which prevent you seeing the station as you arrive; and although each station is announced upon arrival, the recorded message also states the next one, which is confusing if you're listening for one name. As in Moscow, count the stations and carry a map at all times.

TOURIST INFORMATION AND ADDRESSES

Tourist information in the conventional sense may prove to be a problem but this might be alleviated by a planned new Tourist Office, scheduled to open on Nevsky Prospekt, just opposite the Grand Hotel Europe. Hotel service bureaux can advise on travel, entertainment, etc., even if you're not staying at the hotel in question.

Intourist's office is at Isaakievskaya Ploshchad 11, opposite the Astoria Hotel.

The International Youth Hostel gives out a useful map which includes a suggested city tour. They also have a copy of a highly recommended guidebook, *The St Petersburg Times*, which is as thorough and up-to-date as anything else you're likely to find.

POST OFFICE Pochmatskaya Ulitsa 9, 2 blocks south-west of St Isaac's cathedral.
AMEX Conducted through the Grand Hotel Europe, Ulitsa Mikhailovskaya (off Nevsky Prospekt) (Tel. 315 6517)
CURRENCY EXCHANGE All major hotels. The only bank open at weekends is opposite the Grand Hotel Europe. There are exchange offices dealing in many European currencies all along Nevsky Prospekt.
US CONSULATE Ulitsa Furshtadskaya 15 (Tel. 2748568)

SEEING

NEVSKY PROSPEKT, St Petersburg's main street, is very much the city centre and most of the main sights are located here.

The HERMITAGE, one of the world's greatest art galleries, lies a little to the north-east of Nevsky Prospekt, near the river. Foreigners are supposed to pay 25,000 roubles to enter even with a student discount, but it's well worth it. Open 10.30 a.m.–5.30 p.m. every day except Mon., late opening Thurs. It would take days to explore the Hermitage properly, but among its highlights are the Egyptian and Prehistoric collections and the stunning range of European art, including works by Picasso, Van Gogh and Rembrandt. The famous

WINTER PALACE, a huge green and gold building halfway between garish and beautiful, is only one part of the Hermitage. In front of the Winter Palace is the ALEXANDER COLUMN, dominating one of the world's largest squares. Slightly overshadowed by Palace Square is ARTS SQUARE (*Ploshchad Iskusstv*), near the 5-star Grand Hotel Europe (a book in itself). Arts Square is the home of the RUSSIAN MUSEUM, where rates of entry are 35,000 roubles for foreigners, half price for students.

St Petersburg boasts a disquieting number of architectural masterpieces dedicated to the honour of people who've been brutally done away with. One such is the CHURCH OF THE RESURRECTION, also known as the Church of Spilt Blood. Dedicated to Tsar Alexander II, killed by a terrorist bomb here in 1881, this domed building is modelled on St Basil's in Moscow. Around the corner is MIKHAILOVSKY CASTLE, built for Paul I: he was strangled there by conspirators in 1801.

ST ISAAC'S CATHEDRAL, magnificent in itself, offers one of the best views in St Petersburg. For around 3,000 roubles, you can climb to its colonnade (closed Wed.), and for a further 300,000 roubles you can enter the spectacularly lavish interior.

Nearby are 2 celebrated St Petersburg photo opportunities: the ADMIRALTY BUILDING, with the sailing ship spire on its roof; and DECEMBRISTS' SQUARE, with the statue of the bronze horseman dedicated to Peter the Great. Also of historical importance on Nevsky Prospekt are the KAZAN CATHEDRAL (opposite the Dom Knigi bookshop), the CATHERINE THE GREAT MONUMENT and ANICHKOV BRIDGE, with its 4 'horse tamer' statues.

Across the River Neva is Basil's Island, once the city centre, and PETER AND PAUL'S FORTRESS on Zayachy Island: for many years this was a political prison – Dostoevsky and Trotsky both served time there. Open 11 a.m.–6 p.m. every day except Wed. The bridges over the river are raised at night: don't get stranded.

St Petersburg boasts more parkland than any other Russian city; the SUMMER GARDENS, next to the Field of Mars (a monument to the dead of the 1917 Revolution), are worth a visit.

For the evenings, you can get theatre tickets from the central office at 42 Nevsky Prospekt for a few pounds.

SLEEPING

Although St Petersburg is better suited to budget travel than other Russian cities, it's still no easy matter to find a bed. Intourist's cheapest double will set you back £49. Intourist's campsite, Gigno Motel Camping, is notoriously dangerous; there was a shoot-out there 4 years ago. The Soviet youth travel agency Sputnik are sometimes reticent to allow Westerners into their hotels, but it's worth a try: they have a youth hotel 2 bus stops from metro Ploshchad Muzhestra (Tel. 5525632).

The international hostel that opened in St Petersburg in 1992 represented a real watershed in Russian accommodation: run by an American, it was the first hostel in the former Soviet Union and it is hoped that many others will follow. Located on 3rd Sovetskaya Ulitsa 28 (Tel. 329 8018, Fax 329 8019, e-mail ryh@ryh.spb.su), it costs $15–17 per night (breakfast included), plus a $10 reservation fee if you use them for visa support (see **Visas**, above). It seems expensive, but is a superb and friendly hostel and provides the kind of reassurance essential to culture-shocked travellers new to Russia. (It also has the finest showers in the country.) To get there, turn right from Ploshchad Vosstaniya metro station (or Moscow station) on to Nevsky Prospekt, heading away from the city centre, then turn left on to Suvorovskyi Prospekt and right on to 3rd Sovetskaya Ulitsa at the second traffic lights after the Phillips Store. The Sindbad travel agency based at the hostel advertises itself as being able to arrange a variety of local and national excursions.

Elsewhere, it may be worthwhile contacting the University of St Petersburg (Tel. 2000/218 7631) to enquire about accommodation, although student exchange options are best arranged from home.

University dorms require a lot of haggling and probably a little bribery to get into, but again may be worth a try; Plekanova 6 is the best situated, and Grazhdansky Prospekt 28 (metro: Grazhdansky Prospekt) is the more promising. Be prepared to pay in hard currency if you do have any luck.

EATING

Street food is available in abundance in St Petersburg, with dozens of stalls along the main streets selling the usual array of pastry and ice-cream. (For the American version, there is a branch of Baskin & Robbins on Nevsky Prospekt 79, but its allegedly huge range of flavours had been greatly reduced recently.) In the dingy-looking cafeterias that line Nevsky Prospekt below street level, you can get a coffee for the equivalent of a few pence. Bananas, peculiarly enough, are 2 for a dollar from street vendors.

Worth a look are Kafe on Karavan Ulitsa, right off Nevsky Prospekt; Chicken Grill Café, on Prospekt Provishcheniya 84 (metro Gradzhinsky Prospekt); and, for the homesick, there is an English pub restaurant on Nevsky Prospekt.

The Winter Garden restaurant in the Astoria still has a rouble menu – this will almost certainly be the only time you'll ever eat a 3-course meal with caviar in a 4-star hotel for around £5. Along similar lines, the Restaurant Metropol kept its grand decor as a watering hole for Party officials, and is now very reasonably priced (Ulitsa Sadovaya 22). As in Moscow, new restaurants open and old ones close down on a daily basis.

Elsewhere in European Russia

Venture outside Moscow and St Petersburg in Russia and you're firmly off the beaten track. Entering a town which isn't listed on your visa is technically illegal, but restrictions and reprisals are slackening by the day and you're unlikely to find yourself in trouble for going a little out of the way.

An easy trip (by Russian standards) from St Petersburg is north-western Russia. NOVGOROD and PSKOV, 2 of Russia's oldest cities, are situated about 250 km south of St Petersburg. Heading north, you enter the tundra: MURMANSK, on the White Sea, is the world's largest city inside the Arctic Circle, where the sun doesn't rise in December. The Kola peninsula is a region of unparalleled forest scenery.

Within reach of Moscow is the GOLDEN RING, a circle of towns which existed long before the capital. Intourist have been plying these towns for tourism for many years, and with good reason: the old Russian architecture can't be rivalled anywhere else in the country. Suzdal, Vladimir, Yaroslavl and Rostov-Veliky can all be reached from Moscow's Yaroslavl station.

Belarus

There's not a lot in dull Belarus to attract the tourist, and you'll more than likely find yourself hating it after being hauled off an overnight train and forced to spend $50 on a 1-day transit visa. It is not possible to purchase a visa in advance unless you have a letter of introduction from contacts within the country.

The region was badly affected by the Chernobyl disaster in 1986, when 70% of the fallout landed within its borders.

Some people choose to break the long journey from Poland to Moscow in MINSK, a rather bleak city which serves as a potent reminder of the waste of the Second World War. Half of the city's population was wiped out and almost every building has been erected in the last 50 years. It's not beautiful, but it is lively. There are no hostels here, so you'll have to pay official hotel rates.

Also in Belarus is the important border town of BREST. If you have a chance, the huge fortress there, built to resist Napoleon and used against Hitler, is worth taking the time to investigate.

NOTES

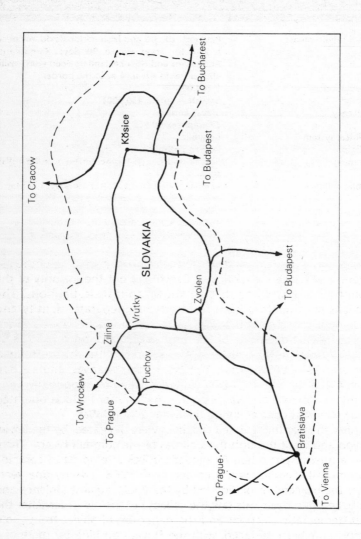

SLOVAKIA

Entry requirements	Passport. UK, US and Irish nationals do not need a visa for stays up to 90 days. Canadians, Australians and New Zealanders need visas, available either in advance or at the border.
Population	5,264,000
Capital	Bratislava (pop.: 435,000)
Currency	Slovak koruna
	£1 = approx 60 Kčs
Political system	Republic
Religion	Roman Catholic
Language	Slovak and Czech (some German and English spoken)
Public holidays	1, 6 Jan., Good Friday, Easter Monday, 1, 8 May, 5 July, 15, 29 Aug., 1, 15 Sept, 1 Nov., 24, 25, 26, 31 Dec.
International dialling	To Slovakia: international code 42 number
	From Slovakia: 00 + country code number

Slovakia as a modern state was formed from the splitting of the old country of Czechoslovakia. The Czech half got the majority of the country's industry and its best known tourist destinations. The Slovaks are therefore keen to assert their separate identity and promote themselves in their own right as a destination for travellers.

The independent state of Czechoslovakia was formed in 1918 by political union of the Czech and Slovak lands of the Austro-Hungarian empire – before that, the Hungarian Magyar empire had dominated the area for many centuries. The first supposedly independent Slovak state was a puppet government which operated under German control during the Second World War.

After the war the reunited republics were 'liberated' by the Soviet Union and went through the traumas of the communist era. There was a brief respite when Alexander Dubček attempted to combine communist ideology with democracy in 1968. Twenty-one years later the peaceful revolution led by the Public against Violence and Civic Forum movements saw the collapse of the old order. After the first democratic elections and the departure of Soviet troops, old ethnic enmities resurfaced, with the Slovaks pushing for more of a say in their own fate. Following the June 1992 election, the Slovaks set up their own parliament in Bratislava and subsequently declared full independence on 1 January 1993.

Much of Slovakia is made up of unspoilt mountains and forests, ideal for hiking, with many picturesque castles scattered about. The beautiful High Tatras are the second highest mountain range in Europe after the Alps.

SLOVAK STATE RAILWAYS

As with other services, the railway has been split between the two states and it will be some time before the Slovak Railway takes on its own identity. At present, assume that most comments on the Czech Railways (see pp.150-51) apply here.

PASSES AVAILABLE Slovakia is in Inter-Rail Zone D, along with the Czech Republic, Poland, Hungary, and Croatia. To tour a single zone for 22 days costs £159. (For further details of the 8 Inter-Rail zones, refer to the Inter-Rail section in Part One of this guide.)

The Euro Domino pass is also valid. See the relevant sections in Part One of this guide for details of outlets, prices and restrictions.

TRAIN INFORMATION

Until the Slovak authorities create their own system, comments made about the Czech Railway will generally apply (see pp.150–51). When reading timetables, bear in mind that the Slovak for Arrival is *Prichod*, while Departure is *Odchod*.

RESERVATIONS Try to reserve well ahead of time to be sure of a seat as trains are busy. This is obligatory on some expresses marked with an R or *míst*. You may be referred to one of the former ARES offices when booking in the larger towns. If travelling on to Hungary it is essential to specify the route you wish to take, the main crossing points being Stúrovo and Komárom.

NIGHT TRAVEL Sleepers and couchettes are operated by the state railway and run on all long journeys. Avoid sleepers, as they tend to be expensive. Beware – numerous thefts from couchette compartments on international routes have been reported in recent years.

EATING ON TRAINS There is either a restaurant car or buffet on selected fast trains.

SCENIC TIPS The lines in and around the High Tatras and between Margecany and Brezno following the lines along the Hailec and Hron rivers are particularly recommended.

TOURIST INFORMATION

The official agency is Satur, though the student travel agency contin-ues, for the time being, to operate as CKM. You can contact Satur's main office in Slovakia: Miletičova 1, 824–72 Bratislava, Slovak Republic (Tel. 63467, 212828).

VISAS At present US and EC nationals do not require a visa. Check with the consular section of the Slovak embassy in your country of origin. Australian, New Zealand and Canadian nationals need to purchase a visa, although this should be available at the border.

MONEY MATTERS 1 Slovak koruna (Kčs) = 100 hellars (hal).

Banking hours are Mon.–Fri.: 8 a.m.–3 p.m. There is no minimum currency exchange and the black market has died down.

POST OFFICES Open 8 a.m.–6 p.m.

SHOPS Typically 9 a.m.–6 p.m., shutting at noon on Saturdays except in large towns.

MUSEUMS Open Tues.–Sun.: 10 a.m.–5 p.m. Generally closed Mon.

SLEEPING

As with the Czech Republic, the accommodation situation is not too good and demand outstrips supply. While Bratislava does not get swamped with tourists the way Prague does, lack of infrastructure still poses problems. Expect prices to rise, reaching Western levels before too long. See the **Czech Republic** section for further infor-mation (p. 152).

Bratislava

The largest city and capital of Slovakia was also, for 3 centuries, the capital of the Hungarian Kingdom, when it was known as Pozsony. Situated on the Danube, close to both the Austrian and Hungarian borders, and influenced by all 3 countries, Bratislava may be reached by train and boat from both Budapest and Vienna, the journey from Vienna taking around an hour by either means. Despite being an essentially modern city, it still has over 400 historically interesting buildings.

TOURIST INFORMATION

Satur, Miletičova 1 (Tel. 212828) will deal with postal enquiries.

The office at Jesenského 5–9 (Tel. 427 36724) deals with personal visitors; open Mon.–Fri.:, 9 a.m.–5 p.m., Sat: 9 a.m.–12 p.m.

The student agency is at Hviezdoslavovo náměstie 16 (Tel. 331 607), open Mon.–Fri., 9 a.m.–4.30 p.m.

The Bratislava Information Service (BIS), is on Panská, in the old town centre (Tel. 333 7151/334 325), open Mon.–Fri:. 8 a.m.–4.30 p.m., Sat.: 8 a.m.–1 p.m. BIS publish a leaflet, *Kam v Bratislave* ('Where to Go'), with English information sections. They also speak some English here.

Tram 113 from the station gets you into the area of all 3 agencies. There are boards around town, with maps on to help you out, although street names sometimes differ from those printed.

ADDRESSES

UK EMBASSY Grosslingova 35 (Tel. 364 420)
US EMBASSY Hviedoslavovo náměstie 4 (Tel. 330 861)
EXCHANGE OFFICES Several banks in náměstie SNP, also at the post office in the town centre.

SLEEPING

Try BIS or the student agency CKM Slovakia, Hviezdoslavovo nm. 16 (Tel. 331 607), for accommodation suggestions, or look at the station for posters on private accommodation and hostels.

The Sputnik Hostel is at Drieňová 14 (Tel. 234 340/238 065). Take tram 8 from the centre to the lake on the outskirts.

There is a YMCA Interpoint hostel at Karpatska 2 (Tel. 493 267), open from mid-July to mid-August. Walk from the station to Malinovskeho Street, then turn left. The hostel is 5 minutes' walk from here and costs 150Kčs.

Two other hostels to try are the Belojansova and the Bernolak, at Bernolakova 3 (Tel. 497725), highly recommended.

For camping, take trams 2 or 4 to the last stop at Zlaté Piesky (Tel. 65170/60578). These are pleasant lakeside sites, which also offer bungalows for rent.

If you're stuck, ask Satur for a list of budget hotels such as the Astra or Sport, where prices start at around $15 per person in doubles.

FOOD AND DRINK

As with the rest of Slovakia, try the wine bars or beer halls for food. Reputedly the largest beer hall in Central Europe is Stard Sladouňa, on Cintorinska. The wine bar Velki Frantiskani at Františknská is in an old cellar; it offers good local food and occasional folk music. The local Slovakian wine is worth a try. For cheap fast-food and drink, try Gurmian at Poštova Str., in the city centre.

SEEING

The city is dominated by the 13th-century BRATISLAVA CASTLE, burnt out in 1811 by Napoleon, rebuilt after the war and now the home of the Slovak parliament and the SLOVAK NATIONAL MUSEUM, featuring Slovakian history and archaeology. ST MARTIN'S CATHEDRAL, with a distinctive golden crown on its tower, dates from the 14th century and is the resting place of several Austro-Hungarian kings and queens. The OLD TOWN HALL, 15th-century, now houses the CITY MUSEUM, with an interesting torture hall. A museum of viniculture is nearby. The SLOVAK NATIONAL MUSEUM with geological and natural history collections is at Vajanského nábr, near the Danube. The TOWN GALLERY, in the Mirbachov Palace at Franiškánske náměstie , has 17th–19th-century art on display. The MUSEUM OF ARMS AND FORTIFICATION is in the St Michael's Tower, the only remaining tower of 4 original medieval ones. Close by is the PHARMACY MUSEUM and the palaces where Mozart and Liszt played their early concerts. A complete contrast is the ultra-modern SNP bridge, spanning the river below the castle. A good view can be had from the restaurant at the top, but do not eat there.

For a spectacular view of the city and environs, catch a bus to Železná Studničká and take a chair-lift through the forest to the summit of Kamzik.

EXCURSIONS There are boat trips to the DEVIN CASTLE ruins, dating from the 9th century, once an impressive fortress of the Holy Roman Empire. The castle is near the borderpoint of Austria, Slovakia and Moravia. Take the boat from Osobne pristavisko, on the river bank, running Sat. and Sun. in summer. Trips by boat are also available in summer to Vienna and Budapest.

To get to the HIGH TATRA mountains, take the train to the industrial town of Poprad-Tatry and then a local service up into the hills (Thomas Cook timetable 885a). Trains go to Stary Smokovec and Tatranska Lomnica, where there is a campsite.

Košice

The second largest town in Slovakia is the eastern region's capital and the administrative hub of the republic. The city dates back to the 13th century, when it was an important centre within the Hungarian state. The city Tourist Office, Satur, is at Rooseweltova 1 (Tel. 23123) at one end of the main square. Open Mon.–Fri.: 9 a.m.–5 p.m., Sat.: 9 a.m.–12 p.m.

Ask at the Tourist Office or CKM Slovakia, the student agency, for details of private rooms or campsites, all of which are on the outskirts of town. There are a few 2-star hotels, but these tend to be fairly busy.

The biggest church in Slovakia, and probably the country's finest example of Gothic architecture, is ST ELIZABETH'S CATHEDRAL, which dominates the centre of the old town. Standing nearby is ST MICHAEL'S CHAPEL and the URBAN TOWER, decorated with old tombstones. The RAKOCI PALACE, now a technical museum, stands in the courtyard of the intriguingly named EXECUTIONER'S BASTION, which once formed part of the city's defences. Also worth a visit is the MIKLUS PRISON, now a museum.

NOTES

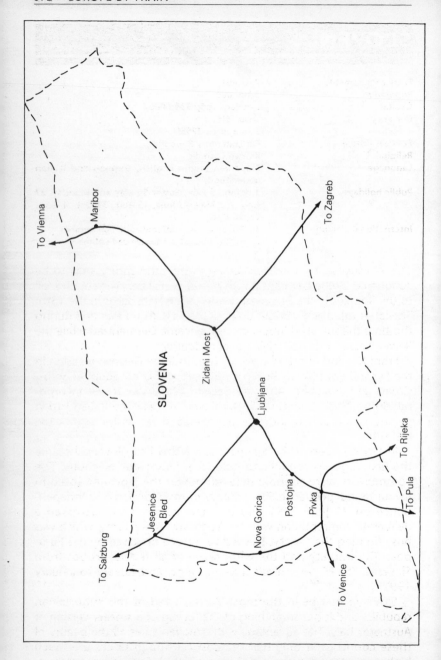

SLOVENIA

Entry requirements	Passport
Population	2,100,000
Capital	Ljubljana (pop.: 330,000)
Currency	Tolar (SIT)
	£1 = approx 270SIT
Political system	Parliamentary Republic
Religion	Roman Catholic
Language	Slovenian (some English, German and Italian understood)
Public holidays	1, 2 Jan., 8 Feb., Easter Sunday and Monday, 27 Apr., 1, 2 May, 25 June, 15 Aug., 31 Oct., 1 Nov., 25, 26 Dec.
International dialling	To Slovenia: international code 386 number
	From Slovenia: 00 + country code number

The Slovenes first settled this region in the 6th century, only to be conquered by the Germans less than 100 years later. The country fell to the Romans in the 9th century and to the Habsburgs in the 13th. The latter ruled almost right up until the First World War and during this time the so-called 'upper classes' became Germanized while the 'lower classes' retained their Slovene identity.

From the end of the First World War until the German invasion in the Second World War, Slovenia was part of the 'Kingdom of Serbs, Croats and Slovenes'. After the Second World War it was incorporated into Tito's Communist Yugoslavia. In 1947 the Italian Istrian peninsula was added and Slovenia gained access to the sea for the first time.

In 1990, 10 years after the death of Marshal Tito, Slovenia became the first Yugoslav republic to hold free democratic elections. The communists were soundly defeated when the Slovenes voted in favour of independence. The country formally declared its independence on 25 June 1991 and the new government provoked a deliberate confrontation with the Yugoslav federal army, which was busy fighting the Croats. This led to a truce brokered by the European Community and the withdrawal of all federal troops from Slovenia. The EC recognized Slovenia's independence on 15 January 1992.

Slovenia had been the most Westernized of the Yugoslavian republics and it has something of the feeling of a smaller version of Austria or Italy. The advantage is that Slovenia has all the beauty of these countries at only half the cost (although prices are much higher now than they were in the early 1990s). The Slovenes are very welcoming to tourists and although obviously most keen to attract those visitors with plenty of money, they still cater well for budget travellers.

SLOVENIAN RAILWAYS
(SLOVENSKA ŽELEZNICE, SZ)
The trains in Slovenia are mostly old rolling stock from the Yugoslav State Railway, though most of it is of better quality than what you would find in Eastern Europe. The expresses between Ljubljana and Pula or Zagreb are modern, electric and air-conditioned. Unless you want to see every little town in the country, stick to express trains between cities wherever possible.

PASSES AVAILABLE Slovenia is in Inter-Rail Zone G, geographically the largest of the 8 zones, along with Italy, Greece and Turkey (which includes the ferry service between Brindisi and Patras). For further information, see the Inter-Rail section in Part One of this guide.

A Euro Domino pass for Slovenia is quite cheap, but hardly worth the effort as the rail network is not that extensive.

TRAIN INFORMATION
Avoid the *potsniki* (slow trains) unless you want to stop at every single station. For express services, see the *IC* or *ZV* ('green train') entries on the timetable. Larger towns and tourist areas like Ljubljana and Postonja will usually have a tourist official who can speak English; otherwise German and Italian will get you by. Failing this, write down the city, train and time you want and pass it over the counter. In smaller towns, there are no information offices, so keep a map and timetable handy. Both of these can usually be had for free in the information office at Ljubljana station.

RESERVATIONS These are only necessary on the international expresses and it is best to make both your inward and outward reservations before entering Slovenia to avoid inevitable language problems.

SUPPLEMENTS Only on EuroCity trains.

NIGHT TRAVEL The country is too small to need sleeping facilities, but international expresses have berths and/or couchettes. Trains between Munich and Zagreb, which stop at Ljubljana, have pull-down seats.

EATING ON TRAINS EuroCity trains have dining cars run by the Germans, while the night trains usually have snack or trolley services. Food and drink are expensive, however, and you would be better off bringing a picnic with you.

SCENIC TIPS The best route is the line between Jesenice and Nova Gorica through the Julian Alps. The line from Ljubljana to Zagreb is also worthwhile and follows the Sava river along its gorge. Sit on the right on the way to Zagreb and the left on the way back.

TOURIST INFORMATION

There are Tourist Offices in all major cities and tourist areas, and most have English-speaking staff members. Here you can get leaflets and maps of the local area and sights.

ISIC BONUSES Many sights and museums give student discounts so be sure to ask first or show your ISIC card before buying a ticket.

MONEY MATTERS The only unit of currency is the tolar (SIT), but because of the inflation problem many tourist services are quoted in Deutschmarks (somewhat curiously abbreviated to DEM).

Banking hours are generally Mon.–Fri.: 8 a.m.–6 p.m. (some banks are closed for lunch from 12 noon–2 or 3 p.m.) and Sat.: 8 a.m.–12 noon. Many tourist agencies will change money and are often open longer hours. Cash will usually receive a better rate than traveller's cheques, and the Deutschmark is the preferred foreign currency.

POST OFFICES Open Mon.–Fri.: 8 a.m.–8 p.m. (and half-day on Sat.). Stamps can also be bought at newsagents'. While the postal service is quite good, *letters without an airmail sticker will be sent by surface mail*. Post should be addressed to you at Poste Restante, 61101 Ljubljana, which goes to the main office on Slovenska Česta 32, across from Tourist Information.

SHOPS Open Mon.–Sat.: 8 a.m.–8 p.m. (outside Ljubljana, shops may close for lunch 12 noon–2 or 3 p.m.).

SLEEPING

Hostels are a bit thin on the ground here and the only one open year-round is in Bled. Hotels are expensive, so in the off-season your best bet is camping – provided you have a tent. In the summer, student dormitories (*Studenski Dom*) are opened as hostels. Your only other alternative is to ask the Tourist Office (or better still, write in advance to the Centre for Tourism, Igriska 6, Ljubljana 61000 (Tel. 125 6172)) for lists of private rooms.

EATING

The food here has a decidedly German flavour to it. Many of the restaurants tend to be expensive, catering to the upper class, but if you wander round the smaller streets you will inevitably find a few cheap eateries. There are plenty of takeaway stalls and farmers' markets where you can put together a good picnic. If you are short of cash, go for a *burek* (a greasy pastry filled with cheese or meat), which is universally cheap and filling. Ask for the tourist menu.

Ljubljana city phone code: 061

STATION FACILITIES

The train station is on the north side of town with bus ranks directly in front of it. Inside the station is a Tourist Information office which will exchange money, including Croatian dinar, at competitive rates. The left-luggage office is on the platform beside another *bureau de change*; it costs 50SIT per bag with a mandatory passport check and is open all night.

TOURIST INFORMATION AND ADDRESSES

The Tourist Office is located at Slovenska 35 (Tel. 215412). From Apr.–Sept. open Mon.–Fri.: 8 a.m.–9 p.m., Sat.–Sun.: 8 a.m.–12 noon and 5 p.m.–7 p.m. From Oct.–Mar. open Mon.–Fri.: 8 a.m.–7 p.m., Sat.–Sun.: 4 p.m.–6 p.m.

POST OFFICE PTT, Coporaulica 11; open Mon.–Fri.: 8 a.m.–8 p.m.; Sat. 8 a.m.–2 p.m.

AMEX c/o Atlas Ambassador, Mestni trg. 8; open Mon.–Fri.: 8 a.m.–7 p.m.; Sat.: 8 a.m.–1 p.m.

UK EMBASSY Trg Republike 3, 61000 Ljubljana

US EMBASSY Pražakova 4, 61000 Ljubljana

Many of the street names are being changed, so if you can't find a particular street, enquire at the main Tourist Office.

SEEING

You can see most of the city in a day, but Ljubljana has a certain charm which grows on you and makes you want to stay longer. The city is primarily industrial-based (they've even modernized the castle!) and the most picturesque spots are in the OLD TOWN along the banks of the Ljubljana river. Turn right out of the train station and walk down to Slovenska cesta (formerly Titova cesta) and go left. This is the main street of the new city and the Tourist Office is about 5 minutes down on your right. The post office is a little further down and a left turn here will take you to the 17th-century FRANCISCAN CHURCH the river. Cross the bridge and walk left along the river to the LJUBLJANA CATHEDRAL on your right. Slightly further along is the colourful vegetable market.

To get up to the CASTLE, or *Grad*, go through the market and follow the street that leads back towards the cathedral, keeping an eye out for a staircase hidden behind a car park. The castle itself isn't too interesting, but the views from the clocktower (70SIT with ISIC) on a clear day are worth the climb.

Come back down the path near the ticket booth and you should wind up at ST JOHN'S CHURCH. Cross back over the river here and you will come to Gosposka ulica, where a right turn will take you to the LJUBLJANA MUSEUM. Continue on past the university and turn left through the park to the URSULINE CHURCH on Slovenska cesta.

SLEEPING

There are student hostels here in summer, but they change location, so check with the Tourist Office. Otherwise, try Camping Jezica at the north end of Dunajska cesta on the outskirts of town (Tel. 371 382), or ask at the Tourist Office for a private room. Either way you're looking at £7–10.

EATING

Cheap eating is an easier proposition: there's plenty of choice, from the excellent *burek* stand outside the train station to the self-service restaurants in the new town and the dozens of small eateries in the old town. Some of the latter look fairly dingy but are good value – just use your common sense. For our North American readers, there's a Dairy Queen (similar to McDonald's) on Slovenska cesta just past the Tourist Office.

EXCURSIONS The POSTONJA CAVES make an excellent day trip. Buses leave from Ljubljana station, cost about 180SIT each way and drop you in Postonja's city centre, about a 20-minute walk from the caves. The Postonja train station is a further 15 minutes outside of town. No buses go directly to the caves. Entrance is around 1800SIT (with ISIC discount) but the tour lasts a couple of hours and is worth the money if you enjoy natural wonders. You travel by electric train and on foot, the formations here being second only to Carlsbad Caverns in the USA. It can get quite cold inside (10°C) so be sure to bring something warm to wear or hire a cloak for 100SIT.

Also nearby is the PREDJAMA GRAD. This castle is built against a cave in the cliff and has recently been restored. Entrance costs about 1500SIT, which includes access to the cave, and you can catch a bus from the Postonja bus depot for about 120SIT each way. Ask the bus driver to let you off at the *Grad* and it's a further 10-minute walk along dirt roads which are well signposted. There are buses every hour and the first sight of the castle as you come round the bend will make you grab for your camera.

Lake Bled

One of the most famous postcards in Slovenia shows a church on an island in the middle of Lake Bled. Bled is at the foot of the Julian Alps, near the Austrian border, about 56 km from Ljubljana. The hourly bus service takes 90 minutes and costs about 150SIT each way. There is also a less regular train service, though the station is 5 km away.

Bled has been a spa resort for many years, though this has not detracted from its character or charm and it remains as popular in summer as in winter. You can get some spectacular views of the island from the CASTLE and MUSEUM (300SIT admission) on the hill overlooking the lake, or take a boat out to the island itself. The boats let you off for about half an hour and cost around 900SIT. A better option is to find a couple of fellow eurorailers and rent a rowboat for about the same price.

The youth hostel at Grajska cesta 17 (Tel. 6478230) is open year round and is conveniently located next to the bus station. Prices are around 1500SIT. The hostel and its surroundings are excellent, but there are only 58 beds, so try to book ahead.

If you get stuck, stay at Camping Zaka (summers only, Tel. 741117) on the west side of the lake (the side nearest the train station).

South-West Slovenia

NOVA GORICA There is absolutely no reason to visit this town, it just happens to be on the end of the scenic line from Jesenice. Our advice is to keep going south to Koper.

KOPER This is Slovenia's main port, and as such, it is very industrialized. However, in the darkest places are the best jewels found – and this is one. Only 16 km south of Trieste, the town was Italian before the Second World War and has a very 'old world' feel to it in places.

From the train station, enter the OLD TOWN through the MUDA GATE. Continue past the bridge fountain, veering to the left, until you come to Cevljarska ulica, which will take you to the town centre. Here you will find the TOWN TOWER, the 15th-century CATHEDRAL, the PALACE, the LOGGIA and the ROTUNDA; all of which are distinctly Italian – except for the rotunda, which is Roman. Further rambling around the twisting streets will open up a variety of interesting buildings, shops and eateries just waiting to be discovered.

Unfortunately, cheap places to stay are non-existent. Try either Slovenijatourist or Kompas for private rooms, and insist on staying in the old city, as rooms here are cheaper and more interesting.

NOTES

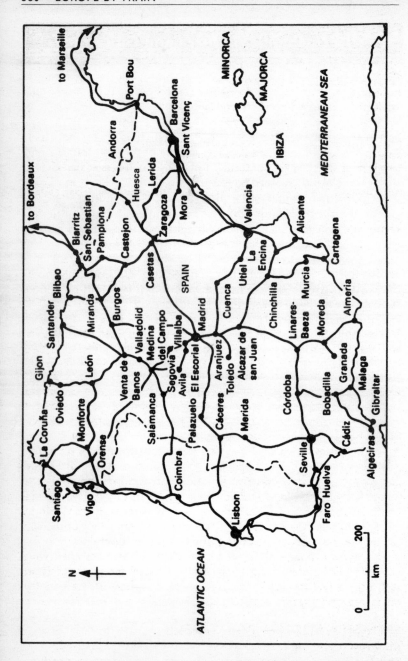

SPAIN (including Andorra and Gibraltar)

Entry requirements	Passport.
Population	39,100,000
Capital	Madrid (pop.: 3,250,000)
Currency	Peseta
	£1 = approx 250ptas
Political system	Constitutional monarchy
Religion	Roman Catholic
Language	Spanish, Basque and Catalan (some English spoken)
Public holidays	1, 6 Jan., Maundy Thursday, Good Friday, Easter Monday, 1 May, 15 Aug., 12 Oct., 1 Nov., 6, 8, 25 Dec.
International dialling	To Spain: international code 34 number
	From Spain: 07 + country code number

Spain is the third largest country in Europe and culturally one of the most diverse. The Phoenicians, Greeks, Celts, Carthaginians, Romans, Visigoths and Moors have all left their mark here. Throughout the long period of Christian reconquest from the Muslims, Spain consisted of several independent kingdoms. They were united in 1479 by the marriage of Ferdinand of Aragon to Isabella of Castille, who celebrated by sending a sailor named Christopher Columbus off to discover the New World. Shortly after reunification, the new king, Charles I, landed well and truly on his feet by inheriting the Netherlands and becoming Holy Roman Emperor in 1519. At the same time his *conquistadores* were bringing enough gold and silver back from South America to make Spain a major world power.

The defeat of the Spanish Armada in 1588 began a slow period of decline which ended in the loss of Spain's colonies after the Napoleonic Wars. More recently, the abdication of the king was followed by a left-wing republic which gave rise to the Civil War of 1936–39 and the rise of the dictator Franco. After Franco's death in 1975, King Juan Carlos steered Spain towards democracy and since 1986 Spain has been a member of the European Community.

The popular image of Spain is sometimes of beaches lined with concrete block hotels packed with badly-behaved foreign tourists. In fact, only a few resorts fit this stereotype and most of the country offers a fascinating mix of history, landscape and culture.

SPANISH NATIONAL RAILWAYS
(RED NACIONAL DE LOS FERROCARRILES ESPAÑOLES, RENFE)
The last few years have seen significant investment to produce

improvements on RENFE, and this is still going on. Unfortunately, supplements are required on all fast trains. You often have to change trains at the Spanish border, so don't go for a sleeper from France unless you're travelling on a *Talgo* which adjusts its wheels to the broader gauge. Check carefully in the timetable to see if you will have to change. The *Automotor* trains which cover the medium-haul routes at semi-fast speeds are both comfortable and air-conditioned, and are a better bet than non-air-conditioned expresses. It's safe to say that all non-supplement trains are pretty slow and crowded, but they'll get you there in the end. The *Tranvías* and *Correos* (locals) crawl along and are only for the stalwart. Some routes are now impossible without supplements being paid, Algeciras–Madrid being an example. The RENFE computer is linked to the International Rail Centre at London Victoria, so you can book ahead from the UK, either at Victoria station or through appointed travel agents.

A word of warning: RENFE has set up a department to oversee areas within the network which are ripe for redevelopment. This could result in substantial price rises and cuts in services on some of the less profitable routes. However, don't be too discouraged: at the moment most fares are quite cheap and the system of supplements is confusing rather than costly.

NON-RENFE LINES A few lines in Spain are not run by RENFE and do not accept rail passes. They are the narrow-gauge lines from Hendaye to Gijón, Gijón to Ferrol, Palma to Inca, Valencia to Gandia and Barcelona to Montserrat.

PASSES AVAILABLE In such a highly developed, tourist-led country as Spain the choice of passes, rover tickets and discounts is enormous. These include 'blue days', 'red days' and the *Chequetrén*, which is available for families or individuals and gives a discount of 15% if you spend enough pesetas.

RENFE operates a discount for all standard fares on about 300 days per year called 'blue days' (*días azules*) when you can expect a 25% or so reduction (50% with a RENFE Youth Pass). The number of blue days varies according to the time of year, with all of February included but only 16 days in June.

There is also a straight 20% reduction for individuals taking return journeys of more than 100 km, which is applicable to all types of train and all classes.

On the other hand, on a red day or public holiday you'll have to pay 10% more for your ticket.

A Euro Domino ticket is available and Eurail passes are valid (see

Part One of this guide for details), and the Inter-Rail scheme applies here. Spain is in Zone F, along with Portugal and Morocco.

INTER-RAIL BONUSES
REDUCED FARE
20% reduction on the ferry crossings operated by Trasmediterranea between Algeciras–Tangier, Barcelona–Palma de Mallorca and Valencia–Palma de Mallorca.

TRAIN INFORMATION
English is not always spoken, so it pays to have a Spanish back-up prepared. Expect long queues. Due to ETA terrorist attacks, left-luggage facilities at Spanish stations are sometimes withdrawn, or subject to security checks such as X-ray examination. There are normally alternative non-official facilities though; usually in the form of some little fellow posted by the station door or in the nearest café who'll guard your luggage for the same hours at the same fee. If in doubt, ask at the station.

RESERVATIONS If you can face the queues it's always advisable to reserve a seat in Spain. Unfortunately, if you decide not to reserve there's no way of telling if someone else has, as reserved seats are not always indicated. On many occasions you settle down in an apparently empty compartment, only to be thrown out just when you thought you were safe. *Reservations are obligatory on all expresses.*

NIGHT TRAVEL Spanish couchettes sleep 6 and are sometimes very old and dirty – you might be better off sleeping on the floor. Sleepers are cheap, however, so all's not lost. For a journey under 550 km, a berth in a tourist-class sleeper will cost about 2,000ptas.

SCENIC TIPS Entering from France, the most scenic route is from Toulouse over the Pyrenees, arriving at Barcelona, although if you return to France by this route you can expect to be searched thoroughly, especially if travelling from Barcelona. The main line from here on to Madrid takes in much that is typically Spanish without you having to go out of your way.

If it's mountains you're after, then it's best to head towards the north-west (León–Tuy) or the south (Córdoba–Málaga, Granada–Almería).

TOURIST INFORMATION

The government-run Tourist Office has branches in all major towns and at many stations. They have an excellent collection of free handouts on all the regions of Spain. In addition, there are local city Tourist Offices which supply maps and more detailed information.

ISIC BONUSES Reduced entrance to the Prado and Bellas Aries museums. For further information, contact Viajes TIVE, Fernando el Católico 88, Madrid (Tel. 543 0208).

MONEY MATTERS 1 peseta (pta) = 100 centimos (c).
   Banking hours are generally Mon.–Fri.: 8.30 a.m.–1.30/2 p.m., Sat.: 8.30 a.m.–1 p.m. From June–Sept. banks may be closed on Saturdays. Shop about, as there's no set rate of exchange, and commission rates are high. The La Caixa bank rate is very poor.

POST OFFICES Open Mon.–Sat: 9 a.m.–2 p.m. and often later in larger cities. *Lista de correos* = poste restante.

SHOPS Open Mon.–Sat.: 9 a.m.–1.30 p.m., 5 p.m.–7.30/8 p.m. (closed Sat. p.m.), but the department stores in large provincial capitals may be open 10 a.m.–8 p.m.

MUSEUMS Vary considerably; most open 10 a.m. and shut again for lunch 12.30/1 p.m., opening again at 4 p.m. till 7 p.m.

TIPPING Tipping is said to be on the way out as most restaurants now include a service charge: however if you want favourable treatment when you next come, round up to the next highest unit of currency above this. Otherwise add 5–10%. Give a small note to porters and attendants. It's common practice to go into a bar or café to use the WC – leave a tip on the bar if there isn't an attendant.

SLEEPING

Every large town in Spain has a Brujula office to help find rooms for a small fee. In addition the Tourist Information office issues lists to help freelancers. You shouldn't have any problems as there's always plenty of cheap accommodation around the stations, all of which is inspected and graded by the government. By law, prices must be shown behind the door of each room and of late hoteliers seem to be obeying the law. During the summer it's legal for prices to be increased by about 15%, so don't get too excited until you've worked it out.
   Hotels start at about 1,200ptas for a single and prices are nearly

always charged by the room, not per person. *Pensiones* and *Hostales* are officially graded (Hs = *hostal*, HsR = *hostal residencia*, P = *pensión*, CH = *casa de huéspedes* and, cheapest of all, F = *fonda*). For the bare necessities, expect to pay about 900ptas per person. Always check to see if breakfast is included in the price; don't assume the management will tell you. Hot showers are another extra which can cost up to 250ptas. Remember that these prices apply to the least expensive areas; in popular towns or resorts expect to pay at least 2,500ptas for a room.

If you think you're being done, the mere mention of *libro de reclamaciones* (complaints book) or *factora* (receipt) should sort out your problems. One of our researchers tried this out in a few establishments and found that the heavy-handed management backed off instantly.

To use any of Spain's 70 youth hostels, you'll need an IYHF card. At 1,300–1,700ptas a night, they are amongst the cheapest accommodation you're likely to find.

If you are thinking about camping, go to ANCE, Principe de Vérgara 85, 2 Ocha, 28006 Madrid; they will give you a map and a *Guía de Camping* (campsite guide). Prices start at about 275ptas per person per night. Sleeping on the beaches is another alternative, but don't make it too obvious or you'll attract trouble from the police or worse.

EATING AND NIGHTLIFE

Spain offers some of the most affordable restaurants in Europe. Give your stomach a chance to adapt to the excess olive oil, and don't have too much seafood to start with. Once you've adapted to local conditions, there's an endless variety of regional specialities to sample, all at reasonable prices. Go for the tourist or house menu where possible, as it's usually a safe bet and works out a lot cheaper than ordering individual dishes. Expect to pay anything from 900 to 1,500ptas for your evening meal and remember that the Spaniards don't eat until at least 9 p.m.–10 p.m. If there's no fixed tourist menu, ask if they do *combinados* – an all-in feast on one plate which often includes something to drink as well. For those low in funds, try *tapas* – delicious and varied titbits available at most bars – but be warned that these are not usually free. The 'Pan and Company' chain in large cities does good *bocadillos* (sandwiches). Local wine is cheap at about 180ptas a bottle, and is a much better buy than beer, though it's often rough and tastes like weak sherry. Spanish cider is excellent. Wine cellars and bars are cheaper and have more local colour than the discos, which make their living by fleecing tourists at the resorts.

The bullfighting season runs from March to October and is

recommended only for the bloodthirsty. Anyone who wants to see one, but is put off by the violence, should head for Portugal, where it is illegal to kill the bull.

Madrid city phone code: 91

Although Madrid was the 1992 Cultural Capital of Europe, it is not one of Europe's most attractive capitals and is certainly not to everyone's taste. It was founded in 1561 by Philip II and he put it in the middle of a hot, dusty plateau to show that because he was king he could do exactly what he wanted. The old town has charm, the nightlife is amongst the hottest in Europe and the Prado is definitely one of the world's great art galleries, but the sprawling concrete districts and lack of major sights entice one to leave Madrid in favour of Toledo or Seville. Still, sleeping and eating aren't a problem and many argue that Madrid is worth the trip for the *tapas* and nightlife alone.

STATION FACILITIES

Madrid has 3 stations: Chamartín, serving the north-east, France and eastern Spain; Atocha, serving Portugal and the south of Spain; and Norte (also called Principe Pio) handling what's left. Some trains, e.g. the Paris–Algeciras express, pass through more than one of them. There are interconnecting trains every 20 minutes, and also an underground service. Atocha station is a tourist attraction in itself: a nineteenth-century iron and glass palace which includes a tropical garden, cafés, bars, a restaurant and a venue for exhibitions!

Because of bomb scares, a system by which the left-luggage lockers could only be used after your kit had been X-rayed was brought in in 1995. If this is in force again it's tough luck at Chamartín, but at Atocha head for some of the bars behind the station (round Calle de Rafael de Riego), and deposit your rucksack for 150ptas.

Don't be surprised if in addition to your rail ticket you get given a Metro-style ticket. This is used to pass through barriers to get to platforms.

There is a Tourist Information office at Chamartín. Trains occasionally may be diverted from Atocha to Chamartín due to railway works – check locally.

Daily trains to Bilbao, Paris, Zaragoza, Barcelona, Valencia, Alicante, Granada, Córdoba, Seville, Lisbon.

TOURIST INFORMATION

The main regional Tourist Office is at C. Princesa 1, Torre de España (Tel. 541 2325) and there's another one at Duque de Medinaceli 2. Both are open Mon.–Fri.: 9 a.m.–7 p.m., Sat.: 9.30 a.m.–1.30 p.m. The municipal (city) office is located at Plaza Mayor 3 (Tel. 366 5477), open Mon.–Sat.: 10 a.m.–2 p.m. Pick up a free map and information leaflets here including a very good list of pensions. There is also a special student information office at the Puerta del Sol metro station.

ADDRESSES

POST OFFICE Palácio de Comunicaciones, Plaza de Cibeles; open Mon.–Fri.: 9 a.m.–10 p.m. and Sat.: 9 a.m.–8 p.m., Sun.: 10 a.m.–1 p.m. *Poste restante* and telegraphs here.

AMEX Plaza de las Cortes 2 (Tel. 429 5775); open Mon.–Fri.: 9 a.m.–5.30 p.m., Sat.: 9 a.m.–12 noon

UK EMBASSY Fernando el Santo 16 (Tel. 319 0200)

IRISH EMBASSY Claudio Coello 73 (Tel. 576 3500)

US EMBASSY Serrano 75 (Tel. 577 4000)

CANADIAN EMBASSY Núñez de Balboa 35 (Tel. 431 4300)

AUSTRALIAN EMBASSY Paseo de la Castellana 143 (Tel. 579 0428)

NEW ZEALAND EMBASSY Plaza Lealtad 2, 3rd floor (Tel. 523 0226)

EUROTRAIN José Ortega y Gasset 71 (Tel. 401 1300)

GETTING ABOUT

For price and speed, the metro is the best means of getting about. It runs till 1.30 a.m. and has nine lines: the *Let's Go* guide to Spain includes a metro map. Buy tickets from machines at stations, individually or in 10s, or from kiosks. Hang on to your ticket till you've finished the journey. Buses are pretty efficient; microbuses are the more luxurious versions of the same theme and both cost the same as the metro.

SEEING

The PRADO MUSEUM is the reason why thousands of art-lovers descend on this city each summer. There are over 3,000 masterpieces here, mainly collected by the Spanish royal family in the 17th and 18th centuries. The old Spanish masters (El Greco, Goya, etc.) are well represented, and there's a fair number of Flemish works collected by the Habsburg kings of the 16th century. There's such a glut of genius here, you'll need to pay 2 or 3 visits at least. The entrance is reasonable at 400ptas, and ISIC holders are free. Near the exit is a shop selling very reasonably priced reproductions, postcards and books. The Prado is open daily, except Mon., May–Oct., Tues.–Sat.: 9 a.m.–7 p.m., Sun.: 9 a.m.–2 p.m., Nov.–Apr., Tues.–Sat.: 10 a.m.–5 p.m., Sun.: 10 a.m.–2 p.m. Your ticket to the Prado also admits you to the CASÓN DEL BUEN RETIRO, near Retiro Park. Also well worth visiting is the REINA SOFIA MUSEUM of 20th century art. Go here to see to see Picasso's famous painting *Guernica*. Open Tues.–Sat.: 9 a.m.–6.45 p.m., entry 700ptas, Sun.: 9 a.m.–1.45 p.m., when entrance is free.

The ROYAL PALACE is the only other 'must' in Madrid. A 45-minute guided tour will take you through the various apartments and the Royal Armoury, which is considered one of the world's best collections of medieval weapons. The palace gardens, especially the CAMPO DEL MORO, are particularly fine and make good venues for regal picnic lunches. Entrance costs 950ptas, but with a reduction for ISIC holders and free admission on Wednesdays for European Community citizens with their passports.

The BOTANIC GARDENS, near the Prado, is also a nice place to have a quiet picnic. Entrance costs 50ptas. Parks are, in fact, Madrid's speciality, very busy and colourful on Sundays. The RETIRO PARK in the city centre is huge and, apart from its rowing lake, theatre, fountains and statues, the CRYSTAL PALACE of the Bourbon kings is here. North-west of the palace is another park on 10 times the scale of the Retiro, which young Spaniards tend to patronize at weekends: the CASA DE CAMPO has among its attractions a zoo, amusement park, swimming pool and outdoor theatre.

OLD MADRID lies between PUERTA DEL SOL (known as the centre of Spain) and the Crystal Palace; notice the descriptive pictures above the street signs to help the illiterate 17th-century locals. These narrow winding streets are the most colourful and interesting in Madrid. If you're feeling particularly penitent you can even buy a hair shirt here.

The taverns in the alleys off the PLAZA MAYOR are good starting-places for your evening's pub crawl, Madrid-style. On Sunday mornings there's a flea market (the Rastro) off the southern corner of the square, where gypsies often congregate and put on street shows.

SLEEPING

Cheap beds aren't a problem here, even in summer. The Tourist Offices will advise you on accommodation, but won't arrange it for you. Brujula, a private placing agency with branches at Torre de

Madrid and plaza España, will do this for a small fee, but you must visit in person. In fact, you shouldn't need their help as there are hundreds of suitable places, many near the centrally located Atocha station, in streets like Calle Toledo. Try the Hotel Residencia Finistere at no. 113, where you can expect to pay around 2,500ptas for a double with a shower. Also recommended is the Hostal Córdoba at 21 pts. Santa Maria de la Cabeza (Tel. 227 3189); 1,400ptas for a single room with shower.

If you're really cutting corners and don't mind other people's nocturnal 'goings-on', or the odd bed-bug, the area south of Puerta del Sol will produce some very inexpensive (from 1,000ptas upwards) *casas de huéspedes*. The university let out rooms to those wanting to stay 5 or more days, and there are 2 youth hostels which aren't too far away from the centre. One's at Calle Santa Cruz de Marcenado 28 (Tel. 247 4532) and the other's at Casa de Campo (Tel. 463 5699) in the park there. You need IYHF membership, and a bed will cost about 500ptas.

The street with more cheap beds than anywhere else is Gran Vía in central Madrid. Hostal Alcázar-Regis, on the 5th floor of no. 61 (Tel. 247 3549), is good value for what you get; La Costa Verde (9th floor) is cheaper, and Buenos Aires (Tel. 247 8800) on the 2nd floor have singles for around 2,000ptas and doubles for 2,900ptas. Hostal Amayo (Tel. 222 2151) on the 1st floor of no. 12 and at no. 38, Hostal California (Tel. 222 4703) and Don José (Tel. 232 1385) have good rooms, and Hostal Margarita at no. 50 (Tel. 247 3549) is reasonable, with singles from 2,200ptas.

Ask at Turismo for the camping leaflet and don't risk the parks unless you're desperate. Camping Madrid (Tel. 202 2835) is reasonable, but a long way out. Take the metro to Plaza de Castilla, then bus 129.

EATING AND NIGHTLIFE

Tapas (tasty snacks served in infinite varieties to accompany your drink) are at their best in Madrid. Most Madrileños spend between 6 p.m. and 10 p.m. on the *tapas* circuit in either Pasaje de Matheu or the area round Plaza Mayor. Mussels, mushrooms, omelettes and filled rolls are some of the savouries with which to bridge the gap till dinner, washed down with sangría or wine. The main meal of the day is eaten at lunchtime (2 p.m.–4 p.m.) and dinner, around 10 p.m., is quite a light affair.

Argüelles, on the metro, is the city's main student quarter. Make for this area to eat cheaply and meet the university students. The bars along Calle de la Princesa are a safe bet to make friends, and back in the centre Calle Echegaray and Ventura de la Vega, off Calle San

Jerónimo, also have cheap restaurants. Restaurant Copatisán, Calle del Barco 16–18, is very cheap and very good. Closed Aug. For a good paella try Restaurant El Parque, Fernando el Católico 78.

The nightlife starts with the pub crawl and continues in the *salas de fiesta* (nightclubs), winding up around 3 a.m.–4 a.m. At weekends, things are twice as lively and the *discotecas* (which are on the expensive side) hold afternoon as well as evening sessions to cope with the insatiable demand ('afternoon' in Spain seems to mean 7 p.m.–10 p.m.); try Archy's at Marquis Riscal 11. The *salas de fiesta* shows range from awful cabarets to sex shows.

Two list of current events in the *Guía del Ocio* is all you need. Avoid the heavily advertised flamenco shows, as they're incredibly commercial and plastic, and ask about for the best discos, etc., in the bars along the Aurrera in the Argüelles quarter. The Colectivo de Gais y Lesbianas, Calle Carretas 12, 3rd floor (Tel. 522 4517) has free information, shows films and publishes a newsletter of gay and lesbian events and activities.

EXCURSIONS Forty-eight kilometres from the Norte or Atocha stations is the huge granite palace of EL ESCORIAL. This was King Philip II's country house which it took over 20 years to complete. In fact, it looks more like a high-security prison than a palace. The guided tours take you round the museums, library, church, art gallery and royal apartments for 950ptas. Open 10 a.m.–1 p.m., 3 p.m.–7 p.m.

A few kilometres further on is the VALLE DE LOS CAIDOS – a memorial to those who died in the Civil War, and where Franco is buried in a huge underground basilica complex.

Or, if you just want to cool off, stay in the train to Cercedilla and take the branch line up into the Sierra de Guadarrama mountains.

ARANJUEZ If you are *en route* south to Córdoba or Seville, it is worth a stop-off here to see the ROYAL PALACE, the SAILOR'S HOUSE, the PRINCE'S GARDEN and the FARMER'S HOUSE. The campsite here, Solo del Castillo, will entice you to stay a while as it's about the best one in Spain.

San Sebastián (Donostia) city phone code: 943

This was traditionally one of Spain's major holiday resorts for the rich and famous. Its position as one of the main Basque cities makes it a slightly less safe bet for a family holiday today, due to terrorist attacks, but the choice is yours; the odds of anything nasty happening are weighted heavily in your favour and the political graffiti are interesting. It's an attractive place; the beaches are good and it will break up a run from Paris to Madrid nicely.

TOURIST INFORMATION AND ADDRESSES

TOURIST OFFICES Calle Fueros 1, and Reina Regente (ground floor, Victoria Eugenia Theatre); open Oct.–May, Mon.–Fri.: 9 a.m.–l.30 p.m., 3.30 p.m.–7 p.m., Sat.: 9 a.m.–l p.m.; Jun.–Sept., Mon.–Sat.: 9 a.m.–8 p.m., Sun.: 10 a.m.–1 p.m. (Tel. 481166)
POST OFFICE Calle Urdaneta 9 (Tel. 464914)
FIRST AID *Cruz Roja* (Red Cross), Calle Matías 7 (Tel. 214600)

SEEING

The SAN TELMO MUSEUM, in a 16th-century Renaissance monastery on Plaza Ignacio Zuloaga, will fill you in on the differences between the Basques and the Spanish or French; or visit the AQUARIUM down on the port to see the collection of sea creatures. The FISH MARKET is well worth a visit, as is PLAZA DE LA CONSTITUTION SQUARE, a former bullring. You can rent a boat and go over to the beach island of SANTA CLARA (there is also a half-hourly ferry in summer), or else just laze about on the beaches of ZURIOLLA, LA CONCHA and ONDARRETA. On the coast is the living sculpture *Comb of the Wind* by Eduardo Chillida.

SLEEPING

During the summer, cheap beds are hard to find. Try the excellent campsite on the Carretera de Monte Igueldo (about 8 km from the station – take the Barrio de Igueldo bus from Alameda de Boulevard) or the 2 youth hostels at La Sirena (Tel. 310268) and Parque Ulia Mendi (only for groups: Tel. 452970). The best pension deals are at Pensión La Perla, Loyola 10 (Tel. 428123). The cheapest you'll find is Fonda Aruaga at Narrica 3 (Tel. 420681) with singles from 2,000ptas. It's also possible to sleep on the beach, but more risky.

EATING AND NIGHTLIFE

It's not easy to cut corners in San Sebastián for 2 reasons: first, there are hardly any places with tourist menus in the eurorailer's budget range; and secondly, the food is so good you won't feel like living off bread, cheese and fruit. This is one Spanish town where the food is consistently good and, of course, the fish dishes are excellent. The city actually has a Gastronomic Academy, and the exclusive and chauvinistic male-only dining clubs frequently sponsor eating contests. There are several bars and restaurants in the central square, Plaza de la Constitución, but watch the prices here.

For pre-dinner *tapas*, or *pinchos* as they're known locally, try the bars along Calle Fermin Calbertón and, for dancing, Botaplan (on La Concha) and Beartzana (in Plaza Easo) are meant to be pretty hot. There are festivals all summer, the most interesting being the Basque folklore one, the jazz festival (July) and the international film festival (September). Ask at Tourist Information for details.

Northern Spain

This region runs from the foot of the Pyrenees to close to Portugal. It is one of Spain's least touristy areas, and the lush forests, good beaches and historic towns make it worth exploration. The Basques – possibly the oldest ethnic group in Europe – have their own very separate history, culture and language. After Franco's death, the ETA (Basque Liberation Front) became increasingly active in their terrorist acts of bombings and murder, and the issue is still not fully settled. 1996 saw the first tourist casualties, but by and large things are fairly quiet today.

PAMPLONA The picturesque old town is well worth a visit for the Festival de San Fermín (6–14 July), better known as the Running of the Bulls. A favourite of Hemingway, the festival is a week-long spectacle of singing, dancing and, most of all, drinking. It is arguably the best street party in Europe: the whole town is bedecked in red and white and in fiesta mood.

The actual bull run begins at 8 a.m. when a group of bulls pursues crowds of people to the bull-ring. Although it may be tempting to prove your machismo and run with the bulls, bear in mind that it is dangerous (because of the crowd of runners as much as the bulls) and, in the event of injury, your insurance cover will probably be invalid. Anyway, the best part of the fiesta is the exuberant nightlife around Plaza del Castillo and Calle Navarrería.

If you can tear yourself away from the festivities, the MUSEU DE NAVARRE has some excellent murals. The CATHEDRAL, with its beautiful Gothic cloisters, and the CITADEL are also worth a look.

Tourist Information is at Calle Duque de Ahumada 3 (Tel. 948 220741), open Mon.–Fri.: 10 a.m.–2 p.m., 4 p.m.–7 p.m.; Sat.: 10 a.m.–2 p.m. They will help with accommodation, but you will have to be extremely fortunate or resourceful to find a bed during the fiesta. Try Fonda La Montanesa, Calle San Gregorio (Tel. 948 224380) which has doubles at around 3,000ptas, or the similarly priced Casa Huéspedes Santa Cecelia, Calle Navarrería 17 (Tel. 948 222230).

The nearest campsite is Camping Ezcaba (Tel. 948 330315) with excellent facilities and a free swimming pool, 7 km away but with bus connections.

If you're out of luck, do not be tempted to sleep rough in the unsafe Plaza del Castillo, but head for the other side of the bull-ring to a park. Showers are available at Calle Eslava 9, open Tues.–Sun.: 7.30 a.m.–9.30 p.m. and are widely used by bedless travellers.

SANTANDER The port of Santander is wedged between the Basque and Galician regions in the province of Cantabria. This part of northern Spain is mountainous with a rugged coastline, and contains some of the world's best prehistoric cave art in the ALTAMIRA CAVES.

The beaches at Santander are the main reason to stop off, particularly the ones at EL SARDINERO, COMILLAS and LIENCRES. The area by the harbour is the 'new town' and this is where the restaurants and bars are located.

Tourist Information is at Jardina de Pereda, open Mon.–Fri.: 9 a.m.–1.30 p.m., 4.30 p.m.–7.30 p.m.; Sat.: 9 a.m.–12 noon (Tel. 42 216120). There are plenty of cheap *hostales* or campsites outside the town.

An interesting excursion from Santander is inland to the picturesque village of MEDINA DE POMAR with its fascinating monastery (open 10 a.m.–1.30 p.m.) and collection of churches.

SANTIAGO DE COMPOSTELA This is the main town in the beautiful province of Galicia, though if you really wanted to explore the dramatic Atlantic coastline you'd be better staying at La Coruña, on the main line to Madrid. Santiago was a popular place of pilgrimage in the Middle Ages for up to 2 million Christians a year who made the journey here to see where the Apostle St James is buried, and today the pilgrimage journey is still followed by hundreds of walkers and cyclists.

The CATHEDRAL dominates the town, but it's difficult to isolate other main sights as the whole inner town is a national monument, and deserving of it. The cathedral was started in the 11th century but encompasses many architectural styles. The student quarter lies between the cathedral and the university and this is the best area to head for at night.

The Tourist Office is at Rúa del Villar 43, closed Sat. p.m., all day Sun. and 2 p.m.–4 p.m. daily (Tel. 15 84081), and they have a list of the pensions with their prices posted up, but once you're at Turismo you're already in Santiago's main hostel street. Try Hospedaje Santa Cruz at no. 42, or Pensión Lens at no. 73; you should get away with not having to pay much more than 2,000ptas for a double. The only time you may have trouble is during the annual festival of St James (15–31 July) or around religious feast days when pilgrims flock into the town. Casa Manoló near St Benedict's church is the best cheap place to eat.

Andorra

This small autonomous principality of 65,000 people lies between France and Spain in the Pyrenees. Andorra was founded in AD 784 by Charlemagne and is under the joint suzerainty of the Bishop of Urgel (Spain) and the French President. The official language is Catalan and both French francs and Spanish pesetas are used. Coming from France, Andorra can be reached by train from Toulouse to L'Hospitalet-Près-l' Andorre and then by bus or from Perpignan to La Tour de Carol and then by bus as well. Coming from Barcelona there are buses three times a day. Whichever way you come, it's a dramatic road journey round hairpin bends to the Andorran capital ANDORRA LA VELLA. The buses don't connect with all the trains, so check the timetable first.

The scenery on the way to La Tour de Carol is fairly dramatic and, once inside Andorra, the mountains are equally spectacular, making for a few days' good hiking.

The Tourist Information office is at Carrer Dr Vilanova (Tel. 820214). They'll provide you with maps and accommodation lists. There are no IYHF hostels in Andorra, but finding a room in a *Residencia* should be no problem. Check the Official Price List for hotels: prices start at around 65F. The owner will take your passport for registration with the police.

Because of Andorra's duty-free status, Andorra la Vella is extremely commercialized, resembling a Spanish costa resort. One consequence of this is that you can pick up extremely cheap duty-frees, for example, a litre of Polish vodka for £3.50! Goods tend to be priced in pesetas, but you can pay in either francs or pesetas and when changing money you can get your cash in whichever currency you want. This can be handy if you are visiting only France or only Spain.

The main sight in Andorra la Vella is the 16th-century CASA DE LA VALL, the seat of the Andorran government. The visit is free with an official guide, but you may need to reserve a place (Tel. 829129).

Aside from Andorra la Vella there are a number of small, less commercialized towns in Andorra which could be used as a base for exploring the countryside. The National Festival is on 8 September with a pilgrimage at the sanctuary of MERITXELL.

Barcelona city phone code: 93

Situated across the Pyrenees from France and on the Mediterranean south of the Costa Brava, Barcelona seems to have as many links with France as with Spain. It's proud of its position as capital of Cataluña, and the language you'll hear in the streets, Catalan, is derived not from Spanish but from the French *langue d'oc.*

The old quarter of BARRIO GÓTICO with its medieval streets is particularly lively, though the whole city is bustling and vivacious Regarded as the literary capital of Spain, and with an important university, Barcelona has the added attraction of its proximity to the Mediterranean and good beaches.

1992 was a particularly big year for Barcelona, as the host of the summer Olympic Games. Literally thousands of millions of pounds were spent on ancillary projects to make Barcelona a great centre for urban tourism.

STATION FACILITIES
Barcelona's main station, Sants, handles most major trains; some also stop at the smaller Paseo de Gracia station nearer the city centre (there are connecting trains every 20 minutes).

Daily trains to: Paris, Geneva, Valencia, Zaragoza, Madrid, Irún.

TOURIST INFORMATION AND ADDRESSES
TOURIST OFFICE Regional office at Gran Vía de les Cortes Catalanes 658 (Tel. 301 7443), open Mon.–Fri.: 9 a.m.–7 p.m., closed Sat. p.m. and Sun. Ask them for their list of budget accommodation, along with your map and leaflets. Also the city office at Plaza Catalunya 17S (Tel. 304 3134).

POST OFFICE Plaza d'Antoni López, open Mon.–Sat.: 8 a.m.–9.55 p.m., Sun.: 10 a.m.–2 p.m. Stamps from the basement.

AMEX Paseo de Gracia 101, open Mon.–Fri.: 9.30 a.m.–6 p.m., Sat.: 10 a.m.–12 noon (Tel. 217 0070)

UK CONSULATE Avenida Diagonal 477 (Tel. 419 9044)

US CONSULATE Paseo Reina Elisenda 23 (Tel. 280 2227)

CANADIAN CONSULATE Pg. de Gracia 77, 3rd floor (Tel. 215 0704)

AUSTRALIAN CONSULATE Gran Vía Carlo III 98 (Tel. 330 9496)

GETTING AROUND
Although walking is the best way to see Barcelona, there is good public transport by bus and metro. Plaza de Catalunya is the main

terminus. Bus and metro rides cost around l40ptas, but you can save money by buying a multi-ticket at metro entrances. A T–1 card for 740ptas allows 10 trips by bus and metro, whilst a T–2 card for 720ptas allows 10 trips on the metro only.

SEEING

Head for the BARRIO GÓTICO and look out for the GREAT ROYAL PALACE in Plaza del Rey, the CATEDRAL DE SANTA EULALIA and the DIPUTACIÓN PROVINCIAL (council buildings). The hub of the city, however, is LAS RAMBLAS. This collection of streets starts at the port and runs to the city centre at Plaça de Catalunya. For sheer entertainment value you can't beat Las Ramblas. It's the Piccadilly Circus of Barcelona, so popular that you pay for a folding chair to spectate, come nightfall.

The incredible and unmissable cathedral of TEMPLO EXPIATORIO DE LA SAGRADA FAMILIA is the work of the Catalan architect Gaudí; however, his death before construction was completed put a spanner in the works, as he didn't leave any plans. Work is now proceeding, however. Open daily 9 a.m.–9 p.m. in high season, 9 a.m.–7 or 8 p.m. in quieter months, with an admission charge of 800ptas.

South of Barrio Gótico is MONTJUIC PARK, the setting for the Olympics. The buildings originally erected here for the 1929 International Exhibition were refurbished specially for the Olympics. The model town in PUEBLO ESPAÑOL is worth seeing, as it shows all the different regional styles of architecture in Spain, although it is a bit 'touristy'. Open Sun.–Mon.: 9 a.m.–8 p.m., Tues.–Thur:. 9 a.m.–2 p.m., Fri.–Sat.: 9 a.m.–4 p.m., 950ptas. Take the funicular up the hill, and admire the view over the port and city. For even more dramatic views take the tram up to TIBIDABO, north of the city. There are also good views from the Palau Nacional and Mirador de L'Alcade (near Parc d'Attractions).

The PICASSO MUSEUM is at Calle de Montcada 15 (open Tues.–Sat.: 10 a.m.–8 p.m., Sun.) 10 a.m.–3 p.m., entrance 500ptas, half price Weds.) and has lots of his works from the early sketches to his final masterpieces.

There are numerous other museums and art galleries – some of the more interesting ones are the BARCELONA FOOTBALL CLUB MUSEUM at their ground (Oct.–Mar., Mon.–Sat.: 10 a.m.–6.30 p.m., Sun.: 10 a.m.–2 p.m., Tel. 496 3600), GAUDI'S HOUSE at Ctra del Carmel 23 in Parc Guell (Sun.–Fri.: 10 a.m.–2 p.m., 4 p.m.–6 p.m., Tel. 219 3811) and, if you aren't too disapproving of bloodsports, the BULLFIGHTING MUSEUM at Gran Vía de los Cortes Catalanes 749 (May–Sept., Mon.–Sat.: 10.30 a.m.–2 p.m., 4 p.m.–7 p.m., Sun.: 10.30 a.m.–1 p.m.) Check with Tourist Information for a full list.

SLEEPING

The youth hostel on Passeig Pujadas 29 (Tel. 300 3104) charges 1,500ptas, breakfast extra. Reception is closed 10 a.m.–5 p.m. but you can leave luggage and reserve a bed after 3 p.m. It has only 68 beds and gets very crowded, so get there as soon after 8 a.m. as possible; its big drawback is the midnight curfew. There are also youth hostels at Passeig Mare de Déu del Coil 41–51 (Tel. 210 5151), Numancia 149–151 (Tel. 410 2309) and the summer only 'Studio' hostel at Duquesa d'Orleans 58 (Tel. 205 0961). The latter are a long way from the centre of town, however.

For camping, there are quite a few sites but they are all a few kilometres out of town. Camping Masnou, Calle Camilio, Fabra 33, El Masnón (Tel. 555 1503), has a free swimming pool and lively bar.

The university at Calle Mestre Nicolau 14 (Tel. 250 1419) offers both sexes bed and breakfast for 800ptas.

Your best bet for cheap *casas* and hostels is in Las Ramblas. Pension Fernando, Calle Ferran 31 (Tel. 301 7993), is cheap and friendly. Hostal Noya, Ramblas 133 (Tel. 301 4831), and Hostal Canaletas, on the 3rd floor (Tel. 301 5660), start around 2,300ptas for singles and are situated right in the city centre.

Although it can be quite rowdy, the Kabul Young Budget Hotel is cheap and central at Plaza Reial 17 (Tel. 318 5190). Mixed dormitories and free (but cold) showers. There is no curfew or lock-out and it costs only l,200ptas or so. Although you get breakfast and can buy sandwiches at the bar, you are better eating around the Plaça de Sant Jaume.

Some distance out is the youth hostel Ocata at El Masnou. To get there, take a suburban train from Plaça Catalunya metro station to Ocata station (20 minutes). Turn right out of the station, left at the Banco de Bilbao and head up the hill. If all else fails, there's a Brujula (accommodation-finding kiosk) at Término station, and if you arrive exhausted in mid-August this is your best move.

EATING AND NIGHTLIFE

The Catalans eat late. Dinner time averages 9 p.m.–11 p.m. There are plenty of places offering *menu del día* in Barrio Gótico, and if you get a chance to sample the regional speciality, Catalan stew, *escudella i cam d'olla*, do so. Casa José, Pl. San José: Oriol 10, is the cheapest, though not friendliest, feed in Barcelona. Cosmos, at Ramblas 34, does a good meal with coffee for about 800ptas. If you're feeling extravagant, go to Barceloneta, the area of colourful winding streets down by the port, and savour the fresh seafood concoctions in Casa Costa on Juicio. Vegetarians should head for Restaurante Bio Centre on Calle Pintor

Fortuny 24, open afternoons except Sun., or for Comme-bio.

If you've money to blow, go to the nightclubs and discos like Georgia, Pelayo 58, or El Cordobés on Ramblas Capuchinos. The Cafe de la Opera at Rambla 74 is the trendiest café if you've got the cash to spare, but for our money strolling through the Ramblas, stopping at a few cafés *en route*, is as good value as anything.

It gets quite lively at the top of the Montjuic on summer evenings, but if that's too sedate for you, head down to El Barrio Chino (near the docks). By Spanish standards some of the shows down there are pretty hot stuff, but bear in mind that this is the red-light area and can be rather sleazy. Be wary of your valuables.

Gays and lesbians should visit the specialist Complices bookshop at Calle Cervantes 2 (metro: Liceu) for a map of venues. Open Mon.–Fri.: 10.30 a.m.–8.30 p.m.; Sat.: 12 noon–8.30 p.m.

EXCURSIONS If the oppressive heat of the city is getting you down, you've not far to go to get to the good but crowded beaches of the COSTA BRAVA and the COSTA DORADA. LLORET DE MAR is infested with package tourists but pretty, while S'AGARÓ is the St Tropez of the Costa Brava. Stay at SAN FELÍU DE GUIXOLS and travel in the 3 km to S'Agaró to save yourself a fortune. Buses run to these and other, closer resorts from Estación del Nord at Ali-bey 80, near metro Arc de Triomf, or from Vergara 5, Barcelona. The bus company is Sarfa.

MONTSERRAT The town, 61 km from Barcelona, is reached by Catalan Railways (from Plaza de España – about £5 with Inter-Rail discount). Set among the mountain peaks, there is a Benedictine monastery, a Gothic basilica and a nice collection of early paintings by Juan Miró and Picasso. It's a good day trip away from town.

TARRAGONA This city lies about 100 km south of Barcelona, on the Costa Dorada. Although touristy and surrounded by oil refineries, the culture vultures may wish to stop off here and visit the ruins of the provincial Roman capital of Hispania. If you are coming from Barcelona, sit on the right-hand side of the train for a visual extravaganza!

You can pick up leaflets with lots of useful information at Tourist Information, Fortuny 4 (Tel. 23 3415), open Mon.–Fri.: 8.45 a.m.–2.35 p.m., Sat.: 9 a.m.–2 p.m. Rambla Nova is the main street in Tarragona, and along this long, tree-lined avenue you will find an information kiosk and the post office, as well as countless places offering cheap food.

The ARCHAEOLOGICAL MUSEUM has a fascinating collection of mosaics and is one of the most important in Spain. It is part of the CYCLOPEAN WALLS, which run for about 1 km along the highest part of town, starting at the end of Rambla Vella, which runs parallel to Rambla Nova. The wall, which varies in height from 3.5 to 12 m, was built around 600 BC. Also visit the ROMAN AMPHITHEATRE and the 13th-century CATHEDRAL in the old town.

The youth hostel is at Avenida President Companys s/n (Tel. 977 24 0195). It normally has 90 beds, but in July and August the number jumps to 190. There are also a number of cheap hotels south of the Rambla Nova and the campsite is a few kilometres east of the town. Take bus 3 or 3a from the Rambla Nova.

PORT BOU Just over the border from France, situated in a natural amphitheatre and nestling beside the Mediterranean, Port Bou is a delightful spot for the travel-weary eurorailer to relax and toast for a day or two. The vast railway station is out of all proportion to its surroundings but it is only a short walk to hotels and the rather pebbly beach.

Tourist Information at the harbour is open throughout the day Mon.–Sat., but only in the mornings on Sun.

Although there is no youth hostel and the locals don't like you sleeping on the beach, the Hôtel Juventas is highly recommended at around 2,400ptas for a double with washbasin and shower next door. It is at Avenue de Barcelona 2. There isn't really much to do in Port Bou but lie on the beach and watch the skinny-dippers. There are plenty of good cafés, but, although the seafood is good value, the prices are not all that cheap.

Valencia city phone code: 96

If you're taking a detour off the railway to visit the Balearic islands of Majorca, Menorca or Ibiza, Valencia is logically *en route*, so you may feel like.stopping off here. There's nothing very exciting here, but it is the point of departure for steamers to the islands, as are Alicante and Barcelona.

TOURIST INFORMATION AND ADDRESSES
MUNICIPAL TOURIST OFFICE At the Town Hall: Plaza Ajuntament 1 (Tel. 351 0417)
REGIONAL TOURIST OFFICE Estación del Nord, Calle Xàtiva 24 (Tel. 352 8593)

POST OFFICE Plaza del Pais, Valenciano 24
AMEX Duna Viajes, Calle Cirilo Amorós 88 (Tel. 374 1562)
US CONSULATE Calle de la Paz 6 (Tel. 351 6973); open Mon.–Fri.:
10 a.m.–1 p.m.

STATION FACILITIES

Valencia Término has daily trains to: Barcelona, Alicante, Córdoba,
Madrid. It also has automatic luggage lockers and a helpful
information office.

24-hour telephone information line: 352 0202

FERRIES TO THE BALEARIC ISLANDS Transmediterránea, Avenida
Manuel Solo Ingeniero 15 (Tel. 367 6512)

SEEING

The PALACE OF THE MARQUÉS DE DOS AGUAS is about the most interesting
building around. It's 18th-century rococo and contains about the best
collection of Spanish pottery in Spain (closed 2 p.m.–4 p.m. for siesta,
closed Sunday p.m. and all day Monday).

The GOTHIC CATHEDRAL is also worth a look. Climb its tower for a view
over the city and visit the museum, which claims to hold the Holy
Grail; open daily 10 a.m.–1 p.m., 4.30–7 p.m.; 100ptas.

Apart from these, the MUSEO PROVINCIAL DE BELLAS ARTES is the only
other place really worth visiting, with works by Goya amongst others.
Free entry, open Tues.–Sun.: 10 a.m.–2 p.m., closed Mon.

The best beaches are further south at BENIDORM and ALICANTE, but
there are closer ones on the Costa del Azahar accessible by bus.

SLEEPING, EATING AND NIGHTLIFE

The youth hostel is at Avenida del Puerto 69 (Tel. 361 7459) on bus
route 19. Open July–September. Round the Plaza del Mercado are
plenty of grotty *casas* and *fondas* with beds around 800ptas. The
cleanest and cheapest is Hostal del Rincón at Calle Carda 11 (Tel. 331
6083), which has doubles from 1,800ptas, singles for 1,300ptas.

The Barrio del Carmen is the area both for cheap eating and for
nightlife. Rice dishes are the Valencian speciality, but you often have to
watch the prices. There are lots of spit 'n' sawdust bars in this area
which vary from colourful and 'ethnic' to grimy and revolting.

Central Spain

About 2 hours from Madrid lie 2 towns which should ideally be included on any Spanish itinerary: ÁVILA and SEGOVIA.

ÁVILA Famous because of Saint Teresa, this town has some of Europe's best-preserved medieval battlements, dating from the 11th century, and other buildings from this same period.

Tourist Information is at Plaza de la Catedral (Tel. 91821 1387) open Mon.–Fri.: 9 a.m.–8 p.m., Sat.: 9 a.m.–3 p.m., Sun.: 11 a.m.–3 p.m. There's no problem finding cheap rooms.

SEGOVIA This has a ROMAN AQUEDUCT antedating Christ, a 14th-century ALCÁZAR (palace) (rebuilt in the 19th century), and dozens of churches in different architectural styles.

The Tourist Office is at Plaza Mayor 10 (Tel. 911 430328), open Mon.–Fri.: 9 a.m.–2 p.m., 4.30 p.m.–7 p.m., Sat.: 9 a.m.–2 p.m., and there are plenty of cheap rooms nearby. Try Fonda Cubo, third floor at Plaza Mayor 4.

Other towns well worth a detour

TOLEDO This is the town which can show you the past 20 centuries of Spanish history and culture in 1 or 2 days. From the Roman circus, through Moorish and Visigothic mosques and synagogues to Renaissance buildings reminiscent of the Spanish Inquisition, every architectural style is represented and wonderfully preserved. It's interesting to note that Toledo was one of the world's few centres of Arab, Jewish and Christian co existence. It's possible to make Toledo a day trip from Madrid (it takes 1½ hours) but you'll kill yourself trying to see all the sights in just one afternoon.

Perched up on the high town are buildings such as the MOSQUE OF THE CHRIST OF THE LIGHT (10th century), the SYNAGOGUE OF SANTA MARIA LA BLANCA, the incredible medieval CATHEDRAL; and dominating the violet-coloured sky is the ALCÁZAR which once housed El Cid. El Greco lived in Toledo, and his HOUSE AND MUSEUM can be seen (these were closed in 1997 but hopefully should reopen in 1998 or 1999). Many of the sights take a long siesta and don't reopen till 4 p.m – one that doesn't is the MUSEUM OF SANTA CRUZ.

There are many more things to see: go along to Turismo, just outside the Puerta de Bisagra and pick up your glossy leaflets and map. The office is open weekdays 9 a.m.–6 p.m. (9 a.m.– 7 p.m. on Sat.: 9 a.m.–3 p.m. Sun.).

From the station (at the foot of the hill) take the bus marked Santa Barbara to the centre. For accommodation, there are 2 campsites: Camping El Greco (Tel. 925 213537) and Circo Romano (Tel. 925 220442). The first (1½ km out of town on the N401 road) is the better, and charges 350ptas per person.

Tourist Information will suggest pensions, of which perhaps Pension Descalzos, Calle de los Descalzos 32 (Tel. 925 222888), is the best. Fonda Lumbreras, Calle Juan Labrador 7 (Tel. 925 221571) is another good bet.

Shop around for your meals and eat at the fixed-price menu places near the central Plaza de Zocodover if possible. This is where it all happens in Toledo, especially at night.

The youth hostel is in a castle 10 minutes' walk from the station and town centre. It's at Castillo de San Servando (Tel. 925 224554) and is beautiful inside with a super pool, though slightly more expensive than a normal Spanish hostel.

SALAMANCA Further down the line from Ávila is Spain's oldest university town, Salamanca. The main reason for going there is to see Spain's most beautiful square, the PLAZA MAYOR, built by Philip V in the 18th century. From the station take bus 1 to the centre of the town where Tourist Information is at Gran Vía 41 (Tel. 923 268571), closed Saturday afternoon and all day Sunday.

An afternoon should be long enough to take in the main sights: the square, university, OLD AND NEW CATHEDRALS, and HOUSE OF SHELLS, but if you come in term-time you might want to stay a night for the active student nightlife.

Look for a room round the Plaza Mayor and Calle Meléndez, which are also the main areas for cheap food.

BURGOS Most Madrid–Paris runs go through this old 10th-century capital of Castile. Franco was declared military commander here in 1936 and as none other than El Cid is buried here. It's the CATHEDRAL that you should head for, as the rest of the town has nothing spectacular in it. Entrance around 300ptas.

Tourist Information is at Plaza de Alonso Martínez 7 (Tel. 947 20 31 25); open Mon.–Fri.: 9 a.m.–2 p.m., 4.30 p.m.–6.30 p.m., Sat.: 10 a.m.–1.30 p.m.

The youth hostel is at Avenida General Vigón (Tel. 947 22 03 62) or try Hostal Victoria, Calle San Juan 3 (Tel. 947 20 15 42), near the Tourist Office.

The nearest campsite is large and well equipped, but a 3km bus ride from the centre. It's at Fuentes Blacas (Tel. 947 221016) and costs 325ptas per tent, 375ptas per person.

A short walk away is the Carthusian monastery, CARTIYA DE MIRAFLORES, which is open Mon.–Fri.: 9.30 a.m.–1 p.m., 3.30 p.m.–6 p.m., Sat. and Sun.: 12 noon–2 p.m., 3 p.m.–6 p.m., and has some ornate tombs.

VALLADOLID Just over an hour from Burgos is the university city of Valladolid. If you take a break here, visit the 16th-century house of Miguel de Cervantes, who wrote *Don Quixote*, off the Calle Miguel Iscar, the CATHEDRAL, the cloisters of the 16th-century S. GREGORIO COLLEGE and the UNIVERSITY.

Tourist Information is at 3 Plaza de Zorrilla (Tel. 983 51810).

CUENCA If you're heading for Valencia and the Costa del Azahar, and fancy a short break in the 5-hour journey from Madrid, take an hour or more off at Cuenca, about halfway up the line. Walk round the old town, starting at the PLAZA MAYOR, and take in the CITY HALL, the CATHEDRAL and the incredible 14th-century HANGING HOUSES on the banks of the Hutecar River.

Turismo is at Dalmacio Garcia Izcara 8 (Tel. 966 22 22 31); open Mon.–Fri.: 9 a.m.–2 p.m., 4.30 p.m.–6.30 p.m., Sat.: 9.30 a.m.–1 p.m.

Pensión Centrale (Tel. 966 211511) at Calle Alonso Chirino 9 is good for a cheap bed. More expensive but with great views is Posada de San José (Tel. 966 211300) at Calle Julian Romero 4, near the cathedral.

Andalusia (Andalucía)

This region is one of the most beautiful in Spain and includes not only the cities of Seville, Granada and Córdoba but a wide variety of incredibly scenic and typically Spanish towns. Here you find real flamenco and bullfights, along with Moorish palaces and hilltop villages.

GRANADA Bus 3, 4, 6, 9 or 11 will take you from the station to the city centre. The Tourist Office is at Calle Mariana Pineda (inside the monument Corral del Carbón) (Tel. 225990); open Mon.–Sat.:10 a.m.–1 p.m., 4 p.m.–7 p.m., Sun.: 10 a.m.–2 p.m. There's another at Plaza Mariana Pineda 10; closed on Sundays and Saturday p.m.. For train information call 223497. The post office on Puerta Real is open 9 a.m.–2 p.m., 4 p.m.–6 p.m., closed Saturday p.m. and Sunday (Tel. 224835). AMEX: Calle Reyes Católicos 31.

Once you've found accommodation and disposed of your baggage, visit the huge Arabic fortress on the hill dominating the city: the ALHAMBRA. It's one of the world's best-preserved Moorish palaces. The ALCAZABA and WATCH TOWER go back to the 9th century, and you should visit GENERALIFE, the summer house of the sultans, the 14th-century palace, and see the incredible mosaics and examples of Muslim art. If you want to see the whole lot – castle, Generalife, royal palace, as well as the remaining grounds – then go early in the day to get its full atmosphere. The Alhambra is open daily 9 a.m.–8 p.m., price 725ptas, but if you are here on a Tuesday, Thursday or Saturday, do head up there in the evening when the whole inside is lit up from 10 p.m. until midnight

Opposite the Alhambra is ALBAYZÍN, the hilltop Arab quarter with its crowded, winding streets, and on the other hilltop is the gypsy quarter of SACROMONTE.

Down in the town take in the Renaissance CATHEDRAL (250ptas) and ROYAL CHAPEL, with its elaborate tombs. Culture fans may be interested in the HUERTA DE SAN VICENTE, the house museum of Federico Garcia Lorca in Calle Arabial: open 10 a.m.–2 p.m. and 5 p.m–8 p.m. and with free entry on Sundays and public holidays.

The youth hostel is the best deal in Granada, although it's a little way out at Calle Ramón y Cajal (Tel. 284306); bus 11 or a 30-minute walk from the station. Other hostels abound near the station in Calle San Juan de Dios. For pensions, try round the station on Avenida Andaluces, or the road up to the Alhambra, Cuesta de Gomérez. Hostal Residencia San Joaquín, Mano de Hierro 14 (Tel. 282879), is excellent, and the Sierra Nevada campsite at Carretera Madrid (Tel. 150062) is OK; take bus line 3, 5 or 10.

Round Cetti Meriem is the place for cheap meals. La Riviera at no. 5 starts meals around 1000ptas and has a good selection. Las Girasoles on Calle San Juan de Dios 24 is also excellent value. Depending on your taste, you can try the Tourist Office recommended 'gypsy flamenco' at Sacromonte or head instead for the bars in the centre. As far as serious nightlife is concerned, save your pesetas and go for a nocturnal stroll up by the Alhambra instead. The old Arab quarter, Albayzín, has atmosphere and most bars serve cheap food, but you should watch your valuables at all times.

CÓRDOBA The Roman and Moorish remains are the reasons to include Córdoba in an itinerary. This was the 8th-century capital of

Moorish Spain, though in many ways today's Córdoba looks as if it's had its heyday.

The main area to concentrate on is the JUDERÍA (old Jewish quarter) with its maze of narrow, twisting streets. Here you will find the MEZQUITA, built in the 8th century; it was the largest mosque in the world before the Christians made it into a cathedral in the 13th century. The structure has an incredible array of decorated arches and pillars, and if you climb the tower you'll see how big the mosque must have been, as the cathedral fits into its original centre. During the summer it is open Mon.–Fri.: 10.30 a.m.–1.30 p.m. and 4 p.m.–7 p.m. and at other times 10.30 a.m.–1.30 p.m. and 3.30 p.m.–5.30 p.m. Entry is 750ptas.

The 14th-century SYNAGOGUE, where the city's one remaining Jew still lights prayer candles on Friday evening, isn't exactly riveting, and the MUSEO MUNICIPAL could be missed out too unless you're keen on bullfighting.

The ALCÁZAR, the palace of the Catholic monarchs, is at its best floodlit at night. It's on the banks of the Río Guadalquivir and the Moorish gardens, towers and fountains make it an interesting place to take in. If you do want to go in, it's open Mon.–Fri.: 10 a.m.–2 p.m. and 6 p.m.– 8 p.m.; last entry is at 7.30. Entrance is free on Tuesdays, otherwise 425ptas.

The Tourist Office is at Calle Torrijos 10, open Mon.–Fri.: 9.30 a.m.–2.30 p.m. and 5 p.m.–7 p.m., Sat.: 9.30 a.m.–1.30 p.m. (Tel. 957 471235). The municipal Tourist Office at Plaza de Judas Levi 3 (off Manriques) is open Mon.–Fri.: 8.30 a.m.–1.30 p.m. (Tel. 957 200522). There's a post office at Cruz Conde 15, open 9 a.m.–2 p.m., 4 p.m.–6 p.m., closed Sat. p.m. and Sun.

The biggest selection of cheap pensions are on Calle Rey Heredia and off the Plaza de las Tendillas. La Milagrosa at no. 12 (Tel. 957 473317) charges from 3,500ptas per person. Check out the Hostel Lucano, Calle Lucano 1 (Tel. 957 476098), which has doubles from 3,000ptas per person. The IYHF hostel is Residencia Juvenil Córdoba at Plaza de Judas Levi (Tel. 957 290166) and charges only 1,500ptas for bed and breakfast. It is a sparkling new building with marble floors, in the heart of the Judería. Highly recommended.

There's camping about 1½ km out at Carretera Córdoba-Villaviciosa (Tel. 957 275048). Buses run every 10 minutes from the campsite to town.

Tourist menus are found most easily in the old quarter and for *tapas* and bar crawls, try the Jewish quarter (round the Mezquita). Flamenco here is among the best in Spain, but avoid the expensive private shows: the bar on Calle La Luna is a good place to see students gathering; to sing, play the guitar and dance flamenco.

RONDA The main line from Córdoba to Algeciras passes through this delightful town impressively perched on a gorge. See the CASA DEL REY MORO and the RENAISSANCE PALACE. Also take a look at the 18th-century bridge spanning the deep gorge beneath the town, as well as the former Moorish fortress and baths, and the cathedral.

For a room, try around the Tourist Information office at Plaza de España. Open Mon.–Fri.: 9.30 a.m.–2 p.m., 5 p.m.–7 p.m., closed Saturday afternoon and Sunday (Tel. 871272). There is plenty of budget accommodation.

ALGECIRAS The Tourist Office at Juan de la Cierva is open Mon.–Fri.: 9 a.m.–2 p.m., Sat.: 10 a.m.–1 p.m. Hostels are cheap and plentiful, so accommodation shouldn't be too much of a problem here and you may prefer to stay here rather than in more expensive Gibraltar. There is a campsite at Playa Rinconcillo (Tel. 661958), about 3 km from the town centre. Take the Rinconcillo bus.

If you are using Algeciras as the departure point for a trip to **Morocco**, buy your ticket from the first office selling ferry tickets to Tangier or Ceuta. Although there are a number of operators on this route, they all charge roughly the same and are quite expensive. It's no cheaper to buy at the ferry terminal than at any of the offices in town. A cheaper crossing is to Ceuta for around 1,440ptas single, which also avoids Tangier, though if you do take this trip remember to *get your passport stamped* during the voyage.

The town itself is rather unremarkable and down at heel, but does have good views of Gibraltar, which you can reach from here by bus for around 250ptas.

Avoid the overnight Paris–Irún–Algeciras train (particularly on Thursday and Friday nights) as it is very overcrowded and full of Arab immigrant workers returning to North Africa. Consequently the return route will be just as busy. The guard has a permanent escort of 2 armed security guards – which says it all!

Seville (Sevilla) city phone code: 95

If Madrid disappointed you, head for Seville. It's a great city to visit: typically Spanish and colourful, and as alive at night as in the day. There are plenty of sights and cheap beds and it seems impossible to hit a day in summer when the heat doesn't drive you into the nearest shady park for a siesta, no matter how dedicated a sun-worshipper you might be. The railway station is called Santa Justa.

TOURIST INFORMATION AND ADDRESSES

TOURIST OFFICE Avenida de la Constitución 21b (Tel. 422 1404); open Mon.–Fri.: 9.30 a.m.–7.30 p.m., Sat.: 9.30 a.m.–2 p.m.

POST OFFICE Avenida de la Constitución 32, open Mon.–Fri.: 9 a.m.–9 p.m., Sat.: 9 a.m.–2 p.m.

AMEX c/o Viajes Alhambra, Teniente Cotonel Segui 3, open Mon.–Fri.: 9.30 a.m.–1 p.m. and 4.30 p.m.–7.30 p.m., Sat.: 9.30 a.m.–1.30 p.m.

UK CONSULATE Plaza Neuva 8 (Tel. 422 8875)

US CONSULATE PEU Paseo de las Delicias 7 (Tel. 423 1885), open 9 a.m.–1 p.m., 2 p.m.–4.30 p.m., closed Wed. p.m., Sat. and Sun.

FIRST AID Avenida Ménendez Pelayo (Tel. 441 1712)

SEEING

The CATHEDRAL and ALCÁZAR complex should be your first stops. The cathedral, the third largest in the world, is built on the site of a former mosque, and the Moorish tower, LA GIRALDA, is a leftover from this period. Also included is COLUMBUS'S TOMB; joint admission to the cathedral and tomb costs 550ptas (200ptas students).

Leave the cathedral at Puerta de los Naranjos, cross the plaza to Puerta Oriente and you'll come to the 14th-century Alcázar palace with its combination of Moorish and Gothic architecture (600ptas, free with ISIC).

PLAZA DE ESPAÑA and the nearby parks offer romantic settings for an evening stroll, and you can hire out boats at reasonable rates and row round the Spanish Square taking it all in.

Behind the cathedral is the picturesque old Jewish quarter of SANTA CRUZ. There are guided tours, but you're better off wandering around by yourself.

SLEEPING

Concentrate your efforts on finding a cheap pension (there's no convenient campsite or central youth hostel). Down from the Plaza de Armas station or in the Santa Cruz area are your best bets, especially around Calle Mateos Gago. Rooms start from about 3,000ptas single. Try to get fixed up early, as Seville's popular with Inter-Railers and Spaniards alike.

The hostels on Archeros are among the best in town. Try Pérez Montilla at no. 14 (Tel. 436 1740) or Casa de Huéspedes Orellana (Tel. 436 2259) at no. 19. Another good street to try is Calle San Eloy, with the Hostal La Gloria at no. 58 (Tel. 422 2673) among the best.

Sleeping rough in the parks is a dicey proposition as you have not only the police to contend with, but also the local rats.

The out-of-town youth hostel is at Calle Issac Peral 2 (Tel. 461 3150). Take bus 34 from opposite Hotel Alfonso XIII to the last but one stop.

EATING AND NIGHTLIFE

Prices in Seville tend to be over the top, but there are plenty of central places with fixed tourist menus, and there are even a few fast-food places creeping in now. Again, the area round the Plaza de Armas station isn't bad, and you can eat for about 900ptas, but some of these places aren't too fussy about hygiene.

The Barrio Triana is a good place to make for to try the local *tapas*, though some bars seem a bit hostile to women coming in on their own. Casa Manolo at San Jorge 16 in the Barrio Triana is cheap and lively. But best value is El Diamante, Constitución 10, where an all-you-can-eat buffet costs under 900ptas. Speciality dishes can be found everywhere but are especially good at Mesón La Barca at Calle Santander 6.

Going to a flamenco is *the* thing to do in Seville. There is no shortage of venues, and by and large they're good value. Avoid the heavily advertised ones and try and make your drinks last as long as possible, as they're (surprise, surprise) overpriced. Los Gallos at Plaza Santa Cruz 11 charge about 2,800ptas for entrance, including your first drink. This is about average, but the entertainment here is above average.

If you fancy an evening at the fair, the new Isla Magica theme park stays open until 1 a.m. during the summer season. A 1-day pass will set you back about 3,100ptas.

EXCURSIONS The sherry capital of JEREZ DE LA FRONTERA is about 2 hours from Seville. If you're in this region in the first week of May go down for the fiesta. There are free guided tours and liberal samplings at the bodegas of Sandeman, Gonzalez Byass, etc.

CÁDIZ, another 50 minutes away, hasn't much to commend it unless you're after a heavy nightlife scene.

If you are going on to Portugal, take the train to Huelva, then a 15-minute walk to the bus station for the bus to the ferry at Ayamonte (about 500ptas).

Costa del Sol

This exploited cement-heap of coastline, best reached via Málaga, is all that you'd expect. It's difficult to know you're in Spain, the food and nightlife are plastic and often vulgar, and you'll begin to understand the background to the jokes about package deals to Torremolinos. Don't come here to look for quiet fishing villages, deserted beaches or friendly locals. However, if you're low on cash, keen to rough it on the beach, meet Europeans and pick up a tan, then you'd be hard pressed to find a better deal in Europe. Also, if you avoid July and August and the main package-holiday resorts, you'd be amazed how different a picture can emerge.

MÁLAGA Don't stay in Málaga too long: not just because you run a higher risk of getting mugged here than anywhere else in Spain, but because the resorts are often crowded, and it's advisable to make for one and get established first, then head back for a day trip to see this city's sights.

Tourist Information in Málaga is at Calle de Larios 5 (Tel. 952 213445), open 9 a.m.–2 p.m. (1 p.m. on Sat., closed Sun.). If you feel you're being followed from the station, turn round and take a good look, then stick to major streets. The instances of eurorailers being followed from station to Tourist Information and being mugged *en route* are amazing. Whatever happens, don't even think about sleeping out at Málaga station. We realize you'll probably know plenty of people who have and have come out unscathed, but we also know scores who've had their rucksacks actually cut off their backs and been threatened at knife-point to hand over their valuables. Honestly, it's not worth the risk.

The British Consulate is at Edificio Duquesa, Duquesa de Parcent 8 (Tel. 952 217 371), in case anything nasty happens. The US one is at Avenida Fuengirola (Tel. 952 461865).

Tourist Information will give you a leaflet on Málaga's sights. Take in the ALCAZABA Moorish palace and GIBRALFARO CASTLE if you can. El Corte Inglés, the big department store, is useful to stock up in. Usually its toiletries, etc., are cheaper than at the resorts, and its cafeterias are worth a visit too. If you must stay, try Hostal Residencia Chinitas, Pasaje Chinitas 2 (Tel. 952 214683).

THE RESORTS The coastal towns to the east of Málaga are less exploited, but the beaches aren't so good. In places like CASTELL DE

FERRO and TORRENUEVA you'll avoid the package tourists, but will find the facilities basic. It's easier coming down from Granada to get to the eastern resorts and use the bus for the last lap.

West of Málaga, the electric train runs as far as FUENGIROLA, stopping at Torremolinos, Benalmadena and Los Boliches *en route*. This train is free on Inter-Rail, but to get on to Marbella or further west, you have to resort to buses.

TORREMOLINOS is the most commercialized centre. Look for rooms in hostels leading down to the beach. As far as eating and nightlife goes, you'd have a job actually to miss the tourist menus, bars and discos, so there's no problem there. Tourist Information is on Bajos de la Nogalera (1 p.m.–4.30 p.m. siesta). If this doesn't appeal, move on to other resorts till you find a suitable one.

MARBELLA is slightly more 'up market', so prices can be higher here. There's a good youth hostel here on Trapiche (Tel. 952 771491) but it may be closed temporarily. As for pensions, try the Hostel Gallardo in the old town; it's cheap and central, with doubles at 2,600ptas. FUENGIROLA is a good compromise between them and, with its 6 km of beaches and many cheap beds and restaurants, an attractive proposition to the footsore eurorailer.

Gibraltar

The British colony of Gibraltar, strategically located at the gate to the Mediterranean, has always had a troubled and bloody history. Named after the Berber Chief Tariq ibn Siyad who captured the Rock in AD 711, it was the object of skirmishes between Muslim and Christian forces until the arrival of the British in 1704. Gibraltar remains dependent on Britain to this day, although there is a strong desire on the part of the largely self-governed colony to become more self-sufficient.

Gibraltar enjoys an unusual fusion of Mediterranean, British and Arab culture, making it an interesting place to prepare for a trip to North Africa, or, as is more often the case, to recover from the culture shock so often experienced in Morocco. Diplomatic relations with Spain are often strained, so when approaching Gibraltar be prepared for frustrating delays when crossing the border. The easiest way of getting there is by bus from Algeciras to La Linea (210ptas). Then simply stroll across the border, which is only a stone's throw from the bus station.

Tourist Information centres are easy to find. The main one is housed within the Duke of Kent House at Cathedral Square (Tel. 74805).

Stock up on cheap cigarettes and alcohol before you leave – prices here are the lowest in Europe. Spanish pesetas are accepted everywhere, but the pound (sterling) is preferred currency.

A ferry runs to/from **Morocco** on Mondays, Wednesdays and Fridays (£35 return). Check the timetable as it changes frequently.

SEEING

Despite being only 6 km long, Gibraltar has a lot to offer. Visit the UPPER NATURE RESERVE; the view from the top, with Africa in the distance, is truly spectacular. Here you can see the famous BARBARY APES (local legend has it that if they ever leave then British rule will also end on the Rock). The nature reserve is also home to ST MICHAEL'S CAVE, an immense grotto which has played host to concerts and gala shows in the past. The UPPER GALLERIES can also be visited. Excavated by the British during the Great Siege of 1779–83, they provided an impregnable line of artillery within the actual north face of the Rock. An exhibition called *Gibraltar: A City under Siege* can be found on the descent from the Upper Rock (it includes 18th-century graffiti). Also worth a visit is the TOWER OF HOMAGE, sole survivor of a huge Moorish castle now buried beneath housing estates. Recently reopened to the public, it also doubles as the local prison.

A general Rock Tour, including the above sites and more, can be arranged with local taxi drivers for around £10 per person, or you can walk and pay entrance fees at each individual site (which works out cheaper). Another option is the excellent cable car to the top of the Rock (£5.00 return).

The town of Gibraltar with its narrow, winding streets, is charming in itself. Visit the museum, built within the walls of an ancient Moorish bath house (£2.00). Relax under the shade of pine trees in the beautiful Alameda Botanical Gardens. If all else fails, go for a swim off one of Gibraltar's 5 beaches.

SLEEPING

The one drawback with Gibraltar is the high price of accommodation. The cheapest you will find is the Emile Gibraltar Youth Hostel on Line Wall Road (Tel. 51106), where single beds cost from £10. Next best is the Queen's Hotel, 1 Boyd Street (Tel. 74000): singles £23, doubles £33. Most travellers stay in La Linea, across the border in Spain. (If you are intent on staying in Gibraltar, try sleeping on the beaches – but be sure to hide from the police as this is frowned upon by the authorities.)

NOTES

....

....

....

....

....

....

....

....

....

....

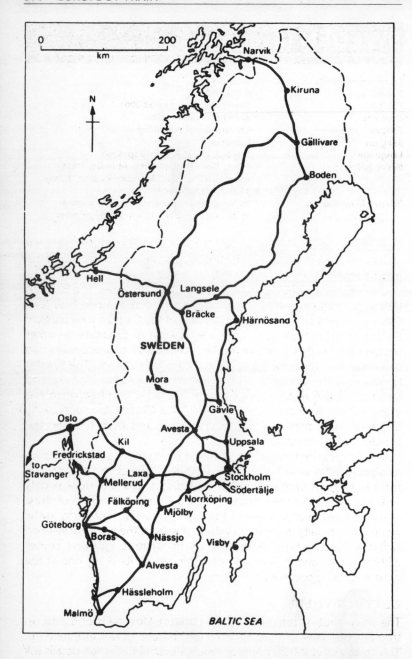

SWEDEN (Sverige)

Entry requirements	Passport
Population	8,400,000
Capital	Stockholm (pop.: 1,600,000)
Currency	Krona £1 = approx 12kr
Political system	Constitutional monarchy
Religion	Lutheran
Language	Swedish (English widely spoken)
Public holidays	1 Jan., Good Friday, Easter Monday, 1 May, Ascension Day, Whit Monday, 20 June, 1 Aug., 31 Oct., 25, 26 Dec
International dialling	To Sweden: international code 46 number
	From Sweden: 009 + country code number

Over half of Sweden's land surface is covered by forests and lakes, an area larger than the whole of the British Isles, yet with a fraction of the population.

Geographically isolated in the 9th and 10th centuries, the Swedish Vikings pushed eastwards down the Russian rivers to trade their furs. This trade eventually caught the attention of the German merchants of the Hanseatic League, who were always keen to capitalize on other people's labour. By the end of the 14th century, all of Scandinavia had had enough of these foreigners who controlled so much. The Swedes hoped that the Union of Kalmar between Sweden, Norway and Denmark (1397) would change things; instead all that happened was that Denmark took over as top dog. In 1523 Gustav Vasa successfully defeated the Danes and was elected king, and from then on the Swedes never looked back.

Sweden reached her zenith in the 17th century under Gustavus Adolphus, who won her a Baltic empire. Defending this position meant constant warfare until the 1800s; it was therefore widely welcomed when Sweden declared herself neutral at the 19th century.

Today Sweden enjoys one of the highest standards of living in the world and a quality of life to go with it, thanks to the highly developed social welfare system. Unfortunately for visitors, nothing comes without a cost and in Sweden's case this means its being one of the most expensive countries in Europe.

GETTING THERE

The main routes from the UK are London–Dover–Ostend and up through Germany, or from Harwich to the Hook of Holland, then up. This takes about 22–25 hours to reach Stockholm. For full details ask

British Rail or NSR Travel, 21–24 Cockspur Street, London SW1.

By sea there are sailings five times a week from Harwich to Gothenburg and twice a week from Newcastle to Gothenburg in high season. Also, another ferry from Harwich to Esbjerg in Denmark connects up to a through-train to Copenhagen, and a line operates from Newcastle to Esbjerg. These routes are all operated by Scandinavian Seaways, which gives 50% discounts to Inter-Rail holders (unless you want a cabin).

SWEDISH STATE RAILWAYS
(STATENS JÄRNVAGÄR, SJ)

Swedish trains are efficient, clean and comfortable. They are very rarely late and run frequent services (every hour or so) to most of the major cities. The journey from Stockholm to Malmö takes only 6 hours, and to Narvik in the far north of Norway 20 hours. The long-distance InterCity and Rapid trains are the fastest, followed by the expresses, which are used on regular routes. The local trains are not as slow as in some countries, but still stop at every station. Modern fast trains (the X-2000s) travel at 130 mph, and the trains have audio channels in seats and outlets for computers! From Stockholm to Gothenburg takes under 3 hours, and from Stockholm to Malmö less than 5. There are supplements on these and on City Express trains, but see 'Reservations'. Ask at stations for a free copy of SJ Tågtider timetables.

PASSES AVAILABLE Sweden is in Inter-Rail Zone B, along with Norway and Finland. (For further details of the Inter-Rail zones, refer to the Inter-Rail section in Part One of this guide.)

Eurail passes are also valid and a Euro Domino ticket is available.

The popular ScanRail Pass is valid for 21 days or one month in Sweden, Denmark, Norway and Finland for unlimited free rail travel and reduced fares on ferry services within Scandinavia. For details see Part One of the guide.

The *Inlandsbanan* is valid for the Inland Railway travelling 1,288 km down the backbone of Sweden from Gällivare in the north to Kristinehamn in the south, with one short stretch involving travel by bus. The card, which gives unlimited travel on the line, is valid for either 14 or 21 days. It costs 995kr for 14 days.

INTER-RAIL FERRY BONUSES

	FROM	TO	REDUCTION %
Stena Line	Gothenburg	Frederikshavn	50
Silja Line	Stockholm (1)	Helsinki (1)	50
	Stockholm (1)	Turku (1)	50
TT-Line	Trelleborg	Travemünde	50

(1) A ticket bought for Stockholm–Turku is not valid for Stockholm–Helsinki.

EURAIL BONUSES

FREE SERVICES Steamer service of the Silja Line between Stockholm and Åland Islands–Turku. (Full fare is charged for cabin space and reservation is compulsory between Sweden and Helsinki.)

Ferry crossings operated by the Swedish and Danish State Railways between Helsingborg and Helsingør (Denmark).

Ferry crossings operated by Stena Line between Gothenburg and Frederikshavn (Denmark).

Ferry crossing from Trelleborg to Sassnitz (Germany).

Ferry crossings operated by Silja Line between Umeå–Vaasa and Sundsvall–Vaasa.

Bus between Boden and Haparanda or vice versa.

REDUCED FARES

50% reduction for Eurailpass holders on the hydrofoil of the Flyvebâdene Company between Malmö and Copenhagen (25% for Eurail Youthpass holders).

50% reduction on normal fares for the ferry crossing Trelleborg–Travemünde (Germany) on the TT-Line.

50% reduction on the full fare of the TR-Line for the ferry crossing Trelleborg–Rostock.

50% reduction on the Danish Navigation Company, Øresund, on the hydrofoil between Malmö and Copenhagen (reservation compulsory).

TRAIN INFORMATION

No problems here, as everyone speaks perfect English and queues are never too long.

RESERVATIONS Compulsory at a cost of 30–100kr. Tickets bought at stations in Sweden automatically include a reservation. On all trains apart from X-2000 services, for which advance purchase is essential, you can board without tickets or reservations and buy them from the conductor, although you still have to pay the charge on the train.

NIGHT TRAVEL This is relatively cheap in Sweden at about 85kr for a couchette and about 165kr for a second-class sleeper.

EATING ON TRAINS All long-distance expresses have a bistro or dining car.

CINEMA COACH A new service on the night train Luleå–Stockholm is the cinema coach, with a film saloon and bistro. Films change regularly and cost 55kr entry. Check before you pay the supplement that the films are in a language you can understand.

SCENIC TIPS Any line north of Stockholm is of interest, particularly from Östersund onwards, either to Trondheim in Norway or to Kiruna in the far north.

BIKES Bikes go as luggage as Swedish trains have no guard's vans. This means that your bike may not travel on the same train, so to be sure it arrives with you, send it 3 days in advance. Cost per bike is 125kr.

TOURIST INFORMATION

Every Swedish county has a tourist board in addition to the local Tourist Information offices called *Turistbyrå*. They are very helpful and always have a good selection of maps and brochures.

ISIC BONUSES Few reductions here; the main one is 20% off tours and day trips to historic places. For further information, contact STF, Stureplan 4c, Box 25, 10120, Stockholm (Tel. 08 4632280).

MONEY MATTERS 1 krona (kr) = 100 öre.

Banking hours are Mon.–Fri.: 9.30 a.m.–3 p.m. Bank charges are high for traveller's cheques (approximately 50kr) so it makes sense to cash large denominations. Forex offices, found in the major cities, will change traveller's cheques at a much cheaper commission rate, however, and are worth looking out for. Credit cards are widely accepted in Sweden.

POST OFFICES AND SHOPS Post offices open Mon.–Fri.: 9 a.m.–6 p.m.; 9 a.m.–1 p.m. on Saturdays. Most shops are open 9.30 a.m.–6 p.m. on weekdays and until 1 p.m. or 4 p.m. on Saturdays. In some larger towns department stores stay open until 8 p.m. or 10 p.m. with some opening Sundays 12 noon until 4 p.m.

The *poste restante* service is free in Sweden and stamps are sold at newsagents' as well as post offices.

MUSEUMS Normally open from about 10 a.m.–5 p.m.

SLEEPING

All regional and local Tourist Offices have free lists of hotels and campsites; many also have a room-finding service called *Rumsförmedling*. They charge a small commission and can find you a room in a private house or in a hotel. In smaller towns and villages look for the sign *Rum* (the Swedish equivalent of B&B, except there's no breakfast). At about 200kr for a single, this represents as good value as you're likely to get – apart from private rooms, which can be booked at local Tourist Offices for around 100–150kr per person, plus a one-off booking fee of 30–50kr. In Stockholm, Malmö and Gothenburg, 300–400kr will get you a package deal which includes bed, breakfast and the city's discount card.

Youth hostels are great and cost about 100–150kr per night; add another 40kr to this if you're not a member.

Camping's no problem thanks to the Allmansrätt law which allows anyone to camp on unfenced land for one night only. Please be careful about fire. Tourist Information will direct you to suitable places. If you prefer your comforts, most towns have campsites with excellent facilities costing about 70–100kr per tent, but these require a camping pass (43kr) obtainable at the site.

EATING AND NIGHTLIFE

Eating out is incredibly expensive in Sweden even at fast-food joints like McDonald's. Always check to see if there's a tourist menu or a cheap set meal (*dagens rätt*) for 45–55kr. More often than not, you'll be eating from supermarkets, which is no bad thing as the quality and choice are excellent. Most of the regional specialities, such as smoked reindeer meat from Lapland, are expensive and confined to the best restaurants. *Smörgåsbord* is cheaper here than in Norway if you feel like a Scandinavian splash-out.

Nightlife is what you make it in Sweden and there's no shortage of things to do. Alcohol and tobacco are expensive and controlled by the government, but there's not much the authorities can do during the midsummer festival when everyone lets rip with non-stop dancing and drinking, particularly in the north.

Stockholm city phone code: 08

All the qualities one associates with the Swedes are reflected in their capital. It's tidy and well laid-out, socially minded and efficiently run, and the high level of money floating around has permitted them to improve their environment with schemes like making the city's waterway safe for swimming and erecting new buildings with more of an eye towards appearance than to economy. The famous Water Festival takes place in August.

It's difficult to make out on a tight budget here, as even supermarket food is expensive, but you'll get by if you follow our suggestions and use your common sense.

STATION FACILITIES

Stockholm Central is well equipped with all the facilities you might expect, including Tourist Information, and there's a 24-hour train information line: Tel. 020 757575 (from overseas 8 696 7509). If you don't have 5kr for the station toilet, there's a free (grotty) one next door.

Frequent trains to Malmö, Copenhagen, Gothenburg, Oslo and all Sweden.

TOURIST INFORMATION

Apart from the station, there's an office in the centre at Sweden House (*Sverigehuset*), Kungsträdgården, opposite the department store NK. Pick up maps and *Stockholm This Week* before visiting the Swedish Institute on the first floor, which has useful factsheets on Sweden, and where everyone involved seems incredibly helpful.

ADDRESSES

POST OFFICE Vasagatan 28–34; open 8 a.m.–8 p.m., Sat.: 9 a.m.–3 p.m., Sun.: 9 a.m.–11 a.m. Also at the central station; open 7 a.m.–10 p.m., Sat. and Sun.: 10 a.m.–7 p.m.

AMEX Birger Jarlsgatan 1 (Tel. 6797880); open Mon.–Fri.: 9 a.m.–5 p.m., Sat.: 10 a.m.–1 p.m.

UK EMBASSY Skarpögatan 6 (Tel. 6719000)

US EMBASSY Strandvägen 101 (Tel. 7855300)

CANADIAN EMBASSY Tegelbacken 4, 7th floor (Tel. 4533000)

AUSTRALIAN EMBASSY Sergelstorg 12 (Tel. 6132900)

24-HOUR CHEMIST Apoteke Scheele, Klarabergsgatan 64 (Tel. 4548130)

SVENSKA TOURISTFÖRENINGEN (STF) For information if you're camping or hostelling in Sweden; write to Box 25, 5-10120, Stockholm, or phone: 020 292929.

GETTING ABOUT

The underground and buses are good and charge by the zone, with individual journeys costing 14kr (plus 7kr per additional zone). Three-day transit passes cost about 120kr (including free entry to some museums and ferries); 24-hour passes cost about 60kr. Buy these at Tourist Information or at stalls in the underground.

The Stockholm Card (*Stockholmskortet*), also known as the 'Key to Stockholm', is available for 185kr per day. An adult and 2 children under 18 can use the same card. It gives you free travel on buses, the underground, suburban trains, museum entrances, many of the sights and a 1-hour sightseeing trip by boat. It also gives you a discount on a boat excursion to Drottningholm Palace.

The banks also hand out free city maps and if nature calls, the best toilets are in the department stores such as NK. Look out for the underground station at Kungsträdgården – it is like a long art gallery of decorated walls.

SEEING

Close to the centre lie the islands of Gamla Stan, Skeppsholmen and Djurgården where the vast majority of sights are located. GAMLA STAN, or the Old Town, dates back to the mid-13th century. The narrow medieval streets are full of trendy shops and restaurants, nightclubs and studios. The 18th-century ROYAL PALACE is in Gamla Stan and parts of it are open to the public till about 3 p.m. daily, except Mon.

There are free guided tours of parliament, in English, at 12.00 noon and 2 p.m..

A new Modern Art Gallery is under construction at SKEPPSHOLMEN and is due to open during 1998: currently it is in temporary premises at Birger Jarlsgatan 57. Stockholm's choice as the 1998 European Culture Capital means that there are loads of concerts, exhibitions and artistic venues.

The NATIONAL MUSEUM is located east of the Old Town at Skeppsholmen, and east of this again is the DJURGÅRDEN, an island almost entirely devoted to recreation. Take the ferry over from Slussen or Nybroplan, or walk from Strandvägen. This is where the 17th-century warship *Vasa* is on view. This flagship of the Swedish navy only lasted 10 minutes on her maiden voyage before sinking into oblivion, till she was rediscovered in 1956 and brought up. She's in a remarkable state of preservation and is well worth the 45kr fee (students 30kr).

If you're heavily into ships and naval history, the MUSEUM SHIPS at Sjöhistoriska museet (Tel. 6664900) will be of interest. Here you can see an ice-breaker, lightship and medieval ship. Open daily 10 a.m.–5 p.m. during the summer.

Stockholm's open-air museum, SKANSEN, is definitely one of Europe's best. It's called 'Sweden in miniature' with good reason, as an afternoon spent there will fill you in more on Swedish folklore, architecture and history than will a week touring the country. There are over 150 buildings of authentic Swedish design, demonstrations of folk dancing, craftsmen at work, a zoo, an aquarium and lots more. Open; May–June: 9 a.m.–8 p.m.; July–Aug.: 9 a.m.–10 p.m.; Sept.–Apr.: 9 a.m.–5 p.m. Entrance costs 30–50kr, depending on the activity.

GRÖNA LUND, or Tivoli, is the amusement park on Djurgården. It is Stockholm's version of the famous Copenhagen Park and is a favourite family attraction.

The Swedish House of Culture (KULTURHUSET) at Sergelstorg is a good example of the country's social-mindedness. Exhibitions of crafts and art are always on and there are free 'creative activities' for anyone who wants to participate so, if you're feeling inspired, jog along and model or paint your masterpiece. There's also a library and access to foreign newspapers and records. It's open in summer, Tues.–Fri.: 11 a.m.–6 p.m. and Sat.–Sun.: 12 noon–5 p.m. The building was temporarily closed in 1997, but should have reopened again.

The only dance museum in the world is at FOLKETS HUS, Barnhusgatan 12/14, while for gay and lesbian visitors, the centre at Sveavägen 57 (Tel.: 7360215) (T-bana: Radmansgatan) has a bookstore, café, restaurant and nightly disco.

SLEEPING

Hotellcentralen (Tel. 7892425) at the central station will give you a map and list of hostels and hotels or find you a bed for a fee of 15–40kr per room. The International Youth Centre will also help out if you're really stuck. You'd do well to make use of these services, especially in peak season, as beds (especially cheap ones) are thin on the ground, though in July many Swedes head south, leaving a bit of space in the city.

Olssons (Tel. 102229) can arrange, free of charge, private accommodation if you're staying more than 2 days, but in general in summer there are never enough to go around. If it's at all feasible to call ahead and reserve, do so; and this goes for hostels, campsites or hotels. (English is widely spoken.)

The most memorable place to stay in Stockholm is definitely on board the *af Chapman*. This youth hostel is a 19th-century sailing ship, fully rigged and decked out, and harboured opposite the Gamla Stan; it costs 90kr for a 'berth' in an 8-bed cabin for IYHF members, non-members pay a supplement of 35kr. You need to pre-book or turn up early – 9 a.m. at the latest – to stand a chance; to reserve, call 6795015.

The other central hostel, open only in summer, the popular and good Frescati Hostel (Tel. 159434; part of Hotel Frescati at Professorsslingan), does not seem to have opened for a couple of years. There's a youth hostel on Skeppsholmen beside *af Chapman* (Tel. 6795017), which is large and good value.

For hotels, try one of the following: Pensionat Oden, Odengatan 38 (Tel. 6124349); Gustavsvikshemmet at Västmannagatan (Tel. 214450); STF Backpackers' Inn, Banérgaten 56 (Tel. 660 7515); or Gustav Vasa, Västmannagatan 61 (Tel. 343801).

Out of the 4 city campsites, the nearest ones are Ängby Camping on Lake Mälaren (Tel. 370420) on underground 17 or 18, and Bredäng Camping (Tel. 977071) on subway 13 or 15 to Bredäng station.

For a list of Swedish youth hostels contact STF, and for student hostels contact YMCA/Kilroy Hotels at Kungsgatan 4, Box 7144, Stockholm (Tel. 234515).

EATING AND NIGHTLIFE

Face the fact, you're going to have to spend twice as much as you would in southern Europe to eat out here. Picnics are the answer, in conjunction with bar meals (*bars* are basic self-service restaurants here). In conventional restaurants look out for *dagens rätt* (today's special) for a slightly cheaper lunch or snack. Buy in supplies at Östermalms Saluhall or Hötorgshallen, the 2 big indoor markets. The central supermarkets also do a good line in groceries and the prices are cheaper than in the indoor markets.

While *smörgåsbord* are filling and tasty, they also tend to be pricey; however, if you arrive in Stockholm Central after a long train journey, treat yourself to the excellent *stora frukost* (eat-as-much-as-you-like breakfast), 6.30 a.m.–10 a.m., closed Sunday. It's about 65kr and will keep you going all day.

At Norrlandsgatan 5, Pk-Building, there is a good vegetarian restaurant where you help yourself and pay according to weight. Hot vegetarian dishes are served all day. If you're cutting all corners and don't mind plastic atmospheres and fast food, there are a number of outlets to choose from. There are several McDonald's beside the Kulturhuset. In the evening the south side of Stockholm tends to be the best area to head for.

There are plenty of pubs and clubs in Gamla Stan, Götgatan and the area around Medborgarplatsen, with bands for around 50kr. For cheaper entertainment, go over to Skansen or Gröna Lund where there's usually dancing, etc. Check with *Stockholm This Week* for current events. The music pub Historia and Café Opera, both on Kungsträdgården, are good places to meet young Stockholmers. The former resembles the bar in the TV series *Cheers*. At midnight the chairs/tables are cleared for a disco to begin. Entry is free before 11 p.m.

A good time to visit Stockholm is the first week in August, when the city's Water Festival produces plenty of fireworks.

EXCURSIONS
UPPSALA
The old university town is 45 minutes away by train. On a day trip here you can see the medieval CATHEDRAL, 16th-century CASTLE, the oldest UNIVERSITY in Sweden, PRE-VIKING BURIAL MOUNDS and the UPPLANDS MUSEUM, which details the city's history and customs. Turn right on leaving the station for Tourist Information at Sit Persgatan 4 (Gamla Torget) (Tel. 018 117500) or try the Tourist Information at Uppsala Castle – open May–Sept. (Tel. 018 153033).

DROTTNINGHOLM PALACE
An alternative excursion is to the residence of the royal family. Built in the 17th century, it lies 8 km west of the capital on the island of Lovön. It's all very pretty: Chinese pavilion, unusual 200-year-old theatre, etc. To get there, either head for Klara Mälarstrand (near city hall) and take the steamer, or take the underground to Brommaplan and then change to Mälaröbuses.

VIEW OF THE ISLANDS
To see at least some of Stockholm's 24,000 islands in the archipelago, take a bus out to the TV tower at KAKNÄSTORNET. This 152m tower is reputed to have the fastest lift in Europe, but the view is worth it once your stomach has settled down. There is also a cafeteria and restaurant with prices which are not as extortionate as you will find in similar towers in other countries. Open 9 a.m.–10 p.m. daily (Tel. 08 789 2435).

Malmö

The southern Swedish area of Skåne with its endless fields and sandy beaches is home to Malmö, Sweden's third largest city. Malmö is a pleasant stop-off and is easily reached by hydrofoil from Copenhagen, or by train from Stockholm or Gothenburg. On arrival, a good place to head for is another of the excellent Inter-Rail centres, on Stortorget 24 (Tel. 118585). They'll help out with free showers, advice and rucksack storage. Your ticket gains you entry.

SEEING

The train station is handily placed just north of the GAMLA STAN (old town), the area to concentrate upon. The STORTORG is a massive market square, built in the 16th century, and the centre of things. Look for the RÅDHUS (town hall) on one side of the square; it is worth the tour inside. Don't miss the LILLA TORG, an idyllic square of medieval houses and cobblestones off the Stortorg, and full of stalls and buskers in the summer months. Take a look at the ST PETRI KYRKA, a Gothic church behind the Rådhus.

The MALMÖHUS is Malmö's castle, once a prison, with Lord Bothwell, Mary Queen of Scots' last husband, on its guest books. The museums here are excellent, and bear in mind that an entry-ticket bought here is then valid for the rest of the day at the other city museums.

There is a good beach south of the Slottspark, further on from the castle.

Tourist Information is at Skepsbron 1 (Tel. 341270), a short walk from the station. The staff are extremely helpful and can sell you the Malmö Card (*Malmökartet*), which costs 16kr for 24 hours and gives free bus transport, free entry to museums and other attractions, and 50% off a boat trip to Copenhagen. Pick up the *Malmö This Month* guide, which is free and widely available, for details of events going on.

SLEEPING

Camping is your cheapest bet in Malmö, as in much of Sweden; bus 11a will take you to Sibbarp Camping at Strandgatan 101.

Otherwise there are hostels at Dahlemsgatan 5, the Kirsebergs hostel (Tel. 342635), or further out at Backavagen 18, where you'll find the IYHF hostel (Tel. 82220).

Gotland

Gotland is Sweden's largest island and is best known for its medieval remains and connections with the Hanseatic League. Take the ferry from Oskarshamn or Nynäshamn to VISBY, the major town on Gotland. Ask at the Tourist Office for connection times and details, but fares are pricey, with one-way tickets costing 270kr (less a 30% discount for students). The Tourist Office here is at Strandgatan 9 at the harbour (Tel. 0498 210982).

While in Visby, check out the OLD CITY WALLS, the cobbled MEDIEVAL PORT, the Viking remains in the GOTLANDS FORNSAL MUSEUM and the ST MARIA CATHEDRAL. The real reason to come to Gotland, however, is to visit the unspoilt countryside. Bicycles can be rented at several places around the ferry terminal and Tourist Office. The going rate is about 60kr per day or 250kr for a week, or you can rent a moped for around 200kr per day.

The high point of the island's calendar is medieval week, traditionally the first week in August.

Gothenburg (Göteborg)

Sweden's second city is about 4 hours from Stockholm, and the detour to the west coast provides an interesting alternative route to get down to Copenhagen, as the direct line running straight down to Malmö is not that interesting. But if you go down that way it is worthwhile stopping off at the pleasant university town of LUND, which has a magnificent cathedral with a moving clock and an interesting outdoor museum (*Kulturen*) with demonstration crafts and old houses. Gothenburg is big on parks, museums and canals – in fact there's a distinct British feel to it, and it is known as 'Little London'. Its harbour is the largest in Scandinavia.

STATION FACILITIES

Göteborg Central has train information available 7 a.m.–10 p.m. daily, with phone reservations Tel. 020 757575, 6 a.m.–11 p.m. daily. Tourist Information is at Östra Nordstan (2 minutes away) in Nordstan shopping centre. Left-luggage, a supermarket, post office and *bureau de change* are available.

Daily trains to Oslo, Stockholm, Malmö, Copenhagen, northern Sweden.

From Göteborg harbour, ferry services to Denmark (daily), Germany (daily), England (3 times/week) and Holland (twice/week).

GETTING ABOUT

You can either buy a 24-hour pass for the excellent bus and tram system for around 40kr, or invest in the 'Key to Gothenburg' (*Göteborgskortet*) which gives you free public transport, museum entrance, a sightseeing tour of the city centre, free sightseeing on the famous *Paddan* sightseeing boats, and many other things, such as a free day trip to Denmark, free entrance to the Liseberg amusement park and much more. It costs around 125kr for 24 hours, 225kr for 48 hours and 275kr for 72 hours. Children pay 50% of the adult price. Always check prices and discounts on offer, and remember to validate your card in the machine on boarding.

TOURIST INFORMATION

Apart from Östra Nordstan, the shopping centre next to the Central station, the main Tourist Office is at Kungsportsplatsen 2, open daily during summer 9 a.m.–8 p.m., otherwise 9 a.m.–5 p.m. Both offer an accommodation service, including private accommodation lodgings. Prices range from 200kr for singles, doubles 150kr per person; their hotels are about twice the price and they take 60kr commission.

SEEING

The centre of Gothenburg is very modern, but if you head off to HAGA, the old district of wooden houses and coffee shops, you'll see a different side of the city. Of the many parks worth visiting try to take in the BOTANICAL GARDENS, SLOTTSKOGEN, with its zoo, lakes and birds, and LISEBERG LEISURE PARK, which has everything from discos to fun fairs. Admission charge: 40kr. The ART CENTRE on Götaplatsen is an interesting place, and for the nautically minded the MARITIME MUSEUM (*Sjöfartsmuseet*) has ships from Viking times to the present day (for groups only).

The KRONHUSET is the oldest building in the city. The neo classical CATHEDRAL is also worth visiting. The FESKEKÖRKA, a 19th-century building filled with fish stalls and vendors, is situated by the moat close to Huitfeldtsplatsen. The 7 a.m. auction in the fish market is worth getting up for.

SLEEPING

The youth hostel is good and not too far out: Göteborgs Vandrarhem (Tel. 031 401050) at Mölndalsvägen is about 1 km from the centre on tram 4 to Göteborgsäng; open summer only. There is a private hostel on board a boat, the M/S *Seaside*, about 300m from the station, along Packhuskajen (Tel. 031 101035) at 175kr per person. There's also a YMCA hostel at Garverigatan 2 (Tel. 031 803962), open 7 July–11 Aug., which is a bit cheaper. Take Tram 1, 3 or 6 to Svingeln. Alternatively, the Nordengården at Stockholmsgarten 16 (Tel. 196631) charges only 80kr in large dorms.

Kärralund (Tel. 031 870200) is the most central campsite and is reached by tram 5 to Welandergatan. It's rather pricey.

EATING AND NIGHTLIFE

Along Kungsportsavenyn (the main boulevard) are restaurants of all kinds and descriptions (from Chinese to Scottish), and alongside them are the increasingly popular fast-food chains. Fish and seafood are naturally in abundance in Gothenburg and often the *dagens rätt* will include a local fish dish. La Gondola at Kungsportsavenyn 4 does good large meals at moderate prices, and they have outside table service. Also strongly recommended is the Figaro bar/restaurant in the Stora Teatern at the Kungsportsavenyn. For picnic food, the markets on Kungstorget are best.

At night, a lot of the young locals seem to gather round Kungsportsavenyn to cast an eye over the visiting talent; otherwise, you're most likely to meet the resident students in the bar at the students' union, Kärhuskällaren, which is near Götaplatsen. Behind the market on Kungstorget is Ölhallen, an authentic Swedish pub, and there are quite a few disco and jazz clubs, though their entrance fees put most of them safely out of the average eurorailer's reach.

Lapland

If you were put off going up to Lapland in Norway, let yourself be persuaded now you're in Sweden. It's easier here: the trains run right up to RIKSGRÄNSEN, just before the border and NARVIK in Norway. From Stockholm to the border is a straight 24 hours, though the conditions on the trains don't make this seem as much of an ordeal as it sounds, and the scenery once you're around Gällivare or Kiruna is breathtaking.

Once you're up there, there's an inland line from Gällivare down through Jokkmokk and Arvidsjaur to Östersund.

It's legal to camp on unfenced land for 1 night, so you can go it alone in a big way, especially out of season. Make sure you leave the place tidy afterwards, though, and treat the plants with respect! Unless you've skin like leather, take with you mosquito repellent of some sort as they're out in force up there. The Svenska Turistföreningen, Box 25, 5-10120, Stockholm, are the people to write to for information on mountain tourist stations and huts, and suggested hiking routes.

To get the most out of a trip to Lapland, plan and book ahead as much as possible. Don't just wander aimlessly on to the train in Stockholm with no food or proper walking boots and expect to pick up relevant supplies once you're there, and don't go with fantasies in your head of great wilderness adventures with Lapps, reindeer and huskies. It's a bit like that, but in reality the towns are a bit grey and morose, and the Lapps (they call themselves *Sami*) are pretty sick of wide-eyed tourists pointing and gawping at them from June to September. If you do go, make sure you have the right equipment with you. Good preparation will ensure you get the most out of this stunning area.

GÄLLIVARE This strategic mining town is at the junction of the main line to Narvik and inland line to Jokkmokk. If you've time to kill here waiting for connections, go to the nearby iron mines at MALMBERGET and take the tour round (check times with Tourist Information), or go to the museum at VASARA where there are skis dating back before the time of Christ. Apart from the ETTORE CHURCH and the largest log cabin in the world, that's about it here.

The Tourist Office is near the station at Storgatan 16, and is open Mon.–Sun.: 9 a.m.–9 p.m. in summer. They'll give you details on how to get up to the Stora Sjöfallet National Park and the surrounding mountains. If you're staying, ask about the private accommodation here. The youth hostel, at Andra Sidan (Tel.: 0970 14380) is 5 minutes from the station. Costs 100kr for members, extra charge for non-members.

If you're travelling up to Kiruna and beyond, consider returning via Narvik and Fauske in Norway. (A bus connects the 2 and Fauske is on the Bodø line.) If, on the other hand, you are heading down to LULEA, take some time out to visit the excellent Museum of Lapp Culture. In addition to being free of charge, you can also get cassettes to wander around with, explaining the exhibits as you go along. The youth hostel, at Örniksvägen (Tel. 0920 52325), is open all year round, take bus 6 from Lulea.

KIRUNA The city itself is fairly unattractive, so use Kiruna as a base for the surrounding countryside. Tourist Information is at Hjalmar Lund-bohmsvagen 42, open 9 a.m.–9 p.m. weekdays, 1 p.m.–8 p.m. Sun. in season.

There's a youth hostel called STF Vandrarhem Kiruna, housed in a big yellow building with an old people's home behind it, at Skyttegatan 16a (Tel. 0980 17195). It only opens from June to August and charges 120kr for members.

There is a campsite about 1½ km from the station, Rådhusbyn Ripan (Tel. 0980 13100). Costs around 60kr per tent, cabins also available from 125kr per person, sharing. Or Tourist Information will get you into private houses for 100–300kr, plus a booking fee.

There are tours of the mines at Kiruna for 65kr.

If you are going on from Kiruna to Narvik, the north side of the train is the one to sit on to see the most spectacular scenery.

JOKKMOKK The SWEDISH MOUNTAIN AND LAPP MUSEUM has special displays on Lapp history and culture and is well worth the 20kr entrance fee. You'll find Tourist Information at Stortorget 4, open Mon.–Fri.: 9 a.m.–7 p.m.; Sat. and Sun.: 11 a.m.–7 p.m., during the summer, mid-June–August. The Tourist Office give out 'Polar Certificates' to prove you've made it to, and crossed, the Arctic Circle (well, your Mum'll like it).

The GAMLA KYRKA (old church) is the other main sight. There's a youth hostel at Stockgatan 24 (Tel. 0971 11977), open summer only, an IYHF hostel at Åsgatan 30 (Tel. 0971 55977) and an official campsite, Notuddens, about 1½ km from the centre.

ARVIDSJAUR The LAPP VILLAGE in the town of Arvidsjaur is still used today by Lapps visiting the town for festivals and gatherings. Tourist Information is at Östra Skolgatan 18, open 9 a.m.–8 p.m. daily in the summer, and they'll arrange private accommodation for you. The campsite at Järnvägsgatan 111 (Tel. 0960 13420) does huts as well as tent sites, and opposite the station is the Central Hotel at Järnvägsgatan 63 (Tel. 0960 10098) with rooms at 300kr single, 350kr double. The youth hostel is at Östra Skolgatan 9 (Tel. 0960 12413), 300m from the station.

NOTES

....

....

....

....

....

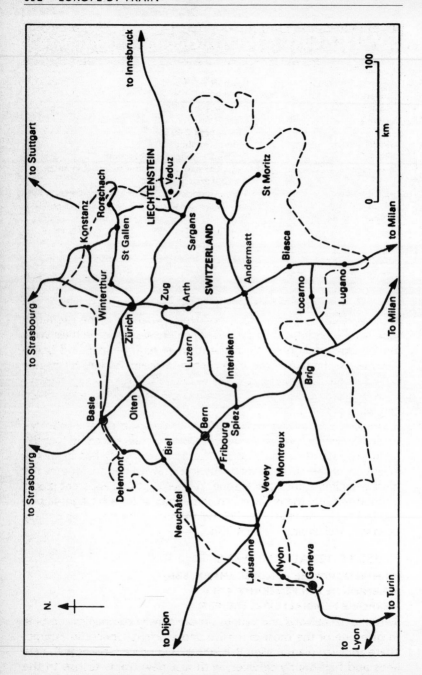

SWITZERLAND, including Liechtenstein

Entry requirements	Passport
Population	6,600,000
Capital	Bern (pop.: 1,600,000)
Currency	Swiss Franc
	£1 = approx 2.40 SFr
Political system	Federal republic
Religion	Roman Catholic and Protestant
Language	Swiss-German, French, Italian and Romansch
	(English widely spoken)
Public holidays	1 Jan., Good Friday, Easter Monday, 1 May, Whit
	Monday, Ascension Day, 1 Aug., 25, 26 Dec.
International dialling	To Switzerland: international code 41 number
	From Switzerland: 00 + country code number

Cross the border from France or Italy to Switzerland and almost immediately you'll notice even the wood-piles are neater. Where the Swiss obsession for punctuality and cleanliness comes from is open to debate, but I suspect it's an ongoing process, started when the Romans cleaned up after the Celts. Then along came the Germanic tribes who brought with them the work ethic we still see in their Swiss descendants, only now it's in the form of high finance and flashy watches. By the end of the 13th century, William Tell and his friends were demanding independence from the Habsburgs. This sparked off a proud tradition of self-government among the cantons which continues to this day.

One of the reasons why the Swiss are so prosperous is the country's neutrality since Napoleon's invasion. Unkind critics have said that the main product of centuries of peace and prosperity has been the invention of the cuckoo clock. Physically, Switzerland is one of the most beautiful countries in Europe. Yet despite these apparent pieces of good fortune, many Swiss can sometimes seem a bit tight-lipped and lacking in the vitality of their neighbours. They have traditionally been very welcoming to the British.

SWISS FEDERAL RAILWAYS
(SCHWEIZERISCHE BUNDESBAHNEN, SBB)
(CHEMINS DE FER FÉDÉRAUX, CFF)
(FERROVIE FEDERALI SVIZZERE, FFS)

Swiss federal railways and various private railway companies combine to give one of the most extensive and efficient services in Europe. There are even plans (called Rail 2000) to improve services with new lines and half-hourly services, with fast new trains to rise to the challenge. The private outfits tend to serve the resort areas, except for the 2 largest. Most notable is the Bern–Lötschberg–Simplon line (BLS), Europe's largest private operation, which runs in friendly rivalry with the federal railway. International and intercity trains are federal-run, and intercity or express trains run hourly between all the main centres, while inland expresses run at least every other hour.

There is a supplement on only 2 inland routes: the Bernina express and the Glacier express. From Chur to Tirano or vice versa it is about 30SFr. each way and from Zermatt to St Moritz or vice versa it is about 15SFr. each way, including seat reservation. A useful spin-off are the free maps and leaflets given out to lure custom.

PASSES AVAILABLE There are a number of rover tickets available in Switzerland, but the most useful is the Swiss Pass. It is available for 4 days, 8 days, 15 days or 1 month (prices: 210SFr, 264SFr, 306SFr, 420SFr in second class) and gives free travel on state railways, steamers, post buses, town buses and trams plus reductions on private lines.

The Flexipass is valid for 3 days within 15 and costs 210SFr in second class. A number of regional tickets are also available. They are valid for 7 or 15 days. With the latter the holder gets 5 days of free travel plus 10 days of half-price travel. Prices vary widely, depending on the region and class and length of ticket.

If you intend to stay mainly in one place and/or use many private lines, consider the Swiss Card, which gives free travel from the border to a destination and back plus reductions on other journeys. It's SFr140 for a month. In general, though, the Swiss Pass is the best bargain.

Euro Domino is also available and both Eurail and Inter-Rail passes are valid. Switzerland is in Inter-Rail Zone C, along with Germany, Austria and Denmark. For details of the 8 Inter-Rail zones, see the Inter-Rail section in Part One of this guide.

INTER-RAIL BONUSES On most private railways of Switzerland, Inter-Rail will bring you a 50% reduction, so always ask first (see Appendix I). One that doesn't is Furka Oberalp.

EURAIL AND EUROPASS BONUSES
FREE SERVICES
Regular steamer services on the lakes of Geneva, Lucerne, Thun, Brigenz, Zürich, Neuchâtel, Biel, Murten, on the Rhine from Schaffhausen to Kreuzlingen and on the Aare from Biel/Bienne to Solothurn. Seasonal services – please consult timetables.

REDUCED FARES

50% reduction on steamer services on Lake Constance between Romanshorn and Friedrichshafen and between Rorschach and Lindau.

35% reduction to the top of Mount Pilatus near Lucerne, by funicular from Alpnachstad, as well as by cable car from Kriens.

35% reduction on entrance fee to the Transport Museum Lucerne, the biggest of its kind in Europe.

25% discount on Jungfrau Region railways.

EUROPABUS A 10% reduction is granted by Europabus on transportation costs only and by local offices in Europe on route 200 St Moritz–Munich.

TRAIN INFORMATION

English is widely spoken throughout Switzerland and most Swiss timetables have an English section. If you have no luck finding anywhere to stay, look out for the travel-aid men with red, white and yellow armbands.

RESERVATIONS Must be made for the Glacier express and the Bernina express. Otherwise it's probably only worthwhile reserving if you are going to Italy, where overcrowding can be a problem or unless you hit a particularly busy weekend. It's not possible to reserve on internal Swiss trains anyway.

NIGHT TRAVEL Wagons-Lits run sleepers on all international routes at their standard rates and couchettes are also available. SBB have no services on any inland runs.

EATING ON TRAINS Most stations are fairly well provided for, which is just as well as even the mini-bars are very expensive. If you've money to burn, the self-service buffet is much better value than the dining cars. Believe it or not, McDonald's have coaches on certain trains between Basel and Geneva, so it's now possible to have a Big Mac, should you feel the urge.

SCENIC TIPS To get to grips with Switzerland's many scenic rail routes would take at least a month and involve paying out vast amounts for private lines. Swiss Pass or Swiss Card holders get round this problem, but most eurorailers have to be content with main-line runs. The possibilities are fortunately endless, without even leaving the main lines:

From Zürich take the train to Chur, then the narrow-gauge Rhaetian Railway to Tikano – Europe's highest line at 2,220m as well as one of the most spectacular. At Chur an alternative is to head towards Zermatt. This line passes over the Oberalp (2,000m) and through the Furka tunnel but it gives no reduction to Inter-Railers.

Lucerne offers the greatest possibilities; foremost among them is the main line to Milan through the 14½ km Gotthard tunnel which took 2,500 men over 7 years to construct in the 1880s. If this isn't spectacular enough, take the branch line to Locarno where you change trains for Domodossola in Italy. This line is a real favourite, passing through some incredible gorges. For the best view, sit on the left-hand side.

Also from Lucerne, the line to Interlaken is equally awe-inspiring. If you haven't seen enough and don't mind paying out, take the private line up to Kleine Scheidegg where, after you change trains, the line goes under the Eiger and on to the Jungfraujoch, Europe's highest station at 3,400m. Private lines also take you up to Mounts Rigi, Pilatus and Titlis from Lucerne.

Bern makes an alternative base for any of these trips, but if, like most eurorailers, you're in a hurry, the main line to Milan via Brig will not be a disappointment. At Brig, if you've spare cash why not head for Zermatt, and take the cogwheel train up to Gornergrat and see the Matterhorn from close up. Approaching from the west, the train follows Lake Geneva as far as Lausanne, where the line splits to enter Bern or Brig – either route is beautiful.

The Martigny to Le Châtelard (and on to Chamonix) route is another classic. Sit on the left-hand side for the best view.

BIKES Can be hired at most SBB stations and some private ones; the cost is approximately 14SFr a day for a basic 6-gear model. Racing and mountain bikes are also available.

TOURIST INFORMATION

Every town has its own well-organized Tourist Offices, usually situated near the station. They keep a good selection of maps and leaflets, as well as running a room-finding service. Ask for the Swiss Holiday Card map: this shows the rail network of the country.

ISIC BONUSES There's a variety of reductions on internal fares and in some museums. For further information, contact SSR Leonhardstrasse 10, Zürich, or SSTE, 3 rue Vignier, Geneva.

MONEY MATTERS 1 franc (SFr) = 100 centimes (c).

Banking hours are Mon.–Fri.: 8.30 a.m.–4.30 p.m. (often closed 12 noon–2 p.m.). Many stations have exchanges which stay open 7 days a week. Switzerland is a good place to change money as few banks charge a commission and rates are generally favourable.

POST OFFICES Open Mon.–Fri.: 7.30 a.m.–6 p.m. (often closed 12 noon–1.45 p.m.), Sat.: 7.30 a.m.–11 a.m.

SHOPS Open Tues.–Fri: 8.30 a.m.–6.30 p.m., and Saturdays until mid-afternoon. Many shops shut for lunch 12 noon–2 p.m., particularly in small towns.

TIPPING Service is generally included in restaurants and cafés, but if it has been good then round up bills to the nearest 5 or 10 SFr – but don't leave money on the table. Taxis usually include a tip in the charge – if not, give 15%. Give porters and WC attendants 0.5–1 SFr.

SLEEPING

Availability and price are the main problems you're likely to face in Switzerland. During the summer, the tourist resorts are packed and then there's always that unexpected conference in town. To avoid paying through the nose for somewhere to stay, arrive as early in the day as possible and start looking right away.

Tourist Offices keep lists of hotels and hostels in the area, and some will find you a room if required for a small charge. Hotels tend to be expensive with singles costing around 40SFr, so think twice before committing yourself. Even a dormitory bed in a student hostel will set you back 30SFr or more. Youth hostels often provide the only answer; there are over 100 of them in Switzerland, most of which are very clean and have excellent facilities. IYHF cards are required and you can expect to pay 30SFr for a bed.

Swiss campsites are among the best in Europe and at only 7– 8SFr per person, you can't go wrong. If you're forced to the hills to sleep out, remember it can get bitterly cold in Switzerland at night, even during the summer.

Free accommodation is listed in a small brochure, *Schlafplätze für Unkomplizierte*, available for a small fee from the Vereinigung Ferien und Freizeit, Wasserwerkstrasse 17, CH-8035 Zürich.

EATING AND NIGHTLIFE

Although Switzerland used to be *very* expensive, prices have not risen so fast here as in other parts of Europe. Budget travellers will find it a bit of a struggle to eat out though. A lot of the regional specialities can be bought from supermarkets (try Co-op or Migros) and prices are certainly not as bad as in Scandinavia. Alpine areas have a good selection of cheeses and cold meats ideal for picnics.

The cheapest restaurants (*Gemeindestube*) don't serve alcohol, so if you want a glass of wine with your meal you'll have to check out the fixed-price menus. Look out for *Rösti* (a filling potato dish from the German area) or *Berner Platte* (a mixture of ham, bacon, and sausage with potatoes and green beans or pickled cabbage). If you can get a group together it's worth going for a fondue. Be aware that if you eat bread put out on the table you will be charged for it – as you will for water.

The Swiss don't exactly specialize in budget entertainment; as a result, most young people take to the bars. From spring through to autumn there are plenty of local folk festivals going on in the mountains, and on 1 August the sky is set alight by fireworks commemorating the founding of the Swiss Confederation..

Switzerland in 1998 is a special Mecca for train buffs - it's the 150th anniversary of Swiss Railways, so watch out for exhibitions, steam trips and special displays. And if you're into museums, it might be worth investing in a Museum Passport, which for 30SFr will give you entry to 180 of them all around the country.

Zürich city phone code: 01

The largest city of Switzerland and home of the 'gnomes' (as Harold Wilson so aptly put it) of the international money market. Walking on the average Zürich pavement, you're literally on top of gold: vaults containing much of the world's gold reserves lie buried beneath them. Zürich is one of Europe's most expensive cities, and doesn't merit more than a day, though there's no denying the old town is picturesque.

STATION FACILITIES

Situated in northern Switzerland, not far from the German border, Zürich handles trains to an impressive number of destinations in Switzerland, France, Germany, Belgium, the Netherlands, Hungary, Austria, 'Yugoslavia' and Italy from its immaculately kept and well-equipped main station (Hauptbahnhof). Female travellers have reported spending a comfortable night in the waiting room here (you need a valid ticket), although I wouldn't officially recommend this option. Train information: Tel. 2115010.

TOURIST INFORMATION

The main office is in the main station. It's open Mon.–Fri.: 8.30 a.m.–9 30 p.m., weekends: 8.30 a.m.–8.30 p.m. There are leaflets on everything here and a free accommodation service (Tel. 2154040).

Though the Swiss Student Reception Service is mainly a travel agent, it does also have information on Switzerland. It's at Leonhardstrasse 5 (Tel. 2423000) and sells Eurotrain tickets.

ADDRESSES

AMEX Bahnhofstrasse 20, open Mon.–Fri.: 8.30 a.m.–5.30 p.m., Sat.: 9 a.m.–12 noon (Tel. 2118370)
BRITISH CONSULATE Dufourstrasse 56 (Tel. 2611520)
US CONSULATE Zollikerstrasse 141 (Tel. 4222566)

SEEING

Getting around Zürich is simple on the modern transport net of buses, trams and S-bahns. Multiple-strip tickets are sold from automated ticket machines, but the best bet is the day card for 7.20SFr which allows unlimited travel on all forms of transport for 24 hours.

To the right of the Limmat River is OLD ZÜRICH with its 16th- and 17th-century guild houses (now restaurants and trendy shops) and nearby are the town's 2 medieval churches: FRAUMÜNSTER on the left bank and GROSSMÜNSTER, the austere Protestant cathedral, on the right. Walking tours of the old town are conducted daily, taking 2 hours and costing 18SFr. For a view over the old town, climb to LINDENHOF just up from the Fraumünster.

BAHNHOFSTRASSE is said to be 'the most beautiful shopping street in the world' – it may well be, but it's certainly one of the most expensive. It runs down from the station to the lake where you can indulge in a boat trip if the weather's up to it. The lake is also great for safe, clean swimming and sunbathing.

The ZOO in the Zürichberg woods and BOTANIC GARDENS at Zollikerstrasse are wonderful picnic spots on good days, and on bad the SWISS NATIONAL MUSEUM behind the station and the RIETBERG in the Wessendonck Villa at Gablerstrasse are excellent. The latter has one of the best collections of non-European art in Europe. The Swiss National Museum opens Tues.–Sun.: 10.30 a.m.–5 p.m.; closed Mondays. Admission free. The Rietberg Museum opens daily (except Monday) 10 a.m.–5 p.m. For the less highbrow, the LINDT CHOCOLATE MUSEUM in Kilchberg is open Wed.–Fri.: 10 a.m.–noon and 1 p.m.–4 p.m., and is free. Also, the Zürich City Festival, which takes place on the first weekend in July every third year (1998, 2000, 2002 etc.) finishes with a sensational firework display on the lake.

There are all sorts of boat trips on Lake Zürich lasting 1½–4 hours which Inter-Railers get concessions on, or there's the trip down the River Limmat which takes you through old Zürich.

From the Hauptbahnhof, take the train for about an hour to SCHAFFHAUSEN, then a further 20 minutes to STEIN AM RHEIN. This beautiful little place with its half-timbered houses and wonderful location can also be reached by boat from Schaffhausen quay. Inter-Railers get concessions and you can take the boat as far as Konstanz.

Enquire at the Hauptbahnhof about the private mountain trains (Inter-Railers: always check whether you can get half price on the line you've chosen) and strongly consider the chance to get up to an alpine village, away from the bourgeois bustle of Zürich.

SLEEPING

It's probably best to forget hotels and keep it as basic as you can. The campsite on the Zürichsee is very good (train to Wollishofen, then 10-minute walk) and works out as your cheapest option. It's at Seestrasse 559 (Tel. 4821612).

Between 27 July and 30 Aug., there's a YMCA Interpoint hostel at Stockerstrasse 18 in Horgen, which is a short train ride out of Zürich; costs 20SFr.

The youth hostel's big and not strictly run. It's at Mutschellenstrasse 114 (Tel. 4823544) and is reached by tram 7 to Morgental (no curfew; reception closes 12 noon–1 p.m.). There is a handy supermarket opposite the hostel, which is cheaper than those in town.

For cheap pensions and 1-star hotels, try the following: Foyer Hottingen, Hottingerstrasse 31 (Tel. 2619315), run by nuns and only for women or married couples; St George's, Weberstrasse 11 (Tel. 241144); Justinusheim, Freudenberg Strasse 146 (Tel. 3613806). These start from 40SFr for singles, 50SFr upwards for doubles. The cheapest place of all is probably the Backpacker Hostel at Niederdorfstrasse 5 (Tel. 251 9015), which charges 30SFr in dormitories.

EATING AND NIGHTLIFE

Round the station is as good as anywhere for cheap places, or use one of the many central Migros cafeterias. Jelmoli, the department store on Bahnhofstrasse, does good meals – the best value is the all-you-can-eat breakfast for 13SFr. There's enough there to keep you sustained till dinner. The Mensa at Rämistrasse 71 and 101 does cheap meals for students (shut during the summer), and there are a few beer halls where you can pick up *Würst* snacks for not too much.

The bars, discos and clubs are all around Niederdorfstrasse. There are also a substantial number of gay bars in the city – the Blue Box Bar at Konradstrasse 13 is reported to be friendly.

Lucerne (Luzern) city phone code: 041

If you can only stop once in Switzerland, make it at Lucerne. It's Switzerland's prettiest, and most touristy, town, and in this country that's saying something on both scores. Set on Lake Lucerne with the Alps in the background, it's beautifully preserved and has everything you always associated with Switzerland. It's 1½ hours from Bern and only 50 minutes from Zürich.

TOURIST INFORMATION AND ADDRESSES

The Tourist Office is a block from the station at Frankenstrasse 1, open Mon.–Fri.: 8.30 a.m.–6 p.m., Sat.: 9 a.m.–5 p.m; Sun.: 9 a.m.–1 p.m (Tel. 4107171). When closed, use room-finding service at the station.

If you're staying a while, consider the Tell Pass, which gives discounts on trips on cable railways and steamers.

Underneath the railway station is a set of shops, including a good but pricey supermarket – open at odd hours and on Sundays.

POST OFFICE Bahnhofstrasse, open Mon.–Fri.: 7.30 a.m.–6.30 p.m., Sat.: 8.00 a.m.–11 a.m.

AMEX Schweizerhofquai 4, open Mon.–Fri.: 8 a.m.–5 p.m., Sat.: 8.30 a.m.–12 noon.

SEEING

The 14th-century covered wooden bridge, KAPELLBRÜCKE, spanning the river Reuss, is the symbol of the town. Walk over it to see the 120 paintings dating from the 16th to the 18th century which tell the town's history. The adjoining WATER TOWER served as a lookout tower, prison and archive store. On Kornmarkt is the beautiful old TOWN HALL, and on WEINMARKT are old painted houses. The SPREUERBRÜCKE is another covered bridge, this time with paintings on the 'Dance of Death'. For a superb view of the town and its surroundings, climb the westernmost tower on the old city wall (closed in winter).

The SWISS TRANSPORT MUSEUM (16SFr) sounds boring as hell, but is actually quite interesting, and gives a discount to Inter-Railers. It's at the end of the park *en route* to the campsite (bus 2 from the station). On Furrengasse is the small but interesting PICASSO MUSEUM (Am Rhyn-

Haus). The WAGNER MUSEUM in the suburb of TRIBSCHEN shows the house where he worked and lived, and some of his possessions. You can get here by bus 6/7 or by the boat from in front of the station (Inter-Rail concession).

The GLACIER GARDEN is a beautiful rocky area formed during the Ice Age. Entrance to it is 7SFr. Unfortunately the PANORAMA (a huge 360° painting) is closed until 1999. Even if you don't go into the attractions, it is still worth walking up the Löwenstrasse to view the beautiful LÖWENDENKMAL, a superb rock sculpture of a dying lion, carved to commemorate the Swiss Guards who died protecting the French king and queen. If you want a view from a slightly higher vantage, the cable car up MOUNT PILATUS (2,132m) gives a third off for eurailers: take the bus to Kriens.

SLEEPING

If you're really intent on a pension or hotel, use the Tourist Office or the station's accommodation service (open Mon.–Sat.: 10.30 a.m.–2 p.m, 3 p.m.–8.30 p.m; Sun.: 10.30 a.m.–2 p.m, 3 p.m.–6.30 p.m) and clearly state your price range.

The campsite is excellent: its situation couldn't be improved – near the beach and the lake – and to get to it you can walk through the park. It's at Lidostrasse 8 (Tel. 370 2146) on bus route 2 and costs 6.50SFr per person and 3SFr per tent.

The youth hostel Am Rotsee on Sedelstrasse 12 (Tel. 420 8800) has over 200 beds and is very reasonable at about 30SFr (35SFr non-members). It's not central and closes 9 a.m.–2 p.m. Bus 18 to the Gopplismoos stop in Friedental, then a 2-minute walk or the more frequent bus 1 to Schlossberg, then a 10-minute walk, will get you there. Try to arrive early, as we've had reports of 1 hour queueing, even at 5 p.m.; the wise arrive early, leave their form and YHA card in the box provided and return before 10 p.m. There is also a 'Backpackers' hostel at Alpenquai 42 (Tel. 360 0420) which charges from 22SFr for a bed in a shared room and has no curfew.

Hotel Weisses Kreuz at Furrengasse 19 (Tel. 410 4040) is an old city hotel within the 90–120SFr bracket, and is as good as you can expect. You can also try the Touristenhotel, St Karliquai 12 (Tel. 410 2474), dorms 55–70SFr with ISIC reductions, or Pension Alpha (Tel. 240 4280). Also try Schlüssel Franziskanerplatz 12 (Tel. 210 1061), singles in the 90SFr bracket, and well located for the old town.

EATING AND NIGHTLIFE

In general both tend to cater for monied European tourists, but if you walk the length of Hertensteinstrasse, you should come up with some suitable pub or restaurant, even if it's just Migros at no. 44, or a fast-food place. The Mr 'Pickwick Pub next to the station has also been recommended.

Apart from the International Music Festival (mid-August–early September), Lucerne is exceptionally sedate. A pub with a collection of eurorailers determined to make merry will probably be your high spot, unless your budget is elastic.

EXCURSIONS The steamer cruises down the VIERWALDSTÄTTERSEE (Lake Lucerne to us) are well worth it. Inter-Railers go half price, and you leave from the quay near the station (ask Tourist Information for details of the alternatives).

The huge glowering mountain dominating Lucerne is MOUNT PILATUS (2,100 m). To get up there, you'd do best to take the boat from Lucerne to ALPNACHSTAD and then travel up on the steepest cogwheel railway in the world. Return by cable car to KRIENS then bus 1 back to Lucerne. It's well worth the effort, and really is an experience you won't forget, assuming you manage to avoid the mid-afternoon crowds and can afford the fare of around 70SFr.

Berne (Bern) city phone code: 031

There's nothing to keep you in Bern for much more than a day if you're a restless type, even though it is the capital of Switzerland. The Bernese hotly dispute this of course; how could anyone suggest that the birthplace of both Einstein's Theory of Relativity and Emmenthal cheese might be just a little bit *boring*? It's pretty but not spectacular, and once you've seen the CLOCK TOWER (daily guided tours of the interior at 4.30 p.m.), BEAR PIT complete with bears, GOTHIC CATHEDRAL and BERNESE HISTORICAL MUSEUM, you've more or less done the rounds – unless you collect Swiss stamps and want to visit the vast POSTAL MUSEUM. The city map from the Tourist Office covers a walking tour which will take in all the sights.

STATION FACILITIES
Tourist Information, left-luggage lockers, baths and showers available.
Daily trains to Brussels, Basel, Milan, Zürich, Lausanne, Geneva.
Train information: Tel. 157 2222.

TOURIST INFORMATION AND ADDRESSES
The main Tourist Office is the one at the station. When they close,

they leave information on accommodation posted up outside, and there's a free phone to make reservations. Open Mon.–Sat.: 9 a.m.–6.30 p.m. (Sun.: 10 a.m.–5 p.m. in winter) (Tel. 311 6611).

POST OFFICE Schanzenpost 1, open Mon.–Fri.: 7.30 a.m.–10 p.m., Sat.: 7.30 a.m.–6 p.m., Sun. 10 a.m.–10 p.m.
AMEX Kehrli and Öhler, Bubenbergplatz 19, open Mon.–Fri.: 8.30 a.m.–12 noon., 1.30 p.m.–6 p.m., Sat.: 8.15 a.m.–12 noon
UK EMBASSY Thunstrasse 50 (Tel. 352 5021)
IRISH EMBASSY Kirchenfeldstrasse 68 (Tel. 352 1442)
US EMBASSY Jubiläumstrasse 93 (Tel. 357 7011)
CANADIAN EMBASSY Kirchenfeldstrasse 88 (Tel. 352 6381)
AUSTRALIAN EMBASSY Alpenstrasse 29 (Tel. 351 0143)

SLEEPING
Definitely avoid hotels here and stick to the youth hostel or campsite. The hostel is at Weihergasse 4 (Tel. 311 6311), near the Houses of Parliament. It closes 10 a.m.–5 p.m., is run quite strictly and costs 25SFr., including breakfast.

Camping Eichholz is down by the river (Tel. 961 2602), a bit out of the city. Tram 9 to Eichholz.

For a central pension, try Hotel Bahnhof-Süd, Bumplizstrasse 189 (Tel. 992 5111), charging from 50SFr for a bed in a shared room, or the Glocke, Rathausgasse 75 (Tel. 311 3771), charging from 80SFr.

EATING AND NIGHTLIFE
For picnic food there are shops in Marktgasse and Zeughausgasse near the station, or there are always Migros for cheap meals. About the only nightspot you can afford, or would find remotely lively, is the Kornhauskeller on Kornhausplatz. It may bust your budget to eat there, but go for the local beer. The only regular gay club is Ursus at Junkerstrasse 1.

EXCURSIONS
FRIBOURG The best day trip you can take from Bern is to this ancient town, only 20 minutes away. The river that runs through it, the Sarine, is commonly regarded as the boundary line between the French- and German-speaking sections of Switzerland. Visit the ÉGLISE DES CORDELIERS with its original St Anthony altarpiece, and take in the view from the bridges that span the river. Most of the sights are on rue de Morat: the church mentioned above, the CATHEDRAL, the 16th-century TOWN HALL and the MUSEUM OF ART AND HISTORY.

The Bernese Oberland

INTERLAKEN The region is stunning in its beauty, but from a euro-railer's point of view, unless you're stopping off to ski or climb, there's not that much to see apart from the scenery.

Balmers Gasthaus, Hauptstrasse 23 (Tel. 033 8221961) is great value: 17SFr in dormitory, 54SFr in doubles, and even provides space under shelters outside when overfull. Contrast the quieter youth hostel further out in Bonigen-Interlaken, at Aarenweg 21 (Tel. 033 8224353), take bus 1 from the station. Most hostels do reasonably priced food.

Only an hour from Bern, Interlaken is a good base for heading off into the Bernese Oberland. Inter-Railers get a 50% reduction on the private railways that take you there.

If you've decided that, now you're this far, you want to spend a bit of time here, consider buying the rail pass from this area's private railways board. For SFr155 you get 5 days' unlimited travel out of 15 on most trains, cable cars and 'gondolas' and the remaining 10 days' travel at half price. It's a lot of money, though, especially when you consider that you can travel half-price on your Inter-Rail.

Try Hüsi's Pub for a good place to meet people from around the world.

Tourist Information is at Höheweig 37 in the Metropole Hotel, as well as at Westbahnhof; and for rooms, look at the bulletin board at Westbahnhof listing the hotel rooms as well as *Zimmer frei* (private rooms). Ask for their free regional budget accommodation guide, which is published separately from their normal hotel lists.

GRINDELWALD This is *the* destination for serious climbers (though LAUTERBRUNNEN is equally beautiful if you're not a climber). What with the NORTH FACE OF THE EIGER, the JUNGFRAU and the MONCH, you won't know where to begin.

There are hourly trains here from Interlaken, though Inter-Rail is only valid on the route to JUNGFRAUJOCH, the highest railway station in Europe at 3,454m. If you get this far, don't leave till you've taken the cable car to MÄNNLICHEN, WENGEN and from Grindelwald up to PFINGSTEGG. From Pfingstegg, walk to STIEREGG. More than likely, this will be the high spot of your travels in this spectacular country.

KLEINE SCHEIDEGG and Jungfraujoch are also in this area and accessible with the help of an extortionately priced mountain railway. If you're staying, try for the youth hostel Die Weid at Terrassenweg (Tel. 036 531009), or camp.

ZERMATT If this has whetted your appetite, you might as well carry on to the MATTERHORN. Your best base for excursions here is Zermatt, which you reach by private railway from BRIG or VISP (Inter-Railers half price). Tourist Information is to the right of the station. They'll fix you up with maps, hiking suggestions and a bed.

Hotel Bahnhof (Tel. 028 672406), opposite the station, is reasonable and has dormitories as well as rooms, which aren't much more expensive than the youth hostel. The youth hostel costs about 20SFr per night (including breakfast). Curfew is at 10 p.m., but can be flexible – check first! (Tel. 028 672320)

Lausanne city phone code: 021

The French Alps are visible from Lausanne, home of the most spectacular Gothic building in Switzerland: its EARLY GOTHIC CATHEDRAL. This is in the old medieval quarter, which is the most interesting (as the rest of the town is very modern) and here you'll also find the HÔTEL DE VILLE and the CHÂTEAU SAINTE MARIE, formerly the Bishop's Palace and now the seat of government tor the canton.

The funicular to DUCHY will take you down to the busy port which looks over to Lake Geneva and the Alps. Of the museums, try to take in COLLECTION DE L'ART BRUT in the Château de Beaulieu, where there are interesting exhibits by psychologically disturbed people, criminals and recluses.

TOURIST INFORMATION AND ADDRESSES

TOURIST OFFICE 2 avenue de Rhodanie, open Mon.–Sat.: 8 a.m.–7 p.m., Sun.: 9 a.m.–12 noon, 1 p.m.–6 p.m., and at the station. They'll kit you out with maps, etc., and arrange accommodation. Ask for the free *Lausanne Official Guide*.

POST OFFICE 43 bis avenue de la Gare, open Mon.–Fri.: 7.30 a.m.–12 noon, 1.30 p.m.–6.30 p.m. (closed Sat. p.m.)

AMEX 14 avenue mon Repos, open Mon.–Thurs.: 8 a.m.–12.15 p.m., 1.45 p.m.–5.30 p.m., Fri.: 8 a.m.–5.30 p.m.

SLEEPING

The youth hostel is down by the lake at 1 chemin du Muguet (Tel. 265782), around 25SFr including breakfast. Bus 1 to Batelière (direction La Maladière), then follow the signs.

The campsite is also by the lake, Camping de Vidy-Lausanne (Tel. 242031) at 3 chemin du Camping and has tents, caravans and bungalows for hire. It is highly recommended.

For rooms or dormitories, try Foyer la Croisée, 15 avenue Marc Dufour (Tel. 204231), or Jeunotel, chemin du Bois-de-Vaux 36 (Tel. 6260222).

EATING AND NIGHTLIFE

Food shouldn't be a problem. There are plenty of grocers' and bakers' shops to buy from, and no shortage of affordable restaurants, but watch out down in Duchy – many restaurants are overpriced, as are many of the small Swiss cafés. Restaurant Manora in place St François is a good self-service restaurant worth a visit. There are a few good supermarkets, open 7 days a week, at the bottom of avenue d'Ouchy.

If you're staying at the youth hostel, consider taking a wander into the park opposite and eating at the café bar next to the tennis courts. Although the menu is somewhat restricted, they do an excellent range of pizzas at reasonable prices and both the staff and the customers are young and friendly. If you've just come off a train after a long journey and can't wait for food, McDonald's is facing the main entrance to the station. But watch the traffic, as the trolley-bus terminal is here and these vehicles are noise-free as well as pollution-free.

There's no unique nightlife here except in the festival and fête in late June, when the town offers plenty to do at night.

Basel (Basle) city phone code: 061

Situated on the crossroads of France, Germany and Switzerland, Basel is the country's second city and is considered the cultural capital of Switzerland. From Basel you can take the train just about anywhere in Europe, from Warsaw to Stockholm.

STATION FACILITIES

As Basel is the border, the French effectively share the station with the Swiss. You'll find information for both SNCF and SBB at the station. French trains stop at the west end of the station. Train information: SBB 6 a.m.–9 p.m. (Tel. 2726767); SNCF 7.30 a.m.–7 p.m. (Tel. 2715033).

TOURIST INFORMATION AND ADDRESSES

As well as one at the station, there's a Tourist Office at Blumenrain 2, open Mon.–Fri.: 8.30 a.m.–6.30 p.m. (Tel. 2615050)

POST OFFICE Nauenstrasse, next to station, open Mon.–Fri.: till 6.30 p.m., Sat.: till 11 a.m.

AMEX c/o Reisebüro Kundig, Äschengraben 10, open Mon.–Fri.: 8.15 a.m.–6 p.m.

SEEING

It's the museums in Basel that hog the limelight. If you're tired of trudging round museums and galleries, just take in the 2 bare essentials: the FINE ARTS MUSEUM and the KIRSCHGARTEN MUSEUM, housed in an old patrician mansion at Elisabethenstrasse 27.

As for the town itself, the 12th-century MÜNSTER (cathedral) is surrounded by medieval houses and stands in an attractive square. The TOWN HALL is on Market Square, and there are still markets held here today; THREE COUNTRIES' CORNER is the spot where the Swiss, French and German borders all meet. Just east of the Tourist Office lies the Münsterplatz, where walking tours start.

SLEEPING

The large and rather institutional youth hostel is at St Alban-Kirchrain 10 (Tel. 2720572). It's clean, friendly and has double rooms and dorms at 23SFr per night including breakfast; a 3-course supper costs 7SFr. Curfew 1 a.m. Take tram 1 one stop, then tram 3 to second stop.

As far as hotels go, try the following, but insist on their cheapest rooms: Hotel Stadthof, Gerbergasse 84 (Tel. 2618711); Hotel Klingental Garm, Klingental 20 (Tel. 6816248).

These 1-star hotels have single rooms (without bath) starting at about 50–60SFr. Cheaper hotels are a short journey over the French border in Mulhouse and the surrounding towns and villages.

EATING AND NIGHTLIFE

You shouldn't have many problems finding shops and cafés to feed yourself from, there are plenty of alternatives. Zum Goldenen Sternen, the oldest pub in Switzerland, at St Albanrheinweg 70, is good for a drink, but watch the food prices.

This Week in Basel will fill you in on events, and if you're there around Shrove Tuesday/Ash Wednesday, you should catch some local festivities.

Geneva (Genève) city phone code: 022

This is perhaps the most international of all European cities, home to dozens of multinational organizations and peace-negotiating bodies such as the Red Cross and United Nations. The town has a rich and well-cared-for air, and is a good place to break up a long haul like Paris–Rome.

STATION FACILITIES

Genève Cornavin station has train information and reservations (Tel. 157 2222), left-luggage lockers, foreign exchange facilities and Tourist Information, and the next building is a post office.

Daily trains to: Lausanne, Basel, Bern, Zürich, Milan, Rome, Nice, Barcelona, Lyon, Paris.

TOURIST INFORMATION AND ADDRESSES

The station office operates all year round. A branch office is at 4 place du Molard (Tel. 311 9827).

POST OFFICE Poste Montbrillant (next to the station)

AMEX 7 rue du Mont Blanc, open Mon.–Fri.: 8.30 a.m.–5.30 p.m., Sat.: 9 a.m.–12 noon (Tel. 7317600)

UK CONSULATE 37–39 rue de Vermont (Tel. 7343800)

US CONSULATE 29 route de Pré Bois (Tel. 7981615)

CANADIAN CONSULATE 1 pré de la Bichette (Tel. 9192000)

AUSTRALIAN CONSULATE 56–58 rue de Moillebeau (Tel. 7346200)

NEW ZEALAND CONSULATE 28a chemin du Petit-Saconnex (Tel. 7349530)

MEDICAL HELP PMC 'Permanence', rue Chantepoulet 21

SEEING

Most of the things to see in Geneva can be taken in on the one main walk. Starting from the station, walk down RUE DU MONT BLANC till you're at the lake, then turn right on QUAI DES BERGUES, cross the river on the FONT DE L'ÎLE to the PLACE BELAIR, then head on to the PLACE NEUVE down RUE DE LA CORRATERIE. Once here, enter the park, which contains the university and the famous statue to the Reformation.

The VIEILLE VILLE is the old cobblestoned quarter round the CATHÉDRALE ST PIERRE, where Calvin preached. On RUE HÔTEL-DE-VILLE is the TOWN HALL where the Geneva Convention was signed, and some 17th-century houses built by Italian religious refugees.

The best museums are the PETIT PALAIS (Impressionist paintings),

INSTITUT ET MUSÉE VOLTAIRE, 25 rue des Délices (Voltaire's house), and the PALAIS DES NATIONS on avenue de la Paix. Don't miss the INTERNATIONAL RED CROSS AND RED CRESCENT MUSEUM at 17 avenue de la Paix. Closed Tues.; open 10 a.m.–5 p.m.

Geneva is the watchmaking capital of the world, so hide your Japanese digital and wander round the superb CLOCK MUSEUM, 15 rue de Malagnou (closed Mon.). Boat trips on Lake Geneva (Lac Léman) are pleasant, but compare prices first. Sunbathers should head for Nyon, on the way to Lausanne, which has a good lakeside beach.

SLEEPING

Summer in Geneva makes affordable beds scarce, so arrive early and immediately aim at getting fixed up. Ask Tourist Information for their list of foyers, dormitories, etc., and phone around.

The large youth hostel is at 28–30 rue Rothschild (Tel. 7326260, 10 minutes from Cornavin station via rue de Lausanne) and costs around 35SFr including breakfast. Reception closes 10 a.m.–5 p.m.

For camping, try L'Arbac (Tel. 796 2101), 6 km out of town on bus 6.

Home St Pierre, at Cour St Pierre, by the cathedral, is a great place. It takes only women and is deservedly popular (Tel. 3103707); singles are dear (around 100SFr) but dorm accommodation is 35SFr.

Contact the Coopérative Universitaire pour Logement for a room in 1 of the 4 university halls of residence (Tel. 781 2598). They charge from 40SFr.

Expect to pay 40–50SFr per person in budget hotels. Ask for the free *Info Jeunes* brochure, which is brilliantly comprehensive and lists all the budget hotels. Alternatively, as is often the case with Swiss border towns, you could opt to stay in France (at Bellegarde), which is much cheaper.

EATING AND NIGHTLIFE

Geneva definitely aims its tourism at the well-heeled, but there are some Migros and budget restaurants dotted around. A picnic down by the lake is your cheapest and most memorable option, but if it's wet, try the restaurant opposite the station on 17 place Montbrillant, or Le Zofage, the university's place at rue des Voisins, with cheap filling *plats du jour*.

Tourist Information will tell you what's on. Geneva actually has the most swinging nightlife in Switzerland, but then that's not hard. Before you get excited, I'm afraid there's probably nothing much you can afford, so content yourself manwatching in place Molard or head for a lively bar like Mr Pickwick's Pub, 80 rue Lausanne. If you enjoy the late club scene, try XS at 21 Grand' Rue, or Le Tube at 3 rue de la Université, which caters for mixed gay and straight clientele.

The Grisons (Graubünden)

From the source of the Rhine east to the River Inn and on to Austria is the canton of Grisons. Here you'll still hear Romansch spoken along with Swiss-German. Chur is the cultural and administrative centre, and such flashy resorts as St Moritz are in this region. The trains are narrow-gauge, but Inter-Rails are valid. Take the CHUR–ST MORITZ line (2 hours), even if you don't get off at the other end, as the scenery is quite beautiful. Accommodation shouldn't be a problem as the canton boasts 28,000 dormitory beds within a 7,000 sq.km area.

CHUR Walk through the old-town streets with their medieval houses and pass through the old gate to the CATHEDRAL, with its pre-Christian sacrificial stone. The HOF (Bishop's Palace) next door is still in use, so don't nose about too much. The pub in there (the Hofkellerei) is a good watering-hole, but a bit touristy in summer.

Tourist Information is at Grabenstrasse 5 (Tel. 081 221818) and there's a good youth hostel at Berggasse 28 (Tel. 081 226563). Ask at the station for a map to get you there.

ST MORITZ The actual town's nothing special and apart from the ENGADINE MUSEUM *en route* to the famed healing waters of the MAURITIUS SPRINGS which reconstructs life of days long ago, there's not much else to see. But people don't come here to sightsee, they come to ski or climb. The general Information Centre is Kurundverkehrsverein on Via Maistra 12, open Mon.–Fri.: 9 a.m.–12 noon, 2 p.m.–6 p.m., Sat.: 9 a.m.–12 noon (Tel. 082 33147).

If your time's short, do just 2 things: take the cable car up the 2,400m MUOTTAS MURAGL and walk the path along the SILS LAKE. If you're going up to altitude, take some warm clothing – best are several relatively thin layers which you can put on as necessary.

If you're staying, try your best to get into the youth hostel at Via Surpunt 60 (Tel. 082 33969). It's beautiful – and cheap by Swiss standards. There's camping at Olympiaschanze (Tel. 082 34090) about 30 minutes from the station. Forget hotels; unless you're flush with cash, you're outclassed here, I'm afraid.

If you are in the money then for 180SFr you can have a piloted ride down the Olympic Bobsleigh run: phone the St Moritz club on 082 34110.

If you're heading for Italy, take the train in the direction of TIRANO on the Italian border (1½ hours), as the scenery around here and on the Passo del Bernina is incredible. Get off at every station and make a day of it, if you've time, as this is the highest line in Europe without cogs or cables.

Ticino

This region, next to Italy and known as the 'Swiss Riviera', has the best of both countries: the scenery, tidiness and efficiency of Switzerland, and the sun, language and ambience of Italy. Lugano and Locarno are the main centres and the area round the lakes of Lugano and Maggiore makes wonderful camping, swimming and walking, away from the crowds. The climate is particularly mild throughout the year.

LUGANO This is a particularly pretty town of sunny piazzas, palm trees and the dominating Monte San Salvatore. It's on LAKE LUGANO and lies on the Zürich–Milan main line. Stroll through the little winding streets on the hill at SAN LORENZO for a view over the town, stopping off at SANTA MARIA DEGLI ANGIOLI to admire the 16th-century frescoes. Walk down to the lake to the Palazzo Civico where the Tourist Office is. They're open April–Oct.: Mon.–Fri.: 9 a.m.–6.30 p.m., Sat.: 9 a.m –12.30 p.m.,.1.30 p.m.–5 p.m., Sun.: 9.30 a.m.–1 p.m. and they'll give you maps, lists of the loccal mountain huts, and arrange accommodation (Tel. 091 9214664). Free two-hour guided walks around the town leave from the Lugano Tourist Office at 9.30 a.m. every Tuesday.

The VILLA FAVORITA CASTAGNOLA houses a fine collection of European and American paintings from the 19th and 20th centuries. It's open from Easter to October, Fri.–Sun., 10 a.m.–5 p.m. From the Paradiso quarter, it's a 10-minute ride on the funicular up MONTE SAN SALVATORE, with a great view over the Alps and lakes. The funicular from Cassarate up to MONTE BRÉ on the other side of the town is another scenic excursion. The MUSEUM OF EXTRA-EUROPEAN CULTURES, on Via Cortivo 24, has displays from Oceania, Indonesia and Africa. Open Tues.–Sun.: 10 a.m.–5 p.m.

There's a youth hostel in Lugano-Crocifisso at 6942 Savosa (at the terminus of bus 5) of an exceptionally high standard (Tel. 091 9662728). Aris Pensione, Via Geretta 8 (Tel. 091 9941478), in nearby Paradiso is a good place to stay or eat, with rooms averaging from

75SFr per person and meals extra. For hotels, try the Montarina which has rooms from 35 to 50SFr and cheaper dormitory accommodation. It's at Via Montarina 1 (Tel. 091 9667272).

There are plenty of markets and food shops offering Swiss-quality Italian food, plus the ubiquitous Migros at Via Pretorio. Commercio on Via Ariosto do great pizzas, or visit the Gabbani *charcuterie* just off Piazza Cioccaro for gigantic salami. In the evening there are often concerts down by the lake, but nightlife here is fairly sedate in general.

LOCARNO From Lugano it's about half an hour to Ticino's capital, BELLINZONA, and from there another half-hour will take you into Locarno, the best place to base yourself for trips round LAKE MAGGIORE. To explore this region you'll need to resort to buses; ask for details at the Tourist Office in Largo Zorzi–Piazza Grande. One of the buses from Locarno station goes through Ascona and Brissago and crosses the Italian border at Madonna di Ponte. Get off at Brissago and make for the island, where there's a beautiful botanical garden.

Back in Locarno itself there's a MUSEUM OF MODERN ART in the Pinacoteca Casa Rusca, with the works of Jean Arp and Filippo Franzoni on permanent display. Funiculars take you up to see the town's landmark, the MADONNA OF THE ROCK (*Madonna del Sasso*). Try the Gottardo (Tel. 093 334454) above the station for a bed.

The private Centrovalli railway from Locarno to Domodossola on the Milan–Brig line is well worth re-routing for. The left-hand side offers the best views of the fantastic scenery.

NOTES

Liechtenstein

Entry requirements	Passport
Population	31,000
Capital	Vaduz (pop.: 5,000)
Currency	Swiss Franc
	£1 = approx. 2.40SFr
Political system	Constitutional monarchy
Religion	Predominantly Roman Catholic
Language	German, English and French widely spoken
Public Holidays	1, 6 Jan., Shrove Tuesday, Good Friday,; Easter Monday, 1 May, Ascension Day, Whit Monday, Corpus Christi, 15 Aug., 8 Sept., 8, 25 Dec.
International dialling codes	To Liechtenstein: int'l code 41 number
	From Liechtenstein: 00 + country code number

This small alpine principality nestles between Switzerland and Austria. It has enjoyed sovereign status as an independent country since the early 1800s, although the Swiss currency is used. There is a separate identity to this little country which makes it worth a stop.

TRANSPORT

The railway plays a subsidiary role in the country as it passes through only a part of it and has only 2 stops. However, the Postbus network is well developed. The best way to enter the principality is by Postbus from either Buchs or Sargans in Switzerland. Services are frequent and the journey times are 30 minutes and 15 minutes respectively. Bus prices are very reasonable: a monthly pass costs 20SFr and few individual journeys cost more than a few francs.

SEEING

The capital, VADUZ, is the seat of government and the home of the Prince of Liechtenstein and his family. The Tourist Information is centrally located at Städtle 37 (Tel. 2321443) and they will provide information and maps on the whole principality and help you with accommodation. You can also get your passport stamped here for just 1SFr, just to prove you've been.

Liechtenstein is a philatelist's dream and the POSTAGE STAMP MUSEUM in the centre of Vaduz has many rare stamps both of Liechtenstein and other countries. It has free admission and is open Apr.–Oct. daily: 10 a.m.–12 noon and 1.30 p.m.–5.30 p.m. There's also a place where you can get a Liechtenstein stamp printed with your own name on it!

The LIECHTENSTEIN STATE ART COLLECTION at Städtle 37 is worth a visit for its fine interchanging exhibitions from the collections of the Princes of

Liechtenstein as well as from other private and public collections. Open 10 a.m.–12 noon and 1.30 p.m.–5 p.m. daily. Admission 5SFr, or 2.50SFr to students with identification. The LIECHTENSTEIN NATIONAL MUSEUM is at Städtle 43, and has the expected displays of archaeological finds, local folklore, history and a good collection of weapons but has been shut for several years. There is also a new museum, the SKI-MUSEUM, but it hasn't been checked out yet.

There is good hiking throughout Liechtenstein; many of the Alpine routes and organized tours start at MALBUN. Another town worth visiting is TRIESENBERG: see the WALSER MUSEUM with its historical collection on the local Walser community. Admission 2SFr, students 1SFr. Open Tues.–Fri.: 1.30 p.m.–5.30 p.m., Sat.: 1.30 p.m.–5 p.m., Sun. (June–Aug. only) 2 p.m.–5 p.m.

BALZERS is also interesting, notably for Gutenberg castle (unfortunately you can't go in) and its varied churches.

SLEEPING AND EATING

The youth hostel here is one of the friendliest we have come across; it's at Untere Rüttigasse 6 (Tel. 075 2325022) and is modern and clean. Showers, sheets and breakfast are included in the 25SFr price. IYHF membership required. Take the Postbus to the stop Hotel Mühle.

Campsites are at Triesen (Tel. 075 392686) or Bendern (Tel. 075 3731211). If all else fails, Tourist Information may find you a room in a private house and many inns have rooms, although both these options are more expensive.

Eating out is expensive even by Swiss standards – which is scary! Your best bet is to put together a picnic at the Denner supermarket on Aulestrasse, or to look out for restaurants offering 'lunch specials'; try and fill up at lunch, as prices are higher for dinner. You should be able to find something decent to scrape by on for 10–15SFr. If you fancy trying the local speciality, it's a sort of small cheese dumpling called *Kasknopfle*, and the local wines are worth sampling.

NOTES

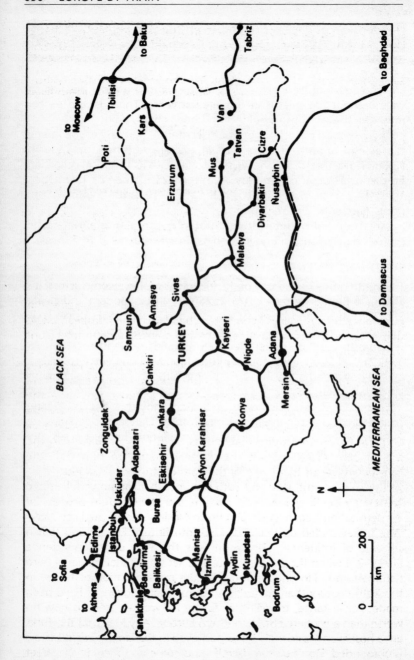

TURKEY (Türkíiye)

Entry requirements	Passport. Travellers have to buy a visa on entry, for £10. Payment must be in hard currency notes – coins not accepted.
Population	57,000,000
Capital	Ankara (pop.: 3,200,000)
Currency	Lira £1 = approx 245,000TL
Political system	Republic
Religion	Muslim
Language	Turkish (German, some English and French spoken in large cities)
Public holidays	1 Jan.–31-day Muslim lunar holiday in spring (29–31 Jan.), 23 April, 19 May, 44-day Muslim lunar holiday in summer (7–10 April), 30 Aug., 28, 29 Oct.
International dialling	To Turkey: international code 90 number From Turkey: 00 + country code number

Only 3% of Turkey is in Europe, the rest lies firmly in Asia – and that goes for culture as well as geography. The Islamic and European blend makes Turkey a fascinating experience and quite different from a jaunt through Europe.

The best preserved remains of its many previous civilizations are to be found on the west and south coasts, the Aegean and Mediterranean. Until 1453 the European area of Turkey was under the umbrella of the Christian Byzantine Empire, but conquest by the Ottomans put a stop to this. From then on there was no looking back and the Ottoman Empire reached its zenith under Süleyman the Magnificent (1520–63); it was largely thanks to him that the Christianity-versus-Islam wars of the 16th century were staged.

It wasn't until the 18th and 19th centuries that this powerful empire went into decline; however, once it did the gradual process of Westernization began. After picking the losing side in the First World War Turkey ended up being divided into British, French and Italian spheres of influence. The result was the War of Independence (1919–23) when the modern state was set up by their national hero Kemal Atatürk. No one did more for the modernization of Turkey in the 20th century than Atatürk and tremendous advances have been made. For instance, travelling in Turkey for women alone is now no worse than anywhere else in southern Europe. Any idea that the Turks are a hostile and unfriendly lot as portrayed in the film *Midnight Express* is unfounded. Don't be surprised if Turks come up to you in the street and ask if they can talk to you to practise their English and if you're befriended by a local, the hospitality they'll show you can leave most Western pleasantries standing.

Do, however, steer very well clear of anything likely to be remotely connected with drugs. In particular, don't carry any loose tablets, even aspirin, and if you do have medicines with you carry a copy of the prescription if possible and the original container.

There has been unrest in certain eastern parts of the country and as a result the British Foreign Office have warned visitors to beware. They have issued a telephone number to contact should the situation give cause for concern: London (0171) 270 4129.

TURKISH STATE RAILWAYS
(TURKIYE CUMHURIYETI DEVLET DEMIRYOLLARI ISLETMESI, TCDD)
In 1990 all of Turkey joined the Inter-Rail scheme ('European Turkey' joined in 1985). Since then there has been a general improvement in services, although you can still expect the journey from northern Greece to Istanbul to take more than a day and the trip from Athens to take up to 40 hours. If you are coming direct from central Europe *remember that you must have a transit visa for Bulgaria* – unless you travel through Serbia and change at Thessaloniki in northern Greece, in which case you'll need a transit visa for 'Yugoslavia'. If you decide to travel through Bulgaria, get your transit visa before you leave home.

Railway services in Turkey are slow. Students can get a 10% discount on train fares (20% on return tickets). Apart from the lines in European Turkey and the Haydarpaşa–Ankara run, you are well advised to use the buses. These are fast, cheap and often modern Mercedes–Benz vehicles. Free drinks *en route* are often included. For a rough guide to the main services, consult *Thomas Cook's Overseas Timetable*.

For short journeys, use a *Dolmus* – these are communal taxis which run on set routes. Stop them by waving. Outside the cities they are usually beat-up Ford Transit or VW vans. Very cheap.

PASSES AVAILABLE Turkey is in Inter-Rail Zone G, along with Italy, Greece and Slovenia. Your Inter-Rail pass also covers the ferry service between Brindisi and Patras. For details of the 8 Inter-Rail zones, see the Inter-Rail section in Part One of this guide.

A Euro Domino ticket is also available (see the Euro Domino section on p. 410 for further information).

TRAIN INFORMATION
English is spoken by the information staff in big cities, while German is more useful elsewhere throughout Turkey.

RESERVATIONS It's always advisable to reserve between Istanbul and Ankara, particularly if you want a couchette or to travel first class.

NIGHT TRAVEL Generally, this is the best way of travelling in Turkey. There are first- and second-class couchettes to choose from.

EATING ON TRAINS Always be prepared with your own drinks. All expresses should have a mini-bar or buffet.

TOURIST INFORMATION

There are Tourist Offices in all the major cities and tourist centres.

ISIC BONUSES 50% off museums, cinemas, concerts, and 10–20% off rail tickets within Turkey. For further information, contact the nearest Turkish tourism and information office and ask for the *Youth Travel Guide*.

NB: Some places will not accept student cards as there are so many Turkish fakes.

MONEY MATTERS Banking hours are Mon.–Fri.: 8.30 a.m.–12 noon, 1.30 p.m.–5 p.m. 24-hour exchange facilities are thin on the ground and there are none at the stations. There is a small exchange office at Istanbul station, if you can find it, at the opposite end of the platform from the station entrance. It is open at weekends and has an average exchange rate.

Inflation is a way of life in Turkey, so bear this in mind when looking at prices. Remember to spend all of your lire before leaving the country as you will find it difficult, if not downright impossible, to exchange – particularly in Greece. It is possible to convert lire back to a foreign currency before leaving Turkey if the original exchange slips are produced, proving it was legally exchanged. Make sure you have sufficient sterling to pay for your visa at the border; US dollars and Deutschmarks are grudgingly accepted.

POST OFFICES Open Mon.–Fri.: 8.30 a.m.–12 noon, 1 p.m.–5.30 p.m. Major post offices stay open till midnight, Mon.–Sat. and 9 a.m.–7 p.m., Sun. Many post offices have exchange facilities; compare the rate to the banks'.

SHOPS Open Mon.–Sat.: 9 a.m.–1 p.m., 2 p.m.–7 p.m., Sun.: closed.

MUSEUMS All museums shut on Mondays, except for the Topkapi Palace which shuts on Tuesdays. Entry usually costs 10,000–25,000TL.

MOSQUES A note to non-Moslems – when visiting a mosque, footwear is removed and normally left on a rack or occasionally with an attendant outside. Women especially should dress modestly. At the better known mosques overalls are provided for those deemed unsuitably dressed.

SLEEPING

There's no problem finding cheap accommodation in Turkey, but we can't guarantee you'll be happy with the standards of cleanliness. Basically, the hotels registered with the tourist board are called *touristic* and are graded *de luxe*, or 1–5 stars. Also there are plenty with no grades at all, many of which are dirty but safe enough. In general, though, discretion is the better part of valour when it comes to a shady set-up. Expect to pay from $10 upwards for a half-decent double (more in Istanbul). Always check the room first and be prepared to bargain if the price seems too high. This tends to be the norm along the Bosphorus, but you can get a reduction with an ISIC card in some places off season.

There are a few *pansiyons* in Turkey and they can be the best places to stay but there still aren't too many of them. Student dormitories are another option and from mid-July to the second week in September there are about 45 youth hostels in Turkey organized by Yurtkur, the student accommodation organization (Tel. 312 431 1100); most of them allow you to stay if you have a student card, but it's best to have an IYHC to be on the safe side.

Campsites are growing in number but are still a bit primitive in their facilities.

EATING AND NIGHTLIFE

Turkish cuisine is among the best in Europe for sheer good value. The variety of dishes is staggering and, as often as not, you're invited into the kitchen to choose your own. (If you don't like the look of things while you're in, now's your chance to skip out with a suitable excuse.) Turkish specialities include *dolmas* (just about anything stuffed with rice) and anything called *şiş* (like *şişkebab*) done on a spit. *Kadin budu* is a concoction of fried rice and meatballs and, literally translated, means 'woman's thigh' (we don't quite see the analogy). Then how about *kadin gobegi* (woman's navel) for dessert? The wine's not bad and the grape brandy, *raki*, is hot stuff. Expect to pay around 25,000–35,000TL for a full meal including wine, though you can eat for a lot less. For a snack, try *lahmacun*, a type of pizza. *Never drink the tap water, especially in Istanbul and Izmir.*

The Turks are big folk-dancers and you should be able to catch each region's favourite without too many problems. The Turkish coffee houses (*Kahve*) are great meeting places, although male only, and, of course, there's always the Turkish bath. This is one way to treat yourself – the pale imitation offered in Western Europe is no comparison. Go and see a belly dancer if there's one advertised, even though they're terribly commercialized these days, but avoid the discos and clubs; although the major cities and resorts are improving, most are still poor Western imitations.

Despite the fact that you will regularly see pairs of males walking along hand in hand, don't be fooled – Islamic law and local custom forbids homosexuality and you could find yourself getting a distinctly cold shoulder if you are too openly gay.

Istanbul city phone code: 1 (Taksim, etc.), 3 (Asian side), 5 (Sultanahmet, etc.)

Incredible mosques share the spotlight with bazaars and the largest Roman building in the world in this fascinating city, and the blend of Asia and Europe makes it quite unique. If you're thinking of a trip to Turkey, make this your destination. It's often dirty and is pretty rough in some parts (women unaccompanied should take extra care), and the intensive train travel will give you ulcers, but there's so much here to catch the eye and imagination that it's all worthwhile. The early morning call to prayer floating amongst the minarets is unforgettable.

STATION FACILITIES

Sirkeci (Tel. 527 0050) is the main station of Istanbul; from here leave the trains bound for Sofia, Belgrade, Athens and the West. Haydapaşa (Tel. 336 0475) is the city's other station, on the opposite shore of the Bosphorus; services to Asia, Ankara, Anatolia, Iran, Syria and Baghdad leave from here.

Facilities at both stations tend to close down at night and there is no bath/shower at either station. Sirkeci station has Tourist Information, exchange facilities and left-luggage. Although this is only a trolley on the platform it is fairly safe as there are many attendants about. Many nearby hotels offer left-luggage facilities but satisfy yourself on their security before committing your luggage.

TOURIST INFORMATION AND ADDRESSES

TOURIST OFFICES 55 Meşrutiyet Caddesi 5 Tepebaşi, Galatasaray (Tel. 245 6875); Divan Yolu Caddesi, Sultanahmet (Tel. 518 1802); entrance of Hilton hotel; Karaköy harbour terminal; Yeşilköy Airport; Sirkeci station; Yalova harbour terminal. Open Mon.–Fri.: 8.30 a.m.–6.30 p.m., Sat.–Sun.: 9 a.m.–5 p.m.

POST OFFICE 25 Yeni Postane Sokak (2 blocks from Sirkeci station). 24-hour currency exchange

AMEX Hilton hotel. Open daily 8.30 a.m.–8 p.m. (Tel. 232 9558)

TOURIST POLICE Across from St Sophia at beginning of Yerebatan Caddesi, open 9 a.m.–8 p.m. (Tel. 527 4503)

UK CONSULATE 34 North Meşrutiyet Caddesi, Tepebaşi (Tel. 293 7540)

US CONSULATE 104–108 Meşrutiyet Caddesi, Tepebaşi (Tel. 251 3602)

AUSTRALIAN CONSULATE 58 Tepecik Yolu Uzeri (Tel. 257 7050)

CANADIAN CONSULATE 107 Buyukdere Caddesi (Tel. 272 5174)

IRISH AND NEW ZEALAND CITIZENS Contact the UK representative.

STUDENT TRAVEL YEDITUR, Inönü Caddesi 37/2, Gumussuyu (Tel. 249 9619/252 5921). Student cards and travel.

MEDICAL HELP For an ambulance call 100 Siracevizler Caddesi (Tel. 144 4998)

GETTING ABOUT

There are cheap buses which leave from Taksim Square. The communal taxis are also a good buy. They have routes between the main quarters, though if you specify you should get dropped off where you ask. Most taxis now have meters, but check, and if there isn't one then agree a price before you start your journey. Even if there is a meter check that the driver turns it on to avoid later difficulties. Frequent suburban trains run along the main line from Sirkeci. Inter-Rail is valid.

SEEING

Basically, Istanbul divides into 2 main areas which are further subdivided into several small districts. The European part of the city is divided by the GOLDEN HORN, and the European and Asian parts are separated by the BOSPHORUS STRAIT. The vast majority of sights are on the southern bank of the Golden Horn.

OLD STAMBOUL is the old walled city across the Golden Horn and it looks like something out of the Fry's *Turkish Delight* advert. For the best panoramic view of the old town, climb the Galata tower. The mosques and palaces are wonderful examples, as good as you'll find anywhere, especially ST SOPHIA, built in AD 347 by Constantine, then rebuilt in the 6th century after a fire, and turned into a mosque after the Turks captured the city in 1453. Today it's a museum, though some of the original mosaics can still be seen. The BLUE MOSQUE, dating from the 17th century, is an amazing feat of engineering, built, as it was, to bend with the force in times of earthquakes – a performance it has done 20 times already. You can go into any mosque in Istanbul as long as you take off your shoes and keep quiet.

Not far from the Blue Mosque is the ornate FOUNTAIN OF SULTAN AHMET. The Roman HIPPODROME was the venue for chariot racing, and today there's a MOSAIC MUSEUM. Nearby you can catch a glimpse of underground Istanbul at YEREB ATAN SARAYI (Sunken Palace), a vast man-made cavern built in the 6th century for water storage should the city be besieged. The GRAND BAZAAR (or Kapaliçarşi) is colourful and entertaining, but barter like mad before buying anything.

The palace of the Ottoman Sultans, TOPKAPI SARAY, is today a complex of museums (entrance 25,000TL with student card); have a look in the HAREM and TREASURY. There's enough here to interest you for hours (open 9 a.m.–5 p.m., closed Tuesdays and half price at weekends). The other notable museums are: the ARCHAEOLOGICAL MUSEUM (entrance 17,500TL for students), the MUSEUM OF THE ANCIENT ORIENT and the MUSEUM OF TURKISH AND ISLAMIC ARTS (both 12,500TL), all of which are self-explanatory.

Another couple of mosques worth taking in on your itinerary are the BEYAZIT, near the university, and the 16th-century SÜLEYMANIY.

As a break from the hot dirty city, take a cruise down the Bosphorus. Boats leave Galata Bridge on 3-hour round cruises between Europe and Asia. They are around £3, great fun and highly recommended. You can also get 5-hour trips which stop off in Asia for 4 hours' sightseeing (fare about £5.50). Boats leaving from the palace end of the quay allow you to visit 4 small islands, the Princes' Islands. There's a round trip every half-hour.

The 'modern' city is on the north side of the Galata bridge and includes Istanbul's underground – the Tunel – with only 2 stations. Tickets are 400TL. The Genoese Galata tower is now a nightclub. Also on this side of the Golden Horn is the 19th-century Dolhambaçe Palace.

SLEEPING

As long as you're not expecting Scandinavian-style cleanliness, you'll cope fine in Istanbul. Beds are cheap and plentiful, and as prices vary little between districts aim for the most central or convenient. Round the station is OK, but a bit on the noisy side. The central Sultanahmet quarter is near the sights and about the best place to head for. Although we concentrate on the Sultanahmet quarter, you may also find cheap places in the Aksaray area and on the Haydarpaşa side of the Bosphorus.

Istanbul youth hostel, 63 Cerrahpaşa Caddesi Aksaray (Tel. 212455), is OK, but hardly central, open only in summer. The only IYHF hostel in Turkey, the Yücelt hostel, is in the Sultanahmet district at 6 Caferiye Sok (Tel. 513 6150/1) and is clean, if crowded. The staff are helpful with onward travel arrangements. Beds from $5. The Orient youth hostel is another worth a try. It is only a 10-minute walk from the station at Yeniak biyik Caddesi 13, Sultanahmet (Tel. 5179493 or 5180780). As well as having 94 rooms available it offers a range of services from cafeteria, hot water, Turkish lessons, TV and video, and information office – and there's no curfew. The Sultan Tourist Hotel on Yerebatan Caddesi (Tel. 520 7676) is good, with doubles around $12, or try the Gögür on Divan Yolu Caddesi (Tel. 526 2319), or the Yöruk at 35 Inçiliçavuş Sok (Tel. 527 6476). Also worth checking out is 'Family Pension' at Piyerloti Caddesi, Kadirga Harman, Sokah no.4, Çemberlitas (Tel. 528 3746). A safe bet is the Hotel Buyuk Sanid, at Hudavendigar Caddesi 35a (Tel. 526 7229). You'll find the rooms as clean and secure as any you'll find in Turkey. Hostel Merih at Alemdar Caddesi no. 20 has been reported to be good for women travellers.

There are several campsites, but Yeşilyurt (Tel. 574 4230) or Atakfiy (Tel. 559 6000) are 2 of the nicest. Camping Florya is excellent, with its own stretch of beach and a cheap restaurant/bar. Take the local train to Florya and prepare for a half-hour walk.

Don't try sleeping rough in Istanbul, it's not worth the risk; there are too many stories of muggings and rape. Don't bother with the black market here either, as police informers are out in abundance, especially in summer, and manage to make a good living out of turning in mugs who accept their offers. The same goes for drugs.

EATING AND NIGHTLIFE

You'll be pleasantly surprised on both scores here. It's possible to eat exceptionally well for next to nothing, whether you eat from the street stalls or at top restaurants. Fish and seafood are particularly good: go down to the Galata bridge where there are dozens of seafood restaurants, or eat from the pavement fish-grilling stalls. If you've saved sufficient by getting into cheap accommodation, treat yourself to a proper Bosphorus meal (about 40,000TL) of *meze* (mixed starters) and fresh fish. You'll have no trouble finding plenty of suitable places to patronize. The area behind the station (Eminonu) is a good one. Our only particular recommendation is the Murat Restaurant on Ordu

Caddesi, Aksaray, which does reasonable menus at good prices, next to the Hacibozan Ógullari Baklavaci.

Don't bother with the fabricated Westernized nightlife of discos and nightclubs. To get a taste of real Istanbul, eat late and wander along Meşrutiyet Caddesi and sample the music in the little cafés. Sultanahmet Square will also be lively but can get pretty seedy late-on. There are a few pubs in the area, however, where you'll meet up with other eurorailers and hitchers. One in particular worth a visit is the Pudding Shop, on Divan Yolu Caddesi (off the Sultanahmet), which is one of Europe's classic meeting places, like Harry's Bar in Venice.

The Istanbul Festival from mid-June to mid-July is no longer so classically minded and now features lots of jazz, folk and rock acts. Ask at Tourist Information for details. If you're after belly dancing, head for the Galatasaray district and Istiklasl Caddesi; or if you've promised yourself an authentic Turkish bath, ask at Tourist Information for their recommendations. Cağaloglu Hamami at Yerebatan Cad in Cağaloglu is excellent – the full works for 50–60,000TL.

North-West Turkey

BURSA This was, for a short while, the capital of the Ottoman Empire. It is a popular resort area because it is only 20 minutes from the sea and is also close to the best-known Turkish ski resort ULUDAG. You can get to Bursa by taking a ferry from Istanbul to Yalova and then a bus.

While in Bursa see the GREAT MOSQUE, GREEN MOSQUE and GREEN TOMB. Nearby are 2 interesting museums, the ETHNOGRAPHIC MUSEUM and the TURKISH AND ISLAMIC ART MUSEUM (entrance 15,000TL, closed Mondays, students half price).

Tourist Information is in the centre of town near the covered market. For accommodation try the Yeni Ankara at 48 Inebey Caddesi, along Tahtakale Caddesi, or camp on top of Uludag at Millipark Camping (take the cable car).

ÇANAKKALE This is the scene of the First World War Dardanelles campaign and the Trojan campaign. The bus from Bursa takes about 5½ hours (costs around £3). In Çanakkale itself there is a museum with archaeological artefacts from Troy and a CASTLE with its First World War artillery and damage. A minesweeper in the park around the castle is now a monument to Atatürk, who was the Turkish commander during the Dardanelles campaign.

The helpful Tourist Office is next to the harbour. The best place to look for hotels is around the town centre. Çanakkale comes to life every August with the Troy festival.

Across the Dardanelles from Çanakkale lies the scene of the bloody campaign, and GALLIPOLI (Gelibolu) itself. You can take a ferry across to ECEABAT and then hire a taxi to look around the battlefield, where the ANZACS (Australia and New Zealand Army Corps) suffered horrendous losses at Anzac Cove in Churchill's ill-fated campaign. The whole peninsula is a vast war memorial and all cemeteries are well signposted and maintained. Full details from the Tourist Office.

Thirty-two kilometres south is TRUVA TROY. There are many buses from the bus station to Troy. The ruins of 9 separate cities are not that interesting in themselves, but with a bit of background knowledge and some imagination they are evocative, especially with the wooden horse replica.

Aegean Coast

KUŞADASI This town has not benefited from the growth of tourism, but it is a good base to explore the fascinating Greek and Roman site of Ephesus. To get to Kuşadasi, either take a train to Izmir and then a 2-hour bus ride or take the ferry straight from Istanbul. The small fortified PIGEON ISLAND is about the only thing worth a visit in Kuşadasi. The Tourist Office is in the port and is very helpful. There are many cheap sea-front hotels and pensions here, the best area being around Aslander Caddesi.

The real reason for coming here is EPHESUS EFES, a huge 2,000-acre site chock full of classical ruins, which can become incredibly hot during summer. To reach the site take a dolmus to Selçuk and ask to get off at Ephesus. It is best to look around yourself as tours can be very pricy. See the GRAND THEATRE, the TEMPLE OF HADRIAN and the FOUNTAIN OF TRAJAN just to name a few. The site is open each day 8 a.m.–6.30 p.m. and admission is about £5.

Three-and-a-half hours east by bus are the amazing white cliffs and thermal pools of PAMUKKALE. There are also ruins of the ancient city of HIERAPOLIS at the top of the cliffs.

Other classical ruins along the Aegean coast are BODRUM HALICARNASSUS and BERGAMA PERGAMON which are well worth a visit.

Ferries link a number of ports to the nearby Greek islands. Although fares are quite steep, this is a way of avoiding the sometimes nightmarish Athens–Istanbul run. Ferry services include Cesme–Chios,

Kuşadasi–Samos, Bodrum–Kos, Marmaris–Rhodes and Ayvalik–Lesvos. The cost of a single ticket is £16–20.

Mediterranean Coast

This coastline has many beautiful beaches and resorts and is a good place to unwind and relax, but beware: there are often thousands of other people there with the same objective. The train runs down to MERSIN, in the eastern part of the coast, which is a bustling place and is best passed through. The Tourist Office is at the harbour, near where Turkish Maritime Lines run a service to the Turkish-controlled NORTHERN CYPRUS (ferry $16, students get a 10% discount). If you go to northern Cyprus, get the immigration authorities to stamp a separate sheet of paper rather than your passport because you may not be allowed entry back into Greece if they see you have been to the Turkish-controlled area of Cyprus.

Small beach towns run along the coast west of Mersin. KOCAHASANLI can be reached by bus and is a large campground right on the beach, a beautiful place. Also try the town of KORYKOS, with its 2 scenic castles, 1 on an island offshore, and beaches. There is no shortage of pensions or campsites here.

Central Anatolia

Central Anatolia is a desolate plateau region of extreme temperatures. It is also home to the capital of modern Turkey, Ankara, and the old capital of the Seljuk Turks, Konya.

KONYA This is an important centre of Islam in Turkey and was once capital of the Seljuks. It is still a big pilgrimage centre. It was here that the famous Order of the Whirling Dervishes started. See the MONASTERY and TOMB OF MEVLANA, the founder of the Dervishes, the ARCHAEOLOGICAL MUSEUM and the MARKET.

The Tourist Office is on Mevlana Caddesi (Tel. 33 111074). For accommodation try the Çata1 Pansiyon (Tel. 33 114981), near the Tourist Office, or Otel Konfor, 51 Eski Garaj Caddesi (Tel. 33 113103). The cheapest beds are likely to be on the rooftop at Otel Mevlana, 1 Cengaver Sok (Tel. 33 119824).

Ankara city phone code: 4

Ankara was once a small, unimportant town, but in the 1920s Atatürk made it the capital of the new Turkish Republic and it has boomed ever since to become a sprawling metropolis which is now Turkey's largest city.

TOURIST INFORMATION

The main Tourist Office is at 121 Mustafa Kemal Bulvari (Tel. 229 2631 or 229 3661; you can also call freephone: 900 447090). There is also an information office at 4 Istanbul Caddesi. Ask for a map and the useful *Ankara Guide*. Both offices are open Mon.–Fri.: 8.30 a.m.–5.30 p.m., and in season 8.30 a.m.–6.30 p.m. and Sat. and Sun.: 8.30 a.m.–5 p.m.

ADDRESSES

POST OFFICE Atatürk Bulvari, open 24 hours with 24-hour currency exchange

AMEX Koc Bank, 58 Atatürk Bulvari (Tel. 418 1804); open Mon.–Fri.: 9 a.m.–4 p.m.

STUDENT TRAVEL Emek Işhani, Kat. 11 no.1109, Kizilay (Tel. 118 1326)

UK EMBASSY 46a Şehit Ersan Caddesi (Tel. 468 6230)

US EMBASSY Atatürk Bulvari 110 (Tel. 468 6110/28)

CANADIAN EMBASSY 75 Nenehatun Caddesi (Tel. 436 1275/79)

AUSTRALIAN EMBASSY 83 Nenehatun Caddesi (Tel. 446 1180/87)

MEDICAL HELP Hacettepe University Hospital, Hasircilar Caddesi (Tel. 310 3545)

STATION FACILITIES

Railway station on Hippodron Caddesi. Overnight services from Istanbul, also connections east.

SEEING

As the city is so sprawling a map is an excellent investment. The bus network is extensive – buy tickets in advance from street kiosks. ULUS is the old section of town where many of the sights are, including the citadel and the Museum of Anatolian Civilizations. The CITADEL is itself a small walled city with winding lanes, a great place to wander. The BAZAAR and a MOSQUE are also within the citadel's walls. The MUSEUM OF ANATOLIAN CIVILIZATIONS is a world-class museum with exhibits from the huge number of cultures which grew up in this cradle of civilization (open Tues.–Sun.: 9 a.m.–5.20 p.m., admission 35,000TL, student card holders half price) and is situated in a restored covered bazaar.

The other main sight of Ankara is the huge MAUSOLEUM OF ATATÜRK, the national hero, in a large park. It is a monument to the man whose adopted name means literally 'Father of the Turks'. There is also a museum of his life and personal effects; open Tues.–Sun.: 9 a.m.–12 noon and 1 p.m.–5 p.m. Also check out the ETHNOGRAPHIC MUSEUM and the TEMPLE OF AUGUSTUS.

SLEEPING

Most of the cheap places to stay are in Ulus. You could try the Cumhuriyet Student Hostel in Cebeci (Tel. 319 3634), open summers. Ask the Tourist Office for a list of hotels. Also try the Beyrut Palas Oteli at 11 Denizciler Caddesi (Tel. 310 8407) or the Otel Bulduk, Sanayi Caddesi 26 (Tel. 310 4915).

EATING AND NIGHTLIFE

Ulus does not have that great a selection of restaurants; try along the Çankiri Caddesi. The bazaar is always a good place to explore. To meet some Turkish students, try the Café Melodi on Atatürk Bulvari.

Eastern Turkey

The east of Turkey becomes wilder and harsher, that is until you get to LAKE VAN, where the land is green and the mountains are beautiful. But keep your eyes and ears open and survey the press for reports of disturbances, especially if you're a non-Muslim.

VAN The city is 5 km from the lake, the largest in Turkey. Outside it is the imposing CITADEL and ANCIENT CITY on the ROCK OF VAN, once the capital of the Urartian empire. There is also a small archaeological museum. The Tourist Office is at 127 Cumhuriyet Caddesi.

Other places to visit around the lake are the ARMENIAN CHURCH on the island of AKDAMAR or the scenic mountains around the town of HAKKARI. The ferry across Lake Van takes about 4 hours.

KARS This town, which lies in the north-east, is not too thrilling itself, but from here you can visit the incredible remains of the ancient Armenian city of ANI, 45 km away. For accommodation try Hayat Oteli, 155 Faikbey Caddesi. The Tourist Office on the corner with

Gazi Ahmed Mukhtar (Tel. 021 223000) will get you the permit you will need to visit Ani as it is very close to the border with Armenia. To get to the ancient city either rent a minibus, get a taxi or catch the early bus (6 a.m.). You have to buy your tickets for the entry to Ani at the museum in Kars. The ruins are very impressive but unexcavated and it is well worth a visit to this spooky abandoned city.

NOTES

....

....

....

....

....

....

....

....

....

....

....

....

....

....

....

....

....

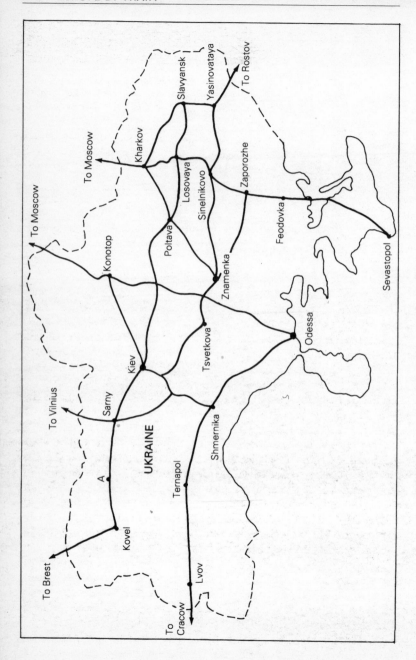

THE UKRAINE

Entry requirements	Passport and visa. All foreign nationals need a full passport and a visa, which should be bought in advance (£15 or $30) as there have been problems buying them at the border.
Population	52 million
Capital	Kiev
Currency	Ukrainian hryvna
	£1 = approx 3.0 hryvna
Political system	Republic
Religion	Russian and Ukrainian Autocephalous Orthodox
Language	Ukrainian, Russian: little English, some German spoken
Public holidays	1, 7 Jan., 8 March; 1, 2, 9 May, 24 Aug., 28 Oct.
International dialling	To Ukraine: international code + 7 + number
	From Ukraine: 810 country code number. International calls may be easiest made through a post office or (more expensively) a hotel.

The Ukraine is now very much its own country, independent of Russia and drifting further from it by the day. It uses a different currency, and you need a separate visa to visit: these are just 2 signs of the Ukraine's full emergence as a nation in its own right. Russia's appalling response to the 1986 Chernobyl disaster, allowing the Kiev May Day parades to go ahead 2 days after the explosion when fallout was over the city, has been seen as a catalyst to the Ukraine's long-sought secession. (It should be said from the start, however, that the risk of contamination to the visitor is minimal.)

With independence came problems: the Ukraine's economy is in as bad a state as Russia's and when visiting you should be aware that it is not a well-organized country. At times, it can seem that officials in different parts of the country, or even within the same city, have conflicting ideas about what the law is. Even more than in Russia, you will find that the locals expect all Westerners to be wealthy; try not to take the attempts of Ukrainians to milk this wealth as malicious. People in this poor country are understandably out for themselves.

Epidemics of cholera and diphtheria both raged in the 1980s. Though these are now under control, you should check your injections; a diphtheria booster is strongly recommended. Beware of the water and be particularly choosy about whom you kiss! You will also need to take your own toilet paper everywhere.

The Ukraine has a lot to offer, for all that many people don't even know where it is. Kiev is a beautiful city, Yalta a thriving resort, Odessa a diverse and fascinating port. Go to the Ukraine and you will have escaped the standard itinerary with a vengeance; go prepared, and a memorable time awaits you.

UKRAINIAN STATE RAILWAYS

Ukrainian trains are similar to Russian ones and most of what is written in the chapter on Russia applies here. This includes the cautionary note on getting out of the country again: you won't purchase a ticket west for anything other than hard currency, and although coupons may get you a ticket to a border town, the price for crossing the border will still be in dollars. Moreover, there are no hostels in the Ukraine which sell rail tickets. If you can't speak Russian, you'll have to write down all your train details on a piece of paper and present it to a station cashier with a pleading grin. If you're the type of person who needs a lifeline when going to a new country, postpone your visit until such time as the Ukraine sorts itself out.

The Ukraine is not in Inter-Rail or any other international rail scheme.

TRAIN INFORMATION

All information given in the Russia chapter applies here. Distances within the Ukraine are large, and many overnight trips are possible. Be prepared for a delay at the border as the track gauge changes.

TOURIST INFORMATION

As in Russia, there's no Westernized system of tourist information. *The Lonely Planet Guide* covers most Ukrainian places of interest, complete with maps, but don't expect accommodation tips: the situation is such that no guidebook can help you there.

VISAS The Ukraine started issuing its own visas in 1994, and the cost is now $30 (£15 if bought in the UK). Theoretically, visa restrictions are less stringent than in Russia, and the application form does not require a strict itinerary or proof of accommodation. You should be able to buy a visa on the border, but in practice this isn't always the case: buy one in advance if you can, and take a photocopy as well as the original. Once in the Ukraine you should register your arrival, either automatically when checking in at a hotel or by going to the local office of OVIR, the government ministry dealing with foreigners.

A cautionary tale: in the course of updating this guide, our researcher, equipped with a full Ukrainian visa, gained entry to the country with no problem. However, while changing money in Kiev, his passport was examined and suddenly he found himself under arrest;

he was escorted to the train station, put on a train by an armed guard, held for several hours at customs and eventually kicked out into Hungary, somewhat disillusioned by the experience. The only explanation he was given was that his visa was invalid, yet the Ukrainian embassy in London claimed there was nothing wrong with it. Unquestionably, this was just bad luck; but the story serves as a reminder that in a changing country the left hand often doesn't know what the right hand is doing: it's easy to get caught up in bureaucracy.

And after that charming tale, the UK address for visa applications is the Embassy of the Ukraine, Consular Department, 78 Kensington Park Road, London W11 2PL (Tel. 0171 229 2712).

MONEY MATTERS Ukrainian coupons, peculiar beasts resembling monopoly money, were introduced in 1993. Although the coupon was meant to be pegged to the Russian rouble, it rapidly went onto free fall, so in 1996 a new currency appeared, the hryvna. You can exchange most Western hard currencies in banks and hotel lobbies. As in Russia, hang on to exchange receipts: you may be asked to show them when you leave the country and coupons cannot be reconverted to hard currency without them (though even with them it's an arduous task). The advice on black-market money changing is that it's not only illegal but also unnecessary and you risk being cheated, it isn't worth it.

POST OFFICES Main post offices are open Mon.–Fri.: 8 a.m.–8 p.m. Many have long-distance phones. The Ukrainian postal system is even worse than its Russian counterpart.

SHOPS Shopping can be a complicated business: you have to go to the cashier's desk, point out what you want and buy a voucher for it. You then take the voucher and exchange it for your purchases. Hard currency shops here are called *kashtan*. Good buys include pottery and, should you have an unusually large amount of extra space in your backpack, rugs.

LANGUAGE Like Russian, Ukrainian is written in Cyrillic, and the 2 languages are very similar. Ukrainian has 2 extra letters which look like small 'i's, both neutral vowel sounds. Eighty per cent of words are similar to Russian, though the ones that aren't include 'yes', 'no', 'goodbye', 'thank you', 'good' and 'hotel' (*gotel*). Russian is spoken everywhere.

SLEEPING

If you're hoping for a trip with no worries about accommodation, either book through Intourist or forget it. Intourist, the state commission for foreign tourism in the Soviet Union, is still officially the agency all Western visitors are supposed to go through, but their prices are so extreme as to be prohibitive. The Ukraine doesn't yet have Russia's slowly evolving hostel network, and the problems Westerners face in Russian hotels are possibly worse here. Ask in Russian how much a bed is in a Kiev hotel and you may hear a price in the region of $2; give away your nationality and you will probably find it increased tenfold. One word of warning for tall travellers; Ukrainians tend to be short and the beds are built to fit!

Hotels run by the Central Council for Tourism and Excursions (CCTE), a domestic tourist agency, will probably charge you around $20 a night per person, and if you can live with that, they have a hotel in most major Ukrainian cities. Many other hotels are not officially open to foreigners and it is impossible to recommend individual ones because of their variability. Try your luck: haggle, look pleading and destitute, and you may get a bargain.

Because of this unpredictability, you may want to seek out locals offering accommodation – many stand outside hotels looking for potential customers. They will charge far less than a hotel, but obviously you have no guarantee of quality, or, for that matter, safety. Use your discretion.

A network of accredited youth hostels is being set up; for details contact Dr I. Fritsky, PO Box 547, 252001 Kiev (Tel. 38 44 2296946).

EATING

The Ukraine suffers the same food shortages as Russia, and has the same profusion of people selling pastries and cakes on street corners. The black market also thrives here. As regards restaurants, the fare is wholesome, if bleak, and the service as erratic as in Russia. Hard-currency restaurants exist throughout the Ukraine, providing a guarantee of assistance (Ukrainian menus aren't easily translated) at a cost. Ukrainians also share the Russian taste for vodka, even if most of it does taste like nail varnish remover.

Kiev (КИЇВ)

Kiev has a lot going for it: historic buildings, a lively atmosphere, a peerless setting on the Dniepr river added to the newfound importance of a national capital. Even if you're having a torrid time of it trying to find your way around the Ukraine, an afternoon spent lazing on the hills overlooking the river can make it all seem quite acceptable.

Most of the sights are located on the Dnepr's hilly west bank. Kiev's main street, Ulitsa Kreshchatik, runs along a valley towards the river, starting in the middle of town and ending at a 5 km stretch of parkland. Outlying Kiev isn't quite so picturesque: away from the old city, which dates back at least as far as the 9th century, the rest of the town is drab, concrete and evidently communist-built.

Lvov (ПЪВЁВ) city phone code: 0322

Lvov is the main city of the western Ukraine, and is more Central European than Russian. Ukrainian nationalism is at its strongest here. It's an industrial city, and suffers from bad pollution, but it is more than a stopping-off point for Kiev. The pleasant hilly setting, historic atmosphere and diverse architecture all make it well worth a visit. Lvov fans out from Ploshchad Rynok, the heart of the old city. Its main street, Prospekt Lenina, is to the west of the Rynok.

STATION FACILITIES

Lvov is the first city you'll reach if you're coming to the Ukraine from southern Poland. You'll also pass through it if entering from Slovakia or Hungary *en route* to Kiev. International trains run from Lvov to Budapest, Bratislava, Prague, Vienna, Belgrade, Bucharest, Sofia and Vilnius. Within the former Soviet Union, they run to Moscow, Kiev, Ternopol, Vinnitsa, Rovno, Chernovtsy and Simferopol (a station you'll visit if you're heading for Yalta). Lvov railway station is 3 km west of the centre, at the end of Ulitsa Vokzalnaya. There's no metro in Lvov, but trams 1 and 9 connect the station to Russkaya Ulitsa in the city centre.

TOURIST INFORMATION AND ADDRESSES

The Intourist Service Bureau is at the Hotel Intourist, Prospekt

Shevchenko 1. It's open 9 a.m.–12 noon and 1 p.m.–7 p.m. There's also a travel agency in the Hotel Dnestr, near the university. The Dom Knigi bookshop on Ploshchad Mitsvekicha sells a tourist map.

POST OFFICE Vulitsya Slovatskovo 1

CURRENCY EXCHANGE Vulitsya Hnatyuka, right off Prospekt Svobodi. Bank at Hotel Dneister, by Park Ivana Franka

SEEING

PROSPEKT LENINA has been an important centre for Ukrainian nationalism over the years, the parkland in the middle being a prime spot for impromptu speech-making. PLOSHCHAD RYNOK was the centre of Lvov life for 500 years from the 14th century. It is home to the LVOV HISTORY MUSEUM (open 10 a.m.–6 p.m., closed Wed.) and is surrounded by houses with a variety of interesting façades. Amongst Lvov's many churches are ST GEORGE'S CATHEDRAL, the former headquarters of the Uniate Church, and the 3-domed ASSUMPTION CHURCH on Podvalnaya Ulitsa. If you're culturally saturated, walk up CASTLE HILL (*Zamkovaya Gora*) for the views, or lie in IVAN FRANKA PARK to the west of the city.

SLEEPING AND EATING

CCTE use the Hotel Turist on Vulitsya Engelsa 103 (Tel. 351065); take tram no. 2 from Russkaya Ulitsa. Phone before turning up: the hotel is primarily for groups and may be full. Alternatively, the Hotel Georges on Ploshchad Mickiewicza 1 (Tel. 799011) may be worth a try. The campsite is 7 km from town on the Kiev road but may be worth a try if you can get out there (Tel. 721373).

Two recommended eateries are Pid Levan at Ploshchad Rynok 20 and Grono on Vulitaya Rileeva 12, but things change quickly in the restaurant business in this part of the world.

Odessa (ОДЕССА) city phone code: 048

Odessa, a busy port on the Black Sea, is also a thriving holiday centre. Endearingly seedy, it's a black market capital made up of a diverse variety of elements; the sort of place you'd imagine to be a haven for movie master criminals. It also has beaches. May and September are the best months to catch a bit of sun in a resort which couldn't be more different from the Costa del Sol if it tried.

The city follows a grid pattern, making orientation easy. It spreads back from the seafront which bends around the north, south and east of the city; the station and most hotels are central.

STATION FACILITIES

Odessa station is on Privokzalnaya Ploshchad, which is at the southern end of Pushkinskaya Ulitsa, one of Odessa's main streets. The station has direct links with Moscow, Kiev, Simferopol, Kishinyov, Izmail and Chernovtsy. Eurotrain are planning to include Odessa as one of their rail destinations.

Ferries from Odessa terminal on Morskoy Vokzal run to nearby beaches at (starting with the nearest) Lanzheron, Arkadia, Chayka, Kurortny and Chyornomorka. Arkadia is recommended.

There's no metro, but a comprehensive network of buses, trams and trolleybuses will get you where you want to go. The railway station is a terminus; so is Ploshchad Martynovskovo.

TOURIST INFORMATION AND ADDRESSES

Dom Knigi at Deribasovskaya Ulitsa 25 (about 10 blocks north from the station off Pushkinskaya Ulitsa) should sell maps, but tourist-orientated ones are a rarity. The official InTourist Office is at ulitsa Pushkinskaya 17, in the lobby of the Krasnaya Hotel.

POST OFFICE The main office is at Ulitsa Gorkovo, some way out, but there are many adequate smaller ones in the city centre, including bul. Sadovaga 8.

CURRENCY EXCHANGE Dendi Exchange, Ulitsa Pushkinskaya 54

MEDICAL Polyklinik, Ulitsa Sudostroitelnaya 21, will accept foreign patients if you're willing to part with hard currency.

TIPPING This is not normally expected, although always appreciated.

SEEING

PRIMORSKY BULVAR is very much the focus of Odessa. It's quite a place: beautiful 19th-century buildings, a strip of park leading towards the sea, and the famous POTYOVKIN STEPS (this is where Eisenstein set the crowd massacre in the film *Battleship Potemkin*). The film doesn't entirely hold true: there's no chapel at the foot of the steps, but a busy and polluted street. The steps start at the Richelieu statue halfway along the Primorsky Bulvar. These days there's an escalator alongside them.

A little way inland is PLOSHCHAD POTYOMKINTSEV; the area abounds with statues and monuments associated with the Crimean War.

Odessa also has several museums, including the ARCHAEOLOGICAL MUSEUM at Ulitsa Latochinka 4 (open daily 10 a.m.–5 p.m.).

SLEEPING AND EATING

Some travellers have reported getting a room in Sputnik's Hotel Bolshaya Moskovskaya at Deribasovskaya Ulitsa 29 (Tel. 22549) for

$4.50 per night, but standard Ukrainian hostel custom applies: it will depend on your approach and, very probably, their mood. The street is 2 blocks back from Ploshchad Potyomkintsev.

CCTE use the Hotel Turist, Genuezskaya Ulitsa 24a (Tel. 614057). Bus 129 from the station to the Ploshchad 10 Aprelya stop will get you there.

Intourist have a campsite at Camping Delfin, Doroga Kotovskovo 29, Luzanovka – 10 km north of the centre. The best way to get there is by ferry to Luzanovska pier, which is about 500m south of the campsite.

Klub-Kafe Chyornomprets on the corner of Pushkinskaya has a reputation for friendliness and the Kafe Kartoplyaniki off Ploshchad Potyomkintsev has also been recommended.

Simferopol, Yalta and the Crimea

The Crimea has been a favourite spot with Russian holidaymakers for over a century. Its popularity continues: millions visit the peninsula every year, focusing on Yalta (ЯЛТА). The Crimea offers beaches and resorts, mountain scenery, and history in abundance. Because of its large non-Ukrainian population, it's now claiming independence in its own right, so keep your eyes and ears open as this could affect prices, facilities, visas, etc.

The train will take you to Simferopol; you have to make your way south to Yalta by road.

STATION FACILITIES

Simferopol station, which is the main station for the Crimea, has connections to much of the former Soviet Union. Moscow is 21 hours away; you can also travel direct to Kiev, Kharkov, St Petersburg, Lvov, Minsk and Odessa. The station lies at the western end of Ulitsa Karl Marxa. If you want to visit the town itself, rich in historical points of interest, the station is about 2 km from the centre. It's a terminus for buses and trolleybuses, some of which stop on the forecourt, others on the road: trolleybus no. 5 will take you into the centre.

There are various ways of getting to Yalta from Simferopol: A metered taxi need not be prohibitively expensive provided you establish a price before you get in: bear in mind that it's 85 km. There are frequent buses and trolleybuses: the number 52 bus goes every 20 minutes or so and costs 3.50hv. Allow up to 3 hours for the trip. Yalta bus station is about 1½ km from the seafront, between Moskovskaya Ulitsa and Kievskaya Ulitsa. Almost any bus will take you into town.

Yalta port offers numerous sailings to Odessa, Sochi and Batumi. The status of foreigners on these passenger sailings is unclear: technically you're not allowed, but that may not make a difference. The sea terminal (Morskoy Vokzal) is at the end of Ulitsa Ruzvelta, which links up with Ulitsa Moskovskaya.

TOURIST INFORMATION

Naberezhnaya Lenina has a *Kashtan* hard-currency shop, a bookstall and post office; the only problem is that its name will have changed by the time this guide is printed. It runs along the seafront from the end of Ulitsa Kievskaya. You can also buy maps at the bookshop on Ulitsa Ruzvelta.

SEEING

South of Simferopol the Crimean mountains begin. The breathtaking scenery is accessible by trolleybus from Yalta. The beaches to the south aren't sandy and the water is polluted, yet they tend to be very full – Russians certainly seem to like them.

In Yalta, most people spend their days on the seafront promenade, which extends west to PRIMORSKY PARK. Many of Yalta's beaches are in front of this. There's a chairlift behind the Kafe Sochi which takes you up to the DARSAN VIEWPOINT.

Yalta was CHEKHOV'S home for his dying years and his house has become a museum. It's at Kirova 112 (open Wed.–Sun. 10 a.m.–7 p.m.). Take bus no. 8 from Sovietskaya Ploshchad.

The town also has a 'fairy-tale glade', POLYANA SKAZOK, full of figures from Russian children's literature cast in iron, concrete or wood. Bus 4 or 8 from the bus station will take you there: it's open 8 a.m.–8 p.m. between mid-May and September, shorter hours the rest of the year.

East of Yalta are the NITSKY BOTANICAL GARDENS (bus 29; closed Thurs. and Fri.).

The coastal area either side of Yalta has resorts and parkland, and trolleybus links make them good day-trips. ALUSHTA, GURZUF, LIVADIA and ALUPKA are all worth visiting.

SLEEPING

Sputnik uses the Hotel Krym, Moskovskaya Ulitsa 1–6 (Tel. 326061), where travellers claim to have got beds for as little as $2.25. Alternatively, try the accommodation bureau, which charges a few US dollars to direct you to rooms in their registered hotels. It's at Roosevelt Ulitsa 6 (Tel. 327873).

There is also a campsite 5 km away, a short distance past Polyana Skazok (see above for directions).

THE UNITED KINGDOM

Entry requirements	Passport
Population	57,100,000
Capital	London (pop.: 7,550,000)
Currency	Pound
	$1 = approx £0.65
Political system	Constitutional monarchy
Religion	Protestant
Language	English, with Welsh and Gaelic in some areas
Public holidays	1, 2 Jan; (17 March in Northern Ireland); Good Friday; Easter Monday; 1st and last Mondays in May; (12 July in Northern Ireland); (1st Monday in August in Scotland), last Monday in August; 25, 26 Dec.
International dialling	To the UK: international code 44 number
	From the UK: 00 +country code number

Even the British get confused about their nationhood, so it's not uncommon to hear 'England', 'Great Britain' and 'the United Kingdom' used incorrectly in conversation. But as a first, can I stress that the island of Great Britain isn't just England; it comprises Wales and Scotland too. Add to this Northern Ireland and you have the United Kingdom, or UK for short. From a traveller's point of view, the United Kingdom offers a diversity of not just geography but of history and culture too – all you'd expect of a country made up of 4 separate nations.

England, the largest of the 4 countries, has been the first target of the majority of immigrants from pre-Celtic times to the present day. The last successful invasion was back in 1066 when the Normans took over. After a power struggle among the nobles the barons were in a position to lay down the law and force King John to recognize their rights in the Magna Carta. By the end of the Tudor era Henry VIII had been through 6 wives and England was a prosperous nation. The 17th century saw a Civil War and England became the first country in Europe to cut off its king's head and try direct rule by Parliament. After a few years they decided it had been a bad move and invited Charles II to come to the throne. The 18th century began with the union of England and Scotland and continued with the development of the British Empire in North America and India. Britain was the world's leader in the Industrial Revolution and became known as 'the workshop of the world'. The economic strain of being heavily involved in 2 World Wars and increased rivalry in the marketplace has led to her decline as a world power.

Physical isolation from mainland Europe is one aspect of British life which no longer exists. After a lot of political and economic huffing and puffing which nearly bankrupted its builders, the Channel Tunnel finally opened in 1995 and although the project has been fraught with setbacks and delays, 'Eurostar' train services are finally beginning to catch on. At present, London, Lille, Brussels and Paris are all now one happy high-speed family, with plans to extend to other French and Belgian stations as well as cities in northern Germany and the Netherlands. It will then be possible to travel direct from, say, Glasgow to Cologne, or even to the south of France.

BRITISH RAILWAYS

British railway services have all been franchised to 25 different operating companies, with the track and stations being owned by another company, Railtrack. The speed and quality of services, as well as the types and prices of tickets available, all vary considerably between the companies.

In terms of speed and comfort, the Intercity 225 and other Intercity services rank almost on a par with France and are certainly as good as in Germany although, as in most other countries, the commuter services could be improved. There are 5 main categories of train:

1. The electric InterCity 225s on the main route from London to Scotland.
2. InterCity 125s, the fast diesels operating at speeds up to 125 mph, are still used on most long hauls.
3. The other Intercity services are either diesel or electric and reach 110 mph on long runs.
4. A network of cross-country trains supplementary to the main Intercity routes and avoiding transfers in London.
5. Local trains which run on more out-of-the-way routes or in the suburbs of the large towns.

There are no supplements to worry about on any of these services. There are also the Eurostar trains through the Channel Tunnel, which need special tickets, and special express trains to the different London Airports, although with the latter you will get better value by getting the ordinary local trains to the same destination

PASSES AVAILABLE The operating companies had to promise to keep the former British Rail's system of passes and through tickets, at least at first; however, there is no guarantee that they will continue to do so in future, or maintain prices. They currently operate several special tickets, depending on how much of the country you want to see. The All-Line Ticket, valid for either 7 or 14 days, costs £250 or £410 respectively for standard class tickets, with children aged 5–15 paying 66% of the appropriate adult fare, and is valid for all stations, for Sealink ferry services to the Isle of Wight, and a 20% reduction on the Windermere Iron Steamboat Company's steamers in the Lake District.

For travel only inside certain parts of England and Wales there are a total of 19 regional rover tickets available for 7 consecutive days between Easter and October, and also FlexiRovers for either 4 days out of 8, or 3 days out of 7, in some areas. They cost from £25 to £64. All prices are standard class, with restrictions limiting journeys to times outside of weekday morning rush hours only.

For visiting or staying in Scotland, the Freedom of Scotland TravelPass costs £99 for 8 days and £139 for 15 days: available only in standard class and giving you free use of some Caledonian MacBrayne ferry sailings. (Note: ScotRail is the name of the train operator in Scotland.)

The Freedom of Wales pass, good for 7 days, costs £54 June–Sept., £49 otherwise, while the Northern Ireland Rail Runabout, valid for 7 days from April to October, costs £25.

The BritRail Pass and Flexipass are available only outside the UK to those under 26 and are valid for 8 or 15 days in a month or 15 days in two months. Another option is the BritRail Pass + Ireland, which covers both the whole of the British Isles, including ferry crossings. For more information and details of prices of these passes, see Travelling Europe by Train: Options.

INTER-RAIL BONUSES

Inter-Railers are entitled to a third off ticket prices in Britain plus discounts on fares from London to most Continental ports. The following ferry services give discounts:

Company	Route	Reduction
Stena Line	Dover–Calais	50%
	Newhaven–Dieppe	50%
	Harwich–Hoek van Holland	50%
	Fishguard–Rosslare	50% (ship); 25% (Lynx)
	Holyhead–Dun Laoghaire	50%
	Stranraer–Larne	50%
	Stranraer–Belfast	50%
Holyman/Sally Ferries	Ramsgate–Ostend/Dunkirk	50%
Hoverspeed (Hovercraft)	Dover Hoverport–Calais	50%
Hoverspeed (Seacat)	Folkestone–Boulogne	50%
Irish Ferries	Holyhead–Dublin	50%
P&O (European Ferries)	Dover–Calais	50%
P&O (European Ferries)	Portsmouth–Le Havre	50%
P&O (European Ferries)	Portsmouth–Cherbourg	30%
Scandinavian Seaways	Harwich–Esbjerg	50%
	Harwich–Gothenburg	50%
	Newcastle–Amsterdam	50%
	Newcastle–Gothenburg	50%
	Newcastle–Hamburg	50%
	Newcastle–Esbjerg	50%

TRAIN INFORMATION

All main stations have their own information counters and there are free timetables for the main-line routes.

RESERVATIONS Compulsory on certain services, as indicated by [R] in the timetable, but advisable on all main lines in summer, particularly on holiday weekends. Cost £1 for standard class for up to 4 people travelling together, £2 each for first class.

NIGHT TRAVEL No couchettes, only sleepers at £27 for standard-class ticket holders sharing a 2-berth compartment, £30 for first class. A bonus is free tea and biscuits in the morning. All sleepers are air-conditioned and modern.

EATING ON TRAINS Expensive restaurant cars run on all main lines, Mon.–Fri. Buffet cars with average-priced snacks run daily on the major routes, while many local trains have trolley services offering a fairly uninspiring range of selections.

SCENIC TIPS There's nothing in Britain to compare with Switzerland or Norway, but the Lake District and parts of North Wales are interesting enough. The really scenic routes are up in the Scottish Highlands, particularly the Inverness–Kyle of Lochalsh and Glasgow–Oban and Mallaig runs. Ask for the *Scenic Rail Journeys* leaflet at the British Tourist Authority.

BIKES There are no facilities for hiring out bikes at British stations, so ask at the Tourist Office for local suggestions. Space to take bicycles on trains is often very limited – you nearly always need to reserve a place in advance and pay a fee.

COACH TRAVEL If you have bought your Inter-Rail Card in the UK or are travelling with a Eurail Pass, you can save money travelling to London and on to Dover with National Express (Caledonian Express in Scotland). They travel to 1,500 locations. A single from Edinburgh to London can be as low as £16. Those under 25 can get a 33% Discount Card for £8. Go to the Victoria coach station in London or any travel agent.

TOURIST INFORMATION

Every major city or town has its own Tourist Information office, and they will fix you up with accommodation for a fee of around £2–4 or 10% and supply you with maps and leaflets. There are also regional and national tourist boards who supply information.

ISIC BONUSES Up to 50% reduction at some monuments where you have to pay, but (in the main) museums and galleries are free.

For further information, contact ISIC, London Student Travel, 52 Grosvenor Gardens, London SW1W DAG (Tel. 0171 730 3402) or NUS Travel, 12 Dublin Street, Edinburgh (Tel. 0131 556 6598).

MONEY MATTERS 1 pound (£) = 100 pence (p).

Basic banking hours are generally Mon.–Fri.: 9.30 a.m.–4 p.m., but most banks now expand on this, particularly in cities, and stay open until 5 p.m. You may find some banks in Scotland opening late on a Thursday, while in England some banks open on Saturday morning. There is widespread use of cash dispensers. Beware of unfamiliar *bureaux de change* which charge high commissions and have poor exchange rates.

Scottish banks issue their own notes and you may get some funny looks if you use them in England, although they are perfectly legal. When leaving the UK try to swap them for English notes, as the others might as well be from Paraguay when it comes to trying to change them in some other countries.

POST OFFICES Open 9 a.m.–5.30 p.m., with sub-post offices generally closing for lunch and closing at 1 p.m. on Saturday.

SHOPS 9 a.m.–5.30 p.m Mon.–Sat. is the basic. Some small stores take lunch breaks, while in London and major cities shops are open late on several days of the week. Most cities have shops that stay open very late and open on Sundays.

MUSEUMS Generally open 10 a.m.–5 p.m.

TIPPING Generally add 10–15% to restaurant bills and taxi fares.

SLEEPING

The wonderful institution of bed and breakfast (B&B) is the cornerstone of accommodation in Britain, and between B&Bs and youth or student hostels you should easily get by. B&Bs average £15–20 (£25–30 in London) and this includes an English breakfast (bacon, eggs, etc.) which should keep you going all day. Always go for small B&Bs where you'll feel like one of the family and will get good value for money. Hotels in Britain are very expensive and are best avoided. Many universities let out their student flats and hostels in summer, and these average about £15 a night. Youth hostels charge according to your age, location and the facilities on offer. Expect to pay £5.65–£12.50. If you're thinking of doing much hostelling, pick up the *YHA Guide to England and Wales*, *Scotland YHA Guide* or *Northern Ireland YHA Guide*, which will show you the locations, etc., of the hostels. It's possible to join the IYHF at most of the large hostels for around £10 (£5 for under-21s). As far as camping goes, the vagaries of British weather may make this a dicey proposition, but if you're keen count on £5 a night and bring mosquito repellent and warm clothes.

The English, Scottish, Welsh and Northern Irish Tourist Boards have guides called *Where to Stay* at £6.95, £2.25, and £2.50 respectively. These aren't bad, though a bit sparse on cheap suggestions. You'll do better getting lists of local campsites and accommodation from Tourist Information, or using their bed-booking service from about £2–4 or 10% commission.

EATING AND NIGHTLIFE

British food has a bit of a bad reputation, but during the past decade or two much has been done to overcome this, and eating out in Britain today is no longer an expensive and tasteless affair. If you've got the cash, go for the traditional dishes like roast beef and Yorkshire pudding, or Scottish salmon or beefsteak. Often you'll find these on the set-lunch menus offered by hotels, and this is your chance to cash in and sample them at a reasonable price (£5 upwards). Always check if VAT (a 17½ % tax) is included in the price, before deciding.

For your picnics, look out for the impressive variety of British cheeses – Cheddar, Cheshire, Wensleydale, Double Gloucester, Stilton, etc. – and shop at stores like Asda, Marks & Spencer, Tesco, Waitrose, Safeway and Sainsbury's, where you can be sure the produce is fresh and reasonably priced.

While in the UK, at least once try to partake in the age-old custom of afternoon tea. This filling snack of scones, jam, cream and tea is often served in even the most luxurious hotels for only a few pounds, and it really gives an insight into the civilized Britain of yesteryear.

It's possible to make out in Britain on very little indeed if you know where to look. All major centres have fast-food chains of some description, and even the smallest village has its own local fish 'n' chip shop where you can fill up for about £2. Chinese and Indian meals are also good value, as (in general) are pub lunches. In towns, many churches open cheap cafés at lunchtime which can give you a good value snack, while the refreshment-rooms attached to the more historic cathedrals are an atmospheric place to try afternoon tea.

The pub is the mainstay of British social life and this is where you should make for to meet the locals. Many pubs, however, are soulless places and don't merit 5 minutes of your time, so be selective and choose either one with a historical connection or those that go to the effort of putting on live music. Pubs open 11 a.m.–11 p.m. (10.30 p.m. in some areas), though some still close between 2 or 3 p.m. and 5.30 p.m. You must be over 18 to drink alcohol. The English and Welsh pride themselves on their 'real ale', the Scots on their whisky and the Irish on their Guinness.

London is the home of British theatre and cinema – but this doesn't mean other cities are dead ducks. Edinburgh's International Festival and Fringe in August puts London in the shade for the 3 weeks it's on. In general, the live music and dancing scene is better in Britain than in most other European countries. Liverpool and Manchester are frequently ahead of London for trend-setting. Pick up the Tourist Board's list of current happenings for whichever town you're in, and remember to try for student discounts on theatre tickets, etc.

London city phone code: 0171 (inner London), 0181 (outer London)

London is a must in any European wanderings. There are 3 Londons to take into account: the CITY of London (the financial and administrative centre), WESTMINSTER (the political, royal and religious centre), and the WEST END (home of the British theatre, cinema, smart shops and clubs). Each area has a different feel to it, and the combination of all 3 with over 1,000 years of history and traditions, plenty of open green spaces and the buzz of Europe's largest city, makes a visit here unforgettable.

STATION FACILITIES

There are 8 major stations in London, all interconnected by Underground or 'Tube'. To ensure you find the right one, here's a quick checklist of destinations served by these stations:

CHARING CROSS Handles suburban lines and the London–Folkestone and London–Hastings trains.

EUSTON Central England and the north-west, Birmingham, Coventry, Liverpool, Manchester, Glasgow and trains for the ferries to Ireland.

KING'S CROSS The north-east, Leeds, York, Hull, Newcastle and on to Edinburgh and Aberdeen. From Newcastle you can sail to Norway, Denmark and Sweden.

LIVERPOOL STREET The area north-east of London, Cambridge, Harwich, Norwich. From Harwich you can sail to the Netherlands, Germany, Sweden, Norway and Denmark.

PADDINGTON The south-west of England, Exeter, Plymouth, Penzance, Bristol, Swansea, Oxford, Gloucester.

ST PANCRAS Trains bound due north, Nottingham, Derby, Leicester, Sheffield.

VICTORIA South-east England, Newhaven, Brighton, Eastbourne, Hastings and Dover, the main gateway to France, and from there to Spain, Italy, etc. The 30-minute train journey to Gatwick Airport leaves from here too. If you're travelling by hovercraft to France, this is also where you depart for Dover Priory. The International travel office is here.

WATERLOO Trains to the south of England, Bournemouth, Portsmouth, Southampton and Weymouth. Waterloo International is also the home of Eurostar connections to Europe via the Channel Tunnel.

TOURIST INFORMATION

The Tourist Information centre at Victoria station forecourt carries information on London. Leaflets, maps, guidebooks, tourist tickets for buses and the Underground, and sightseeing tour and theatre tickets are available. Same-day hotel accommodation can also be booked. The centre is open 7 days a week, 9 a.m.–8.30 p.m. with longer hours in July and August.

Liverpool Street station also has a Tourist Information centre open Mon.–Fri.: 9.30 a.m.–6.30 p.m., Sat.: 8.30 a.m.–6.30 p.m., Sun.: 8.30 a.m.–3.30 p.m. and provides information on London.

The British Travel centre provides information on all of the United Kingdom and is located at 12 Lower Regent Street, Piccadilly Circus, London SW1, open Mon.–Fri.: 9 a.m.–6.30 p.m., Sat. and Sun.: 10 a.m.–4 p.m. (open later on Saturday May–Sept.). Information on Northern Ireland is available from the Ireland desk of the British Travel Centre. The Scottish Tourist Board is at 19 Cockspur Street, London SW1, and is open Mon.–Fri.: 9 a.m.–5 p.m. The Welsh Tourist Board has an information desk in the British Travel Centre.

The City of London Information Centre, with detailed information on the City as well as more general information, is directly across the road from St Paul's Ccathedral. It is open Mon.–Fri.: 9.30 a.m.–5 p.m., Sat.: 10 a.m.–4 p.m. during Apr.–Sept. and 9.30 a.m.–12 noon Oct.–March. There is also a telephone information service on 0171 332 1456 from 9 a.m.–6 p.m. Monday to Friday.

Gay and lesbian information is available by calling in at Gay's the Word booksellers, 66 Marchmont St, WC1.

ADDRESSES

POST OFFICE King Edward Building, King Edward Street (tube: St Paul's), open Mon.–Fri.: 8 a.m.–7 p.m., Sat.: 9 a.m.–12.30 p.m. This is where all *poste restante* mail will end up. The 24-hour post office is at St Martin's Place, Trafalgar Square

AMEX 6 Haymarket (tube: Piccadilly). Exchange open Mon.–Fri.: 9 a.m.–5 p.m., Sat.: 9 a.m.–6 p.m. (8 p.m. in season), Sun.: 10 a.m.–6 p.m. (Tel. 0171 930 4411)

IRISH EMBASSY 17 Grosvenor Place, W1 (Tel. 0171 235 2171) (tube: Bond Street)

US EMBASSY 24 Grosvenor Square, W1 (Tel. 0171 499 9000) (tube: Bond Street)

CANADIAN HIGH COMMISSION MacDonald House, 1 Grosvenor Square, W1 (Tel. 0171 629 9492) (tube: Bond Street)

AUSTRALIAN HIGH COMMISSION Australia House, The Strand (Tel. 0171 379 4334) (tube: Aldwych)
NEW ZEALAND HIGH COMMISSION New Zealand House, Haymarket (Tel. 0171 930 8422) (tube: Charing Cross)
EUROTRAIN Tel. 0171 730 3402, or kiosk at Victoria station (Tel. 0171 630 8132)
WASTEELS 121 Witton Road, SW1 (Tel. 0171 834 7066)

GETTING ABOUT

The tube is expensive and often crowded. Pick up an Underground map, free at any station, and hang on to your ticket till the journey's through, because you cannot get back out without it. Tubes run 5 a.m.–12 midnight. Like the tube, the red double-decker buses operate on a zone system, and you pay the driver or conductor on the bus, while the single-decker Red Arrows are express buses with ticket machines on board. There is an excellent network of night buses which run 12 midnight–5 a.m. on certain routes; all leave from Trafalgar Square.

If you're in London for a while, pick up leaflets on the London Travelcards which are valid on tubes, buses and local train services. Cards vary in cost from zone to zone, and according to whether or not they cover non-Underground rail services in and around London; they are not valid on night buses. Cards for longer periods require a photograph. Most of the sights are in zones 1 and 2; a one-day Travelcard for these costs £3.20. It is also possible to buy a book of 10 zone one tickets for £10, saving £1.

For trips from elsewhere in south-east England an inclusive travelcard is available – get it or a voucher for it before you leave for London. You can get one for a day or a week and it comes with a wallet of discount vouchers. If you won't be taking a tube until after 9.30 a.m., and providing that you want to return to the same place the same day, a cheap day return will save you 30%.

Unless you're in a desperate rush, don't bother with the expensive taxis.

A *London A–Z* (about £3.50) is the best long-term map investment you can make.

SEEING

London has swallowed many villages into its bulk in the course of its development, but even today each village (now district) has its own character and traditions. Soho, Hampstead and Chelsea are as different from each other as individual towns. It's easy to divide London into its 3 sections but this would neglect the areas that fall between, like trendy COVENT GARDEN, or the intellectual centre of BLOOMSBURY, where the BRITISH MUSEUM and parts of LONDON UNIVERSITY are located. Don't forget either the wonderful days out you can have at the maritime centre of GREENWICH, or at the Royal Botanical Gardens at KEW, or HAMPTON COURT PALACE, and many more. This rundown is just a small sample of what you can see, but once you've made your visit to Tourist Information, you should be in a position to work out your own best itinerary.

THE CITY OF LONDON

The London of the 11th century is that area known as 'the City'. In this 'square mile', the wheelings and dealings of the Stock Exchange and big business take place, and the Bank of England and Royal Exchange have their headquarters here.

The sights include the beautiful Renaissance cathedral of ST PAUL'S (the one Charles and Di chose for their wedding in 1981), where Nelson, Wellington and Wren are buried; FLEET STREET, the former home of the British press; the INNS OF COURT and the OLD BAILEY, the heart of the British legal system; and the TOWER OF LONDON, which dates back to William the Conqueror and has served as prison, palace and mint. The Crown Jewels, the White Tower and Tower Green where Henry VIII had Anne Boleyn and Katherine Howard executed are among some of the sights to see here in the splendid Jewel House.

Near the Tower is the famous TOWER BRIDGE. The TOWER HILL PAGEANT, opposite the Tower, takes visitors in computer-controlled cars on a journey back to London in Roman times through to today. At the foot of Tower Bridge, on the southside of the Thames, is the newly developed BUTLER'S WHARF. This incorporates restored historic buildings and modern commercial units such as Sir Terence Conran's GASTRODOME.

The BARBICAN is also in the City (tube: Barbican or Moorgate). This arts centre has concerts, plays and exhibitions as well as the superb MUSEUM OF LONDON, which costs £4 and is open Tues.–Sat.: 10 a.m.–5.50 p.m., Sun.: 2 p.m.–5.50 p.m.

WESTMINSTER AND THE WEST END

Roughly, this stretches from HYDE PARK (the famous expanse with Speakers' Corner, a national venue for impromptu free speech on Sundays) to WESTMINSTER ABBEY, the incredible Gothic church so central to the country's history, where British kings and queens have been crowned for centuries. WHITEHALL and the HOUSES OF PARLIAMENT, the centres of British government and administration, are along here, and so is the timekeeping landmark of London, BIG BEN. To go in and listen to Parliament (a fascinating experience), line up at St Stephen's entrance opposite the abbey.

THE MALL is the boulevard leading from TRAFALGAR SQUARE, home of the NATIONAL GALLERY, to BUCKINGHAM PALACE, the home of the monarchy. The palace's state apartments are open each year from early August to the start of October, 7 days a week. The 18-room tour affords a glimpse of life inside one of the world's most famous homes ('afford' being the operative word: it costs a hefty £9 to get in, and the price of souvenirs is pretty steep too).

The hub of the capital is PICCADILLY CIRCUS with its statue of Eros. LEICESTER SQUARE, London's movie centre, is near here. Just to the north is SOHO; the recent cleaning up of this area means that it no longer lives up to its seamy reputation, except as a rip-off for tourists. London's CHINA TOWN is here, centred on Gerrard Street. To the east is COVENT GARDEN, once a vegetable market, now a shopping arcade. You can normally catch some excellent street performances here, which are well worth waiting around for.

The BRITISH MUSEUM (tube: Tottenham Court Road or Russell Square) is worth at least a day of anyone's time (everything, from the Elgin Marbles to Magna Carta is here). The other main museums are at South Kensington: the VICTORIA AND ALBERT, the NATURAL HISTORY, and the SCIENCE MUSEUMS are all next door to each other. Most of these now charge a donation of £5–6 for entrance (students free).

The ROYAL ALBERT HALL is close by. See the posters outside for what's on. The Proms concerts are held here from July to September and provide an excellent source of cheap classical entertainment. Queues can form up several hours before the doors open; down the steps around the back of the hall, on the opposite side to Hyde Park.

The famous department store HARRODS, where you can buy 'absolutely anything', is in KNIGHTSBRIDGE. Wander round the food hall there – they sell every type and variety of eats you'd ever imagined, and sample tastings are free. Other shops worth taking in for their sheer entertainment value are LIBERTY'S (the neo-Tudor building on Regent Street) and FORTNUM & MASON, Piccadilly. Excellent shopping is also available right along OXFORD STREET.

MADAME TUSSAUD'S wax museum, where the famous are immortalized, is on the Marylebone Road (tube: Baker Street). Shakespeare's GLOBE THEATRE has been reconstructed on its original site on the banks of the Thames at 1 Bear Gardens, Bankside. If you are tired of the city's rush, head into one of the parks – row on the Serpentine (Hyde Park) or look out for the Buddhist Pagoda in Battersea Park. This also has the UK's tallest bungee jump and catapult tower.

SLEEPING

The possibilities are endless, but in the lower price bracket (under £20) you can't expect too much in the way of comfort. London is busy all year, but in the summer it's absolutely packed and advance booking is recommended. The London Tourist Board run an advance booking service from the Tourist Information centre on Victoria station forecourt. Booking can be made by credit card on 0171 824 8844, and on-the-spot booking can be made at the Tourist Information centres. Student and youth hostels average £17.50, halls of residence about £18 and B&Bs £25. Staying with a local family is becoming increasingly popular and there are an increasing number of agencies which will organize this type of accommodation. A minimum stay of a few days may be required, plus a deposit. Ask for details at the Tourist Information centre, Victoria station.

HOSTELS

There are 8 youth hostels: the recently renovated City of London youth hostel (36 Carter Lane, Tel. 0171 236 4965; tube: St Paul's); Holland House (Holland Walk, Kensington, Tel. 0171 937 0748; tube: Holland Park); Hampstead Heath (4 Wellgarth Road, Tel. 0171 458 9054; tube: Golders Green then bus 210 or 260); Earls Court (38 Bolton Gardens, Tel. 0171 373 7083; tube: Earls Court); Highgate (84 Highgate West Hill, Tel. 0171 340 1831; tube: Archway then bus 148, 210 or 271); 14–18 Noel Street (Tel. 0171 734 1613; tube: Oxford Circus), which is perhaps the most central; Rotherhithe (Salter Road, Tel. 0171 232 2114; tube: Rotherhithe); and the newest one, St Pancras (79 Euston Road, Tel. 0171 734 1618; tube: St Pancras).

A comprehensive list of all hostels can be obtained from Tourist Offices. Try some of the following: Tent City, Old Oak Common Lane (Tel. 0181 743 5708; tube: East Acton); Fieldcourt House, 32 Courtfield Gardens (Tel. 0171 373 0152; tube: Gloucester Road); Astor Museum Hostel, 27 Montague Street (Tel. 0171 580 5360; tube: Tottenham Court Road); International Students House, 229 Great Portland Street (Tel. 0171 631 3223; tube: Great Portland Street); Centre Français, 61 Chepstow Place (Tel. 0171 221 8184; tube: Notting Hill Gate).

STUDENT RESIDENCES

If you're staying a while, 2 good ideas are to contact either the London University Students' Union (Tel. 0171 636 2818) or King's College (Tel. 0171 928 2717). Although slightly more expensive than youth hostels, university residences generally have better facilities and are well located. They are obviously not available during term time.

BED AND BREAKFASTS

Some of the cheaper B&Bs are soul-destroying places and you're invariably better off in a hostel, but anyway the areas to head for are Earls Court, Paddington and Bayswater. Homestead Services (Tel. 0181 949 4455) will arrange B&B with London families for between £16 and £35, provided that you stay at least 3 nights.

HOTELS

Some of the better affordable hotels include the Luna & Simone Hotel, 47 Belgrave Road (Tel. 0171 834 5897; tube: Victoria) and the Leinster Hotel, 7 Leinster Square (Tel. 0171 229 9641; tube: Bayswater).

If you feel like treating yourself and are happy to stay a little way outside London, try the award-winning Chase Lodge, 10 Park Road, Hampton Wick, Kingston upon Thames (Tel. 0181 943 1862), which has 10 attractive rooms in the friendly surroundings of a Victorian house and garden.

CAMPSITES

There are 6 readily accessible campsites to London. Ask at Tourist Information for details. Arguably the best is Picketts Lock, Picketts Lock Lane, Edmonton (Tel. 0181 803 4756). Tube to Seven Sisters, rail to Lower Edmonton and then bus W8. Although 16 km from the centre, it is remarkably well equipped.

Overall, Tent City is probably the cheapest at under £5 per person. They have 2 sites: one in Hackney (bus 22a, 38 or 55, Tel. 0181 985 7656) and one in East Acton (Central line tube, Tel. 0181 743 5708). They open from June 1 to Aug. 30 and donate all profits to charity.

With violence on the increase, sleeping rough is not an option and the police are clamping down on the more favourable areas along the embankment at Westminster Bridge and in Hyde Park.

EATING AND NIGHTLIFE

Eating for under £5 is no great problem with the spate of fast-food chains, Indian and Chinese restaurants and very good supermarkets increasing every year. Many pubs serve lunches and, of course, there's always the great British invention, fish 'n' chips. Always check if VAT is included on a menu as this tax can fairly bump up the bill. You can't go too far wrong for fast-food in McDonald's, Pizzaland, PizzaHut or Burger King, but branches of Wimpy vary dramatically. For the best non-European meals, head for Soho and the excellent Chinese restaurants. Marks & Spencer, Safeway and Sainsbury's are all reliable for high-quality groceries, and if it's a good day you can do no better than get a picnic together and head for one of the parks.

For good value Chinese food, try the Man Lee Hong restaurant on Lisle Street near Leicester Square or Wong Kei, 41–43 Wardour Street. In Soho, try Poons, Leicester St Lee Ho Fook, Macclesfield St, and Chan May Mai, Lisle St, all are good value.

For Indian food, try around Bayswater, or, for unbeatable value, the Oval Tandoori restaurant at 64a Brixton Road SW9, which, although out of the centre, is worth the effort to get there.

For excellent crêpes, try Le Shop (formerly the Asterix Crêperie) at 329 King's Road, Chelsea SW3.

Vegetarians can't do much better than try Rhavi Shankar, 133–135 Drummond Street.

For a fairly cheap meal, try the Country Life vegetarian restaurant at 123 Regent Street, W1. Open Mon. 11.30 a.m.–6 p.m., Fri. 10.30 a.m.–3 p.m.

Nightlife and London are inseparable from each other. Your best source of information are the weekly magazines *Time Out* and *City Limits*. The theatre is firmly entrenched in London's nightlife, and you really ought to try and make it along to a show. Pick up the fortnightly *London Theatre Guide* at any theatre or information office. Take along your ISIC to any theatre displaying (S) in its write-up, and you will be able to get cheap standby tickets before the curtain rises. In summer there's open-air Shakespeare in Regent's Park. Expect an average theatre ticket to cost about £9. There's a half-price theatre ticket booth in Leicester Square selling standby seats.

There's music to suit all tastes on offer, from the 'Proms' classics in the Albert Hall to punk in The Marquee, 105 Charing Cross Road. Also try the Wag Club at 3–5 Wardour Street. Ronnie Scott's at 4–7 Frith Street is internationally known for jazz and expensive at £12 entrance (£6 students); rather cheaper is The Bass Clef at 35 Coronet Street.

There are endless lists of pubs and these are as good a place as any to watch the locals in their habitat. Try the Sherlock Holmes, 10 Northumberland St, the Sun in Lamb's Conduit St WC1, or Ye Olde Cheshire Cheese, just off Fleet St. The Firkin chain of pubs are well worth visiting. There are 3 in the city centre and several more spread round the periphery. The Goose & Firkin in Borough Road (tube: Elephant & Castle) has a piano player on Friday and Saturday nights which livens up the friendly atmosphere. The Flounder & Firkin is in Holloway Road in the north, the Ferret & Firkin is in Lots Road, Chelsea, the Phoenix & Firkin at Denmark Hill Station (9 minutes from Victoria) and the Fox & Firkin is in Tavistock Crescent in Notting Hill.

With over 4,000 pubs in London, you're bound to find one to your liking.

If you're after some 'heavy nightlife', a wander through Soho should take good care of that, or if you want to be entertained while having a drink, try the Allsop Arms, 137 Gloucester Place. The Centre at 12 Adelaide St WC2 is a good meeting-place for the under 25s. Leicester Square in particular is crawling with clubs, pubs and buskers.

Southern England

DOVER

If you're arriving from France or Belgium, chances are your first impressions will be of Dover, with its famous chalky white cliffs. It dates back to the Romans and there are still remains to be seen from their time.

If you've a bit of time to spend before making the direct 2-hour journey to London, take in the CASTLE, with its Roman PHAROS, the PAINTED HOUSE (a Roman townhouse off New St, closed Monday). Tourist Information is near Dover Priory Station and at Townwall St. They'll give you help with accommodation if you're staying overnight.

The youth hostel is at Charlton House, 306 London Road (Tel. 01304 205 108), and there's a summer-only YMCA Interpoint hostel at 4 Leyburne Road (Tel. 01304 206138) which costs £5.40.

CANTERBURY

An hour's journey from London, this ancient pilgrimage centre is famous for its CATHEDRAL, where St Thomas à Becket was murdered in 1170, and is well worth breaking your journey for. Note that in the UK, cathedrals and churches don't charge an actual entrance fee but do ask for a 'donation' and will often charge for extras such as nave tours, etc. The remnants of the old city walls can be seen at DANE JOHN GARDENS. ST MARTIN'S CHURCH has evolved from 4th-century Roman villas and is one of the oldest churches in England. There are various remains of long-defunct religious orders: ST AUGUSTINE'S ABBEY outside the city's East Wall, and EASTBRIDGE HOSPITAL on St Peter's Street, open Mon.–Sat.: 9.30 a.m.–5.30 p.m.

Food and beds shouldn't cause you any problems, but Canterbury can easily be seen as a day trip from London. The Tourist Office is at 34 St Margaret's Street (Tel. 01227 766567).

CHICHESTER

Lying 2 hours from the capital on the London–Portsmouth line, this is a charming market town and holds a summer theatre festival worth investigation. The ROMAN PALACE at nearby Fishbourne (open daily 10 a.m.–4 p.m.) has the best-preserved mosaic floors in the country. Tourist Information is at St Peter's Market, West St, open Mon.–Sat.: 9.15 a.m.–5.30 p.m.

WINCHESTER

This is a wonderful place, an archetypal English town. The CATHEDRAL is its pride, and rightly so. Walking down Cathedral Close, you'll come to WINCHESTER COLLEGE, England's first 'public' (private) school, which has nurtured the sons of the élite for 6 centuries. Winchester was the ancient capital of England under King Alfred the Great, and his statue stands at one end of the High Street. A good youth hostel is to be found in the City Mill, near the statue (Tel. 01962 53723).

Not far from here (on bus route 214) is CHAWTON, home of the English novelist Jane Austen, of *Pride and Prejudice* fame. Her house is open 11 a.m.–4.30 p.m.

Winchester is on the London–Weymouth line, about 1½ hours down the line from London.

BRIGHTON

This is an ideal spot for a day trip from the capital. Since the mid-18th century, it has been a popular holiday resort. In 1783 the ROYAL PAVILION was constructed when the Prince Regent came to settle here, and it's here and to the PALACE PIER you should head. Wander round the narrow streets from the Old Steine to West St. Tourist Information is in the Guildhall on the Broadway, open Mon.–Sat.: 9.30 a.m.–6 p.m., Sun.: 2 p.m.–5 p.m. in season.

Brighton has a reputation for hectic nightlife, no doubt influenced by the number of students in the town. Head for the Zap Club, Old Ship Beach, with live events every night.

For a cheap bed, try the reputedly good youth hostel on the outskirts of town at Patcham Place, London Road (Tel. 01273 556196).

PORTSMOUTH

Only 2 hours' journey from London Waterloo, Portsmouth is at the heart of Britain's maritime heritage. The naval dockyard contains a museum and 2 historic ships: HMS *Victory* (Nelson's flagship at Trafalgar) and HMS *Warrior* (Britain's first ironclad). The Tudor warship MARY ROSE is preserved in Portsmouth after being salvaged from the seabed. See SOUTHSEA CASTLE where Henry VIII stood as he watched

Mary Rose sink. Take the local train to Portchester and see the Roman and Norman castle with its huge keep and a church inside the walls.

A ferry leaves from Portsmouth to the ISLE OF WIGHT, which has a completely different feel from neighbouring Hampshire. Take a bus to Queen Victoria's favourite holiday retreat, OSBORNE HOUSE and enjoy the sandy beaches of SANDOWN and SHANKLIN.

SALISBURY

Dominated by its 13th-century CATHEDRAL (the tallest spire in England), the town has lots of character. Take the tour round the cathedral and visit the cloisters and Chapter House. CATHEDRAL CLOSE was a religious city and you can still see some of its buildings, especially MOMPESSON HOUSE, now cared for by the National Trust.

Salisbury is on the London–Exeter and Bristol–Portsmouth lines, 1½ hours from London.

This is the best place to stay if you want to visit the ancient religious site of STONEHENGE, 16 km north of Salisbury. If you know nothing of its history or aren't really interested, don't bother making the trip, as you won't understand what all the fuss is over. All that's there is a circle of stones – and it costs £2.85 (£2.15 for students) to look at them – but they probably date back as far as 2600 BC, and the huge bluestones were dragged around 400 km from Wales, so that makes them rather special. It's thought they were an astronomical calendar, and later on, in 250 BC, the Druids used them for their sun-worshipping festivals.

Another stone circle is at AVEBURY – the village is actually inside the circle, so it is free. Ask at Tourist Information about getting there. The Salisbury CITY MUSEUM in Cathedral Street has a fascinating exhibition which tells you everything but 'why' about the site.

The Salisbury Tourist Office is at Fish Row (Tel. 01722 334956), open Mon.–Sat: 9 a.m.–7 p.m. in season, and they'll help with accommodation. There's a youth hostel at Milford Hill (Tel. 01722 327572) and several reasonable B&Bs.

Bath

Just 15 minutes from the city of BRISTOL, and in the south-west corner of the Cotswolds, lies the elegant Georgian spa town of Bath. This town was second only to London for style in the 18th century; successive generations of the aristocracy came to 'take the waters' and left behind an architectural legacy as rich as you'll find in England. Trains run hourly from London and the journey takes only 75 minutes;

if you're travelling to Oxford you change at Didcot, and Bath's proximity to Bristol means you could also use it as a jumping-off point for Devon and Cornwall.

SEEING

The heart of Georgian Bath is the CIRCUS, the circle of townhouses where the artist Gainsborough lived at no. 17, and William Pitt, the Prime Minister, at nos. 7 and 8. Leaving the Circus at Brock St, you come to ROYAL CRESCENT, considered England's most attractive street. Visit no.1 for an idea of elegant Georgian living.

The MUSEUM OF COSTUME is particularly interesting, housed in the assembly rooms on the Circus. From the abbey churchyard you enter the ROMAN BATHS AND MUSEUM. Take the tour, and visit the PUMP ROOM where the hot spring water is pumped. This complex is open 9 a.m.–7 p.m. daily. If you're there in the mornings and fancy treating yourself to a taste of elegant British life, sit down in the Pump Room for a coffee and enjoy the sounds of The Pump Room Trio (Mon.–Sat.: 10 a.m.–12 noon).

SLEEPING

Tourist Information at The Colonnades (Tel. 01225 462831) will find you a room for a commission, or simply pick up a list of places. Open Mon.–Sat.: 9.30 a.m.–5 p.m. There's a youth hostel at Bathwick Hill (Tel. 01225 465674), about 1½ km from the city (take minibus 18 from Orange Grove, by the Abbey), and a YMCA house at Broad Street Place (Tel. 01225 460471) accepts both sexes. For B&Bs, look around the Wells Road or, for one nearer the station, try Prior House, 3 Marlborough Lane (Tel. 01225 313587), around £12.50 each.

There's a campsite 5 km out, at Newton Mill. It is very good and is served by bus 5 from the bus station (Tel. 01225 333909).

EATING AND NIGHTLIFE

There are plenty of bakers, pubs and supermarkets, so meals shouldn't pose any problems. The city market is good for fruit and vegetables, and Molehill Café, 14 George St, is about the best place in town. After 8 p.m., it becomes a club with live music. Take out a weekly membership for about a pound, if you're staying for a while. The Bath Festival is on in late May. Ask at Tourist Information for the monthly *What's On*.

Devon and Cornwall

Known as the 'West Country', this area is popular with artists and English tourists and is well known for its cream teas and strong cider. Resorts on the Devon and Cornish coasts are the only places in England where it is really possible to surf. The main centres to base yourself to explore the region are Exeter, Plymouth or Penzance.

EXETER

This is the county town of Devon and is dominated by its impressive medieval CATHEDRAL. From the station of St David's, take the bus into the centre. Tourist Information in the civic centre on Paris St (Tel. 01392 265700) will give you all you need on the region, including the national parks of DARTMOOR and EXMOOR.

While in Exeter, take in the 14th-century GUILDHALL and go for a drink in the SHIP INN where Sir Francis Drake went for a jar.

The youth hostel at 47 Countess Wear Rd, Topsham (Tel. 01392 873329), is a short distance out, but good (bus 187 or 356 from Paris St bus station). Alternatively, try the Exeter Student Guest House, 16 New North Rd (Tel. 01392 52493).

PLYMOUTH

A major port since the 14th century, it was here Drake spotted the Spanish Armada and from near here that the *Mayflower* set sail to colonize the New World. Spend an afternoon wandering round the Elizabethan BARBICAN QUAY, NEW STREET with its timber merchant houses and the ruins of the 14th-century castle.

PENZANCE

Right down at the end of the line, Penzance has a history of pirates and invaders, and makes an interesting day trip. The youth hostel at Castle Horneck is highly recommended (Tel. 01736 62666).

Take in the MARKET HOUSE and MORRAB GARDENS where subtropical plants flourish, thanks to the exceptionally mild climate. From Penzance you can sail out to the Scilly Isles, or visit ST MICHAEL'S MOUNT, 5 km east of the town – a castle and mountain where St Michael is said to have appeared. LAND'S END is most definitely worth a visit now you are this far south in England. There are some really scenic walks to do along the rocky cliffs, and you can have your picture taken with a distance post showing how far it is to John o'Groats in northern Scotland, and to your home town.

Oxford city phone code: 01865

Home of England's oldest and most highly prestigious university, which has dominated the town for over 700 years, Oxford lies 45 minutes from London's Paddington station, and can easily be taken in on a day trip from the capital.

TOURIST INFORMATION

Tourist Information is at St Aldate's (Tel. 726871); open Mon.–Sat.: 9 a.m.–5.30 p.m., Sun.: 10 a.m.–4 p.m. Pick up their leaflet on the city and an accommodation list.

STUDENT TRAVEL 13 High Street, open Mon.–Fri.: 9.30 a.m.–5.30 p.m., Sat.: 10 a.m.–3 p.m.

SEEING

Carfax Tower is at the centre, and from here most of the university colleges are only a few minutes away. CHRIST CHURCH, the 16th-century college with its beautiful library, housing the spoils of Henry VIII's monastic plunderings, is down St Aldate's. North of this is MERTON COLLEGE, dating from the 13th century and with a notably attractive chapel; and next door is ORIEL. Take Bear Lane now, then cross the High Street to reach BRASENOSE COLLEGE and ALL SOULS (probably the most prestigious collection of academics around, all specially appointed to the college). At the north end of the square is the BODLEIAN LIBRARY, built in 1602 and containing over 3 million books. The atmosphere in here must be sampled at first hand. MAGDALEN COLLEGE (pronounced 'Maudlin') on the High Street makes a lovely walk through its 15th-century cloisters, and the ASHMOLEAN MUSEUM on Beaumont Street (Italian and English art) is worth seeing. Turn up Cornmarket Street at Carfax and, after the new shopping centre, you'll reach BALLIOL and ST JOHN'S colleges. Opposite Balliol, Latimer and Ridley were burned by Bloody Mary in 1555, with Bishop Cranmer following a year later.

If you want to be terribly traditional, you've managed to hit a sunny afternoon, and you don't mind getting wet, hire out a punt at the CHERWELL BOATHOUSE for about £4 an hour. Oxford is also home to England's first rickshaw service, but it's not that cheap at £15 for a city tour.

Worth a quick mention here is BLENHEIM PALACE, birthplace of Winston Churchill and ancestral home of the Dukes of Marlborough. You can visit the mansion for £5 in season (bus 20 from Cornmarket Street).

SLEEPING

An accommodation search agency called Citycomm Ltd has an extensive database of all types of available accommodation in Oxford and its surrounding area. They will arrange accommodation according to individual requirements for a booking fee of £2.50 per person. The cheapest are likely to be college rooms during the summer from around £7.50. Citycomm is centrally located at 2 Market Street (Tel. 794994).

If you don't use the Tourist Office's or Citycomm's services, try calling in at the many B&Bs in Abingdon Road. The youth hostel is a little too like school to be comfortable; it's on bus routes 72 and Nipper 73 at Jack Straw's Lane (Tel. 62997). There is a backpacker's hostel at 9a Hythe Bridge St (Tel. 721761) and there's camping at Cassington Mill Caravan Park, 8 km out (Tel. 881490) and at Oxford Camping International (Tel. 246551) on Abingdon Road. Mrs Old at 58 St John Street (Tel. 55454) is also worth a try for B&B.

Oxford does get busy in summer, but owing to its proximity to London, it's possible to take it in as a day trip.

EATING AND NIGHTLIFE

There are plenty of places ideal for eurorailers since, though an Oxford student is supposedly a cut above the average, all students still look for the same type of things when it comes to eating and what to do at night.

Brown's Restaurant and Wine Bar seems pretty popular from all appearances. It's at 7 Woodstock Road, and the food and atmosphere are very acceptable. Another place worth a mention is the local for Christ Church college, the Bear in Bear Lane.

There are plenty of pubs; and if you want to meet the students, simply go to the pubs closest to the colleges. The King's Arms in Holywell Street is particularly well attended. Oxford's July–Aug. Festival is fairly classical; to find out the latest events, pick up the *What's On* at the Tourist Office.

Stratford-upon-Avon

About 1½ hours from Oxford lies the Elizabethan town of Stratford-upon-Avon, birthplace of William Shakespeare. The house where he was born in HANLEY STREET in 1564 is charming, or would be if it weren't for the hundreds of tourists trying to get around it. He's buried in Holy Trinity Church. Shakespeare's wife's house ANNE HATHAWAY'S COTTAGE can be visited at Shottery. Americans might also like to visit the Elizabethan HARVARD HOUSE, where the parents of John Harvard (of University fame) lived. The Royal Shakespeare Theatre and the new Swan Theatre put on productions of outstanding quality, though the cheapest tickets are about £5-8 (Tel. 01789 292271 for information on what's playing).

While you're in the area you can pop into Shakespeare's mother's house and complete the family socializing. The HOME OF MARY ARDEN in the village of Wilmcote can be reached by local train in a matter of minutes.

The countryside around Stratford, the COTSWOLDS, possibly represents England at its best: rolling green hills and picturesque limestone cottages. Try to take in the beautiful towns of Broadway and Chipping Camden on a trip from Stratford.

The Tourist Office is at 1 High St (Tel. 01789 293127), open Mon.–Sat.: 9 a.m.–5.30 p.m., Sun.: 2 p.m.–5 p.m. in season. They'll give you a leaflet on accommodation, but the best bets are B&Bs on Evesham Place or Shipston Road. There is a youth hostel at Hemmingford House, Alveston (Tel. 01789 297093); bus 518 from the bus station will take you there. Or for camping, try The Elms, Tiddington (Tel. 01789 292312); also on the number 518 bus route.

Cambridge city phone code: 01223

Oxford's great rival is the similarly ancient market town and prestigious university of Cambridge which dates back to the 13th century and has names like Darwin, Newton, Byron and Milton in its old registers. Cambridge is an hour from London (Liverpool Street or King's Cross), and once you arrive at the station, the bus to Market Square will take you to the centre of things.

TOURIST INFORMATION AND ADDRESSES

The Tourist Office is at Wheeler St (Tel. 322640); open Mon.–Fri.: 9 a.m.–6 p.m., Sat.: 9 a.m.–5 p.m., Sun.: 10.30 a.m.–3.30 p.m. in season. Pick up the *Brief Guide* leaflet and ask about their walking tours.
CYCLE HIRE Nearest to the station and youth hostel is Geoff's Bike Hire, 65 Devonshire Road, £6 a day.
PUNT HIRE Scudamore's Boatyards, Silver Street, or Magdalene Bridge. £9 per hour plus £40 deposit.

SEEING

The area between Magdalene Bridge and Silver Street is the one to concentrate on. The town itself is quite substantial, and the university colleges are set apart, literally in a world of their own. THE BACKS are the meadows and fields on the other side of the Cam, and the best way to drink in this pastoral atmosphere is to hire a punt and view the colleges from the river. An absolute must is a visit inside KING'S COLLEGE CHAPEL, the largest chapel in Europe and one of the most beautiful churches in Britain. Entry to most colleges is possible for a small charge. They are all closed, however, from early May to mid-June, for exams. Take in ST JOHN'S, TRINITY and especially CLARE COLLEGE gardens. A "Guide Friday" tour bus ticket costs £7 (£5.50) for students), but does include the AMERICAN WAR CEMETERY at Madingley, where thousands of World War servicemen are buried.

SLEEPING

Tourist Information will find you a bed for a 10% fee or hand you a list of local registered B&Bs. The best place to find a cheap B&B is near the station at Tenison Road or Jesus Lane in town. Try any of the following in that lane: Mrs Spalding at no. 56 (Tel. 353858), Mrs Day at no. 72 (Tel. 356961) or Mrs Owen at no. 65 (Tel. 60648).

The youth hostel is at 97 Tenison Road (Tel. 353858), conveniently near the station and with cycle hire next door.

There's camping at Cherry Hinton Caravan Site, 4 km southeast of the town centre; bus from Drummer Street.

EATING AND NIGHTLIFE

The picnic bar in Marks & Spencer, Market Square, is the best source for picnic food. The Anchor, Silver Street, next to the river, is a good place to meet students and it does good pub food. The Blue Boar, Trinity Street is also recommended. The Maypole, in Portugal Place, does excellent cocktails.

Ask Tourist Information for the *What's On*, as there's always a round of plays, films or debates. The best value is the Cambridge University Amateur Dramatic Club, Park Street. Their productions are good and their prices low, £1.50–4.00 (Tel. 352000 to see what's playing). In mid-June, 'May Week' is on, when the students are enjoying their new-found freedom after the exams. Many good amateur plays and other events are on, and you may see one of the famous May Balls or a graduation ceremony on at Senate House.

South Wales

CARDIFF, the Welsh capital city, is about 2½ hours from London and an hour from Bristol. It is a reasonably attractive town, with an increasing amount to merit a stop. The CASTLE is an amazing blend of ruins and architectural styles. The CIVIC CENTRE, TECHNIQUEST and NATIONAL MUSEUM OF WALES are all worth a look, while the open-air WELSH FOLK MUSEUM at St Fagan's is fascinating. Take bus 32 out there, it's open Mon.–Sat.: 10 a.m.–5 p.m. (Tel. 01222 569441).

Cardiff Tourist Information is at 8–14 Bridge St and is open daily 9 a.m.–7 p.m. Ask for the free entertainment and visitors' guides (Tel. 01222 222281).

Try the youth hostel at Wedal Road on bus line 80 or 82 (Tel. 01222 462303).

There are plenty of pubs and clubs on and around St Mary Street, but perhaps the most notable are the Philharmonic and the Four Bars opposite the castle, which sometimes has jazz upstairs. The narrow Victorian shopping arcades, interspersed with newer centres, are good for a ramble.

South Wales was once internationally famous as a centre of coal mining and heavy industry, but the shift away from heavy industry in Britain today was reflected in the closing of the last colliery in the Rhondda Valley in 1990. Over the past decade, tremendous changes have taken place in the SOUTH WALES VALLEYS, where vast land reclamation schemes have completely transformed areas of former industrial dereliction and have resulted in the re-greening of the Valleys. Head for the BRYN BACH COUNTRY PARK or the CWM DARRAN PARK to see the beauty of the valleys, where you will find it hard to believe heavy industry once stood in these scenic spots.

The RHONDDA HERITAGE PARK gives a fascinating insight into the regeneration projects and the important cultural and industrial heritage of the valleys. The valley railway lines from Cardiff, which run frequently, make the whole area easily accessible. (Take the line to Rhymney for the first 2 parks, and to Treherbert for the Rhondda park.) A Valley Lines Day Ranger offers unlimited travel for a day.

The BRECON BEACONS NATIONAL PARK is a great place to stop off from a hectic European tour and get some good walking done in lovely countryside. BRECON is a charming unspoilt market town. It is a good base to explore the area, with a main Tourist Information centre (Tel. 01874 611729) able to give details on walks, mountain-bike hire etc. The youth hostel is 1½ km or so out, at Ty'n-y-Caeau (Tel. 01874

86270). Enjoy the mountain views, if you are fortunate enough to get good weather. Brecon is linked by bus 21 to Abergavenny, which is on the Crewe–Cardiff railway line.

Further west and south in Wales, trains will take you from mainline Swansea to Tenby and Pembroke in the PEMBROKESHIRE COAST NATIONAL PARK. TENBY is an unspoilt seaside resort in lovely Carmarthen Bay with an attractive blend of architecture, while PEMBROKE is a fortified town with a magnificently preserved castle as its centrepiece (open daily 9.30 a.m.–6 p.m.). The Pembrokeshire Coast Park contains some of the best beaches anywhere in Britain and a series of dramatic coastlines. The islands just off the coast are homes and breeding grounds to seals and many types of birds.

From Fishguard on the north Pembrokeshire coast and Pembroke on the southern coastline, ferries leave for Rosslare in Ireland.

North Wales

North Wales is an area of dramatic countryside, with a very different character from the south. Welsh is widely spoken in the towns and valleys up here. Fast trains can bring you to the main centres from London, and the coast is also served by direct services from Manchester and the West Midlands.

The SNOWDONIA NATIONAL PARK covers half of North Wales and is one of Europe's best regions for getting away from it all. The terrain is ideal for climbing, hiking, camping and hostelling. A good springboard for ventures into the Snowdonia Park is CARNARFON, reached by taking the train to Bangor, then the bus. Carnarfon is home to arguably the most splendid castle in Britain, the place where the investiture of Prince Charles as the Prince of Wales took place. Other great castles in the area are Harlech, Conwy and Beaumaris on the island of Anglesey (Ynys Mon). Conwy also has Britain's smallest house: Ty Bach is on the quayside with a frontage of a mere 2m.

LLANBERIS is a great place for a base, with plenty of hostels and guesthouses, near to the 1,068m MOUNT SNOWDON itself. Take the privately run SNOWDON MOUNTAIN RAILWAY to the summit for an expensive £12.80 return, or alternatively go up with it and then walk back down yourself.

If you are interested in ecology, conservation and the environment a visit to the CENTRE FOR ALTERNATIVE TECHNOLOGY is a must. Set in a slate quarry overlooking the Snowdon National Park, near Machynlleth, the centre is a maze of windmills, aerogenerators, solar heating panels and water turbines. It is 5 km from Machynlleth station, where you can get a bus to the adjacent village of Pantperthog. Open daily 10 a.m.–7 p.m. (Tel. 01654 2400). Entrance costs £3.50 (students £2).

Each July the small town of LLANGOLLEN hosts the INTERNATIONAL EISTEDDFOD, a Welsh music festival which attracts competitors from over 30 different countries (Tel. 01978 860236). There's also a privately run steam railway here. Buses run from Wrexham and Chirk railway stations to Llangollen.

Northern England

It is said (by Northerners) that you will know you've reached northern England as soon as the beer is drinkable and strangers in pubs start a conversation with you. Although northern England does have more than its fair share of industrialized cities, with all the attendant problems, it does have areas of outstanding beauty, interest and character.

PEAK DISTRICT NATIONAL PARK A 'lung' of green surrounded by the industrialized towns of the north Midlands and by Sheffield and Manchester is this national park in Derbyshire. It was Britain's first national park and is the second most visited national park in the world, so it has to be worth a stop.

A Derbyshire Wayfarer Pass for around £4.50 allows one day's unlimited bus and rail travel within Derbyshire. A good base is MATLOCK at the terminus of the railway from Derby. The youth hostel is at 40 Bank Road (Tel. 01629 582983), a few minutes from the station over the river and straight up the hill. Matlock itself is dominated by the ruined RIBER CASTLE, presently a fauna reserve which has great views. Take a walk along the river to MATLOCK BATH in a limestone gorge for a cable-car ride – from £4.30 up to the Heights of Abraham for more splendid views. An excellent view of the cable-cars, gorge and Matlock Bath can be had from the White Lion Inn at Starkholmes, perched above Matlock and below Riber Castle. Not only does it have unrivalled views and the best beer in the area, it also serves reasonable food and one of our researchers drinks there!

Further north, BUXTON, a former spa town, and CASTLETON, for its caverns, are well worth a look.

The scenery throughout the Peak District is excellent and well suited to walking, but keep to defined footpaths to avoid further erosion of the most popular paths. Tourist Information at Matlock Bath (Tel.

01629 55082) and Buxton (Tel. 01298 5106) will provide information on the best walks, other sights and affordable accommodation.

Liverpool

Liverpool is similar to Glasgow in Scotland in that it has received a lot of bad press internationally and has a bad public image. In fact the crime rate is no higher than in any other major city and the people are renowned for their wit and friendliness. Tourism is a growth industry in Merseyside, and many people who come solely because of the Beatles are surprised to find much more.

TRAIN INFORMATION

Lime Street Station (Inter-City) has daily trains to: London, Manchester, Birmingham, the South-West, Wales, Scotland, Lake District, and Newcastle.

MERSEYRAIL UNDERGROUND: Lime Street, James Street, Central and Moorfields stations in the city centre. Underground and bus information (Tel. 0151 236 7676). Frequent trains to Southport, Chester, Ormskirk, Wirral, North Wales, Manchester.

TOURIST INFORMATION

There are information offices (Tel. 0151 709 3631) in Clayton Square shopping centre and at the Albert Dock. Bus information from the Merseytravel office, Williamson Square.

SEEING

ALBERT DOCK On the waterfront is the largest grade-1 listed building in the country. It has been restored and now hosts an array of small shops, cafés and exclusive apartments. The Albert Dock also hosts the northern branch of London's famous TATE GALLERY. Admission is free although there is often a small charge for admission to special exhibitions. Also at the Albert Dock is the MERSEYSIDE MARITIME MUSEUM – a museum which traces Liverpool's maritime history, and also includes the NATIONAL CUSTOMS AND EXCISE museum and a collection of moored ships. Nearby is the PIER HEAD which holds the three buildings which dominate Liverpool's skyline. From here you can still get a Ferry Cross the Mersey.

Other things to see in the city centre include the two modern Cathedrals. LIVERPOOL CATHEDRAL is a huge Gothic building only completed in the 1980s. It is the largest Anglican cathedral in the world and houses the largest pipe organ in Europe. There are often recitals on bank holidays. In complete contrast at the other end of Hope Street is the Catholic LIVERPOOL METROPOLITAN CATHEDRAL – a concrete and glass circular structure known locally as Paddy's Wigwam or the Mersey Funnel. Inside the spray of light from the stained glass can be quite beautiful; not so the spray of water through the leaking roof when it rains!

If you've come to Liverpool in search of the Beatles, stop off at one of the information shops first. These will give you information about all the walking and coach tours available. The original Cavern club was demolished some years ago but a faithful replica has been constructed a little further down Matthew Street in the Cavern Walks Shopping Centre. If you want to see Penny Lane, Strawberry Fields etc., take a coach trip. Liverpool is famous for its footballing tradition. During the football season, matches can be seen on Saturdays at Liverpool or Everton FCs.

SLEEPING

The YMCA, YWCA and numerous small B&B hotels can be found on Mount Pleasant near the Catholic cathedral and 10 minutes' walk from the station. The Embassy Youth Hostel on Faulkner Square (Tel. 0151 707 1089) is also worth a look. It's in a converted old home and has no curfew.

EATING AND NIGHTLIFE

There are numerous fast-food and fish 'n' chip shops dotted throughout the city centre. Alternatively, make a picnic with food from one of the city centre shops. Liverpool also has a great selection of ethnic restaurants and those in 'Chinatown' are excellent and great value, and especially popular for Dim Sum – the very tasty and varied snacks.

There are some great venues for live music: one favourite is Irish folk at Flanagan's near Cavern Walks, but a local will help out with inside knowledge. Also sample the varied pubs. One of our favourites is the Swan on Wood Street for its selection of good beers and interesting characters. Many of the pubs are spectacularly ornate inside – the Philharmonic on Hope St is a particularly fine example and also does reasonable food.

An hour's train ride away, MANCHESTER is famous for its club scene – the best way to find out what's on is to go into the Corner House arts centre right next to Oxford Road station and look at the leaflets and posters plastering the walls.

York city phone code: 01904

York dates back to Roman times and is considered Britain's best-preserved medieval city with the finest Gothic cathedral. It lies about halfway between London and Edinburgh on the east-coast line, and with the fast 225 Intercity service, it takes only 2½ hours from the capital. A visit is most highly recommended.

TOURIST INFORMATION

The tourist information centre is in Exhibition Square and at the station, and is open Mon.–Sat.: 9 a.m.–8 p.m., Sun.: 2 p.m.–5 p.m. in season. They run a free 2-hour walking tour from the Art Gallery at 10.15 a.m., 2.15 p.m. and 7.15 p.m.

SEEING

There are four main entrances to the city: BOOTHAM GATE, MICKLEGATE, MONKGATE AND WALMGATE, and the city is surrounded by 5 km of defensive walls which make an attractive walk. York MINSTER (the Cathedral which had a tied school) is amazing: the Great East Window is as big as a tennis court, and all the stained glass is medieval. Once you've wandered around the cathedral, visit the CASTLE MUSEUM which is an exceptionally good folk museum with reconstructions of streets, people and implements: go early as 2-hour queues are not uncommon, such is its excellent reputation with visitors.

Real train enthusiasts will like the NATIONAL RAILWAY MUSEUM down by the station – plenty of steam locos, etc. There are many other historic and interesting places, like the TREASURER'S HOUSE, CLIFFORD'S TOWER, the wonderful old shopping streets of medieval York like the SHAMBLES, and the site of the old whipping post, WHIP-MA-WHOP-MA-GATE. Pick up detailed leaflets from Tourist Information. While you're in the area, you might want to visit CASTLE HOWARD, a beautiful 18th-century house which was the setting of the TV version of *Brideshead Revisited*. Ask Tourist Information for the best buses.

SLEEPING

Tourist information will give you lists of B&Bs and hostels, or find you a room for free (with a £4 deposit). York can get very busy in summer, so get fixed up as soon as you arrive. The area round Bootham is not bad for B&Bs, and there's a youth hostel at Water End, Clifton (Tel. 653147), though it's usually packed with groups. Without curfews are Bishophill House, a private hostel at 11–13 Bishophill Senior Road (Tel.

625904) and the International House, 33 Bootham (Tel. 622874) only 300 metres from York Minster. For B&B try Bishopthorpe Road in Bootham, or the Mount area down Blossom Street. The campsite, open May–Sept., is 5 km out of town at Bishopthorpe (Tel. 704442).

EATING AND NIGHTLIFE

There are bakers' shops, markets and pubs a-plenty in York. York Wholefood, 98 Micklegate, do good meals upstairs, and Kooks at 108 Fishergate (closed Mon.) is also worth a try. With over 150 pubs, you shouldn't get stuck for a watering hole. The Black Swan in Peasholme Green is a suitably olde-worlde place, but there are many more dotted around.

Scotland: Edinburgh city phone code: 0131

The elegant city of Edinburgh can't fail to strike the visitor as dramatic: built on extinct volcanoes with a fairytale castle dominating the city, and hills and the sea all around. It's the artistic, commercial, academic and legal centre of Scotland and its history goes back to the 7th century. As soon as you walk up the hill from Waverley Station you're in the centre of things, with the castle and 'old town', behind and to your left, and the 'new town' from the Georgian era on your right, to the north of Princes Street, the main shopping thoroughfare.

TOURIST INFORMATION AND ADDRESSES

The Edinburgh and Scotland Tourist Information Centre is on the top of Waverley Market, just up the ramp and to your right from the station, open weekdays 9 a.m.–8 p.m., Sun.: 10 a.m.–8 p.m. in season (Tel. 557 1700). Ask for the *Day by Day* events listing, published monthly. There is a good Bureau de Change here. Packed with useful information, such as where to eat and what to see, the pocket-sized *Edinburgh City Guide* is one of the best all-round city guidebooks and is good value at around £5 in most bookshops, but there is a slimline "essential" version for 50 pence. The Centre also serves as a ticket-booking agency.

POST OFFICE In St James' Shopping Centre (at east end of Princes Street), open Mon.–Fri.: 8.30 a.m.–5.30 p.m., Sat.: 8.30 a.m.–6 p.m. Currency exchange.

AMEX 139 Princes Street, open Mon.–Fri.: 9 a.m.–5.30 p.m., Sat.: 9 a.m.–4 p.m. (Tel. 225 7881).

US CONSULATE 3 Regent Terrace (Tel. 556 8315).

AUSTRALIAN CONSULATE 23 Mitchell Street (Tel. 467 8333).
MEDICAL HELP: University Health Service, Bristo Square (Tel. 667 1011).
CAMPUS TRAVEL: (EUROTRAIN) 5 Nicolson Square (Tel. 668 3303).
GAY AND LESBIAN INFORMATION PO Box 169, Tel.: 0131 556 4049
PHONE CODE 0131.

SEEING

The medieval ROYAL MILE was so called because it stretches from the CASTLE to the royal palace of HOLYROOD. You can't possibly miss the Castle which dates back to 800AD. It stands on an extinct volcano and can be seen from virtually every corner of Edinburgh. Though entrance is £5.50 (there's no student discount), if you're keen on history it's worth it. The Scottish Crown Jewels are on display here and you can see the 12th-century QUEEN MARGARET'S CHAPEL, the smallest in Scotland and the oldest building in the city. Walking down the Royal Mile, you'll find GLADSTONE'S LAND, a beautifully preserved 17th-Century townhouse in the Lawnmarket, well worth a visit at £2.80 (concessions £1.90), and behind this is LADY STAIR'S HOUSE, known as the Writers' Museum, with Burns, Stevenson and Scott mementoes. ST GILES' CATHEDRAL, the Gothic 1385 High Church of Scotland, is on the right, as are various buildings of the Scottish parliament. Halfway down in the Canongate is JOHN KNOX'S HOUSE and the MUSEUM OF CHILDHOOD, an interesting collection of toys and games from bygone days.

At the foot of the Royal Mile is the Splendid PALACE OF HOLYROOD HOUSE. Open 9.30 a.m.–5.15 p.m. every day in season. Admission is £5.20, students £3.80. It is the official Scottish residence of the Queen and is steeped in past tragedy and history with many good tapestries and paintings. It may be closed from time to time for state occasions, so check if you're going to Edinburgh specifically to see the Monarch's B&B. After a tour of the 16th-century palace, clear your head with a good blast of Scottish air up another of Edinburgh's extinct volcanoes, ARTHUR'S SEAT, or walk to CALTON HILL at the east end of Princes Street to look at 'Edinburgh's Disgrace': the replica of the Athens Parthenon, built to commemorate Scottish dead in the Napoleonic Wars, that ran out of money and remains unfinished.

On one side of Princes Street are the city's main shops, while opposite are gardens and the two neo classical art galleries: the NATIONAL GALLERY OF SCOTLAND and the ROYAL SCOTTISH ACADEMY, both particularly impressive. WALTER SCOTT'S MONUMENT, the huge Gothic tower in Princes Street Gardens, affords a good view from the top, and from here a walk up Hanover Street will take you down to Queen Street where, along on the right, you'll find THE NATIONAL PORTRAIT

GALLERY. Bus 23 or 27 from Hanover Street will take you down to the BOTANICAL GARDENS which are a glorious picnic venue and you'll find the NATIONAL GALLERY OF MODERN ART near DEAN VILLAGE on Belford Road. If you've any time left, search out the GEORGIAN HOUSE in Charlotte Square, the magnificent ROYAL MUSEUM OF SCOTLAND and THE PEOPLE'S STORY MUSEUM, both in the Old Town, the ZOO, one of the finest in Britain, and take bus 41 out to CRAMOND, down by the sea.

During the International Festival and its Fringe in August literally thousands of events are staged: plays, concerts, exhibitions; and every church hall in the city has some group performing in it. Thousands of students descend on the city, as tickets start as low as £5 (some events are free). Running at the same time are the film and jazz festivals, and the bonanza of the MILITARY TATTOO with enough kilts and bagpipes to satisfy even the most ardent American. Tattoo office: Tel. 225 1188, Fringe office: Tel. 226 5257.

Go to INCHCOLM ISLAND in the Firth of Forth for a great day out. The 'Iona of the East' has a beautiful medieval abbey and hundreds of seabirds nest here. It is also home to grey seals. To get there take a train to DALMENY and walk 10 minutes to the pier at South Queensferry, and then a ferry, *The Maid of the Forth* (cost £6.95 return, £5.95 for students), which usually leaves across from the Hawes Inn, where Robert Louis Stevenson is known to have downed a few. Runs May-Sept.

SLEEPING

Aside from late August (Festival time), a bed's not too much of a hassle. For B&Bs, take a bus out to Newington and look along Newington and Minto Streets, or try the Bruntsfield area. The youth hostels are at 18 Eglinton Crescent (Tel. 337 1120) and 7–8 Bruntsfield Crescent (Tel. 447 2994). The University Halls of Residence, Pollock Halls, 18 Holyrood Park Road (Tel. 667 1971), are very good and offer 1,500 single rooms at £23–26 per night. Take buses 21 or 33 to the Commonwealth Pool. The High Street Hostel at 8 Blackfriars Street (Tel. 557 3984) is only a few minutes' walk up the hill from Waverley Station. It costs from £9, you don't need an IYHF card, and it is open 24 hours. There is also a free left-luggage service and showers. To camp, take bus 33 out to Little France, Old Dalkeith Road (Tel. 664 4742).

The Roxburghe Hotel, Charlotte Square (Tel. 225 3921), is a fine, recently refurbished central first-class hotel for the Adult Eurail market. Johnstonburn House Hotel at Humbie, half an hour east of Edinburgh, is a country house hotel of great character and quality, offering traditional comforts and excellent cuisine in an historic setting. The

Adult Eurail market will also find the Greywalls Hotel in Gullane, near Edinburgh a delightful place to dine or spend a weekend. This luxury country house hotel is a fine example of a traditional British estate, and apart from its exceptional restaurant and good accommodation, it has the luck to be situated right next to one of Britain's finest golf courses – Muirfield. Take the train to Drem and a cab from there. Booking ahead in summer is advisable. (Tel. 01620 842144).

The Tourist Information centre can give help with advance booking for the Festival season.

EATING AND NIGHTLIFE

Cheap eats are no problem in Edinburgh and it's possible to fill up for under £3. Pick up the free leaflet from Tourist Information on restaurants. Try the Baked Potato Shop on Cockburn Street. Pubs often offer cheap lunches, and this capital has over 500 to choose from. The University Students' Union at Teviot Row (up the Mound, and George IV Bridge) do meals for about £1.50, or try Henderson's Salad Table, 94 Hanover Street, for healthy meals around £7.50. Also good value is Bell's diner at 26 St Stephen Street in Stockbridge (Tel. 225 8116). It's a very popular eating place, selling home-made burgers, salads, delicious sweet courses and house wines. Also try the Buffalo Grill on Chapel Street for around £8 or the Cellar No. 1 on Chamber Street for a wine bar with good food for around £5. If you are splashing out, try Jackson's Restaurant in Jackson's Close, off the Royal Mile: they do an excellent menu including traditional Scottish food and wine.

If you're here in Festival time, the nightlife position is unmatched anywhere else in Britain. Go along to the Fringe Club, in Teviot Row, off Bristo Square (Tel. 667 2091), where performers, the media and the public gather to socialize (£16 membership for the Festival's duration, bring a passport photo). Be sure to pick up the Fringe programme for the widest range of entertainment you're likely to find anywhere. If you're visiting at any other time, pick up *Day-by-Day* from Tourist Information and combine some events with a visit to some of the city's pubs; a popular pub crawl is along the 19 bars of Rose Street. Many students hang out in the George Square area pubs such as the Pear Tree, Maxie's Bistro, and the up-market, continental wine bar, Negociants, opposite the Teviot Row Students' Union. Café Royal, just behind the large Burger King at the east end of Princes Street, is an outstanding example of a fine Victorian pub. Check out the ceiling in their upstairs bar. They do good bar lunches too, as does the Abbotsford on Rose Street.

Check out what's playing in the Film House (Lothian Road), the

Cameo Cinema, at Tollcross (showing arty films), or the Grassmarket Theatre.

Glasgow city phone code: 0141

Just 45 minutes on one of the half-hourly expresses from Edinburgh is Glasgow, Scotland's largest city and business centre. While it does not have the immediate visual presence of Edinburgh, Glasgow is still a beautiful Victorian city and well worth a visit. Thanks to the 'Glasgow's Miles Better' campaign which started some years ago, it is gradually shaking off an unfair reputation for being violent and dirty. In recent years many buildings have been cleaned and the environment generally improved, although for many years it has had more parks per head of population (780,000) than any other city in Europe – a fact which has surprised many visitors. In Glasgow it's not so much the buildings you come to see (as with Edinburgh) as the people. They are regarded as the warmest, most outgoing lot in Britain, and a visit to a few pubs will confirm that. Previously it has hosted an International Garden Festival and it was the 1990 European City of Culture.

SEEING
When you get off the train at Queen Street Station go straight ahead into George Square and turn right into St Vincent Place. The Tourist Office is on the left-hand side (Tel. 204 4400), where you can pick up leaflets, get information about places to see and book accommodation. Without doubt the major attraction is the BURRELL COLLECTION, an 8,000-piece artistic treasure trove, gathered together over a lifetime of collecting on every continent by Glasgow shipping magnate Sir William Burrell. Entry is free to the collection, which was donated to the people of Glasgow in 1944 but opened only in 1983. The award-winning building housing the collection is situated in POLLOK COUNTRY PARK. Take a train from Glasgow Central to Pollokshaws West and then the free bus from the entrance next to the station. If you don't want to wait for the bus (every 20 minutes) walk through the 361 acres of parkland and gardens and see the herd of Highland cattle near to Pollok House. In Pollok House is one of the finest collections of Spanish paintings in Britain. Entry to both museums is free of charge and they have the same opening hours: Mon.–Sat.: 10 a.m.–5 p.m., Sun.: 12 noon–6 p.m. The ART GALLERY AND MUSEUM, at Kelvingrove, is also worth visiting as it houses Britain's finest civic collection of British and European paintings including Salvador Dali's *Crucifixion*.

The architect Charles Rennie Mackintosh came from Glasgow and many of the buildings he designed can be seen in the city. The Headquarters of the CHARLES RENNIE MACKINTOSH SOCIETY (formerly Queen's Cross Church) are at 866 Garscube Road, open Tues., Thurs., Fri.: 12 noon–5.30 p.m., Sun.: 2.30 p.m.–5.30 p.m. In the city centre you can visit and have tea at the WILLOW TEA ROOM, a famous Mackintosh building recently restored, at 217 Sauchiehall Street (Tel. 0141 332 0521), Mon.–Sat.: 9.30 a.m.–5 p.m.

Well worth a look is the BARRAS at weekends. On London Road and Gallowgate to the east of the centre, this is possibly the world's largest open-air market with an amazing variety of stalls and shops. An interesting look at Victorian life in Glasgow can be had at THE TENEMENT HOUSE, 145 Buccleuth Street, a first-floor Victorian flat furnished with the trappings of a Victorian family. Open Mon.–Fri.: 12 noon–5 p.m., weekends 2 p.m.–6 p.m.

SLEEPING

One youth hostel is near the Art Gallery. Take a train from Queen Street low level 1 stop to Charing Cross and head up the hill following the signs. It's at 11 Woodlands Terrace (Tel. 332 3004). Glasgow's newest Youth Hostel, formerly the Beacons Hotel, has excellent facilities including en-suite facilities for all dormitories, a restaurant and good self-catering possibilities. It is open until 2 a.m. and can be found at 7–8 Park Terrace (Tel. 332 3004). Alternatively, try the University of Glasgow Halls of Residence, bookable through the Tourist Office. An unofficial hostel, run on foreign lines with a relaxed attitude to curfews and duties, it operates each summer. The Glasgow Central Tourist Hostel is situated in the Balmanno Building, 81 Rottenrow East (Tel. 552 2402). It is a few minutes' walk from George Square and Queen Street Station, close to the University of Strathclyde.

EATING AND NIGHTLIFE

In the same area are two restaurants worth seeking out. The Ubiquitous Chip, at 12 Ashton Lane, also specializes in traditional Scottish food but is better known for its wine cellar, reputed to be among the top ten in Britain. Imaginative top-grade food served at medium-grade prices makes this an essential meeting-place for the young, arty crowd (Tel. 334 5007). Glasgow also has a fine selection of Indian and Chinese restaurants around Sauchiehall Street and the university area. One definitely not to be missed is the Shish Mahal, 66–68 Park Road, near Glasgow University. The popularity of this place makes booking more or less essential (Tel. 339 8256) and you'll find well-prepared Indian dishes at reasonable prices, as well as meeting a few Glaswegian students. In the city centre try Babbity Bowster, a café/bar/restaurant which is full of character. The food is excellent and reasonably priced. It is at 16–18 Blackfriars Street (Tel. 552 5055). Pick up *The List*, 80p from newsstands for details of nightlife.

The Highlands

From Edinburgh or Glasgow it's a 4-hour journey up to Inverness, capital of the Highlands. The route is via Perth and Aviemore and, once you're up at Pitlochry, the scenery is wonderful. Perthshire is one of Britain's most splendid regions. Majestic landscapes and pretty villages; neat, clean towns and wonderful old country houses, many of which now serve as deluxe hotels and restaurants, are some of the attractions of this area. Perth and Stirling are the 2 main stopping-off stations, and from there regular buses allow you to explore the hidden corners of this unspoilt part of the UK.

A quick rundown on Inverness is all that is needed, for while it's a pleasant enough place, you should really just use it as a base for the surrounding country. The left-luggage locker facilities at the station are of the excellent modern computerized variety, which are also user-friendly. There's no fine for a lost access ticket as all the lockers can be operated by the central computer which is also good for security. While in Inverness, wander (or take a guided mini-bus tour or cruise) round LOCH NESS where the elusive monster is said to live, and visit CAWDOR CASTLE (19 km east) where Shakespeare set Macbeth.

There are plenty of B&Bs around Old Edinburgh Road, which is also where you'll find the youth hostel, at No. 1 (Tel. 01463 231771), and the Student Hotel (Tel. 01463 236556). There's camping down by the river on the Craig Dunain bus route (Tel. 01463 236920). Culloden House Hotel, 5 km from the town centre, where the station is located, is the recommended luxury hotel in this area of the Highlands. While it is strictly in the 'afternoon tea only' category to most Inter-Railers, those on the Adult Eurail Pass may well consider splurging on a night in sumptuous historic surroundings, enjoying traditionally prepared dishes, and relaxing in the sort of luxury you'd forgotten existed after a few weeks on the road. It's well worth the trip out, even if just to see the 18th-century buildings and enjoy the surrounding countryside (Tel. 01463 790461).

Tourist information at Castle Wynd is open Mon.–Sat.: 9 a.m.–8.30 p.m., Sun.: 9 am.–6 p.m. in summer (Tel. 01463 234353). To get into the corners not covered by rail, rent a bike from Ness Motors or the youth hostel and, armed with a map, head for the north side of Loch Ness and Urquhart Castle. If you're lucky you may even see the monster here.

From Inverness, take the train west to KYLE OF LOCHALSH, a 170-minute journey of beautiful unspoilt scenery through the Wester Ross mountains. From Kyle there's a frequent bus service over the modern bridge to the ISLE OF SKYE, Britain's most dramatic island. The peace and beauty of the Black Cuillin Hills and the haunting cloud formations are quite unmatched elsewhere. PORTREE, the island's capital, has a Tourist Office overlooking the harbour. There's a Backpacker's Guest House (Tel. 01599 4510) on the island, as well as 6 youth hostels.

Skye can also be approached from MALLAIG, and from Mallaig you're back on the main line to FORT WILLIAM and GLASGOW. At Fort William you may be tempted to walk up BEN NEVIS, Britain's highest peak. The Youth Hostel (Tel. 01397 702336) is at the start of the trail, which takes around 7 hours to complete and which affords some fine views. However, this is a tough walk, even for the fit. Never go alone, take proper clothing and make sure someone knows where you're going before you start. A slightly gentler proposition is a walk along the West Highland Way – especially now that there is a van service, Travel-Lite, which for a £25 fee will transport your rucksack for you while you walk (Tel.: 0141 956 6810)

If you were thinking of heading further north, there's a line from Inverness to WICK; but it can be pretty desolate up there, so make sure you're the wilderness type. If it's isolation you're after, try the ORKNEY ISLANDS. These ex-Danish colonies are well worth visiting; the easiest approach is the ferry from John o'Groats. Visit the Stone Age settlement of SKARA BRAE and the Bronze Age STANDING STONES OF STENNESS and RING OF BRODGAR. The Oban–Glasgow run is another favourite for Highland scenery, 3½ hours of it. From OBAN you can visit the beautiful ISLE OF MULL, and from there go to the smaller, more isolated islands of Iona, Staffa, Coll and Tiree. Tourist Information in Oban is at Argyll Square, turn right from the station; and there's a hostel on the Esplanade (Tel. 01631 62025).

No serious trip to Scotland is complete without a visit to a Scotch whisky distillery and some serious sampling. 42 distilleries welcome visitors, details from Tourist Information centres. Most charge admission, but let you subtract the cost from any purchases you might make…

Northern Ireland

More than 25 years of 'troubles' have given Northern Ireland an unfavourable reputation and the situation is definitely volatile. However the political climate here can change rapidly so keep your eyes and ears open if you plan to visit the province. Bear in mind that the media tend to inflate things out of all proportion, and that most of the province is safe to visit, particularly if you're obviously a tourist. However, you may lay yourself open to security-checks from the armed forces in the affected areas and you shouldn't take photos of the security forces or police stations. If you hold strong political views, keep them to yourself and you'll be as safe as houses. That said, the scenery is nice and varied for such a small area, with lots of mountains, lakes, caves, cliffs and some wonderful sandy beaches.

There are two main rail routes from Belfast Central Station (Tel. 01232 230310) – north to Londonderry via Ballymena and Coleraine and south to Dublin via Lisburn, Portadown and Newry. The Dublin-Belfast Express takes less than two hours. Most local services, to Bangor, for the seaside, or Larne, for ferries to Cairnryan (near Stranraer) in Scotland, leave from Great Victoria Street station in the city centre. Belfast–Stranraer ferries leave from Albert Quay, on the northern bank of the River Lagan. There's also a Seacat service from Belfast city-centre to Stranraer.

The Emerald Card and Irish Rover, valid for travel in the Republic of Ireland, are also valid in the 6 counties of the North. There is also the Rail Runabout, which for £25, during April–Oct., offers 7 days' unlimited travel on all rail services throughout Northern Ireland and to Dundalk. Available from the Central Station, Belfast.

Taking the capital, Belfast, as the centre, you'll find County Down and the Mourne Mountains to the south, Armagh to the west, Fermanagh further west and Tyrone inland. County Londonderry is in the north-west corner and County Antrim in the north-east. At Torr Head you're only 21 km from Scotland, and in the northwest of Antrim's coast is the Giant's Causeway, the famous rock formation.

BELFAST: The main things to see are near the UNIVERSITY or in the city centre around DONEGAL SQUARE where the Renaissance-style CITY HALL is located. Well worth a mention are the OPERA HOUSE and the ULSTER MUSEUM and ART GALLERY in the BOTANIC GARDENS. The Ulster Museum is especially noteworthy for its Irish antiquities and for its internationally famous treasures from the Spanish Armada. Admission is free: open

Mon.–Fri.: 10 a.m.–5 p.m., Sat.: 1 p.m.–5p.m., Sun.: 2 p.m.–5p.m. Tourist Information is at St Anne's Court, North Street (Tel. 01232 246609) and is open Mon.–Sat.: 9 a.m.–5.15 p.m. The city bus tours are a good way of seeing Belfast's sights. They take 3½ hours and run from Castle Place, June–Sept. at 2 p.m. Tues.-Thurs. The fare is less than £10. If you've got a macabre sense of enjoyment, many local entrepreneurs are doing tours of the ghettoes affected by the 'troubles'. Despite the accusations of 'political tourism'", it is a fascinating way to get your political 'blinkers' off. Ask locals for details and read the small ads in the Belfast *Telegraph*. There's a youth hostel in the city centre at 22 Donegal Road (Tel. 324733). A look around the university area should turn up a pleasant B&B, but it'll cost you twice the price of a hostel bed.

The ULSTER FOLK AND TRANSPORT MUSEUM at Cultra Manor, Holywood, 10 km from Belfast, is well worth the detour. There are reconstructions of 19th-century life from farms to craft centres.

A trip to Northern Ireland would be incomplete without a visit to the magnificent GIANT'S CAUSEWAY, 40,000 columns of basalt steeped in Celtic legend. At Causeway Head visit the Causeway Centre, open daily 10 a.m.–7 p.m. (earlier closing off-season). The Whitepark Bay Youth Hostel (Tel. 012657 31745) is not too far away, and is situated next to St Gobhan's Church – the smallest in Ireland at 4 ft x 6 lt. Whilst you're there consider a visit to nearby BUSHMILLS, home of the Oldest (legal) Whiskey distillery at 2 Distillery Road. Established in 1608, it is open for tours Mon.–Sat.: 9.30 a.m.–5.30 p.m., Sun.: 12 noon–5.30 p.m. (admission £2.50, last entry 4 p.m.) (Tel. 012657 31521). The visitor centre has many creative uses for the liquid gold.

A particularly scenic excursion can be taken throughout the area on the 'Bushmills Bus', an open-topped affair which runs July–Aug. from Coleraine to the Giant's Causeway via Portstewart, Portrush, Portballintrae and Bushmills. The journey can be broken *en route*.

LONDONDERRY (or just **DERRY**), 2 hours from Belfast, is one of Northern Ireland's most attractive towns. Tourist information at Foyle Street (Tel. 01504 267284). The OLD CITY WALLS have withstood invaders for over 350 years, and while you can walk the 1.5 km circuit to see good views of the city, they are hardly laid out as a walk. The GUILDHALL in Shipquay Place is a neo-Gothic building whose stained-glass windows tell the city's history. The 17th-century Protestant cathedral is notable for stained glass showing scenes of the siege of 1688/89. To hear traditional Irish music and enjoy a pint, try one of the pubs on Waterloo Street: Dungloe Bar, Gweedore Bar or Castle Bar.

Worth a detour by bus, if you're planning to link up with the

Republic of Ireland's rail network rather than heading back to Belfast, is FERMANAGH, the province's lakeland. Buses leave from Waterloo Place in Londonderry, and most go via OMAGH, where you can break your journey by visiting the Ulster-American Folk Park and the nearby History Park.

In ENNISKILLEN, visit the Castle Museum and the tiny Cathedral. Stop for a pint at Blake's of the Hollow: it's genuinely as old as the hills and you'll not be disappointed. Explore the lakes; even from the land the views can be beautiful. Exit Enniskillen via the Shore Road for Belleek – it's worth hitching to stop off at Tully Castle, Church Hill; or the cliffs of Magho. From Belleek it's only 40 km to Sligo (Republic of Ireland), where you can rejoin the rail network.

NOTES

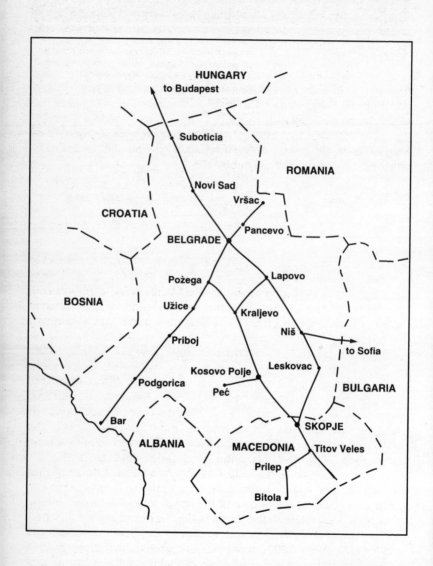

YUGOSLAVIA

Entry requirements	Passport and visa. All foreign nationals need a full passport and a visa, which must be obtained in advance (free of charge at Yugoslav consulates).
Population	11 million
Capital	Belgrade (Beograd)
Currency	new dinar
	£1 = approx 10DIN (with rapid inflation)
Political system	Federation of two Republics
Religion	Serbian Orthodox
Language	Serbian, some German spoken
Public Holidays	1, 6, 7 Jan.,; 1, 2 May,; 4, 7 July, 29, 30 Nov.
International dialling	To Yugoslavia: international code + 381 + number
	From Yugoslavia: International calls are usually made from post offices.

For centuries, the Serbs had a dream – to bring all the Slav peoples in the Balkans together in a single country, with Serbia at its head. They kept on dreaming through most of the Middle Ages, although with the area divided up between the rival empires of the Austrian Habsburgs and the Ottoman Turks it seemed that it was a long way from reality.

Serbia achieved full independence in 1878, along with Montenegro. and the dream moved a step closer. Extreme nationalists were hopeful enough to stage the assassination of the Austrian Archduke Ferdinand in Sarajevo and launch the First World War. Their reward was that when the war was over the victorious Western countries set Yugoslavia up as a nation – 6 different peoples under a Serbian king. The kingdom split during the Second World War, some regions allying themselves with the occupying Nazis while others, under the Communist partisan leader Josip Tito, fought a fierce struggle against German troops. Tito was able to set up a Communist government in 1945 and continued ruling until his death in 1980, never coming under the domination of the Russians like the rest of Eastern Europe.

The federation proved unable to survive the death of its founder and fell apart in the 1990s as one republic after another broke away in a series of bloody civil wars. Eventually all that was left was the rump of Serbia and Montenegro, which disclaimed all responsibility for the actions of the former government. For a while the region was off limits to most people, but today the authorities are keen to encourage tourists, including even eurorailers!

YUGOSLAVIAN RAILWAYS

(JUGOSLOVENSKE ZELEZNICE) (JZ)

There are adequate services along the main line from Hungary down through Belgrade and on to Macedonia or Bulgaria, and a scenic main branch line from Belgrade to the coast at Bar. International trains are reasonable, although slow and often very crowded, while local trains can be pretty dire. Reservations are needed for international services – make them at the departure station as early as you can.

Yugoslavia is in Inter-Rail zone H, along with Bulgaria, Romania, Bosnia Hercegovinia and Macedonia.

TOURIST INFORMATION

There's no general system of tourist information. *The Lonely Planet Guide to Eastern Europe* gives reasonable coverage, and there are municipal tourist offices in the main cities, as well as commercial travel agencies.

VISAS There are Yugoslav consulates in the Eastern European capitals of Bucharest, Budapest, Prague, Sofia and Warsaw, as well as in the USA, Canada, Australia and the UK, all of which should issue visas on the spot. You are unlikely to be able to enter the country without one, and will probably not be able to get one in Slovenia, Croatia or Macedonia. Be warned:Serbian border guards have become quite used to hauling protesting backpackers off international trains and sending them straight back where they came from.

MONEY MATTERS Inflation and hyperinflation has produced devaluations of the dinar in 1990, 1993, 1994, 1996... This means that the 'new' or 'novi' dinar is still distrusted by a lot of people and you will usually be able to use Deutschmarks. Still, changing money is relatively easy: you can do it at any bank, hotel or travel agency and the rate if you change on the street is unlikely to be any better.

POST OFFICES Main post offices are open Mon.–Fri.: 7 a.m.–7 p.m; Sat.: 7 a.m.–12 noon. Many have long-distance phones. The high rate of inflation means that stamp denominations may not always keep up, so it may be safer to go to a post office and have your postcards franked over the counter.

SHOPS Shops keep similar hours to post offices. There are no particular shortages or specialities to watch out for, although you should bring all your film with you.

LANGUAGE Serbian is almost always written in Cyrillic, so you'll benefit from spending an hour or two studying the Cyrillic alphabet – see the Bulgaria section.

SLEEPING

Budget hotels are scarce, and prices are often set in Deutschmarks or US dollars. Your best bet may be to camp or to plan on a long overnight train journey – you should be able to reserve a couchette from Belgrade, but do it early.

EATING

Serbian food has a Balkan feel to it, tending towards hot, spicy dishes such as grilled kebabs. The cheapest sustenance is a *burek*, a pie filled with cheese, meat or potato often available from street stalls. Beer is cheap but not very exciting. Coffee is served Turkish style: sweet, strong, and tarlike.

Belgrade code: 0322

Belgrade is the capital and main city of Serbia. Unlike other cities in the former Yugoslavia, Belgrade avoided suffering during the wars of the 1990s. Not Europe's most attractive or inspirational city, but a useful hub and worth a day or so of your time.

STATION FACILITIES

The main station is on Savski trg, with the main bus station next door. There are frequent trains to Budapest (6 hours), 2 trains a day to Vienna (11 hours), 2 a day to Thessaloniki and Athens (22 hours) and the Balkan Express to Sofia (9 hours) and Istanbul (26 hours). There is 24-hour left-luggage (you'll need to show your passport) and a currency exchange, although check first at the JIK Bank just outside to see if they're giving a better rate. There is a post office on the south side of the station with a telephone centre for long- distance calls. The other thing to do when you get here is to reserve your seat or couchette for the journey out.

Trains to Bucharest (9 hours) go from the smaller Beograd-Dunav station.

TOURIST INFORMATION AND ADDRESSES

The city Tourist Organisation has its main office in the underpass on the corner of Kneza Mihaila and Terzije, and opens Mon.–Fri.: 9 a.m.–8 p.m; Sat.: 9 a.m.–4 p.m.

POST OFFICE Next to the main station, at Takovska 2 or at Zmaj Jovina 17.

SEEING

KALMEGDAN CITADEL is the old fortress which has been at the heart of Belgrade over the years. Surrounded by parkland, it houses a military museum. Take tram No. 1, 2 or 13 from the train station. STARI GRAD, the oldest part of the city is next to the citadel and houses various museums of which the best is probably the ETHNOGRAPHIC MUSEUM, which has detailed explanations in English. A pleasant place to picnic is on ADA CIGANLIJA, an island park in the Sava River.

SLEEPING AND EATING

Budget accomodation is limited at the moment. Most hotels are state-owned and charge an exorbitant fixed rate of around 75DM for a single, 140DM for a double. The Hotel Centar on Savski trg, opposite the train station (Tel. 644 055) charges about 40DM per person in a double room, with bath, but is often full. There are two youth hostels, both about 3 miles out: the Hotel 'M' at Bulevar JNA 56a (Tel. 237 2560/1), take tram 9 or 10; and the Pinorski Grad 'SRC' sports centre at Kneza Viseslava 27 (Tel. 542 166), take tram 23 or 53. Hostel charges are approximately 25DM.

The nearest campsite is 5 miles south-west of the city centre at Kneza Viseslava 17 (Tel.: 555 127), take tram 12 or 13.

A lot of the restaurants tend to be pretentious, but you could try the Grcka Kraljica on Kneza Mihaila, towards the Kalmegdan citadel, or the Polet at Njegoseva 1 if you like fish. There are plenty of fast-food counters and *burek* stands, but watch that the prices are clearly marked.

Bar

It's worth coming to Bar just for the view from the window on the scenic 8-hour journey to reach it from Belgrade. It's also the only practical way for eurorailers to visit Yugoslavia's other republic, Montenegro. The town itself is not wildly interesting, and as one of Yugoslavia's few seaside resorts it gets fairly crowded in the holiday season. A daily ferry goes to Bari in Italy. Most hotel prices are fixed by the government, tend to be expensive, and there is no youth hostel, although you might be able to get a room from one of the tourist agencies at the ferry terminal.

NOTES

APPENDICES

Appendix I

INTER-RAIL DISCOUNTS

SEA OPERATORS (UK and Ireland)

Holyman/Sally Ferries	Ramsgate–Dunkirk	50%
Holyman/Sally Ferries	Ramsgate–Ostend	50%
Stena Line	Dover–Calais	50% (Ship); 25% (Lynx)
Stena Line	Harwick–Hoek van Holland	50% (1)
Stena Line	Newhaven–Dieppe	50%
Hoverspeed	Dover–HoverportCalais	50%
Hoverspeed (Sea Cat)	Folkestone–Boulogne	50%
P&O (European Ferries)	Dover–Calais	50%
P&O (European Ferries)	Dover–Cherbourg	30%
P&O (European Ferries)	Portsmouth–Le Harve	50%
Scandinavian Seaways	Harwich–Esbjerg	50% (1)
Scandinavian Seaways	Harwich/Newcastle–Gothenburg	50% (1)
Scandinavian Seaways	Harwich/Newcastle–Hamburg	50% (1)
Scandinavian Seaways	Newcastle–Amsterdam	50% (1)
Stena Line	Fishguard–Rosslare (Ship)	50%
Stena Line	Fishguard–Rosslare (Lynx)	25%
Stena Line	Holyhead–Dun Laoghaire (Ship or HSS)	50%
Stena Line	Holyhead–Dun Laoghaire (Lynx)	25% (2)
Stena Line	Stranraer–Larne	50%
Stena Line	Stranraer–Belfast	50%
Irish Ferries	Holyhead–Dublin	50%
Irish Ferries	Rosslare–Pembroke	50%
Irish Ferries	Cork/Rosslare–Le Havre	50% (3)
Irish Ferries	Cork/Rosslare–Cherbourg	50% (3)

1. Reservations are compulsory on sailings. Accommodation charges must be paid in full. For Scandinavian Seaways, tickets must be purchased in Britain.
2. Supplementary charge payable in full.
3. In June, July and August the reduction available to Inter-Rail card holders is 65%. Reservations are compulsory during July and August.

EUROSTAR
Inter-Rail 26 Cardholders travel at the Passholder rate.

AUSTRIA (Zone C)

Puchberg Schneeberg–Hochschneeberg	50%
St Wolfgang Schafbahnhof–Schafbergspitze	50%
BB Wolfgangseeschiffahrt	50%
Vereinigte Schiffahrtsverwaltungen für den Bodensee und Rhein	50%
Erste Donau Dampfschiffarhts gesellschaft:	
Gleisdorf–Weiz	50%
Feldbach–Bad Gleichenberg	50%
Chemins de Fer Regionaux de la Styrie (Steiemark):	
Peggau–Deutschfelistritz Übelbach	50%
Unzmarkt–Tamsweg:	50%

DENMARK (Zone C)

Scandinavian Seaways	Copenhagen–Oslo	50%(4)
Hjørring Privatbaner (HP)	Hjørring–Hirtshals	50%
Flyvebadene (Hydrofoil)	Copenhagen–Malmö	40%
Skagensbanen (SB)	Fredrikshavn–Skagen	50%

(4) Inclusive of a rest chair.

FINLAND (Zone B)

Silja Finnjet Line:	Helsinki–Lübeck/Travemünde	approx 10%
	Vassa–Umea	50%

FRANCE (Zone E)

Chemins de Fer de la Corse		50%
Chemins de Fer de la Provence	Nice–Digne	50%
SNMC-M:	Marseille–Ajaccio (in 2nd class)	30%
	Marseille–Propriano	30%
	Nice–Calvi	30%
	Toulon–Bastia	30%

NORWAY (Zone B)

Color Line	Hirtshals–Kristiansand	50%
HSD	Express ferries	25%
Flaggruten	Stavanger–Bergen	50%
Fylkesbaatanei I Sogn og Fjordane	Express and fjord ferries	50%
Larvik Line A/S	Larvik–Frederikshavn	50%
North Norway Express	Narvik–Bodø/Fauske	50%
(except on ferry services)		
Buses in the More, Romsdal, Troms, Nordland and Finmark regions		50%
(majority of services)		

SPAIN (Zone F)

Compagnie de Navegación Transmediterranea:

Barcelona–Palma/Ibiza/Mahón	30%
Valencia–Palma/Ibiza	30%
Almería–Mellila	30%
Málaga–Mellila	30%
Cádiz–Canaries	30%
Algeciras–Tangier/Ceuta	30%

SWEDEN (Zone B)

Stena Line	Göteborg–Frederikshavn	50%
Silja Line	Stockholm–Helsinki	50% (5)
Silja Line	Stockholm–Turku	50% (5)
TT-Line	Trelleborg–Lübeck/Travemünde	50%
Inlandstaget AB	Mora–Gällivare	50%

(5) Stockholm–Turku tickets cannot be used on Stockholm – Helsinki services. Reservations are compulsory for Stockholm – Helsinki services.

SWITZERLAND

All these companies give a 50% reduction:

AB	Appenzellerbahn
AL	Aigle–Leysin
AOMC	Aigle–Ollon–Monthey–Champréy
ASD	Aigle–Sepey–Les Diablerets
BAM	Bière–Apples–Morges
BB	Burgenstockbahn
BGF	GrindelwaldFirst
BLM	Lauterbrunnen–Murren
BOB	Berner Oberland–Bahnen
BOW	Oberdorf–Weissenstein
BrS	Brienzersee
BSG	Lac de Bienne
BTI	Blei–TauffelenIns
BVB	Bex–Villars–Bretaye
BVZ	Brig–Visp–Zermatt
CEV	Chemins de Fer du Veveysans
CJ	Chemins de Fer du Jura
CMM	Chemins de Fer des Montagnes-Neuchâteloises
EBT	Emmental–Burgdorf–Thun
FB	Forchbahn
GBS	Gurbetal–Bern–Schwarzenburg
GFM	Chemins de Fer Fribourgeois
GFM/VMCV	Vevey–Châtel–St Denis–Bossonnens
GGB	Gornergratbahn
GN	Glion–Rochers–de Naye
JB	Jungfraubahn
LAF	Adliswil–Felsenegg
LAS	Les Avants–Sonloup
LEB	Lausanne–Echallens–Bercher
LLB	Leuk–Leukerbad
LLPR	Lenzerheide–Parpaner Rothorn

LSE	Luzern–Stans–Engelberg
LSM	Stockalp–Melchsee–Frutt
LSMS	Stechelberg–Schilthorn
LWM	Wengen–Männlichen
MC	Martigny–Châtelard
MGI	Montreux–Glion
MO	Martigny–Orsières
NStCM	Nyon–Sant Cergue–Morez
OeBB	Oensingen–Balsthal
PBr	Pont–Brassus
RBS	Regional Verkehr Bern–Solothurn
RVT	Regional du Val de Travers
SBN	Beatenberg–Niederhorn
SGV	Vierwaldstättersee
SMB	Solothurn–Moutier
SMtS	St Imiet–Mont Soleil
SNB	Solothurn–Niederbipp
STB	Sensetalbahn
STI	SteffisburgThun–Interlaken (including bus routes)
SZU	Sihital-Zürich–UetlibergBahn
TB	Trogenerbahn
TBB	Thunersee–Beatenberg
Ths	Thunersee
URh	Untersee and Rhein
VCP	VeveyMont Pèlerin
VHB	Vereinigte Huttwil Bahnen
WAB	Wengernalpbahn
YSteC	Yverdon–Ste Croix
ZSG	Zürichsee

Details of discounts are compiled according to information provided by the operators concerned. However, this information may be subject to change without notice.

TRANSPORT MUSEUMS

The following transport museums offer free or reduced admittance to holders of Inter-Rail cards:

Belgium	Railway Museum, Gare de Bruxelles, Nord station
Denmark	Railway Museum, Jernbanemuseum, Odense
France	French Railway Museum, 2 rue Alfred de Glehn, Mulhouse
Finland	Railway Museum, Hyvink
	Narrow Gauge Railway Museum, Jokioinenlm (Minkio station)
Greece	Railway Museum, 4 Siokou Street, Athens
Hungary	Transport Museum, Varosligeti, Korut II, Budapest XIV
	Metro Museum, Metro Station Deák Ferentér, Budapest
	Horse Carrige Museum, Paradfürdo

Norway	Railway Museum, Hamar
Portugal	Railway Museum, Santaren station
Romania	Railway Museum, Bucharest Nord station
Spain	Railway Museum, Palacio de las Delicias, 61 Madrid
Sweden	Jarnvagsmuset, Museum of Transport, Raisgaten 1, Gavle

The following museums offer reduced price admittance to holders of Inter-Rail cards:

France	Grevin Museum of Waxworks, 10 blvd Montmartre, 75009 Paris
	Nouveau Museum Grevin du Forum des Halles, rue Pierre Lesco, Niveau 1, Grand Balcon, 75001 Paris
	History of Touraine Museum, Grand Chaleu Royal, Quai d'Orléans, 3700 Tours
	Museum Grevin Rochelle, 38 cours des Dames, 1700 La Rochelle
	Museum Grevin, Mont-St-Michel, 50116 Mont-St-Michel

INTER-RAIL CENTRES

COPENHAGEN

A special Inter-Rail centre is open from mid May–mid Sept., 7.30 a.m.–12 midnight, at Copenhagen central station (*Hovedbanegard*) and provides information, refreshments, left luggage and showers. Overnight sleeping is not allowed.

LONDON

The City of London youth hostel at 36 Carter Lane, EC4V 5AD offers Inter-Railers a meeting point and information centre and sells refreshments.

OSLO

An Inter-Rail centre is available at Oslo station. The centre offers a lounge, showers, toilets, telephones, left luggage, information and sells sandwiches and beverages. Open 15 June–15 Sept., 7 a.m.–11 p.m. daily. Overnight sleeping is not allowed.

TRONDHEIM

An Inter-Rail centre is also available at Trondheim station. The centre provides a lounge, showers, toilets, left luggage, information, a train reservation service and cooking facilities, and sells beverages. The centre is open 1 July–25 Aug., 7 a.m.–10.30 p.m. daily. Overnight sleeping is not allowed.

IMPORTANT INFORMATION

1. Replacement cards cannot be issued under any circumstances. You are advised to take out insurance to cover you in the event of the loss or theft of your Inter-Rail card.

2. Inter-Rail card holders must pay the usual reservation fees for seats, couchettes and sleeping berths.

3. Supplements are payable on some fast and high-speed trains, e.g. the French TGV and German ICE trains and most high-speed services in Spain.

Appendix II

BRITISH, IRISH AND CONTINENTAL FERRIES

I. English Channel

From	To	Operator	Type	Time hours	Average frequency
Poole	Cherbourg	Brittany Ferries	Ship	4¾	1–2 daily
Portsmouth	St Malo	Brittany Ferries	Ship	9	1 daily
Portsmouth	Caen	Brittany Ferries	Ship	6	2–3 daily
Plymouth	Roscoff	Brittany Ferries	Ship	6	1–3 daily (summer)
Plymouth	Santander	Brittany Ferries	Ship	24	2 weekly
Dover	Calais	Hoverspeed	Hovercraft	35min	6–14 daily
Folkestone	Boulogne	Hoverspeed	Seacat	40mins	3–4 daily
Ramsgate	Ostend	Oostende Lines	Ship	4	6 daily
Ramsgate	Ostend	Oostende Lines	Jetfoil	1½	6 daily
Dover	Calais	P&O	Ship	1½	20 daily
Dover	Ostend	P&O	Ship	3¾	5–8 daily
Dover	Ostend	P&O	Jetfoil	1¾	2–6 daily
Portsmouth	Le Havre	P&O	Ship	5¾	3 daily
Portsmouth	Cherbourg	P&O	Ship	4¾	1–4 daily
Portsmouth	Bilbao	P&O	Ship	36	2 weekly
Ramsgate	Dunkirk	Sally ferries	Ship	2½	5daily
Dover	Calais	Stena	Ship	1½	20 daily
Dover	Calais	Stena	Seacat	45min	5 daily
Newhaven	Dieppe	Stena	Catamaran	2¾	2 daily
Newhaven	Dieppe	Stena	Ship	4	2 daily

2. North Sea

From	To	Operator	Type	Time hours	Average frequency
Sheerness	Vlissingen	Olau Line	Ship	6	2 daily
Hull	Rotterdam	P&O North Sea Ferries	Ship	13	1 daily
Hull	Zeebrugge	P&O North Sea Ferries	Ship	13½	1 daily
Harwich	Esbjerg	Scandinavian Seaways	Ship	19¾	1 daily
Harwich	Göteborg	Scandinavian Seaways	Ship	23	5–6 weekly
Harwich	Hamburg	Scandinavian Seaways	Ship	21½	1 daily
Newcastle (summer)	Esbjerg	Scandinavian Seaways	Ship	21½	2 weekly
Newcastle (summer)	Göteborg	Scandinavian Seaways	Ship	23	1 weekly
Harwich	Hoek van Holland	Stena	Catamaran	3½	2 daily

3. Ireland

From	To	Operator	Type	Time hours	Average frequency
Liverpool	Dublin	IOM Steam	Ship	6½	2 daily
Holyhead	Dublin	Irish Ferries	Ship	3½	2 daily
Pembroke	Rosslare	Irish Ferries	Ship	4	2 daily
Cork (summer only)	Le Havre	Irish Ferries	Ship	22½	1 weekly
Rosslare	Le Havre	Irish Ferries	Ship	21	2–5 weekly
Rosslare	Cherbourg	Irish Ferries	Ship	18	1–3 weekly
Cairnryan (summer only)	Larne	P&O	Jetliner	1	3 daily
Cairnryan	Larne	P&O	Ship	2¼	3 daily
Stranraer	Belfast	Seacat	Catamaran	1½	4–5 daily
Holyhead	Dublin	Stena	Ship	4	1 daily
Holyhead	Dun Laoighaire	Stena	HSS	100 min	4 daily
Holyhead	Dun Laoghaire	Stena	Ship	3½	1 daily
Stranraer	Belfast	Stena	HSS	1½	4–5 daily
Stranraer	Belfast	Stena	Ship	2½	2–8 daily
Fishguard	Rosslare	Stena	HSS	1½	2–5 daily
Fishguard	Rosslare	Stena	Ship	3½	2 daily

Appendix III

EURAIL AID OFFICES

AUSTRIA
BB. Wien Westbahnhöf, A-1150, Vienna
BB, Salzburg Hauptbahhöf, A-5010, Salzburg
BB, Innsbruck Hauptbahhöf, A-6010, Innsbruck

BELGIUM
Société Nationale des Chemins de Fer Belges, Salon d'Accueil,
   Service International, Gare de Bruxelles-Midi, 1070 Brussels

DENMARK
DSB Travel Agency, Central Station, Banegärdspladsen, DK-1570,
   Copenhagen

FINLAND
Valtionrautatiet, Rautatieasema. VR Lipputoimisto, SF-00100, Helsinki

FRANCE
Société Nationale des Chemins de Fer Français, Guichets
   Internationaux, Galerie de Fresques (or Bureaux Informations-
   Réservations), Gare de Paris-Lyon, F-75012 Paris
Société Nationale des Chemins de Fer Français, Service International,
   Gare de Paris-St Lazare, F-75008 Paris
Société Nationale des Chemins de Fer Français, Bureaux Informa-
   tions-Reservations, Gare de Paris-Nord, F-75010 Paris
Société Nationale des Chemins de Fer Français, Bureau SNCF d'Orly,
   Aroport, Cedex A 222, F-94396 Orly-Aéroport
Société Nationale des Chemins de Fer Français, Bureau SNCF de
   Roissy, Aroport Charles de Gaulle, BP 20215, F-95712 Roissy Aéro-
   port Charles de Gaulle
Société Nationale des Chemins de Fer Français, Guichets Billets Inter-
   nationaux, Gare de Marseille, St Charles, F-13232 Marseille
Société Nationale des Chemins de Fer Français, Gare de Nice-Ville, F-
   06000 Nice

GERMANY

Deutsche Bundesbahn, Fahrkartenausgabe, Hauptbahnhof, D-6000 Frankfurt/Main

Deutsche Bundesbahn, Fahrkartenausgabe, Hauptbahnhof, D-6900 Heidelberg

Deutschec Bundesbahn, Fahrkartenausgabe,. Hauptbahnhof, D-8000 Munich

Deutsche Bundesbahn, Fahrkartenausgabe, Hauptbahnhof, D-5000 Cologne

Deutsche Bundesbahn, Fahrkartenausgabe, Hauptbahnhof, D-7000 Stuttgart

Deutsche Bundesbahn, Fahrkartenausgabe, Hauptbahnhof, D-2000 Hamburg

Fahrkartenausgabe, Berliner Zoologischer Garten, 810, D-1000 Berlin

Dresden Hauptbahnhof, Verkehrstelle am Hauptbahnhof, D-8010 Dresden

Leipzig Hauptbahnhof, Fahrkartenausgabe, Georgring, D-7010 Leipzig

GREECE

Chemins de Fer Helléniques, Bureau des Voyages et du Tourisme no. 2, 1 rue Karolou, 107, Athens

Chemins de Fer Helléniques, Gare Centrale des Voyageurs, Thessaloniki

Chemins de Fer Helléniques, Gare Centrale des Voyageurs, Patras

HUNGARY

Magyar Államvasutak, Közönsegszologolati Iroda, Nep Kòz Earasag, Utjah 35, H-1061, Budapest VI

IRELAND

CIE, International Rail Ticket Sales Office, 35 Lower Abbey Street, Dublin 1

ITALY

Ferrovie Italiane dello Stato, Stazione Santa Maria Novella, Ufficio Informazioni, Florence

Ferrovie Italiane dello Stato, Stazione Centrale, Milan

Ferrovie Italiane dello Stato, Stazione Santa Lucia, Venice

Ferrovie Italiane dello Stato, Stazione Termini, Rome

Ferrovie Italiane dello Stato, Stazione Centrale, Naples

Ferrovie Italiane dello Stato, Stazione Centrale, Bari

Ferrovie Italiane dello Stato, Stazione Centrale, Palermo

LUXEMBOURG
Société Nationale des Chemins de Fer Luxembourgeois, Bureau des Renseignements, Gare de Luxembourg, Luxembourg

NETHERLANDS
N.V. Nederlandse Spoorwegen, Bureau Ep 3-32-2, Katreinetoren, Utrecht (in the hall of Utrecht central station)

N.S. International Ticket Office, Amsterdam Central Station, Amsterdam

N.S. Ticket Office, Schipol Airport, Amsterdam Schiplo Airport, Amsterdam

NORWAY
NSB, Billettekspedisjionen, Oslo Sentralstasjon, 0154 Oslo 1

PORTUGAL
Companhia dos Caminos de Ferro Portugueses, Bilheteira Internacional, Estação de Santa Apolania, Av. Infante D. Henrique, P-1100 Lisbon

Companhia dos Caminos de Ferro Portugueses, Estação de S. Bento, Praça Almeida Garret, P-4000 Porto

Companhia dos Caminos de Ferro Portugueses, Estação de Camino de Ferro, Largo de Estação , P-8000, Faro

SPAIN
RENFE, Alcala 44 Madrid, Officina de Viajes

RENFE, Madrid-Barajas, International Airport, Madrid

RENFE, Estación Centrale de Barcelona Sants, Barcelona

RENFE, Calle Zaragoza 29, Seville

RENFE, Plaza Alfonso et Magnanimo 2, Valencia

SWEDEN
Swedish State Railways, Stockholm Central Station, S-105-50, Stockholm

SWITZERLAND
SBB, Reisebüro, Hauptbahnhof, CH-4051, Basel

SBB, Auskunftsbüro, Hauptbahnhof, CH-3000, Bern

CFFS, Gare de Genève, CH-1211, Geneva

CFFS, Bureau des Renseignements CFF, Geneva Airport, CH-1215, Geneva

SBB, Auskunftsbüro, Bahnhof, CH-6000, Lucerne

SBB, Auskunftsbüro, Hauptbahnhof, CH-8021, Zürich

SBB, Auskunftsbüro Zürich Flughafen, CH-8058, Zürich

UNITED KINGDOM
French National Railways, 179 Piccadilly, London W1V 0BA

Appendix IV

CIEE OFFICES

USA

ARIZONA

120 East University Drive
Suite E
Tempe, AZ 85281
(602) 966 3544

CALIFORNIA

2486 Channing Way
Berkeley, CA 94707
(510) 848 8604

UCSD Prince Center
9500 Gilman Drive
La Jolla, CA 92093 0076
(619) 452 0630

1818 Palo Verde Avenue
Suite E
Long Beach, CA 90815
(310) 598 3338
(714) 527 7950

10904 Lunbrook Drive
Los Angeles, CA 90024
(310) 208 3551

394 University Avenue
Suite 200
Palo Alto, CA 94301
(415) 325 3888

953 Garnet Avenue
San Diego, CA 92109
(619) 270 6401

530 Bush Street
Ground Floor
San Fransico CA 94108
(415) 421 3473

312 Sutter Street
Suite 407
San Francisco, CA 94108
(415) 421 3473

919 Irving Street
Suite 102
San Francisco, CA 94122
(415) 566 6222

14515 Ventura Blvd
Suite 250
Sherman Oaks, CA 91403
(818) 905 5777

COLORADO

1138 13th Street
Boulder, CO 80302
(303) 447 8101

CONNECTICUT

Yale Co-op East
77 Broadway
New Haven, CT 06520
(203) 562 5335

DISTRICT OF COLUMBIA

3300 M Street NW
2nd Floor
Washington, DC 20007
(202) 337 6464

FLORIDA

One Datran Center
Suite 320
9100 South Dadeland Blvd
Miami, FL 33156
(305) 670 9261

GEORGIA

Emory Village
1561 North Decatur Road
Atlanta, GA 30307
(404) 377 9997

ILLINOIS

1153 North Dearborn Street
2nd Floor, Chicago
(312) 951 0585

1634 Orrington Avenue
Evanston IL 60201
(708) 866 1767

LOUISIANA

Joseph A. Danna Center
Loyola University
6363 St Charles Avenue
New Orleans, LA 70118
(504) 866 1767

MASSACHUSETTS

12 Elliot Street
2nd floor
Cambridge/Harvard MA 02138
(617) 497 1497

137 E. Franklin Street
Chapel Hill, NC 27514
(919) 942 2334

Cart S. Ell Student Center
Northeastern University
360 Huntingdon Avenue
Bosten, MA 02138
(617) 424 1497

84 Massachusetts Ave
Cambridge, MA 02139
(617) 225 2555

Stratton Student Center
MIT, W20-024
84 Mass. Avenue
Cambridge, MA 02139
(617) 225 2555

MICHIGAN

1220 S. University Drive
Suite 208
Ann Arbor, MI 48104
(313) 998 0200

MINNESOTA

1501 University Avenue SE
No. 300
Minneapolis, MN 55414
(612) 379 2323

NEW ORLEANS
Danna Student Centre
6363 St. Charles Avenue
New Orleans, LA 70118
(504) 866 1767

NEW YORK

205 East 42nd Street
New York, NY 10017-5706
(212) 822 2700
e-mail info@cieee.org;
http://www.ciee.org

35 West 8th Street
New York Student Center
895 Amsterdam Avenue
New York, NY 10025
(212) 666 4177

NORTH CAROLINA

Suite 407
703 Ninth Street
Suite B#2
Durham, NC 27705
(919) 286 4664

OHIO

8 East 13th Avenue
Columbus, OH 43201
(614) 294 8696

OREGON

715 S.W Morrison
No. 600
Portland, OR 97205
(503) 288 1900

PENNSYLVANIA

3606a Chestnut Street
Philadelphia, PA 19104
(215) 382 0343

RHODE ISLAND

171 Angell Street (corner of
Thayer)
Suite 212
Providence, RI 02906
(401) 331 5810

TEXAS

2000 Guadalupe
Austin, TX 78705
(512) 472 4931

WASHINGTON

3300 M. Street N.W.
2nd Floor
Washington DC 20007
(202) 337 6464

WISCONSIN

2615 North Hackett Avenue
Milwaukee, WI 53211
(414) 332 4740

EUROPE

FRANCE

37 bis, rue d'Angleterre
Nice, 6000
(493) 822 333
36 quai Gailleron, 69002 Lyon

GERMANY

64 Graf Adolph Strasse
Düsseldorf D-40212
Tel. (211) 135 029

UK

28a Poland Street
London W1V 3DB
Tel. 0171 437 7767/ 0171 287
3337

Appendix V

TOURIST OFFICES

On the following pages are Tourist Offices listings for countries covered in *Europe by Train*. You will notice a lack of entries for several countries; namely Belarus, Estonia, Latvia, Lithuania, Macedonia, Slovakia, the Ukraine and the new Yugoslavia. Unfortunately, we have been unable to locate functioning Tourist Offices for these countries.

In all cases, if you need to get further information, we recommend contacting the embassy of the particular country.

UK OFFICES

ANDORRA, 63 Westover Road, London SW18 (0181 874 4806 mornings only)

AUSTRIA, 30 St George's Street, London W1R 0AL (0171 629 0461)

BELGIUM, 29 Princes Street, London W1 (0891 887799)

BULGARIA, 18 Princes Street, London W1 (0171 499 6988)

CROATIA, 162-164 Fulham Palace Rd, London W6 9ER (0181 563 7979)

CZECH REPUBLIC, 95 Great Portland Street, London W1N 5RA (0171 291 9920)

DENMARK, 55 Sloane Street, London SW1X 9SY (0171 259 5958)

FINLAND, 3rd floor, 30–35 Pall Mall, London SW1 Y5LP (0171 839 4048)

FRANCE, 178 Piccadilly, London W1 (0891 244123)

GERMANY, 65 Curzon Street, London W1 (0891 600100)

GREECE, 4 Conduit Street, London W1 (0171 734 5997)

HUNGARY, c/o Commercial Section, Hungarian Embassy, 46 Eaton Place, London SW1 (0171 823 1032)

IRELAND, 150 New Bond Street, London W1 (0171 493 3201)

ITALY, 1 Princes Street, London W1 (0171 408 1254)

LUXEMBOURG, 122 Regent St, London W1 (0171 434 2800)

MALTA, 207 College House, Wrights Lane, London W8 (0171 938 2668)

MONACO, 50 Upper Brook Street, London W1 (071 629 4712)

MOROCCO, 205 Regent Street,. London W1 (0171 437 0073)

THE NETHERLANDS, 25–28 Buckingham Gate, London SW1 (0171 630 0451)

NORWAY, Charles House, 5–11 Lower Regent Street, London SW1 (0171 839 2650)

POLAND, 1st floor, 310–312 Regent St, London W1 (0171 224

3692), or Polorbis Travel, 82 Mortimer St, London W1 (0171 637 4971)

PORTUGAL, 22/25a Sackville Street, London W1 (0171 494 1441)

ROMANIA, 83a Marylebone High St, London W1 (0171 224 3692) or 17 Nottingham St, London W1M 3RD (0171) 224 3692

RUSSIA, Intourist, 219 Marsh Wall, London E14 (0171 538 8600); e-mail info@intourus.demm.co.uk

SLOVENIA, 2 Canfield Place, London NW6 (0171 372 3767)

SPAIN, 22–23 Manchester Square, London W1M 5AP (0171 486 8077)

SWEDEN, 11 Montague Place, London W1 (0171 724 5868)

SWITZERLAND, Swiss Centre, 1 New Coventry Street, London W1 (0171 734 1921)

TURKEY, 170–173 Piccadilly, London W1 (0171 355 4207/ 0171 629 7771)

US OFFICES

AUSTRIA, PO Box 1142, 500 Fifth Ave., 20th Floor, NY, NY 10110 (212 9446880);
11601 Wilshire Blvd., LA, CA 90025 (913 477 3332)

BELGIUM, 745 Fifth Ave., NY, NY 10151 (212 758 8130)

BULGARIA, 41 East 42nd Street. NY, NY 10017 (212 573 5530)

DENMARK, 655 Third Ave., 18th Floor, NY, NY 10017 (212 949 2333)

FINLAND, see Denmark.

FRANCE, 610 Fifth Ave., NY, NY 10020 (900 990 0040); 645 North Michigan Ave., Chicago, IL 60611 (312 337 6301); 9401 Wilshire Blvd., Beverly Hills, CA 90212 (213 271 6665)

GERMANY, 122 E42nd St., NY, NY 10017 (212 661 7200); 444 Flower Street, Suite 2230, LA, CA 90017 (213 688 7332)

GREECE, 645 Fifth Ave., Olympic Tower, 5th Floor, NY, NY 10022 (212 421 5777);
168 North Michigan Avenue, Chicago, IL 60611 (312 782 084); 611 West Sixth Street, Suite 2198, LA, CA 90017 (213 626 6696)

HUNGARY, 1 Parker Plaza, 1104 Fort Lee, NJ 07024 (201 592 8585) or 150 E 58th St, 33rd fl, New York, NY 10155 (212 355 0240)

IRELAND, 757 Third Avenue, NY, NY 10017 (212 418 0800)

ITALY, 630 Fifth Avenue, Suite 1565, NY, NY 10111 (212 245 4822);
500 North Michigan Avenue, Suite 1046, Chicago, IL 60611 (312 644 0990);

360 Post Street, Suite 801, San Francisco, CA 94108 (415 392 5266)

LUXEMBOURG, 801 Second Avenue, NY, NY 10017 (212 370 9850)

MOROCCO, 20 East 46th Street, NY, NY 10017 (212 557 2520)

NETHERLANDS, 355 Lexington Avenue, 21st Floor, NY, NY 10020 (212 370 7367);

225 North Michigan Avenue, Suite 326, Chicago, IL 60601 {312 819 0300);

9 New Montgomery Street, Suite 305, San Francisco, CA 94105 (415 543 6772)

NORWAY, see Denmark.

POLAND, 342 Madison Avenue, NY, NY 10173 (212 867 5011);

333 North Michigan Avenue, Suite 228, Chicago, IL 6060l (312 236 9031)

PORTUGAL, 590 Fifth Avenue, NY, NY 10036 (212 354 4403)

ROMANIA, 342 Madison Avenue, Suite 210, NY, NY 10036 (212 697 6971)

RUSSIA, 8 Third Avenue, Suite 3101, New York, NY 10002 (212 758 1162)

SLOVENIA, 122 E 42nd St, New York, NY 10168-0072 (212 682 5896)

SPAIN, 665 Fifth Avenue, NY, NY 10022 (212 759 8822);

845 North Michigan Avenue, Chicago, IL 60611 (312 944 215);

1 Hallidie Plaza, San Francisco, CA 94102 (415 346 8100)

SWEDEN, see Denmark.

SWITZERLAND, 608 Fifth Avenue, NY, NY 10020 (212 757 5944);

250 Stockton Street, San Francisco, CA 94108 (415 362 2260)

TURKEY, 821 United Nations Plaza, NY, NY 10017 (212 687 2194)

UNITED KINGDOM, 40 West 57th Street, NY, NY 10019 (212 581 700);

John Hancock Center, Suite 3320, 875 North Michigan Avenue, Chichago, IL 60611 (312 787 0490);

Plaza of the Americas, North Tower, Suite 750, Dallas, TX 75201 (312 623 8196);

612 South Flower Street, LA, CA 90017 (213 623 8196)

AUSTRALIA OFFICES

AUSTRIA, 36 Carringtlon Street, 1st Floor, Sydney, NSW 2000 (02 299 3621)

DENMARK, 60 Market Square, Melbourne, Victoria 3001 (03 62 33 63)

FINLAND, see Denmark.

FRANCE, 33 Blight Street, Sydney, NSW 2000 (02 231 5244)

GERMANY, Lufthansa House, 143 Macquarie Street, Sydney, NSW 2000 (02 221 1008)

GREECE, 5157 Pitt Street, Sydney, NSW 2000 (02 241 1663)

IRELAND, MLC Centre, Martin Place, Sydney, NSW 2000 (02 232 7177)

MOROCCO, c/o Moroccan Consulate, 11 West Street North, Sydney, NSW 2000 (02 957 6717)

THE NETHERLANDS, 5 Elizabeth Street, 6th Floor, Sydney, NSW 2000 (02 276 921)

NORWAY, see Denmark.

SPAIN, 203 Castlereagh Street, Suite 21a, Sydney, NSW 2000 (02264 7966)

SWEDEN, see Denmark.

SWITZERLAND, 203233 New South Head Road, Edgecliffe, Sydney, NSW 2027 (02 326 1799)

UNITED KINGDOM, 171 Clarence Street, Sydney, NSW 2000 (02 298 627)

If any of the above offices have moved, or if you discover a new one that isn't listed, please help your fellow eurorailers and send us a postcard with the appropriate details to the address on page 4.

Appendix VI

INTERNATIONAL COUNTRY CODES

The following is a list of the telephone country codes for the different countries covered in this book:

Country	Code	Country	Code
Austria	43	Macedonia	389
Belarus	7	Morocco	212
Belgium	32	Netherlands	31
Bosnia	387	Norway	47
Bulgaria	359	Poland	48
Croatia	385	Portugal	351
Czech Republic	42	Romania	40
Denmark	45	Slovakia	42
Estonia	372	Slovenia	386
Finland	358	Spain	34
France	33	Sweden	46
Germany	49	Switzerland	41
Greece	30	Turkey	90
Hungary	36	UK	44
Ireland	353	Ukraine	380
Italy	39	Yugoslavia	381
Latvia	371		
Liechtenstein	41 75		
Lithuania	370		
Luxembourg	352		

Outside Europe:

Country	Code	Country	Code
Australia	61	New Zealand	64
Canada	1	USA	1

PLACING AN INTERNATIONAL CALL

When you want to call another country, you must first dial the international access code for the country you're in. These access codes are listed at the start of each country in the information section. Once you have dialled the access code, then dial the country code for the country you want to call and the phone number. For example:

to call France from the UK; dial 00+33+number.

APPENDIX VII

COMMON CONVERSIONS

LENGTH

1 inch = 2.54 centimetres
1 foot = 0.305 metre
1 mile = 1.609 kilometre

1 centimetre = 0.39 inch
1 metre = 3.281 feet
1 kilometre = 0.621 mile

VOLUME

1 cubic foot = 0.028 cubic metre
1 gallon (UK) = 4.546 litres
1 gallon (US) =3.785 litres

1 cubic metre = 35.315 cubic feet
1 litre = 0.22 gallon (UK)
1 litre = 0.264 gallon (US)

WEIGHT

1 pound = 0.454 kilogram
1 ounce = 28.35 grammes

1 kilogram = 2.205 pounds
1 gram = 0.036 ounce

SPEED

1 mph = 1.609 kilometre/hour

1 kilometre/hour = 0.621 mph

TEMPERATURE

Zero°C =32°F
25°C = 77°F
50°C = 122°F
75°C=167°F
100°C =212°F

DATES

UK/European format: dd/mm/yy
American format: mm/dd/yy

dd=day mm=month yy =year

TIMES

In the 24-hour clock times after noon are as follows;
1 p.m. = 13.00; 2 p.m. = 14.00; 3 p.m. = 15.00; etc., until midnight, which is 00.00.

Appendix VIII

BASIC VOCABULARY

Although it is sometimes possible to get by in English, especially in Germany, Scandinavia and the Low Countries, often it's not. German can often be used in Eastern Europe. We've kept it pretty simple, as theres no point getting too involved in a language you don't know the basics of. If you want a bit more you'll find any number of cheap pocket-sized phrasebooks in most bookshops.

ENGLISH	CZECH	DANISH	DUTCH
Yes	Ano	Ja	Ja
No	Ne	Nej	Nee
Please	Prosim	Vaer sa venlig	Alsatublieft
Thank you	Děkuji	Tak	Dank u
Good morning	Dobry den	Godmorgen	Goedemorgen
Goodbye	Na shledanou	Farvel	Tot ziens
Where is/are...?	Kde je/jsou...?	Hvor er...?	Waar is/zijn...?
Excuse me	Prominte	Undskyld	Pardon
How much?	Kolik to stojf?	Hvor meget?	Hoeveel?
Can I have...?	Chtela bych...	Kan jeg fa...	Hag ik ... hebben
I don't understand	Nerozumim	Jeg forstaar ikke	Ik begrijp het niet
Do you speak English?	Mluvite anglicky?	Taler De engelsk?	Spreekt u Engels?
My name is...	Jmenjui se...	Mit navn er...	Mijt naam is...

ENGLISH	FINNISH	FRENCH	GERMAN
Yes	Kyllä	Oui	Ja
No	Ei	Non	Nein
Please	Olkaa hyvä	S'il vous plaît	Bitte
Thank you	Kiitos	Merci	Danke
Good morning	Hyvää huomenta	Bonjour	Guten Morgen
Goodbye	Nakemiin	Au revoir	Auf Wiedersehen
Where is/are...?	Missa on/ovat...?	Ou se trouve/trouvent...?	Wo ist/sind...?
Excuse me	Anteeksi	Excusez-moi	Entschuldigen Sie!
How much?	Kuinka paljon?	Combien?	Wieviel?
Can I have...?	Voinko saada...	Je voudrais...	Kann ich ...haben?
I don't understand	En ymmärrä	Je ne comprends pas	Ich verstehe nicht
Do you speak English?	Puhutteko englantia?	Parlez-vous anglais?	Sprechen Sie Englisch?
My name is...	Nimeni on...	Je m'appelle...	Ich heisse...

ENGLISH	HUNGARIAN	ITALIAN	NORWEGIAN
Yes	Igen	Sì	Ja
No	Nem	No	Nei
Please	Kerem	Per favore	Var så god
Thank you	Köszönöm	Grazie	Takk
Good morning	Jo reggelt	Buongiorno	God morgen
Goodbye	Viszontlatasra	Ciao	Ha det godt
Where is/are...?	Hol van/ vannak...?	Dov'è/Dove sono...?	Hvor er...?
Excuse me	Elnezest	Mi scusi	Unnskyld
How much?	Mennyi/Mennyit?	Quanto?	Hvor mye?
Can I have...?	Kaphatok...	Posso avere...	Kan jeg fa...
I don't understand	Nem ertem	Non capisco	Jeg forstar ikke
Do you speak English?	Beszel angolul?	Parla inglese?	Snakker Du engelsk?
My name is...	Nevem vagyok...	Mi chiamo...	Mitt navn er...

ENGLISH	PORTUGUESE	SERBO-CROAT	SPANISH
Yes	Sim	Da	Sí
No	Não	Ne	No
Please	Faz favor	Molim	Por favor
Thank you	Obrigado	Hvala	Gracias
Good morning	Bom dia	Dobro jutro	Buenos días
Goodbye	Adeus	Zbogom	Adiós
Where is/are...?	Onde esta/ estão...?	Gde je/su...?	Donde esta/estan...?
Excuse me	Desculpe	Izvinite	Dispenseme
How much?	Quanto?	Koliko?	Cuanto?
Can I have...?	Pode dar-me...	Mogu li dobiti...	Puede darme...
I don't understand	Não compreendo	Ne razumen	No comprendo
Do you speak English?	Fala ingles	Gavorite li engleski?	Habla usted inglés?
My name is...	O meu nome e...	Ja se Zovem...	Me llamo...

ENGLISH	SWEDISH	TURKISH
Yes	Ja	Evet
No	Nej	Hayir
Please	Varsagod	Lütfen
Thank you	Tack	Teşekkür ederim
Good morning	God morgon	Gunaydin
Goodbye	Adjo	Gule gule/Allaha ismarladik
Where is/are...?	Var ar...?	Nerede/Neredeler...?
Excuse me	Forlat	Affedersiniz
How much?	Hyr mycket?	Ne kadar?
Can I have...?	Kan jag fa...	...rica edebilir miyim
I don't understand	Jag forstar inte	Anlamiyorum
Do you speak English?	Talar Ni engelska?	Ingilizce Biliyor musunuz?
My name is...	Mitt namn ar...	Adim... dir

Index

H